Vicious
Circles

ALSO BY JONATHAN KWITNY

The Fountain Pen Conspiracy
The Mullendore Murder Case
Shakedown (a novel)

VICIOUS CIRCLES

The Mafia in the Marketplace

JONATHAN KWITNY

W · W · NORTON & COMPANY
New York

Library of Congress Cataloging in Publication Data
Kwitny, Jonathan.
  Vicious circles.

  Includes index.
  1. Mafia. 2. Organized crime—United States.
3. Crime and criminals—Economic aspects—United
States. 4. United States—Commerce. I. Title.
HV6446.K95 1979   364.1′06′073   78–13183
ISBN 0–393–01188–7

1 2 3 4 5 6 7 8 9 0

Dedication

This book originally was to be dedicated to my father and mother. They will have to wait for the next one.

On June 19,1978, long after most work on the book was completed, Martha Kaplan Kwitny died. She was thirty-three years old.

To an enormous extent, the ideas that molded this book came to me through her, or through experiences we shared. The book probably wouldn't have been written without her; it seems inconceivable that she won't be here to enjoy and defend it when it comes out. This book is about injustice, and Martha dedicated her professional life to fighting injustice. Yet the greatest injustice either of us ever saw happened to her.

In the Perth Amboy schools she was valedictorian, voted "most likely to succeed," editor of the school paper, and president of more organizations than most people ever join. Summers, during college, she handled a full reporting beat for the Perth Amboy paper (where we met—it was my first job). She received high honors through Radcliffe and Harvard Law School.

We tended then to see crooks as victims of the system. We came to realize that they are predators who cheat most the very underdogs we sought to help. I know now that Martha influenced me far more than I her. Her first legal job (except for a summer internship with the U.S. attorney in Manhattan) was on a bail reform program. Then she joined the New Jersey public defender's staff, where she struggled desperately for two years, without success, to find an innocent client. Though she got some satisfaction helping marijuana possessers and others who broke unfair laws, her main job was finding legal loopholes to justify the exoneration of cutthroats. So she switched to trying cases for a country prosecutor, and, later, organizing and conducting complex investigations for the state attorney general's office.

There was no hint of illness. She packed thirty-six pounds on her back for a year as we hiked through Africa and Asia. Then, in 1971, she got pregnant and doctors discovered kidney disease. Our son was born dead at eight months.

Martha went through a depression unlike anything she knew before or after, until we were lucky enough to adopt a daughter. Specialists said Mar-

tha's kidneys would inevitably fail in about five years, but they assured her that new techniques could keep her well, even normal. They also said they could negotiate a pregnancy, hastening the kidney failure only slightly. The birth of our second daughter, in 1973, was Martha's proudest moment.

Her kidneys failed a year later. She reported to dialysis clinics three nights a week, sometimes four. Sessions were five or six hours, often in constant pain. She was hospitalized during periodic crises, nearly died several times, but otherwise rarely missed work. She fainted on the kitchen floor and at the steering wheel, but always after making it home. Her energy level, her emotional patterns, her appearance, her most basic physical drives were altered radically. Many foods and all fluids became taboo. She was thirsty, but couldn't drink. She ached constantly; she sometimes trembled.

Hiding this as she could, she jailed a prominent figure in a local political scandal after a long trial. When a big murder case collapsed because the judge excluded vital evidence (the defendants' voluntary confessions before a hidden tape recorder) she bluffed them into pleading guilty to a lesser crime (illegally transporting a corpse). When a judge ruled that an especially brutal rapist had to be tried separately for each of seven attacks, and the defendant started getting aquitted, Martha devised a ploy to get all seven victims on the stand at one trial. Six of them couldn't mention their attacks, but did challenge the defendent's memory on where he had been when the attacks occured. The jury got the message and voted guilty. She directed and won the first criminal antitrust case in New Jersey history. She commanded a sizable staff, interviewed scores of witnesses, and after a five-week trial, sent to prison the head of a lawn service operation with 450 franchised outlets in four states. She won $145,000 in fines for the taxpayers. The judge agreed to start trial late on the mornings after dialysis. She taught our daughters reading and arithmetic before they started school, told them stories, took them to parks and swimming pools, was patient. Scarcely able to climb stairs, she continued chores around home, insisted on handling all cooking, played tennis until pain (then doctor's orders) forced her off the court.

She got a kidney transplant in 1976. Almost overnight she became her old self. There were a lot of pills to take, and bad side-effects, but the anemia vanished and her general feeling of energy and well-being returned. After two months, her body, against her will, rejected the kidney. Doctors, experimenting desperately to perfect their new process, treated her heavily with immuno-suppressant drugs. There ensued high fever, pneumonia, and more hospital crises. Finally they gave up and took the kidney out. She went back on dialysis. Two years later another doctor offered another kidney, and again the hope of a normal life. This one never really took. Again they applied immuno-suppressant drugs. Then more heavily. They didn't know when to stop. Again the fever, and the pneumonia. She fought for breath for four days and was still fighting when her heart simply stopped beating. But the fight isn't over.

This is for Martha.

Most of the research for this book was done from 1974 to 1977 in the course of various reporting projects for the Wall Street Journal. The bulk of the book was written in 1977, although certain portions were added while the book was being edited during the first part of 1978. It will not reach the bookstores until 1979.

Yet the book is about current events, not history. Most of the characters will no doubt still be around in 1979, and for many years thereafter. Nor are they likely to adopt new habits, if the careers of other such criminals are any guide.

By 1979, some corporations that are mentioned here will have gone out of business or will have passed to new hands. The nature of criminal enterprises requires an occasional change of trade names or managerial window dressing, and it is impossible to continue research ad infinitum. But the death or transformation of a particular enterprise does not mean that the Mob no longer exerts control in an industry. All the criminal schemes that are included in this book are here because they pose a continuing threat.

Extensive material from electronic eavesdropping tapes and grand jury evidence will be found in these pages. Robert Nicholson and Louis Montello, the detectives, would have had access to much of this evidence, and they obviously have contributed much information of a more open nature to this book. Therefore, in fairness to them, I will state that such electronic eavesdropping and grand jury material has been provided to me by others than Robert Nicholson and Louis Montello, and completely without their knowledge.

Jonathan Kwitny
New York City

Contents

PART ONE

MEAT:
The Tummy Ache
Merchants

1

The Meat
That Didn't Moo

Detective Robert Nicholson and his partner Louis Montello sat in a basement in Queens, watched the slow, rhythmic winding of the recording tape, and listened to the sounds of the Mafia. But it was not the Mafia they might have expected, not the Mafia people read about in bestsellers or saw in the movies. Nobody was talking about numbers running or dice games or selling dope. Nobody was issuing hit contracts for other gangsters or having love affairs with movie stars. The people Nicholson and Montello were listening to spoke a language of loins, and hams, and ground beef, and frankfurters. They were meat dealers, some of the biggest meat dealers in the country. They supplied the major supermarket chains and the local butcher shops. They were the men who fed America.

It was 1964, the first of thirteen frustrating years that Bob Nicholson and Lou Montello of the Manhattan district attorney's office would spend trying to break the Mafia's hold on the New York meat market. As much as 20 percent of all the meat in the country changed hands on the New York market (some of it to be processed and shipped out again), making it the world's largest. Every major American packer needed to sell there. And the Mafia seemed to own it—the way the Mafia continues to own a lot of American marketplaces. In fact, more than a decade later, when Nicholson and Montello resigned from the police force in disgust, most of the major criminal figures in their original investigation were still in the meat business.

December had thrown its bleak chill over the city, and nowhere could the onset of winter be felt more than in the dreary Jamaica section of Queens, with its gray rows of factories and warehouses. That was where Nicholson and Montello were holed up in their basement, listening day after day, week after week, waiting for conversations that would incriminate.

Back on November 14 they had planted a bug—a tiny wireless microphone and radio transmitter. The bug was in the office of Norman (Nat) Lokietz, the president and principal owner (if you didn't count the hoods on his back) of Merkel Meat Company, whose headquarters was seven or eight blocks from where Nicholson and Montello sat listening. Merkel was a name known to every supermarket and deli shopper from Perth Amboy to Montauk Point. If you bought processed meat—frankfurters, liverwurst, sliced ham, baloney—Merkel was as likely as any company to have manufactured it. If you bought a sandwich at a lunchcounter, there was a good chance Nat Lokietz was responsible for its contents. Merkel had been an industry leader for more years than anyone could remember. The hoods brought Lokietz in to run it in 1963.

The cops had bugged Lokietz's office in an attempt to prove allegations that corruption in the meat industry was costing the public millions of dollars. But Nicholson and Montello were about to learn—with an explicitness that appalled them—that Mafia control of an industry robs the public of far more than just its money. Their grisly discovery would kindle all the determination they needed to sustain them through the epic investigation that lay ahead.

What Nicholson and Montello had expected to hear in the Merkel office was talk about the extortion activities of the leaders of Local 174 of the Amalgamated Meat Cutters and Butcher Workmen of North America, AFL–CIO. Local 174 was the largest in the five-hundred-thousand-member butchers' union. It had grown out of a local founded in 1934 by a Mafia captain known as Little Augie Pisano (born Anthony Carfano) and his labor side-kick George Scalise. Scalise organized on the Mafia's behalf not only the butchers' union, but also the Building Service Employees Union, the Liquor Wholesalers and Distillery Workers' Union, the gasoline station attendants' union, and a Teamster local, among others. When the Mafia wants to control an industry, the union is usually the easiest place to start.

The officers of butchers' Local 174 had been mere fronts—well-paid fronts —for the Mob from the beginning. All this had been proven in court by the Manhattan District Attorney's Office back in 1940 when Thomas E. Dewey was running it. Scalise even went off to jail in the 1940s on account of his union work, but the system never changed.

Now, a generation later, Nicholson and Montello were trying once again. They were working under the direction of D.A. Frank Hogan and his rackets chief, Alfred Scotti, who himself had worked on the Dewey investigations. In what they attempted and what they learned, Nicholson and Montello would go much further than Dewey's men ever did. Over thirteen years they would track the Mafia's power out of the union halls and into the executive suites of the great supermarket chains and finally to Iowa and Nebraska, and to the chief executive of the largest slaughtering and meatpacking company in the world. They would learn the power of a national crime syndicate over much of a large industry, over the American diet and pocketbook, and sometimes even over law enforcement. What they would see was a cancer choking the American entrepreneurial spirit itself, until the best and most creative of businessmen would accept the Mafia's rules and authority.

Nicholson and Montello were typical of the men who rise to the top of the New York Police Department's detective force. They were exceptionally bright, dedicated, and hardworking cops, yet not in the maverick style of a Serpico, or Serpico's friend David Dirk. They were capable of occasional lapses of genius, such as arranging to secretly tape record a meeting with a suspect and then, with a whole city to choose from, scheduling the meeting in a second-floor hotel room overlooking a construction site so that the rattle of jackhammers overwhelmed portions of the recorded conversation. But they made the tough cases.

Nicholson, stocky, red-haired, freckled, was the brasher of the two. He was deft at conning a fatal admission out of a suspect whose back really wasn't quite to the wall yet. Brooklyn-born, in his early thirties, he was as glib a talker as the bartender he somewhat resembled. But resemblances were deceptive. He had a quick, perceptive mind, and came from a family that also produced the astronomer Thomas D. Nicholson, director of the American Museum of Natural History; they are brothers. Before the meat investigation, Detective Nicholson had been part of the team that exposed massive corruption in the New York State Liquor Authority.

Montello had just helped put mobster Joey Gallo in prison for extortion, a case that grew out of an investigation into shylocking in the garment center. Montello was taller, quieter, older-looking than Nicholson—more the Gary Cooper sort. They made a good team. In fact, according to Nicholas Scopetta, an assistant D.A. who worked on the meat case and later became Commissioner of Investigations for New York City, "We always said that if you just got the lawyers out of their way, Nicholson and Montello could make a case against anybody."

By the time the bug had been secreted inside Nat Lokietz's office in Queens, the two detectives were already six months into their investigation. Their long study of the meat industry had begun because of the honesty of Stephen Shea, executive vice-president of the Great Atlantic & Pacific Tea Company, then the nation's largest supermarket chain. In 1961 the Department of Agriculture had discovered that the A & P and certain other chains were buying "upgraded" meat—that is, wholesale suppliers were labeling lower-grade meat as higher-grade meat, and charging A & P the higher price. Thus shoppers were getting less quality than they bargained and paid for. So the Agriculture Department did an audit, and discovered checks written by one of the suspected wholesalers to Joseph Fazio, an A & P meat buyer. These payments seemed to explain why Fazio accepted upgraded meat on behalf of the super-market chain. So Fazio was promptly fired after thirty-one years on the job.

Fazio's wife, naturally upset, wrote an angry letter to Shea, the executive vice-president, alleging that A & P meat buyers were still taking kickbacks from meat companies. At about the same time, Shea got another letter, anonymous, alleging the same thing. So he hired a private investigator to look into the matter. The investigator reported that nothing was wrong. Suspecting otherwise, Shea brought the letters to the D.A.'s office, where they were given to Nicholson and Montello.

In her letter to Shea, Mrs. Fazio had contended that practically the whole A & P meat-buying department was on the take, including the supervisors who had sacked her husband. Apparently she thought they fired Fazio because he was more honest than the rest, and thus seemed a threat to the system. The truth was, he had been the only one in the department dumb enough to take checks. Others were taking cash or goods, so they didn't get caught.

In June, 1964, after being assigned to investigate Mrs. Fazio's letter, Detectives Nicholson and Montello flew to Chicago. In room 192 of the Drake Hotel with jackhammers pounding in the background, they interviewed Joseph Fazio. They said A & P would "consider" giving him his job back if he'd admit criminal involvement in the payoff racket his wife had described. Fazio acknowledged taking a steady $100-a-week from the South Chicago Beef Company—he could hardly have denied it after the Agriculture Department found the canceled checks. But he said the money came from horse bets that he asked the boys at South Chicago to place for him. They always seemed to have inside dope about which horse was likely to win the race, he said. After much discussion, Nicholson finally cajoled him into a grudging admission that some of the money had been, well, "gratuities." And from then on, what Fazio had to say proved amazingly accurate.

Other meat buyers and executives at A & P were taking as much as $500 a week in cash and merchandise. The larger local packing companies would give color television sets. The smaller ones would give Polaroid cameras. There were also paid-up country club memberships and free trips for the whole family to the New York World's Fair, including airline tickets and hotel bills. A & P executives not only got free cars from meat dealers, but one meat dealer's brother, a mechanic, came around on request to give free repairs on the free cars. As for really big companies like Swift and Armour, Fazio said, they didn't "pay off as far as cash goes. They just take you out and wine you and dine you." Meanwhile, A & P's customers were dining on inferior grades of meat.

From Fazio, Nicholson and Montello got their first lesson in meat kickbacks. So-called "straight beef"—fresh-cut steaks, roasts, and chops—doesn't provide much kickback money unless there is very high volume or unless substantial upgrading is involved. The biggest kickback items are the so-called "specialty cuts," such as briskets, corned beef, and navels (which are ground into hamburger and sausage). As Fazio explained it,

"On straight beef you can't hit 'em too hard, 'cause there's not enough money in it. Most of them [the wholesalers] work a half to a quarter cent a pound [profit]. They can't kick back too much on that. But on the small stuff, navels, briskets," Fazio said, the price went up by six to eight cents a pound to account for bribes—or as he and Nicholson finally agreed to call them, "gratuities." Kickbacks can be bigger on specialty cuts because there is a tighter market, and because the substitution of upgraded, inferior quality meat is less noticeable.

Based on what Joseph Fazio told them, Nicholson and Montello began tailing A & P buyers in the New York area to secret lunch-time meetings with wholesale meat suppliers. Conversations were overheard. The cops learned that a supplier had sent $15,000 in U. S. savings bonds to the home of one A & P meat executive, Walter Kromholtz. When they faced him with this information, Kromholtz broke down and confessed that he was getting kickbacks from seven or eight suppliers, and that others at A & P were doing the same. He provided a list of givers and takers, and agreed to wear a hidden tape recorder in conversations with them so the cops could gather evidence. A considerable number of conversations with A & P men and with suppliers were successfully recorded before Walter Kromholtz decided he had had enough, locked himself in the garage and turned on the car engine. His wife and children found his body.

Most of the talk that was overheard among meat dealers, however, was not about kickbacks to the supermarket executives. A much bigger concern in the industry seemed to be something that Nicholson and Montello hadn't known about—extortion by the butchers' union. In fact, perhaps because 1964 was a contract renewal year, it seemed that whenever two meat executives got together the talk quickly turned to complaints about the bribes that had to be paid to union officers whenever a labor problem arose, and particularly at contract time.

It happened that Nat Lokietz's Merkel Meat Company had been working both sides of the street. Lokietz had been contributing at least $600 a month to the welfare of Walter Kromholtz and the A & P meat department to guarantee that Merkel products would be prominently displayed on the shelves of the giant supermarket chain. But Lokietz was also a prime mover in arranging the behind-the-scenes payoffs to the leaders of Local 174 of the butchers' union. That is why detectives Nicholson and Montello were spending their December days in a Queens basement watching the tape recorder revolve and listening to the conversations in Lokietz's office.

Despite all the evidence of corruption among meat company and supermarket executives, the prime targets of the investigation were now the three top leaders of Local 174—Frank Kissel, Harry Stubach (sometimes spelled "Stuback"), and Karl Muller. Corporate graft had been shoved into the wings and union corruption was brought center stage.

This turn of events didn't reflect any particular prejudice on the parts of

Nicholson or Montello or the district attorney's office. Rather, it, reflected the prejudice of the law, which consistently makes the theft of greater amounts of money by richer people a much less serious crime than the theft of smaller amounts of money by poorer people. The main reason for this is that the legislatures that make the laws are primarily composed of richer people. Thus the crime of commercial bribery, which the meat and supermarket executives were committing, was punishable by a maximum of ninety days in prison (later changed to one year)—a penalty that for all its gentleness is rarely imposed —while the potential punishment for labor union bribery was and is a more sobering seven years, and the penalty for extortion, which the leaders of Local 174 were committing, is a still more sobering fifteen years. Any reasonable cop would rather spend his time working on a case that will result in a fifteen-year sentence than working on a case that will result in a small fine and probation. It is just a fact of life that if you want to stay out of the hoosegow, you are better off stealing money while in the employ of the A & P than stealing it while in the employ of the Amalgamated Meat Cutters' union.

When they decided to plant their bug, Nicholson and Montello still didn't know that the Mafia itself was behind Merkel Meat. They did stop to learn that Merkel had been built up over the years by a family of German immigrants, and then had fallen on hard times under the management of recent generations. Eventually the company was sold to Williams-McWilliams Industries Inc., a Texas-based manufacturer of heavy construction equipment. Williams-McWilliams was looking to diversify. Evidently, it figured that Merkel's losses would provide immediate tax relief as an offset to the profitable construction equipment business, after which Merkel itself could be turned around through more efficient management. The problem at Merkel was the employees, many of whom were operating their own meat businesses on the side with Merkel merchandise. Hams, baloneys, and liverwursts were routinely being snuck out the back door and put on the market without a nickel's profit to Merkel, the manufacturer. Logically enough, Williams-McWilliams reckoned to fire the troublesome employees and straighten Merkel out. But they reckoned without Local 174 of the Amalgamated Meat Cutters' union, which wouldn't let them do it.

Pretty soon Williams-McWilliams sized up the situation. They had unwittingly put their diversification program in the hands of the shakedown artists at the New York butchers' union. Unwilling to pay the price for rehabilitating Merkel, Williams-McWilliams decided to get out of the meat business, and Merkel was sold to a corporation controlled by Nat Lokietz for $2 million. In a year's time Merkel proceded to undersell other provisioners and greatly expand its share of the market, lining up all the major supermarket chains including A & P. Union problems vanished, the result, it was later learned, of a $15,000 bribe.

The real story, however, had stayed secret. Now Nicholson and Montello heard it from Lokietz's own conversation, as he blindly poured history onto their tape recorder. It seemed that the Mafia, for whom the butchers' union local was merely a branch office, had sized up the situation along with Williams-McWilliams, and apparently had decided to put a man of its own choosing into Merkel. For all of its profitability problems, Merkel still had tremendous cash flow, selling millions of dollars of meat to supermarkets, butcher shops, delicatessans, and government institutions. For a mobster, the bottom line on a profit-and-loss statement comes a lot higher than it does for legitimate businessmen. To a mobster, many of the costs of doing business can simply be dispensed with by not paying bills, so that cash flow becomes the paramount consideration.

The particular gentleman who intervened in the Merkel case was Anthony "Tino" De Angelis, who was riding high on Wall Street and whose name was about to become a household word. He was the architect of what has become known as The Great Salad Oil Swindle, one of the biggest frauds in history. In the press reports, books, and legal cases concerning the salad oil swindle, numerous attempts were made to substantiate rumors that Tino—as he is known to all—was in the Mafia. Associations were established, but the conclusions were all tenuous. He has never appeared on the lists of Mafia members (or "organized crime figures") produced by Congressional investigations. He has flatly denied being a "front" for others in the salad oil swindle, and in its investigations the Government never established that he passed loot from the swindle on up any chain-of-command, such as to Mafia bosses. On the other hand, New York Police Department experts on the Mafia suspect that this is exactly what happened. They say they think Tino De Angelis is close to, or part of, the Mafia family headed by Joseph Bonanno. The precise answer, of course, will probably never be known to the public, but the eavesdropping tapes made by Detectives Nicholson and Montello in the Merkel case clearly add a whole new dimension to the De Angelis story.

Until a few years before, Tino had run a hog-butchering operation in New York's Fourteenth Street meat market, where he had done business off and on since the 1930s. What a lot of people still don't know is that Tino really is an expert pork butcher. Some say he's the best there is, a master judge of how to get the greatest amount of usable meat from an animal. To watch him in action in a boning room, you can easily believe it. If Tino had stuck to running a hog-cutting operation for a company that was completely owned and controlled by honest businessmen, he could have made the world a better place. But it wasn't in his nature.

By 1963, he had forsaken butchering and taken a corner on the international market for salad oil—or what the world thought was salad oil. Starting slowly, cleverly conning one Wall Street commodities house after another, Tino began trading in futures contracts and IOUs in ever increasing amounts. He completely outfoxed the American Express Company, which, in exchange for his storage fees, practically turned over to him its huge warehousing facility in Bayonne, New Jersey. Soon Tino had sold literally hundreds of millions of dollars of salad oil for future delivery, and the oil was guaranteed by American Express. According to some accounts, rumors that he had the Mafia behind him actually lured many legitimate investors into giving Tino their money. They figured he would always have the resources to pay them back. They didn't stop to think, though, that the way the Mafia got rich was by skipping out on its debts.

This was the situation in 1963 when Tino began talking business with Nat Lokietz, who was running a Fourteenth Street-area meat concern known as Eagle Brand Products. At this point, Merkel was still owned by Williams-McWilliams. The Mob evidently respected Lokietz, who had developed a reputation over the years for being able to sell hot dogs, baloneys, and hams with an improbably high water content. That he bribed his government inspectors was assumed. Now, Tino, a big public success, was trying to persuade Lokietz to expand. At this point only Tino, a few top employees and possibly some Mafia associates knew the big secret: those storage tanks in Bayonne, the ones the financiers were counting on, contained water and air. There was only enough salad oil to give visitors an occasional peek. It was one of the biggest swindles in American history. But Lokietz, like the financiers, didn't know this when Tino began trying to interest him in buying El Dorado, a meat company Tino owned.

Nicholson and Montello were listening not far away when Lokietz recounted the whole story to a friend over the telephone a year later: "I know Tino very well, and I'll say it on a stack of Bibles, he's one of the nicest guys on earth. He calls me up and says, 'I want you.'

" 'You want me for what?'

"He says, 'I want you to take over the El Dorado plant.' He says, 'We'll take Eagle [Lokietz's company] and throw it into El Dorado.'

"I says, 'But, Tino, I can't do that, because I owe a quarter of a million dollars. I can't just fold up Eagle and throw it into El Dorado.'

"He said, 'What are you worried about? I'll take care of it.'

"I says, 'You'll take care of what?'

" 'I'll take care of the quarter million dollars.'

" 'You take care of a quarter million dollars, you got yourself a boy.' "

Lokietz's lawyer scotched the deal, however, when he found out El Dorado was $7 million in debt, a figure that Tino had vastly understated. "So we left," Lokietz recounted, "and he calls me up a month later. He says, 'How would you like to own Merkel?'

"I said, 'I'd love it.'

"He says, 'You got it.' He was already dickering for Merkel and he was going to give it to us."

In the year between the time Tino made this offer and the day in early December 1964, when Lokietz was recounting it, the world had learned Tino's secret. His Allied Crude Vegetable Oil Company was bankrupted, and so was at least one large Wall Street commodities firm and the American Express warehousing subsidiary. The staggering losses, believed to exceed $400 million, had reverberated throughout the financial world. Tino had been indicted for fraud, and every company Tino was associated with was suffering. Lokietz noted that except for a twist of fate, Merkel would have been bankrupted along with the rest of Tino's holdings. At the closing of the Merkel deal, Lokietz had been required to make an $833,000-down-payment to Williams-McWilliams. Tino had been supposed to provide the money, but there was a last-second argument over legal details. Lokietz came up with his own lender—he didn't disclose who. The day of the closing, he recalled, "was the Saturday before the Monday this thing [the salad oil scandal] hit the papers. Now, ordinarily, he would have been my partner. 'Cause he was the guy that got me the thing. But I finished up all the details. At the last minute, Tino says if I come up with the 833, he don't want no bother with me. We would have been bankrupt."

As Nicholson and Montello listened, Lokietz told a number of callers and visitors how much he admired Tino's fraud with the phantom oil, and he speculated about how much money Tino had salted away. "I spoke to Tino yesterday," he told one person on the phone. "You know how much the take was? What do you think? How much do you think that grab bag was? Four thirty-eight. That's right. Half a billion dollars. That was the grab. And if he has five [stashed away]—if he has *three*—I'd like to be in that position. Packed up and ready to go to jail." (Tino served seven years of a twenty-year sentence, and went back for a while to what apparently was a legitimate hog-butchering operation. Soon, however, he was again soliciting credit on commodities purchases, and people who trusted him were again left millions of dollars poorer. Details are in Part Nine, Chapter Eight.)

The Tino De Angelis story was interesting, but it was not what Nicholson and Montello had bugged the office to hear. The name that the detectives were listening for most intently was that of Frank Kissel, the secretary-treasurer of butchers' Local 174 and its most powerful officer (as the secretary-treasurer is in many butchers' and Teamsters locals). Kissel was a close friend of the mobster Lorenzo "Chappie the Dude" Brescia, former bodyguard for Lucky Luciano. Brescia's brother Frank, himself never identified as a Mafia member or convicted of wrongdoing, was (and still is at this writing) on Local 174's payroll as a business agent. Kissel's name came up soon after the bug was installed, but not in the context the detectives expected.

Lokietz was commiserating with another meat dealer who stopped by his office. The other dealer complained that he was being shoved out of the processed meats and sausage market by the expanding empire of Harry R. "Buddy" White, Sr., who (with his son) owned White Packing Company—and still does.

"He's in Grand Union," Lokietz said disgustedly of White. "He was bumped from Grand Union five times. I pick up the phone to talk to the chief buyer there, he says to me, 'I would like to get Buddy White out of here

tomorrow. But my hands are tied.' He said orders come from headquarters."
And why? "He's gonna be Kissel's brother-in-law," Lokietz said with obvious
irritation. "Frank Kissel's son is marrying his [White's] sister-in-law." The
marriage seemed to seal the fate of White's meat competitors.

The Kissel wedding, apparently a social extravaganza, was a big topic of
conversation among Lokietz and his friends. "There isn't one person that
you've heard about in the meat industry that won't be there," Lokietz marveled. But his parting comment to the same visitor seemed to best sum up his
feelings about Frank Kissel: "Someday you're going to find him dead." There
was a pause. "Of a heart attack. And then everything will blow up."

The conversations in the Merkel office repeatedly shed light on the credit
conditions in the meat industry. After one phone call, Lokietz turned to
someone in the office and said, "That was [unintelligible name]. He had to get
the mortgage. He had to get the money. They threatened to kill him. He had
to get the money this quick."

Another time he talked about the problems of Bill Tynan, who owned Inter
City Provision Corp. "Tynan's in trouble," he said. "He owes real [unintelligi-
ble], about five hundred bananas. They don't let him out."

Talking about Mob loansharks one time, he told his junior partner Samuel
Goldman, "They own two-thirds of the garment district." Replied Goldman,
"I hear 15,000 percent some of these guys are paying."

On another occasion, Lokietz and a visitor to his office were speculating
about how a man they knew with few personal financial resources had just
taken over a packing company.

"You know," Lokietz said, "maybe [the company] is backed by this
bunch."

"Of course," the visitor said. "He has no money."

"So maybe there's financing behind him—the Mafia itself is backing him,"
Lokietz said.

"Most likely. Of course." The visitor observed that Mafia-backed houses
"can charge a penny or a penny and a half more" a pound and still make sales
in competition with other meat dealers. As an example, he cited a firm backed
by Tino that was "practically next door" and had "the same product" as a less
successful firm with cheaper prices.

The names of mobsters were frequently on Lokietz's lips. Once, Nicholson
and Montello heard him talking on the phone to Fritz Katz, another meat
dealer, and heard him exclaim, "Johnny Dio didn't take it, hey? . . . What
happened? . . . Really?" They couldn't hear Katz's responses, because they
were listening to a bug on Lokietz's office, not a tap on his phone. Lokietz
himself lapsed immediately into Yiddish. But they knew that John "Johnny
Dio" Dioguardi was a much-publicized member of the Lucchese Mafia family
and was believed responsible for the acid blinding of journalist Victor Riesel.
Dio's photograph, with a cigarette dangling from one corner of a vicious snarl
as he slugged a United Press photographer outside a Senate committee hearing

room, appeared on front pages all over the country because it so perfectly matched the average man's preconception of what a Mafia member ought to look like. In the 1960s Dio had gone heavily into the kosher meat business, where the huge frauds he perpetrated would result in his imprisonment. At this writing, his underlings are still behind some of the biggest kosher meat firms in the country, with distribution coast to coast (details are in Part Nine).

Then there was the name of Charles "Charlie Callahan" Anselmo, a loan shark with an arrest record for bookmaking and a close friend of Tino De Angelis's. Anselmo, then thirty-eight, had moved in on the meat business through a trucking operation he started—something mobsters can do easily because the Syndicate controls the Teamsters' union. Meat dealers who accepted Anselmo's generous offers of credit soon found that it wasn't like taking out a charge card at Sears. At least one dealer, Seymour Ehrlich, was forced to turn over control of his business to Anselmo. Now, operating as Triangle Meats, a brokerage concern, Anselmo was supplying Lokietz with a lot of the meat that went into Merkel products.

Perhaps these purchases from Anselmo were some kind of quid pro quo to the Mob. Tino had put Lokietz into Merkel to start with, and the deal may have specified where the meat was to come from. At any rate, Anselmo's name was mentioned a lot more reverently than Dio's was around Lokietz's office. A separate detective crew was sent out to tap Anselmo's phone.

"Charlie Anselmo," Lokietz was saying over his own phone November 23, as Nicholson and Montello listened to one side of the conversation through the bug in the room. "It seems that they sent me out a [unintelligable] and they picked it up. It so happens that the company it went to found dirty meat. So fourteen boxes were left behind. It seems that—you know—fucking Anselmo's got people taking all over."

"Taking" was the street word for bribery.

"I wanted to grab the meat," Lokietz went on. "I understand he had the [unintelligible] on 'em. I got the whole information, and as long as I know, [then] I'm guilty of that, don't you understand? . . . I had to send back a trailerload of meat. He's got to pay for it, he knows that. . . . We had to open the meat up, put it into tanks, get rid of the boxes. I still got meat downstairs, twenty thousand pounds. Somebody coming up tomorrow to open them up. . . . I talked to Mr. Callahan, I said, 'Look, Charlie . . . little by little, we're going to try to get rid of it. Little by little . . . Chock Full O' Nuts . . . Shop-Rite . . .'"

Dirty meat? What was going on? Moments later, Lokietz was on the phone with Herman Jukofsky, Merkel's plant manager and the son-in-law of Lokietz's junior partner, Samuel Goldman. "How much meat do you put in?" he asked Jukofsky. There was a pause, as if for an answer. "Eighty pounds meat and twenty pounds of that stinger meat?" he asked. "Seventy-five meat and twenty-five. . . . On the frankfurters, twenty-three. . . . What's his formula on the patties?"

He hung up and told someone in his office: "On the patties, we got eighty pounds of cow meat and twenty pounds of filler. That's the first batch. And you got 22½ percent fat. Then the next batch he did the same way and got 20 percent fat. And they made yesterday, 75% meat and twenty-five pounds of filler. It came out to 22 [percent], fat. And today he made seventy and thirty. On the frankfurters, about 75% meat . . . ."

Everybody knows that hot dogs and packaged meat patties often contain cereal and other fillers besides meat. But Lokietz seemed to be talking about something else. What was stinger meat?

Robert Nicholson was soon on his way to finding out, thanks to a chance investigation that was taking place coincidentally seven hundred miles away. A federal food inspector in Ohio—apparently one of those the Mafia hadn't bribed—walked into a meat warehouse and almost keeled over from the smell. He opened a box of boneless trimmings and handled the meat. He said later that he couldn't get the smell off his hands for two weeks. The meat was traced to a plant in Wisconsin that was licensed to process animal food for mink ranches and zoos. The Agriculture Department began questioning the Wisconsin processor about what his meat was doing stinking up Ohio. The processor quickly passed on warning of the investigation to the customer who had ordered the shipment, and many others like it: Charles Anselmo. For the record, Anselmo had claimed to represent east coast zoos.

Anselmo knew—as the Wisconsin processor must have known, too, and as Nicholson would eventually find out—that the meat was being held over in warehouses en route east, often treated with formaldehyde to get rid of the stench and discoloration, then repackaged for human use. Formaldehyde is the chemical that morticians use to preserve human bodies. It is also used as an insecticide, fungicide, and general disinfectant. Eating it can make you sick, but, toxicologists say, it won't really kill you in small doses—unless you have a heart condition, in which case it *can* kill you. Toxicologists also say that formaldehyde would be hard to trace in meat, even at dangerous levels, so that use of it could easily go undetected. The Mob certainly won't forego a lucrative business just because a few people have heart conditions. How many persons died, if any, because the meat in their liverwurst was treated with formaldehyde, and how many Mob-run meat plants may now be operating under the same system, can only be wondered at.

After the meat had been soaked in this toxic chemical, it was put in boxes and sealed with counterfeit Department of Agriculture stamps that said the meat had been inspected and approved for human consumption at the slaughterhouse of Hyplains Dressed Beef Company in Dodge City, Kansas. News of this would later distress Hyplains Dressed Beef Company, which had never heard of Charles Anselmo. Hyplains didn't even sell the kind of boneless trimmings Anselmo was bringing in. It sold whole beef carcasses, which required a different kind of stamp than the one Anselmo had arranged to have counterfeited. How Anselmo selected Hyplains's name to put on his phony stamps is a mystery.

It's no mystery, however, what Anselmo did when he heard from his Wisconsin supplier that the Agriculture Department was on their trail. Typical of mobsters in business, Anselmo simply couldn't accept the fact that a real businessman occasionally has to cut his losses. Anselmo wasn't going to let the forty thousand pounds go. As soon as he learned that his meat had been impounded in Ohio by the Department of Agriculture, he determined to steal it back under cover of night. He would bring it to his warehouse in New Jersey for whatever treatment and repackaging was necessary.

So Anselmo hired some men, who then broke into his Ohio warehouse at night, stole the meat from the Agriculture Department and hauled it away. This left the Agriculture Department befuddled. But then Nicholson and Montello overheard talk of dirty meat at the Merkel plant, and learned that Anselmo had been discussing plans for the Ohio theft over his tapped telephone. So the detectives began comparing notes with the federal inspection service. With Anselmo's own telephone description of where the stolen shipment was to be taken, and with a little help from their noses, the Agriculture inspectors zeroed in on a warehouse in Pittsburgh where Anselmo's meat lay waiting for the next leg of its journey. Nicholson and a partner boarded the first plane west. Montello stayed behind to keep his ear on the Merkel bug.

For nearly two days in late November, Nicholson and his partner sat in a cold car parked outside the freezer house where the meat was stored, waiting for action. From time to time they would get out and sniff. There was no doubt the meat was still there. Finally, on the morning of the second day, a truck pulled up and men began carrying the meat out of the warehouse and loading it—forty thousand pounds of stinking meat boxed in fifty-pound cartons.

"You could smell it a mile away," Nicholson later recalled.

Poised for a long drive, Nicholson and his partner began to follow the truck as it pulled out. The truck went three blocks, parked, and the driver went into a gin mill. The detectives, dog tired and cramped from so long in the car, parked and waited for him. It was after dark when the driver finally left the bar and returned to his truck. He drove three more blocks, parked again and went to sleep.

The detectives took turns sleeping through the night, in case the truck left. Finally, the next day, they followed the truck to a parking lot in New Jersey's heavily industrial Hudson County. The trailer was detached from the tractor and left behind as the tractor drove away. Some men came and loaded ice into the freezer truck as if preparing it for a long wait. Then they departed. Nicholson and his partner were exhausted. There was no one to relieve them, and it could be days before anyone came for the trailer. They took a chance and went home for a night's sleep. When they came back, the trailer was gone.

Nicholson returned dejectedly to Queens and the sounds of the Merkel bug. There were a lot of unanswered questions. What had happened to the vanished forty-thousand-pound shipment? If Anselmo was buying dirty meat, what was he using it for? Was this the meat he was selling to Lokietz for Merkel sausages? And if so, how were the federal meat inspectors letting it go through?

Was Lokietz paying them off?

In the very first conversation that Nicholson and Montello had taped November 17, 1964, Lokietz had said to a man on the phone, "You gonna be here when they do the inspection? Well, when you come down, I'll explain it to you. I know how to rub the monkey."

Additional conversations after Nicholson was back from Ohio made clear that there was about to be a big changeover in federal meat inspectors, and that Lokietz was plenty worried about it. For one thing, a rival meat company had closed, which would mean a change of assignments. And for another, the supervisor of inspectors was retiring and his replacement, a man named Johnson, was rumored to be a bulldog.

One of Lokietz's senior employees had worked for Swift & Company plants in the south, and was called in for his opinions. He said that inspectors were much rougher in the south.

"How do they get away with all that shit down there?" Lokietz asked.

"They don't," he was told. And the southerner warned him that the new supervisor had better not be the tough one mentioned in the rumors. "He'll kill us. He'll ruin us," the southerner said.

Then, on December 4, the Merkel crowd apparently found out that the Agriculture Department was querying Anselmo about the forty thousand pounds of impounded meat that had vanished. Lokietz and several other persons in the office sounded agitated, especially because of the coincidence of this new investigation with the pending arrival of Johnson, the new meat inspector.

"I always knew it had something fucked up on the scheme," Lokietz said. "Now, we get the [unintelligible] inspection. They're looking for Charlie Anselmo. They're liable to connect this other inspection with [unintelligible]."

Said someone else, "I know Bob Wilson will sit on it. It's gotta be higher than Bob." Wilson was an inspector who was later indicted (and acquitted at trial) on charges he took bribes to let Anselmo borrow his official inspection stamp.

"When are they going to start?" Lokietz asked. "Maybe I ought to tell Charlie to stay away from me. They're phony stamps. . . . What could they do to me? Johnson looks like he's heading for here, huh?"

"Looks that way."

"Could be rough," Lokietz said. "Well, he has a lot more ground to cover."

"He has a lot of territory," the other man agreed.

Then they began questioning a third man. Obviously, from his answers, he was a federal meat inspector. The inspector said he was fifty-seven years old and would retire at sixty on three-quarters pay. "That's not bad," Lokietz said. The inspector said his house was paid for and that he gave money to a woman who lived next door to have his evening meal ready for him when he got home. Then he began discussing Johnson.

"See, when they bring in a supervisor," the inspector said, "they'll bring in kind of a stranger. They go out and send this guy. They sent him down from Boston."

"How's [another inspector]?" Lokietz asked.

"He's all right."

"You can get along with [the inspector]?"

"Yeah."

"You can take care of [the inspector]?"

"I don't know."

"He don't squeal?"

"No."

"He's a regular guy. This Johnson would turn me in like that [Lokietz snaps his fingers]."

"That's right."

Most of what the detectives heard was mundane. There was constant order-taking for hams, liverwursts, and baloneys, dickering over prices, inquiries about the health of a friend who had just undergone surgery, and even Lokietz's futile attempts to teach a dog how to sit up. Nothing seemed to be evidence of butchers' union extortion, or even of the actual use of improper meat. But on December 10, the recorder began to fairly sizzle.

Suddenly there were sounds of a group of men bursting into Lokietz's office, talking excitedly so that their voices could scarcely be distinguished.

"I don't know. I couldn't tell a phony even if they turned it [over] to a laboratory. I'm not gonna get involved in it."

"No one can tell—not even [unintelligible]—unless you send it to a laboratory."

"When we were in Belgium during the Second World War there was a lot of horsemeat."

"Nobody ever checked this stuff from them . . . sent it to a lab?"

"Nope."

"From now on . . ."

"I'm a little worried."

"It can't do anything." That sounded like Lokietz.

"Yeah, but this could be publicized. You know what I mean?" That sounded like a meat inspector worried they might get caught.

"Don't worry about it," Lokietz said.

"But I don't want horsemeat. It could be publicized. There could be trouble. You better be careful. We're in the same boat."

"Good-by, Dave. Don't bug me. I'm gonna be careful," Lokietz said.

"It's for your own good."

Footsteps went away and a door closed. A phone was dialed and Lokietz's clearly identifiable voice said, "Did you get any meat from Anselmo? Good. Today? What'll you need, one load?" He hung up and said to someone else in the room, "This is the rip-off. Who could we trust on a [unintelligible]. The thing is, I don't want to pinpoint this too much."

He dialed the phone again. He was calling Charles Anselmo. "Hello. . . . Listen, who do you *think* it is? . . . Yeah. Is your wire clear? Not tapped? This meat in Jersey, you know why they're looking for it? We just got the report. On the Q.T. Is this horsemeat? Well, I'll tell you, I'm going to check this one out myself. I'm going to do it my own way in a private lab. But if it is, we can't have any part of this thing. The other thing I don't give a shit about. ["The other thing" Merkel was using, as Nicholson and Montello would learn later, was meat from diseased cows, a far greater actual health hazard than the horsemeat was.] But," Lokietz continued, "this thing here [the horsemeat] definitely cannot come into this house, if this is what it is. You better be honest with me."

Anselmo was stalling him off.

"I just *told* you what they're lookin' for," Lokietz exclaimed. "I got this on the Q.T. Let me know in a hurry. The part I didn't know before don't bother me, but this, any part of it, Charlie, I gotta check on this." Anselmo still wouldn't be specific about whether it was horsemeat.

In his frustration, Lokietz finally posed the question this way: "Does it moo?"

"Well," said Anselmo, as his voice was picked up elsewhere over a wiretap, "some of it moos, and some of it don't moo."

"Very bad, Charlie," Lokietz said. "What do you mean I don't need to worry? . . . They got your name, don't you understand? I got it today from [name omitted—a meat inspector]. He told me I'm all right, but they got you down flat. They got you down as Triangle. . . . Yeah, but you don't seem to want to understand one thing. If they pick it up here, it will be publicized. It's definitely gotta go out the window. You gotta make sure that it don't come in anymore. . . . You say 10 percent. I want it to be 100 percent. . . . This is supposed to be all—is this all, or just 10 percent? . . . You're not there to see it, huh? What's this meat that came in today? . . . Please, Charlie, the other one's gotta be stopped."

Lokietz hung up. Then Nicholson and Montello listened to the improbable spectacle of several meat company executives and a federal meat inspector trying to find out if anyone can prove that the product they are falsely labeling and selling is horsemeat. Diseased beef, which might cause serious illness or even kill people, that was a nuance they could handle. But horsemeat would capture the public's attention, and bad publicity could kill the business. Finally one of them volunteered that his son, Dennis, could "look it up in his library —he's had chemistry."

"You can't hold no money on a boy with a book," someone scoffed.

"No? If the book says you can tell the difference, you can tell the difference. By analysis."

At one point a secretary was told to make lunch, and apparently reached for the wrong package of hot dogs. "Oh, no, not those," came the horrified exclamations of men afraid to eat the product they were selling to the public.

"They didn't kill so many horses . . . just a couple . . . that's all . . . it's 10 percent," the voices said as they argued back and forth.

"The government is onto it," Lokietz declared. "Let's get rid of this meat. How much is left? You must have got a whole load. How long will it take us to clean up?"

He was told that it would take about a week before Merkel had stuffed enough sausages to exhaust the load that contained horsemeat. He decided to get rid of it faster by selling some off to other sausage processors.

"Call Philadelphia," Lokietz said. "Call every broker you know—what's his name, who was handling it for awhile in New Jersey. I'll call the guys I know."

"It's not a calamity, but I wouldn't bring any more of it in," someone said.

"That's exactly it. We'll finish up [what we have]."

"Listen," one man told Lokietz, "there's plenty of reason you don't sleep, but not for this."

"That's right," Lokietz responded. "They [apparently Anselmo and the Mafia meat sellers] save you over four hundred dollars a week. You got to be out of your fuckin' head [not to buy from them]."

Nicholson and Montello knew something Lokietz didn't. The Agriculture Department was a long way from Merkel's door. The federal inspectors had already had the meat in their hands twice, and lost it. The New York cops were the only real heat around. They leaned closer to the speaker of the tape recorder. Lokietz called Anselmo back. "Charlie, don't come in with any meat tomorrow. Because before you ship, I got to talk to you. Because I don't think —we're gonna finish up what we got, and that's it. Charlie, don't talk to me on the phone. You'll see me Monday morning."

For a businessman to cancel a deal with a Mafioso can be dangerous. When the deal blows up, the Mafioso starts to worry about what the businessman can testify to. Then the businessman has to worry also. Death is not an uncommon reward for potential witnesses. Lokietz began to reassure Anselmo. "I'm honest with you," he said. "The one thing about me is I'm always honest. I've got $5 million tied up here, so I'm not going to look for any problems."

Lokietz wanted horsemeat left out of future shipments, but not because of remorse. His mind was still on Johnson, the new supervisor of inspectors, and what Johnson's arrival would do to Merkel's profits. Clearly he intended to go on selling lousy Mafia meat, even if from now on none of it actually neighed. When a newcomer entered the office, Lokietz immediately demanded, "Any news on the Johnson situation?"

"Not a single solitary damn thing," he was told. "You better start putting on your thinking cap."

At this point, Lokietz and several associates hatched a plot so astounding that merely reading it, one might think they were kidding. But their voices, as recorded on tape, were in dead earnest.

"The only thing we can do here," Lokietz began, "seriously, have you got a smart cunt in the place—somebody that under pressure won't wilt? When he comes in—as of January 6, he's gonna be the supervisor. . . . What we gotta do—they could hurt us. We could go to jail for this. Find a cunt that won't wilt under pressure. He'll [Johnson] be the fall guy. We got to get a cunt, in the place, and rip her dress. And say that this guy Johnson tried to molest her. You got one from inside the place? You can't bring one in from outside, you know, 'cause then they'll know it's a plant. It's gotta be a girl in the place that's been here a long time."

Somebody started to describe a girl. Lokietz immediately demanded, "Is she Jewish?"

"No," he was told. "She's the most quiet, nice, respectable girl in the place."

"I don't care," Lokietz said. "She could make herself some money. We need her help. She's got to sidle up near him with a ripped dress on, very bad. You know, the guy's a psycho."

Others started to contribute to the plan. "She don't have to tell him what she's doing," said one. "She came into work and the guy molested her."

Another man with a deep, gruff voice began to disagree. "Does anybody know where he lives?" the man demanded. "Just get me his home address. That's all. Just get me his home address."

"Maybe when he walks, maybe somebody'll mug him," Lokietz offered.

"Knock him on the head," said the gruff man. "Just get me his home address. I may be able to work something out on the street."

Others spoke up that they preferred the plan with "this fucking broad."

The man with the gruff voice, who clearly considered getting rid of inspectors to be his area of expertise, said, "I'm thinking it over. Can she be my assistant?"

"Yeah," Lokietz replied.

"All right. Monday morning she reports to me."

The meeting broke up, and a little while later Lokietz got on the phone to Buddy White. White was the meat dealer whose success in Lokietz's opinion was attributable to his son's having married into the family of Frank Kissel, the head of the butchers' union.

"We've got a little problem," Lokietz told White. "This new supervisor . . . I don't care what it costs, but we gotta get this guy before he gets to the area. But you have a little connection more than I have. To you, they probably will listen. You get ahold of Kissel. We got to stretch out. Over the weekend, together, me, you, Trunz [Charles Trunz, another meat dealer], who else is into this? [He names two others.] Then we put some money together and get somebody to get him out of the area. Shit, it's gotta be done. We gotta work on it now. He's due in the sixth [of January]. This guy works nights. Yeah, he works night and day. . . . You're never sure of this guy. I tell you, you're gonna have problems. Me, you, Trunz, we got to get together with a few of these people. We got to do something to this guy. I spoke to Charlie Trunz last week. Well, he wasn't sure the guy was coming in. [Evidently, Trunz didn't like Lokietz's ideas.] I don't understand Charlie, but he's got as much to worry about as we have. Let's not dilly-dally about this thing. The idea is to reach a Congressman, or [Senator Jacob] Javits or somebody."

Buddy White's phone wasn't tapped, so Nicholson never learned what his response was. It would be interesting to find out, however—because at this writing, White still operates White Packing Company, a large processed meat concern in North Bergen, New Jersey. His in-law, Frank Kissel Jr., son of the union leader, runs Eat-Well Provisions, another large processed meat supplier, located in Jamaica, Queens, in the exact same quarters once occupied by Merkel Meat.

Back then, White was told by Lokietz exactly what had happened. The Agriculture Department was investigating Anselmo and Lokietz had found out about it in time—so he thought—to get rid of the evidence and escape detection. Lokietz started out by assuring White that not all government meat inspectors were as bad as Johnson. Some, he said, were "wonderful guys." For example, he said, "you can always find the truth of the matter out from [name omitted—a meat inspector assigned to Merkel]." The inspector, in Lokietz's words, "got a call from downtown" about a load of meat designated by the federal lot number 3490. The inspector had asked "if we're getting it."

"I says, 'Yup.'"

"He says, 'It's horsemeat.'"

Then, Lokietz said, the inspector "brings up a piece in a piece of paper. I'm no expert, but these hairs and all this shit. . . . Meat that's not inspected is one thing, but this is horsemeat."

There was a final bit of irony at the end of the Lokietz-White conversation, as Lokietz turned philosophical. "I wonder if government inspection is worthwhile having, believe it or not," he told White.

Nicholson and Montello were not amused. They now knew how Merkel had suddenly turned around its financial fortunes in the past year. The supplies Merkel was buying had come a lot cheaper than clean, inspected beef. Nicholson and Montello also knew how little chance there was of the Agriculture Department's intervening to stop Merkel. The inspectors were more loyal to Merkel than to the government. And Lokietz was arranging to get rid of the evidence and keep himself clean till the heat died down.

The detectives were in a terrible quandary. It was the end of the day, a Thursday, December 10, 1964. They knew where there was a load of illegal horsemeat and other uninspected meat—perhaps even the same stinking load Nicholson had followed east from Pittsburgh. They knew that the men who had this meat were eagerly stuffing it into various kinds of sausage for sale to the public through major supermarket and restaurant chains, and that these same men were desperately trying to unload the unused portion to any other wholesaler who would buy it—not because it was unfit for consumption, but because it was "hot" and might cause bad publicity.

Nicholson and Montello couldn't let this poisoning of the public go on. But on the other hand, if they raided the Merkel plant—if the police came in—then the cover would be blown on their entire operation. Their bugs and wiretaps would have to be disclosed prematurely. The evidence hadn't been developed to nail Frank Kissel and the other corrupt union leaders. There wasn't even enough explicit taped evidence to make payoff cases against particular meat inspectors. Anselmo's exact connections to the Mafia were still a mystery. But the detectives couldn't let Merkel send its sausages to market. Whatever they did might have repugnant consequences. And they would have to act fast.

2

The Merkel Scandal

It was early afternoon, the next day, Friday, December 11, 1964. Nat Lokietz, the boss, was out to lunch. But suddenly there were sounds of general consternation in the Merkel office. The words came in raspy shouts, loud enough to show panic, muted enough to show fear. Men from the city Markets Commission were raiding the cooler.

For several minutes, Nicholson heard the staff debating whether it would be illegal to flee. It was just the city commissioner, some argued, not the police. Before they could make up their minds, an agent found his way into the office and announced in a pompous voice of the sort that belongs to law enforcement bureaucrats, "I'm acting under orders of the Commissioner of Markets. In the freezer you have over fifty and up to one hundred frozen cartons of boneless beef from establishment 262 of Dodge City, Kansas [that was what Anselmo's counterfeit stamps said; actually, the meat had never been near Dodge City]. There's also a quantity of fifty-pound cartons in the same, uh, warehouse, marked, uh, trimming, beef trimmings. Same plant. Now we're gonna put a green seal on it and the Department of Agriculture's men, meat inspector, is gonna put a cease and desist order from removing it. And then take samples. But the City of New York is putting a green seal on the door, plus this certificate, which we'll give your firm here with instructions to hold that pending whatever action the commissioner—"

Finally Lokietz's son Sheldon, officially the assistant treasurer of the Merkel corporation, broke in with a simple question: "Can you tell me what this is all about?"

The pomposity of the agent quickly dissolved. "If I knew," he began, and then laughed as if embarrassed. "The green thing is an official seal," he said. "Now what they're after, I don't know. The meat inspector is the only one."

"Is anything wrong?" someone asked.

"They didn't tell me," the agent replied.

Nicholson could have been forgiven for smiling at that. Neither the agent in the Merkel office nor Markets Commissioner Albert Pacetta himself knew what the case was all about. But they were necessary tools in a clever plan.

As soon as Nicholson and his partner Louis Montello had overheard the previous afternoon that Merkel was grinding up horsemeat and other unapproved products to use in its sausages and hot dogs, they had taken the news to Al Scotti, the first assistant district attorney. Scotti could have told his detectives to get a warrant, raid the Merkel plant and arrest the operators. That would have guaranteed a lavish publicity coup for the D.A.'s office. But it also would have forced disclosure of the hidden bugs, and their purpose, and thus would have squelched the union bribery investigation, which was still far short of success. So Scotti gave the glory to the markets commissioner, Pacetta.

Nicholson was sent to tell Pacetta to check Merkel for contaminated meat. The markets commissioner wasn't told why the D.A.'s office was suspicious. The real cops didn't have enough respect for the markets commission to trust it with the information. And their disdain was justified. Two years later, Nicholson would have occasion to burst into a New York meat plant immediately after a team from the markets commission had inspected it and pronounced it in apple-pie order; Nicholson found not only large quantities of rancid beef and chicken and mislabeled meat patties, and large quantities of a toxic chemical used to make rancid meat appear fresh, but he also found 116 bales of hot gingham cloth that had been stolen in a truck hijacking two weeks before. Then the owner of the plant blatantly tried to bribe him, giving him some indication of why the markets commission men might have overlooked all the violations. In 1976, Pacetta himself would face an indictment charging he took a $35,000 bribe to influence him as a public official; apparently he beat the rap, though it's impossible to find out how, because all public record of the case was wiped out through a bizarre loophole in the New York criminal law that erases court histories in cases that don't reach conviction.

In the Merkel case, however, Scotti figured that Pacetta would have to act decisively because there was pressure from the D.A.'s office. The meat would be impounded and the publicity would kill Merkel. The crooks would assume that the Agriculture Department, after finding a shipment of bad meat destined for Anselmo, had tipped off the commissioner of markets. And that is exactly what they did assume. The union investigation stayed secret.

But if Pacetta's raiders were in the dark about what was really going on in the meat industry, Detective Nicholson still knew very little of it himself.

Soon after the commissioner's men had left the Merkel office, he began to hear evidence of new levels of criminality. He began to sense that the horsemeat scandal was not an isolated case of fraud, but part of a vast network of corruption.

While Nat Lokietz was out to lunch, the Merkel crowd sounded like a bungling, if disgusting, set of crooks—a real gang that couldn't shoot straight. Dennis, the schoolboy they had consulted, had issued his report, to the effect that a chemist can tell the difference between horsemeat and beef by the amount of protein in the meat. Most of those in the Merkel office were disinclined to believe this news, but Denny's father insisted that the boy had taken "double chemistry every term."

Lokietz's son wanted to know "What is the worst that can happen?" and was finally reassured that the markets commissioner couldn't do any more than issue fines.

Then Charles Anselmo called. He was told not to come over for at least an hour, by which time Nat would have returned, and then to phone from across the street first to make sure the coast was clear.

For a while the group talked about how to pass all the blame to their boss, Lokietz, if the investigators started asking more questions. Then Lokietz arrived. He quickly got the bad news and a lot of advice about what to do: "Tell them you bought the beef in good faith," someone said. "This could put us out of business, they have to protect us. . . ." "This would put five hundred men out of work. Call Bobby Kennedy and tell him," offered someone else.

Nat, however, didn't need advice. He started giving his own orders. "We bought it from a legitimate source. I don't want no publicity. This is what we gotta put the snafu on. I don't know who the fuck to call. They got an order here says we can't move it, but I want it out of here—this fucking meat."

He ordered a quick inventory of how much suspect meat was on the premises. If there was exactly a full truckload—forty thousand pounds—he would say it was the first such shipment received and that none of it had been used. But the report came back that some of the latest truckload had already been put into the grinder, as Lokietz himself had instructed the day before. There were 790 fifty-pound boxes left.

Lokietz's first idea was to sneak the 790 boxes of bad meat out of the cooler that night and replace it with 790 boxes of good meat. The commissioner's men had already taken samples of the Anselmo shipment, but Lokietz knew that the horsemeat was carefully hidden in the middle of the boxes. The samples, taken from the outside, would probably turn out to be 100 percent beef. A switch would assure that any future samples would also pass inspection. He began calling friends in the business, beginning with Buddy White, the meat dealer who had married into the family of the head of the butchers' union. But apparently he couldn't cajole White or the others into opening their warehouses to the illegal meat.

Lokietz decided that a more extreme measure had to be tried. Bribery. They had to—in Lokietz's words—"reach Pacetta." (That reassured Nicholson, if he had any doubts, that the Merkel crowd was totally unaware the district attorney's office was behind the horsemeat raid.) Names were mentioned of people who might know Pacetta. None of them satisfied Lokietz. "We gotta get higher," he insisted.

Then a voice popped up: "We gotta get Herbie. Herbie knows somebody, don't you understand?"

"Moe Steinman," another voice agreed.

At the time, the names meant nothing to Bob Nicholson. He didn't know that "Herbie" was Herbert Newman, the business front man for Moe Steinman. And he had never before heard the name of Moe Steinman, the corruption kingpin of the New York meat market, the man who kept the butchers' union and the supermarket executives paid off and in the service of their true masters, the Mafia. Over the next dozen years, Moe Steinman would become to Robert Nicholson almost as the white whale was to Captain Ahab. But this was the first mention to him of Steinman's name.

Someone tried to reach Herbie Newman on the phone to bring Steinman into the picture, but Newman was away. A message was left.

Then Lokietz began calling others. He told one friend (name unclear on the tape) that he had been out visiting a customer and had returned to find "five guys here from Commissioner Pacetta's office. . . . They were looking for horsemeat. . . . We don't sell any horsemeat. . . . Well, they had a tip that we bought 700 and some-odd boxes of meat yesterday, and it's horsemeat. . . . Yeah, I did buy 700-odd boxes. It was a steady deal, a steady supplier. . . . All I got down here is the 790 boxes that came in yesterday. . . . Providing that it is [horsemeat], I told them that I want this meat out of here, 'cause I don't want no publicity. I got five hundred people. I'll lose this whole business. I'll lose everything with it." Then he asked the friend to find "somebody who can reach Pacetta and tell him to lay off."

At that point, Lokietz's secretary piped up, "Watch what you say on the phone." It was good advice, but Lokietz didn't take it. "This guy Pacetta could give me a lot of publicity that Merkel uses horsemeat," he went on. "And we haven't used it at all. This meat is intact. I haven't used any of it at all. . . . I had no knowledge of this thing," he told the friend. Just one day after Nat Lokietz had assured Charlie Anselmo that "the one thing about me is, I'm always honest," he was telling bald-faced lies to a friend to try to con his way out of a jam. What the friend replied wasn't recorded.

Then one of the other men in the office reported back that he had gotten through on the telephone to Herbie Newman, Moe Steinman's front man, and that Newman had said, "I got a connection. I got a connection to Pacetta."

"What'd you tell him?" Lokietz asked.

"I told him I need a favor of the biggest importance. . . . He says, 'Call me back in fifteen minutes and I'll let you know what I can do. . . .' This is gonna cost you maybe ten bananas."

Meanwhile, Charlie Anselmo had called from across the street, as instructed, and was invited up to the office. He arrived, still trying to bluff his way through. "That's good meat—I mean that's beautiful coloring," Anselmo insisted. "I buy it the way it comes in."

"Where?" Lokietz demanded.

"That's what they been asking me all over," Anselmo replied. "The guy comes in and we give him cash."

Lokietz laughed out loud. "Oh, my God," he said.

"I pay cash, straight dough," Anselmo insisted. "I don't give no checks to nobody. . . . I don't know myself [where it comes from] to tell you the truth."

"Don't be a shmuck, Charlie," Lokietz told him.

"I don't know," Anselmo kept on. "I don't pay the truckman. It comes directly from the plants. A & R, R & A; I think it's A & R."

Someone in the office confirmed that the meat was brought in by R & A Trucking Company. Nat asked for a copy of the bill from one of the loads, and his aide said there was none—pointing out that Merkel, too, paid cash for the shipments.

"The meat was all right," Anselmo repeated. Then he got on the phone to Herbie Newman as Newman had asked. "It's very important," Anselmo told Newman. "Nat'll appreciate it to the end. . . . What do you think? . . . You sure the guy could do something? . . . Positive? . . . All right, I give you the jurisdiction to get hold of Moe. And let him reach Pacetta." Note the language. Moe Steinman's direct tie-in was to the Lucchese Mafia family through John Dioguardi, while Lokietz was tied in through Anselmo to the Bonanno family. Favors between families clearly had to be approved according to protocol. 'I give you the jurisdiction to get hold of Moe. And let him reach Pacetta,' Anselmo had said.

Then Lokietz took the phone and told Newman, "I'm in the clear. The only thing is—who, Moe?—well, the thing is, I'm in the clear. The only thing I'm worried about is, I don't want no publicity on this stuff. I never even knew about it. We buy meat from inspected houses. . . . We're helping Charlie out, buying a lot of meat from him."

Moe Steinman, however, couldn't be reached that day. It was a Friday in December, a time Steinman often prefers to be on a golf course in Florida. So Lokietz and Anselmo resumed laying plans for a transfer of meat out of the Merkel plant by truck that night, while still looking for a political fixer. And soon they found that fixer, who really did reach out with the big bribe. He was the very next man on Lokietz's list of potential octopuses: Tino De Angelis, the great salad oil swindler who had set Lokietz up in business in the first place.

Tino had plenty of political contacts, including Congressman Cornelius Gallagher of New Jersey. Gallagher's district included Bayonne, where Tino had his phony oil storage tanks. According to a *Life* magazine exposé, (which proved devastatingly accurate in every confirmable detail), Gallagher received $50,000 in legal fees from Tino during the time the salad oil swindle was in operation. After the scandal was exposed, *Life* reported, Gallagher engineered a $300,000 loan from a bank he was director of, to enable Tino's associates to start a tallow and lard business; that business then used phony merchandise receipts as collateral for big loans, just as Tino's salad oil business did. In 1977, a Congressional investigation into the Government of South Korea's bribery of American officials disclosed that as late as 1974, Congressman Gallagher had arranged for Korean money to finance a pork business, apparently Tino's.

When Nat Lokietz called, Tino proved he could handle New York City as well as New Jersey. "Listen," Lokietz asked him, "you got any connections in the City of New York? . . . It's a whole lot of things. Have you? . . . To put a cabosh on Pacetta. To reach Pacetta. Do you know anyone? . . . Hah? . . . And it could be done? . . . It's a very big problem. . . . This thing could spread like wildfire. . . . You're going to be in the motel? . . . When are you going to be home? . . . You think you got somebody, right? . . . Tino, see, I don't want to talk to you on the telephone. I'm not looking to fence with you. . . . We buy meat from Charlie Anselmo . . ."

Tino De Angelis said he knew a Brooklyn lawyer who was counsel to a state legislative committee. He said he'd check with the lawyer and call back. A little while later Tino reported that J. Louis "Jack" Fox, an eighteen-term Democratic state assemblyman from Far Rockaway, Queens, was the guy who got Pacetta his job. Pacetta was also from Queens. Tino said he had arranged an appointment for Lokietz that Sunday at Fox's house.

Tino De Angelis was never charged with this bribery plot. The D.A.'s lawyers eventually decided that without a tape recording, there was no proof of what De Angelis and Fox had actually said to each other. But Nicholson knew there had to be a bribery case against someone in what he'd heard. On Sunday, December 14, he followed Lokietz to Fox's house, then followed him back to his own house and heard him call his partner Sam Goldman on the telephone—which Nicholson had wiretapped. Lokietz told Goldman that Assemblyman Fox would take care of Pacetta for $10,000. The first half was to be paid the following morning at ten o'clock in Fox's law office. The bribe would be split fifty-fifty between Fox and Pacetta. Armed with a tape recording of that conversation between Lokietz and Goldman, Nicholson located a D.A., who located a judge, who granted a judicial order on Sunday evening to bug Fox's office. Nicholson and a partner spent all night picking the lock, installing the microphone and transmitter, then locating and setting up a listening post. With the first rays of dawn they sat back to wait for ten o'clock, and, they hoped, the sounds of an indictable crime.

They heard Lokietz ushered in, and heard Fox say he had talked to "my people on Saturday afternoon . . . Unless the complaint originated from some other department, like the commissioner of investigations, or unless it came through the mayor's office," Fox said, the matter could be taken care of to Lokietz's satisfaction. "If it originated within his [Pacetta's] office, that's one thing. If it originated outside his office, that's another thing. This is the whole crux of the matter," Fox said.

The explanation apparently satisfied Lokietz, for the sound of his response was the sound of shuffling currency. There was a lot of shuffling, after which Lokietz said, "You got twenty-five in the quarters and twenty-five in the fifties, right?"

There was a long pause, and then came the stupid, unthinking voice of greed, providing Bob Nicholson with the sure proof he needed. Assemblyman J. Lewis Fox said, "I'm short one."

Just in case the eavesdroppers had missed it, Nat Lokietz prompted Fox to repeat himself. "Hmmm?" Lokietz asked.

"Short one!" Fox insisted.

"Count it again!" Lokietz demanded, answering the detectives' prayers for explicit conversation. There was more shuffling of bills and the unmistakable voice of Jack Fox counting, "one . . . two . . . three . . ."

The $5,000 was all there. Fox then promised that two of his "friends" would meet Pacetta at the commissioner's office at 1 P.M. "These guys have much tighter connections, believe me," Fox said. "If he [Pacetta] can do it, he will do it . . . Let me assure you that he is not going to publicize it until he gets his laboratory report, and assuming that 1 percent [Lokietz's estimate at the beginning of the conversation], that it is [horsemeat], why should he publicize it?"

Despite having just paid a bribe, cash on the barrelhead, Lokietz felt it necessary to uphold his ethical reputation. "I'm an honorable businessman," he assured Fox. "I'll cut corners to make a living, but I won't do nothing crooked." He told Fox about all the money he had lost at his old pork business before Tino came along with the Merkel deal. "All these years we paid city gross taxes, city sales . . ." Apparently Lokietz felt entitled after all the taxes he had paid to throw a little diseased meat on the market.

Fox then described previous legal clients he had represented in the meat business while serving as an Assemblyman. He seemed to feel no pangs of conscience from having collected legal fees while sponsoring legislation in Albany that would help his clients.

Nat Lokietz was impressed. "If this thing blows over," he said, "we're looking for a noninspected plant. If you got good connections . . ."

Fox reassured his guest that things would be taken care of at one o'clock, and that Lokietz would be notified shortly thereafter. The two of them became chummy as Fox escorted Lokietz to the door, even willing to discourse in oblique terms about the Mafia.

"I've learned a lesson," Lokietz told Fox. "Ah, to do business with these guys doesn't pay. Fuck it."

No sooner was Lokietz out the door than Fox called in his secretary. "I have $5,000 in cash," he told her. "You don't have to count it. Just put it somewhere so that we know where it is." Then there were a couple of additional shuffles of paper. "There's forty-eight hundred left," he said, apparently having pocketed $200 in case he saw something he wanted. The secretary put the rest in a tin box in Fox's filing cabinet. He promised to call her from Albany to tell her what to do with it.

Robert Nicholson was euphoric. He had the perfect bribery case on tape. It was too late to bug Pacetta's office to see what would happen there, but it didn't matter. Nicholson had Assemblyman Fox by the balls.

The euphoria didn't last long, however. The laboratory report had come back on the meat samples that were taken from Merkel. The report said they were 100 percent pure beef. Nicholson was dumbfounded. He knew what was in those boxes. But how do you argue with science?

Nicholson sent Pacetta's men back to the sausage factory to take more samples of the contaminated meat. Once again the samples came back from the lab pronounced 100 percent pure beef, infuriating Nicholson. Determined to prove what he knew, Nicholson insisted on posing as a markets commission inspector and getting a third sample personally. Thinking over some comments he had heard Anselmo make on the tapped telephone, Nicholson decided that the horsemeat had intentionally been frozen into the center of the boxes of meat so that routine samples chipped away from the outside wouldn't tell the tale. So the detective went in with a band saw and sliced his way to the heart of the shipment. This time the laboratory confirmed the presence not only of horsemeat, but of another unidentifiable variety of animal flesh that was suspected of being kangaroo meat from Australia (a possible explanation for why Merkel's sales had increased by leaps and bounds).

With the new lab report, Nat Lokietz's worst dreams came true. On Friday, December 18, 1964, the headline that covered the top half of the front page of the New York *Daily News* read, "MOB FLOODS U.S. WITH FAKE BEEF—Find 20 Tons in Queens Plant." On page three was a picture of commissioner Pacetta standing grim-faced behind a table of raw meat, and a story that began, "Organized mobsters using a bootleg packing plant have deluged New York and other cities across the country with horsemeat and other 'unidentifiable' meat labeled as beef, Markets Commissioner Albert S. Pacetta disclosed late yesterday." Pacetta was quoted as saying, "The people from whom Merkel bought this stuff are in a mob-operated enterprise. Obviously there is a bootleg meat fabricating plant where they bone, chop and package this meat. The ring has facilities for transporting and storing its product. It has to be on a national scale."

But at the same time, Pacetta also began a subtle campaign to whitewash Merkel and Nat Lokietz. "Merkel officials told me the firm had been duped," Pacetta told reporters. "They said they did not suspect they were getting bad goods. They accepted the stamps as genuine."

Though the D.A.'s office had no evidence that he was even offered any of the bribe money from Assemblyman Fox, Pacetta would continue to defend Lokietz. Pacetta took steps almost immediately to counteract the supermarket order cancellations that had forced Merkel to announce a shutdown. On

Sunday, December 20, 1964, two days after the scandal broke and one week after Lokietz put in the fix with Fox, some two hundred butchers' and Teamsters' union pickets appeared outside Pacetta's home to protest the layoffs that would result from Merkel's closing. Pacetta welcomed representatives inside and half an hour later he emerged to read a statement to the pickets and the press emphasizing confidence in Merkel. "This is probably a one-shot situation," he said. "I know that none of this shipment, not even one ounce, has got out of Merkel's warehouse. . . . There is no reason to cancel orders because of this incident." The *Daily News* reported that Pacetta said his inspectors "got full cooperation at the [Merkel] plant and no effort was made to hide anything."

The next day, Monday, just three days after the horsemeat finding was made public, Pacetta again met with newsmen, this time in his office, and released a letter he was sending to all Merkel customers assuring them that they could buy from Merkel in safety. Calling the seized horsemeat "an isolated shipment," he said he was telling the Merkel customers that "not one single ounce of this adulterated meat was used in the Merkel products."

Pictured in the next morning's papers alongside Pacetta at the press conference was Karl Muller, president of Local 174 of the butchers' union, one of the three men the D.A.'s office was trying to nail for extortion. A Merkel shop steward was quoted as saying that the adulterated meat couldn't possibly have been used for franks, sausages, or bologna because of the careful quality control tests that Merkel always applied to shipments of meat as soon as they were defrosted.

And, finally, Merkel itself issued a press release saying that "as a result of Commissioner Pacetta's statement this morning, public confidence has been restored in our company and its products and we are getting a number of orders. In fact, many who canceled orders have restored them." Merkel said it was rehiring the five hundred furloughed employees.

Merkel's revival lasted only a month, however, because regardless of what Commissioner Pacetta said, Nicholson and Montello were weaving an ever-tightening noose around Nat Lokietz's neck. Now that the fake beef case had erupted in public under the aegis of the markets commission, the D.A.'s men could pursue it openly without blowing their still-secret bribery and extortion investigation.

The detectives found that adulterated meat had been coming in to Merkel regularly at least since December, 1963, shortly after Lokietz had taken the company over. The bad meat had been distributed not only to supermarkets, where it was often sold under the supermarket house brand name, but to other Merkel customers including the New York City school system, state hospitals and prisons, the Army, the Air Force, restaurants, and hotels. It had been shipped to Merkel from two primary sources, one in Wisconsin, the other in Utica, New York.

Both sources were ostensibly suppliers of food for mink ranches, and in early 1965 Nicholson found himself learning quite a lot about the care and feeding of minks. It seems that minks are exceedingly carnivorous, and if they are at all hungry they will eat each other. Since this cannibalism would tend to drastically reduce the output of coats, minks must constantly be fed meat while they grow. Fortunately for the mink ranchers, the minks aren't very particular about what kind of meat they eat, so the ranchers can get away with buying the dregs that could never be approved for human consumption even in the lowest grade of canned chili.

Long ago, mink ranchers found that their need for a constant supply of low-quality meat meshed perfectly with a problem that had always plagued dairy farmers: what to do with old, sick, sometimes already dead, cows—animals known in the trade as "downers," because they literally dropped down in the fields. So wherever there are a large number of dairy farms in an area, there tend to be mink ranches. And wherever there are mink ranches, there tends to be an abattoir specializing in processing downers.

Bob Nicholson found abattoris in Alma Center, Wisconsin, and Utica, New York, selling their product not only to local mink farmers, but also to Charles Anselmo. Prices were cheap because costs were minimal. Normally, a healthy cow that can pass inspection even for the lowest grade of beef will bring several hundred dollars to the owner. But the going rate for downers was as follows:

If the cow was already dead, you could take it away free.
If the cow was sick and couldn't walk—three dollars.
Sick but could walk—six dollars.

Did the mink food dealers know when they sold to Charley Anselmo that he was feeding people instead of minks? At the very least, they had reason to be suspicious. The detectives located one of the dealers by grabbing a truck driver who hauled the meat east from Wisconsin. The driver, Joseph Hasenberg of Jim Falls, Wisconsin, was given a deal that he wouldn't be prosecuted if he would help get the goods on the mink food supplier, Orland "Buster" Lea of Alma Center, who had a firm called Lea Brothers. Hasenberg agreed to wear a hidden microphone to a meeting with Lea, which Lea then set for an abandoned truck stop in Mosston, Wisconsin, late at night. All electronic eavesdropping must be carefully monitored to qualify as court evidence, and at the abandoned truck stop in Mosston there was only one place to monitor from. So while Hasenberg suckered Lea into describing his operation, a detective from the Wisconsin attorney general's office had to stuff himself into the trunk of Hasenberg's car for two hours.

The detective heard Lea try to argue that, as far as he knew, he was just selling food for eastern mink ranches and zoos. First he had sold to a man named Gasparello—who Nicholson later learned was Ralph Gasparello, a Boston meat dealer who sold meat to Anselmo. Later, Lea said, he had been approached by another friend of Anselmo's, who described himself as a mink rancher in Pennsylvania, and who announced that he "was the big fish from now on—he made the deals."

Hasenberg, the trucker, earned his escape from prosecution by steering Lea into several tacit admissions. Lea evidently knew that the meat was going on to New Jersey from Pennsylvania, and that the deals were handled with haste, surreption, and cash. There were no bills of lading or other records. He knew that higher than standard trucking rates were charged, and instructed Hasenberg not to tell the New York investigators about the higher trucking rates. And he admitted having met Charles Anselmo on a trip to New York after the hauling began—not only having met him, but having brought him sixty animal skins from Wisconsin as a present because Anselmo had said he wanted a fur coat for his wife.

The other major supplier for the fake beef operation was Dominick Gerace of Utica, an area known for dairy farming, mink ranching, and an extremely high per capita level of Mafia activity. Nicholson and Montello tracked down Gerace with information from the Anselmo wiretap and evidence picked up during the raid on Anselmo's warehouse. The District Attorney's office said in court that Gerace had a "powerful underworld leader in the upstate area" as "a silent partner" in his Party Packing Corp. Party Packing regularly sold mink food to Charles Anselmo, who didn't have any minks except for the skins Buster Lea brought him from Wisconsin.

Nicholson went to Utica and with local and state police staged a surprise raid on Gerace's three plants there. They turned up the horsemeat and sub-par beef one would expect to find at an animal food factory. But they also turned up something one would not expect to find: counterfeit U.S. Department of Agriculture stamps saying that meat had been inspected and approved for human consumption. Because of those counterfeit stamps, Gerace's companies had been able to sell animal food to Charlie Anselmo—and perhaps others— at substantially higher than animal food prices. Exact records weren't available because Anselmo always paid cash, but there were indications the shipments had been going on for more than a year, maybe much more. Anselmo may have been distributing mink food to other sausage makers even before Lokietz was established in Merkel.

Now the cops had a strong case against Lokietz, Anselmo, Lea, Gerace, a slew of truck drivers, and some of the other officers in the Merkel plant including Goldman. The next logical step was to call in the federal meat inspectors who were supposed to prevent this sort of thing from happening. Presumably they were the monkeys whom Norman Lokietz was adept at rubbing. Six inspectors assigned to the Merkel plant and the assistant inspector in charge of the meat protection program in the New York area were brought before a grand jury January 6, 1965, and asked to sign a waiver of immunity —a voluntary surrender of their Fifth Amendment rights against self-incrimination. Such waivers are routinely requested of government officials and other persons in high positions of public trust in matters concerning the conduct of their duties. The theory is that while the Fifth Amendment protects a person's right to stay out of jail until there is independent proof of a crime, nevertheless the amendment does not protect a person's right to stay in public office if he won't testify about his activities there.

All seven meat inspectors refused to sign the waiver. Among them was the man Nat Lokietz said had tipped him off to the pending investigation, allowing Lokietz to try to get rid of the evidence. District Attorney Hogan and his chief assistant, Al Scotti, fired off a report to the Department of Agriculture, expecting that the seven inspectors would be suspended from work and ultimately discharged if they still refused to talk. But the Agriculture Department kept all seven men on the job. The district attorneys were livid. "It couldn't happen in New York City if city employees were involved," Hogan fumed to a reporter. Replied the national director of the meat inspection service from his office in Washington, "We've no reason to take any action against the seven. I see no reason to question their right to make such a decision. We have found no wrongdoing. Absolutely none."

Since much of the criminal activity occurred outside New York, Hogan's office shared its information with the United States Attorney in Manhattan, Robert Morgenthau, who could prosecute interstate crimes. (In 1974, Morgenthau would be elected to the D.A.'s job that Hogan had held until his death earlier that year.) On February 23, 1965, Morgenthau's federal grand jury charged Anselmo, Herman Jukofsky (Lokietz's plant manager), Michael Sramowicz (a truck driver), and Madeline Bullard (the owner of a New Jersey trucking company) with interstate transportation of falsely labeled meat products. All but Jukofsky were also charged with conspiracy. At a press conference, according to the *New York Times*, Morgenthau credited the indictments entirely to the work of the Department of Agriculture and to an intensive investigation by his own federal grand jury.

A day later, on February 24, Hogan's state grand jury voted indictments accusing Anselmo of conspiring with Gerace and Lokietz to cause the transportation and sale of improper meat, and of six counts of actual sales.* Then the D.A.'s office turned to the seven suspected meat inspectors who had refused to waive immunity. The mere fact that Lokietz or a colleague boasted on tape of having bribed an inspector was insufficient evidence of bribery. To permit a conviction, the inspector's own voice had to appear on the tape making an incriminating statement. Identifying the various voices from the jumble in Lokietz's office was difficult indeed. But on March 10, 1965, inspec-

---

*Gerace could not be named as a defendant in the indictments, as were Anselmo and Lokietz, because his actions had taken place outside the jurisdiction of the Manhattan district attorney. He was named as an unindicted co-conspirator.

tors Hyman Erdwein and David Fellner were charged along with Anselmo and Lokietz in a conspiracy to obstruct justice by plotting to remove some meat from the Merkel plant the night after Commissioner Pacetta's men had seized it.

The D.A.'s team was anxious to throw everything it had at Lokietz. On April 20, 1965, the Walter Kromholtz tapes were dragged before the grand jury. Lokietz was indicted again, this time for the "corrupt influencing" of an A & P executive, by paying Kromholtz $150 a week to insure that A & P would stock Merkel products. The men who ran eight other wholesale meat concerns in New York were indicted along with Lokietz for also bribing Kromholtz, and the meat director for Dan's Supreme Supermarkets Inc., a local chain, was indicted for perjury before the grand jury.

In May, Morgenthau announced federal indictments against Anselmo, Gerace, and Buster Lea of Alma Center, Wisconsin, for transporting uninspected meat across state lines and for conspiring to do so. Later, more indictments came down, accusing Ralph Gasperello, the Boston animal food dealer who had first recruited Buster Lea for the horseburger business, and Thomas Barr, a big Wisconsin rancher and cattle buyer who hauled meat for Lea.

The month-by-month dribbling out of indictments indicates how much work went into the process. The evidence had been gathered the previous December, but it had to be examined painstakingly to locate each violation of the law the prosecutors could indict on, and to make sure that each indictment would stand up in court as drawn. By the time the indictments were handed down, the evidence compiled by Nicholson, Montello, and others certainly seemed overwhelming.

Nevertheless, the prosecutors did not want to go to trial. It is a popular misconception that lawyers love to march into court and nail an opponent's hide to the wall in dramatic fashion before judge and jury. In truth, most prosecutors see their job as avoiding the costs of a trial wherever possible by getting the defendant to plead guilty. The problem is, this requires a concession from the prosecutor—a bargain. In the purest form of plea bargaining, a defendant agrees to plead guilty to a portion of the charges he is facing, and in return, the prosecution agrees to drop the rest of the charges. Sometimes it can be a good bargain for society, if there is at least one charge the criminal pleads guilty to that carries a stiff penalty—a sentence that would deter others from the same kind of crime.

Often, however, prosecutors seek out guilty pleas at almost any cost. They may be lazy. They may be genuinely overburdened with other work and think they can't spare time for a trial. Unlike the detectives who investigate for them, most prosecutors aren't career men. They know they are soon moving on to private practice or politics, and sometimes become concerned with compiling a statistical record of nominal victories instead of with enforcing a real deterrent to crime. So a prosecutor may let a defendant plead to some minor infraction just to guarantee that the case will end with a conviction. The judge will then pass sentence based on the minor infraction.

Plea bargains can, of course, be a cover-up for bribery. Overt bribery is probably extremely rare among prosecutors these days. But there is a more subtle kind, seldom thought of as such. Either in the front or the back of the prosecutor's mind may be the idea that when he leaves office in a year or two, he will need the lucrative criminal defense or civil work, or the political support, that can be provided by associates of the man he is bargaining with.

Prosecutors argue that they have to allow a lot of bargain basement pleas because the cost of trials is great. But the cost of guilty pleas is often far greater; it just doesn't show up in dollars on an annual budget the way trials do. The cost of cheaply bargained guilty pleas is the perpetuation of crime.

The Merkel case is a perfect example. It involved dealing for testimony, the seamiest kind of plea bargaining. Deal making means giving a defendant lenient treatment not just to avoid trying him, but also because the defendant agrees to "cooperate"—to tattle on others. This is a deadly game. Sometimes it works, particularly against very well insulated Mafia bosses who have learned to evade taps and bugs, and who can't be nailed except by the testimony of associates. Even so, most of the really valuable witnesses from inside the Syndicate, like Joe Valachi and Vincent Teresa (and, more recently, Teamsters Union informer Ralph Picardo), have talked only after they began serving very stiff sentences.

More often, deal making has been a disasterous course for prosecutors who forget the old adage about a bird in the hand being worth two in the bush. Crooks and their lawyers are adept at cheating on these deals. When the time actually comes for their testimony against an associate, the testimony may be made intentionally vague or contradictory, so as to work in favor of the defense and produce an acquittal. And sometimes injustice is produced when a crook, delighting in his new-found role as the prosecutor's pal, leaps at the opportunity to start making up lies about all the people who have ever done him a bad turn.

It was this kind of deal making, even more than simple plea bargaining, that kindled the disgust Nicholson and Montello felt when they resigned from the police force after the close of their long meat investigation. That would come more than a decade later, as they realized that despite all they had done, most of the same people—Norman Lokietz, Charles Anselmo, Dominick Gerace, Tino De Angelis, and others—were still providing America with its meat. But the very first deals, back in 1965, the detectives went along with.

Seymour Ehrlich's deal was relatively easy on the conscience. Ehrlich was a meat dealer who had fallen into debt to Charlie Anselmo, and consequently had allowed Anselmo into his meat business. In the course of gathering evidence, Nicholson and Montello tracked Ehrlich down. They really didn't know that he was involved criminally in the dirty meat conspiracy, but they were certain from business records that Ehrlich knew about the conspiracy and would have some interesting stories to tell about the way Anselmo did business. Without a deal protecting him from criminal charges, he wasn't likely to talk. So they gave him one.

For his part, Ehrlich understood that he was deeply involved in a major scandal, and for all he knew the cops had him as tightly as they did the others. Moreover, Anselmo had cheated and muscled Ehrlich out of his meat business. So when the cops gave Ehrlich the chance to talk and avoid prosecution, he took it.

He told Nicholson and Montello the story of how he had inherited his father's meat business, Ehrlich & Company, and had turned it into a money-loser through poor management. Then had come Anselmo, the friendly truckman, with his easy credit and his offers of a couple of thousand dollars here and there to tide things over. And before long, Anselmo was demanding to be made a fifty-fifty partner. Ehrlich did not have to be threatened explicitly to get the point. Anselmo was going to get his money back and a lot more, and he wasn't going to let the law or the public's health restrict him in how he went about this.

Ehrlich's role was to permit his company to be used as a cover for a dirty meat operation. Whatever meat Anselmo brought in, Ehrlich would box it, label it "boneless beef," and bribe an inspector to stamp it (or to give Ehrlich access to the stamp so he could stamp the meat himself). What happened after that, Ehrlich wasn't supposed to ask.

Ehrlich was there when Anselmo met with Dominick Gerace, the Utica meat packer. Gerace owned Party Packing, which sold meat for human consumption, and another company, C & G, which sold animal food. Party Packing would have provided meat for Anselmo at going prices. C & G could deliver meat at prices more to Anselmo's liking, but that was because the meat was inedible. Sold through Party Packing, however, the same C & G meat could be made to appear fit for human consumption. And there would be only a partial mark-up. When Gerace explained this—in somewhat different language, of course—Anselmo replied, according to Ehrlich, "I don't care what it is we're getting. I don't care if it's downers or horse, so long as we don't get any complaints from the customers."

The business started small, and Ehrlich was able to mix the dirty meat in with greater quantities of good meat that was moving through his shop. The inspectors hardly noticed it. But by late 1963, Anselmo had begun shipping whole truckloads at a time, six to eight hundred cartons. Ehrlich said he had to make special arrangements with a federal inspector, paying up to $100 a day to "borrow" the inspector's stamping equipment. To keep the meat out of sight of other inspectors, sometimes Ehrlich would arrange for one of his trucks to meet an incoming Gerace truck tail-to-tail near the West Side Highway. The meat would be unloaded from the Gerace truck and on to the Ehrlich truck, with Ehrlich's men using the "borrowed" federal stamp to approve the meat as it was being passed over the tailgates. Then Ehrlich's (really Anselmo's) truck would move it directly to Merkel or wherever else it was going.

At first they split the income fifty-fifty as Anselmo had promised. Then Anselmo began to ask himself the question that all mobsters in "legitimate" business ultimately ask themselves: Why give up the other 50 percent? So Anselmo announced early in 1964 that from now on, Ehrlich wasn't a partner any longer. Ehrlich would get one and a quarter cents commission for every pound of meat he obtained a federal inspection stamp for, and an additional penny and a quarter for meat Ehrlich sold on his own. No percentages. By mid-year, Anselmo decided that even this arrangement was too generous. He cut the commission to half a cent a pound. Ehrlich said he couldn't take the risk for so little money. "Well, then, you can forget the deal," Anselmo told him. "I'll see that inspector myself. I'll make my own arrangements."

So Ehrlich's business was now in the hands of Anselmo, lock, stock, and braunschweiger. But Ehrlich had another business to fall back on—and when Nicholson and Montello learned what it was, they cringed. In the spring of 1964, Seymour Ehrlich, Charlie Anselmo's front man in the meat brokerage business, had been awarded a major restaurant concession at the New York World's Fair. And sure enough, the big mover had been—hamburgers. What was in those hamburgers, and how many World's Fair visitors got sick eating them, Ehrlich apparently didn't want to know, and no one else would ever find out.

With Ehrlich in tow, the D.A.'s office would certainly seem to have had the Merkel Meat case pretty well wrapped up. But two more deals were made. First, Gerace came in to Morgenthau, the federal prosecutor, and offered to give information against Anselmo. It is hard to believe that more information against Anselmo was needed, or that Gerace's offer was sufficient evidence of his atonement to merit grace. Nevertheless, for some reason—perhaps a baseless fear that the Anselmo case might be lost without one more eyewitness—the prosecutors took Gerace up on it. Not only was Gerace rewarded by the government's not recommending prison time for him, he was not even required to give information against his upstate godfathers, none of whom was ever prosecuted in the case. Their interests in the meat business in Utica survived intact. Anselmo was left holding the bag. The Mafia family he was believed to be connected to was in a period of decline, which may have had something to do with this. Anselmo's believed overlord, Joseph Bonnano, had been forced from his New York power base, while the family of Stefano Magaddino, which ruled upstate, was on the rise. When Gerace freely offered his testimony against Anselmo, it may well have been with the Mafia's blessing in an effort to cut its losses. We can't really know.

After Ehrlich and Gerace had been dealt with, there was still another test. Despite their commanding position in the Merkel horsemeat case, Nicholson and Montello still didn't have the information they had been seeking when the horsemeat case fell into their laps. They still didn't have a word of usable evidence against Frank Kissel, Karl Muller, or Harry Stubach, the butchers' union leaders. They had indictments pending against eight wholesale meat company executives for bribing the A & P. All eight executives probably knew something about bribing the union, too, since it was all part of the same system. If the executives would testify, then they could break the case against the union. But seven of the eight were unlikely to cooperate for the simple reason that they were unlikely to suffer if they didn't cooperate. Rarely, if ever, does a business executive go to jail for commercial bribery; the maximum fines are relatively small, and often are taken out of business funds eventually.

One of the eight, however, had real reason to quake. He was Norman Lokietz, and he faced numerous charges resulting from the sale of horsemeat and diseased beef, all soaked in toxic chemicals. Lokietz certainly would be susceptible to a deal if the cops wanted to propose it. But how could anyone in conscience offer leniency to Nat Lokietz—the author of a despicable crime against whom the evidence was overwhelming? Somehow, the D. A.'s men resolved whatever problems they had with their consciences.

The law made it easy for them. Although one could reasonably assume that people had died from Lokietz's activity, he couldn't be charged with homicide or manslaughter. There was not even a statute on the books regarding reckless endangerment of health—even though it was the health of millions. Lokietz's crime went under such innocuous headings as transporting or selling mis-branded or falsely labeled meat, and conspiracy to do so—misdemeanors with a maximum penalty of one year in jail.

The charges were numerous, but judges rarely make sentences run con-secutively, even on multiple-count convictions. Ironically, the toughest threats the law had against Lokietz were a possible indictment for perjury—lying to the grand jury the first time he was called in (he didn't know there were tape recordings to prove him wrong)—and for bribery of J. Lewis Fox, a public official. These crimes carry penalties of up to seven years. That was still nothing compared to the extortion term of fifteen years that might be pinned on the union leaders if evidence was forthcoming. Besides, pressing the perjury and bribery cases would require disclosing the wiretaps, which were still secret. And there was one more factor. The criminal plotting in the Merkel office had seemed to encompass much more than just bribery of union officials. The Mafia was obviously heavily involved in the meat industry. Lokietz might be able to deliver targets much bigger than even Frank Kissel. If names like Johnny Dio and Charlie Anselmo were on Lokietz's lips, who knew what cases he might be able to make?

So Nat Lokietz was called in. If he'd talk, at least about the Merkel deal and union bribery, and maybe throw in a meat inspector or two, then Lokietz, the mass poisoner, would get a recommendation of leniency. Nobody could guarantee that the judge would give it to him, but a prosecutor would be up there pumping. Besides, the charges were only misdemeanors, and no other charges would be pressed, so his exposure would be limited.

Lokietz agreed to plead guilty. But he still refused to talk, even about his colleagues who were obviously involved in the Merkel scandal. It was one thing to plead guilty after being caught red-handed; it was another to testify against well-connected men like Charlie Anselmo. Then the D.A.'s office played its trump card; Lokietz's son, Sheldon, would be indicted, too. Only then did Nat Lokietz agree to a deal, and it provided that Sheldon would never see the inside of a cell.

A deal, however, meant that the D.A. had to inform Morgenthau's federal office, which also had charges pending against Anselmo, and which would have to consent to whatever was arranged. When the FBI insisted on interviewing Lokietz, Nicholson became leery. Few civilians realize the bitterness that other law enforcement agencies often feel toward the FBI. Despite the bureau's official contention that it is there to help other law enforcement agencies make cases—which it frequently does—the other agencies often believe, and with good reason, that the FBI is out to *steal* cases. The bureau, it is said, only works on prosecutions it can claim credit for. Over and over, rival lawmen across the country complain in the same metaphor that "communications with the FBI is a one-way street." They say they give the FBI information, but they never get any back. Detective Nicholson liked to use the one-way street metaphor himself, especially after the events of 1965.

Morgenthau's office and the FBI said they needed to talk to Lokietz before they could prosecute the corrupt federal meat inspectors. Their reasoning went this way: Federal courts prohibited the use of wiretap evidence (prior to 1968). Lokietz had been wiretapped extensively. So Nicholson and his men would inevitably use the results of the wiretaps to elicit Lokietz's story, and thus his testimony might be poisoned as evidence in federal court. But if the FBI talked to Lokietz first, without benefit of the wiretap information, Lokietz's testimony in the federal cases would remain pure.

What worried the D.A.'s squad was that the FBI had been informed that Lokietz knew a lot about labor racketeering and the Mafia. That, of course, was the whole reason for the deal. As the D.A.'s men remember it, the FBI agents and Justice Department lawyers "swore up and down" that they wouldn't try to take the racketeering cases away from the District Attorney's office.

Lokietz spent two weeks with the federal agents—a suspiciously long time to talk only about government meat inspectors. But the FBI agents assured Nicholson afterwards, he recalls, that Lokietz hadn't been asked for and hadn't given any information about other payoffs.

Then Nicholson, Montello, and Assistant District Attorney Frank Connelly, who was assigned to the case, began questioning the witness. To their utter amazement, he denied knowing about labor racketeering or any bribery beyond the known outlines of the Merkel scandal. Over and over they questioned him, and he stuck to his story. Finally, after several days, he tired of his own lies. "You guys tell each other everything anyway," he broke down. "I might as well tell you. I told the FBI about the fifteen thousand dollars I paid to the butchers' union."*

The stunned questioners began a whole new series of interviews. It would lead to what became known as "The Kissel Case." Nicholson and Montello wanted to start immediately pursuing Lokietz's information—tailing suspects, throwing up wiretaps. But it would be more than a year before they could do so. There were too many outstanding charges still open on the Merkel scandal.

One peril of deal making is that it snowballs. Once a deal has been offered to a prominent figure in a case, it becomes difficult to refuse the same deal to co-defendants who are less culpable. So Sam Goldman, Lokietz's partner, and Goldman's son-in-law, Herman Jukofsky, the plant manager, were allowed in under the umbrella of prosecutorial grace. So were Michael Sramowicz, the truck driver, and Madeline Bullard, the trucking company owner, who offered to testify against Anselmo.

Lokietz, Goldman, and Jukofsky gave up a meat inspector, as requested. But now, when it counted, they didn't mention the inspector who Lokietz earlier said had tipped him off to the investigation. Lokietz, Goldman, and Jukofsky now told the prosecutors that they had bribed an inspector named Robert Wilson, who had been assigned to Eagle Brand—Lokietz's old company—several years earlier. They said Wilson had been bribed from way back, and that it took only $25 to $100—depending on the size of the shipment— to get him to turn his head while the bribers used his inspection stamp on whatever unstamped meat Charlie Anselmo brought to town.

With this, the plea bargaining and deal making stopped. The remaining defendants were waiting for the opening trial to see exactly what evidence the prosecution had compiled. Thus 1966 dawned, with the curious teams aligned. On the prosecution side were Lokietz and the others who processed the meat, Sramowicz and Bullard who trucked it, and Dominick Gerace who sold it, standing shoulder to shoulder with Bob Nicholson, Lou Montello, Nicholas Scopetta (the prosecutor assigned to try the cases for the D.A.'s office), and Robert Morgenthau (the federal attorney, later district attorney). On the other side, there were Charles Anselmo, Buster Lea, Lea's cattle ranching pal Thomas Barr, Ralph Gasparello (who originally approached Lea to supply dirty meat for Anselmo), Robert Dvorin (who ran an animal food plant in Elizabeth, New Jersey) and the three meat inspectors, Fellner, Erdwein, and Wilson.

The first scheduled trial was of Charles Anselmo, the biggest target on the list. The case was called May 6, 1966. It was over by lunchtime.

As soon as Anselmo heard Prosecutor Scopetta's opening description of

---

*Connelly, Nicholson, and Montello all recall the events this way. The FBI agents involved couldn't be identified.

the evidence and heard that Lokietz, Gerace, Goldman, Ehrlich, and several employees of Anselmo's refrigerated warehouse had become state's witnesses, he began to huddle with his lawyer. Together, they went to Scopetta and agreed to call off the trial. Anselmo pleaded guilty to one count from each of two indictments, for which Scopetta agreed to drop all the other counts of the three state indictments pending against him. The counts all carried a maximum penalty of one year in prison, and Scopetta figured that a judge wouldn't string together more than two one-year sentences anyway. The federal prosecutor agreed to a settlement on similar terms. The most society was going to get out of Anselmo was two years.

It wasn't even that much. On June 2, 1966, they all trooped back to court for sentencing. Anselmo's lawyer opened the proceedings by revealing that his client was really a fine man. Anselmo was married, had four kids, and owned the home where they all lived. Never mind that he risked mass poisoning for profit. True, Anselmo had a prior conviction, but that was eight years ago and it was just for gambling. Besides, the lawyer said, Anselmo had "ceased the meat business," and so was no longer a threat. He had shown "the necessary contrition . . . as is evidenced by the fact that presently he is in this construction business as president [of two corporations], erecting homes." (Heaven help those who have sought shelter from the elements in a house built by Charles Anselmo!)

Scopetta, relying on what Nicholson and Montello had learned, told the judge that Anselmo had sold Merkel more than one million pounds of meat for more than $500,000 in 1964 alone. Contradicting markets commissioner Pacetta, Scopetta said, "All of that meat was eventually processed to stores and supermarkets in New York City and we can assume it was consumed. It was sold as edible meat." Moreover, he noted, Anselmo—despite only one prior conviction—had been arrested half a dozen times in connection with organized crime activities. "He brought a background of loan sharking and bookmaking to the meat business," Scopetta said, "and utilized those means to work his way into the meat business."

Judge Edward R. Dudley responded with the requisite pomposity. "The interest of the people is paramount in cases of this kind," Judge Dudley said. "The interests of the city, of our community, can only be protected if the sentence is both of a punitive and deterrent nature." He then proceeded to award Anselmo a sentence that was neither punitive nor deterrent: a year on the conspiracy count he pleaded to, and six months on the substantive count —a total of eighteen months. A month later, on July 13, 1966, Anselmo appeared before Federal Judge Edmund L. Palmieri, pleaded guilty to two of the federal counts facing him, and got a duplicate eighteen-month sentence that could be served concurrently with the state sentence.

Anselmo entered the federal correctional institution at Danbury, Connecticut, on August 24, 1967, and was paroled four and a half months later on January 16, 1968. A year later he was freed from all supervision, his debt to society paid. He never served time in state prison. As for the contrition he showed by leaving the meat business, Anselmo was scarcely out of the hoosegow before he had set up a new meat brokerage in the Fourteenth Street market, just a few doors from where he had done business before. The new brokerage was called Kaylo Trading Company, and at this writing it is still there. Mr. Anselmo wasn't in when I called, but a woman offered to take a message for him.

After the Anselmo proceedings, most of the other defendants sized up their situation pretty quickly. On the one hand, the government's evidence was overwhelming. On the other hand, nothing serious would happen to them if they were convicted.

On June 15, 1966, Ralph Gasparello pleaded guilty to two counts of unlawfully transporting uninspected meat. Federal Judge Thomas F. Murphy gave him an eighteen-month sentence and then suspended it. Instead of jail, Gasparello went on probation for one year. He walked right out of court and back to his business, a free man.

Later, Robert Dvorin, the animal food manufacturer whose plant Anselmo had used in New Jersey, pleaded guilty to transporting horsemeat not conspicuously labeled. Judge Murphy sentenced him to eighteen months in prison and didn't suspend it. Why his treatment was more severe than Gasparello's is not clear. At any rate, he actually served only eight and a half months before parole.

On August 15, 1966, Buster Lea and Thomas Barr pleaded guilty to two counts of illegally transporting uninspected meat. The plea was entered under federal Rule 20, which allowed them to be sentenced in their home district in Madison, Wisconsin, instead of in New York. Federal Judge James E. Doyle sentenced Lea to jail for six months. He was released in less than five. Barr got one month. They stayed on probation for two years. According to Lee Rubens, the chief probation officer in Madison, "Both remained in their respective businesses and were operating so" when their probation was completed.

On September 28, 1966, Norman Lokietz pleaded guilty in state court to one count of conspiracy. As promised, prosecutor Scopetta was there to praise his cooperation, and Judge Mitchell Schweitzer gave him a six-month sentence with the added courtesy of a two-week grace period to prepare his affairs before turning himself in. Merkel, of course, had closed, but upon his release Lokietz went immediately to work buying and selling meats under the name Regal Provisions Company. (His meat career in the 1970s will be recounted in a later chapter.)

Lokietz's partner Sam Goldman pleaded guilty to second degree perjury for having denied to the grand jury back in December, 1964, that he had discussed uninspected meat with Nat Lokietz. Goldman got a six-month suspended sentence. He never spent a night in jail. He went quickly to work selling flexible packaging materials to the New York meat industry.

On November 18, 1966, Dominick Gerace was allowed to Rule 20-himself to Albany, where James Foley, then and now the chief federal judge of the Northern District of New York, put him on probation. He went right back to his meat packing plants without seeing a jail cell. In 1977, Party Packing was still in operation and its phone number was the same one listed for Dominick Gerace personally. A call to the number was answered by a male who said Gerace wasn't in charge any more. When asked who was, he said it was "confidential information." With or without Gerace the Mafia retained its interests elsewhere in the meat business in Utica.

Charges against Sramowicz and Bullard, who trucked the meat, and Jukofsky, who helped mislabel and move it, were dropped as promised. This was their reward for having agreed to supply overkill testimony against Anselmo, who almost certainly could have been convicted on other evidence, and who served only four and a half months anyway. Sramowicz and Bullard presumably went on about their business. Jukofsky found a job keeping books for the Wilbur W. Whitney Packing Company.

That left the three meat inspectors. On November 22, 1966, Robert Wilson went to trial insisting that he had never taken a bribe and that he had been assigned to work on the docks during 1964 so that his schedule wouldn't have allowed him to rent his inspection stamps to Ehrlich as charged. Lokietz, Goldman, Ehrlich, and Jukofsky—the men who had fingered Wilson in the first place—all testified against him as they had promised to do in exchange for the lenient treatment they received. Their stories were all contradictory, confused, and unpersuasive.

Nowhere did the prosecution introduce into evidence the tape recording of the spontaneous conversation in the Merkel office right after the horsemeat investigation was discovered: "I know Bob Wilson will sit on it. It's gotta be higher than Bob." The tape recordings were still being kept secret because of the union investigation.

The defense offered evidence that back in 1960, Wilson had filed departmental charges against Lokietz's Eagle Brand operation for putting too much water in the hams. Lokietz had solved the problem by switching his ham watering operation to another plant, where Wilson wasn't assigned to inspect. Wilson testified that Lokietz had cursed him and threatened to get revenge. "Thus hangs the tale and the case," the defense said in its summary. "Credibility. Who do you believe?" The jury believed Wilson and acquitted him.

Erdwein and Fellner, the other two meat inspectors who had been charged, hired a clever lawyer who managed to keep delaying the case. It was still untried on June 12, 1967, when the U. S. Supreme Court ruled, on a plea from another man, that New York State's electronic eavesdropping policies amounted to an unreasonable search and seizure. The court said the law permitting eavesdropping did not require sufficient grounds for a warrant, and that the placing of the bug involved an illegal entry onto private property. Therefore, under the Fourth Amendment to the Constitution, the courts from now on would not be allowed to hear evidence derived from leads that were encountered through such eavesdropping. That pretty well destroyed the case against the meat inspectors.

Prosecutor Scopetta wrote the judge recommending a dismissal of the indictment. He could only console himself that the eavesdropping decision apparently was not made retroactive. The prior convictions and guilty pleas still stood. The Constitution thus permitted Lokietz, Anselmo, and the others to go to jail based on eavesdropping evidence presented prior to June 12, 1967, but did not permit Erdwein and Fellner to go to jail because their lawyer delayed proceedings until after June 12. This is the kind of absurdity that leads some detectives and journalists to have less respect for the majesty of the law than some lawyers do.

All the meat inspectors who were at one time or another called into suspicion because of the horsemeat scandal either kept their jobs or qualified for their pensions. Apparently no meat inspector was penalized in the matter, though Erdwein and Fellner were suspended without pay while awaiting trial.

The other seven meat company executives (besides Lokietz) accused of bribing Walter Kromholtz, the A & P meat buyer, received mere fines.

Nicholson and his men came up with a clever ploy to trap J. Louis Fox, the long-time Queens assemblyman whom Lokietz had paid in order to "reach" Pacetta, the markets commissioner. Nicholson had the whole bribe recorded on tape, of course, but back in 1965 he didn't want the existence of the tape disclosed.

Fox was called before a grand jury and was asked a series of questions that would force him either to admit the bribery or commit perjury. He chose the deception, so on January 19, 1966, with Lokietz and the others ready to testify against him, Fox was indicted—not for bribery, but for perjury. That year he was defeated for renomination for the first time in his several decades in office. On June 18, 1968, he pleaded guilty, and on October 14 Judge Joseph A. Sarafite sentenced him to probation for one year. Now, a decade later, it appears that the district attorney's office may have violated Fox's constitutional rights. His conviction clearly was based on evidence drawn from a bugging that the Supreme Court has ruled was illegal. If detectives hadn't listened to the bug, they wouldn't have asked Lokietz about the bribery incident. But if Robert Nicholson has any regrets about his thirteen years on the meat investigation, convicting J. Louis Fox probably is not one of them.

Pacetta himself went on to be indicted for grand larceny and bribery. A judge ordered his acquittal in 1976 on the grand larceny charge, which involved $10,000 in allegedly false insurance claims in connection with an automobile accident. The bribery charge, however, said he took $35,000 from a doctor to influence his vote as a member of the New York State Human Rights Appeals Board, to which he had been appointed. That, too, was scheduled for trial in 1976. Apparently, he beat the rap, but under a strange provision of New York State law, no one can find out what happened. I called William Vanson, the court clerk, to ask about it and was told, "There is no public record of that case. I recall reading something in the paper about it, but officially there is no record of this case."

Thus did law enforcement clean up the meat racket. Convictions were had, but no punishment was imposed that would discourage a basically greedy man from doing it again. Businesses were closed, but the men who ran them quickly went to work in new ones. And corruption in the meat industry, far from being wiped out, was about to grow to proportions that would make the Lokietz sausage operation look truly penny ante.

But Nicholson and Montello, for all their work, had one thing to console themselves with. The price was high, but they had bought a song from Norman Lokietz about the butchers' union. He gave quite a performance, and it resulted in what became known as the Kissel case.

PART TWO

THE MAFIA

The Mafia

In 1976, the *Annals of the American Academy of Political and Social Science* presented an entire issue devoted to "Crime and Justice in America." The only article concerning the Mafia was written by Professor Dwight C. Smith, Jr., director of institutional research at the State University of New York, Albany. Professor Smith's article was entitled "Mafia: The Prototypical Alien Conspiracy," and his thesis was that the Mafia doesn't exist. The Mafia, he wrote, was a phony notion accepted by the United States public because we Americans have a conspiracy phobia—"a recurring apprehension that somewhere 'out there' is an organized secret alien group that is poised to infiltrate our society and to undermine our fundamental democratic beliefs." Professor Smith is far from alone in holding this view, especially among teachers in our colleges.

For Professor Smith, the Mafia scare of the 1960s and 1970s is no different from the Red scare of the 1940s and 1950s. "The precise nature and composition of the conspiracy varies with the times," he wrote. "For the United States the concept of conspiracy has occupied an important and sometimes respected position in our value structure."

On Sicily, Professor Smith wrote, "The phenomenon of Mafia had emerged in response to cultural conditions, not as an organization independent of its surroundings that could decide to export itself. . . . To call it 'organized' required attributing to its practitioners a self-conscious sense of structure well beyond either the necessities of their circumstances or their sense of being."

The Mafia in America, wrote Professor Smith, is merely an invention of the old Federal Bureau of Narcotics, which needed a powerful enemy to explain why it hadn't suppressed the drug traffic, and why it needed an ever bigger annual budget appropriation. The only reason some people admit to being in the Mafia today, Professor Smith wrote, is that the Bureau of Narcotics has made it status-enhancing to call oneself a Mafioso. "For seventeen years the Bureau labored to produce a receptive mood toward a criminal threat and a convincing set of facts that would re-establish 'Mafia' in the public eye." So wrote Professor Smith, the scholar chosen by the American Academy of Political and Social Science to explain organized crime to its members.

It is the thesis of this book that Professor Smith was engaged in an irresponsible act of self-deception. Yet he was merely confessing an attitude that most scholars in the United States exhibit every day by what they don't write and don't teach. On the rare occasions when members of the academic establishment mention the Mafia at all, they customarily explain it away as a phenominon of immigrant sociology—something that happens temporarily, as a matter of course, among the displaced and uprooted. To be sure, the Mafia has long thrived among immigrant communities because new immigrants are particularly helpless and therefore are ideal victims for Mafia racketeers. But the fact remains that millions of Italians, Irishmen, Jews, Russians, Germans, Chinese, WASPs, Africans, and others have immigrated to the United States and found occupations other than extortion, loansharking, professional gambling, rumrunning, arson, armed robbery, bankruptcy fraud, and murder for hire. These criminal activities are not necessary adjuncts of the immigration policy.

The academic establishment refuses to recognize that there are people in society who do evil that other people do not do, and who plan and carry out this evil with each other, and in fact are often blood relatives of each other, to an extent that defies coincidence.

For example: This is not the first book to concern itself with the Amalgamated Meat Cutters and Butcher Workmen of North America. There is another book called *The Butcher Workmen: A Study of Unionization,* which purports to be a full-fledged scholarly history of the union. It was written by David Brody, a history professor at Columbia University, under the sponsorship of a labor-management research project run by Harvard University. I first encountered *The Butcher Workmen* among the textbooks my wife had used during her studies at Harvard, where it was required reading in a labor course taught by John T. Dunlop. Professor Dunlop, who also wrote a rhapsodic foreword to Professor Brody's book, later became the federal cabinet officer in charge of policing the labor field.

Incredibly, Brody's book and Dunlop's course held the butchers' union up as a model of honest American labor organization. Nowhere in the extensive ten-page index is there a reference to the Mafia or to any of its euphemistic aliases. Nowhere is there a reference to Little Augie Pisano, George Scalise, John Dioguardi, Chappie Brescia, Big Paul Castellano, or Moe Steinman, who, as readers of these pages will learn, have played an integral and often dominating role in the operation of the union's largest locals, and who have wielded great influence over the international.

There are two references to Max Block—none to his brother Louis—the men whom Pisano and Scalise selected to run the union in the New York area and who for some three decades did run it while consorting openly with the most bloodthirsty elements of the underworld and selling out their members to anybody who would make a respectable bid. Both references to Max Block depict him merely as a board member of the international union who happened to oppose a long-contemplated merger with the United Packinghouse Workers of America (the merger ultimately took place in 1968). Only coincidental to explaining the board's change of position on that issue, Professor Brody finally mentions that Block "in May 1958 was exposed by the McClellan Committee for misconduct in the affairs of his New York unions, and his association with the Amalgamated came to an immediate end." Professor Brody never goes into the fact that this separation was merely formal, that Block continued to be part of the same clique, which continued to dominate the butchers' union in the New York area, and that Block continued to rake in great amounts of money from his power over the meat industry. (The colleague who replaced Block as official boss of the butchers was the same Frank Kissel against whom Detectives Nicholson and Montello were building an extortion case at the time of the Merkel horsemeat scandal.) Thus do our finest schools deceive their students about conditions in American industry.

Yes, professors, there is a Mafia. It exists not because of the Federal Bureau of Narcotics, but because it offers people access to wealth and power that they can't get legitimately, and because the justice system is unprepared to deal with it. Its existence is grasped anew by each generation of investigators, and each generation has been able to define it more precisely. The Mafia was mentioned in criminal investigations in various cities around the turn of the century. During the Prohibition era, police established many links between the bootleg gangs of New York, Chicago, Detroit, Cleveland, and elsewhere. When Burton Turkus prosecuted the Murder, Incorporated, case in 1940, he was startled to find the same group of men responsible for the deaths of hundreds of persons across the country who had posed some obstacle to the rackets. (Murder, Inc., was a group of contract murder specialists that crossed Mafia family lines; it had close ties to the leadership of the Longshoremen's, Clothing Workers', and Teamsters' unions.)

Ten years later, a Senate committee under Estes Kefauver of Tennessee got an even better handle on the Syndicate, and more details were made public. Moreover, the Kefauver hearings were televised, and the sudden and unprecedented glare of nationwide publicity broke the careers of some powerful individual mobsters.

Then, in 1957, perhaps the most important Mafia-fighter to date burst onto the scene, thanks to the influence of an ambitious elder brother who had become a power in the Senate. Later, in 1961, when his brother appointed him

Attorney General of the United States, many people would say that Robert F. Kennedy was unqualified for the job. No one who said that could possibly have read the fifty-eight volumes of testimony extracted from racketeers and their victims by the relentless questioning of Robert Kennedy as chief counsel to the Senate Select Committee on Improper Activities in the Labor or Management Field from 1957 to 1959. Kennedy's work has to stand as a landmark in the history of criminal prosecution. (Although, as counsel to a Senate committee, he could not directly win indictments or convictions, nevertheless the investigation he conducted and the testimony he elicited were responsible for well over a hundred convictions after the information was turned over to proper state and federal authorities.)

Through years of jet-hop interviewing, wiretapping, and document study, Kennedy made himself the master of detail in the lives of hundreds if not thousands of rackets figures. Aided by perhaps the best investigative staff of its size ever assembled, he stored such encyclopedic knowledge on the tip of his tongue that startled witnesses usually found it impossible to evade him; many made embarrassing concessions, and others pleaded the Fifth Amendment.

Indeed, Robert Kennedy may well have been the best qualified man who ever assumed the post of chief criminal prosecutor of the United States. Certainly he was more ready for it than the two soon-to-be convicted felons who held the job under Nixon, or the well-meaning law professor from Chicago or the civil practitioner from Georgia who would come later. One wonders whether any of them—Mitchell, Kleindeinst, Levi, Bell, or the others—could have named the heads of even five Mafia families if you had asked them point blank on the eve of their assumption to office (with the possible exception of Kleindeinst, who might have known the names from some of his business dealings rather than through law enforcement). But such expertise is not among the demands that Congressional interrogators usually make of nominees for attorney general. It took a lot of people to bust the secret of the Mafia, but if you had to single out one hero, his name would be Robert Kennedy.

The famed rackets hearings of 1957–1959 are a monument not only to a brilliant young prosecutor and his influential older brother, but also to a rather remarkable old senator whose name is forever associated with those hearings. John McClellan never claimed the brainpower of, say, the other senator from Arkansas, J. William Fullbright. Nor the luck. McClellan's first marriage ended in divorce in 1921. His beloved second wife died of spinal meningitis in 1935. In 1943, Max McClellan, the first of the senator's three sons, also died of meningitis while serving with the Armed Forces in North Africa. A second son, John, Jr., was killed in a traffic accident in 1949.

Senator McClellan began drinking heavily and considered retirement. Then the growth of the rackets investigation that his young counsel, Robert Kennedy, was pursuing in the mid–1950s restored McClellan's drive. Clearly a major achievement was taking place under his auspices, and even if it was only the chance of seniority that placed him in control of it, John McClellan had the sense and fortitude to keep it going. Then, in July 1958, just as a final confrontation was building between the McClellan Committee and its arch enemy, Teamster boss Jimmy Hoffa, John McClellan's third and last remaining son, Jimmy, was killed in a plane crash.

The man held on. A lot of people have never forgiven McClellan for maintaining an Arkansas posture on civil rights. But they should never forget what he did for the fight against the Syndicate despite the injustice he saw in his personal life.

The McClellan Committee's findings helped provide the basis for criminal cases that were still reaching the courts more than a decade later. And in the same way, because the hearings explain so well the roots of crime in the 1970s, they provide the background for much that is in this book. They will be referred to throughout. The hearings showed conclusively and as never before the extent of organized crime in America.

Still, the evidence that there was a Mafia orchestrating it all was only circumstantial. The existence of the Mafia is a logical inference from the McClellan report, but the destruction of Professor Smith's position requires irrefutable proof. Based on what he learned in the Senate, Robert Kennedy would go on to provide that proof.

When Kennedy took over the Justice Department, its position in the Mafia war could scarcely have been worse. J. Edgar Hoover, director of the Federal Bureau of Investigation, had long been more powerful in determining the course of law enforcement priorities than was his supposed boss, the attorney general. And Hoover publicly denied there *was* a Mafia!

In his first two decades in office, 1924–1944, Hoover had performed an incalculable public service by creating and establishing a professional quality American law enforcement agency that (so far as anyone knows) couldn't be corrupted. But in the late 1940s he set that agency on an insane and tragic course. Mr. Hoover, in about 1947, let his personal prejudices take him out of touch with reality. He perceived the most important threat to law and order in the United States as coming from the American Communist Party. Shrugging off the Mafia in favor of policing political debate, he unwittingly put himself in a class with Professor Smith. Moreover, he helped chase honest left-wing idealists out of the trade union movement, thereby destroying the one force that would have posed the strongest resistance to burgeoning racketeer control. When Robert Kennedy took over the Justice Department, the FBI's New York office had more than four hundred agents looking under beds for reds and exactly four tracking down the largest American criminal conspiracy since the secession of the Confederacy.*

*Figures from Peter Maas in *The Valachi Papers,* which was compiled with Justice Department blessing and cooperation. At this writing, the Department says it has no other figures.

When a potential big break had materialized in 1957, the federal government had been totally unprepared to take advantage of it. The chance stationing of an alert New York state trooper near Apalachin, New York, in the fall of that year led to the discovery of a convention of Mafia leaders at the rural mansion there of Mob boss Joseph Barbara. State officials investigated, dozens of mobsters were identified, and some were locked up on charges of conspiracy to obstruct justice by fleeing the scene. Officers of the hotel-restaurant workers', hod carriers, Teamsters, mine workers, and jewelry workers' unions were there, indicating that they also were officers in the Mafia. The local cops assembled some potentially devastating information, but couldn't make a strong criminal case and couldn't seriously interest the federals. A division of the Justice Department was set up to deal with Syndicate criminals, but after little more than a year it was disbanded without result or explanation.

Kennedy threw the federal law enforcement machinery into action. Electronics surveillance experts fanned out around the country planting bugs and taps in the offices of the dons. The FBI began to tail the real crooks—although the bureau would continue to divert vital resources to keeping track of thousands of young political idealists (eventually this confusion of priorities would have tragic consequences for law enforcement, including the indictment of FBI officials themselves).

Then, in 1963, a stocky, bull-necked thug walked across the exercise yard at the federal penitentiary in Atlanta, grabbed a hunk of pipe, and bludgeoned a fellow inmate to death. The thug's name was Joseph Valachi. He was known in the streets of his native New York as Joe Cago. Authorities asked Valachi to explain the assault, and the explanation they got was more than they could have dreamed of. Valachi had mistaken his victim—a stranger—for a man he thought was trying to kill him. He thought his death had been ordered by a cellmate, Vito Genovese. And Valachi explained that Vito Genovese could order any man killed because he was the boss of all bosses of the Mafia.

Soon Valachi was unspinning his tale for the Attorney General of the United States. (Robert Morgenthau, the U. S. attorney in the Merkel investigation, was instrumental in realizing Valachi's importance and bringing him to Kennedy.) The tale began in 1930 with a secret initiation ceremony where Joseph Valachi, in front of the major dons of New York, held a flaming scrap of paper in his hands and vowed, "This is the way I will burn if I betray the secret of this Cosa Nostra." And the tale ended with "the kiss of death" planted on Valachi's face by Genovese, a man so powerful he could rule a national criminal empire even while ensconced in a federal penitentiary. When investigators from Kennedy's old Senate committee learned what their former boss had latched onto, they persuaded the reluctant attorney general to let Valachi testify in open hearings about how the Mafia worked. Valachi named hundreds of organized criminals and identified their status in the organization, which he said was called "La Cosa Nostra," or, "our thing."

Like all such accounts, Valachi's testimony probably exaggerated his own importance a bit, protected some friends and threw a few unfair barbs at his enemies. But, by and large, he gave law enforcement and the public its first clear picture of what the country was up against—a thoroughly organized and disciplined criminal cartel. There were, of course, gaps in communication. At one point in the hearings, a conservative Republican senator from Nebraska, rather shocked by the whole business, asked Valachi if there was any Cosa Nostra in Omaha. Valachi leaned over to his Justice Department attorney and there was an exchange of whispers, after which Valachi reassured the senator that he didn't know of any. To onlookers, it appeared that Valachi and the government attorney had been carefully debating just how much it would be safe to disclose. What Valachi actually whispered was, "Where the hell is Omaha?"

To law enforcement, Valachi was a gold mine. The specific information he revealed helped FBI and other agents understand the often confusing esoteric references to Mafia tradition that they were picking up on the bugs and wiretaps. Even more important, the drama of his appearance aroused the public to the cause. But to Professor Smith, Valachi wasn't enough. "Viewed in a more neutral light," Professor Smith wrote in 1976 without further explanation, "Valachi appears to be substantially less knowledgeable than his captors alleged."

If Professor Smith didn't believe Joe Valachi, he probably was just as doubtful of the detailed reports about the Mafia that appeared in the press in succeeding years, particularly in *Life* and other slick magazines—even though it's now clear that much of the information in those articles was coming from reporters' secret access to the electronic surveillance being done by the FBI and other government agencies.

To the law enforcement officers who were clued in, this electronic surveillance provided indisputable proof, enough to convince even the doubters who wouldn't trust an informant like Joe Valachi. Now there was proof from the Mafia's own lips that any man, J. Edgar Hoover or Professor Smith or anyone else, who denied the existence of the Mafia was simply wrong.

For many years, however, this proof was withheld from the public by a powerful political coalition. This coalition consisted, first, of congressmen and senators from Mafia-dominated political machines, which existed in urban areas in the east and midwest. Second, there were Democrats who weren't personally bought, but who feared that a challenge to these Mob-dominated political machines, mostly Democratic, might cause unacceptable damage to the National Democratic Party and its chances for election. And, finally, the coalition included some persons who sincerely believed that electronic surveillance was a violation of civil liberties with worse potential consequences for the country than a continuation of Mafia power, and who therefore believed that all evidence gained through electronic eavesdropping should be suppressed. In the latter group, most importantly, was the chief law enforcement officer of the United States, Attorney General Ramsey Clark.

Clark pulled the bugs Kennedy had ordered installed, which is why many of the transcripts later made public stop in 1965 when Clark took office. So rigid were Clark's views that at one point in 1967 a chief aide to the attorney general apparently perjured himself in effect in public testimony before Congress to prevent this electronic surveillance evidence from coming out. The result was to whitewash the Mafia and at least one corrupt politician.

The aide was Fred Vinson, chief of the Justice Department's criminal division, and the incident occurred as Vinson was testifying before a House subcommittee looking into Mob crime. Vinson's office had been informed that one of the Congressmen on the panel questioning him, Cornelius Gallagher of Bayonne, New Jersey, was the tool of Mafia interests. (Gallagher's relationship with Tino DeAngelis has already been noted.) FBI bugs and taps that were reported to Vinson showed that Congressman Gallagher had dealt intimately on business with a local Mafioso named Joseph "Bayonne Joe" Zicarelli, and that Zicarelli had sought and received favors from the government through Gallagher to protect his gambling operations and certain shady international drug and airline deals. The bugs and taps showed that Gallagher was even friendly with the grisly Syndicate executioner Harold "Kayo" Konigsberg, who later told of disposing of the body of a loanshark found in the basement of the Congressman's house. Back in 1964, when Lyndon Johnson put the handsome, charming Gallagher on his list of possible vice-presidential candidates, the FBI disclosed this information to Johnson, who removed Gallagher from consideration. The chief of the criminal division would have been informed of that, too.

But Vinson was also aware of orders from his boss, Ramsey Clark, that no information gleaned from electronic surveillance could be disclosed publicly. So when Vinson was asked point blank under oath at the public hearing, "How about corruptive influence of organized crime in the federal government? Is there any that you know of?", he replied with what certainly appears to be a lie: "None that I know of, Mr. Chairman." (In two phone interviews for this book, Vinson asked for more details about the incident, which was originally reported in *Life,* but he declined to make any public comment.)

Within a year of Vinson's testimony, however, the dam began to break. Transcripts of conversations overheard by the bugs and taps began to flow into open court for all to see. Local United States attorneys, frustrated by years of covering up for the biggest criminals in the country, used clever devices to get the information before the public. When a mobster facing trial asked (through his lawyer) to see any surveillance information the government might have on him, but inadvertently failed to specify that he wanted the information to be turned over in secret, prosecutors simply dumped onto the public record the results of years of intelligence gathering on hundreds of racketeers and their cronies. These transcripts and other records are still on file for anyone to see through U. S. District Court clerks' offices in Newark, New Jersey, and Providence, Rhode Island.

Many public figures whose names appeared on the transcripts—mayors, lawyers, party leaders—screamed that the massive dumping was unfair, that the mobsters had been invoking politicians' names falsely in order to impress each other. There were probably some cases where this was true, but in general the tapes held up pretty well in light of other evidence. In some cases, like Congressman Gallagher's, the public figure's own voice or the voices of his close aides got trapped on tape. Eventually, Gallagher—who made speeches in and out of Congress staunchly defending citizens' rights to privacy and ridiculing the government's concern with organized crime ("McCarthyism with its new name, Mafiaism")—went to jail for income tax evasion in connection with his Mafia activities. On the other hand, at least one political career was made by the tapes. New Jerseyan Brendan Byrne was elected governor in the next election on the transcribed complaint of a Mafioso that Byrne wouldn't take a bribe.*

At any rate, by 1969 the world had volumes and volumes of transcribed conversations among the mobsters themselves, who were clearly unaware as they spoke that their words were being recorded. For the most part, the participants in these conversations had no reason to lie. Surely grown men would not sit around reminiscing about how they had participated together in various events unless those events really happened. They might exaggerate, but not hallucinate.

The most famous set of these transcripts came from the bug in the office of Simone "Sam the Plumber" DeCavalcante. The FBI listened to Sam and his friends from 1962 to 1965. The tapes became public in 1969 during proceedings surrounding an extortion indictment against DeCavalcante; eventually, he was imprisoned on charges connected to his huge gambling operation.

It is difficult to understand how a reasonable person could read these transcripts—or similar transcripts from bugs on the offices of other Mafia leaders—and fail to conclude that there is across the United States a tight-knit criminal organization with strict regulation of membership and conduct; that it exercises ultimate governing power over its members, superior to the power of country or blood family; and that its sole purpose is making money through illegal activity. The conversations include numerous references to Sicilian titles or names, such as *regime, caporegime, brigata,* and *consiglieri,* now familiar to readers of popular fiction. But these conversations were recorded while Mario Puzo was still an underpaid magazine editor. Many of the conversations were recorded before Joe Valachi surfaced. This is not life imitating art, as Professor Smith and his sociologist friends would have us believe. This is the real thing.

*For some Mafia-related information that, had it been known, might *not* have been helpful to the Byrne campaign, see Part Seven, Chapter One, and Part Eight, Chapter Three.

There are references to orders coming from Sicily or Italy, sometimes passed on during trips that American mobsters made there, sometimes during visits of Sicilians here. This destroyed another article of supposed common sense.

At the risk of being tedious, here are several persuasive passages from the many that are in the transcripts, to convince any lingering doubters; others may skip ahead.

First, to establish that joining the organization is a very real event and not just a loose term, here is part of the transcript of an *udienza,* or formal meeting, that occurred in 1962 between DeCavalcante and Philadelphia boss Angelo Bruno. They met to discuss which of their two families was entitled to "make," or take in, members from South Jersey, and whether families need tell each other when they accept members from a disputed jurisdiction. DeCavalcante was complaining that the Philadelphia Mob was poaching on his territory.

DeCAVALCANTE: Did Philadelphia have the courtesy to ask me anything?
BRUNO: No. Why?
DeCAVALCANTE: When you made people from Trenton?
BRUNO: No, but whoever we made from Trenton, Sam, see, it's people that we've known for a long time. We made Daylight [a nickname].
DeCAVALCANTE: Excuse me, you made a lot of them. Now I know a lot of people, top on down . . .
BRUNO: Sam, wait a minute. Sam, please. Only talk to me about people that were made while I was in charge. That's all. Don't talk to me about who was made before.
[Another mobster, Ignatz, an aide to Bruno, started to butt in.]
DeCAVALCANTE: Wait a minute, Ignatz. I requested this *udienza* . . .
BRUNO: Daylight and Mike, right? Before those fellows were proposed—I didn't propose them, understand?—before they were proposed, do you understand, I went to New York because I wasn't raised [promoted to head of the family] yet. We respect the Commission. Do you understand? And we couldn't do nothing without New York. I said, ah, "We are going to propose these fellows. There's people in the family who want to propose a few fellows. Are we allowed to accept these proposals?" They said, "Yes, you are allowed to accept them. But only the Administration [the leadership within the family] has to know them. Nobody else. . . . The only ones that have to know is the Administration in your family. Not even *gli soldati, soltanto Caporegime, Commissio, La Commissione Nostra, capisce?* [Not even the soldiers, only the captains and our Commission, understand?]" . . . they like me in New York. Let me tell you something. I know before they made people. And Albert [apparently Albert Anastasia, who had recently been shot to death] poor guy, right? And another poor guy. I know this for a fact. They made them and they didn't tell nobody. Not even the families in New York. . . .
DeCAVALCANTE: I know that in New York, even when I was made, Philadelphia was told then. Maybe because I used to hang around Philadelphia, they knew who I was."

But Bruno apparently won the argument, telling DeCavalcante at one point, "That's *Cosa Nostra, Cosa Nostra.*"

Three years later, DeCavalcante called in Bayonne Joe Zicarelli—Congressman Gallagher's friend—for a conversation that makes inescapable the conclusion that there really is a national commission that can supersede the powers of an individual Mafia boss who steps out of line. The Mob boss in question this time was Joseph "Joe Bananas" Bonanno, and the commission was trying to remove him without bloodshed. Previous conversations make clear that the commission had appointed DeCavalcante as an intermediary to try to persuade Bonanno to retire, and that Bonanno had refused, arguing, "This is a *Cosa Nostra* family!" and therefore inviolable. Zicarelli, a close friend of DeCavalcante's, was a senior soldier in Bonanno's gang because Bonanno had "made" him decades ago. So DeCavalcante was trying to persuade Zicarelli to abandon his old boss and become a *caporegime* in the reorganized family, with Bonanno cast out.

DeCAVALCANTE: This guy don't want to listen to reason . . .

ZICARELLI: Well, the man should at least be entitled to the chance to clear himself.

DeCAVALCANTE: Well, does he expect the Commission to come to him? Right or wrong? His own uncle, who is the most respected of the Commission, has pleaded with him to come up and see him.

ZICARELLI: Who's his uncle?

DeCAVALCANTE: Stefano Magaddino [a Mafia boss based in Buffalo]. . . . And they treated him like dirt! This guy was crying to me, the old guy [Magaddino]. He said, "Sam, now you tell me this guy [Bonanno] is a nice guy. I sent for him. He didn't know if I needed him to save my neck." Understand what I mean? Joe, if I call you up in an emergency, and you don't show up—you don't know why I'm calling. There might be two guys out there looking to kill me, right? And your presence could save me.

ZICARELLI: Yeah, right.

DeCAVALCANTE: You can't take it upon yourself to ignore these things. . . . The Commission supersedes any boss.

ZICARELLI: He [Bonanno] ought to know that.

DeCAVALCANTE: Better than anybody.

ZICARELLI: But do they supersede any Boss as far as coming into your family?

DeCAVALCANTE: They can go into your immediate family.

ZICARELLI: This don't make sense to me, and if that's the way it is I don't like it. . . . Who the hell am I to even say it. Now we're talking between you and I. . . . But who are they to come into your house and tell your family? That ain't right . . .

DeCAVALCANTE: Joe, I admire you for feeling that way. But the bosses gave the right to the Commission . . . The Commission can go against it. See, in Magliocco's family. They had trouble in there.

ZICARELLI: When?

DeCAVALCANTE: Joe Profaci.

ZICARELLI: Oh, Profaci, yeah.

DECAVALCANTE: The Commission went in there and took the family over. When Profaci died. Joe Magliocco took over as boss. They threw him right out. "Who the hell are you to take over a *borgata?*" He's lucky they didn't kill him. And Signor Bonanno knows this. When we had trouble in our outfit, they came right in. "You people belong to the Commission until this is straightened out." They done the same thing in Pittsburgh. They made the boss, John, uh—

ZICARELLI: La Rocca.

DECAVALCANTE: La Rocca step down.

ZICARELLI: He's no more boss?

DECAVALCANTE: Oh, it's all straightened out now. But Joe Bonanno was in on that deal. They made La Rocca take orders from the Commission until everything was straightened out. . . . If these people don't enforce what's right and what's wrong, then what's the use of having a Commission?

What happened to Bonanno will be told later.

And finally a selection from another bug, placed in the office of New Jersey mobster Angelo "Gyp" De Carlo, this one illustrating the protocol of murder. In this scene of December 21, 1962, De Carlo is talking with Carl "Leash" Silesia and Joseph "Joe the Indian" Polverino. They are discussing the aforementioned Harold "Kayo" Konigsberg, who had fallen out of favor at a crap game the night before and had narrowly escaped death at the hands of Anthony "Tony Pro" Provenzano. Provenzano had already become head of a large Teamster local, and would rise to one of the top positions in the international Teamsters' apparatus (he will be discussed at length in Part Six). Ironically, in 1978, he would be convicted with Konigsberg for the 1961 murder of his predecessor in Teamster office; Konigsberg had performed that murder at Provenzano's direction. Konigsberg couldn't be a "made" member of the Mafia because he wasn't of Italian extraction (though De Carlo noted, "He said he wanted to be an Italian. . . . Everybody he hung out with was Italian"). Konigsberg was connected through his friend, Joseph Zicarelli (known as "Joe Bayonne"), whom De Carlo says should be consulted before Konigsberg is done away with.

DE CARLO: Tony Pro and that gang condemned this guy [Konigsberg] to death. Who the hell is Tony Pro to condemn him?

SILESIA: Pro can say, supposing I was at the crap game, he would have done the same thing.

DE CARLO: He'd still have to get an OK before he can kill that guy. What do you think? Just because you have an argument with some guy you croak him?

SILESIA: He stabbed him.

DE CARLO: I don't care what he did, he'll still have to get an OK! What do you think? I can go and croak somebody, or—Joe, you think anybody can croak anybody without an okay?

POLVERINO: If this guy had got killed last night, it would have been all over.

DE CARLO: No, it wouldn't have been all over. There would have been a leak

[fuss] about it. . . . You can't kill nobody without an OK from the boss. Not even a *caporegima* can OK a killing. It's got to be OK'ed by the boss . . . Tommy Ryan [Thomas Eboli]. And Tommy Ryan ain't going to do it unless he talks to Jerry [Gerardo Catena, who, with Eboli, was helping run Provenzano's family while its boss, Vito Genovese, was in prison]. . . . The only other guy that can come up to this guy [Konigsberg] is Joe Bayonne. And he can't do it without his *caporegima.*

POLVERINO: They think this guy—

DE CARLO: I don't care what they think or what they do. If he [Zicarelli] asks us to come in there and be the intermediary between them—what do we care whether they kill him or they don't kill him.

POLVERINO: Another thing, Tommy says this guy is capable of—

DE CARLO: I know one thing, if I was in Tony Pro's shoes, and this happened, I'd get an okay from my boss and kill him—Joe Bayonne. . . . It's Joe's fault. He took this kid [Konigsberg]. He never kept him down. He never taught this kid to do the right thing. It's nobody's fault but Joe's. It's Lilo's fault, that's whose it is. [Lilo is Carmine Galante, number two man behind Joseph Bonanno, Zicarelli's boss; in 1977 Galante was said by some to be seeking the title of Boss of Bosses.] Lilo gives his men a wide latitude, tells them they can do anything they want, go anyplace they want. He [Konigsberg] ain't a bad kid after all. Only he was brought up wrong.

It is inconceivable that these conversations were put-ons. They were interspersed with talk of armed robberies, safecrackings, real murders, and other specific crimes—hardly things DeCavalcante and the others would have wanted to clue the police onto. The conversations clearly establish that there is a Mafia.

But exactly what it is, and who is in it, and what role it plays in all of American crime are more difficult questions. Limited answers can be supplied —satisfactory for purposes of this book, but not complete.

A personal note may help at this point. I am not one of those reporters who claims to have sources inside the Mafia. I have talked to persons who apparently are in the Mafia, but usually just brief chitchat while idling away the minutes before a court hearing. Sometimes we have gotten onto the subject of actual crimes, but never has such a person acknowledged to me on or off the record that he had criminal intent or was knowingly associating with Mafiosi. I have read widely, both court transcripts and popular literature, and will try to apply credence appropriate to the source. I talk regularly to law enforcement officials, and will try to use what they tell me with similar discretion. When one of them tells me that there are five thousand "made" members of the Mafia—a figure sometimes quoted—I will take it as an informed guess. No one has yet told me how we can be so certain. Judging from the DeCavalcante tapes, even the mobsters themselves aren't sure.

I will try to be precise with terminology, particularly because so many persons of Italian descent cringe at the word "Mafia." They prefer to use the phrase "organized crime." When Griffin Bell took over as Attorney General, one of his first public pronouncements was to assure everyone that the Justice Department, including the FBI, would continue to ban the official use of the names "Mafia" or "Cosa Nostra," and would refer to the Mafia only as "organized crime."

The phrase "organized crime" is about as vague as a phrase can get. It evades facts that are important to establish, and misleads anyone not tuned in to the code language. After all, any crime carried out by two or more people according to a plan is organized. When one teen-ager occupies a clerk while his friend shoplifts a ballpoint pen, it's organized crime, but hardly an illustration of the Syndicate in action. *Hustler* magazine publisher Larry Flynt was convicted in Ohio under an "organized crime" law, when clearly there were no Mafia or Syndicate people involved in the case; the prosecutor just wanted a law with tougher penalties than exist for obscenity (Flynt got seven to twenty-five years), and found that Flynt technically qualified as an organized criminal. Ignoring the existence of a central criminal organization won't make it go away; on the contrary, acknowledging the organization is a first step in fighting it.

What do members call it? From all evidence, it appears that they usually don't call it anything—just as some orthodox Jews won't write down the word "God" because the mere mention of a holy name seems to profane it. "The Black Hand" was a common term early in the century, when a picture of a black hand appeared at the bottom of many extortion notes. Actually, the symbol quickly became so well established that many people who had nothing to do with the Mafia were putting black hands at the bottom of their threats just to throw fear into the recipients. The trademark could not be protected, and was therefore dropped—although evidently it still carries a certain mystique. Just a couple of years ago, Carol Newman, the wife of a reporting colleague of mine on the *Wall Street Journal,* needed a graphic symbol for the handicraft store a friend was opening in Brooklyn. Since Mrs. Newman had made much of the merchandise with her hands, the simplest and most appropriate thing she could think of was to use a handprint, palm and fingers extended. The handprint, pressed with ink onto a piece of paper, was placed in the window of the store. The effect on the neighborhood was sudden and tumultuous; passersby were horrified. Friendly neighbors quickly persuaded Mrs. Newman to find another logo.

In the 1930s, a popular term was Unione Siciliano. It was preferred by Burton Turkus, the prosecutor of the Mafia in that era. It emphasized a split, very important then and less so now, between mobsters who were born in Sicily and those who were born on the mainland of Italy—the principal mainland crime group was from Naples. Al Capone, for example, was sometimes looked down on by his Mafia superiors because, for all his bravado and the publicity it got him, he was a Neapolitan.

The word "Mafia" is also Sicilian. As for its literal derivation, there are as many conflicting accounts as there are accounts of the derivation of the word "Hoosier" to describe someone from Indiana. But "Mafia" was the name that developed many centuries ago for a resistance movement on an island ruled by one foreign invader after another. The movement changed in its style with each generation, as the enemy changed, and as the style of today's Mafia changes. But the substance of the movement has always been the same: The lawful governing authority is considered illigitimate, and its directives are to be flouted at the pleasure of the Mafiosi.

The Neopolitans had their own criminal organization, the Camorra. There is still some risidual bitterness between the Sicilians and the mainlanders, or their descendants, but the criminal organization in America long ago became one—with the Sicilians usually, but not always, predominant.

The name "La Cosa Nostra" grew popular after Joseph Valachi used it. During the 1960s the initials "LCN" became the accepted shorthand in FBI reports for reference to the criminal group that the FBI is now forbidden by the Attorney General to refer to at all. But "La Cosa Nostra" is by its very nature a euphemism. Literally, it means "our thing." The phrase appears occasionally in the conversation of mobsters as recorded by law enforcement agencies, whereas the word "Mafia" does not. But the phrase doesn't seem to be used as a proper name. It seems rather to be a way of referring to something that the mobsters do not want to call by name. In a similar vein, Sam DeCavalcante referred to another member as *"amico nostro,"* or "our friend." Vincent Teresa, a Boston racketeer, used the term "wise guys," which is now popular with the FBI since it doesn't seem to offend the ethnically sensitive.

The name situation reminds me of a bad joke that circulated around the old cure-all known as Hadacol. The straight line went, "Why did they call it 'Hadacol'?" And the answer was, "Because they Hadacol it something." So it is with the Mafia. The organization definitely exists. Mafia is the name used by most of the people I know who have had experience with it. It's the name used by my long-time friend Anthony Scaduto, a biographer of Lucky Luciano who grew up in Brooklyn buying candy bars from Mafiosi whose stores fronted for the rackets. And so in this book the Mafia will be called the Mafia.

I cannot tell you where or how often the Mafia meets, or precisely what its rules and regulations are. I suspect that it seldom if ever meets officially at all, that it survives quite well on informal gatherings of individuals for some specific purpose, and that its rules and regulations are unwritten and therefore subject to change with the times, like folklore. I have read Joseph Valachi's account of the initiation ceremony with the piece of paper burning in his cupped hands to symbolize the way he would burn if he betrayed the secret of the Mafia. For all I know, every other member may indeed have gone through an identical ritual. But I'd bet that more than a few have escaped it. The Mafia isn't the Boy Scouts, and any organization so founded on basic greed has got to consider certain formalities expendable when they are inconvenient. There are probably battlefield commissions.

Moreover, in this day when run-of-the-mill gumshoes have postgraduate degrees in police science, and wireless microphone transmitters are small enough to fit in your belly button, I doubt that the national commission continues to come together for formal meetings in paneled boardrooms. That doesn't mean, however, that the commission has lost its influence. Polls can easily be taken by couriers, or by a series of small gatherings of leaders near airports in various sections of the country. To conceive of a powerful national commission it is not necessary to believe that every major decision must be brought to a yea or nea before every single member. It would suffice that everyone in the Mafia knew that certain kinds of action couldn't be taken if there was significant opposition among the heads of the most powerful families.

This is my guess as to what happens. It seems unrealistic, for example, that Mafia leaders from all over the country were summoned to a single room to formally vote on the execution of Jimmy Hoffa. But it also seems unrealistic to think that anyone would have proceeded with that execution without having made reasonably sure that the Mafia leadership was behind with the idea. (Another impediment to formal meetings, of course, is that so many Mob bosses are in jail, which has never been an adequate inducement for them to relinquish their power. Probably a lot of Mafia business is conducted on prison visits.)

One other thing about the Mafia: its members are all Italian. This has led over the years to frequent charges that those who seek to identify and fight the Mafia are anti-Italian. Nothing could be further from the truth. For the very reason that the Mafia *is* Italian, a disproportionately high percentage of its innocent victims are Italian. Many of the writers, investigators, and prosecutors who have done the most to fight the Mafia have been Italian—including many who have been involved in the New York meat investigations.

By the same token, many of those who have protested the use of the term "Mafia" have been of suspect motivation. The best-known group was the Italian-American Civil Rights League, founded by Mafia boss Joseph Colombo and run by him until he was gunned down in a carefully planned execution attempt at a "Unity Day" rally of the League in 1971. By his apparent support in the community, Colombo intimidated politicians and reputable civic leaders into endorsing the League. Yet many of the people who attended the Unity Day rally and who had picketed the FBI building on the League's behalf in the preceding weeks were innocent Italian merchants from Brooklyn who were told to attend or they would suffer violence to their property or persons. Goons visited many merchants to insist that they close down on designated "Civil Rights" days. Moreover, FBI bugs in New York's illegal gambling centers showed that the leadership of the Italian-American Civil Rights League and the leadership of the numbers racket were one and the same. There were frequent comments at the numbers banks like, "Hurry up and get the slips tallied, we have to go picket." Since the FBI building is at Third Avenue and Sixty-ninth Street and so much of the illegal betting community was picketing there, the numbers 369 and 693 went into heavy play. Alarmed rackets bosses tried desperately to lay off those numbers with bookies in other cities. Fortunately for them, the numbers never hit during the big picketing drive.

The same interests successfully pressured the Justice Department into preventing Joe Valachi from publishing his memoirs. Commented the surprised Valachi, "What are they yelling about? I'm not writing about Italians. I'm writing about Mob guys."

Italian-Americans haven't produced the most crooks, or necessarily even the best—just the most powerful. Jews, Irishmen, WASPs, East Europeans— all have gotten into the criminal rackets in great numbers. They are well-organized and individually often far more powerful than low-level members of the Mafia. But what isn't understood by the sociologists who talk about "ethnic gangs" as if they were interchangeable, is that these other criminals are not now and never have been as powerful as the Mafia leadership. Even the Jewish gang lords who have worked hand in hand with the Mafia commission have ultimately been subject to Mafia rule: Arnold Rothstein, the criminal financier of the 1930s; Bugsy Siegel, the founder of Las Vegas; Meyer Lansky, who showed the Mafia how to make huge illegal profits from carefully regulated casinos; Lepke Buchalter, the murderous thug who forced the garment industry into submission. These men have stood second to none in malevolence. The Mafia has listened to their advice and usually followed it. Except for the highest level, Mafiosi would do their bidding in matters of business. But ultimately the top Mafiosi retain sole control of the final power—the power over life and death.

That is the bottom line in the criminal rackets. The Italians can kill the Jews, or the WASPs, or whoever it is they are dealing with. Never the other way around. The ultimate distinction has always been that if a non-Italian had a grievance against an Italian, all he could do was complain. The Italians would settle it among themselves. Everybody knew that.

Michael Hellerman, a Jewish financial swindler who made a fortune for Johnny Dio, put it well in his 1977 autobiography. Dio, the kosher meat king from the Lucchese family, depended on the brainpower of Hellerman, who devised their successful stock fraud ventures. He also depended on Hellerman's still unsoiled reputation, so the stocks could be sold. Yet Hellerman got only the cut that Dio allowed him. And Hellerman has always been in fear for his life, even to this day when he is in the federal government's witness protection program. Despite Hellerman's direct connections with some of the highest Jewish ganglords in the country, Hellerman has never for one moment posed a physical threat to Dio. As Hellerman wrote in his autobiography, *Wall Street Swindler*, "A Jew dealing with the Italian mob had to have a protector, a guy who would stand up for you and speak on your behalf when there were disputes over agreements and swindles and money."* The protector was always Italian. The case of Nathan Lokietz and the Merkel horsemeat episode must be read in this light.

Nevertheless, the non-Italians are essential to the profitability of the rackets. There are far more of them involved in operating those rackets than there are Italians involved. A Johnny Dio or a Charles Anselmo operating in the meat industry needs a whole string of non-Italian collaborators like Nat Lokietz and Frank Kissel, the butchers' union leader. "We got Jews, we got Polaks, we got Greeks, we got all kinds," Jackie Cerone, the Chicago mobster, once said. Yet the whole superstructure rests on Mafia musclepower: the threat of death, or beating, or arson.

This criminal superstructure that encompasses all ethnic groups needs a name to distinguish it from the Mafia itself, which is at the core of the superstructure. Again, fishing for a word where any of several might do, this book will refer to the criminal superstructure as the Syndicate, or the Mob. It is connected to the Mafia, but much larger. Segments of it, such as the Jewish groups in Las Vegas and Chicago, appear to be tightly connected. Other segments appear to be independent of the Mafia in varying degrees, but never wholly independent of it. Again, we can only guess at the secret arrangements of other men, but the secrets that occasionally come to light clearly indicate that the entire Syndicate relies on the underlying threat of Mafia musclepower and discipline. And everyone in it who succeeds financially becomes subject to Mafia pressure to give the appropriate don a share of the profits. Often the Mafia takes its profit share by putting a representative on the payroll of a criminal organization that was started by non-Mafia racketeers.

It is impossible to say precisely how this state of affairs came to be. But one reasonable explanation is that the Italians (particularly Sicilians) brought with them to this country a tight-knit, extra-legal organization, whereas non-Italian crooks generally banded together only on an *ad hoc* basis. Any system of justice or discipline relies on the understanding that the system has permanence, and that a transgressor can't simply stall until the system gives up or goes away. Only the Italian groups provided that consistent threat, and thus they predominated.

So there is a Mafia, and there is a Syndicate. And while these are terms of convenience, and other writers have called them by other names, it is essential to realize that they exist. How big is the Syndicate? The most famous appraisal is that of Meyer Lansky back in the late 1950s: "We are bigger than U.S. Steel." As *Time* pointed out a decade later, the usual official estimates

---

*For the record, it should be noted that Hellerman's book is in many ways suspect. The man was convicted for lying and he may still be at it. But Hellerman can *never* be accused of underestimating his own importance. So the statement here is, if anything, conservative. Besides, the trials concerning the Dio-Hellerman stock frauds involved testimony from witnesses besides Hellerman whose testimony verifies the point he's making here.

of income place the Syndicate bigger than U.S. Steel, American Telephone and Telegraph, General Motors, Exxon, General Electric, Ford, IBM, Chrysler, and RCA put together. Such estimates are impossible to make accurately, however. The Mafia doesn't file an annual financial statement with the Securities and Exchange Commission, and the individuals who take the money hide it. As much as possible, they even hide it from their fellow Mafiosi. Normal costs of most businesses, such as executive salaries and overhead, are subtracted before profits are determined; but they aren't subtracted from the usual estimates of the income of the Mafia, since nobody really knows what they are. Nevertheless, there is adequate evidence to presume that the Syndicate is incredibly big, certainly the biggest business in America in terms of gross *or* net.

The most serious public misunderstanding of all—and the one this book is most concerned with—is fostered by many writers who are well aware of the Mafia and the Syndicate, but who, nevertheless, continue to propagate the "willing victim" theory: that is, the idea that the Mafia only serves a natural demand for pleasures that have been made illicit, and that "they only kill each other." It is the purpose of this book to prove that nothing could be further from the truth. Yet the theory continues to receive support from people who should know better.

Nicholas Pileggi, many years a crime reporter for the Associated Press and now a writer for *New York* Magazine, certainly is no blind apologist of the Dwight Smith or Neil Gallagher sort. He has written at length and often very well on the Mafia. But he has allowed himself to be caught up in the "willing victim" defense. In the *Saturday Evening Post* he once wrote, "Without question the success of the Mafia in America today depends upon the excellence of its services; but more important, it depends upon the loyalty of its millions of satisfied customers. From businessmen interested in hiring its loophole lawyers and double-book tax accountants to high-school graduates looking for their first scalp-priced tickets to a sellout Broadway show, the Mafia has been dependable, ubiquitous, and a friend to those in need. It has provided a combination of unique services that millions of citizens insist upon enjoying. It has filled a gap between the letter and the spirit of unrealistic, unenforceable, and unpopular laws. . . .

"It does not take clever businessmen long [Pileggi wrote] to find out that Mafia trucking rates are lower, its laundries wash whiter, its bars serve bigger drinks, and its restaurants have crisper vegetables, fresher fish, and better cuts of meat. . . . Mafia bankers will always lend money and though their interest rates are high . . . they are not much higher than, say, the revolving-credit plan of one of the country's largest department store chains, which socks its customers with an interest rate of 36 percent a year. And Mafia bankers are businesslike: 'Nobody comes and puts a gun to your head and makes you take $10,000,' one old-time Seventh Avenue garment tycoon conceded."

Taking off from there, Pileggi even proceeded to condemn the "growing tendency today to blame all crime and corruption in America on the Mafia. It has been accused of causing Irish gang wars in Boston. . . . It has been blamed when bankers abscond, inflated stocks collapse. . . . Even when perfectly legitimate businesses are founded by the sons and relatives of known Mafiosi, the firms are soon labeled 'Mafia-infiltrated' by U.S. Attorneys."

In fact, no less an authority than Vincent Teresa, the Boston racketeer from an old-line Mafia family who has now become a government informer, has described publicly in detail exactly how the Italian bosses *did* intervene with force to settle an Irish gang war in the 1960s because the conflict was hurting business. Anyone who doubts the way the Mafia has manipulated stocks or intimidated bankers ought to go to the clerk's office at the United States District Court in Manhattan and read the trial transcripts of the Dio-Hellerman stock fraud cases, or to the same office in Newark and read the transcript of the Robert Prodan case (described in Part Seven). As for sons and relatives of Mafiosi in "perfectly legitimate business," the reader is invited to consider the stories of Tommy Gambino and his cheese business in Part Four, Joseph Franzese and his securities business in Part Seven and Thomas Plumeri and his kosher meat business in Part Nine—all good examples of how a younger generation can be used to provide a clean front for a dirty racket.

Pileggi has some highly reputable company in stating the "willing victim" defense, however. Gay Talese's 1971 bestseller, *Honor Thy Father,* is in many ways an invaluable study of the Mafia—certainly it is the best read nonfiction book on the subject. It has been justifiably heralded for its research and writing, but it collapses on the willing victim issue. The subjects, Mafia boss Joseph Bonanno and his son Salvatore "Bill" Bonanno, are brought movingly and sympathetically to life as heroes, loyally clinging to honor and tradition in the midst of the Mafia's purported decline as an organization. They are pictured as helpless victims of FBI agents who are merely looking to make trouble where none exists.

Writes Talese, "Most of the men [in the Mafia] were primarily involved in gambling, which, although illegal, was part of human nature. The numbers racket, off-track betting, prostitution, and other illegal endeavors would go on whether or not there was a Mafia. The Mafiosi were really servants in a hypocritical society. . . ." To be fair, there is a suggestion preceding this passage that Talese is indirectly relating the thoughts of the Bonannos. But the argument is presented without criticism and is maintained throughout the book. *Honor Thy Father* talks about the killing only of rival gang members in the struggle for political power within the Mafia; thus even violence and murder become, like gambling and prostitution, crimes against willing victims.

In May, 1977, John Tompkins and Laurence Barrett, two fine reporters for *Time* magazine, spoiled one of the magazine's several well-executed cover stories on the Mafia with the following prefatory remarks: "The morality of the Mob is somewhat closer to the morality of the average American citizen than it used to be. The Mafiosi always said they were no more corrupt than anyone else, and today more and more people might agree. The public is a willing victim of organized crime—buying blackmarket cigarettes and participating in illegal gambling. It's also difficult for people to think of some racketeer—who lives in a nice house, has a nice car and sends his kid to Harvard—as the enemy."

At least in the passages quoted above, Pileggi, Talese, Tompkins, and Barrett—four talented writers of unquestioned integrity—are simply wrong. They are fuzzing up a distinction that isn't fuzzy at all. The suave fellow with the conservative suit who moves gracefully through business society handling sports bets and booking free rooms in Las Vegas—the clean Mafioso—just doesn't exist. There may be such a fellow who is *working* at arm's length for a Mafioso, and who keeps himself clean. But the Mafioso, however he dresses and whatever he rides around in, is a gunbearing grisly who probably has and will kill on orders, and almost certainly is engaged in robbing innocent people of their money through force or fraud.

Mafia trucking rates *aren't* lower—except in certain instances provided for by a system of extortion, bribery, larceny, and murder that ultimately raises prices sharply (a system described in Part Six). Mafia laundries *don't* necessarily wash whiter, although most of them probably do wash with the cheapest materials available without regard to safety, and they may charge more because they often work as a cover for extortion payments to protect their commercial customers from being burned out or otherwise destroyed.

If Mafia vegetables are crisper, it may well be because they've been treated with something that is illegal because it causes cancer. If Mafia bars serve bigger drinks it is often because they're watered, or poured from mislabeled or hijacked whiskey. The Mob sometimes buys contaminated seafood from overseas that has been rejected for American import, then cleans it out in formaldihyde plants in Latin America and brings it back to the U.S.—fresh indeed. Readers of Part One already know what kind of animal food can go into the "better cuts of meat" the Mafia is reputed to serve. *New York Times* restaurant critic Mimi Sheraton has written a devastating review of the unpalatable cuisine that at least one Mob-run steakhouse serves up.

The truth is that every time an American gets diarrhea, he ought to think about the food inspector who was bribed to approve what he just ate. *That* might lead to a helpful attitude about the Mafia.

As for comparison with department store revolving charge rates, which seldom run more than 18 percent a year now, I have never heard of a Mafia loanshark who didn't charge at least 2½ percent a week, or about 125 percent a year, loan interest. Most such "juice" loans ("juice" refers to interest, which is collected weekly; the principal is due whenever the borrower has it) run from 3 percent to 5 percent a week, or from 150 percent to 250 percent annually, judging from court cases. For smaller, fixed time loans, the usual arrangement is six–for–five, or six dollars paid back one week later for every five dollars borrowed, which works out to an astronomical 1,040 percent a year.

Sometimes borrowers really *are* forced to take such loans with a gun at their head, as is the case with a businessman trapped by gambling debts. More pitiable are those, like some meat dealers, or the pizzeria owners described in Part four, who are so trapped by Mafia control of an industry that they have little real economic choice about the suppliers who will provide their credit.

Talese, in his book, fleetingly mentions in several places that the Bonannos own a cheese factory, or a string of cheese shops, but they are given as examples of legitimate enterprise. He offers no indication that the Bonannos' cheese business is a racket from which countless innocent individuals suffer.

This book is concerned with the Mafia, but not with the so-called victimless crimes that, according to popular conception, the Mafia lives on. I have no dispute with prostitutes, pornography, football betting cards, marijuana or other pursuits of the nonviolent adult population. This book is not the argument of a killjoy or religious moralist. It is, rather, the argument of one of millions of Americans who would like to buy food, clothing, and other goods without paying an overcharge to support a network of thieves; who would like to start receiving the guarantee of minimum quality and safety supposedly provided by protective laws; who would like to patronize merchants who freely choose their products on the basis of quality and cost, without the interference of bribery or physical intimidation; who would like to be able to take a job in any industry and join an honest labor union that would negotiate in the workers' best interest; who would like taxes reduced to cover only the actual cost of services of an honest government, without additional expenses for contracts puffed up by bribes, or for excessive repair work because substandard materials have been used on roads, buildings, and other projects; and who would like to expel from society a class of persons who live like kings but whose only contribution is to innovate new ways to steal from the wealth produced by hard-working citizens.

PART THREE

MEAT–THE UNION

Solidarity Forever: The Union, the Management, and the Mafia

By the Spring of 1965, Detective Robert Nicholson and the Manhattan District Attorney's squad had the witness who could unlock the mystery of the corrupt New York butchers' union. Nat Lokietz knew plenty about how the payoff system worked, and about the mobsters who were in control. This was his story:

The union had divided the wholesale meat industry in New York into two negotiating groups: the fresh beef companies, and the pork and processed meat companies such as Merkel. At every contract the groups were shaken down, and the contracts were staggered so the union leaders had a constant source of extra income. Lokietz professed to know only about his own group, called the Meat Trade Institute, whose contract with the union had last been renewed on July 1, 1964. The date was a crucial bargaining tool in the hands of the union, because the July 4 weekend was the biggest of the year in the picnic meats business, and huge stocks were built up by the end of June. If the companies were shut down by a strike on the June 30 contract expiration date, tons of meat would rot.

And that, according to Lokietz, is exactly what the union bosses had threatened would happen if the Meat Trade Institute didn't make the customary payoff to the leaders of Local 174: Frank Kissel, Karl Muller, and Harry Stubach. In 1964, the ante was set at $60,000. The companies had no choice but to pay, and they paid.

Convinced that Lokietz's story was the break they had been looking for,

Nicholson was anxious to throw wiretaps around the butchers' union office to provide corroborative evidence, especially because the FBI might also be on the trail. Nicholson was furious at the federal men for questioning Lokietz about the racket when they had promised not to, and then not disclosing his answers. Nicholson didn't want the federal agents to steal the case. With Lokietz's confessions about union bribery, the D.A.'s men now had probable cause to get a wiretap order from a state judge and tear the lid of secrecy off the union.

But until the Merkel case had been dispensed with, the lawyers in the office considered it essential that Nicholson and his men devote all their working hours to helping prepare for the upcoming trials. Most of the facts were known, but additional witnesses had to be found to corroborate them. There was paper-shuffling. Someone had to go through the boxes of subpoenaed documents, accounting for all of them no matter how innocuous, and someone had to gather the records of all interviews done on the case no matter how tangential, so that full disclosure could be made to the defense. When getting ready for a court case, prosecutors often treat even crack detectives as clericals, and tie them down to thankless drudgery.

Finally, in April, 1966, Nicholson was freed to go after the labor racketeers. Taps and bugs were authorized for the headquarters of Local 174 of the butchers union. Once again, though, nothing seemed to happen quite as simply as might have been expected.

On the night of April 11, 1966, Nicholson led a troup of twenty men from the D.A.'s office to the union headquarters on East Eighteenth Street off Union Square. Under standard procedure, extreme precautions were taken to wrap secrecy around the break-in that was necessary to plant the bugs. Patrol cars were sent to each end of the block to deter passersby, and to warn the break-in crew by walkie-talkie of any danger. As the lock on the union office was being picked, other cops from the D.A.'s squad started a mock fight at the opposite end of the street to divert the attention of anyone who happened to be in the area, though at two o'clock in the morning the streets were mostly deserted. A primary concern was the local police precinct, which was never trusted with the information that an eavesdropping was underway nearby. The precinct's radio frequencies were monitored to make sure that no local police squads would wander onto the scene and mistake the break-in crew for burglars (no one knew better than the cops themselves that some police might open fire with minimal provocation).

Once inside the building, the break-in crew proceeded up the stairway—elevators made noise—to the union's office on the fifth floor. An electronics technician went to work on the switchboard. Because the Centrex system of direct dialing hadn't come into use yet, all calls had to go through the switchboard and could be monitored from there. Moreover, by other wiring tricks, lines to the offices of Kissel, Muller, and Stubach, the top officers, could be thrown open so that the telephones in those offices would act as bugs without the use of additional microphones. If Kissel picked up his phone, his conversation would be overhead by the wiretap. When he put the phone back on the hook, everything that went on in his office would still be transmitted via the open line to the bug in the switchboard. (The phone system at Merkel hadn't permitted such wiring, and the microphone had to be planted in the room.) Finally, a big cable packed with fifty pairs of wires—to allow the monitoring of many conversations at the same time—was strung out the back of the union office, across a courtyard and into the back of another office that the cops had rented in a building that faced on Nineteenth Street, directly behind the union building.

When the project was completed, Nicholson and his crew went home for a few hours' sleep, and then returned for the opening of business the next day. Within an hour of the time the office opened, they knew they had made a terrible mistake the night before. As Kissel strolled out into the reception area, the switchboard operator called him over and said, "You know, a funny thing's been happening. Every time you go into your office and talk to somebody, I can hear everything you say over my headset."

Kissel was only briefly taken aback. It had been raining a lot recently, he noted. "All this dampness must have done something to the phone wires. If it doesn't clear up soon, we'll call the phone company."

The police shuddered at the idea that the telephone company might find out what they were doing with the company's equipment. So after a discreet interval, one of the cops called the union and identified himself as a representative of the New York Telephone Company. "Have you been having any trouble with your phones?" he asked.

"Yeah, as a matter of fact," the switchboard operator replied. "Every time my boss goes into his office, I can hear everything he says over my headset."

"A lot of people in your area have been complaining about the same problem," the cop said. "It's due to all the damp weather. We'll have somebody over there right away."

Soon, another cop, in a telephone company uniform, appeared at the union office and went to work on the switchboard. He quickly disconnected the wire from Kissel's office. Lacking the necessary equipment, however, he left the job of rewiring it for another break-in crew to handle that night.

Thinking their job would be relatively simple—just hooking up one bug—Nicholson went back with only two other men that night. They made their way into the building easily, having done it before, and had just started up the stairs when from above them they heard a "thump . . . thump . . . thump . . ." As they proceeded up, the sound got louder. "Bang . . . bang . . . bang . . ." By the time they got to the fifth floor it was obvious that all the banging and crashing was coming from the union office.

The officers flashed their bright lights into the room and illuminated what Nicholson later recalled as "three of the biggest men I ever saw." He estimated them at six-foot-five, 280 pounds each. They had lifted a six-foot, double-door steel safe off its legs and onto its side on the floor, and were attacking it with sledgehammers and crowbars.

"Police! Freeze!" an officer shouted.

The men around the safe looked up and saw nothing but a bright light. One of them threw a metal tool toward the light and started to take off in the opposite direction. The police drew their guns and opened fire. There was a shattering of glass, as windows in the office partitions were hit by the bullets.

"We give up! Don't shoot!" the men screamed.

At that point it would have been hard to say which trio of burglars were the most surprised—the ones with the court authorization to be there or the ones without it. The last thing the three policemen wanted to do on their black-bag job was to stumble on a team of safecrackers. If they arrested the safecrackers, it could blow their secret operation. On the other hand, they couldn't very well tell the safecrackers to just go on home and forget about it, especially after all the shooting.

After much hurried deliberation, the cops decided they would first take time to fix the switchboard, then call the local precinct with the following story: They had been off-duty and out drinking, just passing by on the street, and had heard some noise. So they had broken in to investigate, and had captured the safecrackers.

A squad from the local precinct arrived and was impressed by the story. "We've been looking for these guys for months. They've been breaking in everywhere in the neighborhood," one of the officers said.

So Nicholson graciously offered to let the local precinct men make the arrest on their own. He explained that he and his friends had been with women that night and that if their names got on the arrest report, their wives might find out. The local cops took it from there.

The D.A.'s men didn't know exactly how well their ruse had worked until they tuned in to their bugs the next morning. They heard an office manager explaining to Kissel what a wonderful job the local police had done. "Three cops were just passing by on routine patrol when they heard this noise . . ."

The investigation into the butchers' union had begun. It would continue for a decade.

The Amalgamated Meat Cutters and Butcher Workmen of North America bargains for some 525,000 American workers, including clerks, fish and vegetable canners, and leather workers as well as meat cutters. The union was founded in 1897 after a decade of unrest and protest among employees in the big midwestern stockyards. At the same time, local retail butchers were getting together in many eastern and some midwestern cities, and these organizations often affiliated with the Amalgamated. From the beginning, relations were strained between the packinghouse workers and the retail butchers because then, as now, their short-term economic interests seemed to diverge.

In 1921, the Amalgamated—dominated until then by the packinghouse faction—put nearly all its chips on the table in an armageddon-type strike against the big packinghouses, including Swift, Armour, Wilson, and Cudahy. In the face of rising inflation and a generally anti-union mood in the country, the packinghouses had unilaterally reduced wages and nullified many work rules and grievance procedures that the union had won over the years. The strike merely proved that the companies had the power to do it. Government —from the new Republican administration in the White House down to the cop with his nightstick—supported management. By the spring of 1922, the meat cutters were back in the packinghouses under pretty much whatever terms the packers cared to have them, and the union was a much less respected institution in the midwestern stockyards.

But the union still had a source of strength—the urban retail locals, whose members did cleaner, more highly-skilled service work, and were much less affected by economic and political trends. Cheap labor could be hired and thrown into a slaughterhouse, but the closer one came to producing a retail meat cut, the more training was required. The extra 1 or 2 percent of the meat that an inexperienced butcher might leave on a bone could ruin the profit margin of an entire cutting room operation.

From 1922 on, this retail faction was predominant in the Amalgamated Meat Cutters' Union. The retail locals had been apathetic at best toward the plight of their striking packinghouse brothers—in much the same way that retail locals fifty-five years later, in 1977, were less than fully supportive of the long and unsuccessful packinghouse strike at Iowa Beef Processors Inc., by far the world's biggest meat company.

And the retail butcher locals were increasingly under the domination of the Mafia. Butcher shops were part of the food distribution system, which naturally came under the influence of the Mob whether the food was meat, cheese, or olive oil. Food distribution involved two elements the Mafia thrives on: trucking, which has always been under the Mob's thumb through the Teamsters' union, and ethnic loyalty, which diminishes competition. A sausage is not a sausage; it is an Italian sausage, a kosher sausage (that is, a frankfurter), or a Polish sausage. And in ethnic neighborhoods, people tend to buy sausage from the son of the man who sold it to their fathers. The narrower the market channel, the easier the channel is to plug up.

In Chicago, the retail butchers' local—perhaps the most powerful local in the Amalgamated—was controlled by Mike Kelly, who associated with Capone allies who controlled other local unions in the dairy, alcoholic beverage, and laundry and dry cleaning distribution systems. It was Kelly who installed as leader of the Amalgamated Patrick E. Gorman, the man who achieved and maintained the predominance of the retail locals over the next five decades. Ironically, Gorman hailed from the packinghouse side of the union in Louisville. But Gorman was still in his twenties when Kelly got hold of him, right at the time of the big strike. Gorman bore no responsibility for the disaster, and Kelly figured the affable young man could hold together the divergent packinghouse and retail factions. So Gorman was installed as secretary-treasurer (top officer) on Kelly's authority in the early 1920s.

Gorman did prove to be good glue, but he didn't prove to be a stooge, at least not of the ordinary variety: more than half a century later, in 1977, he still held the union's highest office. By that time, not only was Mike Kelly, Gorman's mentor, long dead, but Kelly's *son*, Emmett Kelly, had announced his own retirement as head of the Chicago butchers, and Kelly's *grandson* was running a private business that administered the union's pension fund. Gorman himself was arranging the inevitable transfer of power to his hand-picked successor (who came from the retail side of the union in Utica, New York, where Dominick Gerace ran his horse-packing operation).

Gorman was a strange creature in many ways. He put the union in the forefront of some broad liberal causes over the years, lobbying in Congress for higher minimum wages and aid to the poor (particularly government food subsidies, which would not so incidentally increase jobs for his members). He even, to George Meany's consternation, lobbied against the Vietnam War. On the other hand, he earlier had helped the McCarthy anti-Communist crusade to wreck the careers of rival labor leaders who had left-leaning backgrounds. And he adopted a curiously nonmilitant stand toward management. His desire to get along peacefully with the meat industry infuriated many packinghouse unionists who believed that some tough talk and an occasional strike might improve wages.

Looking back over his tenure in a 1977 interview, Gorman bragged about the way he had preserved industry peace—"We haven't had a strike against Oscar Mayer in thirty-five years. Swift, in twenty." He said, "An organization runs better by getting the respect of the employers than by telling them, 'You better do this.' " He said, the international leadership sometimes restrains local unions that become aggressive.

The trouble with the Gorman policy of industrial cooperation is that it has discriminated against the relatively low-skilled packinghouse employees who have suffered under often miserable working conditions and low pay. The policy has satisfied the higher-skilled retail butchers, whose jobs are safeguarded by apprenticeship requirements of up to two years, and who can ride the coattails of Mafia-Teamster control of wholesale food distribution.*

The most curious trait Pat Gorman's critics see in him is his support for

---

*Ironically, this control often benefits working butchers more than it does working truck drivers. Teamster muscle brings high-wage contracts, but Teamster leaders often use these contracts merely to extort payoffs from employers. Once the payoffs are made, Teamster members can be hired at wages far below those called for in the contract. Skilled butchers, however, are not as interchangeable as truck drivers and warehousemen, so the butchers often really benefit from their improved contracts. Though some retail-wholesale butchers have worked under "sweetheart" contracts in the true Teamster sense, racketeers in the butchers' union have made their money mostly in other ways—for example, the extortionate strike threat that Norman Lokietz explained to Detective Nicholson.

the racketeers who have infiltrated his union and dominated large segments of it. He has allowed them to plunder at will, he has refused to criticize them, he has visited them in jail when they were sent there and he has welcomed them back into union office when they have gotten free. Why? Some critics say Gorman still owes a debt to the memory of Mike Kelly, who put him in office. Others say that while he never personally has been suspected of taking payoffs from employers, he may need racketeer support so he can continue to enjoy the supposedly legitimate perquisites of his office, including a $75,000-a-year salary, liberal expenses, and having his wife on the payroll as the union's interior decorator at fees of up to $120,000-a-year. Gorman himself, asked why he tolerates open corruption in his union, says, "Let him who is without sin cast the first stone. Every person has his idiosyncrasies, his little faults."

To look at some of the "idiosyncrasies" and "little faults" displayed by butchers' leaders over the years, New York City is a good place to start.

On September 13, 1940, a mobster named George "Poker Face" Scalise went on trial for grand larceny and forgery. He had stolen millions of dollars from members of the building employees' union and other unions he controlled. He shook down employers with threats. He padded union payrolls. His criminal overseer was Anthony Carfano, much better known as Little Augie Pisano, one of the top Mafia captains in New York.

District Attorney Thomas Dewey's star witness against Scalise in 1940 was a Mob labor lawyer, Louis Marcus, who had agreed to testify to save his own neck. The young prosecutor handling the case for Dewey was Murray Gurfein, now a federal judge. After guiding Marcus through a description of how Scalise had looted the building employees' union, Gurfein asked him, "Did you have any further contact with any other union at the instigation or direction of Scalise?"

MARCUS: "I did. . . . He told me that he would like to get a charter for the non-kosher butchers in the Borough of Brooklyn. At that time, I represented the butchers' union in New York and I told him that I would get a charter for the non-kosher butchers in Brooklyn—providing I know who was going to be in this union, because I told him that the butchers' organization will not have anyone but butchers in the organization. He mentioned the name of Max and Louis Block, both of whom I know to be butchers; and I said, 'That's very good. I will get you the proper applications and you will fill them out, and I will do all that I can to get you this charter.' I asked him who, if anybody, was going to finance this proposition, because I told him that the butchers' international would not advance any finances for organization, and he said, 'Augie and myself.' "

GURFEIN: Augie and myself?

MARCUS: That's right.

GURFEIN: That was—was that the same man you referred to as Augie Pisano?

MARCUS: I believe so.

GURFEIN: Now, was a charter obtained for this non-kosher butchers' union in Brooklyn?"

MARCUS: It was.

GURFEIN: [a few minutes later] Did you ever have any conversation with respect to any bosses' association of butchers at or about that time, with Scalise?

MARCUS: Yes. I believe several weeks later Mr. Scalise again called me to his office . . . and told me that he would like to form an association of Italian-American butchers."

GURFEIN: Employers, was that?

MARCUS: That's right.

The jury believed Marcus and convicted Scalise, who spent most of the 1940s in jail and then resumed racketeering.

Thus the Mafia wound up on both sides of the bargaining table in the meat industry, a situation that only extended itself in the years ahead. The local that Pisano and Scalise started through the Block brothers grew and merged, and remains today the central organization of the butchers' union in the New York metropolitan area. It bargains for one of every ten members of the Amalgamated Meat Cutters across the country, and one of every five members of the dominant non-packinghouse group.

Pisano and Scalise chose their lieutenants wisely. Max and Louis Block remained in office through two generations of Mafia leadership. As Jewish immigrants from Europe, they knew other European Jews in the meat business who went on to executive positions in the supermarkets. A club was established of union, management, and Mafia. Through the Blocks, Poker Face Scalise and other mobsters were brought to the same restaurant tables with top officials from such major chains as Bohack, Waldbaum's, Daitch-Shopwell, Big Apple, Finast, and A & P.

Scalise had been a boyhood follower in Brooklyn of Augie Pisano and Al Capone. His prison career began at age seventeen when he entered the federal penitentiary at Atlanta for white slavery (forcing young girls into prostitution). About the time Scalise got out of prison, Capone left Brooklyn to fill a leadership vacuum in Chicago, where within a few years he achieved great fame. Scalise served as bodyguard for Capone's chief New York ally, Frank "Frankie Yale" Uale, until 1928 when Uale was shot to death in his car in Brooklyn (a sign of something, but not necessarily incompetence, on the part of his bodyguard). On Uale's death, Pisano took over many of his rackets and became a top captain in the organization eventually headed by Lucky Luciano and later Vito Genovese.

Pisano's star was at its zenith in the 1930s. Under his patronage, Scalise held control of at least seven unions including the beauty operators, the garbage workers, the ashcan handlers, the building employees, the elevator operators, and the distillery workers as well as the butchers. Membership in these unions increased in multiples under the Mafia's strong-arm organizing tactics. The more members, the more dues, and the more pension and welfare contributions there were; according to testimony, the Pisano-Scalise cut was as much as 50 percent of everything that came in.

How the system functioned is not altogether clear from the old trial transcripts available for study. At times, the mobsters seem to have simply walked off with whatever cash was lying around. At other times, they went to elaborate lengths to cover up their theft, such as by the extensive padding of payrolls. Kenneth Ashley, a union bookkeeper, testified that Scalise "told me to take some names out of the telephone book. I did that, and also made up some. . . . I would endorse the checks, cash them and hold the cash for Scalise in a vault until he called for it." An employer who balked at the demands of a Scalise union was subject to burning, bombing, or shooting.

Scalise lived in a twenty-seven-room mansion on an eighteen-acre estate, with a lake, in Ridgefield, Connecticut. The estate was bought with straight cash, almost certainly union cash. (The straight cash deal for posh houses remains a Mafia hallmark to this day.) Off and on in the 1940s, Scalise also lived in New York state prisons at Ossining and Dannemora, and the federal penitentiary at Atlanta. His power faded somewhat, but in the mid-1950s he still was able to engineer the theft of $540,000 from the welfare fund of the distillery workers and whiskey wholesalers' union.

Pisano's power had faded as well. While Capone was in his glory days, Pisano shared in the wealth from the Cuban casinos and Florida race horses. His gambling and liquor distribution rackets in New York were protected by his father-in-law, Jimmy Kelly (real name John di Salvio), a powerful Democratic political figure. Pisano's companies handled beer deliveries to Tammany Hall political clubs both during and after prohibition. His goons had access to police badges and uniforms in case they needed cover for their dirty work. His beer trucks had access to genuine police when necessary to protect them from the occasional competitive instincts of rival Mafia families. He owned nine limousines and had two rum boats. But by the mid-1940s, links to Kelly and Capone were of small benefit. Pisano's income kept flowing, though, from lingering union and political connections. For example, he and Vincent Rao, consigliere of the Lucchese Mafia family, were associated in a firm called Ace Lathing Company, which presumably had an easy time dealing with Local 404 of the Lath Hoisters Union. Joseph Vento, a soldier in the Lucchese family (according to New York Police Department records and Congressional testimony), was president and treasurer of the local. In about 1967, Ace Lathing received a contract to renovate state-controlled Yonkers Raceway for $200,000; the work was entirely subcontracted at a total cost of $150,000, producing a $50,000 profit.

Finally, the night of Friday, September 25, 1959, fate caught up with Little Augie. He and a frequent companion—a blonde former Miss New Jersey who was married to a minor league nightclub comedian—went out for drinks at the Copacabana and dinner at a nearby restaurant. Their party included Anthony "Tony Bender" Strollo, another Genovese officer, and his companion, the wife of a New York stockbroker. On the way home, Pisano's new Cadillac jumped a curb on a residential street in Queens and came to rest against a utility pole. He and the beauty queen were found dead in the front seat, three bullets in his head, two in hers. A few years later, Strollo himself vanished and is presumed dead.*

Such were the friends of Max and Louis Block, who ran the butchers' union in New York for twenty-five years, accumulating enormous wealth and influence. Max became an international vice-president, one of the three or four most powerful men in the international butchers' union. The Blocks had arrived in New York as immigrants from Poland in 1915 with their mother and three sisters. While Mom opened a grocery store in the Brownsville section of Brooklyn, the boys tried prize fighting. Max apparently confined his pugilism to the ring, but Louis was convicted in 1932 of beating up a policeman in Brooklyn; he got a suspended sentence despite two other arrests. Then came the brothers' butcher shop and the call from Little Augie Pisano to head the union.

At least as important as what the Blocks did at union headquarters was the socializing they did on the outside. On an almost nightly basis, the Blocks brought together the meat industry and the underworld. To accomodate their varied friends, and their own taste for the sweet life, the Blocks acquired a steakhouse in New York, which they dubbed the Black Angus, and a country club in Connecticut, the Deercrest. Scalise and Pisano were regular diners at the Black Angus, as were many other ex-convicts, Mafia murderers, meat dealers, and supermarket chain executives who stopped by the restaurant to greet friends and make payoffs. As Scalise and Pisano faded in power, their replacements as colorful Mob dominators of the meat industry also showed up at the Black Angus. These included the aforementioned John "Johnny Dio" Dioguardi and his friend from the Genovese Mafia family, Lorenzo "Chappy the Dude" Brescia. Another powerful figure, however, Paul "Constantine" Castellano of the Gambino family, seemed to regard the public drinking and dining sessions as indecorous and avoided them. Moe Steinman, the mole-like meat dealer and partner in the Daitch-Shopwell supermarket chain, tended by

---

*The killing of a female companion may seem contrary to Mafia style, but there are indications in this case that the beauty queen, Janice Drake, had involved herself in criminal activities and thus had volunteered for combat duty. A union insurance broker (Louis Saperstein) had testified that he made payoffs of union funds to Pisano in Mrs. Drake's apartment. In addition, several months before her fatal date with Little Augie, Mrs. Drake had gone out with Nat "The Manufacturer" Nelson, who was murdered either in her company or shortly after leaving her. Nelson had been the partner of the mobster James "Jimmy Doyle" Plumeri, whose nephew, John Dioguardi, was the rising star in the labor rackets replacing Pisano's man Scalise. Also, curiously, Pisano's friends told reporters after his death that he had known Mrs. Drake since she was a child in Union City, New Jersey; in 1933, when Mrs. Drake was eight years old, the police had tried to nail Pisano on a charge that he murdered a policeman in Union City during a 1931 truck hijacking, and Pisano had successfully defended himself by contending that he had never *been* in Union City—ever. The past indeed holds many mysteries.

nature toward indecorousness and relished his role as key middleman in the bribery transactions. He could almost always be found at the Black Angus bar in the evenings. Jimmy Hoffa and Paul "Red" Dorfman—the Meyer Lansky of Chicago—went there when they were in town. Albert Anastasia's personal bodyguard rented the apartment upstairs.

Another who showed up at the Black Angus on occasion when he visited New York was the late Senator Joseph R. McCarthy, the Communist witch-hunter the Blocks successfully wooed. Like some other corrupt labor leaders, notably in the Teamsters, the Blocks jumped on the anti-Communist band-wagon of the 1950s as a way of winning public sympathy and knifing their honest opposition. Left-wingers in the labor movement tended to be dedicated unionists and were philosophically disinclined to live in luxury off the members' sweat. This made them the strongest natural barrier to the encroachment of racketeers. So over and over again the racketeers used the anti-Communist movement as a device to seize the upper hand.

In 1955, the leftist but honest Fur and Leather Workers' Union was beseiged by McCarthyist investigators and finally agreed to suggestions that it merge into the butchers' union, which also dealt with slaughtered animals, but which was considered to be politically okay. On the ground that the Fur and Leather Workers was based in New York, the international butchers' president, Pat Gorman, assigned the Block brothers to take control. The Blocks conducted a public purge of the Fur and Leather leadership. They had already done an anti-Communist number on the leftist Food Workers' Indus-trial Union, and now their heroic "decommunizing" crusade against the Fur and Leather Workers was written up prominently in the press. The Blocks re-did the bylaws of the whole butchers' organization in the region to prevent "Communist sympathizers" from holding membership. They even closed the Fur and Leather Workers' upstate summer children's camp, denouncing it as a "Communist indoctrination center."

A former officer of the old Fur and Leather Workers and his wife recalled those days in an interview in 1977. "During the McCarthy years," he said, "they tried to smash us. Everywhere we went they called us Communists. . . . They saw you read a Communist Party paper, it was enough. . . . A lot of locals, they were Catholics. They'd go to church on Sunday and they'd tell them, 'You're in a Communist union.' So they got out. . . . The union we had . . . advocated better conditions. We were the first union to get a thirty-five-hour week, and we were among the highest paid." Many of these benefits were lost in the switchover to the butchers' union, the couple said, which made the employers all the more receptive to the anti-Communist drive. And as for corruption, they said, "We never had any corruption in our union since I joined it in 1925. Until the decent people were kicked out—there was never even a whisper. . . . Now everybody knows there's corruption. . . . Corruption comes down from the top."

At the top, Pat Gorman, also interviewed in 1977, had more sanguine recollections of the McCarthy days. "Max Block is more anti-Communist than anyone you know," he said proudly.

While swathing themselves in luxury with union funds, and while delivering fifty thousand trade butchers and the nutrition of millions of Americans into the hands of the Mafia, the Blocks had the gall to declare that anyone who believed in employee control of the companies they work for was "opposed to the institutions of American democracy." For this and other sentiments, Joseph McCarthy honored the Blocks. Governor Dewey, long having shed his robes as a white-knight prosecutor, appointed Louis to the New York Selective Service Appeals Board. And the Government of Israel and various domestic charities threw lavish testimonial dinners for both brothers at the Waldorf, where the attorney general of New York rose to lead the chorus of kudos.

Meanwhile, the Amalgamated from Gorman on down watched approvingly as the Communist hunters subverted the competing United Packinghouse Workers of America. The UPWA stood for such "un-American" principles as prohibiting any union officer from receiving greater compensation than the highest contract wage in the trade. An affiliate of the old Congress of Industrial Organizations, the UPWA had been founded in 1937 with the support of some midwestern packinghouse organizers, men from the dirtiest, most underpaid segment of the butcher trade, who refused to accept the Gorman policy of getting along with management. Always the underdog against the better-financed Amalgamated with its wealthy retail locals, the Packinghouse Workers was brought to its knees after widely-publicized hearings before the House Un-American Activities Committee disclosed the prior Communist affiliations of some UPWA officials. Winning community sympathy in the conservative midwest had always been difficult. Now it became all but impossible. Some survivors of the struggle allege that Gorman's men actually fed information against the Packinghouse Workers to the House committee, although Gorman denies it. Following a decade of negotiations, the packinghouse workers were merged into the Amalgamated in 1968 under terms that gave Gorman and his cronies total control over the policies of the combined union.

Though the corrupt system survived and prospered, the Blocks personally got their comeuppance at the hands of Robert F. Kennedy and the McClellan Committee in 1958. Kennedy showed how the Blocks financed their private country club in Connecticut with "loans" and contributions from employers. For example, the chief negotiator for the rendering industry chipped in $25,000 for the country club in return for a nine-month delay in the effective date of a wage increase for the workers. More money came in from the owners of Daitch-Shopwell—one of whom was Moe Steinman—in return for which Daitch was given a one-year respite from making any contributions to the union pension fund. Food Fair bought a similar deal, and Connecticut General Insurance Company ponied up a $350,000 mortgage to the Blocks' club in return for some of the union's insurance business. Max Block helped his son-in-law, Martin Zeitler, get started in the paper products business by putting the arm on the Bohack supermarket chain to buy supplies from Zietler, testimony showed. Other family members went on the union payroll and in the committee's words "milked the treasuries" of $241,000 in salaries and expenses and $293,000 more in other "questionable items" during the three years 1955–1957 alone. Harold Lippel, a relative of the Blocks who was on the payroll of one local as its secretary also ran an insurance brokerage that collected big fees placing the union's insurance business.

Max was described as living in a "palatial home" in New Rochelle, while Louis had a "handsome Westchester mansion." Daniel Beatson testified that while he was on the payroll of one local as business agent, his real job was to be Max's bodyguard and chauffeur. He gave quite an insight into the working routine of a Mafia-front labor leader. According to Beatson, Block didn't climb out of bed until 11 A.M. He spent most afternoons at the race track, then went to the Black Angus to spend the evening. People who wanted to see him came to the steakhouse and dropped off some money for a food or drink bill. If Block didn't feel like going home at night, there was a posh hotel suite paid for with union funds permanently available for him a few doors from the Black Angus on East Fiftieth Street. Rarely did he go to the office. According to Beatson, he "ran the union by phone."

Extensive testimony was given about the organization in 1952 of ten thousand A & P clerks. The clerks were agitating for representation, and the Retail Clerks' International Association and other unions were threatening to come in, so A & P wisely went to Max Block for help. Dissident officials of Bronx and Westchester butchers' locals testified that the Blocks had "really rigged" an organization election, "betrayed" the workers and arranged a "sweetheart deal . . . a backdoor deal" for a "company union." According to Fred Cornelius, a former aide to the Blocks, forgery was the source of most of the application cards that A & P and the Block brothers claimed were from workers petitioning to join the Amalgamated. "We signed their names writing backhanded, lefthanded, and every other way," Cornelius testified. "We wrote the names on the cards with pens, with pencils, and some of them even upside down. We made up addresses and put in fictitious social security numbers with the names." The result: ten thousand workers were committed by a new contract to a forty-five-hour work week when clerks in rival stores were winning a forty-hour week. Worse, the A & P workers were never told that an additional agreement had been signed guaranteeing the forty-five-hour week for five years. The deal was kept secret between the Blocks and A & P.

Asked about all this, Max Block pleaded bad memory or equivocated under oath. "I'm not familiar with what you are saying," he told Kennedy over and over, when asked such questions as whether he had paid for certain stock rights that had been given to him by the head of the Food Fair chain. Reporters counted 199 instances of equivocation in response to direct questions. Senator McClellan finally declared, "You are pretending to be the dumbest labor leader I've ever heard of."

The testimony landed on front pages all over the country. Gorman stood by the Blocks at first, and to this day defends them morally. But within two weeks, when the furor wouldn't die down and government action appeared likely, the international accepted the resignations from local and international office of both Block brothers and at least one close relative, Lippel. The Blocks got full pensions, however, and held on to the Deercrest Country Club and the Black Angus (technically, Louis owned it and Max was an employee), which continued to be the real headquarters of the Amalgamated Meat Cutters in the New York area.

The Blocks' biggest locals were placed in trusteeship by the international. To run them, Gorman appointed Irving Stern, who in 1976 would go to prison for income tax evasion as a result of Nicholson's continuing investigation of bribery and corruption. A reorganization of the New York area locals ensued, with Stern remaining in control of the main supermarket local. New "elections" were held to select leadership for a wholesaling and processing local. The logical leadership candidate was Karl Muller, a veteran practicing butcher who was popular with others in the trade. Muller was no angel; he had been a friend and supporter of the Blocks, and events later showed that he was not adverse to seeing money passed around and taking some for himself. But the Mafia considered him inadequately connected to its own power structure—not obligated enough—and so it injected its own man for the number one job of secretary-treasurer, while Muller took the number two job of president.

The Mafia's main man on what became the official slate for the election was Frank Kissel, long a buddy of Chappy Brescia and Johnny Dio, the mobsters, and Moe Steinman, the manipulator. Like them, Kissel frequented the Black Angus. He had been associated with Mob meat dealers in Yonkers. Brescia's brother, Frank Brescio (they spell the name with different vowels at the end), went on the payroll of the Kissel local as a business agent, where he remains to this day.

With the replacement of the Blocks by Frank Kissel, the corrupt system flowed on. This continuity, despite the overthrow of individuals, would be seen again in the years ahead.

2

The Kissel Case

Nat Lokietz had rented an apartment in the London Terrace Apartments on Twenty-third Street between Eighth and Ninth Avenues, a short walk from the Fourteenth Street meat district. There, the whole entourage of bribers and bribees in the New York meat business could come after business hours for card games, or visits with girl friends. If a meat buyer didn't have a girl friend, a meat supplier would bring him up a prostitute. After bugging the union headquarters, Bob Nicholson put a bug in the apartment on Twenty-third Street.

He also wiretapped the telephones at the Fireside Restaurant on Twenty-fourth Street where Johnny Dio and the meat dealers often stopped for food and the handling of payoffs, and on the phones at Pete's Tavern, around the corner from the butchers' union office. Pete's was where Frank Kissel and a subordinate sometimes handled minor matters of dirty business.

Shortly after the listening devices had been fixed at the union headquarters, Kissel got a call there from Johnny Dio, and Nicholson bolted up when he heard it. Kissel said the FBI had been around to see him about payoffs from Lokietz. Ironically, Nicholson and Dio came to the same realization at the same moment: Lokietz had told the FBI in great detail about the payoff system, and now that Lokietz had been publicly identified in court as an informant (in the horsemeat case), the bureau was following up.

"He's singing," Kissel declared, and expressed fear that Karl Muller might also break down and talk when the FBI questioned him.

"You got nothing to worry about," Dio reassured the union leader. "It'd be his word against yours."

"I know. But this guy Muller . . ."

Shortly thereafter, just as Kissel predicted, the FBI called Muller and asked to see him. He put them off. Finally, agents did get in to see Muller, but he said nothing of value.

The FBI didn't know it, but the New York Police Department was now using bugs and wiretaps to monitor federal agents as they broke their promise and began investigating a local bribery case that the police had developed. Apparently no prosecution resulted from the FBI interviews. But the police were learning a lot from the physical surveillance and hidden listening devices. These are some of the things they saw and overheard:

Johnny Dio and other mobsters passed money to Kissel, sometimes in front of Pete's Tavern. Almost every night the mobsters and the union boss met at the Black Angus, where Steinman and the Block brothers (supposedly long out of union office) joined in the discussions. Kissel, in turn, paid off Muller, but customarily cheated him; Muller apparently never realized he was being short-changed. Kissel and the mobsters tried to avoid talking business in front of Muller.

Once, Muller agreed to give in to the Bohack chain in a contract dispute; he had some old friends on the Bohack executive staff and was glad to do them a favor. Kissel was furious—not that Muller had conceded a point to an employer, but rather that he had done so without extracting a bribe, which Kissel would have been entitled to share in. So Kissel beat up Muller, who suffered a broken leg in the incident. Muller, terrified of Kissel and his friends, then returned to Bohack and demanded—and received—the retroactive bribe.

On the other hand, there were times Muller seemed to initiate bribery. He agreed to let one small packing company fire an incompetant worker in exchange for which the packing company paid Muller $500. The worker, however, complained that he was fired unjustly. Muller repeatedly pleaded over the telephone with a union doctor to declare the worker physically incapacitated, which would have solved the problem. But the doctor insisted that the worker was okay. Eventually Muller arranged for the worker to get a less desirable job.

Muller also took a $500 bribe to let a meat company owner's brother, who had kidney disease, go on the union payroll so he could obtain insurance coverage. The police, overhearing talk about this after it had happened, informed the insurance company, which had paid out $30,000 on the fraudulent claims. But the insurance company declined to sue, apparently not wishing to lose the union's business. Since the company was working for the union on what amounted to a basis of costs plus a fixed percentage to cover administration and profits, the company wasn't out any money. The $30,000 in illegitimate insurance claims by the relative of a meat company owner ultimately came out of the pockets of working butchers—plus a profit for the insurance company.

At one point, the Mob evidently decided to get some of its money back from Kissel. At nine o'clock one morning, two men showed up at Kissel's house. When his wife answered the doorbell, they flashed badges at her and said they were policemen who wanted to talk to Kissel about a car accident. She let them in, at which point the men pulled guns and admitted several colleagues who had been lurking outside. The thieves tied up the Kissels and ransacked the house. They took some jewelry, but couldn't find any large amounts of cash. They began to slap Kissel around. "Where is it?" they demanded. He insisted there wasn't any big money at home, and the men finally left.

Later Kissel described the incident to Muller over the telephone.

"Did they get it?" Muller asked.

"No," Kissel said.

"Is it there?"

"No. It's still down there."

"The bank?"

"Yeah."

Afterward, Kissel warned Muller to be careful. Apparently the Mafia was prone to Indian giving.

Kissel was proud of knowing the ropes and not getting caught, and sometimes privately derided the Block brothers for having left themselves exposed. "You never monkey around with the welfare fund," Kissel told one caller in explanation of why the Blocks were now out of office.

Kissel's subordinate, Billy, was less circumspect. He believed in using muscle to shake down the owners of small Spanish provisions stores. He would learn the locations of these stores from a friend on the executive staff of Goya, a major Spanish food distributor. Then he would visit the stores and insist that the owner sign a union contract covering the small workforce. The union wage demands would be exhorbitant, but the storeowner would soon learn that the union would stop making these demands if the right people were paid off.

In one particular instance, a storeowner on Atlantic Avenue in Brooklyn refused to go along with Billy's proposals. So Billy decided to hire someone to burn down the man's store. Nicholson heard the arsonist discussing the matter over the phone, announcing that he already had the gasoline. So if the plan had come off, the police would have been ready. But Frank Kissel also overheard the plotting and angrily called a halt.

"Are you crazy?" he shrieked at Billy. "That's not how you force a guy to join the union." Instead, Kissel proposed going to Moe Steinman with the problem. "Moe Steinman has all the health inspectors on the pad [taking bribes]," he said. "They'll give him [the reluctant storeowner] a summons every five minutes till he joins the union." This more civilized plan seemed to work. There was no arson, and the Atlantic Avenue storekeeper came around anyway.

As the police tape recorders wound on, a grand jury investigation into the bribery was opened. Most of the witnesses, of course, came from the meat industry. Eventually the questions asked by the prosecutors became so specific —"Did you pay $1,000 to Frank Kissel on such-and-such a day?"—that the union officers heard about it and began to suspect that their phones were tapped. To find out, they hired Vincent Gillen, the famed private eye whom General Motors had once hired to lure Ralph Nader into a compromising situation with a woman. An associate from Gillen's firm "swept" the union office with his supposedly sophisticated equipment, while the cops listened to him doing it. "There's nothing here now," he announced to Kissel. The fee was later said to have run into the thousands of dollars. (Gillen and a former associate told me they don't recall the incident, but they were doing lots of sweeps at the time and it could have happened.)

Still suspicious, Kissel ordered all his officers to go buy radios. "As soon as you come into the room, turn the radio on," he directed. As Nicholson later recalled it, however, the radios going full blast only forced the men to shout when they spoke. "The clearest conversations that we got were after they turned the radio on," he said.

Chappy Brescia called Kissel and asked him what he thought the grand jury investigation was driving at. "I know what they're after," Kissel replied. "They're after me. I expected this for a long time and I'm prepared for it." Kissel vowed he would never squeal—and he never did.

Then one day the bartender from Pete's Tavern called Billy. The bartender was proud of having a lot of cops on his list of steady customers and of being able to pry information out of them for conveyance to his hoodlum friends. "Tell [Kissel] you definitely got somebody on your phones. Be careful on your phones," the bartender instructed. He said the message had come straight from the cops who hung out at his bar. Apparently one of them had a contact at headquarters who could obtain wiretap information. After that, telephone conversations by the butchers' leaders grew circumspect. But the bug, which monitored conversations in the office, had long been the most productive device anyway. Then, two weeks later, on September 13, 1966, the bartender called Kissel and told him the exact location of the police listening post. To protect their thousands of dollars of eavesdropping and tape recording equipment, and also for their own safety, Nicholson and his men immediately pulled all the equipment out of the union office and the listening post. At about the same time, the taps began to disappear from Pete's Tavern, the union officers' homes, and the apartment on Twenty-third Street. The cover for the electronic surveillance operation had been blown by disloyal cops.

As it turned out, closing down the bugging operation that fall had its advantages. The next spring, 1967, the U.S. Supreme Court threw out the New York State eavesdropping law (as explained in Part One). Even though wire-tapping itself was still legitimate when done the right way, much of the wiretapping and all of the bugging in the Kissel investigation involved illegal entry onto private property. Therefore it not only couldn't be used in court, but it couldn't even be used to produce other evidence, such as witness testimony, that *could* be used in court. The less bugging they had done, the better it would look to a judge later.

The end of the bugging and tapping operation left Nicholson and his men with some inferior but still viable investigative techniques. For one thing, they could nail the butchers' leaders through the testimony of meat dealers who had paid the leaders off. Thanks to Lokietz, the cops knew who the dealers were, and there was reason to believe they would be willing to talk if the proper guarantees for their protection could be arranged. The reason was that Kissel and his colleagues had offered a particularly bad proposition to the dealers in 1964—not a sweetheart contract in the traditional sense. The employers had in general been forced to give their workers the same wage and benefit increases that would have resulted from fair bargaining. The only thing Kissel had offered the employers for their bribe money was no strike over the big July 4 weekend, with tons of meat to spoil. So the 1964 payoff deal had not been composed of the usual formula of 50 percent bribery by the companies and 50 percent extortion by the union leaders. It was extortion pure and simple. So, given protection, the employers might talk.

But while their testimony would nail Kissel, it wouldn't produce the case Nicholson ultimately wanted to make. Kissel wasn't running the show: Brescia, Dio, and Castellano were—directly and sometimes through their man Steinman. To connect Kissel to the higher-ups in the corruption system without secretly recording their conversations, the cops required something of a miracle. As long as Kissel and the bosses wouldn't talk, some third party would have to see or overhear a transaction between them and then testify about it. For months, Nicholson tried to become that third party. He and Montello and other detectives followed Kissel, Dio, and Brescia to the Black Angus and other haunts. Women detectives went along to make the scene look plausible. One of them was attractive enough that Brescia made a polite pass at her.

A couple of times the cops observed Kissel giving what appeared to be large sums of cash to a Genovese family mobster named Anthony "Buckalo" Ferro, later identified as a middle-level executive in the lucrative Harlem numbers racket. But the detectives never figured out why Kissel was giving Ferro money, or where the money came from. No charges were ever pressed.

The one productive incident during this period was a conversation Nicholson observed at the Black Angus in November 1966. Kissel and Brescia sat down together at a table with Irving Grossman, the head of Local 88 of the Retail-Wholesale Department Store Workers Union in Brooklyn. It looked obvious that Grossman was not the one who had asked for the meeting, and in fact clearly would rather have been someplace else. Nicholson and a partner edged closer. Grossman was being intimidated by Brescia—and who wouldn't be! Tough as Kissel was—and Nicholson already knew he had broken Karl Muller's leg—Brescia was tougher. In the 1930s he had served as personal bodyguard for Lucky Luciano. Then he graduated to chief enforcer for a taxicab medallion racket. In addition to whatever licenses were required from the city, every taxicab driver had to buy a sticker from the Mafia at a price of one dollar a day. If a driver didn't display the sticker, his cab might be burned, or he would meet with bodily harm. Brescia was indicted for extortion in connection with the taxi racket in 1938, and disappeared. He re-emerged in 1945, turned himself in, served a brief jail sentence and went back to stealing.

In 1957, the Nassau County (Long Island) District Attorney's office brought Brescia in for questioning as an "undesirable."

"What business you in, Chappie?" a prosecutor asked him in a formal interview.

"I'm in the meat business," Brescia replied.

"What's the price of meat?"

"I'm only in it a short time. I know that turkey sells for forty-seven cents a pound," the mobster replied.

"Dressed or undressed?"

"No, ready for the oven." [Turkeys often provide a mobster's first exposure to the meat business; hijacking truckloads of turkeys is a traditional part of the way the Mafia celebrates the holiday season.]

Five years later, the same prosecutor brought in Brescia again for more questioning. Brescia greeted him with, "How are you, Mr. [William] Cahn? I'm still in the meat business. Here's the price of meats"—and handed him a list.

Now Brescia glowered across a table in the Black Angus at Irving Grossman of the Department Store Workers' union, while Frank Kissel bawled Grossman out. What was the disagreement about? A wiretap was quickly put on Grossman's phone (legally) to see if he would tell anyone. Conversations revealed that Grossman had been organizing in the meat industry, and Kissel and Brescia didn't like it. At the Black Angus, Kissel declared that Grossman had been warned before about organizing meat workers—and he wouldn't be warned again. Then Brescia himself had said in no uncertain words, "I don't want you in the meat business. Get out or I'll kill you."

Grossman was called before the grand jury and asked about the threat. He denied ever having a conversation with Brescia or Kissel in the Black Angus, or being threatened at all. He was indicted for perjury in 1967. Six times his lawyers requested delays while he stayed on as head of the union. He underwent cancer surgery. Finally, in 1973, he pleaded guilty, and with lawyers still raising the terminal cancer issue, Judge Burton B. Roberts let him off with a $1,000 fine. He remained president of the union local, and sole union trustee of its pension and welfare funds. When the federal pension reform act (ERISA) took effect in 1975, it became illegal for Grossman to continue to serve as fund trustee because five years had not elapsed since his conviction. He appealed to the U. S. Parole Commission for a waiver. Nicholson personally went to court in 1977 and persuaded an administrative law judge to deny the waiver.

So Grossman can't run the pension fund, though he remains president of Local 88 because his perjury conviction doesn't fall under the five-year ban imposed by the Landrum-Griffen Act.

Chappy Brescia also was called before the grand jury and jousted with it, trying to avoid testifying. The prosecutor—at this point Nicholas Scopetta— foreclosed Brescia's effort to take the Fifth Amendment by offering him immunity from prosecution. If Brescia talked, he could explain how the whole racket worked. But he wouldn't. The mobster won postponements on the grounds that his lawyer was indisposed, and then that the terms of the immunity grant weren't quite right. But Brescia's string finally ran out, and on May 25, 1967, he began serving two consecutive thirty-day jail sentences for contempt of court. Sixty days later he went free, having successfully refused to answer all questions.

There is an interesting footnote to the Brescia story: District Attorney Hogan was so outraged at the way the mobster had been able to avoid testifying, at the cost of a mere sixty days in jail, that Hogan went to the state legislature and urged it to upgrade the crime of criminal contempt to a felony. The legislature listened to him and voted a law, still in effect, under which future Brescias must serve a year or more for their silence—if a judge has the backbone to give it to them.

Though thirty or sixty days meant little to a professional criminal like Brescia, it was still a sobering penalty in the eyes of the meat dealers who had bribed Kissel. Lokietz had turned the dealers' names over to the D.A., and now they were being subpoenaed. They faced a real dilemma. They couldn't lie— thirty days for contempt was bad, but seven years for perjury was worse. On the other hand, telling the truth wasn't a promising course, either.

It's commonly thought that the Mafia has only one weapon to keep its charges in line—the weapon usually referred to as a cement overcoat. In fact, the murder of outsiders is resorted to rarely by rational mobsters—the kind who have their heads screwed on tightly enough to run large industrial operations. The murder of outsiders often causes more trouble for the Mob than it forestalls, and far more efficient threats are available. Building inspectors can find violations. Customers can cancel orders. Suppliers can refuse to supply. Workers can strike, or otherwise foul things up.

The butchers' union, which the Mafia controlled, could destroy a business that had taken a lifetime to establish. Long after the grand juries had been disbanded and the prosecutors and detectives had gone on to other jobs, Frank Kissel or someone else the Mob appointed would still run the union, and the meat company owners would have to deal with him. What guarantees, they wanted to know, could the district attorneys give them that if they testified, their businesses wouldn't be ruined, either now or a few years from now?

So the District Attorney promised that the dealers would testify as a group, one after the other. That way the union couldn't retaliate against them without destroying the whole industry. No one dealer would be forced to testify unless all of them agreed to testify. And they would all be given immunity from prosecution.

One dealer, Irving Berger, president of Mogen David Kosher Meats Products Corp., still refused to cooperate. He insisted before the grand jury that he had never spoken to the three union leaders—Kissel, Muller, and Stubach—about a bribe. Berger was indicted for perjury. Eventually the case was dismissed because essential evidence against Berger had come from electronic bugging that was declared illegal under the Supreme Court decision referred to earlier.* But Berger's indictment—along with the one pending against Grossman—evidently had its effect on the other meat dealers. Before the Berger case was dismissed on July 25, 1967, the other dealers all had told their stories to the grand jury. And on August 1, 1967, Kissel, Muller, and Stubach were arrested and arraigned on an indictment for extortion. The charges were limited to the payment of $60,000 in bribes by a group of pork wholesalers in 1964 in exchange for the union's promise not to strike. The statute of limitations had expired on all bribes paid before that. Bribes paid later could be covered by future indictments if the grafters escaped punishment on this one.

There were the usual delays, and the detectives interviewed more witnesses and sorted more papers. Finally, on March 10, 1969, a jury was impaneled. The first important witness was Lester Levy, president of Plymouth Rock Provision Company. Plymouth manufactured sausages and smoked meats, which it sold to the Gristede supermarket chain and various independent delicatessans. Levy, now entering retirement, had started in the meat business when he was eight years old. "I was born over a sausage kitchen," he told the jury. "And my dad had a [meatpacking] place." By 1964, Levy was doing $35 million to $36 million a year volume, with a 1 to 1½ percent profit margin, he testified. He employed nearly six hundred persons, of whom 95 percent were members of Kissel's Meat Cutters' Local 174.

Levy said he had met Karl Muller nearly forty years before, when Muller was working as a ham boner for another provisions company. Frank Kissel was a more recent acquaintance. But Levy was a member of the Meat Trade Institute negotiating committee, so in the spring of 1964 he found himself face to face with Kissel at a negotiating session in the Belmont Plaza Hotel in Manhattan. There, he testified, Kissel took him aside and told him the meat dealers would have to come up with a $60,000 payoff to avert a strike.

There hadn't been a strike in the New York processed meat industry since 1930, Levy said. "It was just before the Fourth of July, which is one of the busiest weeks of the year. We had two, three hundred thousand dollars of perishable inventory and no freezers." He recalled going to his old friend Muller and complaining about the size of Kissel's demands.

"Whatever Frank Kissel does is OK," Muller told Levy, adding that he

*That case, known as Berger v. New York, involved a totally unrelated man, Ralph Berger.

—Muller—couldn't "make any changes."

Kissel later said he'd be around to collect Levy's $6,000 share of the payoff. Levy told his controller, John Gevlin, to make the payment in cash.

Gevlin, the next witness, told how one crime had been compounded into another to facilitate the payoff. Levy's Plymouth Rock Provision Company bought many of the meats it cured from Stoll Packing Company. In a normal week, Stoll would bill Plymouth Rock from $3,000 to $5,000 for these meats. But Stoll, like Plymouth, was a member of the Meat Trade Institute and was involved in the payoff problem. So Gevlin arranged for Stoll to overbill Plymouth Rock some $6,000 by upping the true price of meats. This was stretched out over two weeks to make it less noticeable. Plymouth Rock paid the extra $6,000 to Stoll with checks, and then Stoll cashed the checks and returned the money as cash to Plymouth Rock. This made the bribe tax-deductible because it was added to the cost of meat. Gevlin put the cash in the office safe.

"One morning our receptionist advised me that Frank Kissel was outside to see me," Gevlin recalled. So Gevlin went out, escorted Kissel into his private office and gave him the money in an envelope. Kissel took it and left. Not a word was said by either man the whole time, Gevlin testified.

The next witness, Fritz Katz, was the owner of Stoll Packing—and also of Smokemaster Inc., a ham-maker; Pitchal Packing Corp., a bacon-maker; and J. L. Frederick Corp., an importer-exporter of pork. Katz employed 250 to 280 butchers. He was fifty-six years old and had been in the meat business since he was thirteen. He wasn't any stranger to courtrooms, either. In the course of his career he had been convicted of giving bonds to a meat buyer for A & P (he was fined $500 and the A & P continued to do business with him), and of shipping mislabeled meats into Boston (fined $500), Cleveland (fined $1,000), and Somerville, Massachusetts (fined $200).

Now Katz had the chance to point the finger the other way. He recalled to the jury the first negotiating session, at the Commodore Hotel, where Kissel announced that the new contract had to be agreed upon by the expiration date of the old one or there would be a strike; no extension was possible. Later, he said, Lester Levy of Plymouth Rock had taken him aside and told him, "You know what they want? They want sixty thousand dollars. And they want it before the contract is signed and there is nothing we can do about it."

Katz then "talked to Mr. Kissel. I says, 'Frank, what do I hear there? Sixty-thousand dollars? This is ridiculous. What kind of figure is that?' And I was angry and he was angry. He brushed me aside. And he says, 'Stop chiseling. You get away cheap.' And he pushed me aside and walked into the room. That was it."

Late in May, Katz met at the New York Athletic Club with Kissel, Stubach, and two other meat dealers—Charles Trunz Jr., and Harry "Buddy" White, Kissel's in-law whom Nat Lokietz often complained had a competitive advantage because of the relationship. There were a couple of rounds of drinks, and dinner. Then, recalled Katz, "Mr. Kissel said that he wanted the sixty thousand dollars and . . . he wanted it in one lump. He wanted it before the contract is signed, and if this would not be paid before, there will be no contract. And he also said to me at that time, 'I want you to collect it.'

"And I said, 'Frank, I don't want to collect this. . . .'

"And then he spoke to Charlie Trunz. He said, 'Charlie, how about you collecting it?' And Charlie—Mr. Trunz—didn't want it either.

"He said, 'How about you, Buddy?' We all three didn't want to collect it. And then he said, 'Well, I don't want to go around.'

"We said, 'All right, we'll see what we can do.' "

So Katz and White made a list of pork dealers, and by a rough estimate of their size and financial strength determined who would pay what share. The biggest packers, like Merkel and Plymouth Rock, were stuck for 10 percent, or $6,000. Stoll and White were at the next level, $4,000, and so on down the line.

Katz remembered trying to sell the package to the other meat dealers at one of the negotiating sessions. They complained that the amounts assigned to them were too stiff. Warned Katz, "If a doctor says cancer, you must learn to live with it."

Immediately, he said, Kissel broke in protesting, "I resent being called a cancer."

Katz testified that he set up a meeting with Kissel at lunchtime one day at the Old Homestead restaurant, a popular (and excellent) beef house on Fourteenth Street and Ninth Avenue, right at the edge of the wholesale meat district. Just before departing, he reached into his office vault, pulled out $4,000 cash and later slipped it to Kissel in the men's room. More money probably changes hands in the men's room of the Old Homestead than in many bank branches.*

The propensity of meat dealers to keep large amounts of cash on hand that can be used to pay bribes became even more clear from the testimony of the next witness, Buddy White. White confirmed what Katz had said, and had described his own payoff to Kissel. Then a defense lawyer asked how White had procured the $4,000 cash. Replied White, "Well, I should have some money home. I make lots more than fifty thousand dollars a year."

Where did he keep his cash? In his upstairs bathroom, he said, "under the cabinet in the sink."

"You keep cash in there?" said the defense lawyer, feigning surprise.

"A little bit."

---

*An executive of a major American slaughtering and meatpacking company based well west of the Hudson River once told me of his meeting at the Old Homestead with Moe Steinman's brother and partner Sol Steinman. During a men's room break, the executive said, they were standing at adjoining urinals when suddenly he felt Steinman's hand in his pocket. His first stunned thought, the executive said, was that Steinman must be some kind of sex pervert. Within seconds, however, he realized that bills were being inserted. He says he pulled a couple of $100 bills out of his pocket, returned them to Steinman, and got out of the restaurant as fast as he could.

"How much is a little bit by your lights?"

"Ten thousand dollars sometimes," White responded.

The testimony of other witnesses indicated they did business the same way.

White also said that when word of the investigation leaked out in 1967, Kissel, his in-law, had met him in bars several times and urged him not to talk to the grand jury. Once, he testified, Kissel had demanded that White pack up his entire family and move from their home in Glenhead, New York, to New Jersey in order to avoid a subpoena.

Defense lawyers then took to the attack, and suggested through their questions on cross-examination that the state's case was built around the blackmail of prosecution witnesses. The lawyers already had established that the after-hours party apartment Lokietz had rented on West Twenty-third Street was bugged. Now they suggested that the only reason White had testified was that the D.A.'s men had threatened to tell White's wife and five kids what White had been doing in the apartment. White didn't exactly deny this, either—he just said he didn't recall. Nicholson and the detectives on his team insist to this day that no such tactics ever became part of the investigation, and that the dealers talked because they would have gone to jail for perjury or contempt if they hadn't talked.

What's clear is that fifteen of them did talk, with an overwhelming repetition of detail. Nat Lokietz and Sam Goldman of Merkel Meat were among the witnesses. There was testimony that thousands of dollars were transferred in a parking lot, or, in one case, brought to Muller's Long Island home in a brown paper bag. One dealer boasted of having shortchanged Kissel by $1,000 and gotten away with it. Another, Charles Trunz Jr., said Kissel had pried an extra $1,000 out of him, arguing, "Charlie, I think you can do a little better." There was repeated testimony about how Kissel had desperately gone back to the meat dealers in 1967, when the investigation was heating up, and had begged them not to talk.

The defense never denied that the payoffs took place. It merely argued that the employers had conspired to bribe the union bosses rather than the union bosses having conspired to extort money from the employers. The evidence, however, was so overwhelming that the jury's verdict of guilty was no surprise. What surprised people was Judge Abraham J. Gellinoff's sentencing, which actually would have approached a realistic punishment if it had been carried out. Kissel drew seven-and-a-half to fifteen years in state prison, Stubach five to ten years and Muller—who was sixty-six years old and in ill health—three to six years. Furthermore, Judge Gellinoff ordered them to prison immediately, despite their planned appeals, and they were locked into Sing-Sing on April 18, 1969. The judge's job had been made all the more difficult by the meat industry employers. These men, the very witnesses who had testified against the union leaders at trial, suddenly wrote letters to the judge before sentencing asking leniency for the defendants. In fact the letters praised the extortionists as honorable and trustworthy men! If these letters were the result of union pressure, it was never proven; anyway, they didn't work.

But the union bosses found help elsewhere. Less than two weeks after they were imprisoned, another judge ordered them free on the ground that there was probable cause their appeal would be upheld. Upset, the D.A.'s office unveiled its reserve weapon: a new indictment charging the same three union leaders with a similar extortion scheme against the fresh beef side of the industry during the same period. The new indictment named eleven additional meat companies that were forced to cough up $65,000. Before that case could go to trial, however, the appeal of the first case was denied, and the men went back to Sing-Sing on May 27, 1970. Muller was paroled less than two years later, and given his final discharge from supervision in May, 1976. Stubach was paroled in September, 1973, and died the following spring. Kissel did four years of hard time, then went on a work-release program until his parole May 2, 1975. Records of the State Department of Correctional Services show that Kissel was out working for a Bronx firm that can't be located now. Nicholson insists Kissel was brokering meat in Yonkers while serving his sentence. In the meantime, all three men had pleaded guilty to the second extortion indictment and had received sentences concurrent with their original ones.

Before Kissel even went away, he arranged for Local 174 to be placed in reliable hands. The local was merged with another local, which was operated by Kissel's friend and colleague Albert DeProspoe, who took over leadership of the combined local on Kissel's resignation. Al Scotti, the first assistant District Attorney, suggested that Pat Gorman send a team from the butchers' international headquarters in Chicago to make sure the newly-merged local would be run on the up-and-up. The union promised to do so, the D.A.'s men say, but never did.

Meanwhile, Nicholson had learned from some wiretaps that were kept in place that Kissel, long before his 1969 trial, had set up a clever new system for the on-going extortion. It was called "the baseball game." By the time the 1967 processed meat contract negotiations had rolled around, Kissel had come under heavy fire for his $60,000 shakedown at the previous talks. He apparently realized he would have to come up with something different. The price —$60,000—stayed the same. But no more would it be paid in a lump sum. Instead, each month during the life of the contract, 1967 to 1970, a company would be given a turn "at bat," on a rotating basis. During its month "at bat," each company would make its appropriate contribution to the pockets of the union leaders. With an indictment already pending based on the 1964 extortion from the same companies, there was little that Nicholson or the D.A.s could do about the newer racket. The prosecutors clung to the hope that stiff jail sentences against Stubach, Kissel, and Muller would prod the union into a genuine clean-up. Their hope was obviously misplaced.

Not only did Nicholson become aware of continued bribery and extortion, he also got a reminder of how underworld control of the meat industry affects quality as well as price. Acting on a tip from an anonymous caller, he and

Montello raided the Diamond Wise meat company and Stevens Meat Company, both in the Fourteenth Street meat district and both owned by fifty-eight-year-old, Polish-born Herman Weiser. The firms operated out of a joint warehouse and sold to hotels, restaurants, and steamship companies. Hours before the Nicholson raid, inspectors from the city Markets Commission had gone through the Diamond Wise-Stevens meat plant and had pronounced it fit. But the D.A.'s men found hundreds of pounds of rotten meat, chicken and hamburger, in boxes marked with phony inspection stamps. They also found chemical additives, including dangerous sodium bisulphite, which can make deteriorated meat look fresh. And on top of that, they found the warehouse was being used to store a load of hijacked gingham cloth worth $35,000.

The detectives also found evidence of why the city markets commission investigators might have come away from Diamond Wise with favorable reports. The owner, Weiser, handed Nicholson and Montello $500 each and promised another $500 the next day "if you'll let me get this hot stuff out." According to Nicholson, Weiser also offered to fix him up with a sixteen-year-old girl.

Weiser was charged with a half dozen violations including selling adulterated meat. Arrested along with him in the warehouse was Sidney Seewald, the owner of a long criminal record, but not the owner of the new Pontiac that he was driving. It had been stolen from the Hertz corporation. Police assumed that Seewald had something to do with the shipment of hot gingham, but could never prove it. He was charged instead with grand larceny, possession of stolen property and concealing stolen property—all in connection with the Pontiac.

Weiser cleared up the whole list of charges against him by pleading guilty to one count of attempted bribery. The sentencing judge, Arthur Markewich, looked at the evidence and at Weiser and announced, "This was a way of life for him. . . . I have no sympathy with him in his financial loss (the firm went out of business) because he brought this upon himself. At the risk of uttering platitudes, I would say that this is a real example of the wages of sin." The defense attorney argued that Weiser had suffered two heart attacks and that "any further strain in connection with business would be his death warrant." The judge gave him a suspended sentence, put him on probation, and ordered him to pay restitution—a total of $2,696.29.

Justice Mitchell D. Schweitzer heard Sidney Seewald plead guilty to concealing stolen property and sentenced him to time served—Sewald had spent a night in jail after his arrest before posting bail—and discharged him from custody.

Clearly the meat industry now, in 1969, was no cleaner than Nicholson had found it five years earlier. And the biggest crime of all was still to come.

PART FOUR

CHEESE

1

A Bloody Tale of Curdling

If the Mafia can come to Alburg, Vermont, this dreary, ice-stung, snow-pelted corner of the North Woods, you have to believe it can show up anywhere. And the Mafia was here.

Until the hoods moved in quietly about 1966, Alburg's 520 residents managed to eke a living out of their ragged dairy farms, supplemented in the summer by catering to the needs of a few vacationing campers on nearby Lake Champlain. Then came the Great Mafia Cheese Caper. In 1974, the hoods moved away, but several years later the economy of Alburg still hadn't fully recovered from the devastation. Meanwhile, the cheese caper had come and gone from such other unlikely crime capitals as Luxemburg, Wisconsin, and Hayfield, Minnesota. Every community the mobsters have invaded has suffered—as have the rest of us who consume the chief product of towns like Alburg, Luxemburg, and Hayfield: milk.

The caper works this way: milk is bought on credit; cheese is made from the milk and sold; then nobody pays for the milk. For the cheesemaker, it's a sure-fire way to profit. For the farmer, it's about as rewarding as an outbreak of brucellosis in his herd. Thousands of dairy farmers have been stuck with millions of dollars in unpaid bills in recent years, and at least one large farmers' cooperative outside of Alburg has been driven out of business. Yet the price of cheese for the consumer doesn't go down under the Mafia plan. It goes up.

From all indications, the cheese caper is still operating at this writing. At least many of the principals are still in the cheese business, as their families have been for generations. And in 1978 a rash of new plants seems to be springing up. Why does the law let them continue? As with other Mafia business scams, you can't prove the operation is illegal until after the victims have already been milked dry—in this case, literally. By then, the Mafia will have moved on, and if by chance a criminal charge is brought, the trial evidence will concern only the limited local situation. No jury or sentencing judge will be allowed enough information to understand how the caper actually works, over and over again.

The cheese caper really is just a new wrinkle in an old racket—control of the pizza industry. When an American orders a pizza, the Mafia expects a slice of the pie, and usually gets it. The Mafia, of course, has a predilection for making money off retail industries by cornering the market on some essential ingredient or process; pizza must have seemed a natural, for several reasons. First, there are a lot of independent pizzeria owners who don't have much individual clout against a big supplier. Second, many of them are Italian, and thus inclined to deal with other Italians. And finally, while most of the ingredients of pizza—flour, tomatoes, anchovies, and so forth—are in wide supply, one ingredient, mozzarella cheese, comes from a relatively few factories in dairy centers like Vermont and Wisconsin. Control them, and nobody's going to make a true pizza without you. So a lot of old-line Mafia families entered the cheese business early in this century.

In 1973, when the federal government undertook a big investigation of the Carlo Gambino Mafia family, FBI agents assigned to the case found themselves becoming experts in the mozzarella business. They investigated at least half a dozen major mozzarella makers, and found every one was linked to the Mob. An agent finally went to Kraft, the country's biggest cheese maker, and asked why Kraft doesn't make mozzarella. He reported being told by an official that Kraft was afraid criminal elements might burn Kraft trucks, or commit other acts of violence if Kraft tried to compete. (When I questioned Kraft about this, the company denied that it feels threatened. But it declined to comment on whether the mozzarella industry is controled by racketeers. Kraft said it wholesales mozzarella to supermarkets under its label, but that it doesn't want to disclose the names of the manufacturers whom it buys the mozzarella from.)

There are large mozzarella makers, such as the Meinerz Creamery division of Beatrice Foods Inc. (whose stock is publicly traded), which are apparently free of Mob control. But they sell mainly to other large companies, such as the Pizza Hut chain. Even then, their executives rub elbows with mobsters at trade meetings and regularly do business with them. Says Archie Meinerz, who runs the Meinerz Creamery, "There's been many stories about the heavy boys being involved. We know those folks. We know of their reputation. But there's never been any pressure from them." Still, when Mr. Meinerz's cheese is destined for local pizza shops, his company has sold it through Mafia-run cheese distributors.

The reason is clear. As the FBI discovered in its investigation, Gambino relatives and associates not only run cheese factories in the boondocks, but also control warehouses in the cities and distributorships in the suburbs. They are at least close friends with a major manufacturer of pizza ovens in New York. The Gambino organization establishes its own pizzeria businesses and brings in illegal aliens to operate them. For obvious reasons, the aliens are easy to control. From what the FBI found and from what sources in the industry report, there are literally hundreds of such businesses in the New York-New Jersey area alone, and similar methods have been used elsewhere in the country. Random calls to a dozen or so pizza parlors to find out who owns, manages, or works in them can make abundantly clear that a wall of secrecy surrounds the industry. First names are as much as anyone will provide. The FBI found that the businesses are routinely started with juice (loanshark) loans, usually of $40,000 to $50,000. The Mob covers up for the illegally high interest by overcharging for mozzarella. If the market price is 90 cents a pound, the borrowers are charged $1.30.

Thus pizza prices are kept artificially high and the Mafia maintains control of the industry. Competition and other forms of rebellion are discouraged by the unusually high rate of gang-style killings in the pizza industry. For example, the June, 1973 murder of Antonio Priola, who was shot twice in the head and dumped on a Brooklyn street, was believed to be the result of Priola's activities in the pizza business in Kingston, New York.

The FBI found that many mozzarella sales are made cash and aren't recorded, leading agents to suspect massive income tax violations. The pizzerias also are suspected outlets for drugs and gambling. Shortly before he died in 1973, Paul Gambino, Carlo's brother and a convicted counterfeiter, talked with some relatives about buying a big dairy farm in South America to export dehydrated milk products to the United States. It's doubtful anyone could find a more perfect cover for heroin smuggling than a powdered milk export plant in South America. (As far as the FBI knows, the deal died with Paul Gambino.)

Despite all these findings, the FBI investigation of the mozzarella industry came to naught. The data was turned over to the Manhattan office of the federal strike force against racketeering and organized crime, which chose to concentrate its legal attack against the Gambino family's overall loansharking operations. Numerous family members were indicted, including several who are active in the processing and distribution of meat and other food items. Almost all the defendants were acquitted in 1976 when the key witness chose to go to jail for contempt of court rather than to testify, as will be described in Part Nine. The bulk of the FBI investigation of the pizzeria industry went down the drain with the loansharking case.

The Great Mafia Cheese Caper that devastated Alburg, Vermont, Luxemberg, Wisconsin, Hayfield, Minnesota, and other dairy communities around the country grew out of a merger that took place in the late 1930s and early 1940s, combining eastern and midwestern Mafia cheese interests. The organization of Joseph "Joe Bananas" Bonanno of Brooklyn which is near a lot of Italian cheese stores, teamed up with the old Capone organization in Chicago, which is near a lot of cows. Both families had been in the business independently. The Capones controlled the Milk Wagon Drivers' Union and at least two large dairy companies (a handy arrangement for peaceful contract bargaining), and the Bonannos were major food distributors. While Capone, of course, is long dead, Bonanno is considered by many authorities to be the top Mafia boss in the country at this writing. Ties between the two families went back at least to 1930, when (according to old intelligence reports still in law enforcement files) Bonanno had sold Capone a load of machine guns. The cheese merger, however, may have resulted in more bloodshed than the machine gun deal did.

In 1941, the Capone-Bonanno combine began muscling into Grande Cheese Company, which had addresses in downtown Chicago and Lomira, Wisconsin. Grande is now called Grande Cheese Products Inc., and is based in Fon Du Lac, Wisconsin. It remains a major producer of mozzarella cheese, and it continues to be managed by descendants or in-laws of the Mafiosi who took it over in the forties. Of late there's been no indication of continued strong-arm tactics. The industry is acutely aware of Grande's ancestry, and of the Mafia's interest in the mozzarella business. The managers say the family is clean and law-abiding in this generation, and that they have bought back the last remaining stock held by a Bonanno. Nevertheless, the head of the company still appeared on the Justice Department's latest "Organized Crime Principal Subject List," issued in 1970.

On the Capone side in the original Grande deal were Ross Prio, an archetypal Mafia gangster, and Fred A. Romano, who was an assistant state's attorney for Cook County as well as being a partner of Prio's in ownership of a parking lot and another business in Chicago, the Cook County seat. Prio and Romano illustrate perfectly the kind of chummy relationship that mobsters like to develop with government officials. The Sicilian-born Prio compiled a long record of arrests in this country for assault with a deadly weapon, intimidation by arson, bootlegging, bombing, and murder. He was convicted only once. In 1953, when the *Chicago Sun-Times* exposed the earlier ties between Prio and the prosecutor, the state's attorney's office denied there had been anything improper and accused the *Sun-Times* of "yellow, irresponsible journalism." Except for occasional unfavorable news articles (particularly after Joe Valachi named him one of the seven top gangsters in Chicago), Prio enjoyed his golden years with a healthy nest egg, much of which he owed to the pizza-eating public. He died in 1972.

His partners in the Grande deal, representing the Bonanno side, were several members of the DiBella family, whose patriarch, Giovanna DiBella, was involved with the Bonanno family on Sicily, and may have been related.

Giovanna's brother John, who took over the cheese business, lived for a while at Joe Bonanno's house in Arizona, and was a partner of Bonanno in at least two land developments and a parking lot there. Bonanno sold cheese for Grande, and his wife, Fay, was first on a list of shareholders Grande supplied to Wisconsin regulators in 1966 (the only list of its kind on record). Joe's son Salvatore "Bill" Bonanno once remarked that he was taking care of some business for Grande, according to a law enforcement report. The history of Grande and its affiliates and off-shoots pretty well destroys the notion, advanced by *Honor Thy Father,* that the Bonannos were honest businessmen who simply catered to human vices, or that they left their murderous tactics behind when they entered the public marketplace for legitimate goods like cheese.

Nowadays, it's common for cheesemakers to put wine in their recipes, leaving the product streaked with red. But if cheese from the Chicago area bore red streaks in the 1940s, it may have been because of something other than wine. In Grande's first years under Mafia influence, at least six persons intimately connected with the company, its prior ownership or its competition met with pronounced misfortune. In 1943, Thomas O. Neglia, a partner in a Prio-Romano parking lot enterprise whose name also appeared on Grande's incorporation papers, went in for a shave and was murdered in the barber's chair. The next year, cheeseman Sam Gervasi was killed in a repair shop, and James V. De Angelo, who had claimed an earlier interest in Grande, was found in the trunk of his wife's car with his skull crushed. In 1945, Anofrio Vitale, whose name was with Neglia's on the Grande incorporation papers, was an unexpected product of the Chicago sewer system, and Vincent Benevento, who had been known till then as "the cheese king," was shot five times in front of his place of business in West Bend, Wisconsin. Finally, in 1947, Nick DeJohn, another Italian-American who blundered into the mozzarella field unauthorized, was found in the trunk of a car in San Francisco, and the Bonanno-Capone grip on the cheese business had solidified—or perhaps "coagulated" would be a better word. (By this time, Anthony "Joe Batters" Accardo had assumed leadership of the Chicago Mob, but Prio has retained his good standing under each succeeding godfather.)

It was philosophically, if not geographically, appropriate that Grande's labor ties were to Teamster Local 138 of Vineland, New Jersey, later identified as a branch office for Murder Inc.

Grande was a major national supplier of mozzarella. Evidently it was unable to meet the growing demand, because John DiBella and his brother and sister went on to found Kohlsville Cheese Company of Fon Du Lac, Wisconsin, in 1947; Gourmay [*sic*] Cheese Company Inc., also of Fon Du Lac, in 1954; and Cloverdale Dairy Products Inc. of Fairwater, Wisconsin, in 1957. By the time of the famous raid on the Apalachin, New York, Mafia gathering in 1957, Joe Bonanno's cheese empire had spread to manufacturing plants in Michigan, Colorado, California, and Canada. He also owned (usually with a partner or two to run the place) a laundry, two coat companies, and a very unusual funeral parlor. History may record Joseph Bonanno as the mortician who invented the duplex coffin. That is, he specially designed a burying box with a false bottom and a secret compartment, where his family's hit victims could be laid to rest underneath the displayed body of record. Bonanno supplied muscular pallbearers for tandem burials so the strain of the extra weight wouldn't show, and as William Lambert and Sandy Smith described it in *Life* magazine in 1967, "Bonanno's victims in the lower berths were put underground before police even became aware they were missing."

While the notorious Joe Bananas made this feeble attempt to lead a respectable second life, John DiBella, the cheese tycoon, made a successful attempt. Though he was Bonanno's friend, follower, and possibly relative, DiBella apparently had no criminal record. He reported annual taxable income averaging nearly $40,000 back in the 1950s when that was a lot. He was known among reputable executives throughout the food industry as a prominent, if suspicious, colleague.

Yet there is no doubt that he came from a criminal family. One brother served six years in prison for homicide in the 1920s, and another chose to return to Sicily rather than stand trial for a charge that isn't specified in his police record. When John DiBella himself was returning from a trip to Italy in 1961, police searched him at Kennedy (then Idlewild) Airport and found a black book that served them for a while as a telephone directory of prominent Mafiosi. John DiBella clearly had extensive connections to the violent underworld, and it seems unrealistic to suppose that he bore no responsibility for the bloodshed that established his business—or that his relatives and associates who helped him run it didn't know.

Nevertheless, DiBella died a respected citizen in 1964. He got a proper funeral, attended by colleagues both Mafia and legitimate. Some are still in the food industry today. Carlo P. Caputo was there, and so were law enforcement agents who described Caputo in their notes as head of the Wisconsin Mafia. DiBella's property passed peacefully on to relatives who had been involved in the cheese business since 1950.

Already, however, forces were in motion that would alter control of the Italian cheese industry in the United States. As with control of stores, dress factories, union locals, and many other large enterprises, control of the Italian cheese industry was merely an auxiliary prize in a much larger power struggle for control of a Mafia family. The cheese industry was merely a spoil in the Banana War. Yet it illustrates how simple products that we use every day may hang on the outcome of Mafia violence.

On the night of October 20–21, 1964, two men grabbed Joe Bonanno as he and his lawyer were approaching the lawyer's apartment building at Park Avenue and Thirty-sixth Street in New York. The men hustled Bonanno into a car and he wasn't seen in public again until he unexpectedly strode into the

U.S. Courthouse in Manhattan May 17, 1966. Reporters and law enforcement officials have offered numerous guesses as to what had happened. Bonanno had been scheduled to testify before an investigative grand jury in New York the day after he disappeared, and perhaps other Mafiosi were afraid he might talk. Or perhaps Bonanno arranged his own kidnapping to avoid the grand jury's questions. Then a story came out that Bonanno had let contracts for the murder of four rival godfathers (Carlo Gambino, Stefano Magaddino, Thomas Lucchese, and Frank DeSimone, which would have been about the heaviest single hit list in history). According to this story, the appointed gunman (Joseph Colombo) betrayed the murder plans to the national commission, which then ordered Bonanno's kidnapping (and arranged for Colombo's meteoric rise to boss of his own family as a reward).

Finally, on June 10, 1969, the Justice Department submitted in open court (as described in Part Two) the transcribed product of its bug on the office of Sam the Plumber DeCavalcante, the New Jersey Mob boss whom the national commission had appointed in 1964 to mediate certain disputes with Bonanno. DeCavalcante's taped conversations* make clear that for several months before Bonanno disappeared, the commission had been summoning him to come explain himself.

Sam the Plumber, after talking with other members of the commission, told his underbosses in the bugged office—and there's no reason to think he was lying to them—that Bonanno had staged his own kidnapping, although Sam couldn't figure out why ("Who the hell is he kidding?" DeCavalcante remarked). DeCavalcante mentioned nothing about a mass murder plot. But he cited two other grievances against Bonanno. First, Joe had promoted his son Bill to the high post of *consiglieri* over the heads of more veteran hoods whose noses were put out of joint—Bill Bonanno was looked on by other Mafia members as a pampered, inexperienced brat (or, in Sam the Plumber's words, "a bedbug"). Second, Joe Bonanno had been invading the territories of other Mob bosses—in California, Frank DeSimone, and in Canada, Stefano Magaddino (who is based in Buffalo but claims extensive rights across the border).

The California incursion was led by Bill and forty assigned soldiers. It seemed largely an attempt by Joe to give his son an independent territory to work. The existing boss, DeSimone, still didn't like it, and Bill and soldiers finally went home to Brooklyn. Whether or not Bonanno's cheese factory in California was part of this dispute isn't clear. But cheese certainly was a major part, if not *the* major part, of Joe Bonanno's Canadian adventure.

Giuseppe Saputo & Sons Ltd., Montreal, is today a major Canadian cheese maker, as it was back in 1954 when Joseph Bonanno was allowed to buy 20 percent of the stock for a mere $8,000 (Saputo explained at the time that Bonanno had "been very helpful to us over the years advising us," and there-

---

*While such evidence became public record as it was turned over to defense lawyers for examination, it could never be submitted by the prosecution as evidence before a jury.

fore merited the bargain investment). John DiBella's son Pino went to work for Saputo. Giuseppe Saputo and his sons Emmanuel and Francesco have run several cheese making and distributing companies, including Cremerie Stella Inc. (which the Saputos say is now out of business), Caillette Products, and Saputo Cheese Ltd., whose products are now widely available in American stores and supermarkets. The Saputos also run companies in Montreal that distribute olive oil, salami, and other Italian foods, and in 1978 announced plans to build a large cheese plant in Vermont (in fact, they filed a request for $1.4 million in state-backed revenue bonds to finance it).

In 1963, the year before Bonanno disappeared, a cheese war broke out in Montreal when a man named Santo Calderone went into business in competition with Saputo. According to police reports, Calderone's trucks and equipment were bombed, burned, and vandalized, and acid was dropped in his fermenting milk; he closed up shop. In 1971, the New York State Liquor Authority requested the Montreal police's opinion of the Saputo operation (in connection with a liquor license application by an associate), and got the following answer: "If you want to commit suicide in Montreal, you make riccota and mozzarella cheese. Nobody sells mozzarella cheese in this city unless it's Saputo. The whole operation is Mafia."

The report went on to say that Saputo's accounts, especially at stores that cater to Canada's nearly one million citizens of Italian origin, are lined up by Frank Cotroni, brother of Vincent "Vic" Cotroni, boss of the Mafia in Canada. Police surveillance once spotted Vic Cotroni himself riding in a car with Francesco Saputo. The Cotroni name "strikes fear into Italian shopowners," the report said. "It's a subtle form of extortion, but you can't make a case with it. They won't say they are being pressured. That's how they are getting into pizza parlors and stores throughout the area, and we can't do a thing about it." Asked about the report in 1978, a Saputo spokesman said Cotroni "has never been selling cheese for us."

After Bonanno returned to public view in 1966, he tried to regain control of his Brooklyn rackets and the bullets started flying. At least nine men were murdered—and others died of "heart attacks" under such circumstances that Sam DeCavalcante said he suspected poisoning. Bombs rocked the Bonannos' hideaway in Tucson. Finally, by 1969, some kind of deal apparently had been reached with the commission whereby Bonanno would go into "exile" in Arizona and give up his Brooklyn rackets, in exchange for which the Mafia wouldn't kill him.

Some of the Bonannos' cheese ties appear to have survived Joe's exile. But the main part of the empire—the part that was built around the distribution system headquartered in Brooklyn—changed hands, along with the Bonannos' interests in gambling, loansharking, and other Brooklyn rackets. As in the case of the other rackets, the Mafia family that took over the Bonannos' cheese interests was the one headed by Carlo Gambino. Shortly thereafter, in 1969, on the death of Vito Genovese, Carlo Gambino became boss of all bosses, head of the Mafia national commission.

There were four principal Bonanno associates in Brooklyn who, when they came over to the Gambino fold, brought the cheese business along with them. One was Joseph Curreri, a cousin of the DiBellas. The other three were brothers: Vincent, Joseph, and Matteo Falcone, whose father had been a business partner (lemon groves, vineyards, and hotels) of Giovanna DiBella on Sicily. Vincent Falcone once acknowledged at a liquor license hearing in New York that John DiBella had introduced him to Joe Bonanno, and had described Bonanno as DiBella's "godfather."

2

The Great Mafia Cheese Caper

Murder, loansharking, gambling, drugs, and the use of alien labor—these were merely the more understood and accepted crimes that the Mafia brought to the cheese industry. But along the whey, the mozzarella mob has also learned some additional money-making techniques that are much more sophisticated. It took just such a trick to drive the Mafia's message home to Alburg and other small towns.

What the Mob has learned is what certain economics professors refer to as Drew's Law, after Daniel Drew, the nineteenth-century commodities flim-flammer and transportation tycoon. Before Drew was driven into his final bankruptcy, he had thoroughly soaked the Astors and Vanderbilts, among others. Simply stated, Drew's Law reads: "If you don't pay your overhead, your gross is net."

Among the first to test this thesis successfully with mozzarella were Joseph and Vincent Falcone and Joseph Curreri, the former Bonanno associates. They were soon joined in the cheese caper by some of their new friends from the Gambino family who recognized a good thing when they saw it: Joseph Gambino (Carlo's brother) and his son, Thomas, who already controlled the frozen stuffed clam market.

There are three Falcone brothers, Vincent, Joseph, and Matteo. Joseph was born in 1925, has four children and still lives in Brooklyn. He has testified in court that he dropped out of school after seventh grade to work at an Italian dairy. In 1949, he and his brothers formed their own business, Falcone Dairy

Products Inc., which had various addresses in Brooklyn. "We helped develop the modern mozzarella as known today," he once boasted.

In 1954, Joseph and Matteo Falcone were brought in by the DiBellas to run an east coast branch of the DiBellas' Wisconsin cheese operation. The Falcones' father had been an old business partner of the DiBellas' father on Sicily, where they both knew the Bonannos. Gourmay Cheese Company was founded as a 100-percent-owned subsidiary of the DiBellas' Grande Cheese Company; Joseph Falcone became president of Gourmay, Matteo became vice-president, and John DiBella's nephew Joseph was treasurer.

In about 1960, Joseph Curreri, then forty, went to work for the Falcones, first as a salesman, then as manager of the Brooklyn operation. Curreri, also a Brooklyn family man, has testified that he had completed one year of pre-med at Northwestern before going into the cheese business.

By the mid-1960s, Falcone Dairy Products had acquired a Philadelphia-based subsidiary called King of Pizza Inc., which operated plants or distributorships in Gloucester, Mt. Holly, and Cherry Hill, New Jersey, as well as in Philadelphia. Falcone Dairy was offering not just cheese, but a broad line of restaurant supplies.

Then, about 1966, just when Joe Bonanno's troubles might have interrupted the flow of mozzarella from Wisconsin, the Falcones founded a cheese factory in a converted ice house on the main street of Alburg. The plant was placed under the corporate umbrella of their Brooklyn wholesale business, Falcone Dairy Products. Curreri managed the business in Brooklyn, and they hired a native Vermont cheesemaker, J. Leo Laramee, to run the Alburg operation.

Alburg residents remember that some "New York-looking men" would arrive at the cheese plant from time to time in big black Cadillacs. But the natives never got to know the Falcones. On their trips to Vermont, the Brooklynites preferred to commute from the Ramada Inn at Burlington, forty miles south of Alburg. Their preference is understandable, if my visit in 1977 is any indication.

Alburg is not a wealthy town. The social highlight of the day seems to be ducking out of the blizzard for a cup of coffee at Kay's Restaurant, which is literally a snowball's throw from the site of the former cheese factory. I ordered pancakes, thinking at least to get some local maple syrup, but was served an immitation-flavored commercial brand. The popular topic of conversation at the lunch counter was whose thermometer recorded the lowest temperature the night before. The day I came, the winner was twenty-four degrees. Nobody bothered to call it twenty-four "below," because twenty-four "above" would have been unthinkable. There isn't any dilettante talk about wind-chill factors, either; in Alburg, they've got the real McCoy.

Strangers seldom move to Alburg. "People born here, they stay here," I was told by Isolde Quiser, whose husband repairs CB radios. "There's not much to do," she added. She said she's heard about the Mafia, but still doesn't believe it was ever in Alburg. "We don't have much trouble here," she said. "Once in a while, teenagers come in from Canada."

The big change for Alburg began in 1969, so quietly that few noticed it. By filing certain legal papers, the Falcones made the Alburg cheese operation independent from its former Brooklyn parent. The new corporation, Alburg Creamery Inc., continued to ship mozzarella primarily to Falcone Dairy Products in Brooklyn, but instead of its being an internal transfer of merchandise as before, Alburg creamery began to bill Falcone Dairy. What the local people didn't understand at the time, was that this arrangement would allow Alburg Creamery to go bankrupt without disrupting the prosperity at Falcone Dairy.

By 1971, the first Vermont dairy cooperative had sued Alburg Creamery for lack of payment for milk. The suit was settled, but Alburg kept falling further behind. By early summer, 1973, the creamery owed well over half a million dollars to several cooperatives, including nearly $400,000 to the Milton (Vermont) Cooperative. There were more lawsuits. The jig was up.

What happened next was exactly what you might expect to happen at a Mafia-run plant that is faced with going out of business: There was a suspicious fire that reduced the plant to rubble and destroyed books and records. A state investigation couldn't find physical evidence of arson, so no charges were brought. But if an arsonist was involved, as many suspect, he can brag a long time about the Alburg job, because the creamery was directly across a two-lane street from the Alburg Volunteer Fire Department.

On the night of the fire, July 13, 1973, David McFadden, then a volunteer fireman, was at the Alburg Inn, which is next door to the fire station and across from Kay's (Alburg isn't very big). "I remember I was dancing and I looked out the window and you could see the flames," he says. The creamery was devoured almost at once, before anyone could act to save it.

Questioned before a grand jury, Joseph Falcone acknowledged that he was in Vermont the day of the fire, but offered a staunch alibi witness who he said was with him all day. The witness, interestingly, was Thomas Ocera, whose family ran two businesses that distributed Falcone merchandise to Long Island restaurants, and who fronted for the Falcones in operating a large restaurant and catering house in Merrick, Long Island. The restaurant's liquor license was yanked by the state when the three Falcone brothers became known as the true owners, but in the meantime, according to testimony at the license revocation hearing, the restaurant attracted promotional help from higher-ups in several Mafia families. Ocera's companies eventually welched on large debts. Ocera himself was savagely beaten at the restaurant in January, 1971, supposedly by loansharks. But apparently this didn't dampen his loyalty to the Falcones when Joseph relied on him for an alibi in an arson investigation.

The fire at the Alburg Creamery cost Alburg's insurer, Lumbermen's Mutual Casualty Company, $350,000. It would have cost Lumbermen's a lot more except for the alertness of some U. S. border guards. According to government sources, two big truckloads of stinking, rancid mozzarella cheese had been shipped from Canada the day before the fire, destination Alburg Creamery. If the guards hadn't turned the cheese back because of its condition, the cheese would have been burned up in the fire, and presumably reported as an insurance loss worth about $80,000. The cheese came from Giuseppe Saputo & Sons, the Montreal company that gave 20 percent of its stock to Joseph Bonanno and, according to police, worked with the Cotroni brothers on its accounts. Joseph Falcone's Mafia ties allowed him to call on his friends in Canada for help in a pinch, the same way he could call on Thomas Ocera. If the shipments of two truckloads of useless mozzarella from Saputo's to Alburg the day before the fire wasn't part of a plan, it was one hell of a coincidence.

The local bank that held the mortgage on the Alburg factory had a direct claim on the first $100,000 from Lumbermen's Mutual. That still left $250,000 in additional insurance money, even without the claim for the spoiled mozzarella from Canada. The Falcones were never able to ease their pain with this money, however. Before a penny of it was paid over by Lumbermen's, Alburg's big creditors—three farmers' cooperatives—forced an involuntary bankruptcy, freezing the insurance money.

The $250,000 should have provided close to enough to satisfy the creditors, because on paper the Alburg Creamery was only marginally insolvent. It still had as assets several hundred thousand dollars in accounts receivable from Falcone Dairy Products, to which Alburg was shipping about $1.6 million a year in mozzarella (exact figures aren't available because Alburg's records were destroyed in the fire). Theoretically, the farmers, as creditors in bankruptcy, could sue Falcone Dairy for the money they were owed.

But the mozzarella mob was ready for them. In January, 1974, just as the court was sinking its teeth into the bankruptcy case, Joseph Falcone and Joseph Curreri made a bookkeeping switch. They suddenly remembered that back in the fall of 1971, about half the cheese that the Alburg Creamery had shipped—four hundred thousand pounds of it—had been rancid. So they put retroactive credits on the books, which turned Falcone Dairy from Alburg's biggest debtor into a $48,709.31-creditor. In other words, Falcone Dairy claimed that it had suffered losses because of the rancid cheese, and was entitled to additional money just as the farmers were.

Unfortunately for Falcone Dairy, Albert O. Axten, the FBI's resident agent in Montpelier, had been watching the Alburg Creamery ever since the investigation of the suspected arson. When he saw the Alburg bankruptcy papers, he sensed fraud in the way Falcone Dairy had escaped without paying its bills, and he persuaded the Justice Department to bring charges against Joseph Falcone and Joseph Curreri. (Although Vincent Falcone was fully active in Falcone Dairy's operations, he wasn't on record as having directed the accounting credits for bad cheese, and so he wasn't charged.)

The Falcone-Curreri trial was held in Burlington in 1976. Key testimony was provided by J. Leo Laramee, the hired cheesemaker, who said that he didn't recall anyone mentioning anything to him about half the cheese he made being rancid. Once again, Joseph Falcone needed witnesses to support his story. And in the case of the rancid cheese, there were plenty of witnesses around who were indebted to him. They were Falcone Dairy's customers— Brooklyn-based wholesalers who service New York-New Jersey area pizzerias. And they were willing to offer documents or witnesses asserting that Falcone Dairy had indeed been supplying a lot of bad cheese and had been forced to give refunds for it. The companies that provided evidence for the Falcone-Curreri defense make up a handy Who's Who of pizzeria suppliers in the metropolitan area:

There was Lido Cheese Company, which Joseph Falcone acknowledged having bought "for my son when he left school." It was run by both his sons, and Joseph Falcone himself was the authorized signator of its checks.

There was Campagna Brothers, whose president, Joseph Campagna, acknowledged on the stand that the Falcones helped get him started in the business.

There was Lucille Farm Products, run by Philip and Gennaro Falivene, longtime friends and customers of the Falcones who were actually associated with them in the Alburg Creamery operation in 1971, but later gave up their interest.

And there was Ferro Foods, owned and run by Frank Ferro and Frank Gambino, respectively the son-in-law and the son of Paul Gambino, the convicted counterfeiter who wanted to set up a powdered milk export operation in South America. Ferro and Paul Gambino had worked together in a well-publicized shakedown of the knife-grinding industry in 1959. After the Banana War, Ferro and Frank Gambino apparently were involved in the settlement that brought the Falcones into the Gambino camp. The Falcones set them up in a cheese business, Ferro Foods, with a warehouse on the premises of Falcone Dairy Products, which supplied Ferro with cheese from Alburg. Now, at trial, when the Falcones needed evidence of bad cheese, Ferro Foods provided evidence.

At Ferro Foods, cheese seemed to be going bad even faster than the Falcones could ship it. According to trial evidence, Falcone Dairy's sales to Ferro in the second half of 1971 totaled only $70,027.14, while credits for bad merchandise totaled a more substantial $86,011.42. All told, in the two and one-half years before the fire at Alburg, Falcone's newly-revised records listed $905,474.07 in credits to customers for rancid cheese. This raised the question of what happened to all the bad cheese. If the wholesalers had sold it, after writing it off on the books as rancid, then they, too, would be guilty. The Internal Revenue Service was called in to investigate, but what with the informal nature of bookkeeping in the pizzeria industry, the IRS failed to find evidence that might substantiate criminal charges.

The jury in the Falcone-Curreri case chose not to believe the self-serving testimony of the distributors, however. It convicted both Curreri and Joseph Falcone of bankruptcy fraud—falsely concealing the assets of a company in bankruptcy—and the judge sentenced them to three years in prison. They stayed free on appeal well into 1977.

The Milton Cooperative, which once represented more than four hundred Vermont dairy farmers, went bust because of the Alburg Creamery bankruptcy. More than one hundred Milton members were taken in by the St. Albans [Vermont] Cooperative, which paid off Milton's bank debts and got the money back by deducting ten cents a hundredweight from the real price of the former Milton members' milk sales. By 1977, most of the farmers had completed paying off their debts. One, Alton Bruso of Alburg, who has fifty cows, estimates that he lost $3,500. "Back here, we don't even know what the Mafia is," Bruso says. "Sure, I'm angry, but what can we do?"

Meanwhile, if J. Leo Laramee was really making rancid cheese at the Alburg factory, as it was later claimed, the stink evidently didn't bother the Falcones very much. Right after the fire, Joseph Falcone flew to Vermont to enlist Laramee's services in another mozzarella venture. Accompanying Falcone was the man who some observers think is the real Big Cheese: Thomas Gambino.

There are two important Tommy Gambinos. Neither has ever been convicted of a crime. One, Carlo's son, runs trucking and other operations in the New York-New Jersey garment industry, and will be discussed in Part Eight. The Tommy Gambino who flew to Vermont to see J. Leo Laramee is Carlo's nephew. He, too, is known in some circles as a legitimate businessman, thanks to a large food operation he runs.

Back in 1968, according to reliable reports, Tommy Gambino and his brother Emmanuel, a loanshark who was later murdered, ran across a Long Island bail bondsman and a local deputy sheriff, who, in their spare time had developed a process for making stuffed clams in the bail bondsman's basement. With the help of Irving Behrman, a former supermarket chain owner whom they had already turned into a business front, the Gambinos incorporated Neptune's Nuggets, Inc., which used the process on a large scale. The bail bondsman and deputy were quickly out of it. The Gambinos had extensive supermarket connections—which involve Moe Steinman, and which will be detailed in Part Nine—and soon Neptune's Nuggets was selling baked clams, frozen clams and shrimp to most of the big supermarket chains in the east.

Still, Neptune's Nuggets was only number two in its field. Another frozen stuffed seafood manufacturer, Matlaw's Food Products Inc. of West Haven, Connecticut, was doing better, and apparently with good reason. Thomas C. Renner, a Newsday reporter and author who often writes about the Mafia, bought the products at a supermarket and commissioned a laboratory study of them. The study showed that the Matlaw's product contained 24 percent actual clam tissue, while the Neptune's Nuggets product contained only 9 percent. Moreover, the test showed, the Matlaw's clams had a coliform count (coliform is a bacillus indicating fecal contamination) of 25 per gram, while Neptune's Nuggets had a count of 88 per gram (up to 100 per gram was legally allowable). And a test on all bacteria showed Matlaw's with 44,000 per gram, and Neptune's Nuggets with 37 *million* per gram (100,000 per gram was legally allowable).

Shortly after Renner described Neptune's Nuggets in a 1971 *Newsday* series called "Organized Crime and Supermarkets," Neptune's Nuggets closed up shop on Long Island and merged with Matlaw's. The merger, as it was filed with the State of Connecticut, involved nothing more than a straight stock-swap, with resulting fifty-fifty ownership. This appears, at least on the face of it, to be little more than a giveaway by the original owners of half of Matlaw's assets to the Gambinos. Marvin Gutkin and Bernard Katz, the original owners, continued to operate the firm with the Gambinos. Interviewed for this book, Gutkin and Thomas Gambino declined to say anything of substance over the telephone, or to promise that they would say any more if a reporter journeyed out to visit them. But Matlaw's, under the Gambinos, seems to have had little trouble getting its products into the supermarkets.

And so J. Leo Laramee, the Vermont cheesemaker, found Tommy Gambino, the seafood tycoon, a pretty impressive figure back in 1973 when Joseph Falcone introduced them. The deal that Falcone and Gambino came to Vermont to talk about involved Valley Lea Dairies Inc., a farmers' cooperative based in South Bend, Indiana. Falcone and Gambino had a contract to make Valley Lea's milk into cheese and sell it, and they persuaded Leo Laramee to run their operation again. Laramee was set up at a plant owned by Valley Lea in Hayfield, Minnesota, making Greek-style feta cheese for sale to a distributing company Thomas Gambino set up in West Haven.

At the same time, a Valley Lea mozzarella plant was opening in New Wilmington, Pennsylvania, with equipment owned by United Cheese Corp. of Brooklyn, which also received the plant's product, United Cheese was financially backed by Joseph and Vincent Falcone and their wives, and was located in the same warehouse complex occupied by Falcone Dairy and Ferro Foods, the Gambino family distributorship.

Once again, the dairy farmer was literally left with the hind teat. On November 13, 1975, Valley Lea filed suit in New York State Court, Brooklyn, against United Cheese and both Falcone families. In fifteen months of the mozzarella plant's operation, the dairy co-op's unpaid bills had mounted to $758,531.94. In addition to which, Valley Lea claimed $250,000 in other costs and damages. In an affidavit in court, Valley Lea's manager accused the Falcones of having "misappropriated" collateral and otherwise having violated their credit agreement.

The Falcones' response was familiar. In an answering affidavit, their lawyer (who also does a substantial business incorporating pizza parlors by the score) contended that Valley Lea's plant "was infested with a bacteria which caused all of the cheese which was produced during this period of time to sustain a green mold which would render utilization of the cheese impossible." In fact, the lawyer contended that the Valley Lea dairy farmers actually owed the Falcones more than $150,000, instead of the other way around.

In the fall of 1976, the court forced the sale of the equipment and remaining inventory from the old Falcone Dairy facility, forcing that particular corporate entity out of business. The court received far less than the amount of Valley Lea's claim.

Meanwhile, the Greek cheese plant that Mr. Laramee was running in Hayfield, Minnesota, also turned out to be what you might call an ill-feta'd venture. Elmer Enstad, the manager who now makes Valley Lea's milk into cheese there, says the Gambino firm fell way behind on payments and had its credit cut off. Enstad says an agreement was worked out under which Tommy Gambino would gradually pay off a part of the debt that was defined as his share—about $26,000—in exchange for which he wouldn't be associated with the Falcones in their million-dollar problems with Valley Lea. Enstad says Gambino paid off the $26,000 and was let off the legal hook, though Valley Lea won't sell him any more cheese because it still holds him morally responsible for the whole fiasco. "They kept him (Gambino) fairly clean on paper, though they were partners all the way as far as I'm concerned," Enstad says.

Having milked Valley Lea dry in the fall of 1975, the Brooklyn cheese merchants needed another source of supply, and found it in Luxemburg, Wisconsin. The Badger State Cheese Company there, a cheddar operation owned by a family named Koss, was in financial trouble and the Kosses were persuaded to sell 70 percent of the company to Tommy Gambino, his father Joseph Gambino (Carlo's brother), and some Falcone relatives. In came J. Leo Laramee to help convert the plant to mozzarella and run it.

The result was predictable. In August, 1976 (nearly six months *after* Joseph Falcone was convicted in Vermont), Badger State shut down, with debts estimated at $1.3 million, much of it in unpaid milk bills to dairy farmers. The cheese company, two local banks, a Koss and the Wisconsin Department of Agriculture entered a many-faceted litigation over what should happen to the remaining assets. The FBI was called in, but at this writing no indictments have been forthcoming.

It wasn't until the collapse of Badger State, says Leo Laramee, the cheese-maker, that he knew who his bosses really were. "Tom (Gambino) wanted me to start another one after that," he said across a bar table at the Ramada Inn in Burlington in 1977, "but when I saw those headlines in the Green Bay paper about the Mafia taking over Badger State, I knew right then where I was going —right back here to Vermont." He is now a foreman at International Cheese Company, a variety cheesemaker in Hinesburg, whose owner, Dean Economou, a lifelong Vermonter, says, "I wouldn't even want to appear in the same (newspaper) article with those Brooklyn guys. I won't have anything to do with them."

It's hard not to, though, and be in the cheese business. Even as Economou talked, his company was in partnership with another company, the Swanton [Vermont] Creamery, in a state-backed venture to build a plant that will dry and sell whey (the watery leftover of the cheese-making process). The Swanton Creamery operates in a sparkling new plant on a government-subsidized industrial park eleven miles south of Alburg. It produces two hundred thousand pounds of mozzarella a week, more than double the production of the old Alburg Creamery, enough to coat a whole lot of pizza pies. The owners of the new plant are Philip and Gennaro Falivene, who helped the Falcones operate the Alburg Creamery in 1971.

Even though Falcone Dairy Products' warehouse was cleaned out by court order, a portion of the premises was still occupied in 1977 by the pizzeria supply firm of John Campagna, formerly of Campagna Brothers, which the Falcones helped get started. The other brother, Joseph Campagna, who testified for Joseph Falcone and Joseph Curreri, has a cheese distributorship elsewhere in the area.

Joseph Falcone himself, not wasting time while his appeal was being considered, approached a farmers co-op in Frederick, Maryland, in 1977 about a deal to convert milk into cheese. His partner was the widow of Sam DeStefano, a former Vermont mozzarella manufacturer who Leo Laramee identifies as the man who introduced him to the Falcones. The Frederick deal was attacked in the local press, which learned of Falcone's background. What apparently killed it, though, was when Falcone went to prison for what will likely be a stretch of twelve to sixteen months before parole.

The Saputos are proceeding with plans for a big new cheese plant in Vermont.

Grande Cheese Products out in Fon Du Lac is still an acknowledged industry leader. It's run by a family named Candella, which married into the DiBella family years ago. John Candella (or Candela), the family scion, who says the operation is totally legitimate, appears on a Justice Department list of organized crime subjects.

Thomas Gambino still has his clam-stuffing operation in West Haven. According to the Wisconsin Department of Agriculture, he also is president of Capitol Cheese Company Inc., a mozzarella distributor in Brooklyn that owed Badger State Cheese Company $310,000. The department says it has agreed to write the debt down to $210,000 because of the contention that a lot of the cheese was rancid. The Falcones are involved in Capitol's on-going operations, too, according to Wisconsin officials.

The two Gambino relatives still run Ferro Foods, but have their own warehouse now. Frank Ferro says he doesn't have anything to do with the Falcones or with Thomas Gambino (except that Thomas is his cousin). He says he hasn't been getting much bad cheese at all in recent years from his new suppliers, whom he declines to name.

Women answer the telephone at Vincent Falcone's home. They tell reporters that he's away for a matter of days, and that they don't know where.

And the Falcones' lawyer says he isn't their lawyer anymore, and wouldn't know how to reach them. Like the men who run pizza parlors, of which he has incorporated so many, he says he doesn't want his name mentioned.

In the early morning hours of July 6, 1977, two men lugged 210 gallons of gasoline into Giuseppe's Pizza Restaurant in the Philadelphia suburb of Ambler, Pennsylvania. They apparently planned to light a fuse and watch the fireworks in the rear-view mirror as they sped away in their green '77 Buick LeSabre parked outside. Alas, however, they were working too close to the pilot light on Giuseppe's pizza oven.

Blooey.

There wasn't enough left of one body to identify it right away, but the other body was quickly found to be that of Vincenzo Fiordilino of Brooklyn, the twenty-two-year-old nephew of Giovanni Fiordilino, whom police have long identified as a high-ranking member of the Bonanno Mafia family.

What was he doing there, police wondered. Was the firebombing an insurance fraud arson? Was it an isolated incident of revenge?

Some thought otherwise. For the arson in Ambler was only one of several dozen firebombings, torch jobs, and gas explosions that had been ripping apart pizza parlors in New York, Pennsylvania, New Jersey, and Delaware. To many eyes, a war seemed to have broken out over control of the pizza business in the northeast. Carlo Gambino, the boss of bosses, had died the previous October. Meanwhile, Joe Bonanno's top underboss, Carmine Galante, had been freed from a long prison sentence and was in New York working to resurrect the family, which had been in decline since the boss's two-year disappearance in the mid-1960s. The Bonannos were known to be pushing the Gambinos out of various rackets in 1977, and maybe the cheese industry—the one the Bonannos had most clearly controlled in halcyon days—was one of them.

Clement Seroski, the Montgomery County, Pennsylvania, chief of detectives, who investigated the blast in Ambler, says he doesn't know why it happened. "They have a code of their own," he says of pizzeria operators. "The kind of kitchen equipment they have to use, the kind of cheese they have to use, the illegal aliens they have to hire. It could have been local jealousy. It could have been refusal of the owners to go along on purchasing equipment." The Pennsylvania State Police said they believed the Ambler pizzeria was connected to Gambino interests. But Anthony Guerrelli of Warminster, Pennsylvania, lawyer for the pizzeria's three owners, denies it. "The Gambino Family wasn't involved in this operation," he says. "They're involved in a lot of other operations, I know that, but they aren't involved in this one."

They were, however, involved in the King of Pizza pizzeria in Dover, Delaware. Corporate records list Emmanuel and Giuseppe Gambino, both relatives of Carlo, as officers in the King of Pizza. On the night of November 5, 1977, someone put four bombs and a lot of gasoline on the parlor floor.

Whoever it was proved almost as inept as the Ambler arsonists. The bombs and gasoline were still sitting there the next morning when employees at the nearby Pantry Pride supermarket smelled fumes and called the fire department. The bungled arson made page-one of the *Wilmington News-Journal,* and the state fire marshal announced an investigation. Just two nights later, however, patrons at a nearby bowling alley heard an explosion and saw smoke and flames. The arsonist had returned, and there was one less pizzeria in Dover.

Some local law enforcement officers suspect that pizzeria owners set fires themselves, intending to collect on the insurance. The insurance industry has little information on pizzeria fires. Pizzerias are classed along with all other kinds of restaurants from the Four Seasons on down. "There is no way an insurance company can tell you in regard to [just] pizza," an official of one company explained.

But to federal law enforcement agents the insurance angle seems an inadequate explanation for what's been happening. They suspect there's a lot more to the spate of pizzeria explosions than just a lot of pie in the sky. "My impression is that it had something to do with suppliers and franchising and control," says Wallace P. Hay, special agent in charge of the Philadelphia office of the Federal Bureau of Alcohol, Tobacco and Firearms. "Most of them seemed to be reasonably good businesses, and as far as competition goes, it seems like there's room for more than one pizza parlor." The FBI agreed, and right after the Dover explosion, the bureau began a new investigation of the pizzeria industry.

Agents found that the Gambino pizzeria in Dover had been buying supplies from Ferro Foods, the operation run in New York by two Gambino relatives who were closely associated with the Falcones. They also found that the fastest-growing competitor in the industry in 1977 was Roma Food Service of South Plainfield, New Jersey, which was distributing products to pizzerias as far away as Ohio. Roma is run by Louis Piancone, who says the operation is totally upright. He also says his brother Michael has no connection to Roma. In the early 1970s, however, Michael Piancone was also in the pizzeria business and shared an office with Roma. According to federal lawmen, he sold pizza parlors to aliens who would buy supplies from Roma. Then, in 1974, he was convicted in federal court, Newark, for conspiring to evade the immigration laws. He was put on probation, and the probation was extended in 1977 because of some bad-check charges. Back in the early 1970s, there was evidence that Michael Piancone was on good terms with the Gambino crowd, authorities say. What the situation is now in that regard is a mystery.

It's no mystery, however, where Roma buys its mozzarella cheese. The cheese comes from Grande Cheese Products Inc. of Fon Du Lac, Wisconsin, the company taken over in 1941 by Al Capone and his friend—Joe Bonanno.

PART FIVE

LUNCH

Lunch

Back in 1966, when the Mafia took over the lunch-wagon business in New York, Ralph Stingo and Paul Spector evidently didn't mind. They weren't in the Mafia, but the Mafia protected their lunch trucks, and their gross business increased. All the muscle was thrown against their competitors. Only in the 1970s did Stingo and Spector learn what a monster they were dealing with. And by then it was too late for them to rescue their money. But through a strange twist of fate they did manage to gain a little revenge, and, however briefly, give some other lunch-wagon drivers—and the lunch-eating public—a respite from extortion.

Lunch wagons are a common sight in the East, and, increasingly, in other parts of the country. They are small trucks, usually white or gleaming chrome, with a large window in the back or side through which customers can buy from a variety of pre-made cold sandwiches, milk, pre-packaged cake, coffee, and cold soda pop. Usually there's a tub of hot dogs, and sometimes a grill for fresh hamburgers. At lunch or coffee-break time the wagons pull into factory parking lots, or next to schools, or alongside highways, or in shopping centers. They are as American as baseball, apple pie, and Meyer Lansky.

The overcharges forced on a fleet of lunch-wagon owners may seem a petty matter compared to some of the large corporate rackets discussed in these pages. But the plight of Ralph Stingo, Paul Spector, and their colleagues illustrates the plight of thousands of average citizens in many cities in this country who are trying to earn a daily living at one of a variety of businesses that are harrassed by a force seemingly beyond their power to fight it.

Stingo was just twenty-one years old when he entered the lunch-wagon business. He began by renting a truck from a caterer in the Whitestone section of Queens. He carved out a route in the Astoria section, with stops that other drivers hadn't latched onto yet. The caterer charged him fifteen dollars a day for the truck and·sold him the food.

Then the rent went to fifty dollars a day, and Stingo decided the hell with it. He saw other operators who owned their own trucks were doing better than he was, buying their food from a caterer called Kwik Snack in Plainview, Long Island. So he, too, bought his own truck, began taking sandwiches from Kwik Snack, and, like the other independent drivers he knew, began paying three dollars a week dues to the Workman's Mobile Lunch Association, which had just been organized by a man named Gary Petrole.

Right away, trouble started with Stingo's old boss, the caterer from Whitestone. As Stingo continued to make his rounds in Astoria, but now in his own truck, the resentful caterer began sending other trucks out to try to "bump" Stingo from his stops by temporarily reducing their prices to levels he couldn't afford to match. This seemed terribly unfair, and Stingo complained about it to anybody who would listen. He found a sympathetic ear in Gary Petrole. Petrole began riding with Stingo, and threatened the drivers of the competing trucks. When that didn't work, Petrole dumped out the coffee urns of the competitors and turned off their burners so they couldn't make more. That worked. Soon Stingo was enjoying his old exclusivity again. He stayed loyal to the Workman's Mobile Lunch Association, even when the dues rose quickly from three to six to ten dollars a week.

Paul Spector had been in the lunch-wagon business for six years and owned five profitable trucks that toured Brooklyn, Maspeth (Queens), and Long Island City. He saw no need to fork over a fifty-dollar-initiation fee plus weekly dues to the upstart Petrole and his association. But problems began for Spector when some competitors *did* join the association. These competitors—Robert Frank, Frank Morgan, and Eddie Sedara—jointly owned three trucks. Sedara had known Petrole, and his henchman Joseph "Little Joe" Ochiogrosso for some time. Almost as soon as their new "association" stickers were affixed to their windshields, the trucks of Morgan, Frank, and Sedara began "bumping" Spector's trucks from the most lucrative single spot on his route, the Williamsburg Steel plant in Brooklyn.

Finally, after a few weeks of losing business, Spector decided that maybe joining the association wasn't such a bad idea after all. So Petrole, who had ordered the "bumping" in the first place, advised Sedara that the bumping would have to stop. Since Spector's five trucks would pay more dues and initiation fees than the three trucks of Sedara, Frank, and Morgan, Spector was a more welcome member of the association and would get the Williamsburg Steel stop back.

Sedara, who knew that Petrole was a mobster, took this bad news to his partners and advised them to accept the inevitable. Evidently, however, Morgan and Frank were more naive, and thought they could beat the Mafia. They decided that the Williamsburg Steel stop was a gold mine, and that they did not want to give it up. The unfortunate Sedara was assigned to convey this decision to Petrole, who did not take it lightly. A few days after he talked to Petrole, Sedara returned to his partners and announced that they must come to a meeting in Brooklyn with the "big guy." The "big guy," Sedara told them, was Philip Rastelli.

Philip Rastelli, known as Rusty, was listed in 1963 at the Joe Valachi hearings of the McClellan Committee as a soldier in the Joseph Bonanno Mafia family. The committee listed his specialties as "extortion, strong arm, and murder," and said he was "suspected of being active in narcotics." By 1969, the government Mafia charts showed a promotion for Rastelli to the rank of *capodecina,* or captain. According to the Bureau of Narcotics and Dangerous Drugs, he achieved this elevation in about 1965 by arranging for the disappearance of his predecessor, Frank Mari.

Walter Lotoski, who became an informer for the government in the early 1970s, knew Rastelli fairly well. Lotoski himself had spent half his life in various prisons for such crimes as robbery and hijacking. During one of these stretches he met Vincent "Tappy" Soviero, a heroin peddler who was close to Rastelli. In 1962, shortly after Lotoski was freed from the federal penitentiary in Atlanta, Soviero asked him if he wouldn't like to be the official photographer for Rusty Rastelli's upcoming wedding. Rastelli—whom Lotoski had already met by this time—didn't want a commercial photographer whose negatives might be subject to subpoena by law enforcement. Lotoski agreed.

At the wedding, Lotoski later told the FBI, he met numerous mobsters. Shortly afterward, Soviero set him up running a dry cleaning store at 235 South Fourth Street in Brooklyn. Lotoski's dry cleaning vats must have been stuffed with dark, pin-striped suits, because his store was patronized heavily by racketeers. Among them was Rusty Rastelli, who soon arranged to use the dry cleaning store as a drop-off point for heroin to be distributed in the neighborhood. This was the man who stood behind the Workman's Mobile Lunch Association.

When Sedara told Bobby Frank, his lunch-wagon partner, about Rastelli, Frank didn't want to go to the meeting with the mobster. Finally, when he was convinced that at this point there was no choice but to show up, he insisted they both carry guns with them. According to Sedara, they "expected to get holes in our heads" before it was over. Traveling in a black Cadillac—evidently *de rigueur* for the occasion—they rendezvoused with Gary Petrole at the Hegeman and Holland Dairy near Fifty-sixth Street in Queens, which was where the lunch-wagon drivers met every morning at seven o'clock to pick up their wares.

Petrole led them through the streets of Brooklyn to a storefront. They parked outside. The store windows were soaped over so you couldn't see through them. The door was locked. Petrole knocked and was admitted. Moments later the door swung open again for Sedara and Frank, revealing a sparsely furnished room and two men they had never seen before. One was standing near a table, while the other loitered in the background. Petrole introduced the man near the table as "Rusty," then walked over and stood behind him. Frank later described Rusty as being of medium height, slightly more than medium build, about forty, with a full head of "salt and pepper hair," neatly dressed in a brown suit and tie and silk, ribbed brown sox. The following conversation is reconstructed from what Frank and Sedara told the FBI and what they eventually testified to:

"What do you want to do about this?" Rusty asked.

"Why do we have to give up the stop?" Sedara replied.

"If Spector gets that stop, it means five more trucks in the association and more dues," either Rastelli or Petrole said.

Then Sedara argued. "We're getting screwed. We'll be losing a profitable stop. And how do we know we can trust Spector not to try to bump us off other stops after he gets this one?"

"Don't worry about Spector," Rastelli said. "I'll take care of Spector. We'll try to get you a couple of other stops [to make up for the loss of Williamsburg Steel]."

The sides elaborated their positions for fifteen or twenty minutes. Then the meeting broke up, with Frank and Sedara promising a decision the next day. They noted later that Rastelli "did not come on heavy" to them, that there were no threats. Perhaps that was a mistake on Rastelli's part, because on the way back from the meeting Frank decided they would resist the ploy and not give up the Williamsburg Steel stop to Spector. The next day, when Sedara announced the decision to Petrole, the association decals were ripped off the Sedara-Frank-Morgan trucks, and the fifty-dollar-initiation fees were returned to them.

A few days later, as Morgan was servicing a stop at Neptune Meters in Long Island City, Petrole and Occhiogrosso pulled up. According to Morgan, Petrole announced, "There will be consequences if you guys don't give up the Williamsburg Steel Stop. You better talk to Eddie Sedara. You don't realize what will happen to you." Then Petrole punched Morgan in the face. Morgan fought back, but Occhiogrosso approached brandishing a wrench. The coffee break bell rang and the fight stopped.

A week later, Morgan was making an evening run at the St. Johnsbury Trucking depot in Maspeth. Suddenly he noticed ten or fifteen strange men standing around a car parked by the gate entrance to the parking lot. Seven or eight of them, some wearing gloves, approached the lunch-wagon and began asking what kind of sandwiches Morgan had and how much they cost.

Morgan says he became afraid and asked the foreman, a muscular man named Jimmy, to stay close to him because he expected trouble. Morgan then jumped back in the truck and rushed for the exit. But his escape was blocked by the car he had seen standing outside the gate. He raced back to the loading dock, looking for another way out. He was driving around in circles, trying to avoid the men, who were swinging chains and crowbars at his truck, and yelling, "Join the association, Scab."

Finally, a man standing by the entrance to the parking lot, a man who appeared older than the others, waved his hands and called off the attackers. They left. Morgan's truck had broken windows, dented sides, and a hole in the door. The next morning at 6:30, Morgan showed up at Frank's house, advised him of the attack, and told him they had better bring weapons to work. After discussing it, however, they decided instead to go to the Queen's district attorney's office. They were referred to some police detectives who listened politely to their story.

Later that day, as Morgan arrived at his stop at Zarkin Machine Company, Long Island City, he spotted the man who had directed the attack on his truck at St. Johnsbury Trucking the night before. Morgan quickly called Frank, who called the detectives and then raced to the Zarkin plant himself. Frank didn't find any detectives on the scene, but he did spot Rusty Rastelli, whom he recognized from the meeting in the storefront. When Rastelli saw Frank, he jumped into the passenger seat of a late model Cadillac. The man Morgan said had led the attack the night before climbed in behind the steering wheel and drove Rastelli away. After it was all over, the police showed up and checked out the license number of the Cadillac, which Morgan had alertly taken down. It was traced to a vacant lot. The police left and apparently never paid any more attention to the shakedown racket.

A little while later, as Morgan drove the lunchwagon through Queens and Frank followed him in a car—Cadillac, of course—for protection, they found themselves tailed by a carload of goons. Petrole was in the car. According to Frank, "They got in behind [Morgan] and tried to cut him off the road. And they were speeding down the street. It was really a crazy ride, three of us were speeding down the street and [Morgan] was in the front and they passed me and tried to force him off the road. . . . And I remember that they had to stop for a red light . . . and they had to jam on their brakes and they got in between the truck and myself. And that's when [Morgan] jumped out of the truck and was trying to puncture their tires with an ice pick." Petrole and the goons cornered Morgan and beat him badly, blackening his eye.

In addition to this mayhem, Spector's trucks began bumping the Morgan-Frank-Sedara trucks at various locations. The financial losses mounted. Then Petrole approached again on a friendly basis, and said, "Look, nobody is getting anywhere. Let's sit down and discuss it."

According to Frank, "I did not want to have to go to work and be afraid of someone hitting me on the head with a pipe or some other thing like that. All I was trying to do was make a living, and when they came to us we said okay. See, I felt it was a chance to get these guys off our back. And they set up a meeting."

The meeting was in a bar across from a Queens cemetery. Sedara and Frank quickly told Petrole they would give up the Williamsburg Steel stop to Spector. Petrole told them that in exchange they would get several other stops that were in contention, and that no one would bump them. Shortly afterwards, they rejoined the association. The make-up stops proved inadequate, though, and by June of 1968, Frank, Sedara, and Morgan had moved their lunch-wagon operation to Westchester County.

For Paul Spector, however, the protected routes worked out very well.

Over the next year or two, the association itself underwent a number of changes. For one thing, after the racket had been successfully organized, Gary Petrole was replaced as the guy who collected the dues and initiation fees. The new head of the Workman's Mobile Lunch Association was Louis Rastelli, the nephew of Rusty, the mobster. And replacing Little Joe Occhiogrosso as chief goon was 480-pound Anthony "Tony Deisty" De Stefano, a long-time hanger-on among the Rastelli crime group. De Stefano later claimed he had been elected by the members, although the members denied electing anybody and records indicate that the officers were appointed by a "board of trustees."

Petrole, however, quickly found another source of income by organizing a new branch of the racket. He arranged for a commissary in New Jersey to pay him 5 percent of its gross to haul sandwiches to the lunch-wagon drivers' pick-up stop in Queens. When Kwik-Snack, the Long Island firm, saw that all the drivers who had been buying from it were switching to the New Jersey supplier, Kwik-Snack made Petrole an even better deal. Soon the price was up to 10 percent, and it didn't buy exclusivity at all. It didn't even buy Gary Petrole's delivery service. By 1970 every commissary was paying 10 percent of its gross to Gary Petrole merely for the privilege of selling any food to any lunch-wagon driver, even the ones who had been buying from the same commissary for years. Soon Louis Rastelli and Tony De Stefano were in on this act, too.

George Avadikian and Alfred Conversi, partners in a catering firm called Canteen Associates, were visited repeatedly by all three men in 1969 and 1970 with demands for 10 percent of the gross from the five thousand sandwiches a day they sold to lunch-wagon vendors at the Hegeman & Holland dairy pick-up point, according to what Avadikian later told city detectives. Canteen, like the other suppliers, finally agreed to pay, the only alternative being to close down.

For Kathleen Cardineau, a recent high school graduate who was supporting herself by making sandwiches for truck drivers in her kitchen, Petrole made a special deal. Miss Cardineau happened to be the girlfriend of a cousin of Lou Rastelli's, and on that basis, Petrole let her bargain him down to an eighty-dollar-a-week cash kickback instead of the 10 percent.

William Bruce couldn't get a special deal. His Bruce Vending Company of Queens made sandwiches, coffee, juices, and cakes for coin-operated vending machines, and in 1971 he decided to expand into the mobile lunch-wagon market. His plant was just a block away from where the lunch-wagons loaded up in the morning. "I went to where the mobile trucks loaded," he recalled later in trial testimony, "to contact them to see if we couldn't sell them sandwiches for their trucks. . . . I spoke to numerous drivers. . . . They told me I would have to see the—Gary Petrole and the association. . . . They couldn't independently buy from me without permission. That's what they told me."

So Bruce got in touch with Petrole, and Petrole visited Bruce's office with Tony De Stefano. "Mr. Petrole told me that he was in charge of the sandwich business as far as the mobile trucks were concerned, that he furnished all the sandwiches to the mobile trucks," Bruce recalled at the trial. "And did I realize the scope of the business. . . . I told him I didn't know exactly what the scope was. I knew I saw a truck there and our company would like to furnish sandwiches for them. Mr. De Stefano told me, 'Do you know we have an association and all this has to be approved? Number one, we want to see what your products are. . . . ' " As it was mid-day, this problem was easily solved.

"I think they ate part of a couple of sandwiches," Bruce recalled. After getting a free lunch in Bruce's office, and washing it down with his coffee, the mobsters pronounced Bruce's food "pretty good." Then they threw in the kicker: "I would have to pay 12 percent commission on the total volume of the sandwiches," Bruce says he was told. The hoods were getting a mere 10 percent from other suppliers, but Bruce must have looked wealthy.

"I told them I thought the figure was very high," Bruce said. "I wasn't anticipating paying anything and I was attempting to do a service and to increase my business. . . . They told me—well, they can make an arrangement on the commission if I could pay on a cash basis." But Bruce insisted on paying with checks, and so was stuck with the 12 percent.

After the lunch-wagon drivers began loading in the morning at Bruce's plant, he was able to observe on occasion how the association chased away any non-member lunch-wagon drivers who wandered into an association member's territory. Whenever a driver reported competition, Rastelli, Petrole, and De Stefano would hop in their cars and come back a few hours later telling the drivers, "Look, we have taken care of that situation and he will never be on your stop again." They also instructed Bruce never to sell to lunch-wagon drivers who didn't belong to the association. Bruce was all the more impressed because of the way De Stefano constantly flashed the gun in his belt.

Soon, according to evidence presented later at trial, Bruce discovered that he had a new partner in his business—Bobbie Murtz, Louis Rastelli's brother-in-law. Bruce's office building also acquired two new tenants. One was Modern Caterers, which distributed dry goods (napkins, paper plates, etc.) for the trucks and which was owned and operated by Louis Rastelli and Tony De Stefano. The other new tenant was the Workman's Mobile Lunch Association itself; this provided a new office where Rastelli and De Stefano could conduct their gin rummy marathons.

Although members of the organization say they were originally promised such benefits as group life insurance, medical payments and discounts for group buying, they say they received no such benefits. All De Stefano and Louis Rastelli seemed to do, besides collect dues, was sit around Bruce's office playing gin rummy with each other. The only thing members got for their dues was the guarantee that nobody who didn't pay dues could compete with them.

Michael Campirides of Woodside, who had been in the catering business since 1956, remembers what happened when he got disgusted and decided to stop paying his seventy-six-dollar-a-month-dues to Rastelli. "At that time exactly I tell him I'm going to quit because the money is too much, one of my drivers come back and he says we lost a stop because somebody from the association took the stop. . . . I was bumped. I don't even know the fellow who bumped me. I just get off from the stop and that's it." Campirides quickly let it be known to Rastelli and De Stefano that he was staying with the association.

Then there was David Levy, whose wife cooked such a swell souvlaki that Levy decided to go around in a Volkswagen minibus selling it. That was back in 1972, when Levy still believed the United States had a free economy, before he learned that you have to pay dues to the Mafia to sell your wife's souvlaki. One of the places Levy brought his minibus was the Eden Transportation Company in Long Island City. A lot of the taxi drivers who worked for Eden also thought Mrs. Levy's souvlaki was pretty good, which was a severe blow to the lunch wagon they had been buying sandwiches from before the souvlaki showed up. It wasn't long before Tony De Stefano was called in.

According to a supervisor at Eden Transportation, "Mr. De Stefano told Mr. Levy, 'This is a steady stop,' that the man has his regular route and no other food service vehicle can come in here.

"Mr. Levy said, 'There is enough business for both of us. Why should I have to close my doors?' At which point a number of taxicab drivers that were making purchases from Mr. Levy's truck began to argue, just in general, that they can spend their money wherever they wished.

"Well, Mr. Levy was told just to pack up if he knew what was good for him. Mr. De Stefano [told him that]. Mr. Levy was reluctant to leave . . . because he was there to make a living. Mr. De Stefano made a motion to put his hand in his pocket and when his jacket brushed back he had a revolver on his belt. . . . Mr. De Stefano told Mr. Levy if he knew what was good for him he would close his door and get the hell out."

And that was the last time the drivers at Eden Transportation had souvlaki for lunch.

Every once in a while the Mafia makes a mistake, and Louis Rastelli made a lulu, for which he paid dearly. The mobile lunch drivers association had already been shaking down Ralph Stingo, the lunch-wagon driver referred to at the beginning of this chapter. When Ralph and his brother Augustus (called Gussie) tried to expand into the commissary business with Paul Spector in 1972, Louis Rastelli decided to shake them down again. Apparently he didn't know that there was a third Stingo brother, Paul, who was a New York City police officer, and a dedicated one at that.

On March 27, 1972, Patrolman Paul Stingo went to the city-wide anti-crime unit of the New York Police Department and reported that his two brothers were caught up in a protection racket. Eventually, Ralph and Gussie Stingo also agreed to talk to the detectives, and this is the story they told:

Gus Stingo had worked for the Brooklyn Union Gas Company from 1953 to 1970, when he decided to join his brother in the lunch-wagon business. He bought a truck and a route of exclusive stops from Paul Spector, under an installment contract that called for Stingo to pay dues to the Workman's Mobile Lunch Association. Before long, the Stingos decided to get out of wagon driving and open their own commissary in partnership with Spector, who seemed to have some influence. The commissary would service a whole fleet of wagon drivers.

Their first thought was to buy Canteen Associates, an existing catering firm that was in financial difficulty because of the 10 percent of its gross receipts it had to pay to the Rastelli shakedown operation. Before selling out, however, Alfred Conversi, the owner of Canteen Associates, decided to rebel and stop paying the 10 percent. Shortly afterward, a fire put his commissary out of business. The twenty-five or so drivers who had been patronizing Canteen were directed by the association to start doing business with Bruce Vending instead.

So Spector and the Stingos opened One-Stop Catering, their own attempt to beat the shakedown. They arranged to finance sixteen or seventeen lunch wagons, whose drivers then signed a contract to shop at One-Stop Catering until the wagons were paid off. Another group of drivers who owned their own wagons also agreed informally to shop there. As Gus Stingo would later testify, "Between me, my brother, Paul Spector, and the outside buyers, we tried to put it all in one piece, so we could work out of one commissary with the understanding, speaking to the different drivers, that they were looking for something like this, instead of running around for different things to pick up, cups here, or lids or sugar there, all in one place, so they were all for it. So on the strength of the twenty-five, thirty, forty men that were involved, we went ahead on this. We put it together . . .

"This was good. Until all of a sudden it stopped. We had only our own people [the trucks they financed under contract]. Then we approached Louie . . . Anthony De Stefano . . . and Gary. . . . We said why can't we have all the caterers in our place and we can strike a happy medium. He says it can be done. How can it be done? We had to pay 10 percent on a gross of anything that any of these caterers bought, which is almost impossible to survive. It's almost impossible."

So the Stingos and Spector decided to propose a compromise. Since everyone understood that Philip "Rusty" Rastelli was behind the racket, and since Spector knew Rusty, Spector was sent to bargain the Mafia chieftan down. Of course, Rastelli himself never participated in the actual bargaining, any more than he had participated in the heroin sales from Walter Lotoski's dry cleaning store. Gary Petrole was put forward as a go-between, and when Spector appealed for a cut in the extortion rate to 3 percent, Petrole replied, "It can't be 3 percent . . . Rusty gets 3 percent. That's his cut. It leaves 7 percent for the rest of the people." Negotiations continued.

Gus Stingo testified, "We said, 'You are crazy. You are knocking us out of the box before we start. Let us start and then we'll work out something from there, just to survive.'" But Petrole would show no pity. So Stingo and his partners said, "We have enough trucks [of our own to make a go of it]. We are going to drop out of the association." Then the bumping started.

Money got so tight that Gus Stingo was forced to quit. As his brother Ralph testified, "They more or less put the axe to us, that they knew we had to go under, to make things almost impossible. So we owed them fifteen hundred dollars, which they said was back dues, so we turned around and said, 'Look, all right, we owe it to you. We will start paying you fifty dollars a week, or sixty dollars, whatever we could pay you.'

"This was no good to them. 'Either pay us by Friday or we start hitting all your trucks.' So we turned around, we said, 'Look, you know it's impossible for us to get fifteen hundred dollars. You know what we are up against. . . . Let's not kid each other.'"

De Stefano's answer to that was to tell the drivers who were under contract to One-Stop that the contracts weren't recognized under Mafia law. Spector testified that Tony De Stefano told his drivers "they didn't have to worry about the contract or anything like that . . . They didn't have to buy [from One-Stop]; they could go over to Bruce Vending."

"After that," Ralph Stingo testified, "we went down there and we had a long discussion and it was just lucky that my partner Paul Spector was somewhat a friend of this Phillie Rastelli, and then they agreed to like fifty dollars or sixty dollars a week [installment payments on the back dues]. But we lost a stop in the transaction. In other words, it was a route. Most routes are built around one key stop. This stop was called Alloy-Flange. It was a key stop that served four, five times a day, which is worth almost one hundred dollars, and they know once you hit this big stop and take it over, you lose a route. You lose a driver. You lose a truck."

In the middle of May, 1973, Ralph Stingo was forced by his losses to break his contract with Paul Spector and get out of One-Stop Catering. Fourteen months had passed since Patrolman Paul Stingo had informed the New York Police Department's elite unit about the shakedown racket. Now, Ralph and Gus Stingo agreed to tell their stories to a federal grand jury.

"How much money did you lose approximately?" a prosecuting attorney asked Gus Stingo.

"It hurts my heart to say," Stingo replied. "About eighty thousand dollars that I am still paying."

"Did you receive any benefits at all from this association?" he was asked.

"None."

Despite this testimony, priorities at the United States attorney's office were such that nearly two years passed before the lunch-wagon case was even indicted. During that time the Rastelli extortion operation controlled about 150 lunch wagons throughout Brooklyn and Queens. There were indications of ties to catering operations in Westchester and New Jersey. There were also indications that lunch wagons were being used as outlets for numbers and other gambling activity.

Charges were finally announced in March, 1975. They included conspiracy, violation of the Sherman Act by restraining trade, and violation of the Hobbs Act by interfering with interstate commerce by means of extortion. The defendants included not only Louis Rastelli, Anthony De Stefano, Gary Petrole, and the Workman's Mobile Lunch Association Inc. itself, but also Philip Rastelli.

That the real boss was caught up in the net was due to the exceptional work of the elite unit of New York City cops under the direction of Lt. Remo Franchesini, who, in Queens, seemed to approach his work with the same ingenuity and dedication Robert Nicholson showed in Manhattan. In April, 1974, Franchesini's men persuaded Eddie Sedara and Frank Morgan to cooperate. Unlike other potential witnesses from the ranks of lunch-wagon drivers, Sedara and Morgan could swear that Rusty Rastelli personally had participated in the storefront argument over routes and payoffs back in 1966, and had appeared on the scene once when they were being physically intimidated. This evidence was still far weaker than the evidence that could be presented against the other defendants. But the prosecutors hoped that somehow a jury might understand that Rastelli, the Mafia boss (though he could never be referred to as a Mafia boss in the courtroom), was really behind the racket. Sedara and Morgan were placed in the federal government's witness protection program; they received new identities, were relocated in new cities with new jobs, and they were paid. The government just hoped Rastelli's men wouldn't find them before trial date.

But the Mob guns could not be stilled completely. Shortly after the case was indicted, Louis Rastelli was shot in the stomach from close range, and was paralyzed for life from the waist down. He lost all control over urinary and bowel movements. Believing that a trial would cause needless agony for everyone, the government dropped charges against him. He has never given police any information that might help identify the assailant who almost killed him.

A logical inference from the shooting might be that Louis Rastelli was about to "flip," or become a prosecution witness against his co-defendants, perhaps providing the corroborative testimony needed to nail the case against his cousin Phil. But federal and local law enforcement officers who worked on the case insist this isn't so. They think the Mob got to Louis Rastelli just to punish him for his blunders—blunders the Mob considered responsible for getting Phil Rastelli indicted and for halting, at least temporarily, a lucrative shakedown racket.

When the trial started, April 5, 1976, Phil Rastelli faced it in typical mobster fashion. He hired a high-powered attorney, Roy Cohn. And he hired the usual doctor to plead that Rastelli was too ill for court. The best the doctor could come up with in Rastelli's case was an unrepaired hernia. "He complains of coughing, belching, and occasional nighttime vomiting," the doctor said. The government brought its own doctor to court who gave Rastelli a thorough physical and pronounced him fit. Rastelli complained that food in the Brooklyn federal courthouse was "causing some problems" with his ulcer. The government agreed to bring in special lunches. Intimidation was tried. Rastelli's brother was stationed in the courtroom, eyeing down the jurors and the prosecution witnesses, creating an implied threat. So the government stationed an FBI agent in the courtroom, eyeing down Rastelli's brother, creating an implied counter-threat.

Then there was 480-pound Tony De Stefano. He complained about the chairs in the courtroom. So the government brought in a sofa for his comfort. Only after days of such jousting could the case proceed.

De Stefano and Petrole testified that they had never intimidated anybody. They painted themselves and each other as poorly-paid laborers. De Stefano, born in July 1943, testified that he had been forced to leave high school in his junior year, at age sixteen, to work as a mail clerk for Elizabeth Arden cosmetics. Later he drove trucks, and worked in his parents' candy and stationery store in the Williamsburg section of Brooklyn. The Army turned him down as 4-F because he weighed 270 pounds at age seventeen. He said he had gone into the lunch-wagon business in 1968, buying a truck and route for $7,500, much of which he borrowed from relatives. Gary Petrole and Louis Rastelli were just long-time friends of his, De Stefano said. And he denied that he ever went around armed. The gun Bruce saw, he said, "wasn't a real gun. It was one of these starter pistols that they start races with." As for the canceled checks that clearly showed payoffs from Bruce to him, De Stefano told the jury that they all represented "gin rummy winnings."

Petrole, a forty-year-old father of two from Clifton, New Jersey, admitted he had known several members of the Rastelli family for many years. But he denied any criminal activity. He said the records of the lunch-wagon association would prove his innocence, but that he couldn't produce them because he had given them all to Louis Rastelli. And he denied that he ever carried a gun. On cross-examination, the prosecution is allowed to bring out a witness's criminal record, so it was revealed to the jury that Petrole had been arrested once before for illegal gambling at a crap game in Newark, and had pleaded guilty to a reduced charge of failing to give a good account of himself. But that record had been expunged when the Supreme Court ruled that the failure-to-give-a-good-account law was unconstitutional.

Rusty Rastelli's history of identification by Congress as a Mafia leader had not been expunged, and to keep the jury from finding out about it he declined to testify. That way, there could be no cross-examination. He obviously hoped that the evidence of his connection to actual wrongdoing in the lunch-wagon case was so tenuous that without reference to the superstructure of the Mafia, which the prosecutors were forbidden to talk about, the jury might acquit him.

But somehow the jury got the picture. After an eighteen-day trial it brought back verdicts of guilty against all three men on one count of restraining trade (Sherman Act), one count of conspiracy to interfere with commerce by extortion (Hobbs Act), and two counts of actual interference with commerce. De Stefano was convicted of an additional Hobbs Act count.

Judge Thomas C. Platt also wasn't fooled about who was really running the show. He sentenced De Stefano to four years in prison and a $20,000 fine, and Petrole to five years in prison and a $20,000 fine. But to Philip Rastelli, he handed out a ten-year sentence and $40,000 in fines. The sentences still don't qualify as severe; all the men will be considered first-time offenders, so they will probably be eligible for assignment to a minimum security prison farm rather than a traditional penitentiary, and will probably be released by the time they have completed one-third of their sentences. And the case is still on appeal, so there's always the chance they won't do time at all. But at least the lunch-wagon business in Brooklyn and Queens has been quiet for the past year.

PART SIX

TRUCKING

The Teamsters

On a wintry night in 1976 I sat at the counter of a truck stop along Interstate 71 somewhere between Cleveland and Columbus. Next to me, still wearing his grease-smudged green winter jacket was a lanky, craggy-faced, over-the-road (that means inter-city) truck driver from Akron. His swarthy complexion was emphasized by a day's growth of stubble. I had identified myself as a reporter for the *Wall Street Journal* and had offered to pick up the tab for his midnight snack if he'd tell me what he thought about the Teamsters' Union. He ordered dutch apple pie and coffee, and helped me fill several pages of a notebook that was rapidly running out of space to write in.

I was in the truck stop as the result of a challenge from a long-time associate of James R. Hoffa, the former Teamster president who had disappeared the previous July and was by now generally presumed to have been murdered. Two weeks before he disappeared, the *Journal* had published a series of articles describing the theft of hundreds of millions of dollars from the union's biggest pension fund, and the resultant inability of many of the union's 2.3 million members to collect on their pensions. This money, which was taken by the Mafia-run crime Syndicate, came directly from the pockets of every American consumer. The price of everything that ever traveled by truck—that is to say almost everything—includes a heavy Mafia tax. After the stories ran, tips started trickling in that the pension fund theft was merely part of a vast mosaic of corruption that costs the public incalculably. Then the Hoffa disappearance focused the whole country's attention on the Teamsters.

A search for clues led to the Hoffa associate, who said that Hoffa had been a veritable saint compared to the current office-holder, Frank Fitzsimmons. He said that under Fitzsimmons's administration, the selling of sweetheart contracts and other rip-offs of the membership and the American public had achieved an open acceptance that Hoffa never would have tolerated. Without Hoffa around to protect the members' interests, the associate said, the Mob now had unrestrained power. It could exploit its control of the Teamsters any way it wanted.

Because of what I already knew about Hoffa from my reading of the McClellan Committee hearings in the 1950s and the history of his federal trials in the 1960s, I found it hard to believe that any level of morality was operating in the union in those days, and even harder to believe that things were worse now. In 1967, when Hoffa's last appeals were turned down, he had handpicked Fitzsimmons to fill in as Teamster president until his prison term was over. Fitz was Hoffa's office helper and yes-man. Then, after Hoffa obtained his parole in 1971, he had been outraged that Fitzsimmons refused to meekly give back the power. So in 1975, Hoffa attempted the unthinkable—an open fight for the Teamster presidency in a campaign mounted around corruption charges against Fitzsimmons. And he paid with his life. That, it seemed clear, accounted for the far-fetched contentions I was hearing about Hoffa's sainthood. Finally, exasperated with my skepticism, the Hoffa associate issued this challenge: "Don't take it from me. Go ask the truck drivers. Go out to the truck stops along any of the interstates around Detroit or Chicago or Cleveland or Cincinnati"—admittedly Hoffa territory—"and ask the drivers what they think of Jimmy Hoffa and Frank Fitzsimmons."

I spent several days and nights doing the interviews. I drank a lot of coffee. I learned that apple really is the preferred pie of the overwhelming majority of over-the-road truck drivers. And I learned that the Hoffa associate had been absolutely right about what the truck drivers would say. I interviewed scores of them, maybe hundreds. Hoffa, in his murder, had indeed become a folk hero to them. He may have been a crook, but he looked out for the drivers, they said, almost to a man. And as for Fitzsimmons, their opinions were neatly summed up by the twenty-year veteran from Akron in his dirty green winter jacket: "The guys are tired of Fitz, but we can't vote on him. Fitz is just a patsy between the government and organized crime as far as I'm concerned. The union's got down to the point now where they're not much good to us. They're just there to make money. It's a racket."

It is, indeed, a racket—perhaps the world's biggest, a bigger money-maker for the Mob than all the betting in Las Vegas. In fact, without the Teamsters there might not even *be* a Las Vegas, at least as we know it.

Unlike the butchers' union, where racketeers mix with more businesslike elements in a strange amalgam, the Teamsters' Union is totally, thoroughly, dominated by the Mob. It is by far the largest visible institution to be so dominated. It is, in fact, one of the most powerful institutions in the United States, its membership reaching across many vital industries. It affects the price and availability of almost everything we buy. While trucking accounts for only one-third of the transportation of goods in the United States, almost everything is in some part, at some stage, in the hands of a teamster. Thousands of meat packers are teamsters. Hundreds of thousands of government office workers are teamsters. So are the people who handle freight, including mail, at major airports, where the opportunities for organized theft are great. The Teamsters' union holds mortgages on office buildings, hospitals, and small businesses of every variety all across the country. The Teamsters have invested heavily in the insurance industry and have enjoyed great influence at many banks. They have bankrolled the better part of Las Vegas. The Teamsters sponsor Notre Dame's football games on coast-to-coast radio (what would the Gipper say about *that!*). In the 1970s the Teamsters have even moved into law enforcement and now control the working contracts for tens of thousands of city cops, state troopers, and sheriff's deputies from Connecticut to California and up to Alaska. The Teamsters have bullied their way to influence over many other unions—the butchers, the bakers, and the Longshoremen for example.

And there should be no mistake about one thing: the Teamsters are the crime Syndicate—not the individual truck driver or office worker or policeman who pays dues, but the union officials who control almost every facet of the Teamsters' national and regional administration. The Teamsters are an arm of the Mafia.

The union has been open to corruption from the days when it was formed to represent the drivers of horse-drawn wagons (hence the name "Teamsters"). It was by nature the loosest of confederations. The members seldom worked shoulder-to-shoulder, as in a factory. The employers were small and widely dispersed. Every worker and entrepreneur in the industry was a little guy out on a limb, and therefore easy to intimidate if you had a well-organized shake-down operation. The large, nationwide trucking companies came only after the Mob had a well-established foothold.

For several crucial decades through World War II, the union was run by a doddering Pat Gorman-type figure named Dan Tobin. Like Gorman, in the butchers' union, Tobin was not a racketeer himself, but was totally unwilling and unable to keep a clean house, especially as he approached senility. Tobin maintained the union's international headquarters in Indianapolis, which helped give it a low profile that was much to the liking of corrupt local leaders who remained free to run their own fiefs as they chose.

Tobin was eventually succeeded by Dave Beck, a Seattle leader, who moved the union's headquarters to Washington in 1953. Though, like Tobin, he was not a product of Mafia-style racketeering, Beck was a totally venal man who had become a millionaire by helping himself to hundreds of thousands of dollars from union treasuries and "loans" from Teamster employers; he later went to jail for it. Beck defended his union's retention of officers who took the

Fifth Amendment about their racketeering activities—although he threatened to "bounce any man" who took the Fifth Amendment about whether he had ever been a Communist (he frequently used a stance of militant anti-Communism as a smokescreen for his own corrupt ways). He certainly had neither the position nor the inclination to clean the Syndicate racketeers out of the Teamsters, and under his leadership their influence expanded.

It was during the late 1940s, however, that the Syndicate bought its ticket to eventual full control over the Teamsters. The Chicago Mafia, the old Capone organization, made a deal with a rising young union leader from Detroit —Jimmy Hoffa (by all available evidence, Hoffa was not a Mafia member himself). The Mob would support Hoffa in his campaigns for Teamster power, and he would be their man. The first palpable benefit to the Mob was the huge insurance business that Hoffa's Michigan Conference of Teamsters began placing with agencies and insurance companies controlled by Paul "Red" Dorfman, long a key figure in the Capone labor rackets (he took power after the murder of a predecessor in 1939). After the deal with Hoffa, Dorfman's profits from Teamster insurance quickly ran into the millions of dollars, and presumably were spread around the Mob. Later, when Hoffa achieved regional and then national control, and created the vast Central States, Southeast, and Southwest Areas pension fund, the money rolling in to the Dorfman operation was almost uncountable. By the time Red Dorfman died in 1971, his son and partner, Allen Dorfman, had long since taken over day-to-day command as the Mafia's trustee over the Teamster billions. In 1976 and again in 1978, despite an intervening prison sentence and repeated, well-publicized government investigations, Allen Dorfman was hired anew by the Central States pension fund to handle its vast insurance needs, and at this writing—almost incredibly—he retains his open authority with the union.

The Mafia, meanwhile, had helped elevate Hoffa to power in the 1950s.

Having achieved control of the midwestern region with the help of the Dorfmans and other Capone mobsters, Hoffa needed support from another part of the country before making his assault on the union presidency. The East was the likely source of that support because the Mafia had so much power there. But a large faction in the dominant New York-New Jersey area Teamster apparatus was reluctant to go along. Many local leaders valued the loose-knit confederation of the international union because it allowed them independence. Hoffa's design was centralization; he dreamed of a national master trucking contract, a consolidated national pension plan and a powerful international leadership that would speak for all the Teamsters with a single voice. For Hoffa, this was in part a sincere philosophy of unionism—after all, he had not come to the Mafia through the normal route of street crime; he had been a labor leader since organizing his first warehouse strike at age eighteen. He surrounded himself not only with the usual cadre of thugs, but also with some dedicated unionists. But the drive to centralize may have been part of his original deal with the Mafia—that by consolidating Teamster leadership in the international presidency, he could also consolidate and deliver the enormous potential graft.

Since it wasn't clear whether the majority of New York area locals supported Hoffa, the obvious solution was to create more locals—enough to establish a majority. In regional and national gatherings, Teamster locals are represented equally, regardless of their size, like states in the U. S. Senate. So Hoffa and the Mob set about to create a number of "paper" locals—locals with few if any members—that could swing the balance in New York area voting. To supervise this sham they needed someone who wasn't likely to be argued with. The clear choice was Johnny Dio, a friend of the Dorfmans who was already a powerful influence in many unions, including the Amalgamated Meat Cutters.

Dio controlled what was known as the United Auto Workers-AFL (an organization totally unrelated to Walter Reuther's UAW, a CIO union). Eventually Dio's UAW-AFL changed its name to the Allied Industrial Workers Union, but under all of its guises it was no more than a shakedown operation that kept a lot of ex-cons in Cadillacs. For example, one UAW-AFL organizer, Samuel Zackman, who went to prison for extortion in 1953, later told the McClellan Committee that he had employed one Benny "the Bug" Ross to intimidate both employers and employees in small factories. Zakman testified that Ross, without warning, would "walk into a shop, pull the switch and say, 'Everybody out, we're on strike.' " Bertha Nunez, a Honduran immigrant who was employed with 150 other Spanish-speaking immigrants at a Bronx factory at $38 a week, said each worker was required to pay a $15 initiation fee and $4-a-month dues to the Allied Industrial Workers—on orders of her boss. A Brooklyn plumbing manufacturer who didn't want to pay a $2,000 bribe, testified that his children were threatened by another Dio organizer. When the manufacturer went to the police for protection, he was told instead that he had "better make some kind of a deal." Realizing that even the police wouldn't buck Dio, he paid.

Dio's image was so substantial that at one point he was even called in by David Dubinsky of the supposedly honest International Ladies Garment Workers Union. According to testimony before the McClellan Committee, Dio successfully organized a Roanoke, Virginia, textile plant that the ILGWU hadn't been able to budge. The reward paid to Dio wasn't disclosed, nor were the methods he used in Roanoke; a McClellan witness said Dubinsky got very hot under the collar whenever someone reminded him of the incident.

Dio had much stronger influence, even control, in other unions. With the approach of 1957, the year of Hoffa's planned campaign to replace Dave Beck as president of the Teamsters, Dio engineered the creation of seven new Teamster locals. The extra supply of delegates from these locals guaranteed that Hoffa supporters would control the New York region delegation at the convention. According to testimony before the McClellan Committee, Dio created the new Teamster locals by chartering seven UAW-AFL locals and having them affiliate with the Teamsters. The locals were known as "paper locals" because their tiny "membership" was composed not of working people, but of friends and relatives of Dio.

So thorough was Hoffa's manipulation of the 1957 election that there are persistent rumors—never confirmed and occasionally denied—that Hoffa even leaked derogatory information about Beck to Robert Kennedy, before realizing that Kennedy was about to become Hoffa's own arch enemy.

Kennedy finished Beck all right, with a devastating series of hearings about financial double-dealing that would eventually put the Teamster boss behind bars. But just as quickly, Kennedy went to Hoffa's jugular, too.

Some revisionist historians in recent years have painted Kennedy's pursuit of Hoffa as persecution. These revisionists have been inspired in part by their revulsion at what, retrospectively, were some terrible failings among the Kennedy brothers' foreign policies. They have been abetted by the 1976 publication of Hoffa's self-serving autobiography, by the 1978 movie "F.I.S.T." (which was a thinly-disguised romanticizing of Hoffa's life), and by the martyrdom of Hoffa himself. But they are wrong as can be, and the record deserves a brief restatement.

The only evidence that gives the pro-Hoffa revisionists a leg to stand on is that Kennedy's relentless prosecution of Hoffa occurred in the face of acquittals and hung juries. But these acquittals and hung juries clearly represented nothing more than Hoffa's blatant and often successful attempts to sabotage the judicial system. These efforts are typical of Mafia operations over the years, but they have never been carried out with more appalling brazenness than in the Hoffa cases. Ironically, it was ultimately a jury-tampering conviction that led to Hoffa's imprisonment, suggesting that under the American system, poetic justice is at least as likely to occur as the real thing.

To Hoffa and the Mafia, tampering came second nature. As soon as the McClellan Committee, under Kennedy's direction, began to move from Beck to Hoffa, Hoffa's instinctive reaction was to try to fix the committee. He sidled up to a seemingly vulnerable young lawyer, Cye Cheasty, and proposed that if Cheasty would get a job as assistant counsel on the committee camp, Hoffa would literally quintuple Cheasty's $5,000 committee salary. Cheasty took the news to Kennedy, who promptly hired him. There ensued an investigation that by all rights should have had Hoffa behind bars almost immediately. In fact, had the investigation taken its logical course, Hoffa might be alive today. Twenty FBI agents observed Hoffa handing money to Cheasty and Cheasty handing carefully prepared (by Kennedy) dossiers to Hoffa. They didn't just observe it—some of them took pictures. But the government wasn't ready for the trial tactics that would become a Hoffa trademark.

Under the system, it was fair enough to use money from union dues to hire Edward Bennett Williams, probably the best trial lawyer in America, to defend

Hoffa against charges that he was misusing union dues. But most of the members of the Washington, D. C., jury were black, and the racist publicity campaign put on in the black community was outrageous. A "Citizens' Civic Committee" from Detroit, Hoffa's hometown, invested heavily in the local black newspaper's advertising space. The result was a paper whose editorial and advertising content became devoted to propaganda that Hoffa was being framed. Williams's cross-examination tactics contrived to show that Cheasty was a racist by harping on a minor incident to depict him as having unfairly investigated the National Association for the Advancement of Colored People. Onto the Teamster gravy train went Joe Louis, who, in the days before the emergence of Martin Luther King, was probably the greatest hero among black Americans. Louis—vulnerable because of desperate personal money troubles and a big tax debt—literally paraded before the jury, in the courtroom and in the press, arm-in-arm with "my old friend" Jimmy Hoffa. Finally the slickly engaging Hoffa himself took the stand and told an ingratiating story of persecution. He said Cheasty had hired himself out as a defense lawyer, and had demanded and received much bigger fees than Cheasty turned over to the FBI, implying that the assistant counsel had kept some for himself.

Justice Department lawyers—this was three years before Kennedy took over at Justice—weren't prepared for a thorough cross-examination of Hoffa, and they certainly weren't prepared for an acquittal. Hoffa's cross-examination was bungled and the acquittal came. Kennedy, who knew Hoffa was guilty as charged, would spend his two remaining years as committee counsel, and the four years after that as attorney general, trying to correct the damage done by the Washington jury in 1957.

It wasn't persecution. Hoffa deserved everything he got. His administration was fundamentally corrupt. He worked himself into all sorts of profitable deals where he could effectively be paid off by trucking management. The mobsters whom Beck had only tolerated became Hoffa's knights of the roundtable. Out of the shadows and into such respectability as the Teamsters could provide came the likes of local leaders Joey Glimco (twice arrested for murder) in Chicago, Anthony "Tony Ducks" Corallo (a figure in the Lucchese Mafia family probably superior to, though less well known than, Johnny Dio) in New York, and the murderous Anthony "Tony Pro" Provenzano in New Jersey, to say nothing of Hoffa's own brother Billy, a two-time convict who went on the payroll as a business agent in Pontiac, Michigan. There were numerous creatures who had been to jail for crimes like firebombing and extortion and who were employed by Hoffa's Teamsters to commit these crimes anew.

When the law tried to stop them, the Teamsters provided, as they always do, the best legal counsel, whether it was a superstar like Edward Bennett Williams or a skilled lawyer who specialized in Mob work like William Bufalino, a Hoffa friend, a son-in-law of Detroit Mafioso Angelo Meli and a cousin and friend of Pennsylvania godfather Russell Bufalino. Supposedly, the Landrum-Griffen Act, which grew out of the McClellan hearings, makes it illegal to use union money to pay for the criminal defense of an officer.

But the Teamsters have proven more adept at devising schemes to get around this rule than the government has proven in stopping them. In 1975, for example, William Bufalino represented several New Jersey Teamster officials who were under grand jury investigation; meanwhile he took a retainer from their union local to handle "union business." The crime the grand jury was investigating was the disappearance of Jimmy Hoffa.

With his high-priced defense teams and low-life maneuvering, Hoffa stayed out of jail for ten years after Kennedy began his pursuit of the Teamster leader in 1957. But it wasn't because Hoffa was innocent. He was ultimately convicted, twice, in 1964, and in both cases the evidence was overwhelming. The first conviction was for tampering with a jury that in 1962 had been unable to reach a verdict on yet another charge Kennedy had brought against him, with, again, overwhelming evidence. That charge involved a company owned by Hoffa's wife* that leased equipment to Teamster employers who were really paying for "good will" from the union.

Hoffa and his supporters later created the myth that the prosecution in the jury tampering case relied on the word of a lone witness, Edward Grady Partin, a corrupt Teamster official with a long criminal record of his own. It's true that Partin gave Kennedy's staff the tips it needed to initiate the investigation; he did rat on his boss, Hoffa, and he did testify in the case. But the jury tampering was observed by a four-man FBI surveillance team. It was testified to by several relatives of jurors and others and was backed up by telephone records. Kennedy's Justice Department had in fact been directed to prosecute the matter by the trial judge in the earlier case. After the jury in 1962 had announced that it couldn't agree on a verdict, the judge had remarked from the bench, "From the very outset, while the jury was being selected . . . there were indications that improper contacts had been made and were being made with prospective members of the jury. In one instance the Court was required to excuse a prospective juror . . . after he very commendably disclosed to the Court that he had been improperly approached. After the jury was finally impanelled, and while the trial was underway . . . evidence was presented to the court indicating that illegal and improper attempts were made by close labor associates of the defendant [Hoffa] to contact and influence certain members of the jury." Money had been offered and, at least in one case, handed out, and the husband of one juror, a policeman, was promised a promotion to sergeant. These were typical Teamster-Mafia tactics. Ironically, there were indications—never pursued because of Hoffa's conviction—that similar jury tampering had been attempted with the jury at the jury-tampering trial.

Hoffa's other conviction was for mail fraud involving $20 million of loans from Teamster pension funds and $1 million in related kickbacks. Some of the loans were to Mob-connected figures. The most prominent of the loans went

---

*(also by the wife of Bert Brennan, a business associate. The company was Test Fleet Corp.)

to Sun Valley Inc., a Florida land development concern in which Hoffa personally had a large financial interest. The Sun Valley matter was exceptionally sleazy because the union helped Sun Valley sell retirement lots to Teamster members, and the sales pitches apparently were deceptive. Kennedy's staff found that some of the lots were actually under water.

In the face of all this, it is sometimes difficult to understand why Hoffa, in death, holds the affection of many teamsters, and the respect, though often grudging, of most. There may be several explanations. For one thing, Hoffa and the whole union hierarchy he controlled consistently denied that he had done anything against the interests of the membership—like Hitler's concept of the biggest lie being easiest to swallow. Hoffa invented simple, though phony, explanations, for example, that he was dragged down on the words of a liar like Edward Grady Partin. The truth was complex, because the schemes were sophisticated.

For another thing, a truck driver's daily routine is not likely to encourage respect for law enforcement—in fact, quite the contrary. He is hampered by seemingly unreasonable traffic laws, most particularly in recent years the widely-ignored fifty-five-mile-an-hour speed limit (truckers make impressive arguments that the fifty-five-mile limit actually *wastes* fuel). Meanwhile, the laws supposedly designed to protect the driver's own health and safety—cargo limits, cabin design, rest schedules—are routinely flouted by trucking companies with the seeming complicity of federal and state authorities.

Moreover, corrupt as Hoffa was, and as much as he did to bring Mafia members into positions of power in the Teamsters, he stayed mindful of his constituency in the membership. He gave them at least the cosmetics of representation, and never forgot or let them forget his own days on the loading docks at the Kroger Company. While Hoffa's life was certainly not austere, and he did not lack for comfortable surroundings, neither was his standard of living out of line with his position. There were no fleets of private jet aircraft in those days, no long weekday afternoons on the golf course. While he certainly sold out his membership in some very large ways for some very large amounts of money, he could never be accused of failing to put in a real working day in which he handled most union business rather effectively along the lines the membership would have expected him to. He was always the consummate politician. He was accessible to members and had a computer-like memory for their names and their particular personal problems. He was, in short, always a crook, but also always a Teamster.

Not so with Fitzsimmons. On taking over from Hoffa when Hoffa finally went to prison in 1967, Fitzsimmons dramatically increased the perquisites of the union presidency and reduced its duties. Fitzsimmons's world is one of private jets, golfing resorts, and puffed-up salaries. His formless flab is quite in contrast to Hoffa's loading dock physique. Just hearing him speak one senses a noticeably lesser intelligence. He has delegated the time-consuming handling of union business to local and regional leaders—who, as often as not, are mobsters. Thus the Mob, under Fitzsimmons's casual rule, has tasted undilluted power—and has liked it. Hoffa had always been a force in his own right; he always required a favor for a favor granted. Fitzsimmons is a stooge, albeit a well paid one. Sweetheart contracts can be signed and the union's treasuries and pension funds can be raided free of potential interference. The Mafia chain of command can call the shots, as it prefers to do.

There are a couple of handy guidebooks available that illustrate the close control the Mafia has over the Teamsters union in our own day. One is *Teamster Democracy and Financial Responsibility,* published by PROD Inc., an organization founded by Ralph Nader to provide a rallying post for dissident Teamster members; PROD (short for Professional Drivers Council) says it is now almost fully supported by the dues of 5,400 such men. The booklet can be ordered from PROD's Washington office.

Probably the most devastating evidence of Mafia domination of the Teamsters is a seventeen-page single-spaced confidential memorandum prepared in 1971 for use within the Department of Labor. Unauthorized Xerox copies have made the rounds of newspaper offices for some time, and in 1978 the memorandum was placed on the public record as part of testimony before the House Ways and Means Subcommittee on Oversight. Entitled "La Cosa Nostra Influence on the International Brotherhood of Teamsters," the memorandum contains elaborate lists of Teamsters' officials and their criminal backgrounds and associations. It discusses only thirty-five of the Teamsters' approximately eight hundred locals around the country, but they include some of the biggest and most powerful locals—locals that control the most influential offices in the international union structure. And the list far from exhausts the potential examples of gangster leadership in the Teamsters' union. It could probably be several times as long as it is.

Of course, many Teamster locals aren't themselves corrupt. Many have truly competitive elections and honest leaders. But these locals are deprived of power to influence the international union. As a driver from Cincinatti put it, "There have been good men [officers] in our local. But they come back [from regional and national meetings] and tell you they can't do anything. The international controls every local union."

Some teamsters say the control is exercised through fear—that dissidents may be beaten up or murdered. But there are more practical, everyday controls. Ira Farmer, who retired in 1971 as president of Local 100 in Cincinatti, where he had been an officer since 1962, explains how those controls work: "It's one of those pork barrel things. If you want to get anything for your local you have to cooperate with the [international] vice-president who's in charge of your state. On the [convention] floor you'd probably have the right to vote for anybody, but you'd be reminded of it. The vice-presidents have almost absolute control of their region."

Under the Teamster constitution, locals are required to obtain regional approval for all grievances not quickly settled on the local level. Grievances are an especially persistent problem in a disintigrated industry like trucking where jobs shift frequently. Vice-presidents can punish dissident locals by delaying action on grievances altogether. Not only grievances are involved. Under the constitution, locals must obtain regional authorization before they can strike, declare a boycott, receive financial aid, or even file a lawsuit.

Although vice-presidents supposedly are elected at conventions, most of them are first appointed by the international president to fill vacancies that have been created between conventions. Thus by the time of the election, the vice-presidents already are in power and are part of an official nomination slate; their election is a formality. Voting at conventions is not secret, nor is it cumulative; in other words, if a dissident were to attempt election to any office, he would have to run head-to-head against a particular candidate on the official slate, under circumstances where every delegate's vote would be monitored and remembered by the bosses.

Moreover, under constitutional changes inspired by Hoffa, the international president has broad powers to throw out the elected officers of a local that is giving him trouble, to appoint a trustee in their place and to seize all the local's books and accounts. Such trusteeships are common. The international leadership also can authorize new locals and place their charters in the hands of persons it considers reliable. Thus sympathetic convention votes are created. It can also transfer members out of troublesome locals and into locals controlled by officers more to its liking. Thus it can make sure that dissident locals will remain weak ones.

Local officers depend on support of the regional and international leaders for their own job security, and for their pensions as retired union officers. Occassionally, when a local leader loyal to the international is voted out of office, the international will take him on as an organizer or in some other salaried position. And the perquisites of local office are kept sweet—not unusual is the local that owns or leases half a dozen or more new Cadillacs to keep its leaders mobile.

Many Teamster members whom I interviewed volunteered their concern over constant reports that their union is dominated by the Mafia. They expressed fears that their pensions were in jeopardy because of Mob manipulation of Teamster pension funds. Nevertheless, they defended Hoffa, despite his criminal past and associations, and despite his role as first and foremost manipulator of the pension funds. They credited Hoffa for the relatively high wages and benefits in their National Master Freight Agreement. They know that many trucking companies now get away with paying less than the agreement calls for. But they blame Hoffa's successors for failing to enforce the agreement. Though the historical record shows that Hoffa's purported concern for the welfare of the working man is greatly exaggerated, the typical Teamster would still agree with the sentiment of a Missouri driver, who said: "Hoffa might have been a crook, but he made sure that the bottom man, the driver, got his cut. He worked for us."

That, however, is all past. Overwhelmingly, Teamster sentiments are resentful of the leadership that succeeded Hoffa, in the person of Frank Fitzsimmons. Actually, as most members realize, Fitzsimmons is a stooge with little power and is apt to be replaced at the whim of those who really run the Teamsters. If so, he probably will be replaced as the vice-presidents are, in mid-term, so a successor can be appointed and no open floor fight can occur at a convention.

There are three real power bases in the Teamsters, all closely tied to the Mafia. One is the Presser organization in Cleveland. William Presser ran the jukebox racket in Cleveland in the 1940s. An associate of numerous mobsters, he became an early ally of Jimmy Hoffa. He has been convicted for contempt of Congress and for destroying subpoenaed evidence (the evidence was a payoff list prepared for a Cleveland distributing company; the list included not only Presser, but a federal judge and some political figures). He also has been convicted for misusing $590,000 in Teamsters' money. Nevertheless, federal judges in Cleveland have thus far seen fit to turn Presser back into the community without substantial punishment. He has served only two prison terms, one for about two months and one for six. Now in semi-retirement, most of his titles have passed to his son, Jackie Presser, also a pal of the politicians. Between them, the Pressers run the Ohio Teamsters and have a large influence in the butchers, the hotel-restaurant workers, the bakery and confectionary workers and other unions. Jackie Presser may not be content with his father's backstage role, however, and is said by some to have designs on the international Teamster presidency. Possible evidence of this is seen in the determination by which he recently shed more than 100 pounds from his former 300-pound frame, a grotesque figure for a public person. Nevertheless, when I interviewed him late in 1975, he insisted he had "never even thought about a successor" to Fitzsimmons. He even said Fitzsimmons should be "international president as long as he's alive."

"Fitz is a different type of individual [from Hoffa]; he's astute, he's qualified, he's not a dictator," said Presser about a man who had never been more than a front, first for Hoffa and then for various mobsters after they turned against Hoffa. Presser waxed on about what he said was Fitzsimmons's extensive charity work and his prestige among politicians. Then Presser got down to what else he liked about Fitzsimmons: Fitz didn't interfere, as Hoffa had, with individual grievance or contract problems. He allowed the union to operate through a "chain of command." He had, in short, turned the Teamsters over to people like Presser.

Presser follows the common Teamster practice of holding down paying posts in many locals so that he can accumulate a salary of—according to his press agent—about $200,000 a year (some say it's more). He justifies this sum on the ground that he negotiates against "teams of $500-an-hour lawyers," and asks, "Are you saying as an educated person I don't deserve to get paid the same as those who negotiate against me?" Many Ohio truck drivers, however, talk scornfully about the high-living Pressers.

The second of the three sources of real power underpinning the Fitzsimmons regime is in Kansas City. The leader there, Roy Williams, is another possible candidate to replace Fitzsimmons when the Mob decides it's time for Fitz to go. Like Presser, Williams is a former close ally of Jimmy Hoffa, and the Labor Department study referred to earlier alleged direct ties between Williams and Kansas City Mafia boss Nicholas Civella. According to PROD, the dissident Teamster organization, Williams has been able to maintain various Teamster salaries aggregating around $100,000 a year. Three times the federal government has won indictments against him—twice for embezzlement and most recently for making false entries on reports—but each time he has been acquitted, or the charges have been dropped, twice after key witnesses for the prosecution were murdered gangland-style.

The third major Teamster power base is firmly controlled by the Genovese Mafia family in the East. Though some unsettling events have occurred in the summer of 1978, the Genovese power has been, and still seems to be, exercised through another group of former Hoffa allies, a blood family named Provenzano, originally of New York but now of New Jersey. Three brothers, Anthony, Salvatore ("Sammy") and Nunzio Provenzano have controlled the New Jersey Teamster organization since 1961 through their control of Local 560, a 10,000- to 12,000-member trucking local based in Union City. The Provenzanos also control numerous smaller locals, run by stooges. Many of these locals are used to implement sweetheart contracts with wages and benefits so far below purported Teamster standards that the Provenzanos evidently feel embarrassed to bring them before the membership of their home local. Members of Local 560 are kept reasonably well taken care of, while tens of thousands of members of these satellite locals are treated almost like slaves.

Besides the local and regional organizations, the Provenzanos also control an international vice-presidency.

Anthony, usually called Tony Pro, has been identified before Congress as a member of the Genovese Mafia family, as has one of the Provenzanos' chief aides, Salvatore "Sally Bugs" Briguglio. Their power was cemented by the 1961 murder of Anthony "Three Fingers Brown" Castellito, who until then was boss of Local 560. One night Castellito got into his Cadillac after a union meeting and drove away, never to be seen again except by his killers. The Provenzanos took over.

Some fifteen years later, an intensive investigation of the Provenzano organization was begun because of its presumed link to the Hoffa disappearance. During that investigation, the FBI stumbled on a witness to the Castellito murder who himself had gone into hiding shortly afterward. As a result, in

1976, Tony Pro and Sally Bugs were indicted for killing Castellito, in a plot with their one-time friend, Harold "Kayo" Konigsberg, a well-known Mafia-hired skull crusher who was already ensconced in prison on other charges. In 1978, Provenzano and Konigsberg were convicted.

Until the Hoffa investigation struck him in 1978, Tony Pro's power was so awesome as to preclude any meaningful challenges. Certainly his authority wasn't shaken by his 1963 extortion conviction, and the resultant 1967–1971 term he served at the federal prison at Lewisburg, Pennsylvania (where his prison mates included Hoffa, Tino DeAngelis, and Bonanno underboss Carmine "Lilo" Galante). Brothers Salvatore and Nunzio Provenzano simply played caretaker while the boss paid his debt to society. The Landrum-Griffen Act provided that Tony couldn't return to union office officially for five years after leaving prison for extortion, but when the ban expired in 1976 he quietly slipped back into the top job at Local 560. He was able, however, to spend a lot, perhaps most, of his time at his swank Florida home (the developer, soon after selling him the home, received a $4.6 million loan from Local 560's pension fund).

Death seemed the only likely reward for anyone who contested Tony's power. Even the brother of Anthony Castellito went meekly to work as a salaried vice-president in the Provenzano organization, and stayed on as such after Tony Pro was indicted for Castellito's murder. Throughout most of the New York metropolitan area trucking zone, and on into upper New York State and down the Atlantic coast, not a contract was signed, not a pension fund dollar was invested, not a major grievance was pursued outside the imposing shadow of Tony Pro. The Teamster business office in Union City, New Jersey, operated as a headquarters for loansharking, counterfeiting and numerous other crimes, the most important of which was contract murder. The men whose strings were pulled by Tony Pro were believed responsible for dozens of cold-blooded killings.

Provenzano became a leading suspect in the Hoffa case because Hoffa had told people that Tony Pro was one of three men he was going to meet at a Detroit restaurant at the time he vanished (Provenzano denied having such an appointment). Shortly afterward, Ralph "Little Ralph" Picardo, a former close associate (Picardo said chauffeur) of Provenzano's who had been convicted of murder, agreed to turn informer for the government. He identified Sally Bugs and two other employees of the Provenzano organization as having gone to Detroit and murdered Hoffa.

Even so, none of this was enough to convict anybody of anything, and Tony Pro might have survived had it not been for a vigorous new determination that suddenly surfaced in the Department of Justice. It was unlike anything seen since Kennedy's day. During the Nixon years, somewhat as during Eisenhower's term, federal law enforcement (with important exceptions) had largely turned its back on the Mafia in order to face down a scattered gaggle of adolescent Leninists, a small minority of whom had genuinely volunteered violence. There were also millions of good citizens of all ages who were temporarily aligned with these revolutionaries because of the Vietnam war. When the war ended, the good citizens went back to their business. The Leninists burned themselves out, perhaps their biggest legacy being a dangerous public backlash against the law enforcement tactics that had been misused to pursue them. The Mafia inferno, meanwhile, roared on to perhaps its ultimate moment of defiance: the evident murder of the popular would-be leader of the biggest labor union in America.

The FBI and Justice Department, scandalized by recent revelations of misconduct within, suddenly confronted their true mission. If Mafia guns could wipe out even the appearance of democracy and free speech in the Teamsters, and by a public figure like Hoffa, then whose rights were safe? There might not be proof of who killed Hoffa, but the men who were believed to be responsible had committed many other grievous crimes. If enough energy, skill, and determination were applied, some of the cases could be proven —as they could have been all along.

More than any others, two men epitomized this tough new attitude (if they didn't actually instigate it). They are Kurt Muellenberg, head of the department's organized crime and racketeering section in Washington, and Robert C. Stewart, who heads Muellenberg's special strike force offices in Newark, New Jersey, and Buffalo, New York. The drive they conducted resembled one begun 20 years earlier after another brazen Mafia attack on a public figure, the blinding of newspaper columnist Victor Riesel. The man who authorities believed was responsible for the Riesel attack was John Dioguardi—Johnny Dio—and although they couldn't prove it, they focused in so tightly on Dio that he has spent most of the intervening years in prison for other crimes (he's there now). The parallel target in the Hoffa case was Tony Provenzano.

Late in 1975, five months after Hoffa disappeared, Provenzano was indicted for planning a $2.3 million pension fund loan involving a $300,000 kickback to mobsters and Teamster officials. Six months later came the Castellito murder indictment against Provenzano and his aide Sally Bugs. The kickback case was based on a hard-to-understand tape recording of a 1974 meeting about the loan; the tape, made secretly by an undercover informant, had been lying around the prosecutors' offices for eighteen months and had been regarded as weak evidence. Provenzano's words on it were few and vague. But with new testimony from Ralph Picardo—the informant who had talked about the Hoffa case—and with a brilliantly orchestrated trial in March, 1978, Tony Pro was convicted. (Along with him, the jury convicted his lesser known but important pal Anthony Bentro, who had infiltrated the executive ranks of two large, publicly-held corporations. Bentro [formerly Bentrovato] had been executive vice-president of Chromalloy American Corp., a conglomerate whose shares are traded on the American Stock Exchange. Later he had been accused by the Securities and Exchange Commission of helping the head of SCA Services Inc., a waste-disposal firm whose shares are traded on the New

York Stock Exchange, in a successful scheme to divert $4 million in corporate funds. By then he had qualified for a job supervising hundreds of millions of dollars of Teamster pension fund investments for Tony Pro and other labor leaders.)

Two months after the pension fund conviction, which earned Provenzano a four-year sentence (and Bentro eighteen months), a jury in Kingston, New York, told the stunned Teamster boss that he was also guilty of ordering the murder of Castellito (which had taken place while Provenzano was attending his own wedding in Miami, a thousand miles south of the murder scene). Tony Pro was sent immediately to the forboding New York State Prison at Dannemora. The Provenzanos still did not lose their hold on their Teamster organization, but the first signs of real trouble had begun to surface.

On March 21, 1978, while awaiting trial for the Castellito murder charge, Sally Bugs Briguglio was shot dead on Mulberry Street in Little Italy. Some federal authorities think he was killed because Provenzano and others feared he would talk about the Hoffa case. Briguglio had been convicted of felonies twice in the past, and was under investigation for various new crimes by Stewart's strike force. He was threatened with a long prison stretch. Nevertheless, though subjected to intense pressure from the FBI to become a witness against others in the Hoffa case, Briguglio never broke down and talked (according to reliable reports). At one point, when the FBI seemed to have him on the ropes momentarily, he indicated that his wife, children, and other relatives made him so vulnerable that the government could never protect him. He insisted he wouldn't make a deal, according to the reports.

So, some federal officials offer another explanation for the demise of Sally Bugs: a Mafia power play. They contend that Briguglio had betrayed Tony Pro and had conspired with another top Genovese underboss, Pasquale "Paddy Mac" Macchiarole, to take power in Local 560, either directly or through allies, if Tony Pro went to jail. One circumstance contributing to this theory is that Macchiarole was murdered apparently the same day Briguglio was. So (within a day or two) were at least two other members of the same gang. At the time Briguglio was being shot on Mulberry Street, Tony Provenzano—according to Justice Department Sources—was dining at a restaurant very close by, probably within sound of the gunshots. His dinner partner was Matthew "Matty the Horse" Ianniello, the mobster who controls Manhattan's midtown bar and red light district and has underlings involved in commodities options frauds and other rackets. Some law enforcement officials believe that with the murders of March 21, in a scene reminiscent of the end of the movie *The Godfather,* either Provenzano or Ianniello had just established himself as operating boss of the old Genovese gang (the gang's real godfather, Frank "Funzi" Tieri, 74, was cancer-stricken and believed to be semi-retired).

Whichever explanation for Briguglio's death is correct, it doesn't say much for the kind of people who control one of our largest and most vital industries. A week after Provenzano entered prison, he was replaced as head of Local 560

—not by either of his brothers this time, but by his daughter, Josephine Provenzano, either twenty-three or twenty-six years old depending on which account you accept. The local announced that Miss Provenzano, an office worker on the payroll in the past, had been elected by unanimous vote of the membership. Some observers suspect that this development indicates not unanimity, but discord; they believe Salvatore and Nunzio Provenzano yielded up the office to their niece because they regarded her as less likely to be shot by the opposition.

Late in 1975, I interviewed Salvatore Provenzano—Sammy Pro—in his surprisingly modest office in a run-down section of Union City (actually, almost every section of Union City is run-down). At the time, Tony Pro was still under the Landrum-Griffen Act's mandatory five-year ban on holding union office because of his 1967–1971 federal prison term for extorting money from the employers he negotiated with. So Sammy Pro was running shop, both in Local 560 and as international vice-president for the region, and holding down various other titles at a combined salary—according to Labor Department records—of $83,000 a year. His remarks in the interview were nearly identical to those that Jackie Presser had made earlier.

"Fitzsimmons has the same power Hoffa did," Provenzano said, "but he is willing to concede that issues that fall within the area of the [international] vice-presidents they can decide for themselves. Hoffa was the kind of guy that when he said something, he didn't want anybody to disagree with him. The vice-presidents were just figureheads. He came into their area and by-passed the vice-presidents."

One matter Hoffa tried to remove from regional jurisdiction is pension funds. Hoffa succeeded in nationalizing much of the Teamster pension money around the country under the umbrella of the Central States, Southeast, and Southwest Areas pension fund (under Fitzsimmons, that fund became dominated by the Pressers and a few other midwestern leaders). But many large pension funds—including a couple that the Provenzanos have been accused of manipulating—are still independent, and the leaders who run them want to keep them that way.

The Provenzano power base has been used as an open center for extortion, loansharking, counterfeiting, and murder. It is run by ex-convicts. Briguglio, a convicted counterfeiter who supposedly subsisted on a $31,000-a-year salary as Local 560 business agent, moved a few years before his death into a $125,000 house mortgage-free; records show that his wife (in whose name the house was registered) paid $105,000 cash down, and soon paid the other $20,000 so that the Briguglios owned the house free and clear. Another key figure in the local (though technically not an employee or officer), Thomas Andretta, through his wife bought Briguglio's old house for $90,000, also without having to obtain financing from any financial institution, according to Bergen County, New Jersey, land records. Andretta, who has served two brief prison terms after convictions for hijacking, loansharking, and counterfeiting, is a former truck driver with no apparent legitimate occupation. He spends his time around the Local 560 office, or, according to the testimony that sent him to prison a few years ago, following his loanshark victims' children to school. New Jersey state and federal judges—who are selected through an extremely political process —have had ample opportunity to cleanse the community of these men, or at least to exact some substantial penalty from them, but so far haven't chosen to do so.

Briguglio's brother Gabriel, and Andretta's brother Stephen both have held various Teamster posts in areas where the Provenzanos dominate. All four men have been identified publicly by Justice Department officials as suspects in the presumed murder of Hoffa. The two Briuglios and Thomas Andretta personally killed him, according to the testimony of their former colleague Ralph Picardo. But at this writing none of them has been charged. The government tried to get testimony from Stephen Andretta by granting him immunity from prosecution, but Andretta clung to the Fifth Amendment. He was imprisoned for sixty-three days for contempt of court, and finally testified, but apparently said nothing incriminating.

The Mafia has profitted in many ways from its control over the international Teamster apparatus. The hiring capacity of the giant Teamster organization provides a perfect front. Mafia figures frequent the payrolls of Teamster locals with no-show jobs or at least irregular hours. Teamster members and employers are easy prey for Mafia loansharks or vice peddlers. Since trucking is involved in almost every aspect of American economic life, control over the Teamsters gives the Mafia leverage in almost any business it wants to muscle into. The Teamsters can simply shut off supplies to anyone who doesn't cooperate.

But there have been two very immediate avenues to profitability for the Mob in the Teamsters union: pension and welfare fund fraud, and sweetheart contracts. Directly through the trust funds, and indirectly through the sweetheart contracts, the American consumer has been looted of money that must be in the many billions of dollars. The savage cost to Teamster members is even more easily discernible. But perhaps worse, in the long run, is the palpable blow to the nation's morality; a large segment of American business has been openly compelled to submit to corruption. As for law enforcement, it has usually been impotent, and at times even complicitous.

2

The Mafia's
Private Bank

Every week, $31 of the compensation paid to more than half a million North American trucking workers goes into a Teamster pension fund. It will jump to $37 a week in 1979. A million other Teamster members in other jobs are covered by varying contributions into the funds. The Teamster apparatus controls more than one thousand employe-benefit funds with reported assets of about $9 billion, growing by about $1 billion a year. The largest of them alone now takes in half a billion dollars a year. The employees who purportedly benefit from this money don't see it in their paychecks; often, they don't ever see it at all. The employers who shell it out pass the cost directly on to the people who buy the goods that are being trucked. The price of practically everything rises. And the money flows steadily to the Mafia.

The one largest Teamster fund—the Central States, Southeast, and Southwest Areas pension fund, operated from Chicago*—has compiled a record of abuse that makes other landmark swindling operations—Robert Vesco and IOS, or Equity Funding Corp., or the Tino De Angelis salad oil enterprise— look paltry by comparison. It is perhaps the biggest rip-off in history. Thorough records of the stealing have never been made available, but enough

---

*Figures released by PROD in 1978, after this chapter had gone to the printer, indicate that another pension fund affiliated with the Western Conference of Teamsters—a fund particularly free from corruption charges—has edged ahead of the Central States fund in size. The investment policies of the Central States fund could help explain its failure to remain the largest.

evidence has trickled out in various lawsuits and public filings to show that many hundreds of millions of dollars have been plowed into "loans" to racketeers or businesses related to them. The "loans" have never been paid back and are not likely to be.

In 1975, while preparing a series of articles on the pension fund for the *Wall Street Journal,* I asked a team of auditors from a major international accounting firm (one of the so-called Big Eight) particularly experienced at weighing portfolios of the fund's type, to examine the available records and give an informal opinion. The auditors agreed. For six hours the three auditors pored over the hundreds of pages of Xeroxed documents I gave them. I had been a little nervous that perhaps the outrageous frauds I had suspected wouldn't much impress the auditors, who were wisened to the often devious ways of the legitimate businessmen they dealt with. Mobsters constantly offer the defense that bankers are no more ethical than the Mafia is. But as the auditors turned page after page of Teamster loan records, the atmosphere turned to laughter, sometimes uproarious. There were repeated shouts of "Hey! Look at this one!" We had dinner brought up to the New York hotel suite we were using. There wasn't any drinking. At one point, a hooker—good-looking of the dyed red-haired sort—knocked on the door, obviously as she had at many others, and asked if we had phoned for some sort of assistance. The auditors shut the door on her, eager to go back to the Teamster records for more laughs. This is what they saw:

The overwhelming majority of the fund's investments—89.2 percent—were concentrated in real estate mortgages, mostly to small, speculative businesses. (According to the Institute of Life Insurance, most pension funds invested an estimated 10 to 15 percent of their funds in real estate.) Often the loans were for less than $1 million, which the auditors said was too small to be worth the bookkeeping trouble for such a large fund. Moreover, the real estate involved wasn't exactly prime. Many of the investments were in second and even third mortgages. "I've looked at REIT (real estate investment trust) and bank portfolios for a long time and I've never seen a cemetery before," said one of the auditors late in the evening. Then he summed up the bulk of the Teamster portfolio this way: "I don't see office buildings, I don't see apartment buildings, I don't see good, sound investments. I see motels, hospitals, health spas, bowling alleys, cemeteries—all this may come up roses, but I wouldn't bet on it."

From further records, however, it obviously wasn't coming up roses. Deals accounting for well over a third of the money loaned were listed as delinquent or already defaulted on, with the pension fund acquiring ownership of vast acres of questionable real value in lieu of hundreds of millions of dollars due in cash payments. The true loss figures weren't revealed even in these records because borrowers whose loans were listed as up-to-date had more recently gone into bankruptcy or had their corporate charters canceled for nonpayment of state tax, indicating they were out of business. Moreover, some loans apparently were secured by the same property that secured previous loans, indicating that in some cases loans were kept current by the lending of new money to pay them off. On thorough study, it's easy to guess that more than half a billion dollars in supposed investments were actually just excuses to distribute money to fund insiders, Mafia members and their cronies. And this was only one of many suspicious Teamster pension funds.

The Central States fund has always prided itself on its apparent solvency, based on the fact that income from employer contributions exceeds pay-outs to retirees by $100 million or so a year. The trick, however, is that the pension pay-out has always been held far below what it should be. Reliable figures aren't available on how many teamsters are getting retirement or disability pensions, and how many others are claiming pensions that haven't been paid. But when I went looking, I had no difficulty locating scores of Teamster members and former members who said they were being cheated.

Most often, the complainers had been victimized by one of several technicalities in the fund's regulations that give the fund the right to withhold payment. Applied uniformly, these loopholes could destine hundreds of thousands of Teamsters to lose their pensions. Some of these abuses, though by no means all of them, were in theory cured by the "vesting" provisions of the federal pension regulation law, the so-called ERISA act, that was passed in 1974 and took effect in 1976. Whether, in fact, ERISA has led to any real improvement in the conduct of the Teamster pension funds remains to be seen. The law was really designed to create uniform standards for well-intentioned pension operations. It wasn't designed to enable the policing of true frauds, and so far the Labor Department has shown no signs of being able to use it that way.

Under the Central States pension plan, Teamsters are supposed to be able to retire at age fifty-seven for minimum benefits, or at age sixty or more for full benefits of $550 a month for the best-paid trucking jobs. But I found that Teamsters who expected to start collecting a pension as promised on reaching retirement age often had to wait four to six months after that for the big Central States fund even to respond to an application. And then a common response was a form letter stating that the fund didn't keep records of its members' work histories. The letter called on the individual teamster to prove he had twenty years of industry credits for a retirement pension, or fifteen for a disability pension. Few truck drivers keep such detailed business records.

Several years ago, two Ohio Teamsters went to federal court to try to get an order requiring the fund to pay them the pensions they had coming. The judge turned them down. Their lawyer, Jerry Hayes, became painfully aware of how difficult it is for men to gather the kind of proof the fund demanded. Trucking work by its nature involves frequent job-hopping among a myriad of small companies. "These trucking companies are very little," Hayes complained after his case was lost. "They go bankrupt. They buy each other out. I doubt that 20 percent of the trucking companies are still doing business in the same form for twenty years. So records are simply not maintained. . . . The worker gets his paycheck indicating X-dollars were taken out [for pension fund contribution] but nobody ever knows whether the companies actually send in the money. Teamsters get no annual report on what's been paid in. They can write and they get no answer."

Michael Talatinick, a Minnesota trucker who retired to Cape Coral, Florida, was one former teamster I found whose long-standing pension claim hadn't been approved by the Central States pension fund. The fund said Talatinick had insufficient work credits. At issue were five critical years back around 1950 when Talatinick worked for Eastern Motor Dispatch Inc., an Ohio company now long defunct. In the summer of 1972, Talatinick had submitted his Eastern Motor Dispatch identification card and a photograph of him driving an Eastern Motor Dispatch truck, but the Central States fund returned the card to him with a form letter saying only, "The attached papers are being returned to you."

After more inquiries, the fund finally answered him personally the following February: "Kindly be advised that affidavits must be submitted from fellow workers, owners or supervisors. These affidavits must include the type of work you did, the number of years you worked and the number of hours worked per year. You may also submit your check stubs." Talatinick replied that he didn't know where to turn for the affidavits or stubs after all this time. Nearly three years later he was still trying to get the pension by seeking the support of his old union local (number 120 in St. Paul, Minnesota). The local flatly maintained that Talatinick had never been a member, even though he showed me what certainly appeared to be a copy of his membership card and a receipt for his dues, dated 1954.

Ultimately, many teamsters said, they turned to the Social Security Administration for evidence, which takes many more months and an $87.50 fee. But even if the Social Security records are complete—and sometimes, teamsters say, they aren't—those records don't necessarily prove to the fund's satisfaction that each employer paid the weekly payroll deductions into the pension fund as he was supposed to. For example, Robert Maxwell of Akron, Ohio, showed me Social Security records evidencing work with numerous trucking companies over the course of thirty-two years. But when he inquired to the Central States fund about his pension, he was told—after a delay of ten months—that money hadn't been paid into the fund on his behalf most of the time, depriving him of the necessary pension credits. Many teamsters alleged in interviews, though they didn't have proof, that sweetheart deals permit certain trucking companies to pay less into the pension fund than they are supposed to, which allows the fund to refuse pensions to the covered employees long after the companies have gone out of business.

Constant transfers from one company to another and from one depot to another within the same trucking company caused an additional problem: the transfer of workers from one local to another. At any given time, hundreds of thousands of teamsters are represented by locals without reciprocal deals with the Central States pension plan. Many teamsters frequently rotate into and out of these locals. I found in 1975 that teamsters applying for pensions often are shocked to be told that they must have the minimum twenty years' service with one particular plan, even though they have been members of the same international union for many decades. The new ERISA law has provided that some pension must be paid after a minimum ten years of contributions to a plan, though opportunities for abuse are still great.

One local whose independent plan has caused frequent problems over the years is number 705 in Chicago, which has a fluid membership in the neighborhood of twenty thousand workers. Dorman Vestal joined Local 705 in 1954 after seventeen years with an Iowa local. In 1962 he transferred from truck driving to loading dock work, also as a teamster, but the job switch caused him to transfer into Local 710, where he stayed until his retirement in 1969 at age sixty-one. Apparently none of the three locals recognized the others' pension plans. As a result, Vestal—who died in 1971—didn't receive any pension money, and his widow, who would be entitled to receive it now even if her husband had been credited with only twenty years of his thirty-two years' service, told me she was living off an unemployment check and was "practically destitute." In 1975, Local 705 announced that it had negotiated a reciprocal agreement with the Central States pension plan, though the reciprocity apparently wasn't retroactive for the numerous cases like Mrs. Vestal's. Only time will tell whether the abuses are actually cleared up or whether one device for thievery has simply been replaced by another as is the Teamsters' pattern.

Teamsters said that trucking companies often forced them to switch to non-reciprocal locals because of secret agreements with the union to hold down pension fund payments. The workers cited specific cases where companies—including at least one that had received more than a million dollars in loans from the Central States pension fund under particularly favorable terms—transferred scores of workers to jobs that would require them to join a new local with a different pension plan. The trucking companies denied there was any ulterior motive behind the transfers.

Even Teamsters who built up twenty years' total service with one plan sometimes found they had run afoul of the so-called "break-in-service" provisions. Many teamsters said they were unaware of these provisions until it was too late. For example, the fine print of the rules that the Central States fund filed with the Labor Department says, "If a member did not work under a Teamster collective bargaining agreement requiring contributions to this Pension fund for three consecutive years, he cannot count years of employment before such a break in his total years of service for a pension." In other words, a service break would eliminate all prior credit. This provision has scuttled the pensions of many teamsters who have quit or been laid off during hard times in the trucking business, then taken a factory job and several years later gone back to trucking. It also has scuttled the pensions of men who never left the

Teamsters' union, but who have been transferred into and out of jobs not covered by the Central States pension plan.

One such man, for example, is Lester Black of Akron, who drove trucks from 1935 to 1957 in locals now covered by the Central States fund. Then he went to work for another trucking company, but as a mechanic. Although still a teamster, he was employed under what is called a "miscellaneous contract" and therefore wasn't under the pension program. Later, in 1965, he went back to work as a driver, but when he applied for his pension in 1971 at age fifty-seven, the Central States fund omitted his mechanic duty from his work record, apparently recorded it as a break-in-service, and said, "We haven't any alternative but to place your application in our rejection file."

One way that tens of thousands of teamsters apparently have fallen into the break-in-service exclusion is by becoming "owner-operators." Drivers often dream of one day owning their own rigs. So, many companies offer installment sales contracts through which, at least in theory, the dream can come true. But while the driver is paying off his rig he usually is required to work only on assignment from the trucking company that is selling it to him, and he must be a member of the union. After a few years the assigned work often thins out and the driver's income drops, so he gives up his rig—which is far from paid for—and takes a job driving with another company. Such teamsters often remain unaware that their pension fund will count their owner-operator years as a break-in-service—even if the driver has paid his own pension fund contribution from his weekly paycheck.

In 1972, three former owner-operators sued the fund in federal court in St. Louis. The court ruled that company restrictions on owner-operators are so strict that the men were in effect employees, not self-employers as the fund said. But the ruling required pension payments only to the three St. Louis men. Many other teamsters whose cases appear to fall into the same category have had their pension claims denied and have been unable to finance expensive litigation.

In 1977, an Illinois teamster, John Daniel, seemed to have made real headway. Denied his pension under the break-in-service provision, he found a lawyer who filed suit on his behalf under a novel legal theory: that a pension is really a security and therefore subject to the antifraud strictures of the Securities and Exchange Act. A federal appeals court bought the argument, which might have meant that Daniel could collect his pension because the break-in-service provision had been misrepresented to him. The Teamsters, however, appealed to the U. S. Supreme Court, and in 1978 won a big advantage when the Department of Justice intervened on behalf of the Teamsters. Ironically, while the criminal prosecutors at Justice were working night and day to clean up pension fund abuse, the civil lawyers down the hall were arguing on behalf of the abuse; their fear, not unreasonable, was that if the pension-as-a-security argument became law, it might impose oppressive burdens on many well-intentioned pension funds around the country, as well as on the government to supervise them. At this writing, the Supreme Court hasn't acted.

So what has happened to the $1.5 billion or so that the Central States fund supposedly is keeping watch over, but which it regularly refuses to pay out to retired teamsters? Of all the men alive, Allen Dorfman could probably answer that question best.

Few of the half-million or so teamsters whose employers contribute for them into the fund would be able to say exactly what Allen Dorfman has done for them over the years. But they have sure done a lot for him. And so have the rest of us whose purchase of trucked goods pays the cost of Teamster corruption.

Dorfman's official role as consultant to the fund—a job that has paid him as much as $75,000 a year plus expenses—has been only a small part of his profitable relationship with the union. That job was canceled in 1972 as a result of his conviction that year in federal court, Manhattan, for taking a package full of money, allegedly about $55,000, for recommending approval of a $1.5 million loan. But Dorfman stayed on at the hub of the circle of union leaders, trucking company executives, Mafia members, and their lawyers and cronies who are the real beneficiaries of the impressive-looking pension plans in Teamster contracts. To the surprise of many, his power didn't seem to fade after the presumed murder in 1975 of his longtime ally Jimmy Hoffa, although Dorfman did spend the month after Hoffa's disappearance discretely touring Europe.

In 1978, after a Labor Department task force operating under the ERISA law had supposedly spent two years cleaning up the fund's operations, and had forced a reorganization of its board of trustees amidst ballyhoo that all the crooks were now kicked out, the board—almost incredibly—voted to extend Dorfman's contract! As uncovered by Jim Drinkhall of the *Wall Street Journal,* terms call for Dorfman to process claims for a fee of $450,000 a month, in addition to his other business, including the sale of "add-on" insurance to Teamster members and the sale of property and liability coverage for most of the pension fund's 500 borrowers. The fund in 1978 openly disavowed many other parts of its purported clean-up agreement with the Labor Department. But Dorfman is not the kind of man who needs a title or a salary to wield power and accumulate wealth, anyway. His father, Paul "Red" Dorfman, had been running a large part of the Mafia labor rackets in Chicago since Al Capone days, and had sealed the bargain that helped make Jimmy Hoffa international president of the Teamsters.

Allen Dorfman received a B.A. in physical education from the University of Illinois, and soon afterward, in 1949, obtained an Illinois insurance agent's license. Through the efforts of his father, he was appointed general agent for Union Casualty Company, a relatively small firm that handled insurance for the Chicago Waste Materials Handlers' union, which Paul "Red" Dorfman ran as secretary-treasurer (in 1957, the AFL-CIO forced the elder Dorfman out of that job for misuse of funds and for entering private business deals with the employers).

In 1950, Allen Dorfman scored his biggest coup. The Central Conference of Teamsters—just taken over by Hoffa with the influence of Red Dorfman— threw out the low bid for its group insurance contract. Hoffa argued that the low bidder, Pacific Mutual Life Insurance Company, with assets of $377 million, had a history of financial trouble (a Depression-era reorganization). Instead of Pacific Mutual, the union awarded its contract to the supposedly more stable Union Casualty Company, which had assets of $768,000. And so Allen Dorfman, Union Casualty's agent, went on the Teamster pad. Teamster business soon constituted more than 80 percent of his total income, with premiums running more than $10 million a year. Hoffa and the young Dorfman (who was more Hoffa's contemporary than was Dorfman's father) invested together privately in a lodge in Wisconsin and an oil exploration company in North Dakota.

In 1955, the Central States, Southeast, and Southwest Areas pension fund was born, and it didn't have to shop far for an insurance agent. According to Senate testimony by an insurance expert in 1958, Dorfman charged his Teamster clients three or four times the normal rate of commission. Other witnesses said he paid the premiums of personal insurance policies he obtained for union officials, and helped spend hundreds of thousands of Teamster dollars on travel and entertainment.

Soon Dorfman and a few associates were running a complex of insurance agencies, which eventually was located in the same Teamster-owned building that housed the pension fund itself. In 1967, he got the job of monitoring the insurance coverage of the fund's borrowers—surely a convenient position for an insurance agent looking to pick up easy premiums. One Dorfman company acquired a Grumman Gulfstream (from Frank Sinatra) and leased it to the fund, which used it to fly Dorfman and other insiders around the country. The plane stopped frequently at Rancho La Costa, a southern California resort and land development where Dorfman and others acquired property.

La Costa—which is becoming a popular place for respectable people to vacation—was founded and is run by four men including convicted stock manipulator Allard Roen and former bootlegging and gambling figure Morris "Moe" Dalitz. It has been financed since 1964 with some $57 million in Teamster pension fund loans and commitments (according to 1972 records, which were the latest I could obtain; the figure has been reported much higher, nearly $100 million now). Records showed that some $12.4 million of the La Costa loans had been paid back on schedule, but the team of auditors I consulted called the repayment schedule itself into question. Land development loans are considered relatively risky and short-term, the auditors said, and normally should be paid off completely in three to five years. Moreover, they pointed out, many of the loans at La Costa, as in other Teamster-financed projects, are third-party mortgages, which may indicate that new loans were made to pay off prior ones as they came due. "I don't know of any bank or real estate investment trust that's going into third-party takeouts of land development loans," one auditor said, as the others laughed, emphasizing to me just how absurd they considered the investments to be from a standpoint of financial prudence.

La Costa was far from the only business venture financed by the fund where Dorfman became personally involved. From 1964 to 1971, for example, some $13 million in pension money was poured into Beverly Ridge Estates, a California land development whose promoters transferred two parcels to Dorfman's name. The whole $13 million was still owing when the fund foreclosed on the property in 1972. Three promoters of the project were convicted, two for bankruptcy fraud and one for perjury, in connection with Beverly Ridge. A few years ago the fund sold the development for $7 million—about half of what it had previously mortgaged the place for—to one Allen R. Glick. The fund could not argue that it was merely cutting its losses, because it lent Glick the entire $7 million he needed to pay for Beverly Ridge. And the loan was for twenty-five years at 4 percent interest, far below what banks were getting for their money from prime customers. Even so, in December, 1977, the fund foreclosed on that loan, too. Once again, the pensioners apparently were saddled with a floundering real estate project while millions of the dollars that American consumers had shelled out for the pensioners' retirement was given away.

Glick, the man who had received the money, was just thirty-two years old. He had left the Army in 1969 and spent the next several years working for housing and real estate firms in San Diego. Since then, he has become involved in fund loans totalling about $150 million. Many of Glick's pension fund dollars went to finance a big move into Las Vegas hotel-casinos, including the Stardust, the Fremont and the Hacienda. Nearly half a million dollars in "brokerage fees" for the Las Vegas loans was paid to an ex-convict who associates with mobsters and was recently involved in a stolen Treasury bill scheme.

Observers began to suspect that Glick was fronting for the Syndicate. The government launched an investigation. Two persons closely associated with Glick's business interests were murdered in similar style with .22 calibre weapons. In 1978 the investigation was getting ever more intense, and focusing particularly on the suspected involvement of Chicago Mafia figure Anthony "Tough Tony" Spilotro. In recent years Spilotro has lived in Las Vegas, where authorities believe he manages the Mafia's casino and real estate interests with Teamster money.

According to disclosure statements made at the request of the American Stock Exchange (where the debentures of Glick's Argent Corp. are traded) Argent advanced $10 million of its Teamster dollars to Glick personally and other companies of his without properly disclosing it at the time. Argent said the loans were unsecured and unpaid, and might never be paid. Still, Glick had never been charged with a crime.

In the mid-1960s the Central States fund invested $450,000 in the scandal-ridden Seventeenth Street National Bank of Denver, which was looted into reorganization by swindlers and ex-cons. As compensation for its lost investment, the fund received a large block of stock in Villa National Bank, which took over from Seventeenth Street, and Dorfman was appointed to the Villa board to oversee the fund's interests. The fund lent still more money to the bank, but new financial troubles forced another sale and name change in 1970. In 1972, the fund still carried the Villa debt on its books as an "asset," even though the alleged debtor was no longer in existence; the successor bank, United Bank of Lakewood N.A., says it never assumed the debt to the Teamsters fund. How many other nonexistent IOUs were listed on the fund's books as "assets" is anybody's guess.

Dorfman also acquired twenty-five thousand shares of a corporation that was developing Boca Teeca Country Club Estates in Boca Teeca, Florida, with $5.1 million in Teamster loans beginning in 1968. As of 1972, $4.7 million was still owing on the loans—but Dorfman personally had sold his stock and declared a $49,000 gain on his 1969 income tax return.

Directly or indirectly, Dorfman also acquired interest in three other Florida properties that were financed with millions of fund dollars. As of 1972, at least, most of the money was unrepaid. According to testimony in federal court in 1972, Dorfman and four partners took over one property, a motel, merely by assuming the unpaid $1,550,000 mortgage to the pension fund. Two years later, in 1969, apparently without paying anything on the mortgage, they sold the motel for a $350,000 profit and the fund agreed to transfer the mortgage debt to the new buyer. Three years later, in 1972, not one penny of the mortgage debt had been repaid and the mounting interest left the debt higher than ever.

One Dorfman partner in that motel deal was Alvin Baron, a Chicago lawyer who was receiving more than $100,000 a year in legal fees from the fund in the 1970s and who also acquired land at La Costa. The other three partners in the motel deal, according to testimony at Dorfman's trial were Morton Harris and his two partners at the Chicago law firm of Harris, Burman and Silets, which also was collecting substantial legal fees from the fund. In addition, Harris was an officer of an Arizona company that borrowed $615,000 from the fund and repaid hardly any of it, at least in the first eighteen months. (When I questioned Harris about it, he said his only income from the Arizona deal was legal fees, and that "there's no conflict since the fund in this case was represented by other counsel.")

Dorfman and Baron also acquired large blocs of stock in Bally Manufacturing Company, the slot machine people who are going into the casino business in Atlantic City, and whose operations have relied on some $12 million in Teamster financing. When Bally (then Lion Manufacturing Company) went into the slot machine business in 1964, an important hidden owner was Mafia boss Gerardo Catena, who later bowed out when his holdings became known, according to the Nevada Gaming Control Board. More recent stockholders have included Frank Fitzsimmons, the Teamster president himself; Cal Kovens, a developer whose operations have been heavily financed by the pension fund and who has served prison time for defrauding the fund; and William and Jackie Presser, the Ohio Teamster leaders. (Jackie Presser also was once president of a company that borrowed $1.2 million from the Central States fund to open a bowling alley in Cleveland and then defaulted on the debt, according to widely published accounts that he doesn't deny.)

Over the years, records show, the fund has lent many millions of dollars to companies whose income stands to benefit fund insiders. At least $45.2 million has been lent to employers of Teamster members, more than $35 million of which was still outstanding as of the 1972 date of the only detailed records I could obtain. At least two of the employers who relied on financing from the pension fund have been accused by their teamster employees of unfair labor practices, but in both cases the Teamsters union declined to support the employees' complaints.

In one interesting case, the fund lent $12.3 million to Valley Steel Products Company of St. Louis, a Teamster employer. The president of Valley Steel, until his death in 1974, was the father of Robert Crancer, himself a young executive at Valley. Robert Crancer was also Jimmy Hoffa's son-in-law. When the loans were made, from 1963 to 1967, Hoffa was general president of the Teamsters. In 1966 the truckdrivers at Valley voted to strike after rejecting a contract the union had negotiated for them. According to reports by Jim Drinkhall (then writing for *Overdrive,* a truck-drivers' magazine, and now a reporter for the *Wall Street Journal*), the strike was averted by direct pressure on the local from Hoffa, who insisted that the employees return to work. (Valley insists there wasn't any outside interference.) Some $6.9 million was still owed on the loans in 1972.

Some fund loans have gone directly to companies controlled by mobsters and criminals. For example, beginning in 1963, some $1.2 million went to Valley Die Cast Corp. of Detroit, whose president was Michael Santo "Big Mike" Polizzi, an important figure in the Detroit Mafia. In 1972, Polizzi and Detroit Mafia Don Anthony J. Zerilli were convicted of concealing their ownership of a Las Vegas casino as part of a plot to skim profits. At about the time of the conviction, some $800,000 was still owing on the nine-year-old Teamsters' fund loan of $1.2 million to Valley Die Cast.

The fund lent $1.9 million to the lavish Savannah (Georgia) Inn & Country Club, a kind of east coast La Costa. When the loan was defaulted on, the fund took over the club and in 1971 installed as its manager Louis "Lou the Tailor" Rosanova, widely reputed as a Chicago Mafia associate.

Andrew Lococo, another Mob associate, who, before he died in 1974, had been convicted of burglary, larceny, violation of parole, and perjury, was lent

$2.5 million from 1969 to 1971. The loans were made in the name of the Cockatoo Motel, a Los Angeles nightclub Lococo owned, but according to Justice Department sources, much of it went to finance a large fishing boat Lococo planned to operate.

People who are not mobsters or insiders may still borrow money from the Teamsters. But they often have to pay a mobster or an insider to act as an intermediary. George Horvath, a Massachusetts industrialist, was able to bail out his failing textile enterprises for a while with $16,791,850 of fund loans in the mid-1960s. He paid back only about $250,000 of these borrowings. How he got the money became clear in 1972, when Allen Dorfman was convicted of taking a $55,000 bribe for recommending the approval of a single $1.5 million segment of that huge series of loans. Dorfman served less than a year in prison, the sentence awarded by U.S. District Judge Murray I. Gurfein.

In 1973, a Milwaukee businessman, Leo Roethe, heard that to arrange a $5 million loan from the fund he should hire a local lawyer, Joseph Balistrieri, whose father, Frank, has been identified by the Justice Department as head of the Milwaukee Mafia and has served prison time for income tax evasion. According to an associate, Roethe paid the younger Balistrieri a $50,000 legal fee (neither Roethe nor Balistrieri would comment). The loan was arranged, but was ultimately scrapped when prior creditors attached unacceptable conditions. According to the Justice Department, the Central States fund deposited $500,000 in a Milwaukee bank to persuade the bank to lend $125,000 to the Balistrieris; the Milwaukee Teamster official who placed the deposit argues that the granting of the loan at about the same time was a coincidence.

Another problem of the Central States pension fund is its concentration of investments in several speculative areas. Most spectacular is the Penasquitos land development project in southern California. By 1972, the fund had poured $116.7 million into Penasquitos and committed another $25.6 million for the future. One of the auditors who examined the fund's records informally at my request commented on studying the Penasquitos loan: "Never before have I seen a single loan of this magnitude. If that goes bad, you own San Diego. Hell, you own half of California." Not quite—but the loan did go bad and since 1973 the fund has owned sixteen thousand acres, most of it undeveloped. If the project ever earns enough money to repay the loan, the fund, under an agreement made in 1973, will owe a 20 percent equity interest to the project's former co-owner, Morris Shenker, a St. Louis lawyer who has spent much of his long career representing James R. Hoffa. Shenker says he introduced the fund to Penasquitos in 1965, possibly through Hoffa. He says his 1973 agreement not only absolved him of all debts to the fund, but also "settled" millions of dollars in loans Penasquitos had made with fund money to other Shenker business interests. (Among these interests was Murietta Hot Springs, a purported health spa that was exposed on CBS's Sixty Minutes show as a rip-off of the elderly.) Asked if these other business interests repaid the money to Penasquitos or to the pension fund, Shenker says the situation is "too complicated" to explain.

Penasquitos's management declined to discuss its financial status.

Another big concentration of fund loans and commitments—well over $200 million—is in Nevada, primarily in gambling palaces. There is also a disputed promise of a $40 million advance to Shenker to take over the Dunes Hotel. Under Labor Department pressure, the fund backed away from the promise but Shenker (not without irony) is suing the fund to make good on the loan anyway. Meanwhile he is operating the Dunes on other financing. Besides the Dunes, the Teamsters have backed such well-known Nevada spots as Circus Circus, the Desert Palace, the Fremont, the Lodestar, the Plaza Towers, and the Stardust in Las Vegas; the King's Castle, the Lake Tahoe, and the Sierra Tahoe in Lake Tahoe; the Riverside in Riverside, and the Echo Bay in Overton. As with Teamster loans in other places, the Nevada deals occasionally involve convicted criminals as either brokers, developers, employees, or tenants.

The Central States fund is run by a board of trustees, eight representing union leadership, and eight representing employers. Clearly the union has predominated in being able to obtain management representatives it could work comfortably with. Critics have complained that the trustees have thin experience as investment managers, though some have practiced up on the side. From about 1967 to at least 1972, three trustees—two management and one union—were partners of Allen Dorfman and Alvin Baron (the Chicago lawyer who worked for the fund) in a private investment company.

During the 1976–1977 Labor Department investigation, several cosmetics were applied to improve the fund's appearance, but already by 1978 the warts were showing through again. Equitable Life Assurance Society of the United States was hired to manage the assets, but it was later revealed that important strings were tying Equitable's hands to prevent substantial changes, and the fund had withdrawn a promise not to fire Equitable without permission from the Secretary of Labor. The newly-hired firm of Arthur Young & Company, one of the so-called Big Eight accounting concerns, was just as quickly fired and replaced by a one-man auditing operation. The auditor was Harold Silverberg, and the operation had handled the fund's accounts for many years before the brief tenure of Arthur Young. It had formerly been a two-man auditing operation, but Silverberg's associate, David Wenger, had gone to prison after at least two convictions for misusing the fund's money (in one case he was described in testimony as Jimmy Hoffa's personal bagman for a kickback from a fund loan).

And the professional actuary who had overseen the fund since its inception, A. Maxwell Kunis of New York, was rehired after being replaced in 1976–1977 by two much larger companies. Some twenty-five years ago, Kunis was actuary for Union Casualty Company, the small insurance firm to which Paul and Allen Dorfman steered the heavy business of Chicago unions and later of Hoffa's Teamsters. According to testimony at the

McClellan hearings, Kunis once threatened an insurance executive with the loss of all Teamster business unless huge commissions were funneled to Dorfman, even after Dorfman's license had been yanked by New York State (Kunis, interviewed for this book, denies he issued the threat). Commented Robert Kennedy at the McClellan hearings, Kunis "serves the insurance companies, he serves the broker, and he also serves the Teamsters Union, which purchases the insurance." In 1978, he was awarded a new contract, to serve in place of two large actuarial firms that had been hired in *his* place during the Labor Department investigation.

3

Let Me Call You Sweetheart

Robert Kortenhaus, forty, is vice-president of two large regional trucking firms in the northeast. From his office in Elizabeth, New Jersey, he can look out the window at the crowded docks of Elizabethport and, across the Goethals Bridge, to Staten Island. He sees a modern container port, especially designed so that cargo can make a complete journey in a single sealed container that can be loaded onto a ship or hooked onto a truck tractor without costly packing and unpacking. The whole scene is a beehive of trucking activity. You'd expect it to warm a trucking company executive's heart. But Kortenhaus is angry as he points out the window. "That's the largest container port in the world," he growls. "Every day I look out and see those trucks carrying that freight down the [New Jersey] Turnpike."

He is angry because they aren't his trucks. Most of them are being driven by men who work for less pay and lower benefits than Kortenhaus's companies are required to provide. Kortenhaus's companies—Bilkay's Express and Jersey Coast Freight Lines—are bound to the Teamsters' National Master Freight Agreement, which purports to cover all Teamster trucking locals in the New York-New Jersey area, among others. But many companies pay less, often much less, than the agreement calls for. Since labor accounts for about 75 percent of the costs of a trucking business, the firms with lower wages can substantially reduce the rates they charge. And thus they can lure customers away from companies like Kortenhaus's that adhere to the master agreement. While some low-rate trucking companies operate without any union contracts at all, many have their own private contracts with individual Teamster locals. Bob Kortenhaus and other offended trucking company executives don't hesitate to call these substandard agreements by their most unflattering name: Sweetheart contracts.

The term "sweetheart" was often associated with Teamster contracts in the Hoffa era. Robert Kennedy's investigations revealed many direct payoffs to Hoffa and his associates in and out of the union for the procurement of private deals. But under the reign of Frank Fitzsimmons, sweetheart contracts have enjoyed an open acceptance wherever local leaders want to sell them. The uncontrolled proliferation of these agreements, highly profitable to corrupt local leaders, could be one very important reason that the Syndicate was so intent on preventing Hoffa's return to leadership.

Sweetheart contracts naturally are more prevelant in so-called "commercial" trucking zones where Interstate Commerce Commission rules permit open rate competition among trucking firms. Outside these zones, competitive trucking firms must charge minimum rates set by the ICC, so there's less reason for them to try to save money by cheating their workers. The "commercial," or open-competition, zones are usually within large metropolitan areas; for example, Elizabeth, where Kortenhaus's companies compete, is in the New York City commercial trucking zone.

There is an important exception, however, to the rule about non-competitive minimum rates existing outside commercial trucking zones. The exception is the so-called "private carrier"—a company that is mainly engaged in a manufacturing or retailing business, but which owns or leases its own trucks to transport its own products. One reason that many firms decide to carry their own goods rather than rely on common-carrier trucking companies is that private carriers aren't subject to ICC minimum rates. If they can cut costs, the shippers can save money. So sweetheart contracts are also common among private carriers, including some of the biggest companies in the country.

Trucking executives estimate that 80 percent or so of the trucking workers in the New York-New Jersey area are receiving pay and benefits below the National Master Freight standard. Even some Teamster leaders concede figures almost that high. A professional arbitrator who has been a respected figure in the New York trucking industry for many years says, "You can get any kind of contract you want. You make some kind of a deal with whoever's trying to organize. You'll find the same thing all over the country—St. Louis, Detroit. Chicago's a little better. Nobody's doing anything about it. They go to the international and the international sets up a committee to investigate and they give the committee to the same people that's doing it."

Fitzsimmons has received loud and persistent complaints from Robert Kortenhaus and other trucking executives, but the complainers get scant satisfaction. A joint union-management committee was set up to hear complaints in 1975, but soon afterward the appointed co-chairman from the union side quit, and the committee became mostly inactive. The co-chairman from the union was Salvatore Provenzano.

The National Master Freight Agreement, as amended for the New York-New Jersey area, seems to provide a good deal for those truckers who get the benefits of it. It requires $9.38 an hour in pay (with slight variations depending on the locality and kind of truck) and $62 a week in pension and health benefits, as well as enforcing strict limitations on hours and conditions of work. It often results in substantial overtime pay. But most of the trucks that Robert Kortenhaus sees shuttling past his office between the Elizabeth containerport and the New Jersey Turnpike are driven by men who aren't paid wages at all. They are owner-operators, or, as their detractors describe them, gypsies. Because they own (though usually on the installment plan) or lease their own trucks or tractors, they get paid a fixed amount for a given trip. Although employers sometimes deny it, truck drivers—both salaried and gypsy—say that when the costs of buying and maintaining a rig are discounted, the owner-operators are often left with much less money than they would make with a full hourly wage. Sometimes they don't receive pension and health benefits, paid vacations, and other fringes. Container freight is a particularly easy target for low-budget trucking firms that employ gypsy drivers, because it doesn't require extensive terminals and warehouses.

One trucking firm Robert Kortenhaus was angry about was Malden Transportation of Bayonne, New Jersey. Malden hauls container freight for U. S. Lines, a major ocean shipper. U. S. Lines hires Bob Kortenhaus's firms only rarely, for trips into other zones, where Malden is forbidden by ICC regulations to travel. Malden has a contract with Teamster Local 617, which is a party to the National Master Freight Agreement. The agreement specifically prohibits employers from filling more than 5 percent of their fleets with owner-operators, and says owner-operators can't be used at all until work has been given to all salaried drivers available. But Kortenhaus says that all of Malden's drivers are owner-operators, and U. S. Lines says it knows that at least most of them are. (Asked if that's true, Louis Taylor, president of Malden, says, "I don't see that that's any of your business," and hangs up.) Malden's rates are substantially less than those of Kortenhaus's firms, and Kortenhaus insists there is no way Malden could charge so little if it paid full union benefits. Says W. J. Kelly, senior vice-president of U. S. Lines, "What he pays his drivers is no concern of ours." It was, however, the concern of the union-management committee set up under Salvatore Provenzano to investigate substandard contracts. At a meeting of the committee, management representatives accused Local 617—a local in the Provenzano axis—of having substandard contracts with at least two other trucking companies besides Malden. The committee did nothing. Frank Pinto, president of Local 617, wouldn't return a reporter's telephone messages.

Another competitor Kortenhaus said he regards as particularly painful is

Becker's Motor Transport of Woodbridge, New Jersey. Becker's has hauled freight for such accounts as Coca-Cola, Owens-Illinois Glass, and Budweiser Beer. A copy of the contract between Becker's and Teamster Local 863 (dated January, 1971, amended July, 1973, to expire in 1976), as opposed to a master freight contract then effective, showed driver wages as low as $4.11 an hour instead of about $7 an hour, pension and health benefits of $28 a week instead of $56, and two weeks' vacation after two years instead of three weeks after one year. When I questioned Barry Becker, vice-president of Becker's he insisted that Becker's had cancelled the special agreement and was now operating under master freight terms, although he said he couldn't remember when the change was made and he wouldn't answer any other questions. Then I called Donald Clarick, receiver for Becker's during a recent credit reorganization in federal bankruptcy court (Becker was in bankruptcy proceedings because of problems over its acquisition of another business; it was operating profitably). Clarick contradicted Barry Becker and said the substandard contract remained in effect. He said he didn't see any reason for Becker to ask the union for permission to let it pay higher wages.

The top officer of Local 863, who signed the Becker contract, was Joseph "Joe Peck" Pecora, who never returned my telephone messages. Pecora and his brother, Thomas "Timmy Murphy" Pecora, both have been identified before Congressional investigating committees as members of the Genovese Mafia family, as is Tony Provenzano. Joseph Pecora has been convicted of attempted assault and battery with intent to kill, violation of the Taft-Hartley Act and conspiracy to arrange a labor payoff; all three times he was let off with fines. Both Pecoras also played a part along with a prominent butchers' union leader, in arm-twisting supermarket executives to stock a Mafia-backed line of household soap products. This sales campaign ended after wide publicity over the firebombing of A & P stores and the murder of at least two A & P store managers when the supermarket chain refused to stock the Mafia soap.

Ironically, one company that did buy the soap, as described in Senate testimony, was Vornado Inc., which runs the Two Guys department store chain. In more recent years, Vornado has held a trucking contract with Teamster Local 867 that provides, among other substandard items, driver salaries almost $2 an hour below those of the National Master Freight Agreement. Fred Zissu, chairman of Vornado, acknowledged the contract, but said the drivers did "damn well" with Vornado and that the company would "be out of business" within a year if it had to pay standard industry rates.

Retail or manufacturing companies that hire their own truckers argue that they shouldn't be part of the National Master Freight Agreement because they don't compete with other trucking companies. They, and the Teamster leaders they sign with, will tell you with a straight face that the master freight agreement is intended to cover only long-distance common-carrier hauling, not local pick-up-and-delivery or transportation by a private firm of its own goods. But the agreement itself very clearly spells out that it covers "employees of private, common, contract and local cartage carriers . . . in the jurisdiction of Teamsters Joint Council . . ." (the joint council covers all locals in a given area). And common-carrier trucking concerns like those of Kortenhaus would very much like to get some of the business now being transported by private truckers.

Arguing that he can't fight the low-wage competition, Bob Kortenhaus occasionally threatens to shut down his companies, throwing his 400 Teamster employees out of work. Some in the industry think he's exaggerating, but if he does close down he won't be the first. A nearby firm, M & G Transportation of Perth Amboy, for example, really did go out of business a few years ago. Lee Gutwein, its president, says the death blow came when the U. S. Government itself decided to save money by switching to a trucking firm with a substandard contract after eighteen years as M & G's biggest customer. The General Services Administration, which had relied on M & G for its New Jersey hauling, suddenly switched to Seigle's Express of North Arlington, New Jersey, when Seigle's submitted a lower bid. Says Gutwein, "There's no way this man [Seigle's] could really operate with the kind of rate he put in if he's paying the same kind of Teamster wages we were paying." Richard Riley, president of Seigle's, acknowledges that he employs more owner-operators than the 5 percent allowed under the National Master Freight Agreement. But he says Seigle's separate contract with Teamster Local 418 in Garfield, New Jersey, doesn't contain that restriction. And Al Pascarella Senior, president of Local 418, says the Seigle's contract is one of "many, many—I couldn't begin to tell you how many" Teamster contracts that aren't part of the national agreement. He says his men earn a good wage—though he won't say what it is.

Salvatore Provenzano says there have to be substandard contracts because certain commodities are traditionally hauled at lower rates than others. "If you're saying that every truckman who handles a goddamned truck in New York or New Jersey has to be paying the same rate, you're a fool," he says. Told that the national contract doesn't differentiate one kind of freight from another, he says that's the very reason he quit as the union co-chairman of the committee to investigate substandard contracts. "There's nothing in the contract saying what freight is," he says. "It's just what you think is morally right." Evidently Sammy Pro had a moral disagreement with a trucking executive who complained that a competitor was hauling scrap copper under a substandard contract. Provenzano says he quit the committee over that complaint, because "it was the first time I ever heard of" putting scrap copper under the National Master Freight Agreement.

Law enforcement agencies are well aware of the substandard contracts. Their problem has always been to prove that a *quid pro quo,* or kickback, is involved. Trucking company owners like Bob Kortenhaus, who pay full freight, allege that the kickbacks do exist, often in the form of union officers' relatives holding no-show jobs on trucking company payrolls, or even in the form of union people being secret owners of some trucking companies with substandard contracts. "The problem is, how do you prove it?" says the head of one large trucking company. For Kortenhaus, simple logic is proof enough that bribery of union officers is responsible for substandard contracts. "Why else would they give you one?" he asks. Teamster officials like Sammy Provenzano say there are other reasons—such as helping marginal trucking firms stay in business—but Kortenhaus isn't impressed with the argument.

In 1977, the U. S. Government began an intensive coast-to-coast investigation of what may be the biggest organized sweetheart contract racket in history. The names of the employers involved read like a who's who of business: International Paper Company, J. C. Penney Company, GAF Corp., Iowa Beef Processors Inc., Crown Zellerbach Corp., Monsanto Company, Morton-Norwich Products Inc. (Morton's Salt), Avon Products Inc., AMF Inc., Inland Container Corp., Wheeling-Pittsburgh Steel Corp., Crown Cork & Seal Company, Westvaco Corp., and Continental Group Inc. (formerly Continental Can Company)—how many there are in all can't be determined. But every one of these companies, and more, have arranged contracts through Eugene R. Boffa, a convicted bank swindler from New Jersey who is an associate and, directly or indirectly, a benefactor of powerful racketeers in the union. Because contract terms needn't be disclosed publicly, it's impossible to say for sure whether all of Boffa's contracts are substandard, or whether some companies that have used him in the past have since dropped him. At this writing, the government has spent considerable time and money pursuing evidence, and has beaten back Boffa's attempts to win a court injunction halting the investigation (he says it's hurting business). But the government evidently hasn't found the evidence it thinks it would need to indict him or his companies for a crime.

I first encountered the Boffa operation late in 1976, while studying Iowa Beef Processors and its involvement in meat racketeering. Poring over Iowa Beef documents, I noticed reference after reference to checks for tens of thousands of dollars sent to Country Wide Personnel Inc. of Jersey City, New Jersey. What was Country Wide Personnel? I asked sources in Iowa Beef and in the butchers' union. They would only smile, and say, "You ought to look into that." I found Country Wide's phone number through directory assistance and called several times. The executives were always out. I gave up.

Then, in the summer of 1977, someone from PROD, the dissident Teamster organization in Washington, called and asked if I had ever heard of Country Wide Personnel.

"Yeah," I said. "Who are they?"

"You ought to look into them," I was told.

This time I found Country Wide's principal, Eugene Boffa, and went to see him.

Boffa and a partner run two labor leasing companies—Universal Coordinators Inc. and Country Wide Personnel Inc.—which have demonstrated an amazing ability to hire truck drivers and handle Teamster officials while offering wages, benefits and working conditions far short of master freight standards. For a fee of 8 to 10 percent over costs—which can easily mean hundreds of thousands of dollars a year from a single client—Boffa will insert himself as a buffer between a company and the Teamsters. The same drivers (more or less) will report to the same depots and take orders from the same supervisors as they did before Boffa was hired. But Boffa will send out the paychecks (with money he gets from the company that hired him). And the paychecks will tend to be smaller than before. Workers whom the company regards as troublesome can be dumped regardless of legal justification. And a company that hires Boffa can expect to be free of grievances, picket lines, and bothersome Teamster business agents. Boffa asserts that he can create savings for his clients, because he's an expert in union negotiations. But many of the thousands of truck drivers and warehousemen who have worked under Boffa contracts say they suspect otherwise.

In my interview in his office in Elmwood Park, New Jersey, Boffa said he went to work for Universal Coordinators in the early 1960s after becoming bored with his accounting practice. The labor leasing firm had been founded several years earlier by his partner, Louis Kalmar, a former truck dispatcher for International Paper, he said. Later, he said, in 1971, they founded Country Wide Personnel in an effort to forge a nationwide chain of franchised labor leasing companies.

The records tell a different story, however. Papers in the New Jersey Secretary of State's office show that Kalmar and his wife and Boffa started Universal jointly in December, 1960—right after (according to federal court documents) Boffa had been indicted for swindling the Manufacturers Bank of Edgewater, New Jersey, which had just folded while he was president of it. Boffa was convicted in federal court, Newark, after a long trial in 1961. But he was given a suspended sentence on the ground that his co-conspirators— two Pittsburgh men for whom he had approved large loans based on fraudulent documents—had run off with most of the loot to Brazil. At the sentencing hearing, the judge complained that Boffa and his friends had tried "to bring influence to bear on me in connection with this sentence" by submitting "photographs taken of you and certain very prominent persons, some of whom are or were quite close to me. I resent anybody trying to influence me," the judge said. Then he let Boffa off anyway.

Boffa acknowledged in our interview that he had cordial relationships with Tony Provenzano, Mafia godfather Russell Bufalino, and his cousin William Bufalino who is a Detroit Teamster official. But Boffa resents being asked about them. When Russell Bufalino's name came up, he exploded, "Because I'm of Italian extraction every fuck who comes through the door thinks I know this bastard. I worked like a goddamn horse here for seventeen years and everybody says it's 'cause I'm associated with him." He said his relationships with the Bufalinos come strictly as a necessary part of his job negotiating Teamster contracts, and that the same holds for Tony Pro: "Show me a way to deal with truck drivers in New Jersey without dealing with him," Boffa said. He acknowledged that he owned another company that leases cars to Teamster leaders, and that he often lends a Cadillac or Lincoln and a driver free to Teamster officials from out of town who visit the New York area. "I'm not adverse to doing people favors," he said. But he expressed anger over suggestions that his success comes from anything other than being a good labor negotiator. "Just because we have a leasing business and all these bastards lease cars from me—nobody opens any doors for me," he said. He flatly denied that he had ever had any personal business dealings with, or had given money from his labor leasing companies to, any Teamster or Mob people.

Again, the record proved a little different. In the Bergen County, New Jersey, registrar's office, I found records of a $30,000 loan from Boffa's wife, Marie, to Mildred Briguglio, the wife of Salvatore "Sally Bugs" Briguglio, the Mafioso and Teamster official who was murdered in March, 1978. The loan was dated May 27, 1974, just days after Briguglio had left prison on a counterfeiting conviction. Moreover, there were records that this loan followed some neat legal maneuvering by which Briguglio's property was conveyed from his name to his wife's, and that the lawyer who handled this maneuvering was Boffa's son, Eugene Jr., a partner of criminal defense lawyer Peter Willis in the New Jersey firm of Boffa & Willis. In return for the $30,000, the documents showed, Mrs. Briguglio gave Mrs. Boffa a mortgage on the Briguglios' house. The mortgage was marked cancelled a year later when Mrs. Briguglio sold the house. This was the sale, noted earlier, to Mrs. Thomas Andretta. Briguglio and his brother Gabriel, and Andretta and his brother Stephen, all have held various posts in the Provenzano Teamster organization, and are regarded by the Government as prime suspects in the Hoffa case. In the spring of 1978, about the time Sally Bugs and several of his friends in the Genovese family were wiped out, Boffa discretely took off for an extended trip abroad.

Something else Boffa contended during our interview is also at odds with the record. He said he always paid his truckers and warehousemen "top dollar."

On request, Boffa provided a copy of a contract that his Country Wide firm signed with Iowa Beef Processors. The contract he provided was dated April 11, 1972. Drivers earned 10 cents a mile when loaded with cargo and 8 cents on the empty return run, an average of 9 cents. The comparable National Master Freight wage for Iowa Beef's area was 14.425 cents a mile on all runs, loaded or empty, on April 11, 1972, with an increase July 1 to 15.175 cents a mile—about 70 percent more than the Teamsters let Boffa get away with! In addition, Country Wide workers at Iowa Beef had one less holiday and lower health and welfare fund contributions, and there is no indication on the Country Wide contract of any pension fund contribution; master freight employers paid $13 to $14 a week toward each employee's pension at that time.

Boffa also said he didn't service Iowa Beef anymore, but some would disagree with that, too. In 1973, the contract was picked up by a firm called Country Wide Personnel Inc., the same as Boffa's, but with an office in St. Louis. It is one of at least five firms with the same name located around the country. Boffa acknowledges that he helped these other Country Wides get started and that he now supplies them with payroll services and helps them negotiate with Teamsters. But he says he does this on a contract basis, and that they are really separate companies. Whether the companies are really separate can make a powerful difference, as illustrated by a 1977 case in federal court, Delaware, in which six workers at Crown Zellerbach, one of the nation's leading paper products companies, won back their jobs with full seniority and $14,000 cash damages in an out-of-court settlement. They had charged that quick switches by Crown among three labor leasing companies had flim-flammed the Crown workforce, as described below. Defendants in the suit included not only Crown, Country Wide and Universal Coordinators, but also Teamster Local 326 of Wilmington, Delaware, which the workers said had sold them out.

Local 326 is run by Frank Sheeran, who came to Wilmington from Phila-delphia to start the local in 1967. At the time, he was a fugitive from a Pennsylvania charge of murdering a shop steward who opposed the Teamster leadership in Philadelphia. Sheeran later surrendered and the charge was dropped. He has a long history of being arrested on charges that are later dropped. He was convicted once, in 1947, of carrying a concealed weapon, and drew a year's probation. At this writing he is under investigation by at least three federal grand juries: one in Philadelphia investigating Boffa's sweetheart contracts, one in Syracuse, New York, investigating fraud in Teamster pension funds, and one in Detroit investigating the disappearance of Jimmy Hoffa. Sheeran is considered a prime suspect. He was in Detroit about the time Hoffa vanished; he drove there, apparently in a car leased from Boffa, with Mafia boss Russell Bufalino (there are reports that Sheeran also flew in and out of Detroit just before the automobile trip).

According to depositions and other records in the Crown Zellerbach law-suit, Sheeran once drove a truck on Universal Coordinators' payroll at Inland Container; now, he drives a Lincoln Continental leased from Universal's boss, Gene Boffa. Sheeran says he pays for the car—"top dollar," Boffa says—but by money order, so there aren't any cancelled checks. Meanwhile, the IRS. is arguing in tax court that Sheeran illegally deducted the cost of his car—$2,532 over two years—as a business expense; the IRS says he used it for personal travel.

Crown Zellerbach says it employed Universal in 1966 at the opening of the Delaware plant, which was just before Sheeran came to town to organize the union. Wages were low, but the workers couldn't complain to Crown Zeller-bach. They did, however, finally complain to Boffa, and in December, 1973, at an angry meeting with Boffa present, they threatened to strike if he wouldn't bring them under the National Master Freight Agreement. They say (in their depositions and affidavits) that Sheeran tried to talk them out of it, but they were adamant. So they got the new contract with Universal.

But then, just a month later, the employees were stunned to hear that Universal had broken its contract with Crown, and that a new leasing company was coming in—Country Wide Personnel. Boffa says it wasn't the same Country Wide Personnel he runs in New Jersey, but rather a different Country Wide Personnel based in Turlock, California. This other Country Wide was run by Robert Dewan, a former transportation executive at International Paper who had quit to go to work for Universal Coordinators. Universal had sent Dewan to Turlock to handle some West Coast accounts, including International Paper, Monsanto, GAF, and AMF's Voit subsidiary (according to Boffa's deposition). But then, Boffa testified, Dewan "wasn't too happy with what he was doing, so he went into business for himself. And that's when he formed Country Wide of California," which had the Crown Zellerbach account in Delaware. Other evidence showed that Dewan, Universal, and the new Country Wide all continued to share the same address and post office box in Turlock.

Sheeran immediately signed a new contract with Dewan on behalf of Crown's workers. Sheeran acknowledged in his own court filing that he made "no bargaining demands." Down went the wages again. Moreover, since the workers were now under contract to a purportedly new employer, their seniority went out the window, too. Recalled one worker, Roland Blansfield, in an affidavit, "There was nothing different. Same truck, same supervisor. One month after [Country Wide came in], I received my fifty thousand-mile safe driving award and a one-year safe driving pin [all from Crown Zellerbach]. Only thing different was eight years' worth of seniority benefits were wiped out, such as vacation and earning opportunity. And my pay was cut."

Other workers told the same story. And the noisiest dissidents got sacked altogether—or, more precisely, not hired by the new contractor, Country Wide. So some workers filed a complaint with the National Labor Relations Board against Country Wide. They seemed to be making headway, when all of a sudden, in mid-1975, Country Wide disappeared—at least *that* Country Wide. Crown's trucking was now being handled by the *other* Country Wide, in New Jersey, which quickly hired Robert Dewan as a full-time executive.

Asked during deposition why the name Country Wide had proven so popular among labor leasing companies, Boffa replied, "I can't give you the reason why it's so popular. I wouldn't say there is an association."

So six Crown workers who wanted their jobs or seniority back pooled $3,500 and hired a Wilmington lawyer, Jacob Kreshtool. He tried to prove that Crown, Boffa, and Sheeran had been playing tricks, and that the workers were entitled to reinstatement of their short-lived master freight contract with Universal. But Kreshtool says he ran out of money in 1977. In a compromise settlement, charges against Crown were dropped, Country Wide agreed to rehire the six men with back seniority and pay them $14,000, and the union agreed to abide by the deal (though Kreshtool later accused Boffa of trying to renege. Apparently the plant is still operating under substandard contract terms. It hasn't been disclosed how many other Crown installations around the country employ Universal or one of the Country Wides—though it's known that a number of them do—or what the terms of those contracts are.

But Crown seems pleased. A recent trucking trade publication featured an in-depth interview with a Crown executive who raved about the advantages of driver leasing companies, though not naming Boffa or his companies. "They're experts in Teamster negotiations," he said, and added that paying master freight wages could upset a company's entire labor policy. "Say you're paying plant employees three dollars an hour and truck drivers get seven dollars. You've got a problem," he noted. Obviously Crown thinks it has solved the problem.

Meanwhile, thirteen present or former Crown trucking employees in the San Francisco area have filed a similar suit in federal court there, claiming they were "defrauded and deceived" by Crown's dealings with Universal Coordinators.

Another case that produced enough of a public record to expose some of Universal's dealings involved a Wheeling-Pittsburgh Steel warehouse in South Brunswick, New Jersey. Back in 1970, the nineteen workers at the warehouse managed to throw out a sweetheart contract thanks to the support of two Teamster locals independent enough to fight the power structure of their own international union. One of the independent locals, Local 169 of Philadelphia, had a standard contract with a Wheeling-Pittsburgh warehouse in Philadelphia. Then, in 1969, that warehouse suddenly closed and a new one opened in South Brunswick doing essentially the same work. As if by pre-arrangement, Universal showed up at South Brunswick to handle labor contracting and Teamster Local 84 showed up to sign a contract. Local 84 was run by the late Teddy Nalikowski, a close ally of Tony Provenzano. Before the bulk of the workforce was even hired, Local 84 signed a deal with Boffa containing the exact terms laid down earlier in a contract between Wheeling-Pittsburgh and Universal.

Soon, however, workers at the warehouse encountered members of nearby Teamster Local 701, a non-sweetheart local. They all realized that Wheeling-Pittsburgh was paying much less than the standard Teamster contract called for. Moreover, according to affidavits filed later with the National Labor Relations Board, the Wheeling-Pittsburgh workers were completely unaware that they were working under a contract signed by Local 84, which had never consulted them. So they petitioned for membership in Local 701, and a 701 business agent went to Wheeling-Pittsburgh to arrange a representation election.

The next thing the workers remember, according to their statements, someone from Local 84 and someone from Universal arrived together at the warehouse and announced that all employees would either sign Local 84 membership cards or be fired immediately. Protesting, the workers signed. But Local 701 filed a complaint with the NLRB. Salvatore Provenzano, Teamster executive for the region while his brother was barred from holding union office, immediately declared that Local 84 had prior jurisdiction. He ordered Local 701 to drop its NLRB complaint. International president Fitzsimmons backed Provenzano up with an implicit threat to put Local 701 in trusteeship and appoint new officers if the local persisted.

The cavalry arrived, however, in the form of Local 169 of Philadelphia, which had lost the Wheeling-Pittsburgh jobs when the company moved its warehouse to New Jersey. The Philadelphians had finally caught on that Wheeling-Pittsburgh was now paying $2.43 an hour for work still under contract to Local 169 at $3.01 and higher, with additional big savings on pensions and other fringes. So Local 169 filed its own complaint with the NLRB. Apparently sensing that Local 169, with its already signed contract, would open new and more threatening legal ground, the Teamster apparatus backed off and said it would allow Local 701 to organize the plant. Suddenly faced with a local that wouldn't sign a sweetheart contract, Wheeling-Pittsburgh decided that Universal's services weren't needed anymore. The company signed directly with Local 701 for higher wages and fringes. Asked for comment, Wheeling-Pittsburgh says that nobody involved in the decisions to hire and then fire Universal is still with the company, so it doesn't know why Universal's contract was ended. But the workers think *they* do.

The question arises: What is the obligation of large American corporations when they are offered the opportunity to sell out their own employees by making a deal with a convicted felon like Eugene Boffa who is financing the activities of hired killers like Sally Bugs Briguglio? Many of our largest, most respected corporations—and the list at the beginning of this chapter is quite certainly far from complete—obviously have decided that their obligation is to cut costs and increase profits. They know very well who they are really dealing with in these labor contracts, or if they don't, it's because they don't want to know.

When the corporations mentioned here were called for comment, not one of them spoke up in outrage or condemned the Mob's grip on the trucking industry. Some said they had stopped doing business with the Boffa company they were under contract to, but only because of unsatisfactory service. Most of those acknowledged they had merely signed up with other labor leasing companies that operated the same way and that may, for all they seemed to know, have been operated by the same people. Some Boffa clients openly acknowledged they were paying far below master freight standards on their labor lease deals; others said they weren't sure, but not one accepted an invitation to provide figures to prove that master freight terms were being met. They obviously preferred not to talk about it. Said a transportation manager for Morton-Norwich, "I'm not aware of any such involvement. I'm not saying it does exist, and I'm not saying it doesn't."

4

The Enforcers

When Jimmy Hoffa disappeared, there were widespread reports of a possible relationship between his disappearance and the Teamsters' lucrative pension fund rackets. So the Labor Department began what was supposed to be a massive investigation of the Central States, Southeast, and Southwest Areas pension fund in Chicago. Eventually, Labor investigators delved into some other funds. While auditors were on the scene, and books and records were seized, the outflow of money to the Mob clearly slowed. The Central States fund slapped on some cosmetics to try to improve its public image and make the government people go away. A new executive director was hired from outside the union, and he promised to start answering public inquiries. Maxwell Kunis was replaced as actuary after a quarter of a century. Allen Dorfman's contracts were allowed to run down. A large reputable insurance company was hired to advise on investments.

It was all a sham. By 1978, the Labor Department inquiries had bogged down with little apparent result. The fund's new executive director had gotten the boot. The big insurance company was handcuffed and threatened with dismissal. The policy of answering public inquiries—never a meaningful practice—became no longer even a policy. Max Kunis was back. And so was Allen Dorfman (who had never really left).

Justice Department officials were furious. In public statements they blamed the Labor Department for footdragging, and said indictments were being impeded. Privately, officials railed against the Labor Department, and claimed that its investigations were subject to political influence. The Justice Department announced a redesigned investigation that would short-circuit the Labor Department roadblock, and promised indictments and convictions, not only regarding the Central States fund, but also other funds, particularly in the east. The emergence of Anthony Provenzano and his underlings as prime suspects in the Hoffa case had led investigators to the pension funds in New Jersey and New York, where massive fraud had been going on quietly in the shadow of the well-publicized Central States fund racket in Chicago.

Whether this new optimism at the Justice Department pans out remains to be seen. There is, however, substantial reason to question it in light of past performance. Veteran professional enforcement agents at the Labor Department have long had similar complaints about inactivity at Justice, and have alleged the same kind of political motivation.

During my interviews with Teamster rank and filers in the midwest and east in 1975 and 1976, they often volunteered bitter complaints about the lack of prosecution of Teamster officials who were caught in what seemed to be criminal acts. They left no doubt that corruption was a source of deep concern to them. Most of the recent cases they cited had been uncovered by Labor Department and insurance regulators. Under the law, these regulators could only file civil actions and turn the matters over to the Justice Department with a recommendation for prosecution. In case after case, no prosecution was forthcoming. These are some of the cases the Teamsters themselves complained of:

Richard Fitzsimmons, son of president Frank Fitzsimmons, and vice-president and business agent of Local 299 in Detroit—Hoffa's and Frank Fitzsimmons's old local. In the early 1970s, a Labor Department audit turned up what the department considered evidence that young Fitzsimmons embezzled money by submitting false expense vouchers. The Justice Department got a report, but didn't prosecute.*

Norman Mintz, longtime business agent for Local 332 in Flint, Michigan. The Teamsters have long had close ties to the Hotel, Motel, Restaurant Employees' and Bartenders' Union (Jackie Presser is an officer of both), so when hotel-restaurant Local 794 of Pontiac, Michigan, was put into trusteeship by its international leaders, Mintz and another Teamster official were called in to run it. In 1974, an audit showed what the Labor Department considered was evidence that Mintz had been embezzling money from Local 794. The Justice Department got a report, but didn't prosecute. "We alleged embezzlement, but that doesn't mean the Department of Justice is going to buy it," says Louis Woiwode, area director

---

*After the Hoffa case stirred up Justice, Richard Fitzsimmons was prosecuted for his involvement with an ex-convict Syndicate financier named Louis Ostrer in selling a grossly overpriced insurance plan to various Teamster groups. In 1978 a federal jury acquitted Fitzsimmons of criminal behavior in the matter.

of the Labor-Management Services Administration in Detroit. Mintz later left Local 794 of the hotel-restaurant workers and returned to Local 332 of the Teamsters. He declined to comment on the embezzlement allegation.

George Vitale, president and business agent of Teamster Local 283 in Detroit. He pleaded guilty to accepting a loan from an employer and was convicted also of taking a union Cadillac for his own use. Not only did he avoid prison, but the U. S. Parole Board (in the Department of Justice) voted him a special exemption from the five-year ban on holding union office required by the Landrum-Griffen Act for taking union property; so he stayed in his job.

Roland "Red" McMaster, convicted in 1962 of taking payoffs from employers while serving as business agent for Local 299 in Detroit. He was allowed to return to union office on his release from prison (the Landrum-Griffen ban applies to extortion, a crime that requires proof either of favors granted in exchange for the payment, or use of force; McMaster was convicted only of taking money). In 1970 he became secretary-treasurer of the local, allied with Fitzsimmons. When an aid of McMasters' beat up another officer of the local who had stayed loyal to Hoffa, the local threw McMasters out of office. Fitzsimmons immediately hired him as an organizer for the international. In October, 1975, he was charged in Bay County, Michigan, with felonious assault and carrying a concealed weapon. The charges were dropped.

Billy Hoffa (Jimmy's brother) and Don Fitzsimmons (Frank's son), hired as organizers by Teamster Local 614 in Detroit—Hoffa in 1967 and Fitzsimmons in 1973). Their employment was ordered by the union's international office in Washington, which forwarded money specifically to pay their salaries. The Labor Department reported this to the Justice Department as a misuse of funds. Justice didn't prosecute.

Local 295, Long Island. The New York State Insurance Department filed civil charges in 1974 against convicted stock swindler and thief Louis C. Ostrer and ten officials of the local. They were accused of creating an insurance plan that allegedly cost Local 295 members $1.2 million more than it should have, and which was inadequately funded despite the overpayments. The department said Ostrer solicited and won the local's business even though his license had been revoked for taking $700,000 of another client's money. The department said it found similar Ostrer-linked plans at six other New York locals, and the plans also are known to have been sold to locals in Michigan, Missouri, and perhaps elsewhere. Ostrer has said the plan was backed by Frank Fitzsimmons. By several accounts, including the one in Jimmy Hoffa's autobiography, Fitzsimmons's son Don helped sell the plan and profited from it. The insurance department relayed the case to the Justice Department in 1974, but years later nothing had been done.*

(The Justice Department declined to comment on all these cases.)

---

*In 1978, Fitzsimmons's son Richard was acquitted of charges relating to the sale of a similar insurance plan in Detroit. Ostrer was in prison for other crimes.

There is, perhaps, an even more relevant, and more discouraging precedent for the Justice Department's current inquest into pension fund fraud. In the early 1970s, the department undertook a similar challenge—a major investigation of the Central States, Southeast and Southwest Areas fund. With a myriad of enticing leads to choose from, the team of investigators, based in Chicago, decided for a number of reasons that the most promising case was a series of unrepaid loans made to run a continually insolvent factory in Deming, New Mexico. The story of the Deming loans, which totalled $6 million, reveals not only how the pension fund racket works, but also why the Justice Department hasn't been able to smash it.

The Central States fund got involved in Deming in 1959, when it put up about $3 million to finance a new plant there for Auburn Rubber Company, a toy manufacturer formerly of Auburn, Indiana. By 1963, the fund had pumped an additional $1.5 million into Auburn. Meanwhile, some $350,000 in bonds backed by the fund's loans were issued, apparently as kickbacks, to a mobster with a long arrest record who arranged the deal and to Teamster officials the mobster dealt with. In 1969, Auburn Rubber folded, owing the fund $4.9 million with interest. So the Teamsters foreclosed on the loan and wound up owning the toy factory.

Soon afterward, the original Auburn borrowers started a competing toy factory across the street, using tools and machinery taken from the Auburn Rubber plant—apparently without payment to the fund, which held a mortgage on the equipment as collateral for its loans. For a few months in 1970, a new group moved into the old Auburn plant, operated it, and left—apparently without paying the Teamsters any rent. Thus for eleven years, people had been allowed to make money selling toys on $5 million of Teamster financing without ever having to pay the Teamsters fund—only, under the table, the Teamsters' bosses—for the opportunity. And $5 million, taken from the pockets of American consumers to help pay pensions for truck drivers and cargo handlers, had instead been diverted elsewhere.

But if any of this was illegal, the statute of limitations had expired by the time the Justice Department found out about it. The case that eventually went to trial concerned the takeover of the Deming plant by a third group in 1971 with new pension fund loans that reached $1.4 million (in addition to the money already lost).

When the Justice Department started looking into the Deming situation early in 1973, it found that the Postal Service and the I.R.S. were already investigating. So the three agencies decided to pool their efforts and make one big case that would spearhead a broad attack on the fund administration. The government expected that if convictions could be won, the prosecutors would go after other indictments in connection with other loans, and a change in the fund leadership would result.

A major attraction of the Deming case, in the government's eyes, was that witnesses were available from inside the conspiracy. Two men who ran companies that received some of the loan money had agreed to testify that they were part of a scheme to defraud the pension fund. One was Harold Lurie, a thrice-convicted long-time business front for Chicago Mafiosi. In 1971, Lurie, in an effort to avoid further prosecution for income tax evasion, had consented to let an IRS agent pose as his bookkeeper, observing transactions among the mobsters. The Deming case was only one of several that Lurie helped deliver. The second prospective insider witness, Daniel Seifert, ran a company that helped channel Teamster loan money to Joseph "The Clown" Lombardo, identified by the Illinois Crime Investigating Commission as a Mafia loanshark collector. Over the years Lombardo had been charged with, and acquitted of, burglary, loitering, and kidnapping.

Even more than the presence of two insider witnesses, the Deming case appealed to the government because of the prominent cast of alleged wrong-doers it involved. Besides Lombardo, they included:

Allen Dorfman, the kingpin of the pension fund.

Felix "Milwaukee Phil" Alderisio, the most active Mafia captain in Chicago. Hidden FBI bugs had caught him boasting of a sadistic murder. Police knew him as the "King of Scam," scam being the street term for planning the bankruptcy of a legitimate business by taking all the money out so it can't pay creditors.

Anthony "Tough Tony" Spilotro, who, Lurie said, had boasted of being Alderisio's heir. He had been arrested—and acquitted—for robbery, burglary, gambling, and murder.

Spilotro's murder acquittal, in 1973, had been particularly galling to authorities because the state had two good eyewitnesses ready to testify. One, Charles Crimaldi, a turncoat mobster, told the jury in great detail how he, Spilotro, and two others killed Leo Foreman, a stolen goods fence who was suspected of cheating on Mob accounts. This was Crimaldi's testimony:

> Mario [DeStefano] and I drew our guns and . . . the two of us fired. . . . Another shot rang out and . . . I seen Tony Spilotro standing there with a gun in his hand. . . . He [Leo] was lying on his side . . . moaning, "Oh, my God. . . . Please don't. . . . Oh, my God." . . . Mario picked up a butcher knife [and] stabbed him a few times. I kicked him. Tony kicked him. Mario gave Tony the knife and Tony stabbed him, and Leo was still moaning, hollering, "Oh, my God." . . . Sam DeStefano [Mario's brother] . . . put a gun up his buttocks and shot him. . . . Mario stabbed him a couple more times and Leo stopped moving.

The other witness the state was bargaining with to corroborate Crimaldi's story was Sam DeStefano. But he never made it to the jury. One morning, shortly before trial, as Sam DeStefano entered the garage of his house, his head was blown off with a shotgun.

Mario DeStefano was convicted in the Leo Foreman case on Crimaldi's testimony. Although DeStefano had served fourteen years in prison on a previous murder conviction, Circuit Court Judge Robert A. Meier III of

Chicago, who had heard Crimaldi's every word, immediately freed DeStefano on bail while he appealed his second murder conviction and a twenty to forty year sentence. He died of a heart attack while the matter was still in the courts. Tony Spilotro, however, presented several witnesses to testify that he was buying furniture the day of the murder. The jury believed them instead of Crimaldi, and Spilotro was acquitted.

In addition to Lombardo, Dorfman, Alderisio, and Spilotro, the Deming case involved Ronald DeAngeles, long suspected of being the Syndicate's electronics whiz. In 1970, federal agents had burst in on him aboard a converted Coast Guard minesweeper cruising near the Chicago Police Department's lakefront radio headquarters. The yacht was laden with radio intercept equipment and the agents theorized that DeAngeles might be a counterspy for the Mafia. Unable to prove that, the agents noticed an oil slick behind the yacht and convinced a federal grand jury to indict DeAngeles for polluting Lake Michigan. After a year of legal maneuvering, the pollution case was thrown out of court. Lawmen had also tried to link several radio-control bombing murders to DeAngeles, but without success.

Finally, the cast of characters included two of the pension fund's sixteen trustees: Albert Matheson, a Detroit labor lawyer, and Jack Sheetz, head of a Dallas-based trucking employers' association. Matheson and Sheetz had traveled to Deming to see the factory, and therefore were indicted as part of the alleged conspiracy. The indictment came down in February, 1974, naming Matheson, Sheetz, Dorfman, Spilotro, Lombardo, DeAngeles, and Irwin Weiner, a Chicago bondsman who wrote bonds for the fund's trustees and who, according to testimony, had long-standing business ties with Lurie and Alderisio. Alderisio himself had died of a heart attack while in prison for another crime.

The stage was set for the big trial.

Then, on the morning of September 27, 1974, Daniel Seifert, one of the two key government witnesses, entered his office at International Fiberglass Company in a Chicago suburb, accompanied by his wife and son. Two men in ski masks, surprised to see the entire family, shoved the wife and son into a lavatory and shot Seifert. But he escaped into a hallway. There he encountered another man, with a shotgun, and turned to flee. A buckshot blast ripped away the back of his head, but Seifert continued into the fiberglass plant. The two men in ski masks chased him with bullets, yelling for the startled employees to "Hit the deck!" They did. But Seifert escaped out a back door. There, he encountered another man with a shotgun, who fired at him point-blank. None of the witnesses has come forward willing and able to testify against the killers, though the FBI reportedly knows who all three gunmen are.

Seifert's murder cast a pall over the U. S. attorney's office. Prosecutors decided to drop charges on Lombardo, against whom Daniel Seifert had been the primary witness. The other defendants went to trial February 3, 1975.

Matthias Lydon, chief of the government's three trial attorneys, quickly found that he had many problems besides the lack of a second insider witness to corroborate Lurie.

First, the jury was getting a very different picture of the defendants than the one being published in Chicago newspapers, which the jurors were forbidden to read. Defense attorneys presented DeAngeles and Weiner as independent businessmen who wanted to go into plastics manufacturing in Deming. They presented Spilotro as a businessman who wanted to borrow money from his friend, DeAngeles. So long as the three men didn't testify—and none of the defendants did—the prosecution couldn't apprise the jury of their backgrounds. Said prosecutor Lydon afterward, "Probably the greatest problem of the case was not being able to explain who all these characters are and what they were doing together in the first place."

Another prosecution problem was that the IRS and Postal Service investigators had left elephant tracks around Deming after beginning their investigation in February, 1972. This tipped off the alleged schemers that a criminal case was in prospect. So, late in 1972, new accountants were able to reorganize the plastic factory's books. Money that the government believed had been stolen was reclassified as loans. Then many of these loans were repaid—some by means of a $20,000 salary bonus that was suddenly given to DeAngeles and charged off against loans to him and others. This new accounting left the jury with the impression that only a small portion of the pension fund's money wasn't properly accounted for.

Moreover, the rules of evidence prevented the jury from learning of the fund's checkered history, including its earlier losses at Deming. For the jury, the alleged fraud scheme began in the fall of 1970 at Gaylur Mercantile Company, a Chicago salvage firm. Harold Lurie, Gaylur's proprietor, testified that a broker he sometimes dealt with had told him about an inventory of toys left at the old Auburn Rubber plant in Deming, New Mexico. The broker said the toys might make a profitable salvage job for Gaylur, and observed that the Auburn plant and inventory belonged to the Central States pension fund. So Lurie called his friend Weiner, who he knew was a friend of Allen Dorfman's. Everybody (except the jury) knew who Allen Dorfman was.

At this point, however, there was an important gap in Lurie's testimony. The jury wasn't allowed to learn that Gaylur Mercantile was a front for the Alderisio Mafia gang (what's better than a salvage company for disposing of stolen or hijacked goods?). It wasn't allowed to learn that the Deming deal was directed if not actually conceived by Alderisio himself when Lurie visited the Mafia boss in prison. Nor was it allowed to learn that Alderisio used Gaylur as a "wash" for his illicit profits, or that DeAngeles and Spilotro were sometimes on Gaylur's payroll. Before telling his story to the jury, Lurie had testified about all this at a hearing in the chambers of Judge William J. Bauer, who would determine, under the rules of evidence, what the jury could and couldn't be told. There, Lurie was asked this question by Weiner's lawyer, Thomas Sullivan, and gave this answer:

SULLIVAN: Do you recall that Mr. Alderisio had sent word from prison that he wanted you to run the operation because he said you were the only one he has outside [of prison] to run the operation who has any brains?

LURIE: Yes, I remember that.

But Judge Bauer agreed with the defense lawyers that Alderisio's notoriety might prejudice the jury. So the jurors wouldn't hear any testimony involving the dead mobster even though he had overseen the entire operation. Nor would the jury learn that the government had relocated Lurie with a new identity to protect him, nor that another important witness in the case, Daniel Seifert, had been murdered. It was decided that these facts, too, were prejudicial.

The jury was permitted to learn that in November, 1970, Lurie and Weiner visited the plant in Deming to investigate the toy salvage proposition. They decided that they could not only make money from the toy sale, but they could also make money running the plant. So they met with Dorfman, who told them that obtaining a pension fund loan to take over the plant "shouldn't be too much of a problem" (as Lurie recalled it). At the same time, Lurie testified, the three men agreed to split the projected $30,000 profit from the sale of the toy inventory, $10,000 apiece. Documents showed that the toys were sold for $31,687.75, and that Weiner later submitted a check to the fund for $7,169.49 representing sale of the inventory. The prosecution argued, on Lurie's testimony, that the remaining money was pocketed by Lurie, Weiner, and Dorfman. The defense argued that the money was plowed back into the business.

Evidence showed that Dorfman promoted the project exuberantly at a meeting of the pension fund trustees in June, 1971. The trustees, unaccustomed to arguing with Allen Dorfman, approved a $600,000 advance to a new company, Gaylur Products Inc., headed by Weiner, to resume production at the Deming plant. Right after this, a strange parade began through Lurie's Gaylur Mercantile warehouse of salvaged goods, picking out television sets, tape recorders, refrigerators, freezers—even such items as urinals and volleyballs. Among those who received goods from Lurie without paying for them, according to undisputed testimony, were Dorfman, his mother, his lawyer, and a children's charity Dorfman favors. Lurie testified that Weiner told him to charge everything "to the Deming account," which would be reimbursed from the fund loan.

Meanwhile, Tough Tony Spilotro, who somehow got invited into the deal, convinced Ronnie DeAngeles to take charge of cleaning up the Deming plant. DeAngeles also was to convert the machines there for the manufacture of plastic products. DeAngeles got a $190,000 budget and a salary that reached $500 a week, *after* withholding. He also got a house, an airplane, and a Cadillac, which the government charged he should have paid income tax on, but which the defense said he was holding in trust for the company. Soon after starting to work, DeAngeles reported that the plant needed repairs far more extensive than had been anticipated. This sent Weiner back to the trustees for an additional $298,000, and Dorfman was supporting him all the way. At the trial, the prosecution presented testimony from people on the scene who said that most of the necessary repairs had been made under the supervision of a prior caretaker, and that anyway, the repairs cost much less than $298,000. This led to literally weeks of arguing before an impatient jury over who made which repairs, when, and for how much. Defense attorney Sullivan seized on this atmosphere of nit-picking to help his cause. "It really is incredible," he told the jury in his summation, "that in Chicago in 1975 we spent about a week on the question of whether a roof leaked down in Deming in 1971, but we did. Well, that's all right. It's the taxpayers' money. . . . We finally decided it only leaked when it rained."

The roof wasn't the only thing accused of leaking. Extensive evidence showed that hundreds of thousands of borrowed dollars were used for purposes other than resurrecting the plant in Deming. Some of them:

Before the IRS appeared in Deming in February, 1972, Weiner pledged $149,000 of Gaylur Products' money from the pension fund to secure bank loans for his personal business interests. Some $113,000 of this borrowed collateral was foreclosed on when the bank loans weren't repaid. But later, in 1972, after he knew he was under intense scrutiny, Weiner repaid the money.

Weiner sent $33,000 to help Spilotro and his wife resettle in Las Vegas and open a gift shop (in the Circus Circus hotel-casino, which was funded with money from the Central States fund, and which some believe Spilotro has a hand in managing). Judge Bauer wouldn't let the jury hear about cash sent by Weiner and delivered to Spilotro in a briefcase, because the defense contended there wasn't any proof that the money came from Gaylur Products; it couldn't be traced (which is probably why it was delivered in cash in the first place).

Gaylur also "invested"—and lost—$42,000 in what was purported to have been an unsuccessful venture to market, of all things, mobile lunch trucks (see Part Five). The lunch truck firm, called Weenie-Wagon, shared an address and two of its principals with Weiner's bonding company. It was also linked by testimony to Dorfman and Joe the Clown Lombardo.

Gaylur also bought several dozen long-haul trucks and gave them to a firm run by DeAngeles. The DeAngeles firm was then paid to haul goods from Deming in the trucks bought with the Teamster loan money. When the Deming operation folded in 1973, the trucks were driven to DeAngeles's new home in Florida and left there, apparently without payment to Gaylur or the Fund. But the jury never learned this. The government had been unaware of the truck deal at the time the indictment was drawn and so, at trial, Judge Bauer refused to let prosecutor Lydon "gum this [trial] up with proof of another crime."

The jury did learn of checks written on the borrowed money for $6,000 to pay criminal defense fees for DeAngeles and one Sam Battaglia (though the jury didn't learn that this was the notorious "Teetz" Battaglia, or that his fee was ordered paid by Alderisio); $1,080 to complete payments on an Oldsmobile for Battaglia's son; $2,200 for equipment to tap the phones of Weiner's children, whom he suspected of narcotics involvement; $15,000 to help a friend of DeAngeles buy a trucking company (the money was later repaid from the trucking company's cash); and $24,000 (later repaid) to a bonding client of Weiner's.

Then the jury heard Moe Shapiro, a longtime friend of Weiner and DeAngeles, testify that on July 7, 1971, he was chatting with DeAngeles and said, "Gee, I need forty-five hundred dollars if somebody could borrow it to me." Then, Shapiro testified, "Ron, my friend, says, 'Moe I would be happy to borrow it to you.'" The loan was made at once, with Gaylur money, and Shapiro never repaid it.

The court was, in fact, getting an accurate look at the way the Syndicate operates. Any money available is used for any purpose that comes up, with total disregard for normal business propriety or responsibility to creditors. Nevertheless, all the nit-picking simply wore down the jury. The defense cross-examined at length to try to make each item look pretty benign. The main issue at the trial wasn't petty chiseling. It was whether Weiner and his associates willfully misstated their intentions when they obtained the loans. Their application in 1971 (which Lurie testified was inspired by Spilotro) proposed three products for manufacture at the Deming plant: eight-track tape cartridges, five-gallon pails, and malamine dishes. Each item would contribute about equally to a projected $1.6 million annual profit, the application said.

The government contended that the tape cartridge proposal was misleading; the expert whom Weiner had said would run the operation testified that he had already rejected the plant as "totally inadequate" when Weiner put his name down. The dish proposal was based largely on a letter from a Panamanian company promising large purchases; Lurie testified that he had forged the letter at Weiner's request. The pail proposal cited a "contract" for purchase of two million pails a year; the guaranteed purchaser turned out to be a company owned by Weiner's cousin, which went out of business before Gaylur began large-scale pail production.

Nevertheless, the pail business eventually became genuine. In interviews after the trial, jurors said this was a major factor in their deliberations. U. S. Gypsum Company became a major customer, and pails accounted for most of the $1.5 million in sales that Gaylur (later renamed American Pail Corp.) recorded from 1971 until it closed in the fall of 1973. (Most other sales were of toy swim masks and fish fins, a product line Gaylur inherited from the old Auburn Rubber Company.)

But the genuine pail business with U. S. Gypsum didn't materialize until late in 1972, after the Gaylur gang knew they were under investigation and had to come up with something. By then, so little remained of the original $900,000 in fund loans that Weiner went back to the trustees for $500,000 more to buy material for pails. And then, during its supposed boom period in early 1973, Gaylur suffered big operating losses because it was selling the pails for only 85 cents each, a lot less than the $1.11 it cost to make them—and the $1.11 included no rent or debt service to the fund, because Gaylur didn't pay any. This generosity in pricing may be why Gaylur was able to obtain U. S. Gypsum's business, and, with it, a respectable record of gross sales.

The defense argued that costs would have dropped if Gaylur had been able to maintain production as planned. But in mid-1973, Amoco Chemical Company, one of two main suppliers, cut Gaylur off from the petrochemical needed to make the pails, causing a slow-down and then a shut-down. The jurors, however, weren't allowed to learn the real reason for the material cut-off; if they had, it might have turned the whole trial around. The reason Amoco stopped sending materials to Deming is apparent in the internal correspondence of the Amoco credit department. In 1973, an Amoco executive had come across a series of articles in the *Chicago Tribune* exposing the local crime Syndicate. He had clipped the articles and sent them to his boss with a cover memo pointing out that the characters involved were "our 'friends' in New Mexico," and urging that Amoco take "a hands-off attitude" toward Gaylur. A reply memo from a superior concurs, "due to their very questionable background."

Judge Bauer refused to allow prosecution attempts to introduce the memos into evidence on the ground that they would prejudice the jury. The defense was allowed to argue in court that the 1973 petroleum shortage was responsible for the cut-off of materials to Gaylur—a seemingly logical explanation, even though everyone in the courtroom except the jury knew it was a lie. This tactic by the defense forced the government to come up with a lie of its own so as not to appear to concede the point. The prosecutors argued that Gaylur hadn't paid its bills on time. But the defense was able to show otherwise, which impressed the jury.

It is not uncommon in American jurisprudence for the judge and both litigants to conspire to deceive the jury, quite possibly a reason for the system's frequent failures. At one point in the Deming case, defense attorney Jerris Leonard unabashedly protested to the judge—away from the jury, of course—that the truth might have been hinted away by certain remarks in court. "This jury now knows there is something behind this whole situation other than the two reasons which have been given, one by the Government that it's a credit problem, the other by the defense that it was . . . the energy crisis," he argued. But Judge Bauer assured him that the jury lacked such "clairvoyance," and added, "We have conducted side bars on various matters, precluding evidence from going in, both on behalf of the prosecution and on behalf of the defense." Eventually everyone was satisfied that the jury had been adequately misinformed.

Perhaps the backbone of the defense was a two-day presentation of a detailed—but not certified—accounting done by a team of auditors from Arthur Young & Company, one of the Big Eight accounting firms. The auditors acknowledged that the accounting relied largely on information supplied by previous bookkeepers, who in turn had testified that *they* relied at least in part on information given them by Weiner and DeAngeles. But the Arthur Young team, on its big charts, was able to account in some way for almost every penny of the loan money. Howard Doherty, a partner, testified that Arthur Young was receiving $150,000 for its work, to be paid by two law firms representing the defendants. But minutes from the Central States pension fund board of trustees meeting of October 4, 1974, show that a motion was carried for the *fund* to hire and pay Arthur Young to audit Gaylur Products. Thus the minutes indicate (though the jury never learned about it) that the backbone of the defense in the Chicago trial was paid for with money from the pension fund—which was supposed to be the victim of the alleged fraud! (Arthur Young still says it understood the money was coming from the defense law firms; the fund wouldn't comment.)

This confusion between victim and perpetrator dogged the entire trial. According to interviews with jurors, it heavily influenced the verdict. To speak for the purported victim, the prosecution put on the stand one Thomas J. Duffey, a trucking company lawyer and fund trustee. But Duffey was also a partner of defendants Dorfman and Matheson and two other persons connected to the fund in a private investment company. At the trial, Duffey's testimony consistently seemed more helpful to the defense than to the prosecution. As chief prosecutor Lydon listened in disbelief, Duffey, on cross-examination, said that once the fund made a loan the borrower was free to use the money as he saw fit, regardless of the purpose stated in the application (which isn't exactly the philosophy of your typical banker). Duffey also testified that the trustees had been satisfied with Gaylur's unaudited financial statements. The defense leaned on this testimony in its summation, along with other testimony from the fund that its own accountant and efficiency expert had gone to Deming and approved Gaylur's operation of the plant.

The effect of all this on the outcome of the case is illustrated by one juror's comment in an interview: "For fraud to exist, the person being defrauded must be somewhat naive. These pension board members weren't that naive. Some of them were lawyers. Some of them were trucking company executives." The jury never learned that during Duffey's thirteen years on the fund board, the fund had lost incalculable hundreds of millions of pension dollars in bad loans, or that trustees were partners of the defendant Dorfman in an investment company on the side.

At any rate, the trustees wound up in a much better position than the prosecutors did. After the expenditure by the government of millions of dollars and thousands of man-hours, the trial ended April 10, 1975, ten weeks after it began, with the acquittal of every defendant on every count of the indictment.

Matheson and Sheetz continued to supervise the pension fund. DeAngeles and Lombardo continued to carry on as Anthony Accardo, the local godfather, wanted them to. Weiner continued his bonding business. Dorfman was rehired by the fund and his companies continued to collect millions of dollars in fees. And Spilotro stayed on in Las Vegas, where authorities believe he now supervises the Mafia's gambling interests, largely financed by the pension fund.

As prosecutor Lydon quietly observed to me after the trial, while downing two bottles of Michelob at a bar near the courthouse before moving on to gin, "I'd have to say that in a loss like this, there's probably substantial discouragement for any future investigations. I'm not so sure that the office would want to put this kind of time in again."

Then came the murder of Jimmy Hoffa, and slowly the government began to gear up once more. Whether it is still on the treadmill, or whether it will finally gain some ground, only the future will tell.

PART SEVEN

BANKING AND FINANCE

1

The Banks

Mafia bigshots always used to have politicians in their pockets to help them take care of their banking needs.

The crowd around Bayonne Joe Zicarelli had access to the Broadway National Bank of Bayonne through Congressman Cornelius Gallagher, who was a director of the bank and whose law partners owned controlling interest. Anthony "Little Pussy" Russo, a Vito Genovese underboss who ran the rackets along the New Jersey shore, did his banking in the 1960s through the politically powerful Wilentz family.

Democratic National Committeeman and former state attorney general David T. Wilentz was director and legal co-counsel of First Bank & Trust Company of Perth Amboy (now the National State Bank), and his son Warren Wilentz, former county prosecutor and U. S. Senate nominee, was director and legal counsel of the Edison (New Jersey) Bank. The two banks financed Russo's land speculation with more than $800,000 in loans, with the Wilentzes' law firm acting as attorney. Most of the money was defaulted on. Russo did repay one $165,000 loan, but only after the State of New Jersey condemned some land and bought it from Russo for three times what he had just paid for it. One of the Wilentzes' law partners represented Russo (or his company) in these profitable condemnation proceedings, while Attorney General Arthur Sills, a former Wilentz partner whose name was still above the law firm's door, represented the taxpayers.

When the local newspaper tried to expose Russo's dealings, David Wilentz

—a powerful force in the community—talked to the publisher. The story, which had taken six months to develop, was killed on the eve of publication. The reporter (who took the story to the *New York Post,* which published it as a five-part series) was fired. I was the reporter.

Nowadays, many of the old style urban political machines that produced these cozy banking relationships are disintegrating. But the Mafia has found new ways to break the banks. Where no politicians are available, there are still unions. What happens is this: the leader of a Mob-dominated union local approaches a fledgling bank whose officers are dreaming of the big time and drooling for a few heavy depositors to get them launched. The union leader offers to deposit hundreds of thousands of union dollars in the bank—money from pension or severance funds, or the union treasury. The interest rates are negotiable, which means the bank can pay less than top dollar to get the deposits. In return, however—sometimes by tacit understanding, sometimes even by a blatant formal agreement—the banker promises to approve loans for some new "customers" the union leader says he'll be recommending. Sometimes this kind of tit for tat arrangement sneaks up on the banker subtly; he gets the big deposits, the union leader brings around some loan applicants and the banker simply knows better than to turn them down. Sometimes there is nothing subtle about it; the banker gets a cash kickback to sweeten the deal.

In 1976, the United States attorney's office and the FBI in Newark began investigating a series of Mafia banking raids that so far has caused the failure of at least four banks in New Jersey alone. Since 1973, at least $10 million and maybe much more had been lent out to, and not paid back by, a parade of characters whose names read like the index to the Valachi hearings. Some banks large enough to withstand the onslaught without actually going out of business were still in trouble, and there are clear indications that the same racket has been practiced in Ohio (where one bank closed) and probably elsewhere.

The "borrowers" have included loansharks, alleged murderers and ex-convicts of all types. One borrower, a reputed Mafioso named Patrick Pizuto, a twice-convicted armed robber and suspect in a gangland murder, actually got his loan from the State Bank (now closed) of Chatham, New Jersey, while serving a seven-to-ten year sentence in Trenton State Prison. Pizuto came into the bank and applied for the loan one day while out on a work release program. Then, so he could spend the money he borrowed, he commuted his own prison sentence. To achieve this feat, he had an accomplice slip him a blank form of the kind used in Appellate Court decisions; then he forged three judges' names to it and mailed the "court order" for his release to the warden, who promptly released him. He picked up his loan money the same day. Pizuto went back behind bars eventually on his original conviction (U. S. District Judge Herbert J. Stern gave him a suspended sentence on the bank fraud), but his return to prison isn't the only reason his loan is still outstanding. A lot of other mobsters who also borrowed from the State Bank of Chatham, and other banks, are still walking around free, and they haven't paid back their loans either.

Pizuto "borrowed" only $2,500. Most of his criminal colleagues took in the neighborhood of $30,000 to $40,000, because that tends to be the limit on an individual bank officer's authority to approve loans to one customer. Some hoods have incorporated themselves under a variety of phony business names so they could go back for numerous $30,000 to $40,000 loans. One set of loans from the State Bank (now closed) of Manville, New Jersey, reached about $750,000, all benefiting a firm run by Robert Gooding, a convicted extortionist and sometimes partner of Mafia enforcer Anthony "Tony Tumac" Acceturo.

Some series of loans seem to be arranged by a single loanshark or bookie, who is apparently authorized to bring around his recalcitrant clients to borrow cash to pay their debts to him. Thus the customers who were welching on the loanshark can welch on the bank instead. Presumably the mobsters who arrange for the bank to make these "loans" get a cut of the take. Sometimes the identified borrower may be a mere front for a mobster, who then gets almost all of the take.

When the banks fail, there are three sets of losers. First, there are the local small businessmen or professionals who have invested their savings to help capitalize a new banking venture in their community. Second comes the Federal Deposit Insurance Corporation, a government agency that has to bail out the depositors. And third are the union members whose aggregated dues or pension money may not be entirely reimbursable by the FDIC.

At this writing sixty-four persons have been indicted so far in the Newark inquiry. Most of the prosecutions seem to be proceeding successfully toward guilty pleas or convictions, but punishment has hardly been awesome. Of the first twenty persons sentenced, only nine have received jail terms, the longest being eighteen months to five years—even though the looting scheme brings in far more money than armed robbery of the same banks ever could have produced.

The Mafia, on the other hand, may be imposing its own sentences, on figures in the investigation who have cooperated with the government, welched, or otherwise gotten out of line. Two borrowers have been shot to death, one outside his produce store and the other in a Manhattan parking lot, in what seem like classic Mob hits. One victim, according to acquaintances, was murdered hours after leaving the FBI office in Newark, where it's believed he opened up about his loanshark friends. One bank officer, who was giving information to the government while under indictment in the case involving Robert Gooding, died in the crash of a small private plane he was flying—a crash that law-enforcement officers term suspicious. The death of a second bank officer who was involved was ruled a suicide. And the FBI reportedly has a tape recording of a conversation in which the former president of the State Bank of Chatham, Alexander Smith, who has pleaded guilty to misapplication of bank funds, was warned by a prominent lawyer, "We're gonna lay you out alongside Hoffa."

The lawyer who allegedly uttered this threat is George Franconero, who pops up repeatedly in the scandal. Franconero is living evidence that top New Jersey politicians continue to bear links to the Mob, even in the late 1970s. Franconero is the former law partner of Governor Brendan Byrne. His lawyer in the banking mess is Martin Greenberg, another former member of the Byrne law firm, who is also a Democratic state senator and confidant of the governor. One client of the Byrne-Franconero law firm back in the early 1970s was mobster Thomas "Timmy Murphy" Pecora. The firm represented him extensively in civil matters and successfully fought to get him free from jail on reduced bail when he was arrested on a gambling charge. He identified Byrne personally as his lawyer at the time. Pecora and his brother, Joseph, known as Joe Peck, have been identified before Congress as members of the Genovese Mafia family. Joe Peck runs Teamster Local 863, whose pension fund had six-figure deposits in the State Bank of Chatham just before the bank went under because of bad loans in 1975.

Franconero pleaded guilty to submitting false data on a loan application. His sister, singer Connie Francis, came to court to support him. U. S. District Judge Herbert J. Stern sentenced him to probation after announcing that Franconero had agreed to give the government information about other culprits in the scheme. Judge Stern specifically noted, however, that Franconero had been exempted by the government from ever having to testify in court on these matters, which certainly limited his usefulness as an informant.

According to the uncontroverted testimony of others, Franconero had been the attorney for a purported leasing corporation, which issued phony documents that were vital to the bank frauds. The documents certified that the leasing corporation had delivered industrial equipment to various companies set up by the racketeers. Actually, the industrial equipment didn't even exist, but the racketeers could use the phony documents to collateralize loans, which they supposedly obtained to pay for the equipment. Through this method, mobsters and alleged mobsters helped cause the loss of some $4.5 million by the Bank of Bloomfield, New Jersey. The bank was wiped out. In addition, Franconero helped introduce banks to some of the bad borrowers, and also was attorney for a land title company that bank president Smith said was used to channel kickbacks from the Bank of Chatham. The title company allegedly billed the bank for services it didn't perform, and kicked back at least some of the money to Frank Rando.

Frank Rando ran Local 1262 of the Retail Store Employees' Union, based in Clifton, New Jersey, which deposited hundreds of thousands of dollars in various banks just before they started lending money to mobsters. Local 1262 had been put in trusteeship by its international in 1958 and again in 1967 because of alleged corruption among its leaders. Rando, the longtime kingpin of the local, holding various titles over the years, pleaded guilty in 1977 to having an illegal deposits-for-loans deal with the State Bank of Chatham. He was put on probation and was fined $2,500 by Judge Stern. The union says he is no longer connected with it.

Franconero also is close to the key figure in the other union local whose money most frequently has gone into banks at about the time mobsters have taken money out. That is Local 945 of the International Brotherhood of Teamsters, a large local that covers employees of (among other things) the garbage collection industry, in which the Mafia has long been involved. The key figure is Ernest Palmeri, whose title is only business agent, but who comes from a blood family that is prominent in the Mafia, and who obviously weilds a lot of clout. According to the New Jersey Alcoholic Beverage Commission, Palmeri and Franconero shared hidden ownership in a bar and restaurant in Bergen County and improperly employed an ex-con to run it.

Palmeri's father, Paul, now dead, had a long arrest record and attended the famous Mafia convention at Apalachin, New York, in 1957, indicating he was pretty high in the organization. Ernest's brother Frank assisted Mob boss Jerry Catena in a much-publicized attempt to monopolize the supermarket sale of detergents, which culminated in the firebombing of some A & P stores and the murder of store managers a decade ago. Like Rando's Local 1262 of the Retail Store Employes' union, Ernest Palmeri's Teamster local, 945, also was put into trusteeship by its international in the late 1950s because of a corruption scandal. To "clean up" the local, Teamster overlords sent in outside leadership: Mafia underboss Anthony "Tony Pro" Provenzano. When Provenzano had Local 945 running to his liking, he turned it over to the current leadership. Disclosure statements of total bank balances and total interest income show that both Local 1262 and Local 945 keep hundreds of thousands of dollars in low- or non-interest-bearing accounts. Disclosure of the terms of specific accounts isn't required.

At this writing, Palmeri hasn't been charged with a crime, although the government has stated in open court that Franconero confessed to kicking back money to Palmeri, and Palmeri obviously is a target in the continuing investigation. In a brief telephone interview, he said the local's bank deposits are handled by the treasurer, not by him (although others involved say Palmeri personally set up many deals). "I don't want to talk to you or anybody else about it," he said in the interview. "It's a crock of bull."

What makes a bank officer go on approving crooked loans even after he realizes that they are costing his bank more than it can make from union deposits? The presidents of some banks are easy targets for bribe proposals because their own salaries are surprisingly low—sometimes only about $30,000 a year, even though they are empowered to lend out more than that with a stroke of their pen.

Ralph Stein, a business associate of some Mafia loansharks, has used many kinds of influence. He has been sentenced to jail for helping wreck the Springfield State Bank by extracting more than $300,000 in phony loans. The bank president, Donald Spears, was pretty clearly influenced by the Teamsters' deposit of several hundred thousand dollars in his bank. But Spears also has pleaded guilty to accepting bribes from Ralph Stein. In the case of another bank, Stein used blackmail, according to a knowledgeable banking association official. Visiting a difficult loan officer, Stein is said to have casually walked off with the officer's briefcase. Inside he found love letters indicating that the loan officer, who was married, was having an affair with a woman employee of the bank, who also was married. The briefcase was returned without the love letters, and the loan officer suddenly became cooperative. The situation came to light, the source says, when the woman spoke up in a successful effort to protect the loan officer against impending prosecution.

The individual shady bank loans that have turned up over the past few years are far too numerous to set down. What follows are brief accounts of how two of the hardest-hit banks were moved in on.

Shortly after the State Bank of Chatham opened on March 21, 1972, Alexander Smith, its president, was introduced to Frank Rando of the Retail Store Employees' union, by George Fiore, a bank director. (Fiore was indicted later for conspiracy and misapplication of funds, but the charges were eventually dismissed.) Smith had been senior vice-president at the National Bank of North America in Manhattan when he heard that the top job was available at Chatham. Now he was enthusiastic over the chance to run his own bank, and threw $45,000 of personal savings into the pool of capital put up by local investors to start the State Bank of Chatham. Anxious to make a success of it, he says he was delighted to learn over lunch that Rando not only had purchased a certificate of deposit at the bank, but also was prepared to line up some good loan customers. That same day, Smith recalls, he accompanied Rando to a jewelry store run by Anthony Cilli, a friend of Rando's. Cilli pleaded guilty in 1976 to conspiracy in connection with the use of an estimated $100,000 of Chatham bank loans for loansharking. But at the time, Smith says, "I didn't think he was a Mafia type. He didn't look like a hardened person." (Cilli must also have impressed Judge Stern, who sentenced him to mere probation.)

So the bank agreed to make loans to Cilli and other of Rando's friends, in return for deposits of union funds. Soon, Smith says, the Retail Store Employees' deposits jumped from $120,000 to around $360,000, and Smith began making the rounds of other unions to drum up more deposits. It happened that when he came to the Teamsters, he and Ernie Palmeri discovered a common bond. Smith had known Palmeri's sister before, when they both worked for the same bank. On this quick rapport, money started pouring in from the Teamsters and, ultimately, other unions.

Meanwhile, Rando's friends were already coming around for loans. One was Henry Rudnitsky, a produce market owner, who is believed to have used more than $100,000 of bank borrowings to pay off debts to Syndicate figures. When the federal investigation started, Rudnitsky was one of the first potential witnesses approached, and he agreed to cooperate. Shortly after leaving the Justice Department office in Newark one day, he was shot to death in what looked like a Mob "hit."

Smith had quit his $34,000-a-year Chatham Bank presidency in 1975 to become president of another New Jersey bank. After news of the investigation broke, he resigned that job. The stockholders in the Chatham Bank, who were left holding the bag when the bank folded, filed suit in New Jersey State court against Smith, Franconero, and George Piccola, a business partner of Franconero's. The suit accused the three men of, among other things, conspiring to defraud the bank by having it lend money beyond the amount permitted by law, and by making loans that were financially unsound, inadequately secured and in disregard of the bank's interests; the suit sought to reclaim the missing millions. To settle these charges, Smith agreed to repay the bank $1 million (obviously an empty promise—he claims he's broke) and also signed an affidavit admitting moral culpability. The statement says he concealed from the bank's directors that solely on the recommendation of Rando and others he was approving loans to borrowers who lacked good credit records and a demonstrated ability to repay. And, he conceded, "some of the loans were for illegal purposes." He then confessed to similar crimes in federal court and received a suspended sentence. When Jim Carberry of the *Wall Street Journal* and I interviewed him in the fall of 1977, he said he was unemployed.

Franconero also settled the lawsuit out of court, but the terms weren't disclosed and he declined to be interviewed. Piccola, without admitting wrongdoing, agreed to repay the bank nearly $129,000.

The stockholders of the fledgling Bank of Bloomfield, New Jersey, sealed their own fate in 1973 when they invited Robert Prodan to head the operation. Prodan had been working at the much older and larger Franklin State Bank in Newark. The Bank of Bloomfield's board chairman happened to be a loan customer of Prodan's, and when the president of the Bloomfield bank retired, Prodan was invited to succeed him. Almost as soon as he arrived, Prodan set out to bring Bloomfield into the major leagues of banking. He went looking for big depositors, and pulled in at least $1 million from various Teamster groups, including Palmeri's 945. Then dozens of hoods, big-time and small-time, from New England to Michigan to Florida, lined up at the Bank of Bloomfield's door for loans that drove the bank into receivership with the Federal Deposit Insurance Corp. in December, 1975.

Much of what happened was the work of Arnold Daner, who had met Prodan in 1967 when both worked as young accountants in a small commercial finance concern. When Prodan took up a career with large New York area banks, Daner founded an import firm. They remained friends, and Prodan invested heavily in Daner's import firm, which failed. Daner moved to Florida in 1972 and started a company that arranged financing for leases of industrial equipment (similar to financing installment purchases). Daner says Prodan stayed on as his partner; Prodan has said he considered that, but declined. Right about the time that Prodan took over the Bank of Bloomfield, however,

Daner moved his leasing business to New Jersey.

Daner has since pleaded guilty to conspiring with Prodan and their Mafia buddies to loot the bank. He agreed to testify against others, and was relocated by the government for his protection. He also got a two-year prison sentence from U. S. District Judge Herbert J. Stern. Prodan denied his role at first and went to trial. The jury was hung, and eventually he pleaded guilty to conspiracy and was sentenced by Judge Stern to eighteen months to five years in prison, a sentence longer than any of the mobsters involved have received so far. According to the government charges, both Daner and Prodan got tens of thousands of dollars in illegal kickbacks. The scheme worked this way:

Over nearly two years, the mobsters signed $6 million in equipment leases with Daner's firm. As they were signed, the leases were sold to the Bank of Bloomfield, which shelled out $4.7 million cash for the right to collect on the leases—the difference being the bank's interest on its money. This is a common way of handling such transactions. The trouble was, in the Bank of Bloomfield's case, millions of dollars of equipment that supposedly was being leased didn't exist. Equipment that did exist was inflated in value. So the lease money could be spread around among the crooks, and the bank had no collateral. Much of the phony equipment was in the garbage collection, disposal, and recycling field. The private cartage business has long been infiltrated by mobsters, so there were plenty of Mafia-owned garbage firms ready to file phony leases. Also, Daner had persuaded a garbage equipment manufacturer in Florida to give him documents in blank, which Daner could then fill in, thus making it appear that a piece of equipment was delivered to a company when actually it wasn't. (Judge Stern gave the garbage equipment manufacturer a suspended sentence.)

Two mobsters, Dominick Troiano and Charles Musillo, moved in as Daner's partners. Musillo, an ex-con, and his son Michael, twenty-one, financed a loansharking operation with vast sums taken in from leases on nonexistent garbage equipment. They pleaded guilty; Judge Stern sentenced the father to a maximum of four years in prison, the son to a maximum of eighteen months. Troiano helped bring in lease customers, including his relatives. He also pleaded guilty, and Judge Stern sentenced him to a maximum of eighteen months. Among the many Bank of Bloomfield lease patrons familiar to law enforcement authorities were Thomas Milo, a Westchester County garbage carter whose father, Sabato, and uncle, Thomas Senior, were cited in the Valachi hearings as members of the Genovese Mafia family specializing in gambling, loansharking, and narcotics; Anthony "Buckalo" Ferro, identified in the same hearings as a Genovese soldier in gambling and shylocking (Ferro also had been observed earlier collecting cash payments from butchers' union leader Frank Kissel at the Black Angus restaurant); convicted felons Joseph and William "Skippy" Scappatone (who used $50,000 in bank funds to pay loan sharks, according to Daner); and a Detroit garbage firm, Central Sanitation Company, founded by Raffael "Jimmy Q" Quasarano and Dominick

"Sparky" Corrado, whose respective narcotics and labor racketeering deals have been recounted at length in Congressional testimony. (Only Thomas Milo could be reached for comment. He said he is paying back two loans and that papers for a third loan were forged and he never received the money.)

According to Daner's undisputed testimony, Palmeri had a part in some of the leases, including the one to Central Sanitation for $85,000, which involved real garbage disposal equipment. When Central Sanitation failed to make initial payments in the summer of 1975, the bank's outside directors became suspicious and the entire scheme was threatened. Daner testified that Prodan brought him to Palmeri in a restaurant and "told me that Ernie was a very powerful man in New Jersey, told me that nothing goes on in the state in the garbage business without his blessing . . . told me that he [Palmeri] would be able to collect the money if he had to break the guy's head with a pipe." Still, the Central Sanitation lease wasn't paid, and the Detroit firm was in bankruptcy proceedings in 1977.

There is an interesting footnote to the Central Sanitation story. Investigators in the Jimmy Hoffa disappearance have spent long hours trying to figure out where Hoffa's body might have been disposed of. Speculation centered mostly on two sites. One was a garbage dump in Jersey City (simply because Hoffa's suspected killers had dumped other bodies there in the past), the other was the garbage compacting equipment at Central Sanitation, which had a pick-up spot near where Hoffa was last seen. An FBI informant reported that Jimmy Q Quasarano, who founded Central Sanitation, had dined with Frank Fitzsimmons at a Detroit restaurant just a few days before Hoffa disappeared, though that story has been denied by Fitzsimmons and is unverified. Quasarano was also close to Anthony "Tony Jack" Giacalone, a prime suspect in the Hoffa case. Thus, ironically, Jimmy Hoffa's interment may have been financed by the Bank of Bloomfield, and, ultimately, the Federal Deposit Insurance Corporation.

Not all of the lease payments at the Bank of Bloomfield were welched on. Some $500,000 of the money that Daner (and his silent partners) received was plowed back into making early payments on the bank leases so the operation would seem to be working and more money could be drawn out. The Daner company also financed $150,000 in equipment—apparently genuine—for the restaurant that Palmeri and Franconero are alleged to have had an interest in. Daner testified that Franconero was legal counsel for the leasing firm.

Daner also testified, without being disputed, that he and Prodan met for dinner once in New York's Little Italy with famed mobster Matthew "Matty the Horse" Ianniello and other mobsters, including Charles Musillo. Daner said they discussed forming a garbage company in Florida with New Jersey bank money. Prodan acknowledged cosigning a $20,000 loan at another New Jersey bank to help finance the resulting garbage company, which he said Musillo was involved in, though he didn't mention Matty the Horse. Daner also told how $25,000 in funds from the Bank of Bloomfield went indirectly, through loansharks, to Carmine Galante, who some people think is the most powerful Mafioso in the country (or, at least, the chief aid of the man who is —Joe Bonanno).

Late in 1977, the banking scandal began to spread interstate. When the New Jersey investigation was extended to the Trust Company of New Jersey, the state's fourth largest bank, investigators found a major out-of-state Mafia figure, Dominick E. Bartone. Bartone had been helping himself to the Trust Company's coffers, after having employed the same scheme with a major bank in his hometown. The hometown was Cleveland—appropriately enough, considering that the two most authoritarian empires in the Teamsters union are in New Jersey and Ohio. In March, 1977, Bartone had been convicted of various federal charges involving $830,000 in "loans" from the now defunct Northern Ohio Bank in Cleveland. In New Jersey he was charged with conspiracy, misapplication of bank funds, filing false statements with a bank, and interstate travel with intent to bribe a bank officer in connection with about $1.4 million of allegedly fraudulent loans. The government said he actually received $565,000 from those loans, while a Florida man, Murray H. Michael, was accused of having received $833,000.

According to PROD, the dissident Teamster organization, both the Trust Company of New Jersey and the Northern Ohio Bank held substantial deposits of Teamster money. Bartone had a twenty-year history of association with top Teamster officials, and was a prominent figure in Senate hearings into the Syndicate. He was on close terms with John Nardi, a Cleveland Teamster boss who was murdered by a car-bomb during a Cleveland Mafia war in May, 1977. Back around the time of the Cuban revolution, Bartone was convicted twice of Caribbean gun-running. He also served prison time for tax evasion. Murray Michael, the co-defendant, had been indicted for federal crimes at least twice before. He was convicted in 1962 in Maryland of embezzlement, larceny, and fraud, but the case was reversed on appeal.

The Trust Company of New Jersey insists that the fraudulent loans it made had nothing to do with Teamster deposits, but rather were solely the result of kickbacks to a single crooked bank officer, James N. Neveras. The indictments say Bartone and Michael had agreed to pay Neveras 10 percent of the loans he approved. Neveras is named in the indictments as an unindicted co-conspirator, indicating that he may be cooperating in the investigation.

At this writing the facts of the story are still unfolding. But the lesson can already be drawn: the Mafia has gained effective control over a number of banks, and probably holds sway over many more of them than has thus far been disclosed.

Stocks and Insecurities

In its edition of August 30, 1968, *Life* Magazine devoted twenty-seven pages to a relentlessly detailed account of the activities of a stocky, bullnecked cutthroat named John "Sonny" Franzese and the men around him. The article, by James Mills, was a masterpiece of journalism.* It certainly leaves no doubt about who and what Sonny Franzese was and is. It recounted his bloody rise to power in the Colombo Mafia family. When the article appeared, Franzese, then forty-eight, had not yet begun serving a fifty-year sentence in federal prison for masterminding a series of armed bank robberies pulled off by underlings. He is serving it now. The article noted the bank robberies, but mainly concerned Franzese's trial—and acquittal—for the brutal murder of another underling, and how the laws of evidence cheated the jury out of hearing information that almost certainly would have convicted him. It was one of the longest articles *Life* ever published.

One week after the article appeared, the Wall Street brokerage firm of Dean Witter & Company, now Dean Witter Reynolds Inc., second largest in the country, hired Sonny's nephew Joseph Franzese to fill a lowrung position on the executive ladder. Joseph Franzese was subjected to a routine background investigation, and received what Dean Witter says was "a favorable report" from "an independent business report firm"—despite the fact that the *Life*

---

*As good as I've encountered. It deserves to be searched out and studied by every aspirant to the profession.

article was probably on the newsstands while the report was being made. As Franzese worked his way up that executive ladder, no one at Dean Witter knew that he was related to a notorious leader in a secret criminal organization that is built largely on blood relationships—or at least no one objected. After the FBI finally caught up with Joey Franzese and his multi-million-dollar securities fraud schemes in November, 1976, an official corporate spokesman for Dean Witter told the *Wall Street Journal* he had never heard of Sonny Franzese.

The Franzese-Dean Witter case raises several interesting and important questions. Should there be guilt by association? How should business deal with Mafia kin who have no criminal records, or with employees who are known to befriend members of the Syndicate? The case suggests an answer to these questions. But before turning to it, let the record establish that the Franzese-Dean Witter matter is no isolated example.

The Mafia has infiltrated the stock brokerage business since at least the early 1960s, when Carmine "the Doctor" Lombardozzi discovered that some of the inveterate gamblers who fell prey to his loanshark racket by night, by day worked with embossed pieces of paper worth far more than the $50 bills stacked around the crap tables. Once the Mafia realized it had stockbrokers in its control, it began figuring out ways to capitalize on this resource. The first schemes were simplistic indeed. Stock certificates were stolen and turned over to the mobsters, who didn't know quite what to do with them. Openly selling them on the stock market may have worked for a while, but obviously wasn't a permanent solution. By the late 1960s, major brokerage firms realized that they had been caught napping. Stock forms had been left lying around, entrusted to messengers. But once Wall Street discovered that stock was being stolen, it didn't take long for the brokerage firms to start keeping better track of serial numbers. One could no longer expect to sell a stolen stock certificate on the open market—without being caught.

So more ingenious schemes were required, and the Mob quickly latched on to another organized network of criminals, a group whose supply of schemes seemed endless. These were the professional securities swindlers referred to in an earlier book as *The Fountain Pen Conspiracy.* They have no lasting formal structure like the Mafia, but are freelancers who, because of the nature of their trade, are constantly in touch with each other, and often in partnership. They know how to take stolen stock and place it in the assets of a business firm, or an insurance company, or a trust of some sort, where the serial numbers won't be examined. Then the business, or trust, on the basis of its increased "assets," may qualify to receive a bank loan or complete a business deal that might otherwise have been denied. The trick is to think up a deal in which the sucker, often a bank or small businessman, will put up money on collateral of the securities without actually taking possession of them so the serial numbers can be checked. The value of stock used in this manner is much less than the market value, but it can still be enormous. Many instances of such fraud are set down in the other volume. For example, Anthony "Hickey" DiLorenzo, a Mafia-connected Teamster boss who helped Johnny Dio control labor at New York's Kennedy Airport, was convicted for supplying stolen IBM stock used in a clever insurance swindle in Pennsylvania. Carmine Lombardozzi's brother John was convicted for helping promote a worthless stock issue known as Picture Island Computer Corp.

Early in 1978, an undercover investigation by the Queens district attorney's office broke up a major fencing operation at a Mob-controlled trucking company near Kennedy Airport (fencing is selling stolen goods).* Although the hoods in the trucking warehouse dealt mainly in cargo stolen from the airport —cameras, wearing apparel, electronics equipment, and appliances—police found that they also dealt in stolen Union Pacific Company stock certificates. According to police, a computer manager for Union Pacific had befriended someone connected with the fencing ring. This led to a plan by which the computer manager lifted blank stock certificates and either forged them or had them forged so that they would appear to have been properly issued. They sold for 10 percent of market value. (He pleaded not guilty and at this writing is awaiting trial.)

Once the Mafia had discovered that stock certificates were a lot like money, it quickly began doing with stock some of the things that it does with money —like counterfeiting it. How much of the stocks and bonds now listed as assets by various companies big and little are really stolen or counterfeit is anybody's guess. But enough cases of this kind of hidden funny-money have come to light to indicate that the problem is real.

The Syndicate has also moved into numerous small and medium-sized stock brokerages. Sometimes it controls the whole brokerage firm. Often the gimmick is to take a stock offering for a small new company and manipulate it by reporting phony sales to the National Daily Quotation Service. The companies issuing this stock, if they have any legitimate business operations at all, are frequently small and financially troubled. The manipulators make the price appear to rise as they peddle the stock to the public, and then, when the shares are unloaded, the phony supports are taken away and the stock price plummets. (Johnny Dio's takeover of a New York brokerage firm and his manipulation of several stocks in this manner will be recounted in a later chapter.)

Sometimes the Mob has managed to cause havoc in the stock of a well-known company. Early in 1978, Yiddy Bloom, a Miami Beach crony of the almost legendary Syndicate financier Meyer Lansky, pleaded guilty in federal court, Philadelphia, to conspiring to manipulate the stock of Magic Marker

---

*The undercover investigation, in which police purchased stolen goods in order to find out who was selling them, was run by Lt. Remo Franchesini, the same investigator who put Philip Rastelli in jail in the lunchwagon case.

Corp. in nearby Cherry Hill, New Jersey. Bloom's son, Jerrold Bloom, had gotten a job as a broker in the branch offices of some large Wall Street firms —Shields & Company and Harris Upham & Company (now part of Smith Barney, Harris Upham & Company). Two other figures who pleaded guilty in the scheme were brokers at the Washington, D.C., office of Hornblower & Weeks Hemphill, Noyes Inc., another major Wall Street firm. One of them was the office manager. With more than one firm involved, trades could easily be manipulated. According to the indictment, some eighteen conspirators in all caused the price of Magic Marker common stock to rise from $5 a share to $31 a share in nine months. It soon fell to about $2 a share. The same conspirators also manipulated the stock of a smaller firm, Uni-Shield Corp., a packager of hardware and household supplies in Bucks County, Pennsylvania. U. S. District Judge Clarence Newcomer sentenced Yiddy Bloom to one year in prison for the manipulation, and sentenced Jerrold Bloom to probation. He also fined the two a total of $15,000 and ordered them to contribute a total of $65,000 to charity, which apparently has the advantage over fines of being tax deductable.

Infiltration of stock brokerages also has become a natural part of the manipulation of giant union pension funds. Some good examples were provided in testimony before Congress early in 1978 by Robert Windrem, research director of PROD, the dissident Teamster organization. Windrem testified, without contradiction, to the following: Teamster Local 282 in Elmont, New York, has seven thousand members who deliver building materials to construction sites throughout the metropolitan area, and deliver beverages and groceries on Long Island. Its president and administrator of its pension and benefit funds, is John Cody, a convicted burglar and robber (a further conviction for extortion was overturned on appeal). Cody selected Carlo Gambino, the Mafia boss of bosses, as official greeter for his son's wedding reception in 1973. The IRS is after Cody for back taxes on what it says was kickback money he took in connection with the funds' investments (he denies it; the case is pending). And the fund—Windrem testified—has lost millions of dollars because of mismanaged investments.

In 1972, Cody's brother-in-law, Morris Tarica, and another man, who employs Local 282 members, formed a brokerage firm, Tarica & Company, which bought a seat on the New York Stock Exchange. The brokerage hired Cody's son Michael and another man—the brother of the president of Teamster Local 707 in Queens—and began handling business for numerous Teamster pension and benefit funds. In 1975, Tarica & Company sold its seat on the exchange, but its key personnel went to work for two other New York Stock Exchange member firms, Bear Stearns & Company (a major broker) and R. W. Presspich. Presspich also hired Ross Provenzano, the son of Nunzio Provenzano and nephew of Anthony Provenzano, officers of Teamster Local 560 and part of the Genovese Mafia clan. Presspich and Bear Stearns proceeded to attract considerable Teamster business.

One might expect some consolation in all this—that the union members' money might at least be invested in stock exchange companies instead of shady real estate deals. But not so. Even as Windrem testified, the Local 282 fund, run by Cody, was preparing to lend $33.5 million—60 percent of all its assets —to Hyman Green, a New York real estate speculator whose firms have defaulted on at least two loans from the Central States, Southeast and Southwest Areas pension fund in Chicago. The government was preparing legal action to try to prevent the loan.

So we return to the Dean Witter-Joseph Franzese case, described at the beginning of this chapter, and the question of business attitudes toward Mafia relatives and associates who themselves have clean records. The answer is *not* that Dean Witter should have refused employment to a young man just because his name was Joseph Franzese. The answer *is,* however, that business ought to be aware of the high tendency of Mafia kin to follow the criminal path, and, when dealing with them, take a few unusual but relatively simple precautions.

Joey Franzese was leading a double life, but the dark side of it really wasn't hidden at all. The information about him that has emerged since his indictment indicates that if anyone had made inquiries, or followed him around for even one evening during off-duty hours, the Mr. Hyde in him probably would have been revealed. But not until 1976, eight years after he had begun at Dean Witter, did an outsider view his other life and choose to expose it. By that time, Franzese had risen to a key managerial position at Dean Witter (there's dispute now about his exact title and powers, but clearly he had enough authority to cause Dean Witter's computer to issue huge checks).

The unlikely outsider who spoiled Franzese's racket was an immigrant British printing salesman named Peter Trott. Trott represented printing concerns, and his task was to hunt up people who needed printing done and line them up with the printer best suited to their needs. In March 1976, a broker in the business introduced him to Imar Publications, a small New York firm that was setting about to cash in on the Off-Track Betting craze in New York by publishing a new horseracing magazine called "Off-Track." Imar Publications turned out to be owned and operated (entirely or in substantial part) by one Jerry Franzese, whom Trott would later learn was a nephew of Sonny, the convicted bank robber and acquitted murderer, and a cousin of Joey, the Dean Witter executive. Trott hadn't heard the name Franzese any more than the spokesman for Dean Witter had. He says Jerry Franzese offered the Off-Track Betting Corp. (a public agency) itself as a reference, and that OTB offices on Long Island told him they would indeed distribute the magazines (which they ultimately did).

Granted, it would be hard to contemplate a better authority on off-track betting than someone from the Colombo Mafia family. Nevertheless, from Peter Trott's point of view, it was unfortunate that Jerry Franzese was running the magazine. Trott signed Imar up with Holiday Press of Olive Branch, Mississippi, a subsidiary of Holiday Inns. After two issues, Imar still hadn't paid its printing bills, which had run up to $47,000. Holiday Press refused to extend more credit, and Imar became defunct.

Holiday Press was none too happy with its salesman, for Trott, by his own admission, was personally responsible for having talked the company into letting Imar work on credit. The printing firm, Trott says, directed him to stay close to Imar in hopes of discovering assets that could be seized by court order to cover at least part of the debt. So he repeatedly visited the Imar office on Forty-fifth Street near Sixth Avenue, and met with Jerry Franzese. "I took that debt very personally," he says, "because for the first time since *Saturday Review* went down, I got stung with a heavy debt."

Finally, in August, Jerry Franzese took a new tack. (This account comes from Trott's court filings and interviews with him and with federal officials. Jerry Franzese couldn't be reached for an interview.) Franzese told Trott that he was involved with a crime syndicate. He told Trott who Sonny Franzese was, and that Jerry was his cousin. "I can do you favors —I'm connected," Jerry reportedly said. "I owe you a favor. I cost you forty-seven thousand and cost you your credibility. I can take care of it." So Jerry Franzese introduced the printing salesman to his cousin Joey, the Dean Witter executive, and promised they would bring Trott into "a good deal." In retrospect, it seems likely that Joey had reached the point in his scheming when he needed a respectable businessman on the outside to help him cash some of the big checks he was planning to draw, and that Trott had been sized up as somebody who could play this role. Just how much Jerry knew of the scheme then is open to question, and he hasn't been charged with a crime.

Apart from their last name and their black, wavy hair, the cousins seemed very different to Trott. Jerry, the magazine publisher, was a handsome six-footer, he says, while Joey, then thirty-one and apparently the younger of the two, was homely, stocky, and a mere five-foot-six or so. "They looked like Laurel and Hardy," Trott says. Jerry wore mod-style dress jeans with colorful silk shirts and lots of jewelry. He rode to his midtown office in a chauffeured limosine, at least until his chauffeur wrecked it in August 1976. He liked to keep good-looking young women nearby. Yet he lived in what Trott calls "a derelict Italian area" in Brooklyn, in a home where "the furniture looked secondhand." Jerry was married and had "two lovely kids," Trott says. But he says Jerry's conversational responses were limited mostly to, "Yeah, yeah, Man. I dig, I dig."

Joey, the stock brokerage executive, dressed conservatively at work. By contrast to Jerry's limo, Joey puttered about in a Volkswagen beetle or a Chevy wagon. By contrast to Jerry's Brooklyn neighborhood, Joey had a modern house in the Brighton section of Staten Island. But, says Trott, it was "a development house—$95,000 and not worth it." Trott describes the decorations as "showy, no-taste. White and gold curtains with ropes. Plastic on the sofa and plastic runners on the carpet." Joey was taking a business course at night to try to complete his B.A. requirements. According to Trott's understanding, he was "manager of the margins desk" at Dean Witter's home office at 2 Broadway. ("Margin" is the term used in the securities industry to refer to credit; because federal laws tightly regulate how much credit can be allowed in the purchase of securities, margins accounts at many firms are handled separately from cash accounts.)

"He functioned normally from nine to five," Trott says. "He had a nice wife and family. But he just didn't look at life like that. All he wanted was to make a big score so the money could go out and earn 'vig'." Vig is short for "vigorish," or the weekly interest that must be paid on a loanshark account without reduction in the principal.

Trott began to find out what "vig" meant from his periodic visits to the New Hope Club, a Staten Island "social club," where the Franzeses hung out. The bigwig in the barroom seemed to be Tutti Franzese, a very large older relative of Jerry and Joey. The first thing Trott remembers noticing about the club is that when the men opened their jackets, they sometimes revealed glimpses of pistols sticking in their belts. The big hit on the jukebox was the theme from *The Godfather*. "Any time the theme from *The Godfather* came on," Trott says, "there was like this feeling of euphoria. He [Joey] mellowed —like he was born to be a crook. Everybody cried in their beer. But they all carried .22 automatics, in their sox, belt, wherever.

"The club is a dillapidated old house. It's very dark. There's a long bar. People came in and asked, 'Did you pick up the vig tonight?' I was told there were prostitutes operating by call from there. The place was full of young girls. They gave them mescaline, cocaine. There was a room with a bed in it, right off the main bar, and couples would go in. When a guy came out, everybody would applaud.

"It's a pathetic thing," Trott says. "They really think they're big Mafia types. Joey and Jerry are trying desperately hard to be accepted into the family. I think Joey basically is a very intelligent man. Jerry, too. But all they say is, 'Yeah, yeah. I dig, I dig.'

"I have a very low opinion of the Mafia," Trott continues. "They've got a bunch of shmucks working for them. I came to this conclusion after just listening to their conversations about vig, and the big show of armament, and screwing around with second-class women. Before I met them I thought they were very, very polished people, with manicured fingernails, Yves St. Laurent suits, driving flashy vehicles, living in nice spots, ruthless, would kill on the spur of the moment. That's what Hollywood made me believe. The newspapers. But I find them loudmouthed, ill-educated, almost illiterate, in very lowlife businesses like garbage pick-up. Frankly, I find it hilarious. *I* could be a bigger crook than they are.

"They're pathological liars," he continues. "They'd call and tell me, 'We need you here [at the New Hope Club] in twenty minutes.' It would turn out to be nothing. Either they're living in a dream world or they're testing all the time." They may indeed have been testing, and apparently Trott passed the test, because in early fall, Joey made his pitch.

By September, 1976, Trott says, "they were constantly coming around at all hours of the day. I realized I had new partners." Then the Franzeses explained to Trott (as specifically recounted in the complaint of a lawsuit he filed) "that Joey prepared computer programs at Dean Witter which controlled the record keeping of . . . customers' accounts. They explained that, because Joey occupied a primary position on the [Dean Witter] margins desk, he could generate accounts for nonexistent customers and negotiate fictitious securities transactions for these 'customers.' Joey assured the Plaintiff [Trott] he was in a position at Dean Witter to effectively control the . . . computer run-outs, and if necessary to destroy files in any fictitious account he generated, so that any illegal disbursements of Dean Witter's funds would either go undetected or, even if detected, could not be traced to him."

Joey told Trott that he had repeatedly managed to defraud Dean Witter's excess funds accounts in the past. (Excess funds are unclaimed accounts. Some persons, for example, may put money in the stock market without telling anyone, then die; after a given time, the money in the account reverts to the brokerage.) Franzese apparently was able to learn from the computer which excess funds accounts were about to pop up for automatic cancellation, and whenever a good $10,000 job appeared, he would empty the account himself before Dean Witter got to it. For obvious reasons, however, there are limits on how much one can steal from unclaimed accounts. So Franzese had thought up a new scheme, and it went like this:

He would create a phony account on the computer, and have the account sell nonexistent securities. He would have Dean Witter write a check to the account representing the proceeds from the make-believe sale, and he would cash the check for himself. Then he would program the computer to forget all about it. Joey even showed Trott a $547,000 check from Dean Witter payable to Globe Ltd., a ficititious account Joey said he set up. "That's how much control I have over Dean Witter," Joey said. Trott was used to handling big checks in his business. If he would help cash this one, he was told, the $47,000 printing debt would be paid, and more.

Trott says he thought at first that Joey was lying, and passed it off. But he repeatedly saw checks drawn on Dean Witter that Joey had taken out, not cashed, and later redeposited. He says Joey didn't try to cash the $547,000 check because Tutti had seen it and was demanding most of the proceeds from the deal for himself.

In October, 1976, Joey came up with a $750,000 check. He wanted Trott to go to Switzerland to cash it with a banker Joey would supply. As a commission salesman, Trott's time was pretty much his own. Trott agreed to go, and says he intended to inform the authorities and abort the scheme. The trip never came off, however. On October 22, 1976, Franzese told Trott that the Swiss banker had backed out and wouldn't cooperate. The $750,000 check had to be either cashed or returned to Dean Witter before the next audit period (or it would look a bit peculiar) so the check was returned.

On the same day, however, a new plot was substituted. Franzese would create an account in the name of Peter B. Simpson, and Trott would be supplied with a set of identification for Simpson. He was to go to a New York coin dealer with this identification, explain that he was in the process of divorce and wanted to hide his assets from his wife. So, Trott would say, he was planning to sell his large portfolio of securities through Dean Witter, and wanted to arrange with the coin dealer for an exchange of the Dean Witter checks for gold Krugerrands. The asset sale was to occur in two waves, each represented by a check. First Trott would swing a Krugerrand deal for about $285,000. And once credibility had been established, they would go for Big Casino—another $2.5 million in one check.

Trott was to open a post office box in Simpson's name. On November 2 or 3, he would receive the check at the box number. He would have it certified at a bank, exchange it for Krugerrands with the coin dealer and be picked up by Joey Franzese in a limosine. They would transport the coins to a bank on Staten Island. On November 1, as recounted in Trott's lawsuit, he "secured the mailing address-post office box number, made the preliminary arrangements with the coin dealer, and advised Joey that 'all systems were go.' "

There was one important thing the Franzeses didn't know about Peter Trott at this point. Several years before, a scandal had occurred at American Airlines. The executive who supervised the airline's in-flight magazine, *The American Way,* was convicted of demanding and taking kickbacks in the awarding of contracts for various things—including printing. And the name of the printing salesman who had turned the executive in to the government and started the whole scandal was, unknown to almost everyone involved, Peter Trott. In that case, Trott had dealt with one of the top agents in the New York office of the IRS, Tony Lombardi.

Now, on the eve of a far bigger swindle, he went again to Lombardi, who has long experience chasing Mafia types, and didn't need much educating about who the Franzeses were. Lombardi explained to Trott that the Dean Witter scheme didn't involve tax dodging as the kickbacks at American Airlines had, and so shouldn't be investigated by the IRS. In a selfless move that not every law-enforcement officer would have made, Lombardi brought his valuable informant to the FBI, which clearly had jurisdiction in the Dean Witter matter.

The check, which totaled $284,981.51, arrived at Trott's post office box at 8:30 A.M. November 3. By 8:45, it was in the hands of the FBI. Agents examined it, and told Trott to have it certified as Franzese had instructed. Trott was able to have this done "in two seconds," he says, at a window at the Irving Trust Company. Two FBI men were loitering one hundred feet away. Then they rigged Trott up with a body tape recorder and microphone, and were listening in when Trott told Franzese the deal was set. Trott arranged additional conversations, so there was plenty of evidence against Joey Franzese when he was arrested the next day, before the Krugerrand deal was ever consummated.

Trott's life was clearly in danger. The FBI and a couple of Justice Department lawyers had told him this on the day he first called Lombardi. They advised him to go into the federal witness relocation program with a new identity and a new job, and he did. As with other persons in the program, all Trott's belongings were shipped first to a warehouse in Washington, and then forwarded to wherever he lives now. He says only half of his possessions arrived. Bills piled up.

Trott figured he had done Dean Witter quite a favor, saving it several million dollars now and who-knows-how-much in the long run. So he went to the big brokerage house for help. "I wasn't looking for a goddamned reward," he says. "All I wanted was for them to split my bills with me. I lost my job. I didn't want a job from Dean Witter, but job *references.*" Dean Witter refused. "He's as guilty as Joey Franzese," a spokesman reportedly told Trott's lawyer. "Just chickened out at the last second."

Trott sued Dean Witter. Dean Witter fought the suit. U. S. District Judge Morris E. Lasker, declining to decide the facts, threw the suit out of court on the ground that even if everything Trott said was true, there was still no law that would allow him to collect from Dean Witter.

But at least Joey Franzese was brought to justice. Faced with the FBI's tape recordings of his conversation with Peter Trott, he pleaded guilty to mail fraud. Federal sources say they also found evidence that Franzese had indeed stolen from Dean Witter's excess funds accounts in the past in amounts of about $10,000 each, just as Trott had said. Dean Witter says it can't confirm or deny this. It objects to the courtroom characterization of Franzese as controlling its computer. Dean Witter says his title was Supervisor of the Foreign/Institutional Margin Department at Operations Headquarters.

U. S. District Judge Charles L. Brieant sentenced Joseph Franzese to probation, and fined him $1,000.

The Mafia's involvement in the securities industry certainly is not limited to stocks. The insurance business has long been heavily infiltrated. Sometimes hoodlums take over agencies, and sometimes whole companies. The Angelo Bruno Mafia family of Philadelphia did both in recent years, through its young financial wizard, Bruno's nephew Michael Grasso, Jr. Grasso and four henchmen operated several insurance agencies that wrote tens of millions of dollars in performance guarantee bonds. That means that the insurance company was guaranteeing various third parties (such as employers of contract labor, or suppliers of materials) that work would be completed and materials would be paid for, even if the bond purchaser went broke or skipped town. Posting such bonds is a common business requirement, particularly in the construction industry. Grasso's agencies wrote these bonds on forms issued by Wisconsin Surety Corp., American Empire Insurance Company, and American Fidelity Fire Insurance Company, but without passing the premiums on to the companies or even notifying the companies that the bonds had been written. Thus either the third parties who accepted the bonds were unprotected, or else the insurance companies were in jeopardy of tremendous losses without knowing it. When the Wisconsin Insurance Department threatened to close Wisconsin Surety down because of its shaky financial condition, Grasso sent in money to take it over and, through an accomplice, ran the company. Scores, maybe hundreds, of small businesses were victims of this racket, not to mention churches, libraries, savings and loan institutions, and the United States Government itself, as well as the state governments of New York, New Jersey, and Pennsylvania and numerous cities and towns, all of which accepted the bonds. There were millions of dollars in claims filed against these bonds, each handled as an individual matter. Based on interviews with attorneys in 1978, it appears that in some instances the insurance companies shelled out on these claims, but that the great bulk of losses—unpaid debts supposedly covered by the bonds—had to be absorbed by innocent victims who took the bonds in good faith.

In March, 1977, Grasso was convicted of mail fraud after a five-week trial. He appealed and a new trial was ordered. In December, 1977, he was convicted again. When he appeared for sentencing before U.S. District Judge Joseph S. Lord III, he was already on five years' probation for an earlier conviction for making false statements to the Federal Housing Administration. Judge Lord wasn't about to give Grasso probation for the multi-million-dollar insurance fraud. He gave Grasso six months, and then set him free pending yet another appeal.

Then there's the commodities business.

Throughout 1977 and on into 1978, every night, Sunday through Thursday, more than ten thousand small businessmen, corporate executives, professionals, and farmers around the United States were receiving surprise telephone calls urging them to put their savings into commodities. The calls came via WATS lines from Miami, Toronto, or one of several other cities. But the caller usually identified himself as an expert from Wall Street. Then he explained how his listener could become richer by investing in coffee, rubber, sugar, or cocoa options or other commodities deals.

Most of those who took the bait, however, didn't become richer. They became poorer—by about $5,000 each, and sometimes much more. Unknown to the prospective customers whose names popped up on a computer list, the phone calls came from firms run by ex-cons, de-licensed stockbrokers, and persons connected with Mafia organizations of such well-known hoods as Matthew "Matty the Horse" Ianniello (boss or underboss of the old Genovese Mafia family) and Charles "Charlie the Blade" Tourine.

Commodities options are a highly speculative kind of security. They are rights to buy or sell a commodity future at a given price on or before a given date. The future, in turn, is a contract for actual delivery or receipt of the commodity at a given price on or before the date. Futures are a common investment, but few reputable brokerage houses handled commodities options at all, and rarely if ever sold them to small investors.

The high-pressure phone calls from shady outfits, however, were raking in millions of dollars a month. An official of the Commodities Futures Trading Commission said it might be "the biggest fraud problem in the country right now." He complained that his agency's effort to stop the Syndicate's sale of commodities options had been hampered by weak laws, frugal budgets, and unsympathetic judges. Other law enforcement officials contended that the CFTC itself was inefficient and therefore responsible.

The one thing sure was that the commodities options salesmen were playing with a stacked deck and for the most part getting away with it. Prospective customers didn't know much about the options. Commodities options hadn't been legal on American exchanges since the 1930s, when Congress outlawed them as too speculative. They were considered vulnerable to manipulation by swindlers. They obviously still are.

But while the options were illegal here, they continued to be traded in London. And American investors, battered by the stock market in the 1970s, were easily persuaded that world-wide inflation would keep commodities prices moving higher. So the London options were pushed in the United States. Most of the deals turned out to be losers, of course. And even winners didn't pay off when the firms marketing them simply pocketed the money instead of investing it in London. To project an aura of respectability, many firms had an office or mailing address in the Wall Street area. But they did their selling from the hinterlands, where costs were lower. Miami and Fort Lauderdale, long centers for various frauds, have many retirees to man the hundreds of WATS lines. By the fall of 1976, authorities in South Florida began to suspect that the Mafia was in the business.

On the surface, the hoods seemed a little out of place as investment advisors to conservative Midwesterners. Matty the Horse Ianniello had built his reputation on being czar of the Times Square combat district; police normally look for his men behind the cash registers of "massage" parlors, topless bars, and porno shops. Yet Philip E. Simon and Joseph Alter—both identified by New York police as long-time Ianniello associates—were dealing with a clientele that doesn't usually come near Times Square. It was still nudity, all right, but while the rest of the Ianniello gang sold naked women, Simon and Alter sold naked options. Naked options, as they are known on Wall Street, are basically just uncollateralized IOUs issued on the credit of the issuer. A legitimate options seller, after taking out his commission, would either use the customer's money to buy an option guaranteed by the London exchange, or would segregate enough money in a special account (varying as the price of the commodity fluctuated) so that a futures contract could be bought any time a customer so instructed. Naked options sellers put all the money in their own pockets.

Simon and Alter had been running a telephone solicitation land sale racket in Miami. Then a court injunction closed the operation down in 1976. So Simon and Alter changed their trade name from Property Resale Service Inc. to Crown Colony Options Ltd. The new business apparently was better than the old. Police say the number of WATS lines was increased to eighty, each manned in two three-hour shifts a night by salesmen cajoling strangers into sending money to an account number (Crown Colony's) at Chase Manhattan Bank (it helps to use a prestigious name).

One Crown Colony customer, for example, was a fifty-five-year-old retired seaman from New York City who has had three heart attacks.* He lost $3,700 on a rubber option. "It was explained to me that it was something like stock options," he says, "and they were guaranteeing that rubber would go up to 80 cents or 90 cents a pound" from about 37 cents. Sure enough, rubber did move up to about 45 cents a pound within the option period, and the seaman had what looked like a modest profit even though he had been overcharged for the option. "I tried to exercise the option, but I couldn't get in touch with the people. They were never in," he recalls. "They said they'd call back, but they never did. Once they get your money, they do what they want with it. I didn't know I was dealing with thieves."

Florida authorities were well aware of what was going on. They knew Simon had a record of three felony convictions. They investigated and learned that Crown Colony was pulling in $1 million a month and that the firm, to say the least, wasn't spending the funds as its customers had been led to expect. But the local authorities say they couldn't close down Crown Colony because neither the options being sold nor the victims were in Florida. The FBI was called in, and so was the CFTC. In June, 1977, the CFTC won an injunction in federal district court in New York that forbade Crown Colony from continuing to engage in fraud. But while the CFTC boasted that it had shut Crown Colony down, Florida officials say the telephone sales office in Miami continued to operate in full swing, and was still doing so many months after the injunctive order. And according to the CFTC's own computer records, Joseph Alter continued to be registered to sell options in the United States, and his firm continued to be listed as Crown Colony.

Many similar firms were springing up at around the same time, some with interlocking personnel. One was Barclay Commodities Corp., whose Las Vegas sales office was frequented, law enforcement officials say, by Ari Leo Fromm, whom they call a close associate of Charlie the Blade's son, Charles "Chuckie Delmonico" Tourine, who himself served time in federal prison for

---

*Names of the victims of this racket have been left out because they appear to be entirely innocent, they never sought publicity, and they cooperated in furnishing information that could prove embarrassing.

interstate transportation in aid of racketeering. Fromm served time in Germany in connection with a securities fraud there, authorities say. Barclay insists that it never "misrepresented or lied to people," and said only one customer had ever complained to the CFTC about Barclay.

I talked to four investors with formal complaints against Barclay pending before the CFTC, and authorities say they are just a tiny portion of those who lost money. Three of the four said they were deceived into buying "sure-fire" options for up to $8,500 each that proved to be losers. One seventy-six-year-old of Casper, Wyoming, says she scored an $11,100 paper profit on a timely $4,400 investment in coffee. But she says that when she called her salesman to cash in, he told her that he had reinvested her earnings—against her specific instructions, she says—in a higher-priced option, which was a loser. After she complained, she says, Barclay sent her a check for about $1,200, the purported difference between the profit from the first option and the cost of the second one. Authorities say this "reinvestment" story is common. They also say the phone peddlers charge 40 to 300 percent over the true price of the option on the London market.

A shoe-store owner in Hoffman Estates, Illinois, contends that the high price he was charged—$8,500—for a coffee option in effect defrauded him of his money. "Coffee was $1.79 a pound," he says. "I thought I was getting $110 for every point it went up"—the salesman's projection, the shoe-store owner says. "But I didn't realize that was just getting back $110 of my original investment. In paying the price I paid, coffee would have to go up to $2.55 before I made one penny." Actual prices for similar options in London ranged from $3,480 to $3,700, less than half what the shoe-store owner paid, according to some reputable New York commodities brokers.

I went to Miami to see some of the telephone solicitation operations for myself. They were easy to find because they advertise in the *Miami Herald* for telephone salesmen. I saw five very similar operations. Each office had one or two cluttered telephone rooms, sometimes with small desks jammed together and sometimes with phones on counters running along the walls where salesmen sat shoulder-to-shoulder. Managers looked to be in their twenties or early thirties. They wore either a T-shirt and cotton pants or fancy leisure suits with gold jewelry. Several managers (thinking I was an applicant for salesman) showed me big piles of "tap cards"—names and addresses they said were purchased from Dun & Bradstreet. These were the customers who would be called. There were printed scripts for the salesmen to read. The wording varied only slightly from shop to shop. On the walls were posted statements for use in rebutting the arguments of reluctant prospects. Most shops had two scripts, a "front" pitch designed to get the prospect to accept an information package in the mail, and a "drive" pitch used a week or two later to get him to send money. I was told that I would have to fill out a CFTC registration form and wait six weeks for clearance before I could "drive" customers, but one shop said I could start "fronting" right away for partial commissions. The CFTC runs applications through the FBI and SEC, and generally approves those that don't turn up criminal or securities violations.

According to law enforcement authorities and former salesmen, prospects are usually referred to as "mooches," and supervisors exhort salesmen with such rallying cries as, "The mooch has your money in his pocket!" Sales figures for each phone man often are posted on a wall, and managers openly say they won't tolerate salesmen who can't bring in at least $20,000 a month. One house is reliably reported to have brought in a prostitute each night at eleven o'clock to give what was announced as "a blow job to the night's top salesman."

Phone time is considered precious. One shop said it keeps two salesmen on hand for every WATS line so that as soon as a light on any telephone button flashes off, someone is ready to use the line while the previous caller is jotting down results. Many WATS lines serve other purposes during the day. Crown Colony's office was occupied daytimes by a telephone wig-selling operation also controlled by the three-time convict and pal of Matty the Horse, Philip E. Simon.

As of June 1, 1978, however, Crown Colony and other options houses may have had to look for something else to sell in the nighttime, too. On that date, the CFTC declared, the sale of commodities options in the United States was once again illegal. While some doubted the ability of the CFTC to enforce this ban, it seemed to have substantial effect. By spring, soon after the ban was announced and several months before it took effect, there were already reports that the telephone sales firms were switching to yet another investment fraud —raw diamonds, usually of a size and quality below investment grade, and at prices far above wholesale cost.

On June 29, 1978, Crown Colony Options Ltd., and its president, Allen Goldschmidt, pleaded guilty in federal court, New York, to criminal charges resulting from the fraudulent sale of London commodity options. The CFTC was pressing a civil suit against Barclay Commodities Corp., also charging fraud and misrepresentations. The suit sought receivership for the company and a return of its profits (allegedly $7.8 million) to the customers. Barclay denied the charges and at this writing no date had been set for a hearing.

PART EIGHT

MISCELLANEOUS INDUSTRIES

1

The Docks

No one volume could hope to cover all the ways in which the Mafia has infiltrated the marketplace. But several industries have been infiltrated by the Syndicate for so long, and play such a large part in everyday life, that they require brief mention here, before this book moves on to a final dramatization of a major corporate surrender to mobsters.

In 1953, Budd Schulberg gave the world a classic exposé of endemic corruption on the big city docks. It was a movie, *On The Waterfront,* a work supposedly of fiction. Nevertheless, it confronted Americans with a stark and accurate view of a world they depend on but seldom see. It showed a tribe of muscular but utterly helpless men, assembling each day at hiring halls to beg work from bosses who were interchangeable, whether they came from the International Longshoremen's Association (the industry's major union) or from the stevedoring companies.

Ten years later, in 1963, the *Saturday Evening Post* sent Schulberg back to the docks to write a piece called "The Waterfront Revisited." In it, he said: "Ties between political and waterfront leaders have always been close. To see how close, you only had to study the guest list of an I.L.A. president's testimonial dinner. There, prominent city officials and judges sat jowl-by-jowl with the 'labor leaders,' shipping executives, stevedore bosses, racketeers, and killers—one big happy family of despoilers gathered together in tribal ceremony, flaunting their power over the harbor and the city it serves and controls."

Schulberg recited in his article a long list of high-ranking union officials and the various crimes they had been convicted of. He rattled off case after case of conflicts of interest, where union officials or their families got rich from the profits of stevedoring companies. And in reference to the open and seemingly well-organized theft of cargo from the docks, he wrote, "The piers of the port are like supermarkets with no checkout counters."

Nevertheless, Schulberg saw a silver lining. For one thing, the New York-New Jersey bistate Waterfront Commission, which had been created largely in response to exposes by Schulberg, newspaperman Malcolm Johnson, and others a decade earlier, had survived political attacks by the union. It had imposed licensing requirements, it had changed the crooked and demeaning hiring hall procedure, and it seemed to be making headway toward correcting other problems. Most of all, Schulberg seemed favorably impressed by Anthony Scotto, the new head of the New York Longshoremen and a growing power in the international union. At first glance, Scotto's background was a little alarming. He was only twenty-eight years old, and got where he was by marrying the daughter of his predecessor, Anthony "Tough Tony" Anastasio. Anastasio was the brother of Albert Anastasia (they spelled the name slightly differently), the widely-known Lord High Executioner of Murder Inc. Anastasio rose to power in the union via the Mafia, and he hand-picked young Tony Scotto as his successor. Scotto had married Anastasio's daughter in 1957, the same year Albert Anastasia was massacred in his Manhattan barber's chair in one of the best-publicized gang slayings of the century. Carlo Gambino—head of Anastasia's Mafia family—had attended the wedding ceremony.

Scotto, however, didn't (and doesn't) look or talk like the popular conception of a mobster. The son of an immigrant laborer, born a few blocks from the union hall, he used the money he earned on the docks as a youngster to put himself through Brooklyn College. He impressed Schulberg as "modern, intelligent, forward-looking." Scotto declined to lead a campaign to clean the Mafia off the docks, Schulberg wrote, only because he wanted "to win by patience and attrition what he could lose through precipitous opposition." Scotto has favorably impressed many other people as well. His union and community influence have been enormous. His switch in support away from another candidate was a large factor in the successful re-election campaign of Mayor John Lindsay. He helped push Hugh Carey to the governorship of New York. In 1976, the campaigning Jimmy Carter came out to the docks to shake his hand. Among many of his men, he has the same kind of tough, caring image that Jimmy Hoffa developed.

In Scotto's case, however, first glances may not have been deceptive after all. In 1969, a Justice Department list of Mafia figures was placed in the Congressional Record, and there on it, as a captain in the Gambino family, was Anthony Scotto. Reports based on Congressional releases identified Scotto's wife as the owner of the Englewood (New Jersey) Country Club, where numerous high-ranking Mafia figures including Thomas Eboli, Eugene and Jerry Catena, and Angelo "Gyp" de Carlo were said to come frequently.

In February, 1970, Scotto, by then an international vice-president of the union as well as its leader in New York, was given a chance to reply to all this in hearings before a New York State Joint Legislative Committee on Crime. When asked whether he was part of the Mafia, he declined to answer on the ground that to do so might incriminate him. He and his wife also declined to answer questions about the country club, and also about CC Lumber Company, a major dockside concern that was about to break into the news. Throughout 1970, the Waterfront Commission held hearings on whether to de-license CC Lumber, the largest marine carpentry company in the Port of New York and New Jersey, on the ground that its major stockholders, Joseph and Leo Lacqua, "lacked good character and integrity." Scotto's wife—Anthony Anastasio's daughter—was Leo Lacqua's niece and Joseph Lacqua's cousin. The facts presented before the commission involved Newbrook Enterprises Inc., a real estate company solely owned by the Lacquas and Mrs. Scotto. Anthony Scotto—whose union represented the Lacquas' waterfront employees—was said to have personally intervened to persuade the King's County LaFayette Trust Company to lend Newbrook Enterprises $245,000. The union deposited substantial funds in the bank, and a bank officer testified that these deposits (and the implicit fear of losing them) were used to obtain numerous extensions of the loan's repayment schedule. Bank records submitted as evidence contained such remarks as, "In view of our relationship with this account and others controlled by Anthony Scotto, the writer agreed to recommend a two months renewal," and, "We have additional related business, namely various ILA accounts controlled by one of the guarantors, Anthony Scotto, averaging approximately seven hundred thousand dollars."

On this evidence, the Waterfront Commission de-licensed CC Lumber. Its decision was upheld by the New York Court of Appeals, which specifically found that Scotto had "breached his fiduciary obligation as a union officer under Section 723 of the Labor Law" and had committed "illegal acts." Scotto has continued to defend himself in the press, saying he hasn't been charged with any criminal violations.

CC Lumber wasn't the only major port enterprise whose owners were linked to the Mafia and which seemed to get special benefits from the Longshoremen's union. Erb Strapping Company, which handles the work of opening and resealing cargo for inspection by customs officials and others, was owned by the boss of bosses Vito Genovese himself. Since his death in 1969, it has continued to do business under the operation of Genovese's family and associates. According to lengthy de-licensing hearings before the Waterfront Commission in 1970, Erb Strapping fell into Mafia control in 1955. It had been founded and was run by Arthur Erb, Sr., until his death in 1945, then was taken over by his son, Arthur Junior, who developed a serious drinking problem. Needing help, he called on his sister, Eleanor Erb Pica, and her husband,

Vincent Pica, a bartender and postal worker. Pica knew just where to go for help—his old neighborhood buddy from childhood, Vito Genovese, who could solve just about any problem. Genovese put Arthur Erb into Alcoholics Anonymous, and put Erb's company into his own pocket. For $245 Genovese received 49 percent of the stock, and became vice-president and a director. When he went to prison on a heroin rap in 1960, he transferred the stock and his hefty salary to his brother Michael Genovese.

The Picas were very close to Vito Genovese socially (according to the evidence at the Waterfront Commission hearings), and when Vito was on trial in 1959 he lived at the Pica home in Teaneck, New Jersey. Mrs. Erb testified that after the famous Apalachin Mafia convention was raided in 1957, she had talked to Vito about it. "He said he attended an innocent barbecue—that's all it was," she said. From 1955 at least through the time the hearings were going on in 1970, Erb Strapping employed nonunion men in violation of its Longshoremen's contract. Its pay scale was not only below the requirements of that contract, but below the requirements of the federal wage and hour law. It paid commercial bribery in the form of a gift membership in the Englewood Country Club (the one said to be owned by the wife of Anthony Scotto, the head of the union). Erb Strapping bought its insurance from a broker named Saverio Eboli—the son of Mob chief Thomas Eboli. And, perhaps most significant, under the Genovese regime it expanded its operations. Erb Strapping opened offices in Philadelphia and Miami. It started offering an "expediting" service, meaning that a company could pay Erb Strapping not to do any physical work of packing or unpacking, but just to see that cargo didn't sit around too long or get sent to the wrong place. On this basis, the business grew from a gross of $100,000 in 1955 to a gross of $1.5 million in 1970.

As in the case of other forms of Mafia corruption, every penny that is stolen on the docks ultimately comes out of the pockets of the people who buy cars, radios, cameras, food, and other items that are imported, or could be. The cost is incalculable.

When the Waterfront Commission began its investigation in 1968, discretion caught up with Michael Genovese and he sold his interest back to the Erbs for $160,000, plus interest, which worked out to payments through 1977 totalling $199,000. Despite his exit, the commission carried out its de-licensing of Erb Strapping. The commission's powers, however, were limited to banning Erb from doing business within one thousand yards of the New York waterfront. In other cities, Erb Strapping kept operating, and in the Port of New York it simply opened doors in a new location in Jersey City just outside the one-thousand-yard limit, where many of its operations can continue. Dun & Bradstreet reports as recently as 1977 indicate that Erb Strapping is still going strong, and that Arthur Erb, Jr. is president, Eleanor Erb Pica secretary-treasurer, and Vincent J. Pica general manager. Dun & Bradstreet says that Erb Strapping declined to disclose its finances.

One major business Erb Strapping has definitely been into recently is meat inspection. Erb Strapping is one of several locations in the New York area approved by the Department of Agriculture where importers or exporters of meat can bring their product to have government inspectors pass judgment on its purity.

By 1977, word had swept the waterfront from New York to New Orleans that a mammoth federal investigation was underway. So many people had been interviewed, and so many grand jury subpoenaes had been issued, that report-ers were able to piece together a pretty good picture of what was going on. This was no narrow probe into a few particular instances of graft. Rather, the Justice Department had determined to try to end criminal control over the importing and exporting of goods from the United States. This enormous undertaking was under the supervision of Justice Department attorneys, as all such investigations are, and scores of investigators and back-up personnel were involved. But sources indicated that to an unusual degree, the waterfront investigation was the work of one FBI agent, Ray Maria, who had developed a reputation as a rackets-buster in Chicago. On the wharfs of the Great Lakes, he ran into the wall of corruption that had been erected by the maritime union leaders, and by the shipping companies whose profits were protected by a monopoly that derived from the corruption. When Maria was transferred to Miami in the mid-seventies, he set about to break the racket. His modest comment now: "A chimpanzee could have put the case together. The facts were there." Nobody did put the case together, however, until Maria.

His investigation took a classic course, beginning with a secrecy phase that included widespread electronic eavesdropping and undercover work, and then, when the secret could no longer be kept, a publicity phase in which tremendous pressure was applied to persuade suspects to become government witnesses. FBI agents serving grand jury subpoenaes once even brought along a casette tape recording, so that the person receiving the subpoena could be stunned on the spot by hearing his own voice in an incriminating conversation. In the background was the long trial in federal court, New York, of Fred R. Field, Jr., vice-president and general organizer of the International Longshoremen's Union. Field was convicted in 1977 of shaking down officers of United Brands Company (formerly United Fruit Company) for $125,000 over several years to ensure the proper handling of the company's Chiquita brand bananas and other imports. He was sentenced to one year in prison and fined $50,000 by U.S. District Judge Morris E. Lasker.

Once Maria's waterfront investigation became public, federal officials openly acknowledged that Anthony Scotto was a key target. At this writing, the government hasn't charged Scotto with a crime, and he has stated that he's done nothing it could charge him with. The rest of the industry, however, hasn't come away so clean. In the first of what were expected to be several indictments coming out of the investigation, eleven executives of stevedoring or other dock-related companies, ten Longshoremen's union officials and one accountant were accused of racketeering through the demand for and payment of hundreds of thousands of dollars in bribes. The 128-page indictment painted a grim picture of how business is done on American docks. Some twenty-one companies operating in the ports of Miami, Mobile, Jacksonville, Savannah, and Charleston were implicated in the gross manipulation of interstate and international commerce. Obviously, from the picture the government drew, you couldn't ship unless you paid off. Among the union leaders indicted were four international officers of the ILA.

The system has survived so many years that it's no longer possible to say who is the most responsible, the shipping companies that buy the special privileges or the union leaders who take payoffs. As in the meat and trucking businesses, the Mafia is often on both sides of the bargaining table. What is clear is that the situation constitutes a racket that robs us all, and despite the current investigation it's still going on.

2

Clothing

One hot afternoon in the summer of 1977, I stood on the corner of Eleventh Avenue and Twenty-fourth Street in Manhattan, on the fringe of the West Side area known as the Garment Center, and watched what seemed to be a very busy and modern trucking operation. A constant stream of large trucks pulled away from the loading docks packed with boxes that evidently contained the shirts and pants and dresses that would clothe America. The docks looked just built, and most of the trucks freshly painted. It was as spic and span a trucking operation as I had ever seen. Except for one thing: who controlled it.

I had been sent to the corner by a trucking company owner who was helping me and another reporter get started on what was supposed to be a long and thorough investigation for the *Wall Street Journal* into Mafia control in the garment center. "Six months ago, that was a nothing building," the trucking executive—call him Ed—told me in an angry voice. "Within a month they put a million dollars into it. It seemed like it went up overnight." Who was *they*, I wanted to know. "Two Gambino sons in their middle or late twenties," Ed said.

Ed's company hauled fabrics. For long-distance haulers the trips to New York from the southern mills were plagued by the normal problems that befall companies dealing with Teamster truckers—heavy payments to corrupt pension funds, and the threat of competitors' getting sweetheart contracts. But at least the long-distance haulers could go after customers as they saw fit, and make a living as relatively independent businessmen. At the doors of the metropolitan area, however, all that stopped. Somewhere near the Hudson River, either in New Jersey or Manhattan, the cargos had to be turned over to the Mafia. The fabric was left at a warehouse, to be picked up by a Mafia-approved truck for delivery to garment factories that had no choice about which trucks would bring in the fabrics or which trucks would carry out the finished goods, or how much the fees would be. Trucking was just one of many tools the Mob has used to control the garment industry, but in the 1970s it is probably the most important one.

Everything Ed said jibed with what others had said and written for years. It tended to confirm the opinions of the editors at the *Journal* that it was time for a new look at the industry. The figures who ran the garment center back in the 1930s were almost legendary. Lepke Buchalter died in the electric chair. The mere mention of the name of Buchalter's brutal pal, Gurrah Shapiro, could still wipe the smile from the lips of old-timers. Johnny Dio cut his teeth as a garment center terrorist. Dio's crime boss, the late Thomas "Three Fingers Brown" Lucchese owned some garment factories and was a familiar figure in the district. So was the Genovese family underboss Thomas "Tommy Ryan" Eboli until his murder in 1972. Ed even pointed out the coffee shop on Thirty-sixth Street near Seventh Avenue where Eboli did business.

Nowadays (I knew from my work in the meat industry) Johnny Dio's brother and partner Thomas Dioguardi was reachable at a garment factory he ran. Mob boss Russell Bufalino had long been in the apparel business in his native Pennsylvania (as was Lucchese) and was said also to have extensive interests in the New York garment center. But the new kingpin in the district was said to be Thomas F. Gambino, the son of don Carlo Gambino and the cousin of the other Thomas Gambino who keeps watch over the frozen clam and Italian cheese markets. The Thomas Gambino in the garment center carries a double-edged sword. He is not only Carlo Gambino's son, he is Thomas Lucchese's son-in-law.

A few months before I went to see Ed, I had talked with the father of a friend of mine, an important figure in the New York area garment business until his retirement a few years ago. Call him Sam. Sam said that Gambino had been involved with a dress factory in the garment district, and more recently had moved into dominance of garment center trucking with the help of Hy Ruff, a businessman who had agreed to take Gambino and his brother Joseph on as partners. (Records later verified this.) In the previous few years Ruff had taken over several garment industry trucking companies, Sam said. One company he mentioned was Greenberg's Express, originally of Newark but now moved into New York. The name "Greenberg's Express" was painted onto many of the trucks I saw pulling into and out of the trucking depot at Twenty-fourth Street and Eleventh Avenue. According to Sam, Ruff became a leader in the association that controls garment center trucking, and Tom Gambino showed up personally at meetings with a "bodyguard."

Sam explained how corruption in the center worked. He said the monopolistic practices of the Mob-controlled "associations" went far beyond control of truck traffic, and into the basic work patterns in the industry. Conveniently for the Mafia, the work of manufacturing garments is divided among two kinds of firms, each of which performs a distinct but essential role. Some firms, known as jobbers, design the clothes, buy the cloth, and ultimately sell the clothes to retailers. But for the important middle step—the sewing—they send the cloth out to other firms, known as contractors. Thus contractors employ the most labor, while jobbers make the most decisions. Lucchese and Gambino both were jobbers, Sam explained.

Long ago, the International Ladies Garment Workers' Union put a clause in its contracts requiring jobbers to register a select number of "permanently designated" contractors, and forbidding jobbers to switch from one contractor to another unless there is extreme provocation, which has to be proven. One typical clause reads, "Dress production shall be distributed equitably only among permanent dress contractors. An employer shall have the right to discharge a designated permanent contractor for the following reasons only: (a) general poor workmanship, (b) general late deliveries, (c) general inefficiency which unreasonably increases the Employer's cost of production."

The union rationale for this handcuffing of individual entrepreneurs was to stabilize the jobs of workers, most of whom were employed by contractors. But such restraints obviously play perfectly into the hands of the Mob. Upstart companies are prevented from luring customers away from competitors by offering better service or lower prices. And, as with the sweetheart contracts in the trucking business, the Mafia can hold power through its reputation for being able to obtain favors. Sam, for example, told a story about a friend of his who did contracting work for a jobbing concern owned by Thomas Lucchese (known in the garment trade as Tommy Brown). Lucchese wanted to switch to another contractor, for reasons of his own. This was against the rules. But a goon was sent around to Sam's friend to warn that if he tried to enforce the ILGWU contract and stop the switch, he would find real trouble. Sam said his friend agreed to back off. The union, of course, didn't complain either.

Sam also told about the union local that represents garment center trucking employees (other sources had told me about it when I was researching the Teamsters Union). The local is affiliated not with the Teamsters, but rather with the ILGWU. The distinction, however, seems to be a fine one. Sol C. Chaikin, the president of the ILGWU, has been quoted as saying, "We have never been able to control 102." The Teamsters and the Mafia, however, at times seem to have had better luck.

The longtime manager of Local 102 was Sam Berger, a close friend of Johnny Dio and other Teamster-connected mobsters. In 1957, Berger was indicted for conspiracy and extortion, and the ILGWU insisted he resign from his job for taking the Fifth Amendment (he was eventually acquitted on that charge). He found other work—as executive director of the Master Truckmen's Association, the group of trucking employers that negotiates with Local

102. A vacancy had conveniently been created in the Master Truckmen's job when the incumbent was murdered. The job switch from one side of the bargaining table to the other presented few conflicts for Berger, because, from all appearances, he was still taking orders from the same bosses—Johnny Dio and Tommy Lucchese. In 1964 he was one of a group including Lucchese family member James Plumeri and two Teamster officials who cut up a $250,-000 kickback on a $1.5 million loan from the Teamsters' Central States, Southeast and Southwest Areas pension fund. In 1969 Berger was convicted of conspiracy in that matter, which also involved officials of the Teamsters and the International Brotherhood of Production, Maintenance, and Operating Employees. He was sentenced to five years in prison by U.S. District Judge Walter R. Mansfield. Berger died a few years later.

His long-time assistant in the Master Truckmen's Association, Frank Wolf, succeeded Berger in running the association. In 1976, Wolf was acquitted by a jury of federal charges of extortion, along with his friend and co-defendant Matthew "Matty the Horse" Ianniello, a top leader in the Genovese Mafia family.

In early summer, 1977, news articles carried on the wire services and in several major newspapers seemed to confirm much of what Sam and Ed had said about the Gambino family's seizure of power. Two top officials of the Interstate Commerce Commission staff were suspended in connection with an ongoing grand jury investigation into organized crime influence on ICC decisions. Specifically cited were decisions to approve and expand the authority of two trucking operations—Greenberg's Express and Consolidated Carrier Corp.—whose officers were listed as Hyman Ruff, president; Thomas Gambino, vice-president; and Joseph Gambino, secretary-treasurer. The articles also noted that ICC records showed Ruff and Tommy Gambino as owners of several other trucking firms. As far as can be ascertained, none of the three men has ever been charged with or convicted of a crime.

But the names of the firms mentioned in those articles were the same names I saw printed on the sides of the trucks entering and leaving the loading docks at Twenty-fourth Street and Eleventh Avenue. According to Ed, the Gambinos' garment center trucks brought goods to the way-station I was watching, where other Gambino trucks carried them either to area retailers or to designated warehouses where they could be transferred back to the outside world of competitive interstate trucking companies for shipment out of the area.

The cost to the public of this kind of arrangement—the amount added on to the price of clothing in the United States—had to be enormous. The workmanship of contractors who know that within wide limits they can't be replaced must surely take its effect on quality. And, so, the performance of trucking companies that have similar protection—not to mention the enormous opportunities for carefully planned "hijackings" that such a system allows for (in other words, trucking companies can steal the goods they are carrying, sell them on the black market, and cover for the loss by reporting an armed hold-up).*

Having seen and heard all this, I started going to law enforcement sources to find out what they knew. I began with a police officer who had contributed information for earlier stories and who I knew had done some work on Project Cleveland, a joint federal-state undercover investigation into the garment center in 1973. An ex-convict named Herman Goldfarb had been set up in a garment center trucking business with federal money. His office and his person were wired for sound, and he was assigned to trap mobsters in their extortionate ways. The operation was closed down prematurely amidst great controversy. A top city cop, a prominent journalist, and Goldfarb himself openly charged that there had been mismanagement by William I. Aronwald, first assistant and then chief of the Manhattan office of the federal strike force against organized crime and racketeering, who had directed the project. The major cases the project was supposed to produce—including the one mentioned earlier against Frank Wolf and Matthew Ianniello—ended in acquitals (although evidence gathered almost as a byproduct of the garment center investigation did result in the 1978 pension fund kickback conviction of Teamster boss Anthony "Tony Pro" Provenzano).

While Project Cleveland didn't clean up the garment center, however, it did corral a lot of valuable intelligence about what went on there. And the information—as relayed by the trial evidence and by the officials I talked to—went right along with what I had heard from Ed and Sam.

The *Journal's* investigation of the garment center was supposed to keep two reporters busy for months. Instead, the investigation lasted about four days. It took only that long for us to become convinced we were following a well-worn trail. Every law enforcement source I was talking to apparently also had been talking for months to three reporters from *Women's Wear Daily,* who were on the verge of breaking a mammoth series of exposés. Our team decided to wait and see what *WWD* would come up with. It turned out to pretty much pre-empt the field. The three reporters—Tony DeStefano, Thomas Moran, and Allen F. Richardson—produced a most imposing series of articles that began on the paper's front page every day for two weeks under the heading, "The Mafia: S.A. [Seventh Avenue]'s Silent Partner." It began August 22, 1977, with the news that the Cosa Nostra—our thing—"could call New York's multibillion dollar apparel industry their thing, because virtually every piece of clothing made here is touched by the hands, or the money, or the influence of organized crime."

The articles identified at least twenty firms in the garment center as being under the control of Syndicate figures. The figures named were mostly familiar

---

*Neither Greenberg's Express nor Consolidated Carriers has ever been accused of such fake hijackings.

—Bufalino, Gambino, Lucchese, Eboli, Dioguardi, Plumeri—but the detail was staggering.

"Most of the legitimate businessmen in the industry simply accept the mob as they accept traffic-clogged streets and high taxes," the articles said. "Leading New York banks and textile firms apparently have no qualms about dealing with mob-controlled firms, and major department stores don't mind buying from them. Local garment manufacturers and union officials often sit down with mobsters in the discreet darkness of the Mannequin Restaurant on West Thirty-sixth Street or in the Mini-Pub on West Thirty-fifth Street and amiably discuss the day's race results or late deliveries from a contractor. Others, if they're well-connected but having problems with things like late deliveries, will ask favors from powerful Mafiosi such as Frank Tieri. . . . But there is always a price.

" 'If you ask for certain favors, one of the conditions is that you put one or two names on your payroll,' explained New York City Police Detective Gerry Panza, who worked undercover as a coat manufacturer for over a year. 'Those persons don't do any work. They may come in from time to time. Eventually they may start telling you how to run your business.' "

The articles contained extensive examples of how overall Mob control in the garment center facilitates loansharking, shakedowns for "labor peace" and professional truck hijackings.

The articles also explained how the industry avoids antitrust prosecutions under its no-competition arrangements. Years ago the government started making inquiries about possible antitrust violations in trucking, and the industry simply stopped keeping written logs of which truckers were wedded to which companies. Now the arrangements are simply "gentlemen's agreements. They are no longer put in writing."

One trucker was quoted as saying, "When I first joined the association I asked if I had to register my accounts and they said, 'No, we don't do that any more. It's illegal.' "

3

Beer, Wine, and Liquor

"Of all the crimes that e'er have been, sellin' whiskey is the greatest sin," begins a folksong from Indiana. And so many people have seemed to believe. From the excise taxes that led to the Whiskey Insurrection of George Washington's day, through the bootlegging era of the 1920s, Americans have considered booze a special business, and have encumbered it with special and often hypocritical laws. And partly because of such laws, the liquor business has been especially susceptible to corruption. Its history is checkered with scandals and there has been recent evidence of corruption from coast to coast.

From 1974 to 1977, New Yorkers got a better-than-usual picture of exactly how racketeering in the industry works, because a bright and ambitious young politician, Michael Roth, was appointed head of the State Liquor Authority. Roth had determined to make a name for himself as a corruption fighter (at this writing he is campaigning for election as state attorney general on his record with the liquor authority). Roth didn't send anybody to jail, and he didn't close down any major operations. But given his limited number of investigators, and given the political priorities under which the investigators had to be in go-go bars much of the time making sure the dancers all wore pasties on their nipples, Roth did a remarkable job of exposing real wrongdoing. He levied some substantial fines and tub-thumped for changes in the anti-competitive price-fixing laws that encourage the corruption.

According to Roth's charges, the biggest brand name success stories in the industry in the 1970s were the beneficiaries of big kickback operations. Until the corruption story broke, Madison Avenue had been taking all the credit for catapulting Schaefer beer and Dewar's White Label scotch from also-rans to number one in their fields in the New York market. But the F. & M. Schaefer Corp. admitted to the liquor authority that it made $160,000 in "questionable" payments to "numerous" retailers for pushing the beer, and agreed to pay a $50,000 fine. Schenley Industries Inc., a subsidiary of Rapid-American Corp., was accused of paying $500,000 in illegal kickbacks from 1973 to 1975, the very years that its White Label brand was overtaking J & B and Cutty Sark as the number one selling scotch whiskey in the state by most estimates. At this writing, Schenley has declined to comment and the charges haven't been settled. Accused with Schenley were five independent whiskey distributing companies through whom the payments were allegedly passed.

It is the distribution network that appears to handle the corruption and to tie the industry to the Mafia. When Prohibition was repealed in 1933, state governments considered applications for liquor distribution licenses. And the people best prepared to enter the business were the ones already in it—illegally. Says Roth of today's big distributors, "All those guys were in bootlegging. That's how they got into the wholesale liquor business."

Probably the largest wine and liquor distributor in the New York area is Peerless Importers Inc. of Brooklyn, which has subsidiaries throughout the state and in Connecticut, and which was one of the distributors accused by the liquor authority of handling kickbacks for Schenley. Peerless's principal owner and president, Antonio Magliocco, is the brother of Joseph Magliocco, who was caught by law enforcement authorities at the famous Mafia gathering in Apalachin, New York, in 1957. Joseph Magliocco, underboss of the old Joseph Profaci Mafia family and close to Joseph Bonanno, lost his beer distribution license after the Apalachin affair when the liquor authority ruled he was "not a fit and proper person." His brother Antonio, however, has enjoyed a much better public reputation, even though New York Police Department files list Anthony, or Antonio, Magliocco of Brooklyn as a member of the Colombo (formerly Profaci) Mafia family, and he was identified as such in the press during a 1972 furor over mobsters in business in New York City. His name also appears on the Justice Department's 1964 and 1970 lists of organized crime figures.

This notoriety has brought heavy investigative attention to Antonio Magliocco, but so far, the liquor authority emphasizes, the repeated investigations in recent years haven't turned up evidence that would justify criminal charges. During the Prohibition era, Antonio Magliocco was arrested six times for possessing and transporting liquor, maintaining a nuisance, and disorderly conduct. Each charge was dismissed in court. In recent years, Magliocco's companies have suffered several license suspensions and fines for kickbacks and other pricing violations. But there have been no charges against him personally. "If we could get something on Magliocco we could all be heroes," says one investigator.

In 1977, Brandeis University held a testimonial dinner at the Plaza Hotel in New York for Magliocco, and named him Brandeis "Man of the Year," a designation that has been awarded to a long line of reputable industrialists. To anyone's recollection, Magliocco was the first such honoree whose name appeared on the Justice Department's lists of organized crime figures. But a spokesman for the university said, "Being on lists, that's not really the thing. We're going on his charitable record. They [the Magliocco family] have been among the most charitable people in the wine and spirits industry—not only for Brandeis but all over."

Joseph Magliocco died of an apparent heart attack in 1963, although a Mafia colleague once remarked in front of a hidden FBI microphone that Magliocco had probably been poisoned. According to some published accounts, Magliocco, shortly before he died, had plotted the murder of some rival Mob bosses. At the time of his death, according to the New York State Commission of Investigation, Joseph Magliocco owned stock in two liquor distributing companies that now are subsidiaries of Peerless, and in a real estate company that now is Peerless's landlord.

Among Antonio Magliocco's apparent charitable activities, besides his gifts to Brandeis, are his efforts to help ex-convicts find jobs. A Treasury Department agent in 1970 found twelve employees at Peerless's Brooklyn operation who had recently been convicted of felonies or serious misdemeanors, including grand larceny, receiving stolen goods, possessing counterfeit money, possessing heroin, possessing burglary tools, and felonious assault. Some were repeat offenders who apparently were hired fresh from jail. The Treasury agent, along with the FBI and New York police, was investigating a rash of hijackings of trucks carrying liquor from the Brooklyn wharves to the Peerless warehouse. At least six trucks, each carrying nearly $100,000 of merchandise, were hijacked in an identical manner within a few blocks of each other in broad daylight, and so many other truckloads were hijacked under other circumstances that the agent said he couldn't give a total. In six cases, the driver was taken at gunpoint from his truck near Meeker and Henry streets by men he could identify later only as "white," and was dropped off by car unharmed in another part of the city. In each case the hijackers pinpointed loads of expensive, major label merchandise. Believing the hijackings were staged, a federal grand jury indicted three Peerless trucking employees for tampering with the seals on their trailers. But a trial judge directed a verdict of acquittal for lack of evidence in one case, and the other two cases were dropped. No charges were filed against Peerless or Magliocco.

Another Treasury agent did an inventory check of Peerless's warehouse in 1970 and reported "a shortage of sixty thousand gallons," but no charges were filed. In 1972, the liquor authority warned Peerless that it was keeping inadequate books and records that made it "not possible to reconcile" the large quantities of liquor bottles reported broken or destroyed on the one hand, with federal tax stamp numbers or individual retail accounts on the other. The warning said action would be taken if there were further incidents, but apparently there were none.

The unions representing many of the workers in the liquor industry also have had long connections with unsavory characters. The Distillery, Rectifying, Wine, and Allied Workers International Union of America was the product of the same minds that created the New York area butchers' union—Little Augie Pisano and George Scalise. In 1955, together with union official Sol Cilento, they were indicted in a $300,000 kickback scheme with distillery workers' and liquor salesmen's union insurance funds. The indictments were overturned on the unusual legal ground that "a trustee of a union welfare fund . . . is not chargeable with a crime for violating his trust, even though he simultaneously be an officer of the union."

Many salesmen complain that their union is too cooperative with employers. Their chief evidence for this charge is their longstanding complaint that the union allows them to be the fall guys in the kickback racket, the ones who have to pass the dirty money in order to keep their jobs and who have to cheat on their income taxes (which many of them privately admit doing) to cover up for the lost money.

Because of the prejudices mentioned at the beginning of this chapter, liquor is probably the most regulated legitimate business in the country. Kickbacks and other rackets that are rampant in the industry often work just because of these regulations. In New York, for example, it is illegal to sell liquor for less than a 12 percent mark-up over the wholesale price, which in turn is regulated by law according to the basic price posted by the distiller (for domestic brands) or importer (for foreign ones). Most state governments fix liquor prices to some extent. Thus actual retail prices usually are fixed by law (although some stores can successfully charge more than the legal minimum because of an exclusive location or some other advantage). It takes kickbacks and other rackets to keep price competition alive.

Salesmen carry cash from store to store in satchels to give kickbacks to retailers. Wholesalers ship retailers free loads of whiskey, then account for the missing whiskey by reporting a warehouse robbery. Wholesale firms lard their rosters of salesmen with persons who are doing other work but whose accounts are credited with tremendous sales commissions; this leads other salesmen to suspect that in some cases the commissions are really cover-ups for illegal kickbacks to retailers who patronize these special sales accounts. For example, one large wholesale firm run by the son of a convicted Prohibition era bootlegger attributed an indicated annual sales volume of at least $1.5 to $2 million to the account of a "salesman" who really was working fulltime as a reporter for the *New York Daily News.* The reporter's brother-in-law was a vice-president at the wholesale firm. Another big commission man is by trade an author; his father and uncle own large-volume retail liquor stores that do their ordering through him. Yet another big earner is the wife of the general manager of one of the city's busiest liquor stores.

It's questionable whether any of these persons would be padding payrolls as "salesmen" if the law allowed liquor producers and distributors to price their goods as the market indicated and to give volume discounts as the savings justified such discounts. But when it comes to beer, wine, and liquor, the law forbids the kind of pricing mechanisms that other industries take for granted. Defenders of the law argue that the introduction of price competition would wipe out a lot of mom-and-pop liquor stores, unfairly robbing the owners of their life savings, which they have invested in costly state liquor licenses. But the current system is really rooted in the notion that liquor is a "special" business, because it is basically immoral, and therefore that price competition would be unseemly. Surely the mind of man could devise some system for compensating mom-and-pop owners who would want to turn back their liquor licenses rather than face price competition. It would not be illogical to suppose that the chief support for the current system really comes from the Syndicate and the politicians friendly to it; at least the Syndicate seems to be the chief beneficiary.

A change in the law probably still wouldn't force the racketeers out of the business, at least not overnight. But it would almost certainly make life more difficult for them, and easier for law enforcement. It would create a much more meaningful distinction between the good guys and the bad guys in the industry. Right now, the system of minimum pricing and kickbacks, with its heavy overhead for graft, keeps prices to consumers artificially high. It causes some brands to be pushed at the expense of others. And it robs the public tax coffers of millions of dollars a year (because those who get the kickbacks almost certainly don't report them, and those who give them often doctor their own tax returns or expense accounts to reflect their true net income).

Several large wholesale liquor firms in the New York area have distributed printed lists among their salesmen showing how much money was available to be kicked back illegally to retailers for purchases of various amounts and brands of liquor. One list, for example, showed forty-two brands of wine and liquor, the minimum number of cases that must be bought to qualify for a rebate, and the percentage of the price (or in some cases the dollar amount per case) to be rebated. Mickey Sabatino, a salesman at Magliocco's Peerless Importers, took a look at this list and said that he and hundreds of other salesmen for several major firms have received lists just like it. He said kickbacks are higher on some brands because they are being pushed harder than others. The one list showed 1½ percent for a kickback on purchases of Cutty Sark or Black & White scotch, but 5 percent for purchases of White Horse. "This is done by the distiller," Sabatino said. (He uses salesman's lingo; technically, in the case of scotch, it's the importer.) "Somebody comes over and says, 'We're stuck with White Horse. We have to get rid of a thousand cases. We'll give you a little extra for it.' "

William Rosenthal, controller of Peerless, denied that his company had issued the particular list in question, but acknowledged that Peerless periodically gives its salesmen lists of "bonuses" that will be awarded for selling certain brands. "Unless you give bonuses from time to time, certain items get lost in the shuffle," he said. "We want the salesman to know it will be worth his while to push this particular item." He says the bonuses are perfectly legal, and appear on the salesmen's checks. The question, of course, is whether the salesmen kick the money back to buyers. Said Michael Roth when he was running the liquor authority, "I don't know for a fact that the sales managers tell the salesmen to give back [to the retailers] the point and a half [1½ percent]. But you don't have to. He knows he's got to meet his quota."

Some salesmen, having been promised their names wouldn't be used, admitted they give kickbacks. Some retailers, given the same promise, admitted they receive kickbacks. But for a long time during the investigation, persons in the industry who *would* be quoted denied that kickbacks existed. E. Vincent O'Brien, vice-president and general counsel for Joseph E. Seagram & Sons Inc., which makes many brands and imports many others including White Horse, said his company absolutely forbids it.

Finally, in 1976, the heat got too strong. In addition to what Roth was doing in New York, Matthew Feldman, the president of the New Jersey state senate, pleaded guilty to federal charges of having bribed buyers on behalf of the whiskey wholesale company he was vice-president of. The investigations, expanding now to two states, smoked out the head of the liquor salesmen's union for what must be one of the most extraordinary performances in the whole history of the labor movement. Joseph Matranga, longtime president of Local 2 of the union, which is affiliated with the Distillery, Rectifying, Wine, and Allied Workers International, AFL-CIO, called a meeting of his twelve hundred members in a dingy Queens boxing emporium. Nearly one thousand salesmen attended. So did the executives of several wholesale firms. The air was thick with the odor of cheap cigars.

Matranga—after years of complaints by his members and denials by the union that there was a real problem—openly acknowledged that "almost everybody" in his union was involved in a "filthy, immoral" kickback racket. He then announced that the racket would end immediately. Henceforth, he said, wholesalers would be required to sign monthly affidavits disavowing "kickbacks, inducements or rebates" including any form of free goods. Matranga said his own members would be required to sign similar monthly affidavits. "Any wholesalers who won't go along will be picketed," the union's attorney added. "Beautiful, beautiful," the membership shouted back, applauding loudly. Then Matranga told his membership, "I directly order you all" to stop the kickbacks.

Calls to several wholesale companies, however, still failed to produce any acknowledgment that there were kickbacks—or any enthusiasm about Matranga's affidavits. And the New Jersey Wine and Spirit Wholesalers Association denied that bribery was commonplace there, as Matthew Feldman, the president of the state senate, said it was when he pleaded guilty.

U.S. District Judge Frederick B. Lacey fined Feldman $1,000 and didn't even bother to put him on probation. Feldman stayed in office. Governor Brendan Byrne, a fellow Democrat and the chief law enforcement officer of the state, defended Feldman on television with the incredible statement that "We all commit about the same amount of crime. It's all a question of what kind and whether we get caught." (Byrne said he was quoting an old law professor.) The New Jersey investigation never followed through beyond the Feldman case.

In New York, Roth, a lame duck Republican appointee in a Democratic state administration, left office with his clean-up work far short of completion. When Roth's successor, a Democrat who had previously administered veterans' affairs, was appointed, the main thing the *New York Times* could find to say about him was that various legislators were criticizing the appointment as a "political favor" to the Queens Democratic organization. Aides to the new man confided in 1978 that he had a weak knowledge of the industry, but was working hard to learn about it. So far, however, there have been no new actions announced, and there's been no indication that life in the industry is any different.

PART NINE

THE CORPORATION–
The Anatomy of Bribe

1

Steinman

On April 25, 1970, a scruffy, half-literate little manipulator named Moe Steinman shuffled into a suite at the elegant Stanhope Hotel overlooking Central Park in Manhattan, pulled the blinds, and within a few hours assumed a stature that even the most celebrated racketeers in history hadn't dreamed of.

Other mobsters had gone only partway. Gurrah Shapiro had controlled the garment center, and Joe Bonanno the Brooklyn dairy products district. Steinman had also gone partway—he had dominated the Fourteenth Street meat market. Some racketeers before Steinman had persuaded the heads of rival Mafia families to unite behind a single organized shakedown system. Thus had Steinman united racketeers from three powerful Mafia families, Genovese, Gambino, and Lucchese, and become the meat industry front for all of them. Other racketeers, before Steinman, had achieved nationwide control over certain specialty products, like mozzarella cheese, or over an atomized industry, like trucking.

But on this day, Moe Steinman, as a front for the Mafia, would achieve what no one else had achieved, even in the days of Al Capone or Lucky Luciano. Moe Steinman, who had risen from the gutter only by his lack of scruples, would tighten his fist around one of the biggest corporations in the country, a corporation that dominated a major national industry. It was an industry that almost every American depended on almost every day. It was an industry—unlike trucking—that was clothed with all the garments of Wall Street respectability.

Into this darkened room at the Stanhope Hotel, Moe Steinman would summon Currier J. Holman, founder and head of Iowa Beef Processors Inc., by far the largest meat company in the world. Then, as now, Iowa Beef's name was listed in the upper levels of the Fortune 500 ranking of largest corporations. Its shares were traded on the New York Stock Exchange. Its financing was handled by a syndicate of the biggest banks in the country. Then, as now, its sales were in the billions of dollars, and its food was on the tables of millions of Americans from Bangor to San Diego.

And Currier J. Holman, the tall, graying Notre Dame alumnus and widely-recognized business genius who organized and ran this mammoth operation, was to come crawling all the way from the Great Plains, bringing with him his co-chairman, his executive vice-president, and his general counsel, all at the beck of a foul-mouthed alcoholic hoodlum.

Iowa Beef, though founded only in 1961, already in 1970 dominated the meat industry the way few other industries are dominated by anyone. Since then, in partnership with Steinman and his family and friends, Iowa Beef has grown more dominant still. It was as if the Mafia had moved into the automobile industry by summoning the executive committee of General Motors, or the computer industry by summoning the heads of IBM, or the oil industry by bringing Exxon to its knees. Moe Steinman and the band of murderers and thugs he represented had effectively kidnapped a giant business. Its leaders were coming to pay him the ransom, a ransom that turned out to be both enormous and enduring.

As a result of the meeting in the darkened suite at the Stanhope that day in 1970, Iowa Beef would send millions of dollars to Steinman and his family under an arrangement that continued at least until 1978. After the meeting, millions more would go to a lifelong pal of Steinman and his Mafia friends, a man who had gone to prison for using slimy, diseased meat in filling millions of dollars in orders (he bribed the meat inspectors) and who wound up on Iowa Beef's board of directors. Consequent to the meeting in the Stanhope Hotel, Iowa Beef would reorganize its entire marketing apparatus to allow Steinman's organization complete control over the company's largest market, and influence over its operations coast-to-coast. In 1975, Iowa Beef would bring Moe Steinman's son-in-law and protégé to its headquarters near Sioux City to run the company's largest division and throw his voice into vital corporate decisions. But, most important, a mood would be struck in the Stanhope that day —a mood of callous disregard for decency and the law. Iowa Beef would proceed to sell its butcher employees out to the Teamsters union, to turn its trucking operations over to Mafia-connected manipulators, and to play fast and loose with anti-trust laws.

Because of their hold on Iowa Beef, the racketeers' control of other segments of the meat industry would expand and harden. And as a result of all this, the price of meat for the American consumer—the very thing Currier Holman had done so much to reduce—would rise. Meyer Lansky once said that the Syndicate was bigger than U. S. Steel. When Iowa Beef Processors caved in on that April day in 1970, the Syndicate, as far as the meat industry was concerned, *became* U. S. Steel.

Moe Steinman is not impressive to look at. He is of average height, but seems shorter. He isn't fat, but there's something overweight about him. He has a sad, doberman-like face, that is pockmarked and ruddy like a drunk's. Steinman is often drunk. His clothes are sometimes flashy, but seldom tasteful. He is appallingly inarticulate when he talks. But everybody knows what he means.

Detective Bob Nicholson once stood near the bar of the Black Angus restaurant and saw a slightly tipsy Moe Steinman point his stubby finger at John "Johnny Dio" Dioguardi, the foremost active labor racketeer in the Lucchese Mafia family. "You listen here, Johnny," Steinman said. "You don't tell me how to run my business. I tell you." The boast rocked Nicholson (and Dio may not have cared for it, either). Ultimately, the Mafia retained its power, through its violent system of justice. But the fact that Steinman was allowed to get away with such bragadoccio—and he did it repeatedly—showed just how indispensable he had become to the Mafia's designs on controlling the marketplace. There is a story in the industry that once in the late 1960s Steinman brazenly cheated Peter Castellana, a relative and high aide of boss Carlo Gambino. Steinman is said to have short changed Castellana on the sale of a load of hijacked turkeys. And nobody raised a finger.

Industry sources also talk about a speech Steinman gave in 1970 at a retirement party for a Grand Union supermarket executive. The party, naturally enough, was at the Black Angus, which was owned by a retired executive from the rival Bohack chain, who had acquired it from the family of the retired head of the butchers' union. While the departing Grand Union official was guest of honor at the party, the center of attention was Johnny Dio, who also was about to depart, in his case for prison, where he was being sent as a result of illegal deals in the kosher meat industry. Steinman, it's said, stood up before the assembled guests, openly recalled how close he was to Dio, and assured everyone that he personally would "take care of the business" while Dio was away.

Only once, in the mid-1960s, is Steinman said to have suffered Mob disfavor. There are reliable reports that he was beaten up once in a supermarket warehouse, and hospitalized. Nobody who is willing to talk seems to know for sure what the beating was about.

Bob Nicholson had been impressed the first time he heard Steinman's name, back in 1964 in the Merkel horsemeat scandal. When Merkel's boss, Nat Lokietz, wanted a connection in government so he could bribe his way out of trouble, he had called Moe Steinman. Steinman didn't arrange the bribe meeting—Tino De Angelis did—because Steinman was out of town. But after the bribery attempt backfired, Lokietz went to Steinman again in a last-ditch effort to keep Merkel afloat. In the spring of 1965, Steinman had met with Lokietz at the Long Island home of a Big Apple supermarket meat buyer, who acted as intermediary. The buyer was in Steinman's pocket; he would later plead guilty to evading income taxes on payoffs he took from Steinman. Through subsequent conversations that were wiretapped, police learned that Lokietz had asked Steinman to get the Mafia to rescue Merkel. Some money, some political clout, and Lokietz could be back on his feet again. Steinman huddled with Dio over the idea one night at the Red Coach Inn in Westchester County, but with the horsemeat scandal all over the papers and Dio involved in some promising new rackets, they decided to let Merkel go on down the drain.

As a result of these meetings, however, Steinman was called in for questioning before the Merkel grand jury. Nicholson was sent to serve the subpoena, and thus got to meet the racketeer for the first time. Immediately Nicholson saw the arrogant conniver that was Steinman, a man who thought he could wheel and deal his way out of anything.

Nicholson found Steinman at the Luxor Baths, the famous old establishment on West Forty-sixth Street where the wealthiest of New York's European immigrant community used to go. There they relived the old-country male ritual of a steam bath, a massage, and a nap. Numerous business and entertainment celebrities had visited the Luxor over the decades. But by the late 1950s, the clientele had cheapened a bit and mobsters were more in evidence. The bathhouse was a frequent hangout for the likes of Johnny Dio, Anthony "Tony Bender" Strollo, and Lorenzo "Chappy the Dude" Brescia. Wiretaps would later reveal that the Luxor served as a convenient location for underworld plotting and the passing of payoffs. It was at the Luxor that Steinman often took care of supermarket executives and butchers' union officials. In 1975, the Luxor Baths closed, and reopened as a house of prostitution.

Nicholson remembers going into the lobby of the Luxor with his subpoena in 1965, and paging Steinman. The stocky (but not fat) racketeer came down in his bathrobe and turned on his crude charm.

"Can you tell me what this is about?" he asked Nicholson.

"Sorry," he was told. "I can't discuss it."

"Why don't we sit down to talk?"

Nicholson looked around at the well-appointed lobby, and then at Steinman in his bathrobe.

"Come on into the steam room. We'll have a nice bath," Steinman said.

Nicholson turned him down, but kept him talking. Maybe there would be an open offer of a bribe.

"After we have a bath," Steinman said, "we can talk. We'll have a few drinks, maybe we can go out to dinner."

Nicholson kept him talking.

"Are you married?" Steinman went on.

Nicholson said he wasn't.

"Do you have a girlfriend? Maybe I could get you a girlfriend. I'm a nice guy. You'll like me."

"I had to say, 'No, thanks,' " Nicholson recalls now. "Anything further would have been a compromise. But that's the way Moe Steinman operates. He never gets caught."

Others have noticed the same phenomenon. Says a partner in a large and long-established New York meat supply company, "Steinman bribes people in the bank not to sign him in or out when he goes to his safety deposit boxes. He has boxes all over the city. Once I was with him on a trip overseas and he bribed the guy at the airline counter $20 to avoid a $50 overweight charge. He didn't need the money. It's just a game with him."

Steinman was wrong when he thought he could bribe Bob Nicholson. But there were ways over Nicholson and around Nicholson. Even when the law had Steinman absolutely dead to rights in 1975, he was able to manipulate his way out of trouble. Bob Nicholson was right about one thing: "He never gets caught."

Moe Steinman has declined numerous requests for an interview. His communications to the author have consisted mostly of grunted greetings and monosyllabic comments in the hallways of various courthouses. There was also a very pregnant stare one day in a visitors' room at the federal Metropolitan Correctional Center in Manhattan when Steinman showed up at what I had been told would be a secret meeting between me and a cellmate of his.

Much of Steinman's story, however, can be told from the public record. He has testified several times about his background (while his veracity has not been constant, certain facts can be verified). And many persons in the meat industry, including his son-in-law Walter Bodenstein, have contributed information to the following sketch.

Steinman was born in Poland around 1918. He came to the United States with his parents at age eight. His father, a butcher, settled in Brooklyn. He quit school after eighth grade and ran off to be a porter or carny worker at the Chicago World's Fair in 1933. He returned to Brooklyn, where a young greengrocer named Ira Waldbaum had decided to lease out sections of his stores to meat dealers. This was, of course, long before Waldbaum's became the major regional supermarket chain it is today.

A dealer who had leased the meat departments in two Waldbaum's stores hired young Moe Steinman to run them, and the budding hoodlum was on his way. Steinman bought his first meat from Sam Goldberger, who would later go to prison for selling adulterated meat and bribing federal food inspectors. And Steinman made connections with two other Polish-Jewish immigrants, Max and Louis Block, who had just left their own Brooklyn butcher business to organize the Amalgamated Meat Cutters' union under rights obtained through mobsters Little Augie Pisano and George Scalise. Pisano and Scalise were of an older generation, but there was a younger, more contemporary Mafia figure whom the Blocks and Steinman and Goldberger began to meet —Johnny Dio.

Soon Steinman was expanding his meat counter operations to the Bronx and Westchester County. When the war came in 1941, Steinman quickly got classified 4-F. He has testified that he doesn't remember why he flunked his physical, though others have observed that if he didn't find a way to put the fix in on the Selective Service System, it would have been uncharacteristic. At any rate, Steinman's 4-F status allowed him to achieve fame and fortune while still in his twenties.

From 1942 to 1945, Steinman was known among meat dealers throughout the five boroughs as "Black Market Moe," the man who never asked for ration coupons and who always had meat to deliver. As Walter Bodenstein, his son-in-law and protégé, put it, "My dad during the black market was in the bakery business. He told me as a boy he had been offered large sums of money for sugar and stuff like that. And he would throw the people out. I guess Moe didn't throw people out."

"If you had meat during the war, there was no problem making money," recalls one prominent wholesaler. He and others in the industry say Steinman was almost certainly a millionaire by the time peace finally forced him to look for other rackets.

The racket he found was one he stayed with a long time. Essentially, it was a disguised way of taking kickbacks from supermarket chains for insuring "labor peace." This he could guarantee through his connections with the labor unions and the Mafia. The disguise required two hats.

First, he would hire himself out as a supermarket executive who could handle "labor problems." Because all the chains were supposed to be competing with each other, for the benefit of the consumer, he could be a payrolled executive for only one of them (it was Shopwell Inc.'s Daitch-Shopwell chain). But in industry-wide bargaining, he would act as lead negotiator for the group of them. One chain alone, however, could not supply Steinman with all the money he would need for the required under-the-table payments to union leaders and Mafiosi, as well as for his own not particularly modest style of living. So it came to pass that the chains all bought substantial quantities of meat from a particular wholesale brokerage firm, and that the firm was controlled by Steinman. The firm would overcharge for its meat, and the overcharge would create enough money to provide for all the people who had to be paid off. This payoff list soon grew to include executives at the various supermarket chains and their relatives, because if the executives were going to participate in graft it seemed unfair for them not to be able to take some of it for themselves.

Steinman's wholesale meat firm would overcharge equally to all the supermarket chains, so that none of them would get a competitive advantage—even the chain for which Steinman was a salaried executive. The customer would pay through the nose for everybody's high living, but that was all right. If any upstart supermarket manager tried to offer the customer a better deal, he would feel the pain of the organization's cleaver in his back. Either the Block brothers' butchers or Johnny Dio's truckers would start making trouble. There could be excessive grievances, or slow-downs, or, if necessary, even a strike.

And this is the way the supermarket system in the New York-New Jersey-Connecticut area works. It is the racket that Moe Steinman began running shortly after the war, when he opened his Mo-Jo meat wholesale business and simultaneously went to work for the Shopwell supermarket chain (now Daitch-Shopwell). It is the same racket that Steinman was running, with different corporate styles, when Bob Nicholson began chasing him in 1971. And as this is written, there are still trappings of the same deals involving some of the same people and the same corporations that were doing business earlier, and the same Moe Steinman. But in the absence of wiretaps and court subpoenaes, it is impossible to say exactly who is paying how much to whom and for what.

Steinman has always needed a partner to mind his meat operations while he was out engaged in the real business of making payoffs and manipulating the cost of food. In the original Mo-Jo wholesale meat concern, Steinman's partner was Joseph Weinberg. Court testimony later showed Weinberg's close connection to members of the Gambino and Genovese Mafia families, and perhaps it was Steinman who introduced them.

Paul "Constantine" Castellano was the brother-in-law of boss of bosses Carlo Gambino, and succeeded Gambino as head of the Mafia family when Gambino died in 1976. Like Steinman, Castellano was involved in wholesale and retail meat firms in Brooklyn in the 1930s. Others of his blood family also entered the industry, and the Castellanos now own many stores and distributorships in Brooklyn and Manhattan. They have a long record of welching on debts; of suffering suspicious hijackings, which can lead to insurance claims; of selling goods that were later found to have been stolen off docks or trucks, and of cheating other firms by receiving the assets of companies about to go into bankruptcy proceedings.

One typical bankruptcy fraud revolved around Steinman's partner Weinberg. A veteran meat dealer, Weinberg was able to open Murray Packing Company in 1959 with a good credit rating. A few months later Joseph Pagano, a young Genovese henchman and convicted narcotics trafficker, became an executive at Murray Packing. (Joseph Valachi testified that Pagano and his brother murdered mobster Eugenio Giannini in New York on September 20, 1952.) Meanwhile, Gondolfo Sciandra, a Gambino soldier and relative by marriage, opened another new meat concern and it began buying supplies from the Weinberg-Pagano company. So did the Castellanos' own company, Pride Wholesale Meat and Poultry Corp. But these favored customers always paid less than Weinberg and Pagano were charged by their own suppliers. For example, Weinberg's Murray Packing would buy hams for fifty cents a pound and sell them to Pride for forty-five cents a pound. Naturally, no business is designed to continue losing money this way.

Murray Packing quickly stepped up its rate of buying meat, but fell further and further behind in paying its bills. Soon the "float" of unpaid-for meat had reached $1.3 million. At that point, in 1961, the creditors sued. Murray Packing was declared bankrupt and there were no assets around to pay the bills, because the Gambino-Castellano firms had received the meat. (The basic concept behind all this is the same one that other Gambino operatives applied to the cheese business in Vermont and elsewhere.)

The exceptional part of the Murray Packing case is that it was prosecuted (because the new U.S. Attorney in Manhattan, Robert Morgenthau had an unusual interest in crimes of high finance). Joseph Pagano, the young Mafia subordinate, tried to take the entire rap himself by telling a federal court that he had withdrawn some $800,000 from Murray Packing illegally, and had lost it all gambling. The jury dismissed this story. Peter Castellana, scion of the Castellano family,* drew five years in prison; it was the only time in at least four similar bankruptcy cases that Castellana was brought to justice at all. Sciandra got eighteen months, and Weinberg, who contended he was just an innocent dupe, got one year. They were released after serving much less.

Pagano, however, was stunned by civil bankruptcy judge Sidney S. Sugarman, who also refused to believe the gambling story and ordered Pagano to jail for contempt of court until the $800,000 was repaid to Murray Packing's suppliers. Finally, in 1970, after almost six years, the court accepted the Mob's offer of a deal. A lawyer appeared with $75,000—one can only imagine where it came from—and Pagano was released and forgiven the rest of his debt. Over the years, the court had collected just $8,244.30 from the others who helped steal $1.3 million. According to law enforcement reports, Pagano immediately was given command of a big Mafia move into the now illegal business of factoring Medicaid claims; members of Steinman's family also were heavily into the business at that time, as will be described later.

Pride Wholesale Meat & Poultry Corp., the Castellano firm, had to go out of business as a legal entity in order to avoid civil claims in the Murray Packing bankruptcy. But Pride continues to be a trade name of the Castellanos, who are still major distributors of specialty meats and chickens, and occasional creditors in bankruptcy court. Among other things, Peter Castellana runs Ranbar Packing Corp., the region's largest distributor of Paramount chickens (the ones touted on television by Pearl Bailey). Ranbar alone reports annual sales of $30 million.

Moe Steinman's supermarket chains were at the heart of another Gambino family rip-off in the meat industry in the late 1950s. Paul Gambino (Carlo's brother) and Frank Ferro (who later became part of the Gambino cheese operation described in Part Four) briefly took over the business of sharpening knives for retail meat sellers. Their operation, though, amounted to little more than a shakedown of the knife grinders who had previously handled the work. After a brief time in business, the racketeers offered to quit if the knife grinders'

*Slight variations of name spelling are common among Mafia kin.

organization would pay them $300,000. The organization paid, and the chain stores sent their knives back to the original grinders. (Questioned about this before the New York State Commission of Investigation, Gambino and Ferro invoked the Fifth Amendment right against self-incrimination.)

The Gambino family's long-established ties with Moe Steinman and his partners probably have been useful to other members of the family. For many years, Paul Castellano, Jr., and Joseph Castellano have operated P & H Rendering Company in Brooklyn. P & H buys fat and other meat byproducts from supermarket chains and meat wholesalers, then reprocesses these wastes into cooking lard, or soap, or perhaps an ingredient for pet food. Paul, Jr., and Joseph are first cousins of Peter Castellana, and sons of Paul, Sr., known as "Constantine." All were thus related to boss of bosses Carlo Gambino.

The biggest Castellano racket, by knowledgeable accounts, continues to be loansharking. This high-interest emergency money lending isn't limited to the meat industry, but the Castellanos have used it there to increase the family clout. They are believed to control a large percentage of the independent meat companies in the Fourteenth Street market because of the debts owed to them.

From right after World War II and through the 1950s, while Joseph Weinberg was taking orders for Steinman's Mo-Jo meat firm, Moe Steinman was pursuing a rather unusual career as a supermarket executive. Exactly how his deal worked probably can't be learned at this late date, but clearly he was burning his candle at both ends.

At a court hearing once, he gave the following suspicious version of the story: After the war, he owned and operated eighteen independent meat outlets in Westchester County. In 1949, the owner of the Shopwell supermarket chain asked him to take over the chain's independently-owned meat concession by buying out the existing concession-holder. This Steinman did, for $65,000. Then (Steinman testified), in 1953, Shopwell decided to take over ownership of its own meat departments and bought Steinman out for Shopwell stock. The deal involved no cash, and so presumably left the thirty-five-year-old Steinman a major holder in the Shopwell corporation. He also became a salaried executive at about forty-five thousand postwar dollars a year. Steinman wasn't asked, and didn't choose to tell, what relationship if any his Mo-Jo meat firm had with Shopwell after he became a salaried executive.

The principal owner and manager of the Shopwell chain back then was Lou Taxin, who has long since retired. In an interview for this book, Taxin said he simply did not remember when or how Steinman became associated with Shopwell. He said he also didn't remember whether Steinman, while employed as a salaried meat buyer for the chain, was buying meats from his own wholesale firm. Old-time meat wholesalers say that's exactly what Steinman was doing, and that his unusual status was widely understood throughout the industry as a cover-up for graft. They also say the arrangement dated back to shortly after the war. When Steinman's name came up in criminal charges in

1973, Shopwell was quoted in the press as saying he had been with the company since at least 1947, not 1949 or 1953.

At any rate, the record is clear that by no later than 1953, Steinman had become Shopwell's director of meat operations. He also became its very first "director of labor relations." Everyone noticed that Steinman spent a lot of time with the heads of the butchers' union and the racketeers who controled various unions. When Moe Steinman was involved in the contract talks, labor problems disappeared. The supermarket chains he protected sometimes went more than a year without paying pension fund contributions for their employees, as the contract required, and the unions didn't object.

In 1956, Shopwell merged with Daitch Crystal Dairies to form the Daitch-Shopwell chain that is a leader in the eastern market today. Daitch's stock shares were traded on the public market, so shares of the merged corporation, which was known as Shopwell Inc., were also publicly tradable. For many years they have been listed on the American Stock Exchange. In recent years, even before Steinman's 1975 "retirement," Shopwell's disclosure statements filed with the S.E.C. contained no reference to Steinman as a top officer or major shareholder. What has happened to the major block of stock he apparently once held in Shopwell can only be wondered at. Despite more than a dozen attempts to interview them on this point for this book, Shopwell's senior officers—Herbert Daitch, Martin Rosengarten and Seymour Simpson—refused to come to the phone or respond to messages.

Whether Steinman helped engineer the Daitch-Shopwell merger wasn't learned either, but the merger was certainly fortuitous for him. Since 1956, the company has been headed by Herbert Daitch, who has been a staunch defender of Steinman throughout various troubles with the law. Daitch could hardly have been a more gracious employer. There certainly wasn't any clock-punching required. Steinman has testified that "I was in for six hours, I was in for an hour, I didn't come in at all sometimes." The detectives who followed him around, or tried to, in the early 1970s, say the six-hour days were rare if they ever even existed.

He slept late. Afternoons he spent with a girlfriend in a hotel, or in an apartment he kept in Queens. For his long-time girlfriend, Steinman picked the wife of an old friend. It was the subject of wide speculation in the industry whether the old friend knew about this liaison—especially after the old friend's name popped up on Steinman's illegal payoff list when it was made public as part of an indictment in 1973. Apparently the old friend was getting $250-a-week "salary" from a Steinman brokerage firm while doing no work for the firm and while his wife, a busty, good-looking brunette, was sleeping around town with Steinman.

What business Steinman did, he did at bars—most frequently the Black Angus, where his hosts were the Block brothers. Though revelations at the McClellan hearings had forced them to resign after twenty-five years' running the butchers' union, they were succeeded in office by men of their choosing, and continued to exercise authority from behind the bar of their restaurant.

Steinman also frequented other bars, notably the Bull & Bear at the Waldorf Astoria Hotel. It particularly infuriated Bob Nicholson later to see the way Steinman cowed the staff at the prestigious Bull & Bear, where some of the most reputable businessmen in town gather for lunch or a six o'clock scotch. "They bowed down to him," Nicholson recalls with disgust. "The Maitre D' protected him at a table in the corner where he used to sit and talk with union people. Nobody could sit at a table next to him. We (the detectives assigned to follow him) couldn't get near him. He was a big tipper. That was his philosophy. You could get anything you want if you paid for it. He was crude. He had no manners. But when he wanted something"—Nicholson shakes his head—"then he was the charming Moe Steinman."

One law officer puts it this way: "All he [Steinman] ever did was drink, and eat, and fuck."

Well, not all. Steinman negotiated labor contracts with as many as eighteen different locals. Most of the terms were set over the telephone or across a bar table. Formal "negotiations" were staged later in hotel suites, but they hardly appear to have been conducted at arms' length. Steinman became lead negotiator in many labor dealings for a large group of supermarket chains, supposedly competitors, based in or near New York. The owners and executives of these chains were by and large of similar background. They were friendly with each other outside of business. They hung out at the same country club (of course they may have had to do that—the club was owned by the head of the butchers' union).

The membership in this clique of supermarkets was not fixed. Some chains showed more independence than others. But by and large they bought their meats, at least certain cuts, from whatever company Moe Steinman told them to buy from. And the extra money they paid for the meat kept labor problems away, and fattened their own incomes through kickbacks. The chains that supposedly competed with Shopwell, but which were later found to have executives on Steinman's payoff list, included Big Apple, Bohack, Food City, Sloan's, First National Stores (Finast), Foodarama, King Kullen, Shop-Rite (a cooperative whose current central management has refused to deal with Steinman, though many of its stores are run by his cronies), and, of course, Waldbaum's, Steinman's first employer. Food Fair, Grand Union, Great Eastern, Hills, and Key Food were other chains cited in court evidence as being under Steinman's influence, although none of their executives were ever convicted.

The executives who *were* convicted were almost all from the vice-president level. Where were the chief executives all this time? Where were the principal owners of the supermarket chains? None were ever accused in court of getting money from Moe Steinman, or of conspiring to bribe union leaders by overpaying for meat. But human nature has led many people in the industry to assume that at least some of the bosses got their money indirectly. The middle management officials who were convicted had received such enormous payoffs—sometimes more than $100,000 a year each—that it is easy to speculate that they were spreading this money around the office. People in the industry frequently remark that the president of such-and-such a chain "had to know . . . had to be getting part of it." It hasn't been proven.

One of Moe Steinman's illegal payoff lists was later found to contain the names of close relatives of Herbert Daitch and Martin Rosengarten, the chairman and president of Daitch-Shopwell. (Because the relatives evidently paid taxes on the money they received, they weren't charged with any crime.) Steinman's business protégé and son-in-law, Walter Bodenstein, has stated that the basic decision to buy certain Steinman-promoted products was made directly by the chief executives, even at the largest chains.

But nobody cared—as long as the money was coming from the people who shopped in the supermarkets, and as long as there was no effective competition. (A & P was never part of the clique, but its executives were caught up in similar scandals operating independently.) Because the heads of the supermarkets were not involved directly, they could continue to run their supermarkets, even after Steinman was caught up in a scandal. As of 1977, at least, they were continuing to buy meat from Steinman family brokerages.

While Steinman was at the Black Angus, or the Bull & Bear, or the Luxor Baths, passing out envelopes, his brother Sol handled meat buying for Shopwell. Moe's "boss," Herbert Daitch, evidently was content to settle for a pinch hitter if his last name was Steinman. Then, around 1961, while Moe's wholesaling partner Joe Weinberg was deep in the Murray Packing Company scandal, Sol left Daitch-Shopwell to take over another meat wholesaling operation, Trans-World Fabricators, Inc. More properly, Trans-World was a brokerage. From its office in the Fourteenth Street meat district, Trans-World took telephone meat orders from supermarkets (and other retailers) and made telephone purchases from meat processors to fill the orders. For the most part, there were no warehouses, where product was moved in and out. The firm just took "commissions" on what the supermarkets bought. And if the commissions weren't paid to Trans-World, often the meat couldn't be sold.

Trans-World had been started a couple of years earlier by Herbert Newman, a long-time side-kick of shady characters in the meat industry. He had been partners with Sol Steinman in another meat company in the early 1950s, and also at one point had been involved with Charles Anselmo, the bookie, loanshark, and chief supplier in the Merkel horsemeat scandal. Sources in the industry say that Newman (who died of cancer in 1974) went to jail in the 1940s as a result of meat dealings, though no record of that could be found.

A couple of years after Newman started Trans-World, it was foundering. Newman, a heavy gambler and all-round big spender, effectively gave the company over to the Steinman brothers. He testified once that he needed the Steinmans' help in order to sell meat to supermarkets. Moe, on the other hand, testified that Newman needed better credit, and the people just naturally trusted the Steinmans. At any rate, after Weinberg was gone the Steinmans needed a new commission firm and in Trans-World they got one, without investing so much as a dime. According to Newman's testimony later, the Steinmans simply "declared" that they were partners, and nobody was about to argue with them. For a while, Trans-World shared an address at 408 West Fourteenth Street with Anselmo, who was, at that time, busy trucking diseased meat into New York for Merkel sausages. Anselmo still operates from there; Trans-World eventually found another office around the corner on Gansevoort Street.

True to expectations, the Steinman family brought Trans-World a quick upturn in business. Large orders were placed with Trans-World by Waldbaum's, Hills, King Kullen, Bohack, Grand Union, First National (Finast), Sloan's, Food-O-Rama (which became a large part of the Shop-Rite chain) and, of course, Daitch-Shopwell, where the Steinmans, as official meat buyers, were all too happy to feather the nest of their own meat supply firm with money that belonged to Shopwell's public shareholders. These were the names that came out in testimony as Trans-World customers; undoubtedly there were others. Prices, as always, were puffed up to create a huge kitty for pay-offs to all concerned, including various Mafiosi. The shoppers paid for that. Soon, other commission companies were established under the same ownership, assertedly for tax reasons.

Back in the early 1960s even Moe Steinman probably didn't dream he could grab a commission on *all* the fresh meat that came into chain stores in a three- or four-state area. To accumulate money to handle his payoffs, he claimed the right to commissions on certain easily identified specialty meat items. These included mostly the parts of the cow known in the trade as "offal" (pronounced "awful"); livers, oxtail, tripe, and flank, or "skirt" steak. All of this is meat that does not come from the four standard fresh-meat cuts—the chuck, the ribs, the round, and the loin. But the biggest specialty item by far for Steinman was the brisket, which comes from the belly of the cow, and which most frequently winds up on American dining tables as corned beef.

At first, Steinman simply required that independent corned beef makers buy their briskets from him as part of his control of the offal market. Since corned beef requires processing, which is usually done locally, it was an easy item to control. If the processors didn't buy their briskets from Steinman, the supermarkets wouldn't buy the processed corned beef from *them*. This produced an easy $1 a hundredweight (or $1 commission for every one hundred pounds of corned beef sold). But when Steinman saw how easy it was to control the corned beef market, he decided to nail the manufacturers both coming and going. "You don't sell to the supermarket anymore, you sell to me," he told them.

One New Jersey corned beef maker later told police he had been selling under an exclusive contract to a particular supermarket chain. Then one day

Steinman arrived and said, "You can't sell this account any more."

"What do you mean?" demanded the stunned manufacturer.

"Look," Steinman instructed him. "From now on you deliver your corned beef to Trans-World. *I'll* deliver it to the supermarket."

Steinman eventually testified, with his figures scrutinized by federal prosecutors, that he pumped from eight to ten cents a pound into the price of every corned beef sold in a supermarket anywhere near New York. But even that wasn't enough. Steinman also saw that something unusual happens to the corned beef market during the second week in March: every Irish bar and restaurant in town has to have corned beef for St. Patrick's Day, and in New York around St. Patrick's Day every successful bar and restaurant at least pretends to be Irish. So Steinman began holding back corned beef from the market and storing it in coolers well ahead of time. Then, come the second week in March, there was almost no limit to what he could charge for it. To put it simply, by the late 1960s Moe Steinman had put a corner on the corned beef market for much of the northeastern United States. He so restructured the market in New York that Lorenzo "Chappy the Dude" Brescia, Moe's Mafia friend, sent his son into the business, manufacturing corned beefs and selling them through Moe.

It wasn't hard to figure out where Steinman's hold on the supermarkets came from. He controlled the unions. In the words of one meat dealer who started to lose his market until he joined the system, "The union personnel, the foremen, they made certain that nothing but Steinman meat was acceptable. I could sell Bohack meat at fifty cents a pound and it would be rejected. They had to pay Steinman fifty-five cents a pound."

Usually the pressures were subtle, but when disagreements arose, Steinman could interject a heavy hand. Hills, for example, was one chain that apparently tried to buck the system on occasion. Once in 1968 Steinman decided that Hills hadn't been coughing up enough commission money. So, just before Thanksgiving, the unions threw up a picket line around a Hills' warehouse full of turkeys. According to Robert Goldman, a lawyer for Hills' meat buyers, Steinman "demanded that Hills purchase seven hundred barrels of corned beef a month and thirty thousand pounds of flank steak." That or no turkeys on Thanksgiving. Hills chose to sell the turkeys, and by the end of the year had become Trans-World's largest customer.

One Fourteenth Street wholesaler recalls a time when a customer of his with several stores was trying to resist unionization. The butchers' union had been defeated in an employee election supervised by the National Labor Relations Board. So the union asked wholesalers to refuse to sell meat to the small chain until it consented to organization. When the wholesaler in question continued to provide supplies, he began getting calls from his major supermarket chain customers: if he didn't stop selling to the boycotted chain, the major chains would stop buying from him. The buyers apologized for this threat, but said the union had given them no choice. "We got people working in our stores using a band saw that aren't supposed to," the big chains said. "We got weighers putting meat in the case. If we run into problems we'd have to put in three or four people per store, and we can't afford it." So the wholesaler fell in line.

In 1967, a big money-making opportunity arose for Steinman. It bore a prophetic similarity to the Iowa Beef Processors shakedown that began three years later. Holly Farms Inc. of Wilkesboro, North Carolina, hadn't been able to break into the New York market even though it was the nation's largest chicken producer. Holly Farms packaged its chickens by a new cryovac process that eliminated the need for re-packaging in the stores. This meant less work for butchers, so the butchers' union barred Holly Farms's product.

Steinman saw an opening. He arranged for Daitch-Shopwell to try the Holly Farms chickens for a few weeks. The union apparently "understood" and didn't complain. Daitch-Shopwell's president, Martin Rosengarten, was delighted, according to Steinman's testimony later: "He called me in and he told me, 'Here is a package that's great. It's beautiful. You can throw it in the case when it comes in. The only problem is, I don't know if the unions will allow it.'" He should have had more confidence.

Steinman immediately went to Al DeProspoe, the man Frank Kissel had selected to run Local 174 when Kissel went off to jail. They made a deal. As described later, the union would let in cryovac chickens if the supermarkets promised not to fire any butchers because of it.* By the time Steinman broke the good news to Holly Farms, however, there was more to it. In his own words, "Now I turn around, which my president [Rosengarten] knew about it, and I said to my president that I want to ask them [Holly Farms] for the brokerage for the New York territory. He said, 'If you can get it, go ahead.' I didn't hide anything." Nor did Rosengarten seem to object to Steinman's design to sell the new product to all the chains in town, even though this would cost Shopwell—Steinman's employer—its competitive advantage. Steinman's commissions came first.

Holly Farms, of course, was delighted at what Steinman had pulled off, and was easily persuaded to let him have an exclusive brokerage contract—so much for every pound of Holly Farms chicken sold in or near New York. Details of the deal have never been made public. Rather than cut Newman in on the profits, Moe sidestepped Trans-World and set up a separate brokerage firm, Cedar Rapids Fabricators Inc., to receive the commissions from Holly Farms. Then, in his word, he "gave" Cedar Rapids to his son-in-law, Walter Bodenstein, to operate. Holly Farms also was somehow persuaded to hire Bodenstein, a lawyer, as its New York legal counsel, on substantial retainer.

---

*I tried repeatedly to reach DeProspoe for comment, but he failed to return messages left with the union and with his daughter.

A similar practice would be followed three years later with Iowa Beef.

Bodenstein had married Steinman's youngest daughter, Cookie, six years earlier. He had gone on to Brooklyn Law School and had spent the previous several years moving from one small law firm to another, and spending some time in between practicing out of his home. Evidently Steinman decided his daughter's husband needed steadier work. Putting commissions on chickens wasn't the end of it, either. More deals were set up by which Bodenstein could profit from the supermarket chain connection. J. B. Brokerage was established to sell them sawdust powder to clean floors. Linden Overseas Ltd. was established to sell dishes imported from Japan as a sideline. Onto the payroll of these ventures went about two dozen relatives and friends of Steinman and his supermarket employers.

The deal with Holly Farms apparently continues to this day, though the amount of money it involves has been reduced, through no fault of the Steinman family. In the mid-1970s, Frank Perdue's catchy advertisements created a name brand competition that cost Holly Farms its market leadership. Holly Farms' chickens don't carry a brand name in the supermarket case. Perdue's chief brand name competition came from Paramount Chickens, the brand preferred by Pearl Bailey and Carlo Gambino, whose Mafia family distributes them.

In all likelyhood, the Holly Farms deal was worth millions over the course of the decade. The sawdust powder and dish deals, however, apparently were too trivial and petered out, especially after Nicholson and his men started looking over everybody's shoulders. By then, though, Bodenstein had found his way into other shady deals, some of them involving Johnny Dio, who had an office at the same Park Avenue address where Bodenstein operated his law practice and chicken brokerage.

In 1968, Frank Kissel was packing his bags for jail, which left a vacuum of bribery in the wholesale meat industry. After more than a dozen meat wholesalers had testified against Kissel and his union colleagues in 1967, union officials were getting edgy about taking money directly from the employers. So Steinman, who already had a lock on the retail (supermarket) end of the corruption, volunteered to fill the vacuum by becoming a middle man in the wholesale industry. "I'll deal with the companies, and you deal with me," he told the union officials.

The threat Steinman used over the wholesalers was not primarily labor trouble, but supermarket trouble. Sure, he controlled the unions, but he also controlled the buyers. Recalled one wholesaler later, "I was already in the chains. Suddenly Moe comes around to me and tells me I have to pay one thousand to this guy, fifteen hundred to that guy, five hundred to that guy. . . ." The wholesalers didn't know with certainty where the money was going. But a huge pool of cash was being accumulated, and problems were being taken care of.

The arrangement depended on phony sales to wholesalers by Steinman's Trans-World brokerage firm. "Moe would bill me for merchandise I didn't get," one wholesaler explained. "I'd pay with a check. . . . I got 10 percent of the cash and Moe would distribute the rest in bribes." (The 10 percent may have been an added inducement to cooperate, or it may have been a way of making sure the wholesaler was taking money illegally and thus wouldn't talk.)

Other wholesalers have explained the same pattern; wiretaps placed later by Nicholson's men confirm it. Of course, Moe kept a goodly share of the bribe money for himself and his Mafia friends. With the help of Steinman's supermarket network, the Mafia moved into waste hauling, soap distribution and even, of all things, the mass-produced bagel industry. First on the scene, as always, was Johnny Dio.

John Dioguardi was born in New York City April 28, 1914. He grew up on Forsyth Street in Manhattan's Little Italy. His father, Dominick, owned a bicycle shop. But young John apparently became closer to his uncle and neighbor on Forsyth Street, James "Jimmy Doyle" Plumeri, a prize fighter, racketeer and Mafia member. By the time Dioguardi graduated grade school in 1929, he had learned to terrorize pushcart owners by dumping their wares until they paid him.

In 1930, he got a lesson in justice. One Giovanni Dioguardi, thirty-five, presumably a relative, who lived a few doors down on Forsyth Street, was shot six times and killed on a street in Coney Island. He and the man police arrested for shooting him had recently been acquitted of murdering a widow to steal her jewelry. Now, police said, they were feuding over how to divide up the jewelry. It had been Giovanni Dioguardi's second murder acquittal. The only punishment he ever received was from his fellow criminals.

After a year and a half at Stuyvesant High School, Johnny Dio got work in the garment center through his uncle, Plumeri, assisting the vast shakedown racket headed by Lepke Buchalter and Gurrah Shapiro. Dio and Plumeri ran a trucking association, and garment manufacturers were well advised to hire only truckers who paid dues to it.

In 1932, Plumeri and another mobster were wounded in a shoot-out, which brought a police investigation of the association. Dio and Plumeri were indicted for coercion, but were acquitted. The next year they were indicted again, for extortion, and again were acquitted. The state was having trouble getting victims to talk. Finally, in 1937, Dioguardi got a three-to-five-year stretch at Sing-Sing after being convicted with Plumeri and several other mobsters of extortion and attrocious assault.

Evidence was that they had been getting $500 from every truckman in the garment district, plus a tariff on every suit and coat made in New York. From the *New York Daily Mirror:* "At the trial, frightened witnesses testified how recalcitrant employers and employees were beaten when they refused to pay. . . . One man said he was confined to bed for two weeks after an assault.

Another said the hoodlums had threatened to cut off his ears." Midway through the trial, Dio and Plumeri stopped the flow of revelations by pleading guilty.

In 1944, Dio was indicted for operating an illegal still, but the charge was dismissed.

In 1954 he was indicted and convicted for failure to pay state income tax in connection with his continued shakedown receipts in the garment center. The judge gave him sixty days.

It was about at this time that Dio became close to Jimmy Hoffa, as Hoffa sought New York support for his takeover of the Teamsters. Newspaper columnist Victor Riesel began writing about their activities, until, on April 5, 1956, he was permanently blinded in an acid attack outside Lindy's restaurant. Dio was accused of ordering the blinding, but was never convicted of it, although of the five men who took part in the attack, four were convicted and the fifth was murdered by his accomplices a few weeks after the attack. Those convicted served long prison terms, including years of additional time for refusing to testify against Dio (except for one man who did testify as to all he knew).*

In November, 1957, Dio went on trial with some Teamster officials for shaking down the owners of various stationery stores. The store owners had been picketed and told that if they wanted to break the picket they would have to sign their employees up with Teamster Local 295, and hire John Dioguardi's "labor consulting" firm, Equitable Research Associates, for a $3,500 retainer and $200 a month. After a four-week trial, Dio was convicted and sentenced to two years' in jail.

In 1958, while in prison for the stationery store shakedown, he went on trial again on similar charges involving shakedowns of the owners of electroplating shops. This time Dio was sentenced to fifteen to thirty years. But one year later, an appeals court overturned the first conviction, and, implicitly, the second, on the ground that Dioguardi never personally issued any threats. In a decision that seemed to legitimate the whole purpose of the Mafia, a divided court ruled that "Extortion cannot be committed by one who does not himself induce fear . . . but who . . . receives money for [the] purpose of removing or allaying . . . pre-existing fear instilled by others."

---

*The Riesel attack was one of only two carried out over the years against newsmen, the other being the 1976 murder of Don Bolles, a reporter for the *Arizona Republic* in Phoenix. In both cases the attacks backfired badly. Stiff justice was meted out not only to the actual attackers, but to persons at least as high as the middle level of the conspiracies. Perhaps more telling, though, the attacks brought a swift and heavy increase in the very scrutiny and publicity they were designed to squelch, and resulted in far more damage to the Syndicate's activities than Riesel or Bolles could possibly have caused had the attacks not occurred. Despite all the other crimes he's been convicted of, Dio is still best known as "the man who blinded Victor Riesel," and that reputation more than anything else assured that the police, the FBI, and the press would never leave his heels, and that he would spend most of the rest of his prime years in prison for other crimes.

Johnny Dio walked out of jail a free man on June 24, 1959.

In less than a year, the federal government yanked him back to court on charges that he failed to report taxable income from three dress manufacturing companies (all of them non-union) and two labor union locals. By the end of 1960 he was in the slammer again, this time the federal penitentiary in Atlanta, supposedly for four years. But two years later, in March, 1963, he was free again on parole, and in October of the same year he was discharged completely.

That was bad news for Kosher meat lovers. Dio's parole had been granted on the contention that he had a good job in legitimate industry—as a salesman for Consumers Kosher Provision Company in Brooklyn. Of course, no industry remains legitimate for very long with people like Johnny Dio involved in it. What had happened was that Dio and several fellow mobsters had managed to convince two rival kosher meat manufacturers that each needed its own group of mobsters to compete effectively with the other's group of mobsters. It was a trick that had worked decades earlier in the garment district. On Fourteenth Street, which supplies kosher meat coast to coast, it worked so well that the *Daily News* took to calling Dio and his colleagues the "Kosher Nostra." They are among the biggest kosher meat suppliers in the country to this day.

Herman Rose, the owner of Consumers Kosher Provision, had let someone in the Dio organization know that he was desperate over the inroads recently made by his chief competitor, American Kosher Provisions Inc. Consumers had been losing many orders to American, which had clearly become lead brand in the supermarkets. It wasn't hard to figure out why. The year before, American had signed up two free-agent sluggers of real all-star class for its sales force: Max Block, who had just been forced to resign as head of the butchers' union but who still exercised effective control over it, and Lorenzo "Chappy" Brescia, the Genovese family Mafiioso who had long been close to the union. Who would say "no" to them?

Block received $50,000 a year and a substantial chunk of American Kosher stock. Brescia got $25,000 a year. A good indication of their influence is the fact that their supposed "boss," the sales manager, was getting only $15,000 a year, and later testified that he never saw Block or Brescia except once when the president of the company introduced him to them at a dinner table at the Black Angus.

Dio's son, Dominick Dioguardi, then about twenty-one, and James Plumeri's son Thomas, thirty-two, convinced Herman Rose that in order to compete against the likes of Block and Brescia, Consumers would have to hire Johnny Dio himself—which Rose agreed to do in 1963 for $250 a week. This served, first, to get Dio his parole (the honest job) and, second, to give the Mafia power over not one but two kosher meat companies. As usually happens in such cases, Consumers only fell deeper into debt as the mobsters tried to milk it in every way they could.

It's unlikely the mobsters ever contemplated the kind of competition Rose thought he was buying. Block, Brescia, Dio, and Moe Steinman—whose hands were directly on the strings of the supermarket buyers—had all been buddies for many years and continued to be buddies.

Herman Rose died in July, 1964. The Kleinberg family, which owned American Kosher Provisions, had already been shoved aside. In August, 1964, Dio announced that Consumers and American were going to merge. This allowed for a transfer of assets—namely meat—back and forth. Pretty soon, other firms were created or taken over—First National Kosher Provisions, Mizrach Kosher Provisions, Tel Aviv Kosher Provisions, Finest Provisions Company. Meat again was transferred back and forth. Supermarket chains went from one to the next as lead supplier. In instance after instance, a kosher firm's debts for meat purchased would climb, and then the income of the debtor company would be cut off by a switch in supermarket loyalties before bills could be paid. The suppliers—western cattle firms and unlucky local wholesalers—took a bath.

In January, 1965, Consumers' suppliers threw the company into involuntary bankruptcy proceedings. The very next month, Consumers was declared formally bankrupt, with tremendous losses. Within a year, American was in bankruptcy proceedings. A few months later, First National's remaining assets were sold at auction to satisfy judgments.

Mizrach became the lead Dio brand, Its trade name was taken from a company that had been producing kosher salami, frankfurters, and baloney for forty years. When the original Mizrach went into reorganization under the bankruptcy law, it became an easy target for a Dio takeover. Milton Sahn, an attorney representing Mizrach's creditors, quickly accepted an offer from Dio whereby young Plumeri would sign on customers for Mizrach in exchange for 5 percent of the gross. Plumeri brought in more than $50,000 a week in new orders. One creditor, at a meeting in March, 1966, objected, "Why do we have to deal with Dio?" According to *New York Post* reporter Marvin Smilon, someone answered him, "Shut up and sit down. You ask too many questions." (Sahn, the attorney who effectively approved Dio's takeover of Mizrach, now represents the wholesale meat industry trade association in New York, and repeatedly put obstacles in the way of this author's efforts to get information from meat dealers. Sahn's co-counsel for the Mizrach creditors, Fred I. Zabriskie, later represented the Castellanos' meat interests.)

While the lawyers marched in and out of bankruptcy court, Dio, with the help of his man Steinman, maintained control of the industry. They had a solid one-two punch, the unions and the supermarkets. Dio took time to develop a close personal relationship with Chaim Horowitz, generally known as Chaim Yiddle (pronounced "Yoodle"). Horowitz was the long-time head of the Kasruth Supervisors Union, an affiliate of the Amalgamated Meat Cutters, until his death in 1976. The say-so of the rabbis in Horowitz's union is what transforms meat into kosher meat. Though they never found evidence that Horowitz or his men actually took money from Dio, the detectives saw the mobster and the rabbi together often.

Meanwhile, the supermarket chains switched suppliers in perfect step to Dio's needs. An official of American Kosher Provisions later testified that one day, buyers from "many" supermarket chains simply declared that American Kosher was out. American Kosher's managers "were never told who was to replace them or anything of that nature," the official said.

As in other cases, the Hills chain tried briefly to buck the trend. Hills had switched from American to Mizrach with the others. But in 1966, after American had gone through bankruptcy proceedings, the Kleinberg family (its owners) tried to resurrect the company independent of the Mob. They persuaded Hills to switch its business back to American. Moe Steinman immediately announced to George Gamaldi, Hills' meat buyer, that Gamaldi had made a big mistake. Gamaldi found out just how big the mistake was when the butchers' union struck his supermarket chain. Herbie Newman, Steinman's brokerage partner, quickly called Gamaldi and announced that Moe could help straighten out the labor situation. Gamaldi apparently got the message.

Aaron Freedman of Waldbaum's testified that he had switched to Mizrach because of complaints from shoppers about American Kosher's products; he also testified that he had no idea his friend Johnny Dio was behind the Mizrach and Tel Aviv brands he switched to.

Complaints from shoppers may well have occurred. When a Dio brand was getting ready to go off the shelf, its final orders were filled with the cheapest product around—usually spoiled meat. The supermarkets had to sell the product, because Dio's companies expressly forbade returns. One route salesman for Consumers and later American testified that he suddenly started getting merchandise that was "light in color, sometimes green and at all times sweaty." He added that it was "so patently inferior to anything we have had that this is an atrocity to perpetuate on our customers. There is no question in my mind that this is the worst merchandise I have ever seen."

In April, 1966, the federal government filed bankruptcy fraud charges against Dio, his son Dominick, Tommy Plumeri, and David Perlman, a fifty-three-year-old kosher butcher without whose practical advice the racketeers might not have been able to slice a salami. (According to the prosecutor, Moe Steinman lied and risked a perjury charge before the grand jury to try to protect Dio.) In 1967, all but Dominick Dio were convicted of diverting some $200,000 in assets in the Consumers bankruptcy (the other bankruptcies weren't included in the charges). The men stayed free during four years of appeals.

Those were halcyon days for Dio. He tended flowers at his lavish home in Lookout Point, Long Island (it cost $75,000 in the early 1960s). He came to town in blue sharkskin suits, monogrammed shirts and a diamond ring, and at the funeral of an important Teamster leader he sat quietly among the political dignitaries. His business front, the supposed source of his high income, was Jard Products, which still does business today from the same office at 260 Fifth Avenue. Jard sells promotional items to commercial establishments—ashtrays emblazoned with a restaurant's name and similar items. Its customers have included major supermarket chains like Daitch-Shopwell and Waldbaum's. Obviously, Jard would be a perfect cover for a shakedown of retail businesses by someone like Johnny Dio who controlled unions. But Jard has never been involved in any of the corruption charges against Dio.

Other businesses in the family, however, were quite frequently the subject of accusations. Dio's brother Frank and an in-law were sentenced to prison in 1966 after being caught with 209 pounds of heroin. Johnny Dio himself was in a circle of mobsters who controlled the import-export trucking business in New York, particularly around John F. Kennedy Airport. Dio's partners were two Mafiosi who had been convicted for smuggling, loansharking, larceny, and assault, and a Teamster leader who was eventually convicted of labor racketeering. Together, the racketeers controlled Teamster Local 295, which represented the labor, and also controlled the association that represented, whether they liked it or not, the eighty or so trucking firms that did the employing. Whatever its faults, this arrangement certainly saved time at the bargaining table. The Teamster leader, Harry Davidoff, put thirty airlines on notice that their cargo wouldn't be handled in New York unless they employed trucking firms that paid dues to the Mafia-run "association." Despite extensive exposure by the New York State Commission of investigation in 1967, the system carried on long afterward. When Davidoff was finally forced out of office by his troubles with the law, he was replaced by his son, Mark, who runs the union local today. Young Davidoff has never been convicted.

Other persons close to Dio were engaged in retail bankruptcy scams. They would open stores or distribution companies, order large amounts of merchandise on credit—everything from television sets to razor blades—sell the merchandise and then go out of business without paying for it.

But perhaps the most bizarre business situation John Dioguardi ever found himself in was the Great Mafia Bagel War of the late 1960s. It began one morning when Dio, a high-ranking member of the Lucchese Mafia family in New York, and Thomas "Tommy Ryan" Eboli, a high-ranking member of the Genovese Mafia family in New Jersey, each woke up to discover that he had acquired power over almost half of the ever-growing east coast bagel market. And each discovered that he had only one major competitor—the rival Mafioso.

There occurred an unusual series of sit-downs—not over plates of spaghetti with clam sauce in Little Italy as tradition would have it, but rather over bagels and coffee in little Jewish bakery shops in Teaneck, New Jersey, and Brooklyn. One interesting result of these meetings was that Dio got his come-uppance; Vito Genovese was still alive then and still boss of bosses, and his man Tommy Eboli effectively got Johnny Dio kicked out of the bagel business—which was less of a blow to Dio than it was to the unfortunate Jewish bagel-maker, Ben Willner, who had staked his career on Dio's influence. Eboli's own Jewish bagel-maker, one Arthur Goldberg, had found a better mobster.*

But there was an even more impressive show of power in the bagel war. It became obvious that the real man in the driver's seat, for business purposes, was Moe Steinman, who had both Dio *and* Eboli over a barrel. No matter who the Mafia decided was going to *make* the bagels, he was going to have to come to Moe Steinman to *market* them. In fact, when Eboli finally won the struggle, Dio's bagel-maker, Ben Willner, was allowed to keep the wolves from his door by going to work for a factoring company operated by Steinman's sons-in-law.

It was a long drop for Ben Willner, who, in 1966, had become a pioneer of the automated bagel. His new machine could turn out bagels for about 50 to 55 cents a dozen, whereas traditional hand-rolled bagels cost about 65 cents a dozen (wholesale prices to supermarkets). Naturally, the membership of the Bakery and Confectionary Workers' Union wasn't overjoyed with the new machine. But an officer of the union introduced Willner to Steinman, who introduced him to Johnny Dio. Dio straightened the union problems out, and pretty soon Moe Steinman's supermarket chains were stocking bagfulls of automated bagels. Daitch-Shopwell alone sold between $3,000 and $4,000 worth a week. Dio also saw to it that the trucks that carried the bagels would be the same ones that carried his kosher provisions.

Meanwhile, however, Eboli and several henchmen had come to the rescue of Goldberg and some partners who were also having union problems. The mobsters wound up owning a whole chain of bagel shops with on-site bakeries around the New York area. Eventually they sought supermarket accounts, thus creating the crisis with Dio and Willner.

After Dio caved in, in December, 1968, Willner's automated bagel factory went out of business, and the Eboli-backed group promptly took it over. The Eboli group then expanded its chain of bagel shops to several states, established a corporation known as Bagels USA, headquartered in Miami, and sold stock to the public. Certain irregularities in the way this stock was sold got Bagels USA into hot water with the Securities & Exchange Commission, and the firm eventually went out of existence. It has been replaced, however, by a successor company run by at least two of the same principals; this corporation is Bagel Nosh, and at this writing in 1978 it operates stores in many states. Thomas Eboli has since been murdered, and thus he certainly isn't part of Bagel Nosh. But two former prison inmates—Leo Vittorio, a convicted robber and gun violator, and Thomas F. Smith, a convicted stock swindler—are. Both came from the old Eboli bagel operation. After reporter Jim Drinkhall of the *Wall Street Journal* began asking questions about them in 1978, a telephone receptionist at the company said they had resigned as top officers and were now just "consultants."

In November, 1970, Johnny Dio and Tommy Plumeri finally ran out of

---

*Prior to the bagel business, Eboli's most famous excursion into the marketplace for legitimate goods involved the recording industry, where he had been a business partner of the head of Roulette Records.

appeals and went to prison. Dio had always been able to run his operations from jail. Plumeri served two years and returned to Mizrach, which soon became the second biggest kosher food supplier in the country, topped only by Hebrew National, a division of the Colgate-Palmolive Company. In the mid-1970s, industry sources say, Plumeri and Dominick Dio moved their loyalties to a Bronx firm known as Mogen David Kosher Meat Products, and it became number two in the country, while Mizrach, still operated by the mobsters' former partners, became number three. (Interviewed by phone, a spokesman for Mogen David said the mobsters weren't "employed" there, but that the president of Mogen David "is friendly with him [Plumeri]. I know they talk to each other." In 1978, Mizrach was taken over by new owners who say they have nothing to do with Plumeri or the Dios.)

Most non-Mafia racketeers who want to be part of the Syndicate wind up tying their wagons to a particular Mafioso. If this patron goes to jail or is otherwise waylaid, the outsider can be in trouble. But racketeers of Steinman's stature are much bigger than that. He had many Mafia ties. Those with the Genovese family—the family of Tommy Eboli and his fellow sub-bosses Gerardo and Eugene Catena—involved his close relationship with the Catenas' friend, Irving "Izzy" Kaplan, who, until he retired in 1977, was head of the New Jersey butchers' union and a high-ranking vice-president of the international. Insiders report that he still runs the union in New Jersey even after formal retirement. Bob Nicholson and his detectives frequently saw Steinman and Kaplan huddling together at the Black Angus and elsewhere. Later, when Steinman gave the government damaging information on certain people in the meat industry in exchange for lenient treatment for himself and his family, he never accused his really close friends—and Kaplan was among them.

Kaplan's most widely-publicized duty for the Genovese family was selling soap products promoted by the Catena brothers. The Catenas got into the soap business by offering assistance to a floundering detergent company. Its products were of relatively low quality, and the company's best hope was to market them as "house brands" under the labels of any supermarket chains that would agree to take them. The Catenas were able to summon some pretty effective salesmen—not only Kaplan, the head of the butchers' union, but also Joseph and Thomas Pecora (commonly known as Joe Peck and Timmy Murphy), who are powerful Teamster leaders in New Jersey and have themselves been identified in Congressional hearings as members of the Genovese family.

As Donald Gray, investigator for the Senate Commerce Committe, summed it up, "To get goods into a store, the first guy you'd go see isn't the purchasing agent, but the labor representative." The Steinman-dominated supermarket chains had already stocked a brand of sausage made by the son of an official in Kaplan's union. Now, with the men who negotiated trucking contracts also involved, the Catena gang sold its soap to (according to a

Commerce Committee report) Grand Union, Bohack, E. J. Korvette, Harsh Foodliners, Gimbels, Shop-Rite, First National (Finast), Food Fair, Hills, Sears, W. T. Grant, and other chains. The soap was in thousands of stores. The one food chain that wasn't buying was the one chain that Steinman never had any direct influence over, the A & P. The Mafia detergent, known as Ecolo-G (because it contained no phosphates) badly flunked A & P's quality control tests. In fact, it ranked lowest of twelve products tried. There's evidence that it also failed to meet quality control tests elsewhere.

When Gene Catena heard that A & P wasn't going to stock his soap, even after personal sales pitches from Izzy Kaplan and Joe Pecora, he exploded and touched off one of the most violent (and one of the stupidest) campaigns the Mafia has ever waged. Barking out orders in his office to Kaplan and brother Gerry (and to a hidden FBI microphone he didn't know was there) Gene Catena shouted, "We'll kick A & P's brains out!"

Sure enough, immediately thereafter the A & P chain was hit with a series of explosions and arsons in stores and warehouses all over the metropolitan area. Real damage was estimated at well over $7 million, and more than $60 million in facilities were knocked out of commission. Worse, A & P store managers were being viciously beaten and two of them were murdered. One murder occurred at a manager's home after he had gone to police and identified from photographs the arsonist he saw trying to burn his store. He was found in front of his house with bullets in his stomach and heart and two in his head. After that murder, the FBI bug recorded Gene Catena as saying, "When is A & P gonna get the message?"

Unfortunately for justice, the FBI recordings could never be used in court. Only one alleged arsonist was indicted and none were convicted. Finally, the Justice Department, frustrated, started harrassing Catena with grand jury subpoenaes. Kaplan was indicted with some fellow union officers on a charge that never held up.

So the campaign against A & P stopped. As a peace token, Kaplan signed a new labor contract with the chain just days after Catena's grand jury appearance. It was a management offer he had previously rejected. Nevertheless—and this may be the most shocking part—despite all the publicity about the bombings and murders, and despite detailed Congressional hearings, the Mafia soap products continued to appear on the shelves of hundreds of Steinman-manipulated supermarkets throughout the region. Bohack, for one, continued to use the soap for its own private-label detergent. Even as late as 1971, seven years after the campaign started, the Mafia-backed manufacturers were taking in $8 million a year from these low-cost products. Finally the Food and Drug Administration stepped in and did what the Justice Department could not do; it ruled that the soap was "corrosive" to the skin and "a severe eye irritant" and the product was eventually yanked off the market.

The arsonists and thugs who were identified—though never convicted—in the A & P war all came from a Mafia group based in Westchester County and headed by Nicholas Ratenni. Ratenni was associated with the Genovese family. He was also associated with Moe Steinman, at least as far back as the 1940s when Steinman owned eighteen meat stores in Westchester County. Ratenni's main involvement in the marketplace has long been the garbage collection industry. Many supermarket chains employ companies connected to Ratenni to handle their waste. Old-time meat wholesalers assert that these deals were set up by Moe Steinman, a golfing partner of Ratenni's.

The A & P war is only one instance of the violence, and, mainly, the threat of violence, that has helped racketeers like Steinman keep the meat industry in line over the years. The A & P war simply got out of hand. Usually the strong-arm was applied more subtly and judiciously, and therefore more effectively. But few meat dealers doubt that it is there, which has made the job of law enforcement officials—and of reporters—much more difficult.

One particularly well-publicized incident was the gunshot murder of two meat wholesalers at the bar of the Neopolitan Noodle restaurant in 1972. The public and the meat industry got very different versions of what happened. The story put out by police was that the shooting was part of the Gallo-Colombo intra-family war then raging, and that the Mafia gunmen (never identified) in the Neopolitan Noodle had mistaken the meat dealers for two rival Mafiosi who had been standing at the bar earlier in the evening. The story persisted despite the fact that the two murdered men were in a party of eight—four meat dealers and their wives (the other two men were wounded by bullets), and that witnesses said the men had been talking loudly in large doses of Yiddish. The shooting of upstanding businessmen, supposedly innocent bystanders with no connection to organized crime, was roundly condemned.

But a Congressional investigator experienced in Mafia affairs expressed doubts. "Are you going to believe," he asked me in 1974, "that a Mafia hit man can't tell the difference between four Colombo soldiers and four Jewish businessmen out to dinner with their wives and talking loudly in Yiddish?"

Clearly a lot of people in the meat industry don't believe it. Several prominent wholesale and retail meat executives pointed out the incident to me without prompting two years after it happened. They noted that one of the murdered men was Sheldon Epstein, salaried manager at the time of Empire Veal & Lamb Company. Epstein, however, had announced plans to start a new veal business, in partnership with a prominent veal grower in Wisconsin and a prominent retailer in New York, both of whom had reputations for avoiding the industry's shady deals. The new business would have competed with Empire, which, according to Senate Commerce Committee documents, had paid large sums to Frank Kissel "and other union officials in order to avoid a shorter working week," and had even bought $470 in airline tickets to send Kissel on a trip to Florida. Epstein's new company also would have competed with two Bronx concerns that sold through Moe Steinman's brokerages. The new Epstein business never got started.

According to Walter McFarland, the Wisconsin veal grower who would have provided the merchandise for the business, "We needed Shelley to run the thing because he knew all the buyers." According to Thomas Burke, manager of the Northeast Veal Growers' Association, "Shelley had the ability and the knowledge to become the biggest man in the industry." Maybe he was becoming too big.

The other murder victim at the Neopolitan Noodle was Max Tkelch, manager of Flushing-Zeger Meat Company, which, according to Senate Commerce Committee documents, had also been paying off the butchers' union. What was Tkelch's sin? Nobody I could find seems to know about that.

Other incidents have been reported by authorities as one thing, but have impressed meat dealers as something else, perhaps related to their industry. One is the 1972 slaying of Joan Kramer, a twenty-four-year-old college coed in New Jersey. The police identified her millionaire father as a meat dealer. What was never pursued was that her father made his money running the Tantleff Beef Company in Newark, and was the brother-in-law of Jules Tantleff, the former Bohack executive, briber of union officials, and owner of the Black Angus restaurant where almost every crooked deal in the industry was discussed and where Johnny Dio, Moe Steinman, and various union officials kept what was effectively their office. The police pinned the murder on a sex maniac. What they never really dealt with was the family's complaint that shortly after Miss Kramer disappeared, they received several telephone calls from a purported kidnapper who successfully extorted a $20,000 ransom from them before their daughter's body was found. The police simply discounted the kidnapping story. In 1975, they charged a man with the crime on the sex fiend theory, but he was acquitted at trial.

A third incident that impressed the industry was the 1968 murder of Dominick Lombardi. For the record, Lombardi was just a truck driver for Daitch-Shopwell. But Lombardi didn't drive a truck at all. He chauffeured a limousine and provided armed protection for the supermarket chain's vice president—Moe Steinman. Lombardi was killed at the Roundtable, a Manhattan nightclub, and police announced at the time that he was shot in a dispute over another man's wife, a belly dancer at the club. The Roundtable, however, was directly across the street from the Black Angus, where Moe Steinman was drinking at the time of the shooting; the limosine was parked in the street between the two restaurants. Moreover, sources in the meat industry say that Dominick Lombardi wasn't screwing around with the married belly dancer at all—Moe Steinman was. And the sources doubt that jealousy had anything to do with the shooting; they note that Steinman has on other occasions gone out of his way with money to create friendly relations with the husbands of his paramours, and that Lombardi's killing may well have resulted from his activities in the meat rackets. The belly-dancer's husband was quickly arrested and indicted for the murder; he was just as quickly released on bond. More than six years later, not one move had been made to prosecute him. After an article appeared in the *Wall Street Journal* pointing out the rather unusual delay (it "really should have been tried a long time ago," a prosecutor confessed), the case was resurrected. But witnesses had disappeared and the accused man was acquitted.

The men in the meat industry say they know of others who were threatened or worse for getting out of line. Said one wholesaler who wouldn't go into detail, "I don't want to wind up in a box. Moe Steinman's connections go straight to the heart of the Cosa Nostra. I've known too many people who wound up in cement shoes or close to it." Said another about his colleagues who wouldn't talk, "It's not themselves they're afraid for so much, it's their families."

Newsday, the Long Island newspaper, ran a series of articles in 1971 about the Mafia in the supermarkets, and quoted one chain store buyer in these words: "If a product like clams, or bread, or soap, or what-have-you is being sold by a salesman with the last name of Dioguardi or Gambino or Pecora, you know damn well who they are and what they represent. . . . It's just not smart to say I'm not going to take it. . . . You'd worry about every car that passes you by, not to mention the pressure they'd bring to bear on the labor front."

Robert Nicholson recalls hearing the complaint of two Hungarian immigrants in 1968. The men had fled their homeland after taking part in the fight against the Soviet invasion in 1956. Meat dealers by training, they jumped at an advertisement they saw for someone to run a corned beef plant in the Bronx. They didn't know there was anything wrong with the owner of the plant, John Dioguardi, or that Dioguardi's man Moe Steinman had cornered the corned beef market. Dio told them, "I'll deliver the product [briskets], you make the corned beef, I'll deliver it to the stores," and they'd be partners.

The plant was run-down and the product wasn't very good but it was the best the two men could produce. There was no union, and no government inspection. They didn't know where the corned beefs were going. Soon Dio began holding back on the money he owed them. Then, after three months, they found the plant padlocked with a sign advertising for a new manager. They went to Dio, who told them he didn't want them as partners anymore, and wouldn't pay them.

Nicholson told the men who they were dealing with in Dio, but he told them it could be very important to law enforcement if they would agree to wear a hidden tape recorder to a meeting with the mobster. When he warned them of the danger, they said they didn't care. One Hungarian stepped forward, pounded his chest and said, "Me not afraid of Russian tanks, me not afraid of Johnny Dio."

Then, however, Nicholson had trouble locating the men. When he did, they said they had talked to some people and changed their minds about cooperating. Then Nicholson couldn't locate them at all.

That's the way the meat industry was in New York when Currier Holman rode in out of the west with the best idea a meat man ever had.

2

Holman

Currier J. Holman was the other meat industry leader in the darkened suite at the Stanhope Hotel that April day in 1970. He presented quite a contrast to Moe Steinman. His features were even. His whole bearing was distinguished. He looked like the very tintype of the midwestern business success that he had become.

It had been less than ten years since Holman, a veteran cattleman, had founded Iowa Beef Processors Inc. But he had spent a quarter of a century developing the vision behind Iowa Beef. In all that time, Currier Holman had watched packing plants ship whole swinging carcasses of beef around the country, just as they had for a hundred years. Holman had sensed that butchering beef at the slaughterpoint, then shipping it out in boxes, would result in enormous economies. By 1970, after just nine years of actively pursuing this idea, he had built Iowa Beef into the largest meat processing firm in the world.

When Iowa Beef was founded, the industry was dominated by the so-called Big Five packers: Swift, Armour, Wilson, Morrell, and Cudahy. Before the end of fifteen years, Iowa Beef had become bigger than Swift, Armour, Wilson, Morrell, and Cudahy *put together.* It had even fostered a host of immitators, including the number two packer in the industry, MBPXL Corp. (originally Missouri Beef Packers), which also had edged ahead of Swift. In 1977, MBPXL was slaughtering thirty to thirty-three thousand cattle a week. Iowa Beef was slaughtering *eighty to ninety thousand* cattle a week. This three-to-one ratio between number one and number two is among the biggest in any competitive industry in the United States today.

Meat dealers everywhere will tell you that Iowa Beef offers a consistency and availability of product that competitors can't come close to. "Another company may offer me six or eight carloads of meat, but if I need twenty carloads right now there's only one place I'm going to go," says one large buyer. And an eastern distributor for a rival firm complains, "I don't like competing against them. They have the highest quality, but they have the largest quantity, too." (Quality here refers to consistent size and leanness of the same cut on each shipment, rather than to tenderness, flavor, or purity, which are considered mostly standard in the industry.)

In an amazingly short time, Iowa Beef has changed the processing and marketing habits of an industry. It has influenced the eating habits of a nation. And yet, despite all of its innovations, and all of its genius, Iowa Beef found itself unable to stay in business at all without selling its soul to the Mafia.

Currier Holman—Currier is his mother's family name—was born in 1911 in Sioux City, Iowa, an area that his grandfather had helped pioneer. Holman's father had accumulated enough holdings in real estate and banks that neighbors considered the Holmans well-to-do, although family members insist they were poor-to-average. The elder Holman died in a flu epidemic in 1918. Currier moved with the rest of the family to California. His elementary school was Hitchcock Military Academy in San Rafael. After that he was packed off to prep school at Shattuck Military Academy in Faribault, Minnesota, where his mother had attended a sister school. About his private schooling, Dr. Clifford Bowers, a lifelong friend, says, "His mother was kind of a socialite and those things were kind of important to her."

According to Holman's entries in *Who's Who in America,* his higher education was Notre Dame, '33. Notre Dame says it parted company with Holman for undisclosed reasons during his junior year in 1932. Grant Holman says his brother Currier quit college in disappointment after a broken appendix forced an end to his football career in 1932. George Henry Rohrs, who really did graduate Notre Dame in 1933, says Holman's football career was ended in 1930, not by a broken appendix but by George Henry Rohrs. "I beat him out, I'd say," says Rohrs, who adds that they were competing for the final remaining spot on the last team ever coached by Knute Rockne, who was killed in a plane crash the next year. A roster of all Notre Dame football games ever played doesn't include the name Currier Holman, indicating that he never stepped onto the field. Yet decades later his speeches were peppered with recollections of his experiences on the team, references to Rockne and comparisons between business at Iowa Beef and football at Notre Dame.

"I remember him because we played the same position (end)," says Rohrs. "But I wouldn't say that many people would remember him. He didn't make a big impression then. That's why I was surprised to see in the paper how prominent a position he held. He was a big strong farmboy, and those people keep to themselves pretty well." Other classmates say the same thing. Holman wasn't a standout as a youth.

After leaving Notre Dame, Holman briefly attended the University of Oklahoma. He left there to get married. The marriage was annulled after eight months. A few years later he met and married a Sioux City woman who would remain Mrs. Holman, loyal even through the tribulations of the 1970s.

Even in the depths of the Depression, Holman found work. In a 1975 interview with *Meat Processing* magazine, he recalled, "Every day I'd take my place in the employment line at the Swift plant in Sioux City. Those of us in that long and desperate line would wait the day and usually go home with nothing. Then finally I got the nod. . . ." In a 1976 interview he told me a very different story, but a story more in line with the recollections of his friends. The manager of the Swift plant was a friend of the Holman family whom young Currier had kept supplied with football tickets. So he went personally to the manager for the job and was the only one hired. "I was sort of ashamed," he admitted. "There were men with children who needed work more than I did. But somehow one has to get on with their life."

Swift put him in what was known as the "gut shanty," where his job was stripping the guts and offal from freshly slaughtered carcasses. In the *Meat Processing* interview, he recalled his first night: "About one o'clock in the morning I was hauling a barrel of sheep guts—or what was left of them—over to the rendering works. In the process of moving them from one department to the other on the barrel truck over a slippery floor, I lost my footing and down we went—barrel, guts, and me. I came up on the bottom and the contents of the barrel came up on top. I pulled myself out of that awful mess, leaned against a column and cried real tears. I was tired, all alone on my first night doing clean-up in that big plant."

Even back in those days, friends remember Holman talking incessantly about the inefficiencies he saw. The cattle he was helping slaughter had spent several days en route from the feed lots where they were fattened, and perhaps another day in the pens where they were bought and sold. The wasted time and extra handling resulted in considerable weight loss. The slaughtering operation itself seemed inefficiently organized. And many live cattle were being shipped in railroad boxcars to distant slaughterhouses on the east and west coasts, resulting not only in weight loss but in much greater shipping, slaughtering, and butchering costs than if the kill had been made at a central location.

Recalled Holman in 1976 (it required two years of hounding to get him to agree to an interview with me), "Really, it didn't take anybody very bright working in those packinghouses as they used to be to know the changes that were needed. They were inefficient—multistoried—people would stand waiting for elevators to go from floor to floor for fifteen minutes at a time." Grant Holman remembers his brother, while still in the gut shanty at Swift, talking about the packinghouse he would start one day. "I want to be the biggest packer in the world," Currier Holman told his family even then.

After several years, Swift put Holman into office work, but four months later he left. Armour had offered him the job he really wanted—buying cattle.

Holman saved his money and early in the war years he found an opportunity to buy into an established private cattle trading concern at the Sioux City stockyards. A few years later his partner retired and Holman went on his own. Halfway across the country a man known as Black Market Moe was starting a supermarket racket with his Mafia friends. But Holman had never heard of him. Holman was busy developing his own reputation as the biggest cattle trader in one of the biggest stockyards in the country. Recalls his friend Dr. Bowers, "as an order buyer you can work as many hours as you want and make as much money as you want. He was there fifteen or eighteen hours a day, seven days a week. If anybody wanted to buy cattle, Currier was there to sell them." Another lifelong acquaintance, Neil Tennis, an Iowa banker, adds, "Nobody would work as hard as Currier. A thirty-six-hour day wouldn't be long enough for him. He eats and breathes this stuff. We run into him socially late at night and that's all he can talk about. We can start talking baseball, but it always gets back to the cattle business."

This intense concentration on work took its toll on those around him. "The family isn't happy," says one close relative. "They don't have a father, they've got a business. He has very few friends because he talks nothing but business, constantly."

For fifteen years Holman took phone calls from small slaughterhouses around the United States and bought cattle in the Sioux City yards to fill their orders. But through all that time he never lost the dream of one day starting his own packing company. Finally, in 1953, he began knocking on doors looking for financing.

His idea of challenging the old-line packing companies with up-to-date methods was not entirely novel in Sioux City. Says Dr. Bowers, who became one of Holman's investors, "Quite a few people had thought of it, but nobody had been willing to gamble on it. The general idea was that it would fail because Armour, Cudahy, and Swift were so big." Over the next two years, Holman managed to convince some twenty-five to thirty Sioux City burghers to lay out about $1 million, of which Holman himself put up about $50,000.

The new firm, Sioux City Dressed Beef, started operations in 1955. Though not nearly as revolutionary as Iowa Beef would be a decade later, Sioux City Dressed Beef cut an adventuresome style for its day. Sioux City Dressed Beef accepted Holman's theory that beef and pork were two different businesses, and that the major packers were creating inefficiencies by trying to handle both products at the same time. "Pork is a branded item," Holman declared. "In branded items the consumer pays whatever she wants to pay for an Armour Star or Swift Premium. In beef, nobody knows the difference. Beef is a commodity. In commodities, the low-cost producer has the market." Holman's packinghouse would concentrate on beef.

Also at Sioux City Dressed Beef there were the beginnings of an assembly line. A conveyor chain brought the cattle after slaughter past rows of workmen who methodically hacked the carcass into quarters. Thus Holman pioneered two more of his ideas: first, the use of what he called "General Motors technology," where each butcher in line performs a specific function as the carcass moves past instead of the old way of having one man prepare each carcass; and second, the shipping of beef in quarters instead of in trimmed carcasses, eliminating much waste material from the product before transporting it. Neither idea, however, was carried near its ultimate extension.

Sioux City Dressed Beef met with only limited success, both financially and technologically. One reason was that Holman had been unwilling to bet all his chips on it at the start. Instead of running the plant himself, Holman had his investors hire a manager. He continued full-time in his cattle-selling business. The packinghouse suffered not only from the loss of his management skill, but also, perhaps, from a conflict of interest. Holman was selling cattle to his own company, a practice very similar to what Moe Steinman was doing at the same time in New York.

Within a few years, Holman and the packinghouse manager were feuding. Many of the investors sided with the manager. Ostensibly, the issues were such matters as the manager's desire to branch into pork. Holman later said the break-up was over "improprieties," strongly implying that it was the manager rather than Holman who was guilty of them. But basically, in the words of one person who was close to the company, the issue was that "Currier Holman isn't going to be involved in something without wanting to run the whole show himself."

Holman and the investors who sided with him were bought out by their partners (the company they founded is still operating in Sioux City, though it's been through several changes of name and ownership). After giving up on Sioux City Dressed Beef, Holman went back to ringing doorbells looking for money for a new packinghouse. Meanwhile, he had made friends with A. D. "Andy" Anderson, who had built a pork plant in nearby Dennison, Iowa, in the mid-1950s. Anderson shared Holman's opinions about the need to redesign the packing process to take advantage of modern technology, and they used to talk about it when Anderson stopped by Holman's office at the Sioux City stockyards.

According to a story Holman liked to tell, Anderson used to run a small store and "on Thursday nights Andy would be down in the dumps" because that night he'd have "to scale all those fish" for the Friday trade. Then came frozen, pre-scaled fish. Although they yielded a lower profit margin on each sale (and surely didn't taste as good), frozen fish eliminated the mess, brought an increase in volume, and represented (in their minds) the inevitable march of progress. Why shouldn't the same system work with beef? "You know," Anderson would tell Holman, who would latch onto the phrase, "you can't go back to scalin' fish on Thursday night."

They decided to found their new packing company together and by 1960 they got the money—mostly with the help of the investors who had sided with Holman in the split-up of Sioux City Dressed Beef. Iowa Beef Processors Inc. opened its first plant in May, 1961, in Dennison, Iowa, with Holman and Anderson as co-chairmen. Although the great technological leap forward was still in the future, even that first plant in Dennison represented an important advance. Holman bought the cattle directly from feed-lot owners near Dennison, thus thumbing his nose at industry practice. The rules of the stockyards said that all cattle had to be brought to Sioux City and sold there on the open market. Holman saw that this ritual postponed the slaughter for several days and caused a weight loss of up to 7 percent. Since Holman no longer was a member of the stockyards and was buying cattle only for Iowa Beef, he made his own arrangements with feed-lot owners. Cattle were brought in directly, just when the assembly-line process was ready to gobble them up. As little as two or three hours after the animal left the grain trough, the knife descended.

To make this system succeed, Iowa Beef needed a series of processing plants, each near a feed-lot center. So Holman and Anderson bought a second plant in Fort Dodge, Iowa, and remodeled it to their assembly-line system. It opened in June, 1962. (At this writing, Iowa Beef has ten plants and plans for more.)

In the early 1960s, Holman and Anderson knew very well where they were headed. If it made sense to reduce the carcass to quarters before shipping it out of the midwest, then it made further sense to reduce it to primal cuts (loins, ribs, chucks, and rounds) and eventually to smaller cuts known as sub-primals. That way, a supermarket would have to do no real butchering at all—just unpack a box, take each carefully trimmed piece of meat and slice it off like bread into individual cooking portions that would be placed in plastic trays for the meat counter. Theoretically, Iowa Beef could ship the meat already trimmed down to individual portions and packaged in the plastic trays, so all the supermarket would have to do would be to throw them out on the counter. Holman, however, believed supermarkets would prefer to do their own final packaging so that the customer would continue to identify the meat with the particular store and not with the particular packinghouse. This was part of his theory that beef should be treated as a fungible commodity, and, again, circumstances seem to have proved him correct.

But the foresight Currier Holman had in regard to meat, he lacked in regard to other things. He simply didn't reckon with the Mafia. He and Anderson foresaw only one obstacle to their plan—technology. And they proceeded to deal exclusively with technology. To ship such small cuts, they would need new processes for butchering, chilling, and sealing the meat. The processes called for materials and equipment that didn't exist yet. From about 1962 they began working with manufacturers to design the stuff they'd need. For example, Iowa Beef guided Dow Chemical toward development of a new kind of plastic wrapper that would handle easily, seal in the meat from contamination and yet allow it to continue aging in transit. With machine tool manufacturers, Iowa Beef designed a variety of special saws that would allow assembly line butchers to conduct their individual operations quickly and neatly as the conveyor belt moved on. Holman and Anderson laid out a plant, to be built in the Sioux City suburb of Dakota City, Nebraska, where steers would be reduced to sub-primal cuts, and where the sub-primals would then be cryovacked (carefully reduced to temperatures just above freezing), sealed in plastic, and boxed.

Instead of receiving a swinging carcass, the purchaser would receive a box of what he wanted. A & P could hold a sale on chuck in New York while Safeway held a sale on rump roast in San Francisco. The butchering process would be much more efficient at a central location. By-products that the supermarkets couldn't use, such as bone (which can be ground up for animal food), fat, and hide, could be disposed of centrally, which benefitted both cost control and the ecology.

The first of these revolutionary plants opened in Dakota City early in 1967. It was capable at first of boxing only ribs and loins. Two more years were required to bring the plant up to where it could process an entire steer as Holman had dreamed. And by then, a second such plant was under construction at Emporia, Kansas.

The new system meant an end to the traditional two-year apprenticeship for butchers. Says one Iowa Beef executive who worked directly under Holman and Anderson, "Instead of having to teach every operator how to do a whole lot of things, they now have to teach an operator only how to do one thing, such as bone out a plate. The next operator does something else. One man with a certain kind of saw separates the head loin from the short loin. Then it goes to another operation where a guy with a hand knife separates out the tenderloin. Then another operator on a saw saws the bone off the strip loin to make it a boneless strip." And so on. Trimmings, too, can be rough-ground at the plant into the makings of hamburger and boxed (hamburger looks best if fine-ground just before sale). According to Holman, even more important than the butchering efficiency is the precise refrigeration process, which has limited shrinkage (weight loss) from factory to supermarket to less than 2 percent.

By 1969, Holman and his associates seemed to have the technology well in hand. It would be only a few more years before their process was carried to its logical conclusion and they filled supermarket counters with their meat from coast to coast.

All their calculations, however, had omitted several factors that turned out to be just as important as technology: the butchers' union, the Mafia, and Moe Steinman. Holman never really admitted the *real* way his process saves money. He argued that pre-butchering the meat holds down shipping costs. But the expense of cutting, cryovacking, and sealing the meat largely offsets this savings. In fact, some supermarket executives say these expenses actually exceed the savings, so that meat from Iowa Beef may really cost a little more than traditional carcass meat. The one way that the Holman process indisputably saves money and sharply reduces the price of meat to the consumer is that it eliminates butchers' jobs in supermarket warehouses and stores. If the meat has already been butchered at the packinghouse, then the task of displaying it on the receiving end no longer requires a staff of skilled butchers. The task becomes more like that of a high-school boy who unpacks canned peas from a carton and puts them onto the shelf. What the Iowa Beef formula really amounts to is replacing a large number of highly-skilled, highly-unionized butchers who receive big-city pay rates, with a smaller number of less-skilled, less-unionized butchers who receive rural pay rates.

So the butchers' union had a real cause for concern over the rise of Iowa Beef. It is the commonly accepted belief that the Mafia and Moe Steinman merely exploited that legitimate concern. But Robert Nicholson and others in and out of law enforcement have another theory: that some leaders of the butchers' union were, from the very beginning, part of a mammoth conspiracy to sell out their own members and shake down Iowa Beef as no major company had ever been shaken down before.

3

The Crime

Iowa Beef came under seige in 1969. The developments were so swift and startling, and came from so many different directions, that at first shock it may not have occurred to Currier Holman how they all related.

In approximately January, 1969 (officials have offered conflicting dates), the Dakota City plant began to box whole steers. Until then, the plant had been able to handle only ribs and loins. The plant did have supermarket customers, but ribs and loins are used primarily by the so-called "HRI trade"—hotels, restaurants, and institutions. America's daily at-home diet is the chuck and the round, the shoulders and haunches of the animal, and the backbone of the supermarket meat trade.

Thus it was not until early 1969 that Iowa Beef could really begin the mass marketing retail store campaign that Holman and Anderson had envisioned when they started out. Iowa Beef, it's true, was already at or near the top of the slaughtering business, perhaps the nation's leading supplier of carcass beef to supermarket chains and local processing operations. But the company clearly was going to rise or fall on whether the new boxed beef program went over. Boxed beef in supermarkets had been the whole idea from the beginning.

New York is easily the country's biggest meat market. The New York market traditionally includes everything within a wide sweep of the city—Moe Steinman had been defining his territory as everything within a 125-mile radius of Columbus Circle (at Fifty-ninth Street and Eighth Avenue). This 250-mile-wide area is not only populous, but exceptionally carnivorous. Some 16 percent of all the meat consumed in the United States (according to industry figures) is consumed in this market. Moreover, the market takes in a lot of meat that is processed there and shipped elsewhere, including overseas. And California, the other major population center, has tended to be an island to itself as far as meat is concerned, with the big midwestern packers traditionally not shipping across the Rockies (though Iowa Beef is trying now to change all that).

At any rate, it is not unusual to hear meat men say that New York represents 25 percent of the total market they are shooting at. Clearly, Iowa Beef had to have New York.

To line up the market, Iowa Beef employed an experienced meat salesman, Lewis Jacobs. Under Jacobs, the company won orders fairly quickly from two major supermarket chains in the area, Pathmark (which is operated by Supermarkets General Corp.) and Shop-Rite (a cooperative of individually-owned chains that buy under the name Wakefern). Jacobs later recalled hearing that there was a clause in the butchers' union contract that might prohibit bringing in pre-butchered meat. Butchers' contracts all over the country had such clauses, and in many areas they were quite explicit. In New York, however, the clause was rather vague, and the Iowa Beef idea seemed good. So Aaron Perlmutter, chief meat buyer for Supermarkets General, decided to risk a purchase. He even flew to Dakota City to take a look at the plant and seal the deal.

A half a dozen carloads (a carload is a tractor-trailer full, or about forty thousand pounds) were delivered and used. Then a shipment was rejected by Pathmark on grounds that it was no good.

One carload of meat, worth maybe $40,000, rejected by one supermarket chain, normally wouldn't cause a crisis in a major corporation. But there was nothing normal about this. As soon as he heard about the rejection, Currier Holman knew his whole career was at stake. "Andy and I got on an airplane [a private jet] and went [to New York] that morning. Got there that afternoon," Holman recalled later. Not wanting to get held up by bureaucracy, they waited until 4 A.M., then barged onto the loading dock and opened the boxes. "There was nothing wrong with the meat," Holman insisted. He went to Pathmark as soon as the doors opened.

"Show us what's wrong," Holman demanded. "Why won't you take it in?"

He couldn't get an answer. He and Anderson spent eight hours arguing with underlings. Finally they fought their way to the boss's office. Milton Perlmutter ran Pathmark (he had hired his father, Aaron, to handle the meat end of the business). At first, the younger Perlmutter continued to argue that the Iowa Beef shipment had been of poor quality. Holman, knowing better, searched for another motive.

At last, Holman discovered that Milton Perlmutter indeed had a "hang-up —he wasn't going to buck the union. . . . He said, 'Look, our people on the dock won't unload that. Now it's as simple as that. I'm not going to force them to. I'll bring it up in negotiations.' "

So dedicated to work were Holman and Anderson that they spent extra hours personally trying to dispose of their forty thousand pounds of meat before it really did go bad; Holman says they finally sold it for a five-cent-a-pound loss "in East Cupcake, New Jersey, or some goddamned place." But the real crisis wasn't the forty thousand pounds of meat; it was the future of Iowa Beef, and of the whole meat industry. For many months, Lew Jacobs couldn't sell any more meat to anybody.

In April, 1968, the butchers' union had begun a continuing campaign of diatribe against Iowa Beef and its new methods. A long article in a union newspaper was headlined "The Shape of Things to Come!" and referred to Iowa Beef over and over again as a "monster." It said, "What we see before us are the rapidly mounting technological advancements which have become a Frankenstein monster that in time will swallow and destroy the great majority of . . . our jobs." The article railed against "employer demands that they be given carte blanche to bring in pre-cut and pre-packaged, consumer-ready retail cuts from anywhere in the country." The article was written by Frank Kissel, who was still a major voice in the union even on the eve of his departure for state prison. Under Kissel's leadership, the union put together a movie about the "monster" featuring scenes of the Iowa Beef plant in operation, and began showing the movie to the rank and file.

Right on the heels of this campaign came the Moe Steinman-Iowa Beef shakedown. In the wake of the scandal, the union has contended that it never really opposed the concept of boxed beef at all, and that New York butchers rejected Iowa Beef's product in 1969 out of sympathy for a strike that their fellow butchers were waging over pay in the Dakota City plant. But Iowa Beef's meat was rejected in New York many months before there was a butchers' strike in Dakota City. The Pathmark incident occurred early in 1969, and there was no strike until August.

The union has contended that its contract in New York, unlike its contracts in many other cities, never prohibited boxed beef. It is true that the New York butchers' contract language was vague (it said retail cutting had to be done on premises, but it didn't say whether this meant that *all* butchering had to be done on premises). Nor did the union ever tell Iowa Beef explicitly, on the record, that boxed beef wouldn't be permitted into New York. Nevertheless, the situation was abundantly clear to most of the people involved, especially to Holman.

"Now whether it was in their contract," Holman said, "I never read their contract. The practical aspects of the matter were that there were thousands of dollars worth of meat there that there was nothing wrong with, that the union wouldn't unload. It had absolutely nothing to do with the strike. . . . So it became obvious that we [he and Anderson], a couple of naive midwesterners, had taken on a very big task, because we really did not understand. . . . Every Amalgamated contract in the country [not literally true] has a clause which says that they'll only take carcass beef. Now several years ago, we decided we might someday take that to the Supreme Court because it might be an illegal part of any contract. But we didn't choose to do that before we built millions of dollars worth of new facilities." Lew Jacobs recalled the situation pretty much the same way.

Throughout 1969, they continued desperately to try to sign up a major eastern supermarket chain. There was no success. The factory at Dakota City had a capacity for forty thousand cattle a week; yet production was down to six or seven thousand—in Holman's words, "because we just couldn't sell programs."

On a mid-summer morning of 1969, Benny Moscowitz, a Fourteenth Street meat dealer, sat down for coffee with Herbie Newman at a restaurant on the corner of Fourteenth Street and Ninth Avenue. Such meetings were frequent. Newman was the operating partner of Moe Steinman's meat brokerage business. Moscowitz was one of the meat dealers who had to pay bribe money to union officers and supermarket meat buyers through Steinman. He had been part of that shakedown network at least since the 1950s, when he was a member of the Block Brothers' country club. The way it worked in 1969, Steinman would bill Moscowitz periodically for meat that didn't exist. Moscowitz would pay for it with a corporate check, cash the check himself, put 10 percent in his pocket, and hand the rest to Steinman or Newman for appropriate distribution. But this morning—actually, it was lunchtime in the meat district, where work begins about 6 A.M.—Herbert Newman managed to throw into the conversation the name of Currier Holman. That was interesting, Moscowitz said. It had been a long time since the two had talked, but Moscowitz used to know Holman rather well. Newman nearly jumped from his seat. He was ecstatic. He continued to pump the puzzled Moscowitz for details. The story began in 1945, when the Office of Price Administration had been trying to allocate scarce meat supplies. Moscowitz's stepfather, who was also in the meat business, had gone to Sioux City to try to find a source of cattle. Currier Holman knew where the cattle were, so, through the stepfather, Moscowitz back in New York began buying cattle through Holman. Holman would arrange for the slaughter at a nearby slaughterhouse, then ship the carcass east. After the first load came orders for a second, and a third.

As Holman himself later remembered it, "Then one day he called and said, 'I'm coming out to see you.' So I—he came out to the house for dinner and he was so goddamned uncomfortable." Holman laughed as he told the story: "We didn't have kosher meat, so he couldn't eat. . . . Anyway, he said, 'Jeez, I never made so much money in my life. This is the greatest business I've ever seen. You could get whatever [price] you wanted. They were all lined up in the morning.' " Holman later visited Moscowitz on a trip to New York, and even went to Moscowitz's house for dinner and met Moscowitz's wife. The relationship continued for a few years after the war.

Over their coffee, Moscowitz told Newman this story, and couldn't understand why Newman was so interested. Moscowitz was strictly a small fry, and Holman was a thousand miles away. Yet Steinman's partner was bouncing around the restaurant booth. "Holman—oh, he's terrific," Newman exclaimed. Then he assured Moscowitz, "You'll hear from Moe about this."

Shortly afterward, on August 24, 1969, the Amalgamated Meat Cutters and Butcher Workmen of North America struck the Dakota City plant of Iowa Beef. Officially, the union said it was striking over pay and working conditions—very specific local issues—at the Dakota City plant. That made the strike easier to justify before the public and the government, and the local workers certainly believed it. Iowa Beef had never been a generous employer, and the Dakota City workers had plenty of legitimate gripes.

But the strike was heavily supported by the international union. The union's opposition to the whole concept of boxed beef had been too widely and repeatedly expressed for the issue to be confused now. Holman knew the strike was really over his basic concept. His mistake, if he made one, was to assume that Kissel and other international leaders were sincere in their undying opposition to boxed beef. He did not seem to consider at first that this giant international labor organization might just be setting him up for the Syndicate.

By October, the strike was beginning to hurt. Holman, undaunted, was still out looking for customers. One day, while he was in Los Angeles talking to officials of Young's Market, he got a message that an old friend from New York had been trying to reach him—Benny Moscowitz. Holman returned the call. "He said he wanted to bring a guy out to see me."

Holman immediately told Moscowitz, "We've got lots of problems. Let's talk about it over the phone."

"No," Moscowitz said, "you've got to meet these people. I'll bring them out."

So a meeting was set up at the Rodeway Inn in Sioux City. (The recollections of Holman here are taken from an account he gave to the New York District Attorney's office, which Nicholson secretly recorded, interspersed with additional material from an interview Holman gave to the author in 1976.)

Holman and Anderson "went up to the Rodeway, and, uh, Benny was sitting there, and he said he had some people he wanted me to meet." Unfortunately, Moscowitz's friends were late sleepers, and they weren't dressed yet. Holman had to wait for them. "I get up early," Moscowitz explained by way of excuse. "In the packing business, we're pretty early risers."

Finally Herbie Newman showed up in the lobby. He was a large older man with thick glasses, who, perhaps because of vision problems, kept his head tilted back and tended to look down his nose at people. They chatted awhile.

"And then walks in a guy. . . ." Holman paused, seemingly unable to describe Moe Steinman. "And so we're sitting in the middle of a lobby of a motel, and I said, 'What are you? What's your business?' "

"Er, I do a couple of things," Steinman replied. First, Steinman told Holman, he was a vice-president of the Daitch-Shopwell supermarket chain.

Holman: "I said, 'well, that's interesting.' I said, 'We're trying to sell a lot of meat to the chain stores. We tried to sell your goddamn chain. Maybe you can help us.' "

"Maybe I can," Moe Steinman replied.

Then Steinman said, "I got a interest in another company, called Trans-World." Holman remembered the name. Trans-World had been buying briskets (for corned beef) and other offal (meat not part of the chuck, round, ribs, or loin) from Iowa Beef since the early 1960s. It still did not quite click in Holman's mind that he was looking at the man who, with Holman's meat, fed every drunk in the world's largest city on St. Patrick's Day.

"What do you want to talk about?" Holman asked.

"Well, we want to talk about buying some product from you."

At about this time, Holman suggested that they all go over to the plant. Steinman crowded into the front seat with Holman and Anderson, and they drove across the Missouri River to Dakota City. "We got into a kind of a pissin' match coming out in the car," Holman recalled. "He was talking about being in Trans-World, and being vice-president of Daitch-Shopwell, which I didn't understand. I said, 'Then, well, what the hell—er—how can you be vice-president for Daitch-Shopwell? Do you want to buy them for Daitch-Shopwell or do you want to buy them for Trans-World?' "

"Newman's the one that wants to buy," Steinman said. "I'm here just, er, to help him."

Holman: "I said to him, I said, 'You know, you couldn't work for me.' I said, 'We don't countenance people doing two or three things on the side. . . .' There was a conflict of interest someplace. . . . Well, he laughed it off. . . . He said he didn't consider it that."

At the Iowa Beef office, which adjoins the Dakota City plant, Holman had Newman and Steinman talk to some salesmen about the price of skirt steaks, which Newman seemed to be interested in. Meanwhile, he called Moscowitz aside.

"What the hell are you doing out here?" Holman asked his old friend.

"These people didn't believe I knew you," Moscowitz replied.

Holman: "I said, 'What the hell's that?' It didn't seem like very much of a deal to know me."

Moscowitz didn't explain. Years later, Holman would give it more thought. "I don't know," he said. "Maybe the union sent Steinman out here. There were so many things happening at the time."

He did recall that at one point, Steinman said, "Maybe I can help you in New York City. Maybe I can help you with your labor problems."

"We can sure as Christ use all the help we can get," Holman replied.

Apparently Steinman left his charm back on Fourteenth Street, because he managed to thoroughly insult Holman and everyone else at Iowa Beef by refusing to take the customary tour through the most wonderful meat plant in the whole world. "And it seemed odd to me," Holman said. "I remember he said, when was the next plane out of here. He was here for a couple of hours and wanted to go home!" (On a subsequent visit, Steinman did tour the plant, though only at Holman's insistence, and then he still managed to insult everyone by not taking his sun glasses off the whole time.)

On that first day, and at their subsequent meetings, Holman spent significant time talking alone with Steinman. Sometimes Anderson—who has consistently refused to talk about the whole business—listened to what they were saying, but no one else did. There has never been a really satisfying account of what went on in these conversations. Holman has denied there was anything inconsistent with what he's put on the record. But Steinman must have said something about doing business with Iowa Beef beyond just "helping" Newman. After Steinman left, Holman took time to telephone Martin Rosengarten, the president of Daitch-Shopwell, to ask if he was aware of Steinman's outside activities. Holman later recalled that "Rosengarten said, yeah, he didn't care what he did, 'cause he was very valuable." And at one point on that first visit, after talking to Steinman, Holman told Newman, "We've got a little problem here. You can sure as Christ help us. We're getting killed with boycotts in New York. If you can move any goddamned meat, why we'll sure appreciate it."

Over the course of the fall and winter, the strike began to evolve into a war. Scabs were working at the plant and several of them or their relatives were shot. One woman died of gunshot wounds after rumors started that she had leaked information to company security guards. A bullet was fired through Holman's window while he was sitting in his office. (He kept the window with the bullet hole in it exactly as it was for several years afterward.) Police records indicate thirty-three instances of dynamite either found or exploded, but they don't indicate that anybody ever went to jail for it. The history of law enforcement in Sioux City would not have provided a threatened man much comfort. According to Don Oldis, who tried to operate a reform-oriented newspaper in Sioux City during the early 1960s, the lawmen themselves spent much of their time operating brothels and illegal drinking establishments, and collecting money from private parking lot concessions. After a series of exposés, Oldis's newspaper plant was hit by two suspected arsons, the second of which burned it to the ground. He's now a real estate man in Denver.

While Holman saw his office become an object of siege, with bullets flying and dynamite bursting around the city, Benny Moscowitz kept reminding him of Steinman's visit. Moscowitz called several times and put on the phone people he said were former butchers' union vice-presidents; these men said they could help Iowa Beef resolve the strike. Holman evidently was slow to get the message.

To help deliver it, the Mob-bribed New York leadership sent fifteen hundred workers parading through the Fourteenth Street area urging the cutting shops there to refuse to buy even carcass meat from Iowa Beef. Meanwhile, the Emporia plant opened. That plant has never successfully been organized by any union, and so wasn't affected directly by the strike. But Iowa Beef was now slaughtering more than forty-four thousand cattle a week. It had to have some New York supermarket chains.

Then P. L. Nymann's house blew up. "Gus" Nymann was Iowa Beef's general counsel. He lived at 3905 Sylvan Way in Sioux City. His neighbor on the left was Currier Holman. Said Holman later, "They burned our general counsel's house to the ground. It was intended to be my house, which is immediately contiguous to his, but they just missed. . . ."

"There was no question that it was a professional job," Holman continued. "All week we'd had these problems in the neighborhood that the goddamned garage doors didn't work. I mean in the middle of the night the garage doors would go up, or they wouldn't go up at all the next day." Someone obviously had been experimenting with a radio-control device. "And in doing that they got the wavelength of a garage door, and it was the one next to mine. And some time a bomb was planted there. A woman went out of the house about seven-thirty, took some children to school, drove back at about twenty minutes to eight. About sixteen minutes to eight the goddamn thing—boom! I was looking out the window and I heard the son of a bitch go off."

Police say it's a miracle no one was hurt or killed. The heat from the blast was so intense that a steel lawn mower in the garage was literally melted. No one was ever charged with the crime.

In all his statements, Holman managed to fuzz-over the question of exactly when he caved in and called Moe Steinman. He tried to give the impression that he didn't talk to Steinman again until after the strike was settled the second week of April, 1970. Other statements by him and his associates make it seem likely that he talked to Steinman before that. Gus Nymann, the general counsel, remembers Holman discussing Steinman a lot in the weeks *before* the strike was settled. Later, in court testimony, Nymann tried to recall these conversations: "Mr. Steinman had influence with or could handle union officers," Holman had told him. "I think I'd have to say I was curious. I wasn't sure whether it meant that he'd wine them and dine them or do other favors for them, or possibly the ultimate of paying them money."

Holman has also left fuzzy the date of another significant conversation. At some point in March or April of 1970, he called Fred Lovette, the head of Holly Farms, the nation's leading chicken producer. He knew that Holly Farms had run into problems with the butchers' union in New York just three years earlier, and appeared to have solved those problems by hiring Moe Steinman as a broker.

Holman: "I said, 'Fred, what, er, do you know anything about Steinman?'

He said, 'Yeah, I know him, and, er, he's really responsible for our First National [Finast Supermarkets] business that you saw. I think he can help you in New York if anybody can. . . . If you want to be successful with First National or the other retailers in New York City, it's my opinion that he can do a great deal for you.' "

Several Iowa Beef officers were in the room when the call was made and heard the conversation over a speaker-phone. As Howard Weiner, the treasurer, recalls it, Lovette said, "Prior to their relationship with Moe Steinman they had difficulty getting their product into the New York area, and after the relationship with Moe Steinman they were able to get their product into the New York area." Lovette also told the Iowa Beef men that he had been required to put Steinman's son-in-law, Walter Bodenstein, on retainer as legal counsel in New York.

By April, 1970, with the strike unsolved and the meat unsold, Iowa Beef showed a $9 million loss for the year so far. "The banks were becoming restless," Holman admitted.

Chemical Bank, the lead bank in Iowa Beef's $30 million loan line, wanted to talk it over. So Holman, Anderson, Howard Weiner (the treasurer), and Dale Tinstman (a Nebraska investment banker who was then handling Iowa Beef's securities and who is now president of the company) flew to New York April 10. As Holman recalled the meeting at the bank, Iowa Beef was told, "You people either put $15 million in equity in front of your line of credit, or we want to be paid off."

Holman later remembered his dismay. Iowa Beef would have "gone broke" he said. He told the banker that in "today's market and with . . . the strike we're in right now . . . you know damn well that it's impossible . . . for us to sell one dollar's worth of equity in this goddamn company. What you're saying is that you want out."

"Well, er, you said it," the banker told him.

Two things happened then, apparently that same afternoon of April 10, 1970. A tentative agreement was reached in the butchers' strike. And Holman called Moe Steinman to arrange a meeting. According to Holman, the strike settlement came first. That leaves open the question of why Holman, knowing what he knew, would call Steinman immediately *after* the strike was settled. This is Holman's explanation: "We had trouble. Very deep trouble. [We were] out of cash. . . . So Andy and I decided to come back to New York City and talk to Mr. Steinman . . . to see if he could as a matter of fact help us with the retailers as he said he could."

The morning after the tentative strike settlement and the arrangement for a meeting with Steinman, Chemical Bank backed off from its demands. This gave Iowa Beef some breathing time. But everyone knew that sooner or later the boxed beef was going to have to come into the New York market if Iowa Beef was to survive.

Several days later the Dakota City labor accord was completed. On April 21, 1970, Iowa Beef's top executives were back in New York and settled in at the Stanhope Hotel for an afternoon meeting with Moe Steinman. In the party were Holman, Anderson, general counsel Nymann, and J. Robert Kemp, the new co-chairman who had officially replaced Anderson in preparation for Anderson's early retirement. At lunch beforehand, Holman explained the situation to Lew Jacobs, the company's unsuccessful New York salesman. As Jacobs remembers the explanation, Steinman had "indicated" that his Trans-World brokerage did business with the New York chains, and "would be the company that could best provide sales for the boxed beef product in the New York area." But, Holman told Jacobs, "in view of the fact that a contract existed that stated that beef of this type was not allowed . . . there would have to be some sort of agreement, or arrangement. . . ." Holman also promised to test Steinman's ability first by having him "produce . . . various union officials at a specific time and at a specific place."

Steinman arrived at the Stanhope with his brother Sol and partner Herbie Newman. Holman told him right off that Iowa Beef needed to sell the boxed equivalent of sixteen thousand carcasses a week in New York, more than had ever been sold by one company, and that he needed a "showcase" chain that would convert its meat program to handle Iowa Beef's product exclusively. By Holman's recollection, Steinman said, "I can help you with some of the retailers. I'm not sure I can help you with all." Then Steinman picked up a Yellow Pages and pointed out fourteen chains "that he thought he could help us with." Later he enlarged the number to nineteen chains. Then Holman told Steinman about the union resistance, and Steinman said, "I don't know, but I think I can handle it."

Jacobs doesn't remember so much equivocating. He says Steinman declared that in exchange for a commission from Iowa Beef, "he would guarantee through his influence with union officials that metropolitan New York would be an open city insofar as receiving boxed beef products into the retail chain stores and warehouses."

Then, in Holman's words, Steinman "walked to the corner phone, he made three or four calls—I can't remember whether there were two calls made at the time and then another call—and then two people called him back. After the sequence of phone calls was over, he said, okay, he said, tomorrow noon we will have the union, the vice-presidents, the presidents of the unions that are involved in this territory around Columbus Circle here and we'll talk."

That set the stage for the key Stanhope meeting the next day. The four executives from Dakota City gathered in the suite where they had met the day before and they waited. Almost precisely at noon, they heard a knock on the door. Steinman led them down the corridor to another room where some men were waiting. "It was very dark," according to Holman. "The blinds were closed. I remember I couldn't even see. I was having troubles focusing on the guys' faces down the other end of the room." The faces were convincing testaments to Steinman's power. They belonged to:

> •Irving Stern, international vice-president of the union and director of the New York region, who had emerged from Local 342, the main retail butchers' local in the area;
> •Albert DeProspoe, the man Frank Kissel had picked to succeed him as head of Local 174, which dealt largely with wholesalers but also with some retailers;
> •Irving "Izzy" Kaplan, also an international vice-president and head of Local 464, which covered most of New Jersey (Kaplan was the man who had helped mobster Gerry Catena in the soap sales campaign that resulted in arson and murder at the A & P); and
> •Frank Brescio, an official in DeProspoe's local and brother of Mafia labor extortionist Larry "Chappy the Dude" Brescia, the former bodyguard and driver for Lucky Luciano. (The D.A.'s office says Brescia was there; union sources insist he wasn't. The brothers spell their name differently.)

Also present, waiting for the Iowa Beef men, were two outside lawyers who were defending the union in civil lawsuits Iowa Beef had filed alleging Taft-Hartley Act violations during the strike. The lawyers had been brought to the Stanhope because Steinman promised that the lawsuits would be dropped as part of the overall settlement. But because he was an outside observer, one of the lawyers, Harold Cammer, was able to provide a delightful description of the meeting. He had never before seen Moe Steinman and didn't know who he was.

"He was just a furtive-looking character out of *Guys and Dolls,*" Cammer says of Steinman. "I thought he was a messenger, or a coffee-getter—some greasy, sleazy-looking fellow who never looked you in the eye, who had a hang-dog look about him. I thought he was there to get coffee for the Iowa Beef people. I had no notion until later that I was in the presence of a famous character. This fellow, he looks like a worm.

"The Iowa Beef people," Cammer continues, "when they came in the room I thought they were Texas Rangers. They looked like a bunch of Texas Rangers."

Cammer and his colleague, thinking the meeting had been called to settle the Taft-Hartley case, began talking law. Nymann, Iowa Beef's counsel argued back. At this point, by Holman's recollection, Irving Stern, the union's regional director, exploded. "You goddamn lawyers get the hell out of here," Stern barked. "You get your ass out and don't come back until I call you. They got a room for you down at the end of the hall."

Stern had just come from the Black Angus where he and Steinman had shared an early lunch with lots of drink and food and promises that the union's troubles with Iowa Beef would soon be over. Later, Stern would go to jail for tax evasion after being charged with taking bribes from Steinman. Now, on Stern's command (though he denies he used profanity), the two union lawyers and Nymann padded meekly back to the Iowa Beef suite to wait.

As soon as they were gone, by Holman's account, Stern demanded to know, "Okay, now, what is it? What's the deal?"

Holman replied that he wanted his boxed beef in New York, "and I don't want any more ass-aches like I got hit with out at Supermarkets General [Pathmark]." Holman said he would drop his lawsuits against the New York unions if they would allow his boxed beef to come in.

"And there was silence in the room," Holman recalled.

Steinman broke it. "Okay, you guys go on down to your room and we'll come back to you," he said. Holman and the Iowa Beef crew left.

Holman later insisted that there was no mention in front of the union leaders that Steinman had a brokerage deal in the works with Iowa Beef. But then Holman added, "I'm not saying what happened when I wasn't in the room."

The executives waited, somewhat in awe. "We were impressed," Holman later acknowledged, "that Mr. Steinman could arrange for the union officials to be there. . . . That the night before, he, with a phone call, the next day— and they did appear!"

After about twenty minutes, there was a knock on the door. "Come on down," Steinman said. Holman and his men returned to the darkened room with the union leaders. "Mr. Stern was the spokesman," Holman recalled. "He was pretty cryptic. He said, 'Okay, if you do what you say you're going to do, you got it.' "

Thus the fate of Iowa Beef was sealed. There remained only the small problem of convincing the lawyers to forget about the pending Taft-Hartley suits. The prospect of lengthy litigation apparently had them all envisioning new cars or trips abroad. Holman said they looked as if they were "going to cry, or jump out the window." But he insisted that his only desire was to sell meat, not to pursue damage suits.

The lawyers and labor leaders were dispatched. Steinman joined Holman and Anderson for a drink at the bar, and then went back up to the Iowa Beef suite, where they began hammering out terms of the brokerage agreement. Nymann, who apparently had been waiting for them back in the room with Kemp, remembers that the meeting lasted two-and-a-half hours. He says Steinman was demanding a brokerage fee of thirty-five cents for every one hundred pounds of meat sold, which was substantially higher than Iowa Beef's normal brokerage agreement of twenty-five cents on boxed meat and seventeen and a half cents on carcass meat.

Nymann and Kemp both observed (according to their testimony later) that Steinman repeatedly tapped Holman and Anderson on the shoulder, or on the knee, and retreated with them into the bedroom to consult in private. Apparently Steinman recognized that Nyman and Kemp had reservations about the agreement, and he wanted to deal behind their backs. Kemp remembers calling Holman aside and warning him that Steinman "seemed to be kind of low-class, a low-class individual. He had a pretty raunchy outfit on." (Harold Cammer, the union lawyer, remembers "a loud suit and a florid green tie—he looked like a tout.") But Holman was not dissuaded.

That night Holman and Anderson went to dinner with Moe and Sol Steinman and the two Steinman wives, at the Black Angus. "And they knew everybody there!" Holman later marveled.

On Holman's return to Dakota City, there were numerous meetings of the executive staff to discuss the deal. Howard Weiner, the treasurer, remembers attending them and being told that union people had "recommended or suggested or identified" Steinman as a man who "could open doors. . . . It was discussed that . . . the nature of his relationship with the union was an unusual one . . . being the vice-president of labor relations for a retailer, a management person, and still a close relationship with union people and a friendly relationship. This seemed in conflict with what we were used to as management people."

On the other hand, Weiner notes, "The reputation of New York City preceded our involvement with . . . Steinman. . . . We felt that it was a common practice that people paid other people off to do business in New York City." Weiner remembers open talk "that Moe Steinman's influence and his ability to open doors meant that he was going to pay off union people and meat buyers. This possibility was distasteful to everyone in these meetings, including Mr. Holman. The conversations always came to a conclusion by Mr. Holman's remarks and question: 'Do you want to get your meat into New York? New York is the largest meat market in the world. You want to sell there or don't you?'

"I had said at various times, 'It's a sad state of affairs that Iowa Beef, the 127th largest manufacturing company in the country, the largest beef producer in the world, has to do business with people like this,' " Weiner says.

Roy Lee, Jr., was just taking over as president and chief operating officer of the company (part of the move in which Anderson was retiring and Robert Kemp was being moved up as a replacement). Lee says he objected to the Steinman deal, but that Holman told him "this was the only way to get boxed meat into New York, that because of Steinman's connections he could get 150 loads a week of meat sales quickly. . . . It was indicated that [Steinman's commission] would be used to pay off meat buyers and labor officials."

Did they know they were dealing with the Mafia and with underworld elements? "I never heard him [Steinman] use the words," Holman said. "I just assumed that he would kind of . . ." Holman never finished the sentence.

In May, Steinman arrived at Dakota City with his brother. Characteristically, he started intimidating his hosts before they could even begin to make any demands of their own. First, he dashed Holman's assumption, based on talks at the Stanhope, that he was going to do something tangible for his money, such as set up distribution warehouses for the meat in New Jersey, the Bronx, Manhattan, and Long Island. Holman had told his colleagues in

Dakota City that Steinman would have to invest "some multimillion dollars" to establish his business. But when Steinman arrived, and Holman began to talk about the first distribution center, according to Lew Jacobs, the Steinmans immediately "rejected the idea on the basis that . . . it would entail too much money and they didn't want to get involved with the labor or the facility at that particular time." The executives nodded meekly. Moe wouldn't be handling any meat. Nobody asked Steinman just what it was that he expected to get paid for. Everyone knew.

Next came the discussion of the commission, which Holman had hoped to lower to the normal twenty-five cents a hundredweight or less. But Moe announced that not only was twenty-five cents not enough money, but even thirty-five cents was not enough. Rather than accept a cut, he demanded a raise. In Jacobs's words, "Steinman said . . . that he would need more money, and it was around that time that we were asked to leave the room." Holman, Anderson, and the Steinmans continued the discussions privately.

Moe immediately demanded fifty cents a hundredweight.

"For Christ's sake, I'm not going to pay fifty cents a hundred," Holman responded.

"Well," Steinman said (according to Holman's account), "look, I got to buy a union steward. You had trouble in Supermarkets General. I've got to buy a guy a broad. I may have to buy a chain store buyer and, er, I've got to pay in cash. I can do it for fifty cents and that's it. Take it or leave it."

Holman adjourned to a private office with Anderson, who advised his reluctant partner to pay the money (according to Holman; Anderson would neither testify in court nor be interviewed for this book). "Jesus Christ," Anderson told Holman, "we've paid [another broker] that for years. . . . You know what we do in Las Vegas. We can't sell a goddamn pound of meat out there. You know what [a salesman] said about [a prominent hotel in Los Angeles]. We got to buy the goddamn chef in order to get the meat in there."

Holman later recalled what went through his mind. He was "dealing with a bunch of crooks in New York. Same crooks we deal with in Los Angeles or you have them out in Las Vegas." There was no way around it, he decided. "Anybody that's in the meat business in New York City is a crook. . . . I finally agreed to pay him a half a buck."

Holman was wrong, of course. Not everybody in the meat business in New York is a crook. A lot of New York meat dealers hate Moe Steinman and everything he stands for. They—like their customers—are in the majority, the victims. They have lost money and risked their personal safety to resist Steinman over the years. But there are indeed crooks in the meat business in New York. And Currier Holman was about to do business with them.

Roy Lee nominally the president and chief operating officer, remembers that he and other executives objected to the 50-cent commission. He says Holman overrode them. Lee also says Holman and the other executives tried to get Steinman to accept a quota system, under which he would have to guarantee a minimum level of performance in order to get paid. Moe Steinman would hear none of it. There would be no minimum quotas.

Holman then told Steinman that Iowa Beef needed a "showcase" supermarket chain in New York. If one chain would turn its entire meat program over to Iowa Beef, other chains could see by example how Holman's new boxed beef concept saved money.

"The best one you can have is Waldbaum's," Steinman told him. "They sell the best meat in New York. They got the finest stores."

"What the hell," Holman replied. "Why don't you put it in your own goddamn store?"

"Herb Olstein, he ain't gonna buy boxed beef," Steinman said. Olstein—Steinman's friend and subordinate at Daitch-Shopwell—was and still is head of the chain's meat department. In 1977 and 1978, Daitch-Shopwell centered its advertising campaign around Olstein, and his supposedly superior ability to discriminate between good meat and bad. Olstein's discerning visage constantly peered out from the food pages of the *New York Times,* an enticement to shop at his butcher counters. But back in 1970, Steinman insisted that Olstein was just too pigheaded to perceive the virtues of what Steinman and his family would later contend was the best beef in the whole wide world. On the other hand, Steinman said, Aaron Freedman, the executive who supervised the meat department for Ira Waldbaum's chain, "is the kind of guy that's got an open mind in the meat business." Holman said he immediately assumed that Steinman was paying Freedman off, though he never asked. Evidence later would show that Freedman was indeed rewarded heavily for his loyalty to Moe Steinman and Johnny Dio. Steinman mentioned at one point that if Waldbaum's bought the boxed beef, Freedman might become a stockholder in Steinman's commission company. He didn't though—straight bribery was enough for Aaron Freedman.

Within a month—"as soon as we could get him there," Holman said—Aaron Freedman was touring the plant at Dakota City. Moe Steinman had escorted him there.

Meanwhile, Lew Jacobs, the salesman, was sent back to New York. He was still going to have to do the real legwork. Steinman would earn his commission with a few phone calls, and maybe by ironing out occasional wrinkles over a scotch at the Black Angus. On Steinman's instructions, Jacobs leased an office at 527 Madison Avenue in the name of Cattle-Pakt Sales Inc. ("Cattle-Pakt" was Iowa Beef's trademark for its boxed beef program.) Jacobs sent the lease to Walter Bodenstein, Steinman's son-in-law and lawyer, as Steinman told him to do. Then Steinman began arranging interviews for Jacobs with the same supermarket purchasing executives who had turned a cold shoulder before. Steinman never went along with Jacobs to these meetings, and Jacobs was instructed not to mention Steinman's name. That "wasn't necessary," Jacobs says Steinman told him.

Jacobs was surprised to find, however, that the purchasing executives themselves brought up Steinman's name. On June 3, Jacobs was set up with appointments to see Freedman at Waldbamm's and also Alvin Bernstein, the meat buyer at the Big Apple chain (now part of Shop-Rite). Bernstein later pleaded guilty to tax evasion in connection with charges of taking $268,000 in bribes in 1969, 1970, and 1971.

Both Freedman and Bernstein gave Jacobs the same answer when he asked them to place an order: "I'm going to have to speak to Moe Steinman about it," they said. Bernstein added that he knew Aaron Freedman was about to travel to Dakota City with Steinman and that Big Apple wouldn't buy from Iowa Beef until they got back. All these men, of course, were supposed to be competing with each other for customers. Jacobs was getting an impression of the New York meat industry not unlike Alice's first impression of Wonderland. Soon he wrote back to Holman, "I believe that once we can arrive at an understanding with Moe, we can expect standing orders . . . for chucks or backs from Daitch, Waldbaum's, Hills, and Big Apple. All the accounts will project their promotions [advertised specials] with us and will cooperate as best they can."

It must be remembered that Iowa Beef was asking stores to do much more than just add a competitive product to their existing line of meat. Boxed beef was a whole new product, to be handled in a revolutionary new way, with most of the butchering work eliminated at the retail level. The product would in most cases have to be introduced gradually, but ultimately Iowa Beef was asking stores to convert their entire meat handling operation and to foresake all traditional suppliers in favor of Iowa Beef, either exclusively or else in company only with other packers offering boxed beef.

Back from Dakota City, Steinman met with Jacobs on Monday, June 15, 1970, and told him to go the next day to the Big Apple warehouse office in East Islip, Long Island. There, Alvin Bernstein placed an order for boxed beef.

On Wednesday, July 8, 1970, Jacobs was sent to the office of Food Fair stores. "They told me that as in the past they had no clearance from their local union for permission to handle boxed beef," Jacobs recalls. "I called Moe Steinman and told him about it, and he said that he would look into it. . . . He said that he would take care of it." Evidently, he did—with the help of Irving Kaplan, the butchers' union leader in New Jersey, where Food Fair's regional meat warehouse was located. Kaplan, it seems, went to Food Fair on behalf of Iowa Beef just as he had gone to various supermarkets on behalf of mobster Gerry Catena's second-rate detergent in the campaign that resulted in Mob war against the A & P. Food Fair gave Iowa Beef an order, and Jacobs wrote back to Holman, "Until the time that Moe and Mr. Kaplan cleared the way, Food Fair had never taken the boxed beef product" in its regional warehouse.

On July 18, Jacobs received word that Steinman was ill and had gone into the hospital. There Steinman stayed for six weeks, while messages were passed back and forth between him and Jacobs by brother Sol Steinman.* On August 21, Jacobs was sent to see Aaron Freedman, who placed an order from Waldbaum's for eighteen to twenty loads a week, representing fifteen hundred to two thousand head of cattle, depending on their size. This was the biggest order yet, clearly the "showcase" deal Holman had in mind. Waldbaum's wasn't just sampling boxed beef. It was commiting itself to the Iowa Beef program.

The results, however, were disappointing. "Their gross was going down," Holman later admitted. He attributed this to Waldbaum's lack of experience with a radically different product. "They didn't know how to work with it. We had to teach them," he says. Events appear to have born him out. As soon as Steinman left the hospital in September, Holman himself came to New York to straighten out the problems in talks with Steinman (who, again, was an officer of a rival chain) and Freedman.

On November 11, 1970, Jacobs went to Steinman's apartment on East Sixty-fourth Street, and meetings were arranged over the next two days with Bohack, which became a large buyer, and Big Apple, which moved from an experimental use of boxed beef to a large order. In all these deals and others, boxed meat was flowing into the New York market without union opposition. Jacobs's reports back to Holman continued to reflect the one thing that was responsible for Iowa Beef's sudden new success: it was Steinman's behind-the-scenes talks with supermarket executives when Jacobs; the salesman, wasn't even present.

Until this point, Iowa Beef had been dealing with Steinman on the basis of a handshake agreement. Now that the Steinman commission arrangement had become a big business, Holman and his colleagues decided that a formal contract was necessary. Moreover, with hundreds of millions of pounds of meat now set to move into New York, Steinman's fifty-cent commission (equal to one-half cent a pound) seemed exhorbitant. Even if it were cut back to the originally proposed 25 cents, Steinman would still be raking in millions. Moreover, since Steinman hadn't established a warehouse (let alone five warehouses, as originally planned), only those customers prepared to buy whole carloads from Dakota City or Emporia could place orders. There was no storage facility to service smaller customers, or to service larger customers on the numerous occasions when they would have to fill sudden shortages on brief notice.

So a new meeting was set for December 4, in New York. At 7 P.M., Steinman joined Holman, Kemp, Lee, Jacobs, and Howard Weiner (the trea-

---

*The author has found it impossible to learn whether this particular hospitalization was the one that resulted from a beating, referred to earlier. Sources in the industry say their best recollection is that the beating occurred in the late 1960s. Steinman won't talk. His son-in-law Bodenstein insisted in an interview that Steinman hadn't been hospitalized at all since 1963, when he suffered an illness unrelated to any beating.

surer) for dinner at the Essex House Hotel. Afterward, they all trooped back to a suite at the Hampshire House, where they were joined by Bodenstein. Haggling went on until 3:30 or 4 A.M. Though Holman, the purported board-room genius, had come in determined to wring concessions out of Steinman, the racketeer once more seized the upper hand. Over the objections of Iowa Beef executives, Steinman insisted on—and got—a continued guarantee of commission on all meat shipped within 125 miles of New York, whether or not the shipment resulted from a deal he helped arrange. Only A & P was excepted.

Then came the amount of the commission. Lee and Weiner were especially insistent that it be knocked down to 25 cents—still $1 million a year. Holman prodded them with encouragement whenever Steinman left the room to confer privately with Bodenstein. But Steinman refused to take a pay cut. Weiner: "He stated to me that he had certain expenses that others didn't have, and he needed the [larger] fee. I asked him what those expenses were."

"Well, I have income tax," Steinman replied. (Steinman's quotes are according to Weiner.)

"Everyone has that. That's not unusual," Weiner said.

"Well, kid," Steinman began, "I have other expenses, too. There are three kinds. I pay meat buyers off at 15 percent. I pay union people off at 7 percent. And it costs me 10 percent to convert the corporate money to cash, and I have to deal in cash."

"I said I understood," Weiner recalls. "I just didn't say very much at all after that."

Nor did anyone else from Iowa Beef complain about the morality of the deal—even when Steinman explained in detail that the payments were made the first Tuesday of every month at the Black Angus bar, where he and Holman had eaten dinner together.

Holman recalled the split-up a little differently, but it didn't matter. There was plenty of evidence that money was indeed flowing, to wholesalers, to buyers, and to union officers. Steinman himself clearly had money to burn, and Newman and Sol Steinman were getting their share. And so, to be sure, were Mafiosi like Johnny and Tommy Dio.

Holman and Steinman shouted at each other about whether Iowa Beef could afford to pay the mobster 50 cents a hundredweight in perpetuity, as Steinman demanded. Finally, Lee proposed a compromise. Steinman, he argued, would make more money in the long run if he would give up a little commission. Then Iowa Beef could afford to contract with another meat dealer who had a genuine warehouse, and who could handle orders for partial carloads. Thus many smaller retail outlets could participate in the boxed beef program, and even the big chains could feel more secure. Lee proposed that Steinman receive 50 cents a hundredweight on the first five million pounds, and 35 cents a hundredweight thereafter, on full-carload sales; on sales through another distributor, Steinman would get 25 cents a hundredweight for the first five million pounds and 10 cents thereafter. Moreover, the contract would be for five years—no more.

This exceeded Holman's intentions considerably. Still, Steinman wouldn't take it. He retreated with Bodenstein into a bedroom to talk it over. A little while later, they emerged. Steinman would take Lee's offer, he said—but only if Iowa Beef would also retain Bodenstein as its New York legal counsel. As Weiner recalled it, Steinman said that Bodenstein "could be invaluable to Iowa Beef in the New York area for some of their legal problems if and when they had them. He knew lots of union people and did a lot of legal work for union people and others." Steinman suggested $50,000 a year as a retainer, which made it seem almost magnanimous when he agreed to Holman's counter-offer of $25,000. It was the first time Iowa Beef had ever retained permanent counsel outside Dakota City.

Holman remembered that the Lovette family at Holly Farms had told him they, too, had been forced to take on new legal counsel in New York in order to get their chickens past the union boycott. He also remembered a poignant moment from the previous May. It seems almost a contradiction in terms to imagine Moe Steinman in a poignant moment, but this is what Holman recalled: "The only time I ever saw Steinman where I really thought I understood him, he was in this [Holman's] office, and he walked over and looked out and he said, 'You know, it's been a long, miserable life. I grew up on the streets of New York. I never knew anything like this. Look at that sky. This is clean. I like it. I'd like to have my kids associated with it.' Then we went back to business, of course. I have no doubt that he's done a lot of bad things. But for a moment, he recognized something different."

Those who seek tragic dimensions may find them, even in a Moe Steinman. The tragedy, supposedly, is that he had no choice about what he became (though, in truth, a lot of Jewish immigrants from eastern Europe succeeded in business without turning to the rackets). Tragedy more often has been ascribed to Currier Holman himself; some say he was forced to sacrifice his integrity in order to save his business (though, in truth, other businessmen, even meat dealers, have sided with the law and survived a shakedown episode).

No such pressures, however, fell on Walter Bodenstein. He chose his destiny free from the threat of poverty or business catastrophe. Perhaps, however, this makes him the saddest example of all. He never needed to embroil himself in conspiracies. He is personable, articulate, and bright. He learned law, and he even managed to teach himself the meat trade when he had to. It is difficult to sit and talk business with Bodenstein for very long without concluding that he probably could have succeeded on his own. Unlike Steinman and Holman, Bodenstein does not give one the feeling that he outsmarted the world by his shady dealings; rather, one feels that somewhere along the line Bodenstein himself was outsmarted.

For the first twenty-five years of his life, Walter Bodenstein seemed the very model of a nice Jewish boy. Born in the Washington Heights area of Manhattan in 1936, the son of a bakery store owner, he made it through Syracuse University and Brooklyn Law School, and even spent a summer as an intern at the U.S. Attorney's office. An old college buddy fixed him up with an attractive young woman named Estelle, nicknamed Cookie, who was a friend of the buddy's sister. In 1961, they were engaged to be married. All Bodenstein knew about his prospective father-in-law when he proposed to Cookie was that Steinman was some sort of executive at Daitch-Shopwell. Their wedding in a hotel, with a live orchestra, didn't strike him as excessive, and he still thinks industry people are greatly exaggerating when they describe it as a big Mob-style affair.

Bodenstein soon learned that Steinman was a domineering man who tried to rule the whole family, but he insists that he and Cookie staked out their independence and maintained it. He also learned, however, that his father-in-law knew racketeers like the Block brothers and Johnny Dio. He and Cookie went to dinner with Steinman and his wife at the Black Angus, and he observed the way Moe flitted around various tables, talked on the phone, and spent little time with his own family. At least in the beginning, this behavior offended Bodenstein, who thought Steinman was being downright rude to Mrs. Steinman and Cookie.

Yet, on occasion, Steinman would send him law clients—including Holly Farms and a large rendering concern that dealt with the supermarkets. Bodenstein insists that he gave all these clients their money's worth, and that he attracted most of his law work on his own.

At some point, however, Bodenstein succumbed, either to Steinman's insistence that his daughter be supported more regally, or perhaps to the lure of all the diamond rings and limos he saw at the Black Angus. As described earlier, he allowed Steinman to set him up in various brokerages. He allowed these brokerages to funnel money illegally to relatives of Steinman and supermarket executives.

Then he started doing business with a stock brokerage that Johnny Dio manipulated. Bodenstein knew Dio through the Black Angus, where they sometimes said "hello." Bodenstein also had his law office (and chicken brokerage) at 260 Fifth Avenue, where Dio's Jard Products Inc., the promotional novelty firm, also had an office. Bodenstein says the shared address was just an "unfortunate circumstance," and that he rarely saw Dio there.

Dio, always on the look-out for new rackets, had discovered the boom in fly-by-night stock promotions in the late 1960s and had lined up several shady brokers to front for him. They would acquire the stock of a floundering company for relatively no money, then would rig the market in the stock by reporting fictitious sales to the National Daily Quotation Service. Based on these phony price quotations, Dio and his Syndicate friends could make money selling shares to the public at inflated figures. Then the public would be left holding the bag when the fraud was inevitably exposed and the stock price crashed. Dio was convicted in two of the cases involving stocks called Belmont Franchising Corp. and At-Your-Service Leasing Company.

At a City of Hope charity dinner Dio attended in 1969, Steinman was introduced to a couple of Dio's stockbroker pals. Soon afterward, Bodenstein acquired two thousand shares of Belmont Franchising stock at $15 a share. He sold it after the illegal run-up for more than $30 a share, a profit of more than $30,000. In the subsequent federal investigation of Belmont (which sent Dio and one of his stockbroker fronts to jail), Bodenstein was called in for questioning. After some deliberation, authorities decided not to charge Bodenstein with any crime because there was no proof he was involved in the fraudulent transactions that caused the stock price to go up. But it was, or should have been, a clear warning to him of the quality of people he was dealing with and the possible consequences.

Meanwhile, Bodenstein was getting entangled in still another business that was about to run afoul of the law. When Bodenstein got into Medicaid factoring (or debt collection), it was legal. When Congress observed how Medicaid factors operated, Congress made it illegal. Medicaid factors would buy up bills from doctors who did a large business with Medicaid clients. The factors would pay the doctors immediately at a discount of their true claims, then collect in full from Medicaid. The supposed legitimate benefit was that payment to doctors was speeded up. Many of these doctors, however, operate what have become known as "Medicaid mills" in slum areas. Great numbers of people are shuffled in and out for procedures of questionable necessity, carried out in questionable fashion. The business is believed by city and state investigators to have been heavily penetrated by the Mafia, particularly by Joseph Pagano, who had gone to jail in the Murray Packing fraud with Steinman's partner Joseph Weinberg. In exchange for extortion payments to the mobsters, doctors were promised that other doctors wouldn't compete with them, and that their own offices wouldn't be burned down. In addition, investigators suspected that public officials were paid off to expedite and approve bills submitted by the certain factors. A doctor who agreed to testify for the state against Pagano was shot in the head, effectively ending the investigation.

Bodenstein had set up a company called Computer Health Systems Inc. in New York. It operated largely in the Bronx, where Medicaid mills were rife. Bodenstein says Steinman wasn't involved. Nevertheless, when Computer Health expanded to Massachusetts, Nat Meyerson, Steinman's other son-in-law, who also handled books for Steinman-related meat brokerages, was sent to Boston to run it. In about 1971, Bodenstein tried to sell securities in Computer Health Systems to the public through a stock issue that was to be handled by J. M. Kelsey & Company, the stock brokerage that was fronting for Johnny Dio's frauds. Kelsey & Company was exposed, however, before the Computer Health issue could be launched.

In 1973, Bodenstein was called before a federal grand jury investigating bribes paid to union officials. When he announced that he would take the Fifth

Amendment, he was given a grant of immunity from prosecution so the government could get his testimony. Free from the possibility of prosecution, he cleared the record of other past law violations by talking about them.

Bodenstein confessed that he illegally failed to report income from numerous sources in connection with the Medicaid factoring business. Among the people who gave him money that he failed to report as income, he named a dentist who ran a huge Medicaid mill that had become a focus of a state investigation into Medicaid fraud. He also named Benjamin Willner, the bagelmaker who lost his business when his sponsor, Johnny Dio, gave in to a rival Mafia boss; Willner had been given a job with Bodenstein's factoring operation to console him.

In the time left over from all this other activity, Bodenstein also handled pre-paid legal plans for the memberships of two union locals. He won't identify them, but one was Local 489 of the butchers' union (the union and Iowa Beef were deadly enemies, yet Bodenstein managed to represent them both). Local 489 covered Westchester County. Its leaders had long been under Steinman's thumb. Bodenstein got the lucrative contract under the local leadership of Anthony Maggiacomo, whom Steinman later confessed to bribing, according to sources familiar with Steinman's grand jury testimony. After Maggiacomo died, the Bodenstein deal was terminated, and Maggiaccomo's successor, Joe Bottigliere, refused to pay thirty to forty thousand dollars of Bodenstein's back billings. "I threw him out," Bottigliere says.

When Bodenstein was brought into the Iowa Beef affair in December, 1970, his world was in transition. Johnny Dio had just gone to jail (in October) for the kosher meat frauds. On top of that, Dio and his Mafia overlord, godfather Carmine Tramunti, had just been indicted (in November) for the first of the J. M. Kelsey stock frauds. The handwriting was on the wall for the continuation of the Medicaid factoring business, as the government was about to take the position that it wouldn't pay factors.

Bodenstein says he had heard that his father-in-law was negotiating a contract with Iowa Beef, and he accepted Steinman's invitation to attend the meeting at the Hampshire House. Steinman had introduced Bodenstein to Holman the previous summer at the Black Angus, and the young lawyer says he was deeply impressed by Holman personally and by the idea of boxed beef in general. Within days after the December 4, 1970, meeting at the Hampshire House, it developed that Bodenstein, not Steinman, would handle the day-to-day commission work for Iowa Beef's sales in the New York area. The operation, known as Cattle Pakt Sales (later shortened to C. P. Sales), would be handled out of Bodenstein's law office (and chicken brokerage). Steinman, however, dropped by periodically; he could visit Johnny Dio's office, now run by Dio's relatives, in another part of the same building.

Early in January, it was Bodenstein who flew to Dakota City to finish details on the formal commission contract. But Holman insisted that Steinman's signature be on the contract, too. As Roy Lee, the president, remembers, Steinman "was a significant party to the agreement. . . . It was my impression that he would not be part of the corporate structure, but he'd still be involved."

In the month between the Hampshire House meeting and the signing of the contract, the Iowa Beef executives went through the same kind of hand-wringing they had gone through the previous April, when Steinman was originally taken aboard. Howard Weiner, the treasurer, remembers Holman asking him right after the meeting December 4, "How do they convert the money to cash?"

"I told him I didn't know," Weiner says. "I could guess." Weiner says that on the corporate plane back to Dakota City he tried to tell Holman how the money might be converted for a 10 percent kickback. He remembers that Holman just kept repeating, "It's a shame that the 127th largest manufacturing company in the country has to do business like this. . . . It's a shame that the largest beef producer in the world has to do business like this. . . ."

When they reached Dakota City, Holman explained the news to the other executives. Roy Lee, the president, recalls Kemp or Anderson saying, "Iowa Beef would not be part of any payoffs. . . . We would be paying a brokerage fee to a broker and we wouldn't be involved in any further transactions that might occur. . . ." Lee, however, believes, "everybody in the room knew that it wasn't legitimate."

Gus Nymann, the general counsel, recalls that he told Holman, "This is a dangerous situation." According to Nymann's testimony later, Holman replied, "I know that you lawyers would tell us not to do this, but I'm going to do it anyway."

Nymann also objected to putting a new lawyer on retainer. He testified that he told Holman he was pleased with the law firm that already handled occasional labor matters for Iowa Beef in New York. Holman replied (Nymann testified) that "if we had serious labor relations matters" Iowa Beef would still use the other firm, but "it was important to have this retainer agreement" with Bodenstein and "it was related to the commission agreement."

When the commission agreement was brought before the Iowa Beef board of directors for ratification, nobody objected. But privately, doubts about the agreement persisted for years among the executives under Holman. Largely because of these doubts, on August 16, 1971, Holman fired Roy Lee.

On December 8, 1970, four days after the Hampshire House meeting, Moe Steinman called Lew Jacobs and told him that the Hills supermarket chain was going to start ordering from Iowa Beef. Steinman also said, as Jacobs remembers it, that he had "about completed his rounds" and would call Jacobs each week to tell him when to check with each account to learn its projected needs.

On March 27, 1971, Jacobs met with Holman, Bodenstein, and Steinman. They introduced Jacobs to George Wilhelm, a former salesman for Armour

& Company, and announced that Wilhelm would be working under Bodenstein and doing Jacobs's job. Iowa Beef was sending Jacobs to New England. Jacobs was stunned.

Wilhelm, Jacobs's replacement, says he had long envied Iowa Beef's superior product and had wanted to sell it. Besides, he says, Armour wasn't paying him enough. One day that spring, Wilhelm was approached by an Armour customer, Herb Olstein, head of the meat department at Daitch-Shopwell. Olstein suggested that Wilhelm should go to work for a new brokerage operation that was being set up by Olstein's friend and boss, Moe Steinman, and his family. It didn't seem to matter that Olstein (according to Steinman) wasn't farsighted enough to recognize the advantages of boxed beef. Boxed beef just happened to be the product Wilhelm would be selling.

One month later, a man named Morris Feldman walked into Currier Holman's office in Dakota City. Feldman had been a salesman for a rival slaughtering company, Monfort of Colorado, and had said he wanted to discuss working for Iowa Beef. But when Feldman showed up in Dakota City, he brought with him Sam Goldberger, and introduced Goldberger to Holman as a big customer, someone who had the cash to bankroll Feldman in a distribution venture. Holman recognized Goldberger's name. Goldberger had run a firm in Minneapolis that made frozen entrees and bought a lot of its meat from Iowa Beef. Recently, the firm had been bought out by International Multifoods for several million dollars.

But Holman didn't know, and Feldman didn't mention, that Sam Goldberger had grown up in the meat business in Brooklyn with Moe Steinman and Johnny Dio in the 1930s. Or that Goldberger had sold Steinman his first meat when Steinman took over the meat concession at Waldbaum's, which was now Iowa Beef's biggest New York customer. And Feldman certainly didn't mention what Goldberger was doing from 1947 to 1954.

Anyone who was in the Armed Forces in the late 1940s and who thought the food wasn't very good, or who was bothered by stomach trouble, would be interested in Sam Goldberger. Goldberger's American Packing Corp. had a major contract in those years to supply meat to the Army, not only for its own troops but also for the Navy supply depots in Newport, Rhode Island, and Pennington and Norfolk, Virginia. In 1952, Goldberger was sentenced to three years in prison (he served fourteen months) for swindling the government out of a fortune by bribing Army inspectors to approve millions of pounds of meat far inferior to contract specifications. There was also meat in "insanitary and unsound condition," the charges said.

At the trial, one meat inspector testified that Goldberger "told me in the boning room that it would be worth my while to play ball with them—that's just the words he used." A former employee testified that "there was some meat there that smelled awful bad" and that two nearly successful attempts were made to kill him after he had agreed to talk to the FBI. There was evidence that 280 veal sides the Army had rejected because of their "defrosted, insanitary, and unsound condition" were simply reshipped, passed (or overlooked) by friendlier inspectors, and wound up on the mess tables at Fort Bragg, North Carolina.

At the sentencing of Goldberger and his colleagues, the judge said, "There is very little in this case which would incline the court to leniency. . . . There is not much that I can find to say in mitigation of their offense."

According to Holman, Goldberger did mention—about the time he was invited onto the Iowa Beef board of directors—that he had "got into a squabble over the delivery of Army beef. His problem was he wanted to deliver too high quality meat to the Army and they didn't know enough to take it. This was back in the days of OPA and all that sort of stuff," Holman said.

In about 1968, Goldberger had begun doing business with his old friend Steinman again. Through his firm in Minneapolis, he would sell Trans-World brokerage large quantities of meat, particularly briskets, which he bought from Iowa Beef, and which helped Steinman monopolize the corned beef market. They became friends again, judging from their telephone conversations wiretapped by the district attorney's office. Three months after Steinman signed his contract with Iowa Beef, Goldberger showed up in Holman's office. Holman has denied repeatedly that Steinman influenced his dealings with Goldberger in any way, and Goldberger says the same. If they're right, the visit was a hell of a lucky coincidence for Goldberger.

Goldberger stayed in Dakota City for lengthy negotiations. The distributorship he was supposed to be discussing never materialized. But in the meantime, Goldberger convinced Holman "that Sam knew more about beef patties than anybody else I ever met in my life. He had a deeper knowledge of the meat business than anybody besides Andy Anderson. Sam was brought on board because he could be immeasurably helpful to us in developing a hamburger patty, frozen or otherwise, which is a skill not known to a great many people."

As a matter of fact, the frozen meat patty operation that Goldberger developed for Iowa Beef in 1971 was a total flop. The packages clouded up in supermarket display cases, housewives wouldn't buy them, and supermarket owners shipped them back to the factory. Iowa Beef lost a lot of money. But Holman refused to blame Goldberger, who stayed on the company's board of directors, where he was a firm advocate of doing business with Walter Bodenstein. And before long, Goldberger had assumed a relationship that puzzled observers for many years—a relationship that allowed him to buy millions of dollars of hamburger trimmings from Iowa Beef for much less than other buyers had to pay, and to make a fortune selling the trimmings on the retail market. And the Internal Revenue Service would, in 1978, charge him with making much more of a fortune than he admitted to on his tax forms.

By April, 1971, Steinman, Bodenstein, and Goldberger were in. Just a year after the boycott was broken, Iowa Beef was shipping sixty carloads of boxed beef a week into the New York market (according to figures Lew Jacobs got from Steinman), and the prospects were favorable that this amount would soon multiply.

4

The Investigation

Seven years of investigating the New York meat industry had produced a lot of informants for Robert Nicholson. On a hot day in late summer, 1970, one of them called up.

"Have you got any idea what Moe Steinman is doing now?" the informant asked.

Nicholson said he hadn't.

The informant suggested that Nicholson meet him at Pappas', the popular Greek restaurant (later destroyed in a fire) on Eighth Avenue and Fourteenth Street.

Within the hour, Nicholson was sitting at a restaurant table listening to the informant, a wholesaler, explain how big Iowa Beef was. Iowa Beef, the informant said, was flooding New York with pre-fabricated meat, which was costing him and other wholesalers a lot of money. And Moe Steinman was collecting half a penny for every pound of meat Iowa Beef sold in New York. "They're trying to completely capture the whole meat market and force everybody in New York to buy from Iowa Beef, and they're using the union to do it," the wholesaler said.

Under Nicholson's prompting, he went on to tell how Trans-World Fabricators was arranging for the supermarket chains to pay huge overcharges for meat. He told how Trans-World kicked back money to chain store executives, union leaders, and mobsters. He told how wholesalers in the Fourteenth Street market were forced to make payoffs in order to get their meat into the supermarkets, and how Steinman would raise cash for bribes by billing wholesalers for meat that was never delivered. And the informant told how Herbie Newman managed Trans-World while Moe Steinman lived a life of leisure. In an hour, the informant had laid down the entire bribery, extortion, and racketeering case that scores of law enforcement officers would spend years trying to prove. Nicholson did not doubt a word the man said.

Back at the district attorney's office, Nicholson proposed another mammoth investigation of the meat industry. The three top officers of the fourteen-thousand-member wholesale butchers' local were serving prison sentences thanks to the work of Nicholson and his men. So Al Scotti, head of D. A. Frank Hogan's rackets bureau, was not about to turn aside the judgment of his best investigator. Nicholson got a go-ahead. He also got Lou Montello, his old partner from the Merkel case, back, and a new partner, Detective Jack Carey.

To supervise the investigation, Scotti assigned Franklyn Snitow, who had come to the office fresh out of law school only a month before. Bright but totally untested, Snitow still held the title of criminal law investigator; not until a few months later, in January, 1971, when he passed the bar examination, could he be sworn in as an assistant district attorney. Snitow hardly looked the part of a tough-as-nails prosecutor of the Frank Hogan mold. But despite his youthful face, adolescent voice, and inexperience, he quickly earned the admiration of the detectives. "The Iowa Beef Processors case would never have come about if it weren't for Snitow's persistence," Nicholson observed later. "We had guys in our own squad who said, 'You got nothing. It's a hot dog case.' " But Nicholson knew that in Moe Steinman and Iowa Beef he had the classic example of criminal power over the marketplace. And Snitow stuck with him through half a dozen years of often bitter discouragement.

In order to start throwing up wiretaps, Nicholson and his detectives needed probable cause that a crime was being committed. They figured the first obvious step was to start tailing Moe Steinman. That proved easier said than done. Steinman's behavior seemed calculated to be erratic. He left his apartment building by various doors. He would walk in various directions. Sometimes he would hail a taxi, and sometimes he would be picked up, and by various people, including, sometimes, a man the detectives recognized as Johnny Dio's son, Dominick "Nicky" Dio. Young Dio would chauffeur the meat boss in a Cadillac. Sometimes Steinman would ride from his building to another location, where he might be met by a second car.

He would frequently, but not always, show up at the Daitch-Shopwell office in the Bronx late in the morning, stay awhile, then take off. Rarely did he go to Trans-World brokerage. Afternoons he was regularly seen at an apartment in Forest Hills, Queens, where he met his mistress. He would frequently stop at a bar, Conrad's Cloud Room (whose proprietor was later murdered gangland-style). Toward evening, the routine was more established:

the Bull and Bear in the Waldorf, and, nearby, the Black Angus. But Steinman was always cordoned off by protective (and no doubt well-paid) waiters and hangers-on.

What the team of gumshoes observed might have alarmed the Shopwell Inc. public shareholders. They were paying Steinman at least $50,000 a year in salary and far more in commissions on meat sales from Trans-World, and he was putting in what seemed to be a most unindustrious day of activity. Nevertheless, it wasn't illegal. There was nothing in Steinman's day that might convince a judge to authorize electronic surveillance, let alone convince a grand jury to vote an indictment.

So the detectives changed strategies. As fall turned to winter—about the time the Iowa Beef deal was being formalized in writing—the detectives gave up on Steinman and began trailing his partner Herbie Newman instead. The switch proved fortuitous; the detectives could scarcely have designed a better suspect than Newman. While Steinman had shrouded his life in the manner of some criminal genius from literature, Newman was a classic criminal klutz. If he had been a murderer, one gets the feeling he would have left fingerprints all over the victim's house and then shot himself in the foot drawing the gun out of his pocket. While Steinman slunk unobtrusively in corners, Newman was a conspicuous six-foot, 235-pounder with a bulldog face, a shock of gray hair and big, floppy feet that gave him a funny walk. He wore coke-bottle glasses and kept his head tilted back at an unusual angle to see out of them. Evidently he was hard of hearing because he loved to shout; the cops discovered that they could overhear his half of a conversation from across the room.

Every morning, Nicholson, Carey, and Montello could depend on Newman's silver Cadillac to be parked near Trans-World's office at Gansevoort and Little West Twelfth Streets in the meat district. Every morning between 10:30 and 11 A.M. he would leave on foot for the Manufacturers Hanover Trust branch at Fourteenth Street and Eighth Avenue. On the way he would pass a hot dog stand and buy a hot dog. The detectives came to believe he could never pass a hot dog stand anywhere without buying a hot dog. Inside the bank, Newman would proceed directly to his safe-deposit box. He could not have picked a better time for the police (or a worse one for him); 11 A.M. was the quietest hour of the day at the bank. And he always went to the same cubicle to open his box. Detective Jack Carey was always in the next cubicle, staring idly at his own empty safe-deposit box, which the police department had rented for him as soon as Newman's habits had been reported. The partitions between the cubicles reached only part-way to the ceiling, so a person in one cubicle could easily hear what was happening in the next one, especially if its occupant constantly talked to himself, as Herbie Newman did, in a loud, hard-of-hearing voice.

Carey would wait in his own car outside the bank until another detective, parked in front of the Trans-World office, radioed him that Newman was on his way. Then Carey would dash into the cubicle just in time for Newman's arrival. Every day Carey could hear Newman counting to himself, and the detective began to get the idea that hundreds of thousands of dollars in cash and securities were in Newman's box. Then, one day, Newman brought his son, Richie, into the cubicle with him and gave the young man an inventory, replete with denominations of more than $200,000 in bonds, and an accounting of so many shares of this and that. (This story sometimes sounds suspicious to those who have never heard Newman talk. To those who have heard him, however, it is plausible, and the detectives vow that they learned what they did because of Newman's loud voice and transparent habits. Throughout the whole history of Nicholson's meat investigations, there has never been a hint of unauthorized electronic spying or break-ins.)

After he left the safe-deposit box, usually with some big bills in his pockets, Newman would proceed to another bank. This was the one part of his routine that varied. He picked a different bank every day. Perhaps Steinman had cautioned him. At any rate, the detectives were able to keep up with him frequently enough to observe him handing a $500 bill to a cashier and receiving fives and tens in return, or a $1,000 bill and receiving twenties. Then he would go to another window, usually in the same bank, and change the smaller bills to a check, which he then might change elsewhere to cash, thus covering over the trail from his pocket money back to its criminal origins.

After that—unless he happened to pass another hot dog stand, in which case he would stop and have a hot dog—he would proceed in the silver Caddy to the Ozone Park Bar on Woodhaven Boulevard and Jamaica Avenue in Queens. He would order a beer and go to the pay phone. He would call Steinman. In a loud voice he would say things like, "The people from the union want the money. I got a call from the union. They want their money." Then he would call his girlfriend, Helen, whom he later married, and tell her he was hard at work on a big business deal. This done, he would get back into the Cadillac (while Nicholson followed in his Chevy), drive to Acqueduct race track and head for the $100 window. He would bet like crazy, between $1,000 and $2,000 a day. Sometimes he lost, sometimes he won, but more often he lost.

After the track, he would go to meet Steinman at the Black Angus or the Bull and Bear. Since the Kissel case, when there had been evidence of electronic surveillance at the Black Angus, Steinman was spending more and more time at the bar in the Waldorf. The police could never get close enough to hear what Steinman told Newman at the bar table. But they didn't have to. Newman would immediately leave and go to the pay phone in the lobby. He would call union people, or the head of a meat company and say, "Moe says you gotta do this," or, "I just talked to Moe, and Moe said to tell you it's going to cost you . . ." or, "It's okay to fire so-and-so. Call me from the office tomorrow." Cops would stand behind Newman at the phone as if in line, holding dimes, listening. Once one of them tapped him on the shoulder and asked if he was going to be long.

Sometimes Newman would call people from the track, or from the Ozone Park Bar, to discuss meat sales. Over and over the police began hearing the phrase that would become ever more familiar in the coming year: "street." "It'll cost 75 cents plus third street," Newman would say. Or, "a dollar-ten plus eighth street." Eventually the cops would learn, from sources in the industry as well as their own powers of deduction, that "street" was the code word for the bribe. Seventy-five cents plus third street meant that the actual price of an order of meat was 75 cents a pound, but that the supermarket would be billed 78 cents. The other three cents would be the bribe money. Part would go back to the buyer—typically, one cent for every six-or seven-cent overcharge, or one and a half cents on an eight- or nine-cent overcharge. (This jibes rather well with Howard Weiner's recollection that Steinman said he would pay 15 percent of Iowa Beef's commissions as bribes to buyers.) Of the remaining "street," part would go to union officers, part to the Mafia, and part to keep Newman and Steinman in Cadillacs.

Early in 1971, a corned beef dealer became an informant about conditions in his industry. Steinman had stolen all the business, the dealer complained. There was nowhere to buy briskets except through Trans-World. Iowa Beef, the world's biggest supplier of briskets and every other cut, had two large buyers: Moe Steinman, and Sam Goldberger, who sold to Moe Steinman.

By the spring of 1971, the detectives had given Snitow enough to go to court with. Snitow, the ink barely dry on his bar exam, got a wiretap order for the Trans-World brokerage office. The detectives also wanted to bug Newman's cubicle at the bank. The loud conversations Carey had overheard seemed almost unbelievable. But the bug wasn't authorized because the cubicle was also used by innocent strangers.

Eventually, there were orders to tap and bug Steinman's home, then his Queens apartment, Herbie Newman's apartment, and other likely sites. All this cost money.

In about July, 1971, the district attorney's office took what turned out to be a momentous step. It disclosed the meat industry investigation to the Manhattan office of the federal strike force against organized crime and racketeering.

The strike forces had been set up in 1966 and 1967 in certain major cities with acute Syndicate problems. Originally the work of Attorney General Ramsey Clark, they were even more heavily relied on during the Nixon Administration. The idea was to throw concentrated expertise into Syndicate prosecutions. Selected agents from the FBI, Internal Revenue Service, and perhaps the Postal or Customs services would be specially trained along with selected Justice Department prosecutors to work on organized crime cases independent of the local U. S. Attorney's offices. Where possible, they would cooperate with state and local law enforcement agencies to bring prosecution under whatever law, state or federal, seemed appropriate.

In practice, the strike forces (which have been undergoing retrenchment under Presidents Ford and Carter) were like any other special prosecution unit. They were needed in some places only because the existing prosecutor, the local United States Attorney, was less than fully qualified. The local U. S. Attorneys are the real wielders of power in the Justice Department. Their foot-dragging can frustrate even the best-laid plans of a vigorous Attorney General. Their initiative can bring results even when the administration in Washington is weak. Yet presidents have traditionally used these critical appointments as a means to pay off political debts to local power brokers. Despite the public protestations of Jimmy Carter to the contrary, presidents obviously still do use the appointments that way.

Thus U. S. Attorneys have often been inept, and most have had no career dedication to law enforcement. Where existing local prosecutors were the kind of people they should have been in the first place (for example, in New Jersey after 1969, or Manhattan when Robert Morgenthau was in office), the strike forces weren't needed. They served mainly as a tool that other law enforcement agencies could use to get more money out of Washington, because, like any other hot-shot new idea, the strike forces were bestowed with liberal budgets.

In some locations, however, the appointed heads of the federal strike force, though the product of professional selection within the Justice Department, were themselves inexperienced or possessed of less than the soundest judgment. And that could mean trouble. Worse yet was the situation in a federal district like Manhattan after Morgenthau was removed by Nixon. The succeeding U. S. attorneys, Whitney North Seymour, Paul Curran, and Robert B. Fiske, Jr., though bringing to the office all the requisite integrity and legal skill, were by nature Wall Street lawyers, not gung-ho rackets-busters, and— judging from the evidence—were reticent about initiating investigations and seizing the offensive against the Syndicate. The presence in such circumstances of a strike force leader like William I. Aronwald led to real trouble.

Young Aronwald dominated the New York strike force for most of its existence, first as senior assistant and later as chief. He already had moved swiftly through careers as a college football hero, non-career Army captain and assistant district attorney under Frank Hogan. Determined to make headlines as a rackets-buster, he displayed the aggressive qualities that good cops and FBI agents dream of in a prosecutor, yet seldom find. He devoted his resources to daring and sometimes innovative investigations of the areas that most needed it. He achieved an impressive on-paper record of guilty pleas. Nevertheless, his biggest investigations failed to clean up anything. Key trials ended in debacles. The true villains escaped when they had seemed to be in real trouble. Other law enforcement agencies that Aronwald worked with became infuriated at him. Aronwald was greatly interested in the trappings of his office; he actually packed the pistol his job entitled him to (most prosecutors don't). But by the time he was done, in 1976, the well-known New York City crime writer Jack Newfield was remarking that Aronwald (along with the town's other special prosecutor, Maurice Nadjari) had inadvertently done more to further the cause of organized crime in the city than the heads of leading Mafia families. Such was Aronwald's record that toward the end of his tenure, the Justice Department in Washington began an investigation into the possibility that he might be corrupt, based on the flimsiest of allegations from a convicted con man. The investigation concluded, almost certainly correctly, that he wasn't corrupt. The problems lay elsewhere.

Two explanations have been offered for why the district attorney's office brought its big investigation to Aronwald. Under oath, in a courtroom, with Aronwald staring him in the face, Frank Snitow once testified, "With the advent of the strike force, we believed that our investigation would lead us to both state and federal violations and that it would be appropriate that we brought federal authorities in on the investigation at basically the ground level."

Off the record, sources from the D.A.'s office tell a different story. "We were underfunded and without equipment," says one. "We needed tape recorders, lens equipment, cameras, general operation money. So, contrary to the desires of most of the people in the office, we were required to go to the strike force to obtain money." Another well-placed source agrees. "We needed money and the strike force had it," he says. "We went to them only after we wanted to expand the surveillance. They promised to give us the money and they did—twenty thousand dollars worth of equipment. We got money from the feds to pay for trips to Florida to follow Steinman and Newman. That's what the Strike Force was there for." A D.A.'s source says the investigation got more than one hundred thousand dollars in federal benefits. Aronwald says it was much less.

The wiretap on Steinman's Sixty-fourth Street apartment turned out to be more frustrating than productive, although there were many intriguing calls. Among them were several from Sam Goldberger, who at that time was on Iowa Beef's board of directors. Goldberger, or his son Robert, it seemed, would call Steinman whenever they arrived in town. Sometimes meetings would be arranged in restaurants. Once, the wiretappers overheard Moe instructing Goldberger to put more fat, coloring, or condiments in the meat. "It seemed as though Sam was working for Moe," one detective recalls. "Sam seemed very subservient. They talked about big carloads of meat." Often, too, it was hard to tell who was buying what from whom, or exactly what Goldberger and Steinman were really talking about. The conversations seemed to be in code. For example:

> STEINMAN: How many steaks can you take?
> GOLDBERGER: I can take a thousand steaks.
> STEINMAN: What size sweater do you take?

GOLDBERGER: I take a size eight.
STEINMAN: How were the steaks you got last time?
GOLDBERGER: Oh, they were fine.
STEINMAN: How many do you want this time?

And so on. "We never figured it out," the detectives recall.
Currier Holman probably had no idea this was going on.

There were also lots of calls from local meat dealers and buyers, but little in the way of incriminating discussion. The calls frequently ended with Steinman's admonition, à la Mae West, to "come up and see me." Then a strange thing happened. On a call to Newman's tapped telephone from a pay booth, Steinman told Newman, "I was down in Florida. I saw the people down there. They told me all about the investigation. I'll tell you when I see you."

What investigation? Nicholson's investigation? What people?

Then Steinman began telling callers not to talk to him on his home phone.

The constant admonition to "come up and see me" rang in Nicholson's ears. So the detectives bugged Steinman's apartment. From industry sources who had been there, the detectives learned just where to put the microphone. "He took us into this room," one buyer had recalled. "It had a bar in there. Lounge chairs. He did all his business in there." So that's where the bug went.

Then another strange thing happened. As one detective later recalled it, "From that day that we put that bug in that room, he never went in there. We were listening to emptiness."

The puzzling apparent prescience that Moe Steinman showed about the D.A.'s investigation was only a forewarning of even more puzzling events that were to come.

Despite the frustrations, the stepped up surveillance provided a lot of new insights and some hard evidence. Steinman was seen meeting regularly with Aaron Freedman, the Waldbaum's executive, at Patrick's Pub on Northern Boulevard in Queens (or, as it was referred to in telephone conversations, "the Irish Place"). Sometimes, it was observed, Sal Coletta and George Gamaldi, meat buyers for the Hills supermarket chain, would join them. Steinman and Freedman would take long pleasure weekends in Florida. The wiretaps told how Steinman had just spent $5,000 refurnishing the Queens apartment he shared with his girlfriend most afternoons. Newman, too, liked Florida high-living. He had a $200,000 house on Normandy Isle off Miami Beach. He bought a thirty-four-foot boat for $65,000 and then ran it aground his first day out, wrecking it. Nicholson, Montello, Carey, and several colleagues who joined them off and on overheard all this.

From other conversations, they figured out that Newman was using Robert Donahue, a naive executive at King Kullen supermarkets, to cheat Steinman. Newman would tell Moe, for example, that "Donahue's gonna order three loads, eighth street," but instead of sending Donahue his normal penny-and-a-half share of the eight-cent-a-pound pay-off pool, Newman would send less than half of that, and keep the rest. Once Steinman even bawled Newman out over the phone for giving the King Kullen executive half a cent too much as a kickback (not knowing that Newman had kept the extra for himself). "I'm not happy," Moe told his partner. The King Kullen customers who were paying eight cents a pound extra for their corned beef (or more by the time the supermarket added its own mark-up) probably weren't happy either.

At Waldbaum's, purchasing arrangements would be handled by a junior buyer, and when all the details of the legitimate part of the order were ironed out, Aaron Freedman would come onto the line and say, "What street?"

Executives at another chain once had to run around to their own supermarkets after banking hours to pick up seven thousand dollars cash to meet Steinman's insistent money demands.

By coincidence, the taps on Trans-World were in effect in July, 1971, during the trial of Angelo Vignari, an associate of Charles Anselmo, on loan-sharking charges. The trial ended in an acquittal. Newman's son Richie allegedly had introduced the supposed victim to Vignari, and so was called by the government to testify. This put him in trouble right away, and it was double trouble because the alleged victim hadn't paid the twenty thousand back, and Vignari was insisting that Herbie Newman make good the money.

Newman, afraid for his son—and also worried about the twenty thousand dollars—went to Moe for help. Moe went to Tommy Dio, who said he'd look into it. Dio returned with the news that his colleagues were indeed angry. First, the kid had led them to a bad borrower, and on top of that he had testified against them.

On one tape recording in July, 1971, Richie Newman insisted to Moe, "I didn't hurt them in my testimony. If I had done anything else it would have been worse." Moe told him to go off to Florida for a while. "You'll wind up getting your head blown off," he admonished.

A little later, Herbie Newman went to Moe to see if Moe's Mafia friends could get Vignari off Newman's back. According to Newman (who later testified about it before a grand jury), Vignari was trying to "extort" money from him, including threatening him with a "G", which was the lingo for "gun." So Steinman promised to see Tommy Dio, whom he referred to as "Mr. T." On August 4, 1971, Steinman called back with a report on the big sit-down, wherein Tommy Dio, as Steinman's representative in the Mafia, was able to reduce the bill somewhat, but not to cancel it. Dio had told Steinman that Newman was going to have to pay something to Vignari. As Steinman put it, "Mine [my representative] said to me, 'Play safe and make sure he does it, you know?' "

Other conversations made clear that Tommy Dio had good reason to go to bat for Steinman and Newman. Trans-World brokerage was paying him gobs of money—$78,000 in June and July alone, which Newman thought was way too much. When Newman complained, Steinman reminded him that in May they had paid even more. When Newman indicated that an accountant was asking embarrassing questions about these payments, Steinman suggested getting rid of the accountant by bribing him.

"Take the man," Moe told Newman, "and tell him, 'Look, I don't care if we gotta give you a little extra, it has to be a mistake'."

"Yeah," Newman replied.

"Simple as that, Herb. I mean, am I right?"

Apparently, Steinman discussed the payments with Tommy Dio on August 16, 1971, at an affair that Newman also had attended. The next day Newman asked Steinman on the phone, "Were you with him last night? Tom?"

"Sure, that was him," Moe replied, and then indicated that the Mafia was going to continue taking its big cut.

Newman didn't like it. "You're short close to seventy-eight thousand dollars," he complained. "We are missing seventy-eight in two months. . . . You gotta make money. Where's the money?" There was more argument.

"Well, I can't—I can't explain to you," Moe said. "You know what I'm talking about."

"Yeah," Newman finally agreed.

The detectives became impressed during the course of the wiretaps with the systematic way that Thomas Dioguardi, ostensibly just a garment center executive (Dom-Rose Mills, a $3 million-a-year business), had replaced his brother John since John went to prison. The cops never doubted that John was still giving the orders from his jail cell when Tommy went to visit, but Tommy had clearly become the man to see for anyone who had dealt previously with his better-known brother. Tommy was gruffer, not as handsome or polished as John. He showed up at the Black Angus and Bull and Bear (and sometimes the Belmont Plaza Hotel) to talk business, but not as Johnny Dio had on a regular basis. Rather, it appeared to the detectives, Tommy showed up only when he was summoned by telephone. The number at Tommy's office at Dom-Rose Mills was called regularly by Moe Steinman and other meat racketeers. Usually the message was just a time and meeting place.

Deals with other Mafia groups went on as usual. One series of conversations between Newman and Steinman in September, 1971, indicates that they were trying to persuade Big Paul Castellano (brother-in-law and underboss of Carlo Gambino) to let them sell meat to Key Foods, a chain of stores in Brooklyn, where the Castellanos ruled the roost. Newman was pressing Steinman to get some action out of Castellano.

"I expect to maneuver soon. I should have it," Steinman replied. "I have done him favors. He's trying. He has them, so he's going to try and give me, give them to me, too." Then Steinman told Newman not to be so greedy. "It doesn't mean nothing," he said. "Whether a bit more or a little bit less, it doesn't matter. . . . As long as you got the big chains backing you, that's all that counts."

The detectives didn't understand the significance of it at the time, but the wiretaps made clear that for some reason Moe Steinman was doing favors for a meat dealer named Benny Moscowitz. In the summer of 1971, Steinman was pushing supermarket chains to stock a brand of frozen meat patties that was manufactured by G & M Packing Company, which Moscowitz owned. This sometimes entailed dumping an existing brand out of the frozen meat counter, but Steinman told the other executives he talked to that this was okay with him. It seems obvious now in retrospect that Moe Steinman, enjoying the sudden wealth of the Iowa Beef deal, was trying to do a little something for the man who had provided him entree to it.

This meat patty switcheroo was just one of the manipulations uncovered by an especially productive wiretap set up in late summer, 1971, on the telephone of Julie Tantleff. Tantleff was Steinman's friend of thirty years, a former vice-president and sales manager of the Bohack supermarket chain, and, since about 1967, owner of the Black Angus. The tap was placed on the phone in Tantleff's apartment in the San Carlos Hotel, a few doors down from the Black Angus, after a peculiar meeting at Newark Airport. Nicholson had been to Newark Airport on business a year or two earlier; that time he had observed a Pennsylvania chicken farmer passing a bundle of cash to Harry Stubach and another butchers' union official. The cash was wrapped in a contract to sell chickens to supermarket chains. This time, another meeting was planned to discuss the sale of meat to supermarkets. Present, besides the detectives and police photographers lurking in the shadows, were Stienman, Tantleff and two supermarket chain executives.

One of the executives was George George, who, years before, had worked for Tantleff in the Mayfair supermarket chain. George had gone on to a high position in the Big Apple and Foodarama chains, which merged and traded under the Shop-Rite banner. The Shop-Rite affiliation had cost Steinman's brokerage firm a big account, because Shop-Rite's president, David Silverberg, is a relative Boy Scout in the industry and tries to avoid dealing with Steinman whenever possible. So when Foodarama joined Silverberg's cooperative, it agreed to stop buying from Trans-World.

In the summer of 1971, George was given responsibility for overall operations of Foodarama in New York State (the firm also had stores in New Jersey, Pennsylvania, and Connecticut). Steinman sensed that with a friend of Tantleff's in commmand, there might be an opportunity to recapture a big market. In addition, Foodarama's contract with its store clerks was about to expire, and Steinman could arrange a sweetheart deal with the union. To get the ball rolling, Steinman offered Tantleff 1½ percent on beef liver and 2½ percent on all other items he could persuade George to buy for Foodarama. Of course, Tantleff would be expected to share these "commissions" with George himself —as kickbacks.

So Tantleff met at Newark Airport with Steinman, George, and another Shop-Rite executive. They discussed Foodarama's need for "assistance" in dealing with labor unions. Tantleff mentioned that Steinman could be "helpful in an advisory capacity." Steinman himself volunteered, as George recounted it later, that "he thought he might be able to handle it," and that he "could influence the union." Of course, Steinman said, any assistance with the unions was contingent upon Foodarama's purchase of certain products from Trans-World Fabricators. Tantleff told George he'd split his share of commissions fifty-fifty—after ten thousand dollars was deducted to pay off the union officials.

Next came the labor negotiations George had been afraid of. They involved the Retail, Wholesale, and Department Store Workers' Union. Tantleff and Steinman talked over the phone repeatedly about payoffs to the union leaders (though there was no evidence the leaders received any money and they weren't charged with a crime). When Tantleff was asked to testify about the pay-offs before a grand jury, he pleaded poor memory, which resulted in his conviction for contempt of court. The conversations were conducted, like Steinman's others, in guarded code language, and the code certainly didn't include the word "bribery." Nevertheless, readers can judge for themselves the apparent meaning of the phrase "the truth," which is repeated over and over with no literal sense to it.

From the context of the conversations, George was being offered his choice of two contracts, a hard one and a soft one. "Let him decide which he wants," Moe told Tantleff. "My opinion, I told him, is tell him [the union officer] the truth and take the other contract and get through with the headache. If you don't want it that way, then. . . ."

A week later, Steinman—who, to repeat, was an officer of a purportedly rival supermarket chain—again called Tantleff. "Sam [a union officer who has since died] knows the whole truth," Moe said. "Either they take the 15 on the contract or take the other one." Then Steinman gave Tantleff what amounted to a script George George was to follow at the union negotiations—"the regular procedure," Steinman called it, adding, "tell the truth." He said the union leaders would ask for a decision on a particular problem, whereupon George was to say he had to go back and talk to others—"stall for time," Steinman instructed. "Then Sam will tell me what to tell them, do you get it? Sam told me to tell him this. Sam knows the whole truth."

Then Steinman went on to say that he had discussed the matter with officials from Local 342 of the butchers' union (the retail store local), whom he identified as Nicky and Irving—obviously Nicholas Abondolo and Irving Stern, two men who would go to jail in the ensuing scandal. Steinman instructed Tantleff that Abondolo and Stern had to be given perfunctory treatment so George could go ahead and sign the softer contract with the department store workers' union. "Let him stay with Nicky and Irving and listen to their story," Steinman instructed. "If he doesn't like it and all that, say, 'Look, gentlemen, as far as I know it's supposed to be that way, whatever it is.' And go right to the door."

"Yeah, sure, okay," Tantleff responded. "I'll guide him with it."*

---

*Later, Stern and Abondolo would contend that they were relatively less guilty than other labor leaders in the supermarket industry, and that they were entrapped by Steinman's gang to

A little later, George himself called. First he buttered Tantleff up by saying that Shop-Rite would probably start carrying Benny Moscowitz's meat patties. Then he got down to business. "I'm involved in something now that I need Moe for," he said. The negotiations were underway in Newark as rehearsed, and the union leader wasn't cooperating. "We're prepared to go with the deal Moe told me," he said, and asked to speak to Steinman. Tantleff said he wouldn't be able to reach Steinman until later, but not to worry. "I can only tell you this, George," he said, "that I'm positive as I'm sitting on this chair . . . that whatever Moe said to you would be done will be done."

When the contract was settled, it came time to figure out which items would be overpriced in order to create the kitty necessary for the payoffs. Apparently Foodarama wanted to hold down the price of liver, a normal upcharge item. Sol Steinman called Tantleff September 24, 1971, to discuss it.

"I spoke with him [Moe] on that liver thing," Sol said, "and I mentioned they're looking for something off, like, you know. And I told him that I could safely—if we give them [Foodarama] something else. Where we can make back on something else. He says he is willing to go along with that, if we could add it on to, say, skirts, or flanks, where there is more tonnage, like. Wherever the tonnage to make it back, he says, he is willing to go that way."

Replied Tantleff, "If we could get around it in a different way by putting on a penny or more on the skirts and the flank steaks, corned beef. If, after all, you are taking a hell of a lot more tonnage in a month, month's time, than you would on, on the livers." So Foodarama apparently would be allowed to gyp its customers a little bit on a lot of items instead of a lot on a few items.

Steinman's influence wasn't limited to the butchers' and retail store workers' unions. In October, Foodarama was hit by a wildcat strike of its warehousemen and supervisors, who were members of the Teamsters union. Steinman called George to offer "assistance in breaking the strike" by providing what in George's own words were "goons" and "thugs" to drive trucks through the picket line. Apparently the problem was resolved without such unpleasantness. But Tantleff later assured George that Steinman had a lot of influence in the Teamsters through his friend "Trerola or something." Joseph "Joe T." Treratola is leader of the Teamsters' New York joint counsel.

In December, 1971, came a series of telephone calls that became known to the detectives as "the Christmas Tree conversations." George apparently had sent word that he needed to talk to Tantleff about how much payoff money he should give to the union leaders and how to transmit it. Tantleff called George with the information, and was typically circumspect in his speech.

---

take the rap for the true villains. In this case, at least, Steinman and Tantleff seem to be cutting Stern and Abondolo out of a sweetheart deal in which bribes were planned for leaders of a rival union local who were never prosecuted.

"I was speaking to [another executive] and he told me you might be looking for me," Tantleff began.

"Tell you why," George said.

"About, er, some Christmas trees or something."

"Nothing to do with Christmas trees," said George, obviously puzzled.

"No, no," repeated Tantleff, "I'm talking about *Christmas.*"

"Yeah," George said, laughing as he caught on. "Right!" They both laughed.

George seemed uncertain about how to make the payoffs.

"Well, that's up to you," Tantleff told him. "But I, I, if you remember, I even told you when I was at Bohack I used to handle it personally. Then I'd put in expense slips over a period of two or three months to get it back." Then he added, "Moe is in Florida for the week, and he won't be back until Monday. So nothing should burn your ass anyway . . . Let's wait until he gets back and let him take care of it."

"Yeah," George agreed.

By Christmas, 1971, the investigation was ready to move on to a new stage. Whether or not the wiretap tapes alone could have proven a criminal case in court against any particular individual, the tapes were overwhelming evidence that a mammoth racket was going on. They would clearly justify judicial support for an expanded inquiry. Snitow and Scotti decided the next step would be to obtain a warrant to raid the Trans-World office, seize all books and records and try to trace various payoffs back to inflated meat prices.

A raid seemed all the more urgent because of certain signals Nicholson and his men were picking up that the racketeers might have become aware of the investigation. How this could have happened, despite the tight secrecy that surrounded the wiretaps, mystified them. But during a telephone call in mid-December, George George told Julie Tantleff, "You know, I'm even hesitant even to discuss anything with you on the telephone. But there is rumors flying hot and heavy up where we are that there is a sort of a look into, er, that situation over there. There have been questions up here and, er, on our end."

"Right," Tantleff replied. "I know in New York there's been going on, not like for, er—"

"A specific thing," George said. "It's a specific situation."

"I know there's been talk going on," Tantleff told him. "Around New York there has been rumbles, like, I'd say for the past six months." Six months earlier, the wiretap had gone on Moe Steinman's telephone and Moe Steinman had suddenly started telling people not to call him on the phone.

"I don't have too much information on it," George said, "but Sid brought it to me the other day, er, somewhat upset, and, er, I don't know what if there is any clarification on it."

"As I say, I really don't know," Tantleff said. "I only know that in general there has been rumbles. You know, going on for the past six months, that they are looking into, er, activities of unions and things like that."

"Well, I'll, er, well, someday maybe I'll stop in and we'll talk," George said.

Then Julie Tantleff gave the detectives a clue as to who had the pipeline into the investigation. It was Mr. Fix-it himself. "And I could say," Tantleff reported to George, "the one that could, er, best answer us would be, er, one of the other labor relations men in one of the other big chains. . . . I'd say, he is—he's away now. He's in Florida and he wouldn't be back till Sunday. . . ."

On a cold, snowy January 7, 1972, detectives from the New York district attorney's office burst in on Trans-World's headquarters in an old several-story building on Gansevoort and Little West Twelfth streets. They presented their warrant, but it didn't get them much. The walls and floor of the office were scrawled with red paint. There were swastikas, and the words "Jew Bastard." There were not, however, any books and records. Someone in the office said they had been destroyed in a vandalism attack a few days earlier. And sure enough, the local police precinct had received a report a few days earlier of a vandalism attack on Trans-World brokerage.

Nicholson quickly reported back to Snitow, who accompanied the team of detectives to a meeting in the D.A.'s office with Harry Kurzer, Trans-World's accountant. Kurzer said that he, too, had seen evidence of the destruction after Sol Steinman had called him to report the "attack."

Snotow recalls, "We expressed our disbelief of that, of the circumstances surrounding the destruction of those books and records, and we stated that we had examined the premises, that it was curious that only the books and records of Trans-World Fabricators had been destroyed, in that Trans-World Fabricators shared space with, or locker space with, another firm at that same premises, and only those books and records belonging to Trans-World Fabricators had been sprayed with red paint, and the books and records of the other firm, which were located on a lower shelf, I believe, within that same locker, had been curiously left alone. We explained that we had reason to believe that in fact the material had not been destroyed and in fact it had been taken by Steinman so that we would not be able to conduct our investigation."

Kurzer, the CPA, said he had told Sol Steinman to gather up the "destroyed" books and records and put them in barrels, and not to throw them away. He said he hadn't seen them since. No financial data of any value was ever found regarding Trans-World Fabricators.

So Snitow and Nicholson proceeded to grill Kurzer himself for his recollections. They told him time and again, in Snitow's words, "that we knew what was going on and we wanted Mr. Kurzer to cooperate, and we were willing to give him immunity, notwithstanding that he might have been involved in these crimes. We wanted Moe Steinman. And Mr. Kurzer declined to cooperate in any way, shape, or form. . . . He denied knowledge of any type of inflation scheme.... We said that he wasn't being truthful.... Had we gotten anything out of him ... anything with respect to what ultimately came about ... we would have been in a position to indict Moe Steinman.... I would have been in a position to have him indicted for substantive crimes at that time."

Nicholson had long ago devised the strategy for this investigation. The goal would be different than in the A & P investigation, or the Merkel investigation, or the Kissel investigation. It was a new and more comprehensive goal. And Snitow shared it, and Al Scotti, the head of the rackets bureau, shared it, and Frank Hogan, the D.A., shared it. This time the object would be not simply to jail a few meat sellers, or meat buyers, or union officers, who would then return to business, or be replaced by others who would continue to be used as pawns in the great extortion game that robbed every meat-eating resident in a four-state area. This time the City of New York was out to bust the racket itself—to break the power of Johnny Dio and Chappy Brescia and Paul Castellano—to get the Mafia out of the marketplace.

The mobsters, of course, were well insulated. Except for Castellano's relatively small meat business, which was more or less just a front for his real activities, the mobsters didn't sell the meat, or buy it, or get on the phone to talk price with the people who did. Yet there was one man who tied the mobsters to every crooked deal in the meat industry, one man who could truly break them, and that man was Moe Steinman. Steinman had to be nailed so solidly that he would spend the rest of his life in jail if he didn't talk. Nicholson, Montello, Carey, half a dozen other detectives, Snitow, Scotti, Hogan—they knew their job was to get Moe Steinman.

5

The Surrender

The books and records were gone. The accountant wouldn't talk. The wiretap tapes talked, but not enough. Secrecy and the advantage of surprise had been forfeited, as the "vandalism attack" at Trans-World made plain. The next step was to apply power, to try to make key witnesses talk by putting the screws to them. A grand jury was convened. Snitow called in a secretary and began dictating subpoenaes and, ultimately, indictments.

> The Sixth Grand Jury of the County of New York for the March 1972 Term, having been duly and properly empanelled, has been conducting an investigation to determine whether the crimes of Grand Larceny by Extortion, Coercion in the First Degree, Bribe Receiving by a Labor Official, Bribing by a Labor Official, and Commercial Bribery have been committed and whether there has been in existence a Conspiracy to commit these crimes.
>
> As part of the said investigation, the Grand Jury has sought to determine whether Herbert Newman, Moe Steinman, Sol Steinman, certain labor union officials, certain organized criminal elements and others conspired to cause, through the unlawful use of the influence of said labor union officials, certain agents of supermarket chain stores to purchase meat directly or indirectly from Moe Steinman at inflated prices. . . .

Before the cops could use Moe Steinman to work up to the Mafia, they would have to start with the lowest, sleaziest elements in the meat racketeering network and work up to Moe Steinman. And who was lower and sleazier than

Herbie Newman? Subpoenaes were drawn for Newman and Sol Steinman.

Moe Steinman found out about it and told his brother and his partner to get out of town. Sol did. But Newman went instead to an apartment on Thirty-fourth Street and First Avenue. He had rented the apartment to bring girls to, but now figured it could serve as a hideout. The cops had been following him there for months, however, and now did so again, and immediately served the subpoena. So Newman went to Miami. There he bought a doctor, who mailed letters to the court saying Newman had contracted a fatal heart condition and couldn't travel. This allowed two lucky detectives to escape the New York winter by going to Florida so they could investigate Newman's health. When they returned with photographs of Newman painting his $200,000 house and hauling rocks onto his lawn to build a rock garden, the judge ruled that Newman was well enough to come home and face the grand jury.

The questions the very first morning were enough to terrify Newman. During the lunch recess, he raced to the nearest pay phone and called Steinman. They carefully rehearsed what Newman would say in response to further questions. "I don't remember. . . . It might be. . . . I'm not sure."

"Don't worry," Newman finally reassured Steinman. "I won't tell them nothing."

But he already had. Detective Jack Carey was standing behind Newman at the entrance of the telephone booth, taking careful notes of everything he said.

Newman testified March 13, March 22, April 10, April 12, April 17, April 19, April 25, May 16, May 17, May 23, May 24, May 25, May 31, and June 1, 1972. Then he was indicted for criminal contempt of court for giving "conspicuously unbelievable, evasive, equivocal, and patently false answers" to Snitow's questions.

For example, at one point, Snitow read to Newman from the transcript of a wiretapped conversation of August 17, 1971, in which Steinman reported that he would "be short" $40,000 or $50,000 "to give away."

"Now," Snitow said, "Wasn't he telling you that was what the so-called Mob element demanded?"

"I don't know," Newman testified.

"You deny that?"

"I can't say yes, I can't say no," Newman said. "All I know is that he was the one. . . . You see, Moe Steinman—I explained to you the first day I sat down here, that I'm a molecule, or a atom compared to the man."

Snitow demanded specific testimony about Steinman's Mafia power sources.

"I knew that he knew members of the underworld," Newman said. "I knew that. And Moe Steinman would say something to me that he had to give—I never questioned it."

Snitow wouldn't let go. "Isn't he telling you, 'We have this obligation to pay off these individuals and we have got to give them this money'?"

"That—I can't say that," Newman said.

"Do you deny that he is saying that?"

"I don't know anything about Mob elements," Newman swore. "I know that he's—that he knows them all. I know he associates with them. I can't say that he went and gave this to the Mob. I never was there."

Nicholson, in the audience, winced. He knew Newman was lying.

Snitow played a tape recording of their discussions of the Castellano gang in Brooklyn, and the Key Foods account.

"Do you know whom he's referring to?" Snitow asked.

"No."

"Is he referring to a man by the name of Castellano?"

"I don't know who he was referring to. I never spoke about these kind of people."

"Do you know who Castellano is?"

"He had stores in wholesale, and he also went to jail . . . either for receiving stolen merchandise . . . I'm telling this jury that Moe Steinman knew all these types of people," Newman said.

Snitow wanted names. "When you said 'all these types of people,' let's be more specific. Whom did you mean?"

"He did know Castellano. He knew—"

"Go ahead. Tommy Dio? Larry Brescia?"

"Do you want me to give it to you? Tommy Dio, Johnny Dioguardi. . . . He knew Brescia."

"Known as Chappy?"

"He probably knew other people, but I never met the other people."

Snitow played the tape again. "That is Castellano?" he asked.

"Now there is two Castellanos," Newman suddenly responded.

"Tell us about the two Castellanos."

"There is Peter Castellano*, the one who was in trouble. And then the other one, I don't remember, maybe I met him once . . . Paul Castellano."

"Do you agree that he was referring to a Castellano?" Snitow demanded.

"I can't agree on that because I don't know. . . . It is possible that I knew, but I don't remember now."

Snitow played a tape of Newman and another supermarket executive discussing, in their roundabout way, kickbacks.

"Weren't you paying because he was buying corned beef or whatever the product was at a higher price than you sold to others?" Snitow asked.

"No," Newman said.

"You deny that?"

"I don't know."

*He spells it "Castellana"; the grand jury stenographer took down the more normal family spelling.

"You don't deny that?"

"I don't deny it . . . I don't admit it . . . I just don't remember. . . ." Snitow played Newman a tape recording of Newman's own voice talking to Steinman about "Mr. T" and asked Newman if "Mr. T" wasn't Tommy Dio. Newman said he couldn't remember.

After his indictment for criminal contempt, Newman went back down to Florida. When time arrived for his trial, another doctor wrote back that Newman was suffering from terminal cancer. This time, the doctor was telling the court the truth. Newman died in 1974, protecting Moe Steinman's secrets with his last breath.

As soon as the District Attorney's office saw that it would get nothing out of Herbie Newman—though it continued to offer Newman every opportunity to commit perjury—the office tried another avenue. The whole Moe Steinman investigation had started eighteen months earlier with the Iowa Beef incident. Maybe the investigation would end there. Iowa Beef was fifteen hundred miles away, but it did business in New York, and it had conspired in New York, and Iowa Beef and its officers were subject to the New York courts.

Out in Dakota City, doubts about the Steinman deal still smouldered in the minds of subordinate executives, ready to ignite if the District Attorney's office threw off the right spark. Walter Bodenstein himself had stirred up lingering resentments by attempting to exploit Iowa Beef's name in an audacious new venture. Early in 1972, even while Moe Steinman was telling brother Sol and partner Herbie Newman to lay low, Bodenstein was planning a public offer of C. P. Sales stock, thus cashing in quickly on the new company's potential for future commissions from Iowa Beef. Apparently Bodenstein was still fascinated by the way Johnny Dio and his phony stockbrokers had cleaned up in the securities markets. If Dio could make money selling buffalo chips, think what Bodenstein could make selling blue chips! The C. P. Sales stock prospectus made no effort to conceal the company's only real asset—an exclusive contract with the world's largest beef producer.

Then, in February, 1972, Bodenstein told the world's largest beef producer about this idea. The world's largest beef producer told him to forget it. Holman had taken his chances with the New York City cops, but he wasn't going to throw a red flag in front of the Securities and Exchange Commission. So Bodenstein promised not to use Iowa Beef's name in a public stock registration, at least not "immediately." But the incident left a bad taste in several mouths.

Then, a month or two later, a flurry of grand jury subpoenaes arrived from New York, throwing Iowa Beef's sleepy midwestern headquarters into a turmoil. The D.A.'s office figured that somewhere in a company the size of Iowa Beef, there had to be an honest man—or at least a disgruntled one. Maybe all the subpoenaes would produce a cooperative witness.

It wouldn't be Currier Holman. Holman immediately went looking for criminal defense counsel in Manhattan, and hired Richard Wynn and Jeffrey Atlas, two former assistants in Hogan's office who had recently gone off on their own to do defense work. It is unfortunately true that lawyers freshly departed from the prosecutor's office are often among those most desired as defense counsel. They are believed to have special insights into the way the local prosecutor does things, and to have a special ability to call up their former colleagues and make a favorable deal. They are believed to get increased respect from judges, who consider them to have "graduated." And they are believed to have a pretty good recall of what information is in the prosecutor's files and what targets are on his agenda. All too often, these beliefs turn out to be correct. This not only puts pressure on good young prosecutors to foresake law enforcement for greener pastures in the defense bar, but more important it tends to dillute the loyalty and dedication of prosecuting attorneys to the cause of law enforcement altogether. Even while they are working as assistant district attorneys, they know that eventually their bread will be buttered on the other side, often by the very people they are supposed to be investigating while on the D.A.'s payroll. Many lawyers take a D.A.'s job fully intending to use it as a stepping stone toward work for the opposition. Almost any cop or FBI agent will tell you that this conflict of interest often occurs, and always works in favor of the defense.

The week of May 15, 1972, Wynn and Atlas, Holman's new lawyers, flew to Dakota City to begin preparing a defense against the inquiries being made by their former boss, the district attorney. Holman maintained his complete innocence. But his stonewall began to crumble almost immediately, for the subpoenaes had indeed found some honest men. The first was Howard Weiner, the treasurer. When Wynn and Atlas interviewed him, he laid the whole story on the line.

On Friday, May 19, Holman heard about Weiner's meeting with defense counsel, and immediately yanked the treasurer on the carpet. "What did you tell them?" Holman demanded.

"I told them everything," Weiner replied.

Holman started. "You didn't tell them what I think you told them."

"If you're referring to the Moe Steinman relationship," Weiner said, "I told them everything."

Then, by Weiner's recollection, Holman "became explosive and angry and berated me for discussing this subject with them. He then called Mr. Nymann [the general counsel] into the office with me being present, and told him that he had given me poor advice by telling me to discuss this subject with Mr. Wynn and Mr. Atlas. He then called Mr. Atlas and Mr. Wynn and, I believe, Lew Jacobs [the salesman] into the office—I was present—and he [said he] would go to New York himself to the grand jury . . . and talk to them." But, Weiner recalls, Holman said he "didn't remember the things that Weiner remembers," and added that Weiner could "tell them whatever the hell he wants to."

Then everybody left the room but Holman and Weiner.

"Are you telling me that you didn't hear what I heard at the Hampshire House?" Weiner asked.

"That's what I'm telling you, kid," he says Holman answered.

"Well, you're a liar," Weiner responded, and left.

On the next Monday, May 22, 1972, Weiner asked for a meeting of the executive committee. Holman said everyone was too busy, that anything Weiner wanted to say he could say to Holman. Weiner says he described the New York investigation again, and asked for help "in deciding what posture to take."

Holman, he says, interrupted him with a string of obscenities. Weiner announced his resignation.

Within hours, Gus Nymann walked out, too. Holman's general counsel and next-door neighbor had tolerated having his house dynamited in the struggle. But he couldn't tolerate his boss's flouting the law. "I didn't feel that I could participate in the investigation where it seemed that people were going to say that they didn't remember the events of a significant meeting," Nymann said later. Such were the ethics of the corporate counsel; he preferred to quit his well-paid job rather than defend a lie. Wynn and Atlas, the recently departed law enforcement officers, however, would stay on with Holman to the last appeal, and beyond that, they would explore whether they could rescue the chairman's ego by filing a libel action.

Howard Weiner flew to New York with his private lawyer and told the grand jury his story. It was perhaps the biggest break in the whole Moe Steinman investigation. With the information that Weiner supplied, Snitow was able to summon other officers from the firm and ask them for details—not just their own colored accounts of what went on, but precisely whether so-and-so said what Weiner said he said, or, if not, what actually happened.

By the time Holman himself came to New York July 21, the dam had broken. Everyone at the D.A.'s office expected that Holman would now cooperate. They expected him to testify that Moe Steinman had shaken him down for huge payments to support the continued bribery of supermarket executives and (more important, because the law provided much greater penalties for this) union officials. With Holman's testimony, Steinman could be indicted, and so could every union officer who had been at the Stanhope. And that would be the lever for cracking the whole racket.

What the D.A.'s office still hadn't realized, however, was that Currier Holman's primary concern was and always had been selling his meat. And no matter how many lawyers and detectives Frank Hogan could marshal, Moe Steinman still controlled the New York meat market. Holman was not about to cross him.

"If Holman would have cooperated, we could have had an extortion case against the union officers and Steinman, too," recalls Al Scotti, the head of the rackets bureau, who led the negotiations. "Then we might have gotten somewhere. But Holman wouldn't cooperate. He insisted on giving an innocent version of the whole thing, which is ridiculous. I had Wynn and Atlas, who used to be prosecutors here, in my office, and I offered to let them write their own ticket. But Holman wouldn't go along."

Holman persisted in his story that the talk about bribery had been a bargaining tool to help Steinman argue for a higher commission rate. There was no conspiracy, Holman said; he had understood all the while that Steinman was bluffing, and had merely played along as part of his own negotiating strategy.

But—the prosecutors told him—there actually *were* payoffs. The telephone wiretaps proved that to a moral certainty, whether or not the wiretaps would stand up in court.

Maybe so, Holman and his attorneys countered. But unless the prosecutors could prove that those payments were made with Iowa Beef's commission money, and not out of Steinman's other funds, then the prosecutors didn't have a case. It couldn't be money from Trans-World, or one of Steinman's other brokerages, or cash from Herbie Newman's safe-deposit box. It had to be money from C. P. Sales. True, C. P. Sales was taking in $1 million a year from Iowa Beef, but as long as that money could be accounted for—even by way of Bodenstein's personal high-living—then there was no bribery case against Iowa Beef.

Back in their own huddle, Snitow and Scotti agreed they couldn't charge Holman or Iowa Beef with a substantive crime—not unless somebody came forward with evidence showing that commissions to C. P. Sales had actually gone to pay bribes. And it was quite possible that Steinman had arranged the deal carefully enough that the connection didn't exist, and that the bribe money really *was* paid entirely from other funds. Morally, that might not amount to much of a distinction, but legally, it was everything.

Still, there was another road that the prosecutors could follow. They could charge a *conspiracy* to bribe—there was plenty of evidence of intent. Not only did they have the testimony of the subordinate officers at Iowa Beef, but they had secretly recorded Holman's own interview at the District Attorney's office (Nicholson had hidden a tape machine under the sofa; this was perfectly legal —Holman had been warned that anything he said could be used against him). And while Holman on tape didn't exactly admit a conspiracy to bribe, he did admit that Steinman repeatedly told him there would be bribes paid. And he did admit that his own mental state at the time was one in which he believed that "everybody in the meat business in New York is a crook."

So the rackets squad would charge Holman and Steinman with conspiring with each other, and try to build from there.

In New York State, where a junkie can be sent up for life, the maximum penalty for commercial bribery, no matter how many millions of dollars is involved, was ninety days in jail, and has since been raised to one year. The penalty for conspiracy to commit commercial bribery is still only ninety days.

Labor union bribery bears a penalty of up to seven years in prison, and conspiracy to bribe labor union officials—the worst thing Holman and Steinman could be charged with—carries one year.

That charge alone certainly wouldn't put Steinman as deeply into the corner as the prosecutors wanted him. On the other hand, the year would have to be served at a place like the Rikers Island jail, alongside pimps, junkies, and muggers. And Nicholson had a gut sense that Steinman was terrified of such a place. Moreover, if a year wasn't enough to impress Steinman, it might be enough to impress Holman. The mere threat of a plausible conspiracy indictment might impress him. And with Holman's cooperation, the D.A. could pin an extortion rap on Steinman that would carry a fifteen-year prison stretch.

Finally, there was the power of the federal government. As far as Scotti's men were concerned, Bill Aronwald and the strike force were on their team in this case. All sorts of federal anti-racketeering statutes carried penalties of up to twenty years, including interstate travel to break state laws.

Steinman had been to Iowa at least twice to see Holman, and Holman had come to New York at least three times to see Steinman. Moreover, bribery usually results in violation of income tax laws. So the D.A.'s men once again brought their laboriously assembled case to Aronwald.

In August, 1972, Aronwald assigned several Internal Revenue Service agents attached to the strike force to start questioning the man Nicholson figured was the best prospective witness regarding tax violations: Harry Kurzer, the accountant for Trans-World and other Steinman-related brokerages. In several meetings in late summer, Kurzer consistently denied that anything untoward had taken place in connection with the meat businesses. In an effort to end his reluctance, Aronwald arranged a complicated deal under which Kurzer could receive immunity from prosecution if he incriminated himself while telling any story that turned out to be the full truth. But the denials continued. Interviews broke off that fall while Aronwald tried an unrelated case, but in December, 1972, the agents were back with Kurzer, who finally agreed to throw them a bone.

The books of some of the brokerages contained long lists of employees who were relatives of Steinman, or of his fellow senior executives at Daitch-Shopwell supermarkets. Kurzer acknowledged that these were not bona fide employees of the brokerages. He said he had warned Steinman repeatedly that listing relatives on the employee payroll was a possibly illegal tax dodge, and that if Steinman wanted to give money to his relatives he couldn't deduct it from his corporate taxes as a business expense. He said Steinman had promised to clean up the books, but that Kurzer later discovered that Steinman had merely transferred the relatives to the books of a new firm that received cash from the other firms. The new illegal payoff firm happened to share an address with Walter Bodenstein, who was its principal officer.

In addition, Kurzer conceded to the feds that he had warned Steinman about some other "business expense" deductions that the IRS men had already grown suspicious of: the posh Steinman pad in Florida, for example, and big cars for everybody—and heavy bills at the Black Angus Restaurant and the Tammybrook Country Club, which was operated by an ex-convict meat dealer Steinman was friendly with. All this tax chiseling was petty stuff, of course, compared to the union and supermarket bribery the cops were after. But it was illegal, and carried potentially stiff penalties. The case was moving in the right direction so long as Steinman was being backed into a corner, a corner he couldn't get out of without turning on his Mafia friends.

On March 12, 1973, a joint federal-state press conference announced some indictments that shook the meat industry coast-to-coast. The People of the State of New York had charged Currier Holman, Moe Steinman, and Iowa Beef Processors itself with conspiring to commit commercial and labor union bribery. The federal government charged Holman, Steinman, and C. P. Sales with conspiring to violate a state anti-racketeering law and with interstate travel to carry on unlawful activities.* The United States also charged Moe and Sol Steinman, Walter Bodenstein, and Herbie Newman with filing fraudulent tax statements in connection with the phony employees.

Holman bitterly remembers being hauled down with Steinman for fingerprinting. Steinman, the pro, was in and out. But a computer foul-up caused a "hold" to be put by Holman's name. Evidently his prints were confused with those of some unidentified fugitive. Holman says Snitow exuberantly demanded that the executive be thrown into the city lock-up overnight as any common mugger would be in the same situation, but he says the computer straightened itself out before nightfall and he got to go home. Snitow says the computer didn't straighten itself out quickly at all; he says he went to a judge in an effort to be nice to Holman and obtained the executive's early release against normal court policy that he should have been held.

For the D.A.'s office, it was only the beginning. A new round of grand jury hearings was begun immediately, in an effort to build on the terror that had suddenly seized the meat district. Among the first witnesses to be called were Julie Tantleff and George George. Like Newman before them, Tantleff and George each knew that if he pleaded the Fifth Amendment and refused to answer, he might be given immunity from prosecution. That would mean he would have to tattle on Moe Steinman, or else go to jail indefinitely for civil contempt of court. So both Tantleff and George took the Newman alternative: obfuscation.

Despite the conversations on the wiretap tapes, Tantleff flat-out denied that

---

*Aronwald says he intentionally omitted Iowa Beef from the list of defendants, and tried unsuccessfully to persuade the state to do so in its indictment, because he didn't want to tar the large company with the misdeeds of its leaders. He says that when a newsman asked him about the discrepancy, he covered up the disagreement by attributing the difference in indictments to differences in state and federal law, which, in fact did not exist.

he had discussed paying off Nicholas Abondolo (then and now president of the retail butchers' local in New York), and pleaded poor memory about whether Moe Steinman asked him to have vending machines placed in certain super-markets, or to get the markets to stock Benny Moscowitz's meat patties, or to pay off various other union officers besides Abondolo.

George admitted talking about payoffs to the union leaders, as the tape recordings clearly showed he did. But George refused to concede that the payoffs actually took place. He contended that he talked about them because "we all read newspapers and we go to movies and see this." It was, he said, a "figment of my imagination." He was forced to concede that he had actually handed an envelope full of cash to an unnamed union officer, but—George explained—the union officer had told him that another Foodarama executive "owed him some money."

On May 31, 1973, both men were indicted for criminal contempt of court, as Newman had been, for giving "conspicuously unbelievable, evasive, equivo-cal, and patently false answers," and Tantleff faced an additional charge of first degree perjury.

The indictments of Tantleff and George scared Moe Steinman, Nicholson's sources reported. Right now, Steinman faced just a year on the conspiracy charge. But if Tantleff and George were convicted and decided to talk rather than go to jail, they could testify to extortion, which carried up to fifteen years in a state prison.

Moreover, Nicholson had located Nat Meyerson, Steinman's other son-in-law, who had been involved with Bodenstein in the Medicaid factoring business and who had kept accounts for some Steinman-connected broker-ages. Meyerson's marriage to Steinman's daughter Helene was breaking up, and Meyerson was feeling no particular love for the Steinman clan. He might testify. The meat buyers, too, were beginning to quake in the after-math of the spring indictments. Six years before, a group of industry lead-ers had come over en masse to testify in the Kissel case, and now perhaps, it could happen again. After all, Nicholson reasoned, the small cutting shops on Fourteenth Street were being hurt, not helped, by Steinman's ploy with boxed beef.

Also, the District Attorney's men still viewed the strike force as an ally. Trans-World was handling huge amounts of cash. If the federal government would lay claim on Steinman for back taxes, the bill could run in the millions and overwhelm him.

It was summer, now, 1973, and Nicholson knew exactly what he wanted Steinman to do. It would be more than just talk. Nicholson wanted Steinman to wear a hidden tape recorder in conversations with Tommy Dio, Chappy Brescia, and various members of the Castellano family. The recordings would provide conclusive back-up evidence in court. If Steinman would "wear a wire," he could also nail down cases against meat buyers and union leaders. But the real game Nicholson hunted were the Mafiosi.

Moe Steinman had been scrapping for nearly half a century in New York. He knew better than to leave himself without a way out. In January, 1972, about the time Trans-World's books were destroyed by "vandals," Steinman had found himself a brilliant criminal lawyer, Elkan Abramowitz. Like Currier Holman, Steinman had gone for his defense to someone who used to be on the other side. Abramowitz was a former assistant U. S. Attorney.

But for whatever reason the lawyers were chosen, Steinman made the better choice. While Wynn and Atlas led their client, Holman, into the wired-up lair of the District Attorney to make an on-the-record confession, Abramowitz played the prosecution like a violin. He knew the feuding that sometimes goes on between rival law enforcement agencies. He saw the presence of both state and federal agencies in the meat investigation, and was able to turn the other side's superior numbers to Steinman's advantage (though he modestly denies now that this was his intent).

On one side was Frank Snitow, inexperienced and relying heavily on Al Scotti and Bob Nicholson. Scotti and Nicholson had been chasing the Mafia for years. They had already achieved too many false victories through plea bargaining. This time they were hunting bear. They had an unmistakable bloodlust for Steinman and the higher-ups. If somebody was going to leave a door open for Steinman's escape, it would have to be Aronwald.

Within days of the time the joint federal-state indictments against Steinman were filed in March 1973, Abramowitz dropped by Aronwald's office "to talk preliminarily about discovery and other matters." Marvin Sontag, the IRS agent assigned to the case, sat in on the meeting. The subject of Steinman's possible "cooperation" came up. But Abramowitz says he left the office telling the strike force team that Steinman probably wouldn't want to cooperate because the mobster thought he could defend himself successfully.

Nevertheless, there's evidence that Steinman was secretly preparing even then to deal with the federal prosecutors by squealing on selected bribe recipients, while protecting his true friends. Certainly he would not turn over information on anyone with independent ties to the Mafia—only on those whose criminal dealings were done exclusively through Moe Steinman. That way they couldn't spread the investigation further if they were to start squealing themselves. And the Mob wouldn't be angry.

Irving Stern, the regional butchers' union leader, was just the kind of man Steinman was likely to turn on. Steinman couldn't stand Stern personally. Stern had been a leftist labor organizer at one time, and still preached the language of militancy. Now he was dealing in dirty money, like the others—and yet not like them. Stern seemed out of place in his role as a racketeer, and was privately derided by Steinman and the butchers' leaders Steinman was closest to, such as Irving Kaplan. (That may be why Steinman dealt Stern and his union local out when making bribery arrangements for the Foodarama contract in 1971.)

By May, 1973, word of the investigation had spread to every bar on

Fourteenth Street, and Stern was visibly scared. A lot of people noticed it. Nicholson got an anonymous phone call saying that Stern had cashed a large amount of bonds, supposedly around $200,000 worth, in an effort to hide his bribery hoard. During this period, Stern foolishly went for legal advice to Walter Bodenstein. Bodenstein, who said later that he didn't think he was acting as Stern's lawyer, welcomed Stern to his home in Westchester, then secretly tape-recorded the proceedings as the union leader worried out loud about the loot he had stored up from Moe Steinman. The tape recording basically confirmed what Nicholson had been told about a large amount of bonds. Later it became a valuable tool in Moe Steinman's arsenal for dealing with the prosecutors. It put Stern in a bag that Steinman could deliver at will.

Justice takes a holiday in August. Almost all judges go on vacation the whole month, and if there are no judges there are no courts, and so lawyers often take the month off, too—including prosecutors. As a rule, no business is considered so urgent that it can't wait until September. Frank Snitow assumed it would be no different in August, 1973. When the courts closed, Snitow cleared Moe Steinman from his mind and took his wife to Europe.

For Elkan Abramowitz, however, the August doldrum offered a brilliant opportunity to strike. He called Aronwald's office. Aronwald was on vacation, but Abramowitz got Sontag, the IRS agent. Abramowitz said he wanted to find out what kind of deal he could get if Steinman would give the government some very big cases. Sontag reached Aronwald at home, and the federal prosecutor agreed to come back from vacation the next week to talk with Abramowitz. Not one word of this was breathed to anyone else, particularly not anyone from the District Attorney's office. (Abramowitz says he made the initial call July 16, though he did not meet with Aronwald until at least August 6.)

It so happened that the Internal Revenue Service had been working for some time on an investigation into suspected violations by supermarket chains of the wage and price control act then in effect. Two years earlier, President Nixon had launched his surprise inflation-fighting program by freezing prices and wages. There had followed several "phases" during which prices and wages were allowed to move a little bit according to the strictures of Washington. (Ironically, Irving Stern, the butchers' union leader with the $200,000 in bonds, was appointed by the Nixon Administration to a wage-price board that supervised the controls for the food industry.) In June, 1973, a new freeze was announced, which was to end August 13. There would follow another "phase," and then, finally, prices and wages would go back to being determined by the people who were buying, selling, working and hiring. The problem was that a lot of people had really been operating that way all along, even when it was illegal. And the IRS, which was charged with finding and punishing these people, was having a tough time of it.

The IRS knew good and well, for example, that something funny was going on in the meat business. Data had been gathered from ninety food store chains across the country. As far back as the fall of 1972, an official had told *Supermarket News,* a trade publication, that some stores were suspected of having "a higher mark-up on beef than is permitted. . . . Frankly, we haven't been satisfied that retail prices have been going down fast enough," the official said.

Despite its suspicions, however, the IRS apparently didn't want to assign accountants, lawyers, computers, and clericals to fish for months among meat purchase records with uncertain result. So, with the price freeze now due to expire in a week or two, the IRS still didn't have a case to take to court to punish the food chains. Legally, indictments could be filed after the freeze under the statute of limitations, but practically, they would lose much of their appeal. To newspaper readers, television viewers, and politcal higher-ups the issue would be moot.

Suddenly, in absolute defiance of coincidence, in walked Elkan Abramoweitz and Moe Steinman with an offer of sworn testimony and documents to show that under-the-table agreements existed between New York area supermarket chains and wholesale meat dealers. The excessive part of the payment was to be deferred until after controls went off. Thus the effective wholesale prices were actually higher than the ones posted, which explained why retail mark-ups looked excessive. And Steinman could name a score of supermarket chains that had participated in such deals.

Twenty supermarket chains indicted for overcharging customers! Aronwald had to take note. "He saw the cameras rolling," a lawyer at the D.A.'s office later remarked.

Would Steinman also tell his story of bribery in the meat industry, Aronwald wanted to know? Abramowitz said that Steinman would name some buyers and union officials, but wouldn't identify them until after he got his deal in writing. Would Steinman also agree to testify against any Mafia people? Steinman didn't have any dealings with organized crime people, Aronwald was told. Steinman liked to be seen in their company, and pretended to be friends of theirs, but only because it made people afraid of him. He didn't deal with them, and couldn't testify against them, and if Aronwald wanted his supermarket indictments he would have to agree to take Moe Steinman's word for that. No Mafia. Aronwald agreed.

And, Abramowitz went on, not only would Aronwald have to come across with a sweet deal closing out any existing or prospective federal charges against Steinman, he also would have to get the state off Steinman's back, too. Steinman wasn't about to cop a plea in federal court only to start getting grilled by Bob Nicholson and his men. In order to get the supermarkets, Aronwald would have to deal with Scotti on Steinman's behalf to make sure the mobster was protected on all flanks. (Frank Hogan, for thirty years the nation's most celebrated D.A., was already beginning to suffer the effects of an illness that would prove fatal, and Scotti had taken over much of the responsibility for the office.) And still more: Abramowitz said all charges would have to be dropped against Sol Steinman and Walter Bodenstein.

Abramowitz said he also would like charges dropped against Steinman himself in exchange for the supermarkets. But they all knew that Scotti would never agree to dismiss the state's pending charge against Steinman in the Iowa Beef Case. Scotti would insist that Steinman plead guilty to the Iowa Beef indictment or its equivalent as part of any kind of deal. But the state charge carried a one-year maximum sentence, and the state would not be able to charge Steinman with any other crime if he put his story on the record under a broad grant of immunity.

So how would it be if Steinman also agreed to plead guilty to one federal tax count? Aronwald could then promise to recommend in court that Steinman's federal sentence be made concurrent with the state sentence. As Abramowitz well knew, a one-year concurrent federal sentence would actually be to Steinman's benefit, because Steinman could then serve all his time in a relatively comfortable federal detention center with other tax cheats, and could avoid the ungodly world of pimps, junkies, muggers, and hold-up men to be found in state prison.

Aronwald took the bait. There is a dispute over the exact penalty agreed upon. The D.A.'s office would later charge that the deal guaranteed Steinman no more than a one-year overall sentence. New York State judge Burton Roberts, to whom Steinman offered his guilty plea on the Iowa Beef charge, also stated from the bench that Steinman had been legally guaranteed no more than a one-year total sentence on all charges, both state and federal. Aronwald himself insists otherwise. He points out that the federal tax charge Steinman pleaded to carried a three-year maximum sentence. At least theoretically, under the statute, Steinman could have spent that long in jail, if a federal judge had wanted to send him.

Either way, however, justice was indeed taking a holiday in August, 1973.

During the second week of August, Aronwald called Scotti. Steinman had agreed to plead guilty and cooperate fully, he said. But a formal deal had to be signed immediately, because the price freeze act was about to expire. Scotti, startled, explained that it was Snitow's case, and Snitow would be in Europe for another week. Aronwald insisted it couldn't wait. The deal would be sealed the following Monday, August 13, in Abramowitz's office, and the D.A. was invited to send a representative. Aronwald insists he explained the whole deal to Scotti over the phone and that Scotti agreed to it. "I didn't agree to anything," Scotti says angrily. "They had some kind of investigation in Washington with respect to the price control act, and it was very important that they get this man's cooperation. I insisted that he would have to cooperate with us in our investigation of organized crime figures. That was our major objective."

Scotti says he told Aronwald that he wouldn't intervene in an assistant's case, and begged Aronwald to wait one week for Snitow to return. Aronwald wouldn't do it. At the same time, Abramowitz says that Aronwald was beseeching him to make a separate deal for Steinman with the strike force, leaving the state out of it, but Abramowitz wouldn't do that.

Scotti tried to get in touch with Snitow. Snitow couldn't be reached at his hotels, because his wife, who preferred the charm of small pensiones, had changed their tour arrangements. Scotti went to Interpol, the international agency that was created to aid cooperation among police departments of various countries. Interpol agents began a bizarre manhunt for Snitow across Europe.

Nicholson also was on vacation. Lou Montello was sent to Abramowitz's office August 13 without authority to agree to anything. Apparently he didn't participate in any negotiations, but, as instructed, brought back a copy of the deal worked out by the lawyers. Aronwald says he got a call later that day from Paul Vitrano, head of the D.A.'s detective squad, saying the deal had been approved by Scotti. Says Vitrano, "I don't recall having made that call, and I wouldn't have had the authority to do it. If anybody made a call it would have to have been Scotti." Everyone agrees Scotti didn't make it.

The next day, August 14, 1973, Aronwald signed the agreement on behalf of both the state and federal governments. The agreement was explicit on that point. Abramowitz says that Aronwald told him the D.A.'s office had approved the deal, that Montello's presence led him to believe it, and that once his client Steinman started talking, there could be no further state or federal prosecution beyond the guilty pleas Steinman had agreed to make. The first "de-briefing" session for the mobster was scheduled for 9 A.M. August 15.

Nicholson—back from vacation in midweek—and Montello went to Abramowitz's office, anxious to find out what Steinman would say, disbelieving it would be the whole truth.* They found Aronwald, Sontag, some other federal officials, and Abramowitz, who was presiding over a generous spread of coffee, breakfast cakes, and so forth. They did not find the guest of honor, who chose to be more than an hour late. And when Steinman finally did come through the office door, Bob Nicholson was more disgusted than surprised.

"He'd been drinking," Nicholson recalls. "He walked in with a quart bottle of Dewars in his hand and slammed the bottle on the table."

Then came Steinman's first words to the assemblage of lawyers and investigators who had been waiting more than an hour: "Anybody want a drink? Let's get some ice in here."

Nicholson felt himself filling with rage. The racketeer from the gutter had successfully intimidated the head of the federal strike force and all his men. They were supposed to ridding society of people like Steinman. Yet Steinman

---

*This account is from Nicholson and Montello. Aronwald strongly disagrees with the interpretations drawn, and Abramowitz disagrees with some of them. Both say they don't remember some things that Nicholson and Montello remember, but don't deny them either. Other things they do deny are noted in the text. Sontag's first response to an interviewer also is noted in the text. Later, after seeing the Nicholson-Montello account, he stated that IRS rules forbid him to comment.

was putting on an act designed to cow them, to put *them* on the defensive. And it was working. Nicholson looked around the room at Aronwald and the IRS men, all waiting obediently for Steinman to tell them as much or as little as he cared to. And if Steinman was really going to open up about the Mafia, Nicholson wondered, why hadn't Aronwald invited any FBI men to hear it? None were there. Aronwald could count on the IRS to zero in on pricing violations and be content making tax cases against the people Steinman would say he bribed. The FBI might have had the same designs on the Mafia that Nicholson did.*

Steinman unscrewed the cap of the White Label and took a swig straight from the bottle.** The mobster was in total command, and that didn't surprise Nicholson either. "He drank all day and all night," Nicholson says. "But he could still do business."

The racketeer with the bottle in his hand launched into his life story. "I was a poor boy from Poland. . . . I had nothing. . . . I got to be a big man. . . . I got a lot of money. . . . I'm doing this for my family. . . ." He carried on about his daughters, about how much he loved them. He complained that investigators had been bothering the girls ever since their names had been found padding his payrolls. "I'm not like you people," he rambled on. "I drink. I carry on. I know you all think I'm associated with organized crime and the Mafia," he said. Then he denied it. He said he just "set out to live my life to give that impression." He wanted to be seen with them. But he didn't really know them.

"But I do know about bribery," he said. "I do know about meat buyers, union officers, wage-price . . ."

Nicholson: "He was naming the companies, and whetting everybody's appetite. And I sat there listening to him and the only thing I could think of was, 'You're a liar.' He was dominating the conference. He was running the whole show. The government officials were there joking with him."

Steinman returned a cold stare. "He didn't like me, and I had no love for him either," Nicholson says. Nobody spoke. And then Nicholson and Montello fully realized that the federal men were taking Steinman's side. The two detectives, who had been investigating the meat industry for more than nine years, sat looking at the newcomers who were suddenly pulling their carefully woven carpet out from under them. Everybody in the room seemed to believe what Steinman was saying—everybody but Nicholson, Montello, and, of course, Steinman himself.

"You say you're going to give names, dates, places on bribery," Nicholson

---

*Aronwald notes, correctly, that he called the FBI in on the Iowa Beef case when the D.A.'s office first brought it to him in 1972; but after a brief time the agents disclaimed interest and left the case for the IRS. If the bureau had known Steinman was talking, however, agents probably would have leapt at the chance to question Steinman about his Mob friends.

**Abramowitz says he doesn't remember whether Steinman had a bottle of whiskey. Aronwald says he remembers the bottle, but doesn't want to say who, if anyone, drank out of it.

said. "How are we going to know you're telling us the truth."

"You can get other people in," Steinman said. He said he would provide corroborative witnesses if the government would grant them immunity. There was his brother, and his son-in-law. "I got books, records," he added.

Then Nicholson asked the kicker: "Would you be willing to wear a concealed tape recorder and have conversations with these people about these instances?"

Steinman looked nervously at Abramowitz. Abramowitz showed no expression. Nobody spoke.

"Yeah," Steinman finally said. "I would."

"Would you wear it at the Black Angus?"

"Yeah."

"Would you wear it with Tommy Dio?"

"Yeah."

"Then let's go right from this meeting down to our office and get started," Nicholson said. That would leave no time for Steinman to tip anybody off, or to rig any conversations. It would leave no time for second thoughts. There would be instant proof.

It was Aronwald—not Abramowitz—who leapt up. He went out to the hallway. Nicholson followed, and this is his version of what happened there:*

"Steinman isn't going to wear a wire," Aronwald declared. "It would cause too many problems. Problems with the Justice Department. I got to go to Washington to get permission to let him wear a wire."

"*We* don't have to go to Washington," Nicholson told him. "We [the D.A.'s squad] could do it easily. We can wire him this very day."

"No," Aronwald responded. "That means we'd be making new cases and this thing will drag on forever. The wage and price violations are urgent. We need his testimony. He couldn't testify and wear a wire at the same time."

"I know this man," Nicholson pleaded. "I've had him under investigation for the better part of ten years. This man never told the truth in his life. You have to have some kind of control over him. Send him out with a wire and you'll know soon enough whether he's telling the truth or not."

Aronwald stared back at Nicholson. "I believe him," he said.

Nicholson didn't believe Steinman, and he didn't believe Aronwald believed Steinman, either. "He knew as well as I did that if Moe Steinman went out with a wire we'd have a new investigation going within twenty-four hours. What happened was, he just saw the case slipping away from him and becoming a New York County District Attorney's case again."

Montello and Nicholson agree with this description of the meeting. Sontag says he, too, agrees that the strike force sold out Nicholson's investigation;

---

*Aronwald denies Nicholson's version of the conversations and says he doesn't remember if the subject of Steinman's wearing a wire ever came up. Abramowitz says he remembers that it came up, but he doesn't remember whether Steinman agreed to wear the wire.

then he indicates that he's being sarcastic, and tells an interviewer to believe anything the interviewer wants to believe; then he hangs up. Aronwald denies that Steinman ever agreed to wear a wire when talking to Mafia figures. "Whoever said that is a liar," he says. He says the district attorney's office in its wiretap investigation "produced absolutely no evidence of any criminality whatsoever against Moe Steinman or anyone else." [George George and Julie Tantleff were convicted based on the wiretaps, and Herbie Newman was indicted but died before trial.] About the more general charges that he blew the Steinman investigation, Aronwald says, "I don't care to respond. . . . You're trying to deep-six me."

Later that day, Interpol caught up with Snitow on the canals of Venice. Racing to the nearest phone, Snitow called his office—on his own nickel, he later stressed. Told what had happened, he was furious. He offered to fly home immediately, also at his own expense, to try to straighten things out. He was told it was too late for that. Bill Aronwald's signature was already on a letter agreement with Steinman. The racketeer was already confessing under a grant of immunity. It would be impossible to make further cases against him.

It seemed the news couldn't get worse for Snitow, but it did. When Snitow returned on Monday, August 20, 1973, Nicholson and Montello gave him an account he could scarcely believe. He remembers Nicholson was "livid—we were on Moe Steinman's turf, and Moe Steinman seemed to be controlling things." Snitow asked to be included in the interviews, figuring there might be a way to salvage the situation.* Now that it would be forever impossible to use testimony from Currier Holman to convict Steinman of extortion, as originally planned, at least Snitow might try the reverse. He might get Steinman to help convict Holman in the Iowa Beef case.

So for two or three days of interviews, Snitow probed for Steinman's story —and was shocked to find that it backed up Currier Holman's story. Steinman insisted that he had never intended to use Iowa Beef's commissions to bribe anyone. He insisted that Holman had never believed Steinman would do such a thing. In fact, Steinman insisted that his books and records would show that all his bribes were paid with money from other brokerage deals. The money that went to C. P. Sales could all be legitimately accounted for.

By the end of the first day, Snitow and Aronwald were having words. By the end of the third day, the whole deal had blown up in an explosion of tempers. The D.A.'s office was claiming Steinman was lying, which would have abrogated the agreement. But the deal Abramowitz and Aronwald had drawn up required a mutual decision by federal and state authorities that Steinman

---

*Aronwald and Abramowitz say that Nicholson and Montello continued to attend the "debriefing" sessions the previous Thursday and Friday, which they regard as evidence that the detectives somehow endorsed the deal. The detectives deny that they attended. In retrospect, it's hard to see how any conlusion could be drawn from their presence or absence.

was lying before the deal died. Aronwald stuck with Steinman. Abramowitz gallantly tried to make peace during an afternoon at the D.A.'s office, but failed. Sources who were there recall "an almost violent confrontation" during which Scotti—who Aronwald insists had approved the whole deal—called Aronwald "a liar," and accused him "of allowing Steinman to run the investigation."

The D.A.'s men should have expected as much. Walter Bodenstein, Steinman's son-in-law, whose indictment for tax fraud had just been dropped in exchange for Steinman's "cooperation," was still operating under a contract with Iowa Beef that would soon be worth $1 million a year or more. In fact, just at the time of the Iowa Beef investigation, when Steinman's testimony could have been deadly to Holman, the C. P. Sales contract was being extended for another five years. For that kind of reward, Steinman was not about to turn on Currier Holman.

Says an important figure in the case from the D.A.'s office, "Steinman absolutely boxed us in because of the unwillingness of another law enforcement agency to stand up to him with us. Once Steinman knew Aronwald was willing to believe him, he didn't need us anymore. Rather than get support [from the strike force], we were told, if you don't want to go ahead with it, okay, they believe him, they'll go ahead. It was made to appear as if we were sabotaging the investigation. Aronwald thought he would really get these guys. Moe supposedly would produce and he didn't."

And that was the end of all cooperation between the two offices, and the beginning of two long years of hostility as each tried to pursue its own view of justice.

"The effect it had," said Nicholson, "was that we never again got a chance to talk to Moe Steinman."

As a final irony, the Justice Department in Washington vetoed the prosecution of the wage-price cases Aronwald had been attracted to. The department decided it wasn't worth trying a crime that would no longer be a crime when the trial occurred. Aronwald has argued since then that the wage-price cases weren't the most important part of the Steinman deal anyway—"just the most pressing."

6

The Scraps

For all the evidence he withheld, Moe Steinman did give a lot of usable information to the strike force. Generally, however, it turned out to be less than met the eye.

He quickly provided Nat Meyerson, his son-in-law and bookkeeper (who Nicholson says was already giving evidence to the state) as a corroborative witness. Under a promise of immunity from prosecution, Meyerson told how he went to the office every week and drew up phony invoices for the purchase and sale of meat that never really existed, all as a cover for Steinman's bribe money. If Steinman wanted money from a wholesaler as a contribution to the payoffs, he "sold" the wholesaler meat that was never delivered. They wrote the whole transaction off on their taxes as the cost of meat. On other occasions, Steinman used the cooperative wholesalers to "launder" commission money he had received from supermarkets or packinghouses. The wholesalers would sell *him* nonexistent meat, then cash his checks and return the proceeds. On all transactions, the cooperative wholesalers were allowed to keep 10 percent of the cash.

"If I wanted [to wash] twenty-five thousand dollars," Steinman would later testify, "I was getting it from you, you would give me a ticket, like twenty-five thousand dollars of flank steaks, and you would give me a bill and I would give you a check for it with a statement . . . and in turn you would give me back twenty-two thousand five hundred dollars in cash."

Like Meyerson, most of the other industry figures Steinman brought in received immunity from prosecution. Since the government was now conducting a tax evasion investigation rather than a racketeering investigation, it would concentrate on indicting takers of bribes rather than givers. Benny Moscowitz, the man who brought Moe Steinman to Dakota City, got immunity. Some prominent names in the New York wholesale meat industry were brought in and not indicted, although the government would allege in court papers that they helped pass money around.

Harry Kurzer, Trans-World's accountant, got no such kindly treatment, however. When Steinman and Meyerson revealed that Trans-World had made $9 million in phony meat-purchase deductions in 1972, and that another firm Kurzer kept books for made similar phony tax deductions, Kurzer was exposed for not telling the whole truth before the grand jury earlier in the year. This cost Kurzer his immunity, the government decided, and he was indicted for tax fraud. Kurzer's lawyers disagreed. After exhaustive appellate hearings, the defense won. The court said that even though Kurzer's previous testimony under immunity wasn't *directly* responsible for his indictment (he never mentioned the phony meat sales), nevertheless his testimony *contributed* to his indictment. If Kurzer hadn't testified, the court reasoned, Steinman might not have been indicted for tax fraud. And if Steinman hadn't been indicted for tax fraud, he might not have agreed to turn government witness against Kurzer, so Kurzer might not have been indicted. All of which was true, and none of which said anything about whether Kurzer had illegally cheated the government out of millions of dollars. But Kurzer got off.

Steinman also provided the strike force with the names of numerous supermarket chain meat executives who were taking bribes. He involved Food City, Bohack, First National, Big Apple, Foodarama, Sloan's, King Kullen, and Hills. He was obviously selective in what he said. No chief executives or top-level officials got named. No one from Daitch-Shopwell got named. He conspicuously avoided accusing his old friends Aaron and Barnett Freedman at Waldbaum's. Ironically, one of the meat wholesalers who came in under a grant of immunity let slip Barnett Freedman's name, and so Freedman got indicted anyway. (Aaron Freedman died.)

Says one member of the district attorney's team, "Steinman must have told the supermarket officials, 'Look, I'll tell them so much and no more. You can get off with an income tax violation and maybe a fine. Not bribery of union officers.'" Everything that happened tends to support this position. The executives were charged with failing to pay taxes on illegal payments they took, but there was no mention of their role in creating the illegal kitty to pay off the union bosses and others.

If Steinman had really caved in, one might expect that his reputation as a Mister Fix-it in the meat industry would suffer. Far from it, the proceedings seemed to be *enhancing* his reputation. When defense attorneys for the men Steinman was accusing would show up at various proceedings in connection with required pre-trial disclosure, they were surprised to find Steinman's lawyer, Elkan Abramowitz, not only present but sometimes leading the questioning. Sometimes, they say, Abramowitz seemed to be in charge of the whole situation.

Word was passed that Steinman had practically taken over the investigation. According to one defense attorney, "The night after a guy would testify before the grand jury, somebody connected to Steinman would call them and read back their testimony."

A few defense attorneys complained that Steinman was concocting his accusations to try to explain away nearly $2 million in unreported income that the government had traced to him personally within the statute of limitations. Steinman certainly wasn't concocting the fact that he paid heavy bribes; there is good reason, however, to question the dollar amounts he was reporting to the strike force. The money Steinman said he gave to the supermarket executives and union officials totaled very nearly the amount he was on record as having received in undeclared income. After deducting the bribe money, Aronwald brought an indictment charging Steinman with ducking taxes on a mere $70,000 in personal income in 1970. But everything Nicholson had found out about Steinman in two years of constant surveillance indicated that the racketeer kept far more money for himself (and the Mafia), than he was admitting to Aronwald.

Steinman attempted to account for $1 million of his income by saying he had given it to a dead union officer, Anthony Maggiaccomo, who had run a Westchester County butchers' local. Steinman met with Maggiaccomo's successor, Joseph Bottigliere, and Nicholas Abondolo, president of the retail butchers' local in New York City, at a Chinese restaurant near Gracie Mansion. Steinman was semi-drunk as usual. "I need your help," he said to Bottigliere and Abondolo. "I've got to give up a union." He asked them to agree to testify with him that he had passed huge bribes to Maggiaccomo, who had died a year earlier. Bottigliere and Abondolo refused. Steinman later named Abondolo, his secretary-treasurer Moe Fliss, and Irving Stern, the international vice-president and regional director who had been associated with their local, as bribe recipients.

There was no doubt in Nicholson's mind that Stern, Abondolo, and Fliss were indeed taking payoffs from Steinman. Over a long period, the police had observed all three men beseeching Chappy Brescia for favors at the Black Angus. There was the business about Stern's bonds. But Stern, Abondolo, and Fliss were merely on the fringe of the Syndicate. Other major union figures, who Nicholson was convinced were probably much more corrupt than these three, were not named at all.

Nicholson also resented the way Steinman brought in his friends to testify against his enemies under grants of immunity so that his friends never got indicted, even when they were confessing to serious crimes like bribing union officials. For example, to build the case against Stern, Abondolo, and Fliss, Steinman brought in the chummy crowd from Big Apple and Foodarama.

Foremost was Jack Saker, chairman of the Foodarama board. (Saker became a major stockholder in the Shop-Rite chain when Foodarama joined it.) With Saker came his meat buyers, Milton Cohen and Alvin Bernstein, and his executive vice-president, George George, who had taken a criminal contempt rap for Steinman by stonewalling before the state grand jury.

Saker testified that when he first took command at Big Apple, either Stern or Fliss had told him that the company paid off the three union leaders at $1,000 a month for "labor peace" and "good will." Saker testified that he made his first payment by giving $1,000 cash to Artie Zuckerman, whose family had controled Big Apple. (Zuckerman wasn't charged.) From then on, Saker said he handled it himself. Fliss would call to tell him where to make the payments —often at the Island Inn in Westbury, Long Island—and Saker would comply.

Cohen testified that he and Bernstein were also taking care of Stern and Abondolo by delivering $2,000 a month of supermarket money to Steinman. In turn, Steinman testified, he passed the bribes in cash to Stern and Abondolo at the Luxor Baths, at the Bull and Bear, in the lobby of the Waldorf Astoria, or in Walter Bodenstein's office. George testified that when he took over meat purchasing at Foodarama, Abondolo called him and declared that Saker had fallen behind on his payments. So George went back to Saker and got $2,000 to bring the bribes up to date, they testified.

Neither George nor Saker was charged with a federal crime. Cohen and Bernstein, their subordinates, were required to plead guilty to tax evasion (Cohen on $54,000 in bribes from Steinman in two years, Bernstein on $268,000 in three years). Steinman had promised Aronwald some supermarket executives, and the underlings were sacrificed. After Cohen testified against the three butchers' leaders he was let off on probation. Bernstein, on the other hand, wouldn't squeal, and said he didn't know of any payments to the union men. He got a four-month jail term; there was argument on the court record that he, too, could have obtained probation if he had "cooperated." That's the way the investigation worked.

There was also testimony on the record that Steinman passed $50,000 from Hills Supermarkets to Stern, Abondolo, and Fliss so the union wouldn't object to Hills' plan to erect a new storage cooler. No one was charged with paying the bribe. Benny Moscowitz, who had been involved with the meat crowd for 30 years, also wasn't prosecuted, despite testimony on the record that he had bribed Stern, Abondolo and Fliss (through Steinman) so they wouldn't object to having his pre-shaped meat patties in the stores.

Steinman indeed seemed to have the investigation well in hand. During the winter of 1973–1974, he assured a Hills executive, George Gamaldi, in a tape-recorded conversation, "They're looking for unions. They're not looking for Johnny Dio. They're looking for unions."

Aronwald got his unions in March, 1974. Stern, Abondolo, and Fliss were indicted on charges of racketeering in interstate commerce, illegally receiving money from an employer and tax evasion. At the same time, the government announced the indictment of thirteen supermarket executives (including Steinman, Cohen, and Bernstein) from eight major chains, all on tax evasion charges. The executives tended to be near retirement, and were strictly subordinates, not owner-bosses.

Together, the union and supermarket officials were accused of evading taxes on about $1.7 million in bribes during the three years covered by the investigation; this amount was strikingly close to the amount of untaxed cash the government had been able to trace to Steinman, and thus the chief racketeer was able to avoid a potentially staggering tax liability. The government, by its own indictments, was backing up his contention that he had paid the money out in bribes. Steinman himself was charged with evading only $70,000 in taxes. No doubt Steinman had indeed made heavy illegal payoffs from his brokerage income, not only to the union and supermarket officials he named, but probably also to others and to Mafia figures as well. That was the reason people bought and sold meat through Steinman. But no one at the district attorney's office believed he had kept only $140,000 (the approximate gross for a $70,000 tax bill) for himself. Somewhere, the government had not obtained the full story.

The industry took the news of the indictments in stride. The Amalgamated Meat Cutters apparently never considered removing Stern, Abondolo, or Fliss from office. The three men stayed on, and issued their own statement to the press, saying, "We are shocked. . . . Our innocence will be proven in court." They were wrong on both counts.

Most if not all of the supermarket chains had enjoyed long warnings that their executives were under investigation. Some had the decorum to separate the suspects from power, though at least in some instances with retirement benefits. None of the chains' top bosses burst forth in indignation or demanded a clean-up of the industry. Some stuck by the accused. "He's done a good job handling labor relations for us, and our union contracts," said Herbert Daitch, Steinman's colleague and supposed boss at Daitch-Shopwell. "This was something on his own, nothing to do with us, and I was as surprised as anyone else when this trouble started," Daitch said.

A Bohack vice-president told the *Wall Street Journal* that the company wasn't even aware of the indictments against two recently retired officials, including a vice-president of meat operations who had of late gone into private consulting. Continuing in hypocritical pomposity, the Bohack vice-president added, "One of the things that has been a thorn in the side of anyone who runs a business is that a person who buys can be gotten to by a supplier." He said that Bohack tried to guard against this. He did not add that Julie Tantleff, longtime vice-president and sales manager at Bohack, had been at the center of the racketeering for many years, or that Bohack would continue to rely heavily on Steinman-Bodenstein meat operations.

If anyone was truly in the dark about the government's investigations, it wasn't the supermarket chains. It was the district attorney's office. Nicholson and Snitow had been cut off from all information after they refused to become part of the Steinman deal.

The office still had mopping up to do from its own open indictments. George George was allowed to plead guilty to one count of criminal contempt; Judge Burton B. Roberts let him go with a $500 fine. Julie Tantleff, facing the much stiffer perjury charge, chose to go to trial. He was acquitted of perjury, but was convicted of four counts of criminal contempt, and was sentenced by Judge Arnold Fraiman to four months in jail. The Department of Corrections says it has no record that he ever served time, and industry sources say he has stayed free by arguing that he has medical problems. He won't comment.

In the spring of 1974, in advance of the pending Iowa Beef trial, the D.A.'s men made one last effort to get Moe Steinman's cooperation. Snitow brought the mobster before Judge Burton Roberts to make the guilty plea the Aronwald deal committed him to make. Normally when a judge takes a guilty plea, he requires the accused person to put on the record a full confession of whatever deeds he is pleading guilty to. This record in Steinman's case might create evidence against Holman. But under questioning from Judge Roberts, Steinman steadfastly refused to concede that he or Holman had ever planned to bribe anyone with commissions paid by Iowa Beef. Faced with these assertions, Judge Roberts refused to accept Steinman's guilty plea, and ruled that the state would have to prove the charges at a trial, infuriating Snitow more than ever.

The Iowa Beef case came to trial in June, 1974, and the state had problems. Not only was there no evidence from Steinman, but the case was open to question morally. Holman had conspired to bribe his way into the New York market, all right, but who could argue that Holman and his boxed beef didn't have a right to be in the New York market in the first place? Can you convict a man for what he does with a gun at his head, even if it's only a financial gun?

On the first day of trial, the defense lawyers, Richard Wynn and Jeffry Atlas, made a tactical blunder that may well have cost them the case. They waived a trial by jury, and asked Judge Roberts to try the case himself. They reasoned that consumers were so angry over high meat prices, a jury would want to hang any meat producer it could get its hands on, and that no housewife could give Currier Holman a fair shake. What they ignored was that Holman's only hope for acquittal was the flexibility by which juries can depart occasionally from the legal straight and narrow to allow for moral right and wrong. A jury might be persuaded that Holman had no real choice but to break the law and pay Moe Steinman, that any other man might have done the same thing. Judge Roberts had no such flexibility. His only real option was to rule that Holman had broken the law, and was therefore guilty. And that's exactly what happened.

The trial lasted through June and July, right up to the August break in the court calender. It was a sweltering summer. Rumpled seersucker was the uniform of the day, though Holman added a touch of elegance with his $250 elephant hide loafers from Hunter's World.

The first witness Snitow produced was Howard Weiner, the treasurer whom Holman had cursed out and forced to resign because Weiner had volunteered the truth to Holman's own lawyers. Then came Lew Jacobs, Roy Lee, and Gus Nymann—men who had effectively been shoved out of their jobs because of the Steinman issue. As Holman sat, grim-faced, at the defense table through the long weeks of testimony from these men he regarded as traitors, it became clearer and clearer that Steinman had done more than reach his hand into Iowa Beef's pocket; the racketeer had swung a cleaver through the ranks of the giant company's management, forcing every important officer either to adopt a philosophy of corruption or to get out.

Then came the tape recording of Holman in the D.A.'s office, and the beef tycoon once again had to listen to his own cynical justification for bribery: "Anybody that's in the meat business in New York is a crook." The statement made headlines in *Supermarket News,* and probably didn't do much to endear Holman to the legion of decent wholesalers, butchers, and supermarket officials who desperately want the chance to do business free from extortion.

The defense testimony was relatively brief and irrelevant. Its most memorable feature was a slide show about the advantages of boxed beef. Harold Cammer, a butchers' union lawyer (of all things, Currier Holman calling on the butchers' union for his defense!) testified that although the union contract required retail cutting of beef to be done on premises, this really had never precluded boxed beef from coming into New York so long as the final cutting was done in the stores. George Wilhelm, who was running day-to-day operations at C. P. Sales, testified about how busy he was training supermarket meat buyers to use boxed beef. And Bob Kemp, who replaced Anderson as cochairman, tried to reaffirm his loyalty to Holman, but gave only a slightly more favorable version of essentially the same facts that had been presented earlier by his disgruntled former colleagues. Holman never testified. Nor did Steinman. Nor did Walter Bodenstein, who sometimes sat in on the proceedings from the gallery.

The real defense presented by Wynn and Atlas came in the form of legal argument. The state, they said, had failed in its evidence to preclude the theory that Holman never really intended his commissions to be used as bribes, that Steinman was only bluffing about the bribes in order to bargain for a higher commission, and that Holman had understood this all along. The interesting part about this defense was that it relied entirely on the continued cooperation of Moe Steinman. Steinman had carefully arranged his finances, as he showed them to Aronwald and the IRS, to bail out Holman. The union officials that permitted boxed beef to come into New York were indeed bribed, and the supermarket officials who bought the beef were indeed bribed, *but not with Iowa Beef's money*—according to Steinman's story. If Steinman had ever changed his tune, Holman would have faced additional substantive charges, and his defense would have collapsed. All the more reason that Holman would continue his generosity to Steinman's family and friends in the future.

(Wynn and Atlas also argued that Steinman had dropped out of the broker-age deal after signing it in January, 1971, so that the indictment against Holman, which came down in March, 1973, exceeded the two-year statute of limitations. Judge Roberts agreed with the state that Steinman's role lived as long as the contract did, and the contract was still in effect.)

Judge Roberts planned to spend August in Israel, and so put everyone in suspense by announcing he would reserve his decision until September 16, six weeks after the trial ended. Actually, there should have been little doubt that he would convict. Indeed, the decision was about as favorable to Holman as anyone had a right to expect. Roberts all but made the executive into a martyr.

"IBP's dire financial position made it imperative to him that the fastest and surest way of opening the lucrative New York market to boxed beef be util-ized," Judge Roberts wrote.

> He expressed this necessity often and obsessively. He knew that payoffs had to be made on behalf of IBP to sell its meat in other areas. He was also very much aware that payoffs were considered a necessary cost of doing business in the New York City retail meat trade. He had been in the meat business too long and had come too far not to have seen the handwriting on the wall. It is naive to think that he would allow the fate of the company he built but [which] was now so perilously close to ruin to hinge on the possible success of an honest-to-goodness salesman who had to pound the pavement and knock on doors in hopes of finding a meat buyer who was not already 'on the take' and convincing him of the merits of boxed beef. IBP's survival depended on someone to sell their meat who was capable of satisfying the 'crooks', as he called them, in the New York market. The tribute the unions and buyers were apparently receiving from everyone else would have to be paid by IBP as well. If IBP was to survive it had to sell to New York. In order to sell to New York it had to join the corrupt system there. It was as simple as that and, of course, Holman knew it.
>
> Somewhat to his credit, it was not until the company was on the brink of financial disaster that he agreed to pay the price and when he did so it was with reluctance. But the distaste he had for participating in such methods proves that he made a conscious choice. Sadly, like a modern-day Dr. Faustus, Currier J. Holman sold his soul to Moe Steinman.
>
> Holman's explanation of how he came to entrust IBP's future to Steinman in the capacity of a legitimate meat broker is simply not credible. What is clear is that Holman could see from the beginning that Steinman was the particular kind of 'broker' that IBP needed to bargain with the corrupt union leaders and meat buyers of New York City. From the time he checked Steinman's credentials with Lovette of Holly Farms, Holman knew this was a character who enjoyed a most extraordinary influence in the meat industry, to say the least. And if he was not already sure of it by then, Steinman would leave no room for doubt as to what that influence was based upon. He was a shady character if ever there was one.

He looked and acted like a hoodlum in a grade-B gangster movie. His position with a supermarket chain and his interest in a meat business constituted an apparent conflict of interest. He turned up suspiciously in Dakota City at the height of the strike with the loaded offer of 'help' with IBP's labor problems. His phone calls from a coin booth produced the key union leaders who had been boycotting boxed beef and brought them quickly to the dimly-lit suite at the Stanhope. His meeting with the leaders behind closed doors, after Holman and his associates left the room, preceded the suggestively cryptic declaration of instant labor peace. His return from Dakota City where he had gone in search of increased commissions was required by the meat buyers before they would even deal with IBP's representatives.

Thus, when Steinman specifically articulated the fact in June, 1970, that he needed the higher rate because he had to take care of union officials and meat buyers, there was every reason to believe he was not merely puffing. And when Holman agreed to pay the increase upon such representations he demonstrated his unmistakable intent to concur in Steinman's illegal mission as of that time at the very latest. The sale of his soul to Mephistopholes was complete. All that remained was for it to be formalized and reduced to writing.

This process began with the Hampshire House meeting in December. Once again, Steinman reiterated what his methods had been and would continue to be. Significantly, there was no disbelief and no disavowal. After all, Steinman's secretive contacts with buyers since July had brought the orders for boxed beef rolling in. Almost miraculously, the once-fierce union opposition had ceased. Either Holman believed Steinman had been distributing bribes on behalf of IBP and wanted him to continue to do so, or else he gave Steinman a multi-million-dollar, no-cut exclusive brokerage contract in gratitude for having done little more than being an appointments secretary. The latter suggestion, of course, is absurd. Holman's intent to enter a conspiracy with Steinman and the corporate intent of IBP to do so as well is clear beyond a reasonable doubt.

After concluding reading his written opinion, Roberts stunned Snitow by announcing he would sentence Holman and Iowa Beef immediately. Normally, sentencing awaits an investigation and written report from probation officers and recommendations from the district attorney and defense lawyers.

Snitow said he couldn't make a quick recommendation without approval from Richard Kuh, the district attorney who had recently been appointed to replace Frank Hogan, who had died. Roberts sent Snitow on a hasty chase through the corridors after Kuh, who rushed into court breathless, arguing for stiff punishment to deter other corporations from similar conduct.

Roberts would hear none of it. He declared that Holman and Iowa Beef would be punished severely by inevitable civil lawsuits from stockholders, consumers, and others with whom it did business, as everyone tried to collect for financial losses caused by the Steinman conspiracy.

And when Roberts passed sentence, he was sentencing not Currier Holman, the convicted conspirator, but Doctor Faustus, the fallen hero. "There are very few people in American business who would have acted differently in these circumstances," the judge said. "In a certain sense, this court will always consider you a victim of the extortionate practices" of union officials and supermarket executives in New York. And he gave Holman an unconditional discharge—no punishment.

Nor did Roberts visit any wrath upon Iowa Beef, the corporation, whose profits continued ever upward on the strength of the deal the judge had determined was illegal. Under the law, the maximum amount a corporation can be fined for conspiracy to commit commercial bribery in New York is a ridiculous $2,000. The penalty for conspiring to bribe union officers is $5,000. The law, however, also allows the judge to fine a violating corporation up to twice the amount of any profits it made from an illegal transaction. Judge Roberts did not see fit to apply this provision to the Iowa Beef case. The total $7,000 fine Iowa Beef paid represents the value of about thirteen of the ninety thousand cattle that the company slaughters and processes every week.

Roberts took pains to emphasize his sympathy for the convicted defendants. He said Holman was "now disgraced and may possibly lose his position." (There was no chance of that.) Iowa Beef, he said, was "a corporation trying to do legitimate business within the community," yet "now faces substantial losses from civil suits. . . . If damaged financially, that is the price of morality. Unfortunately, you [Holman] did not have the moral strength. I don't know since Eve ate the apple in the Garden of Eden how many would have had that strength. But American business must have that strength . . . because if you have no givers you can have no takers."

A fine speech. But the civil suits never materialized, and probably wouldn't have succeeded, because Steinman's clever accounting had made it impossible to show that any money from Iowa Beef was used to pay bribes. And Holman remained co-chairman and boss.

After thus writing off the major product of the three-year investigation by Nicholson and the rackets squad (the only other convictions were Tantleff and George for criminal contempt, and both men were still walking the streets) Roberts angrily and blindly lashed out at the massive injustice of it all. But he picked the wrong targets. Incredibly, he attacked Snitow and the District Attorney's office. What he said must have hurt Snitow, Nicholson, Montello, and Carey to the quick.

Rising from the bench in a rage, Roberts castigated the District Attorneys' office for making a deal with Steinman, whom he called "a barracuda," to convict Holman, whom he referred to as "a minow." He accused the D.A.'s office of cooperating in the federal deal to give Steinman no more than a year in jail in exchange for his testimony. He cried that the deal was so outrageous he had been "sorely tempted" to acquit Holman "in the interest of justice" just to show his contempt for the extortionate villainy of Steinman.

Snitow tried lamely to blame the whole business on Aronwald's office, to say that the state wanted to impose stiff sanctions on Holman to create a deterent. But the young lawyer stood no chance in the monarchy of the courtroom. Every time Snitow talked back, Roberts screamed out his denunciations louder.*

This was the thanks Nicholson got for eleven years. But he was still at it.

---

*Roberts was a Democrat, Kuh a Republican, and the Democrats were going after Kuh's job in the election that year. Considering the atmospnere in the courtroom, however, it is unlikely this had anything to do with what happened.

7

More Crime

Bob Nicholson didn't attend the Iowa Beef trial. He was busy tapping Tommy Plumeri's telephone. Plumeri, Johnny Dio's younger cousin and most trusted associate, had gone to prison with Dio in 1970 in the kosher meat scandal, but had a shorter sentence, and was soon free.

Nicholson had been staking out a suspected loansharking operation based in a bar near Thirty-eighth Street and Second Avenue, and thought he recognized Plumeri's face. A check of the license plate on the car parked outside showed it was indeed Plumeri. So the police started following him, and put a tap on the telephone at his apartment at Eighty-fourth Street and York Avenue. They never got him for loansharking. But they did find out he was earning big money selling accounts for two kosher provisions companies, and heard him promise to line up the Daitch-Shopwell account.

Then one night Plumeri got a call.

"You know who this is?" said a drunken voice. It was a voice Nicholson recognized at once. "This is Uncle Moe," the voice said. "I think you and I got to have a talk."

A meeting was set at a restaurant on Third Avenue. Steinman and Plumeri brought their wives. Two detectives went in right after them, but couldn't get a nearby table. The detectives stood at the bar as close as possible to where Steinman and Plumeri and their wives were sitting, and strained to hear. But then Steinman and Plumeri went up to the bar to talk privately, and picked a spot right next to one of the detectives.

The gangsters were discussing an account for one of the kosher meat companies, and Steinman was trying to persuade Plumeri of something. Steinman began rattling off names, apparently listing some mobsters he had dealt with in the past.

"Nobody does nothin' unless I get my cut," Steinman said. Again he seemed to be bossing a Mafioso around.

"What do you want?" Plumeri asked.

"I want fifty thousand," Steinman said.

"You got it," he was told.

They drank on it and went back to the table.

The wiretap had to come off because it wasn't producing evidence of loansharking. But Nicholson says a report of Plumeri's activities and of the bar conversation was sent to the strike force as evidence that Steinman had lied, that he knew mobsters intimately, and that he was still engaged in crooked business. Aronwald says he can't recall getting the report.

At the same time, while the Iowa Beef trial was still going on, Steinman was at the Summit Hotel acting as lead negotiator for a group of New York area chains in contract talks with Retail, Wholesale and Department Store Workers' Unions, Local 338. Local 338 was run by the same Sam Karsch whom Steinman had described three years earlier in a wiretapped telephone call to Julie Tantleff. "Sam knows the whole truth," Steinman had said at the time, as he and Tantleff pulled strings in Foodarama's labor negotiations. Now Steinman was apparently trying to teach Karsch the truth again. The chains Steinman was negotiating for, all the ones covered on this particular contract, included Associated Food Stores, Key Food Stores (the chain he once said was under the Castellanos' influence), Waldbaum's, Hills, Daitch-Shopwell, and Bohack.

When the *Wall Street Journal* reported the situation, Steinman was formally withdrawn as chief negotiator, though he stayed at the table for Daitch-Shopwell and obviously retained his real influence. All the charges could not bring him down. A man in Steinman's position does not need the title of chief negotiator to control negotiations.

Right after the Iowa Beef trial, Judge Roberts withdrew from the Moe Steinman case, which was technically still scheduled to come to trial. Roberts said that after what he'd heard in the Iowa Beef Case, he could no longer be fair. With Roberts out of the way, another judge—Arnold Fraiman—took Steinman's plea of guilty. He was scheduled for sentencing in January, 1975.

Then the letter came. It was four pages; neatly typed, double-spaced, unsigned. It came in a white envelope postmarked New York City, no return address. Aronwald got a copy. District Attorney Robert Morgenthau (the Democrat who had just been elected to replace Kuh) got a copy. And I got a copy (my stories on Steinman had been appearing in the *Journal*). The anonymous letter—and some telephone calls that followed, apparently from the letter writer—offered an appealing and logical explanation for many mysterious twists in the Steinman investigation. This is the story from the letter and phone calls:

In late summer, 1971, the Mafia organization of Paul Castellano heard from two double-agents in the District Attorney's office that Moe Steinman was being investigated. Such spy-type revelations occasionally occurred, because Castellano's people kept a paid pipeline into the D.A.'s detective squad to try to protect their gambling interests (the anonymous writer-caller said). The two double-agent detectives told their Castellano contacts that Steinman's phone was being tapped. As proof, they offered a nugget from one of Steinman's phone conversations with Herb Olstein, the Daitch-Shopwell meat buyer, in which Steinman talked about spending $5,000 to furnish the Queens apartment he shared in the afternoons with his girlfriend. The detectives said that if Steinman wanted, they would meet with him and supply more information.

News of the investigation was delivered by Paul Castellano (the writer-caller said) to Daniel Ciaripichi, a meat executive for the Bohack chain who was later charged with failing to pay taxes on $109,000 in bribes in two years and pleaded guilty. When Ciaripichi learned that Steinman was in Florida, he went instead to Olstein and told him the story. Olstein confirmed the conversation about the $5,000 and gave Ciaripichi Steinman's phone number in Florida. Steinman raced home and met Ciaripichi at the Foursome Diner, Avenue U and Knapp Street in Brooklyn. Soon afterwards, he met with the two detectives, who told him that for $30,000, they would lay out the investigation for him and keep him posted on all developments. Steinman agreed to pay them off in installments.

A simple, logical story. If true, it would explain why Moe Steinman stopped talking over the tapped telephones, why he stopped doing business in the bugged room, and how he was able to stage the mock Nazi attack on his own office just a few days before Nicholson came to exercise a search warrant.

According to the writer-caller, the detectives kept pressing Steinman for more money. He complained about this to a number of people, and finally, in the summer of 1973, just before making his deal with Aronwald, he met one of the cops in a restaurant on Twenty-eighth Street near Broadway and made it clear he was discontinuing payments.

Some twenty-five or thirty detectives in the D.A.'s squad could have obtained the information that was allegedly passed to Steinman. Because the leak was said to have come from that office, the investigation was turned over to Aronwald. He reported that there was no basis for the allegations. Yet what explanation was there for Steinman's ability to stay one step ahead of his pursuers? I called lawyers for Ciaripichi and Castellano. They said their clients wouldn't comment at all about the allegations. I called Olstein. "That's not true," he said, when I told him what was in the letter. "The whole thing is a mystery to me. I don't even know Steinman's telephone number in Florida. I don't know anything about this at all. I don't want to get involved in this." He also said that no one from either the District Attorney's office or the federal strike force had called or visited him about it. I was the only one to ask.

Why, I asked Aronwald, hadn't he gone to Olstein in his "investigation"? He wouldn't discuss it with me.

Because of the anonymous letter, Moe Steinman's sentencing was post-poned till April, 1975, and then, because of new judicial appointments, until June. Before Judge Fraiman in state court, Snitow pleaded for toughness. Steinman, he said, had engineered "a virtual takeover . . . monopoly" of the offal industry, and had coordinated "bribery that can only be described as mindboggling" throughout the meat industry. "No longer are we confronted with the James Cagney coming in to tell one company to buy from another." Now, he said, there is "a cartel . . . an insidious plan . . ." This was "the future of bribery." Steinman was the "central figure," a "corruptor of infinite influence. . . . We would flatter ourselves to say we had brought an end to this form of corruption."

Abramowitz, Steinman's lawyer, was more subdued. He knew that his man almost inevitably faced the one year maximum sentence in state court, where Aronwald couldn't use his influence. Abramowitz spoke briefly of Steinman's cooperation and of his many supporters in the community who had written to the judge asking leniency.

Fraiman then called Steinman the "moving force behind this conspiracy, the person who brought all these people together and served as an intermediary between them." Steinman had, he said, perpetrated "a most serious crime that has in fact cost the consumers of this area millions of dollars at a time when they can sorely afford it."

Then he sentenced Steinman to the maximum: one year in jail and a $1,000 fine.

Riker's Island jail is a hell-hole where a year could seem long. But scarcely had Steinman been driven there than Aronwald rescued him by arranging a federal sentencing hearing a few days later. Before U.S. District Judge Charles Metzner, Aronwald and Abramowitz contended vigorously to see who could heap the most praise on the little manipulator. The prosecutor noted the glowing letter he had already sent to Judge Metzner about Steinman, but said that "more amplification is necessary with respect to the extent and nature of Mr. Steinman's cooperation. Particularly, it has been widely publicized, I think to Mr. Steinman's disadvantage unfairly, that Mr. Steinman was in effect the barracuda, and those defendants indicted as a result of his testimony were smallfry. And this simply is not the case. . . . Somewhat of a distorted picture has been painted with respect to Mr. Steinman."

Aronwald even managed to justify the way Steinman passed around his loot by putting phony employees on the payroll, (which might interest any would-be tax evaders who are looking for a similar way to cheat Uncle Sam): "In effect, what Mr. Steinman was doing," Aronwald told the judge, "was using the corporate monies to take care of members of his family and friends and close associates of his who had fallen upon hard times, rather than taking care of them out of his own personal pocket. I am not saying that what he did was right, but I am saying that Mr. Steinman himself did not personally benefit from the monies being diverted from the corporate entities."

After praising Steinman's cooperation up and down, Aronwald actually offered the everybody-does-it argument in Steinman's defense: "Without in any way seeking to minimize or excuse Mr. Steinman's conduct," Aronwald said, "I believe it is sufficient to say that the kickback arrangements and agreements that were disclosed as a result of our investigation were and regrettably may continue at this very time to be a way of life within the industry."

Then Abramowitz—the man who sold Aronwald this bill of goods—got his turn. It would have been difficult to outdo the prosecutor, but the defense attorney tried. "This man has rehabilitated himself," Abramowitz declared. "He has not committed one crime since 1971. He has been on a period of probation longer than most cases. He has indicated to the government and to this court that he is finished with his life of crime."

Abramowitz may not have known of the reports to the contrary that the D.A.'s office had given the federal strike force. Aronwald says he didn't either.

Also before Judge Metzner were a series of effusive letters pleading for Steinman to get leniency. One was from Martin Rosengarten, the president of Daitch-Shopwell, a publicly-owned company (Shopwell Inc.) listed on the American Stock Exchange. Rosengarten's son, Glen, was on Steinman's illegal payoff list. A second letter was from Steinman's daughter, Helene Meyerson, who also was on Steinman's illegal payoff list. Four other letters came from persons whose last name was on the illegal payoff list, presumably indicating that a family member was getting part of the loot. But this wasn't mentioned to Judge Metzner, who sentenced Steinman to one year in prison rather than the three-year legal maximum.

Whether the three-year sentence had been precluded as part of a secret deal, as Judge Roberts and others have charged, is something we can't know for certain. It is obvious, however, that Judge Metzner's one year sentence was not a penalty for Steinman, but a reward. It meant that he would not have to go back to the brutal city jail, but would be hosteled at the federal Metropolitan Correctional Center in Manhattan, where accomodations aren't exactly up to those at, say, the Waldorf, but are comfortable—better, in fact, than the slums imposed on hundreds of thousands of New York citizens who have never been convicted of anything. One can imagine Bob Nicholson's reaction to Steinman's federal sentencing: "When we put Moe Steinman in jail, Aronwald took him out," Nicholson complained.

When Steinman wasn't needed to testify in New York City, he could survive in health at the government's Allenwood prison farm in Pennsylvania, or even—according to some sources—back at his condominium at Inverarry playing golf with the federal marshals assigned to guard him. The warden of the correctional center in Manhattan says Steinman was kept under a special government witness program so that his comings and goings needn't be recorded. The warden says Steinman received one official furlough, in September, 1975, for the Jewish high holidays. Evidently Steinman was not discriminating about the religions he benefitted from; he was permanently released on parole in time to spend Christmas at home, too. His total time served: six months.

But, as Aronwald noted, he had "cooperated."

At Steinman's sentencing, Aronwald announced that he was dropping all federal charges against Currier Holman on the ground that Holman had been tried in state court on a parallel matter. Holman's legal troubles were over.

By the time Steinman was sentenced in June, 1975, all the accused meat executives had pleaded guilty to income tax evasion except for three from Hills Supermarkets. The three union officers, Stern, Abondolo, and Fliss, also were holding out. But by and large the scoreboard on the Aronwald deal with Moe Steinman was filling up. One could begin to assess the value of his cooperation. It was impressive if you looked at the names and corporate titles of those who pleaded guilty. But if you looked at the details of the pleas, and at the sentences, the record was dismal.

Aronwald's decision about whom to indict implied that the meat executives, mostly vice-presidents of supermarkets, were at the heart of the Steinman racket. If so, they were guilty of puffing up the price of meat to the consumer by from one to ten cents a pound depending on the cut. Yet Aronwald let each of them plead to a single count of income tax evasion. Aronwald insists he did not recommend sentences to judges or make other prejudicial remarks, except to note where a man had cooperated in supplying evidence. But the punishment could scarcely have been more lenient. Here is the record:

Robert Miller, meat buyer for Food City Markets Inc., charged with failing to pay taxes on $22,000 in bribes over three years; sentenced by U.S. District Judge Charles E. Stewart, Jr., to probation and a $3,000 fine.

Robert Labasin, meat buyer for Bohack Corp., charged with failing to pay taxes on $65,000 in bribes over three years; sentenced by U.S. District Judge James L. Watson to probation and a $1,000 fine.

Daniel Ciarapichi, vice-president of meat operations for Bohack Corp., charged with failing to pay taxes on $109,000 in bribes over two years; sentenced by Judge Watson to one month in prison and a $5,000 fine.

Barnett Freedman, director of meat purchasing for Waldbaum Inc., charged with failing to pay taxes on $43,000 in bribes over three years; sentenced by U.S. District Judge William C. Conner to probation and a $7,500 fine.

Peter Pfeiffer, vice-president of Northern Boneless Meat Corp., charged with tax fraud involving $272,000 in two years; sentenced by U.S. District Judge Morris E. Lasker to probation and a $5,000 fine.

Saul Paul, vice-president of meat purchasing for First National Stores Inc., charged with failing to pay taxes on $8,000 in bribes in one year; sentenced by U.S. District Judge Vincent P. Biunno to probation and a $4,000 fine.

Milton Cohen, manager, the meat department, Big Apple Supermarkets Inc., charged with failing to pay taxes on $54,000 in bribes over two years; sentenced by U.S. District Judge Charles Brieant to probation and a $10,000 fine.

Alvin Bernstein, meat buyer for Wakefern Food Corp. and Foodarama Supermarkets Inc., charged with failing to pay taxes on $268,000 in bribes over three years; sentenced by Judge Brieant to four months in prison and a $10,000 fine.

John Pandolfi, vice-president of meat operations for Sloan's Supermarkets Inc., charged with failing to pay taxes on $65,000 in bribes over five years; sentenced by Judge Lasker to three months in prison and a $5,000 fine.

Robert Donahue, meat buyer for King Kullen Supermarkets, charged with failing to pay taxes on $60,000 in bribes over five years; sentenced by U.S. District Judge Orrin Judd to probation and a $3,000 fine.

"I don't understand these sentences," Al Scotti remarked. "These judges must be living in a different world."

He was commenting not just on the sentences given to the supermarket buyers and others involved in the meat scandals, but on the general pattern of sentencing in American courtrooms today. And he was expressing a dismay that is common among those who have given long service to law enforcement.

Sentences clearly are not designed to deter a person who knowingly sets out to make money by violating the law. Nor are they designed to provide equal justice to rich and poor, black and white. Most prison terms—almost all terms of more than a year—are meted out with the idea of separating a dangerous person from society. Someone who appears dangerous to a judge from across a few feet of desk and a railing is likely to be someone of a different race and social class who has a history of violence.

Yet far more money can obviously be made by supermarket executives in a well-coordinated plot to jack up prices than can be made by a thousand hold-up men who pull guns on check-out girls. Moreover, the executives probably give a lot more thought to what they do and are a lot more fearful of going to prison. The principle of deterrent prison terms would be especially effective with them. As it stands now, punishment for so-called white collar criminals is rare and minor—no more than a petty cost of doing business. The amount of money involved in the theft carries little weight in sentencing. A big reward clearly outweighs the risk. That is why the ranks of white collar criminals are now heavy with Mafiosi and other people who are also capable of violence when it serves their interest.

What accounts for this pattern of leniency? In some cases, of course, judges are simply bought, cash on the barrelhead (although there is no indication of judicial bribery in the meat cases just cited). In most cases, two other factors are at work.

First, most judges in the United States are politically selected. This doesn't necessarily exclude fairness and competence from the bench, but it doesn't encourage them either. The average judge is more apt to be a hail-fellow-well-met than a scholar or introvert who might do a better job. The judge has shown his ability to gain popularity at political gatherings and to court the "influential"—i.e., rich contributors. The defendants in big-money crime cases are apt to be the very kinds of people the judge seeks to be popular with. It isn't regarded as nice in those circles to send businessmen to prison, and at trial time even a Johnny Dio is displayed as very much the businessman.

Moreover, in many areas of the United States, anyone who has worked his way up in politics has already been compelled to raise his threshhold of indignation fairly high. There is very little in the way of nonviolent shenanigans that he has not already blinked at. He has seen and ignored that government employees are required to kick back part of their salaries to the party machine, either overtly, or by the more subtle method of the forced purchase of exhorbitantly-priced tickets to political fund-raisers. He has seen and ignored that government contractors do the same. He has seen and ignored that some persons in his party, whom he has been forced to at least tacitly endorse, are on friendly terms with reputed gangsters. He has probably tried hard not to find out more about it.

A judge who has risen through politics will be obligated to a lot of people. He may want to advance to a higher court, or run for office. At sentencing time, convicted racketeers or their businessmen colleagues often look for some mutual friend to approach the judge by mail or phone with a subtle pitch for leniency. Even the most notorious gangsters can call on the heads of charities they have assisted, or on others who occupy prominent positions in the community, and politically-bred judges are simply not inclined to be contentious with such people. On occasion, a judge will even note such contacts on the record before meting out a wrist-slap. Probably more often, the pressure is put on and never disclosed.

Many judges caught in this trap would probably like to avoid it and do the honest thing. A law setting out strict minimum sentence requirements might provide such judges with the excuse they need in order to reject pressure for leniency. Moreover, if the minimum penalties were to increase with the amount of money involved in the crime, they might create a true deterrent to the really major rackets. (Any mandatory sentencing law should have an escape hatch for the unusual circumstances that inevitably arise; but to invoke the escape hatch and give a lesser sentence, the judge should have to spell out his reasons for considering the case extraordinary, and the prosecutor should have the right to appeal.)

There is, however, a second sentencing problem, which involves neither bribery nor politics. A lot of judges seem to be incredibly naive about the moral difference between professional criminals and honest citizens. The professional criminal finds it easy to disguise himself in the clothing and manner of the judge's neighbors. He usually has two years or more after learning that the law is about to come down on him before he faces his actual sentencing (these delays, caused largely by the slowness of judges in dealing with dilatory defense tactics, are themselves great roadblocks to a strategy of deterring crime). Thus the criminal has plenty of opportunity to prepare a sympathetic scenario. He can start a business or get a job with someone else's business. He can develop a medical history—rare is the racketeer without a heart condition, cancer, or at least psychiatric problems in the family at sentencing time.

The prosecutor's office will have spent the intervening years pressing the active indictment against the defendant, rather than investigating his ongoing criminal activities. Defense lawyers could claim that a continued investigation was interfering with the crook's right to a fair trial over his previous crime. So in court, as in the case of Moe Steinman, the offense at issue is made to appear ancient, and the recent record is made to appear clean. Judges tend either to believe this distorted picture, or to feel that they must accept it for sentencing purposes.

Moreover, the judge knows how horrible many state prisons are. Without thinking of himself as bigoted, he will hesitate to send the neatly dressed white man in front of him to the same overcrowded dungeon to which he has just sent a parade of scruffier men who might be stopped and questioned on sight if they dared set foot in the judge's neighborhood. We need new prisons. A system of decent prisons where a man could be sent without great fear for his health, and where he could lock himself in a private cell to protect him from the more violent animals confined within the same walls, might ease the minds of judges and encourage truly deterrent sentences in so-called white collar cases. Prisons can be made safe and sanitary without being turned into country clubs.

Many judges are also incredibly unaware of how quickly and easily convicts get out on parole. The parole system effectively shaves away two-thirds of a sentence, and, coupled with additional time off for good behavior or work credits, can reduce the sentence in some states to one-fifth of what it originally was. Moreover, parole offers one more opportunity to con the system, or to bribe it, if you are a racketeer or white collar criminal. It is one more example for the lower-class inmate of how he is discriminated against. Parole rules are made to order for the gangster, who can always find a legitimate-looking front for his operations, and they ignore the deterrent purpose of the original sentence. If parole were abolished entirely, it might lead to much more certain knowledge by a prospective criminal of exactly what penalty he faced. Discipline in prison could be maintained by other means, such as the award or withdrawal of privileges.

Right now the only thing certain is that many intelligent people have decided that crime pays. The justice system is equal only in its ineffectiveness.

The government brought George Gamaldi to trial November 17, 1975. Gamaldi was the first of the three Hills' supermarket executives who had pleaded not guilty. Probably not coincidental to their decision to fight, they were the three charged with taking the most money—Gamaldi $267,300, Blase Iovino $297,800, and Salvatore Coletta $306,174, all over four years. Even persons who were convinced that the three men did take kickbacks doubted that they could have pocketed such staggering amounts. They had asked for and received the right to separate trials. But the evidence against them was similar, and the Gamaldi case was regarded as a bellwether. It was the first courtroom test of the credibility of Moe Steinman, the man whose testimony was bought by the government at so high a price. The case against Gamaldi rested principally on the testimony of Steinman and his brother Sol.

Nicholson and Montello had caught Gamaldi in some potentially incriminating conversations back when they were wiretapping Moe Steinman. But a federal judge refused to allow the tape into evidence, because Snitow, too soon out of law school, hadn't understood the proper proceedures and failed to have the tape sealed in time by a state judge (early in the investigation, when Gamaldi was overheard, Snitow thought the sealing could wait until the particular wiretap order expired, whereas in fact it must occur within a few days). Nicholson had also made some interesting observations of Gamaldi meeting with Steinman and Aaron Freedman at Patrick's Pub, on Long Island. But the state and the strike force hadn't been cooperating, and the government, perhaps forgetful of what Nicholson knew, never called him to testify.

So the case was almost entirely up to the Steinmans. But were the Steinmans up to the case?

Gamaldi had hired Robert Goldman, a talented and reputable defense attorney, who, in the manner in which these things go, had recently become a law partner of Richard Kuh. Kuh was the outgoing District Attorney, who would have had access while in office to all of Nicholson's files. Of course it would have been unethical for Goldman and Kuh to have discussed such matters, and Kuh and Goldman are probably well above average in their observation of legal ethics.

"We will prove to you," Goldman said in his opening statement to the jury, "that Mr. Steinman was the man that controlled the meat business in the entire city of New York. No meat moved in New York unless tribute was paid to Mr. Steinman. The biggest wholesalers in the United States couldn't move their meat into New York unless they first paid Mr. Steinman. . . . Mr. Steinman did not have to pay a nickel to a buyer to effect sales. He had other methods, and you will learn from a long history of criminal association and activity that he had far more effective ways of obtaining sales at any time he so chose. . . . We will prove to you that Mr. Steinman at no time would either part with such [large sums of] money or had any occasion to part with such money. . . . Moe Steinman . . . needed victims to get him out of the predicament in which he found himself. . . . He victimized George Gamaldi. . . ."

The courtroom prosecutor assigned by Aronwald to draw out Steinman's story was Barbara S. Jones, an uncommonly patient and crafty questioner who in later years would knock off such Mafia heavyweights as Russell Bufalino and Anthony Provenzano. But with the Gamaldi case she was in the impossible position of a fairy-tale princess ordered by some mad monarch to weave straw into gold. Steinman on the witness stand was exactly as Bob Nicholson had always described him. He fidgeted, he mumbled, he looked devious, he contradicted himself, he interposed awkward pauses so it looked like he was making things up. You would not have believed him if he said it was raining outside and you heard the drops on the roof.

Steinman said he had been paying off Gamaldi, the chief meat buying executive for Hills, since the early 1960s. In 1968, the first year covered by the indictment (because of the statute of limitations), Hills bought out Great Eastern Supermarkets, whose own meat executives, Blase Iovino and Sal Coletta, took over meat buying for the entire chain. Steinman said he had them all on the payroll. The first week or ten days of every month, he said, he delivered an average of $23,000 a month (but sometimes $28,000 to $30,000 a month) at Patrick's Pub, at Steinman's apartment, at the Luxor Baths, and at a Long Island motel. He testified that he kicked back eight to ten cents on every pound of corned beef, and seven to eight cents on every pound of flank steak and skirt steak. (This may have been a figure for total kickbacks to everyone, not just supermarket buyers; Steinman was never a beacon of clarity on the stand.) He said the payoffs stopped in January, 1972, because he learned he was under investigation.

Goldman took Steinman through a merciless cross-examination. Steinman was pitifully unable or unwilling to be specific about his own financial history. He seemed to be hiding something when he talked about the deals he arranged for himself and Bodenstein. And he was even less specific about how much money he had given Gamaldi, Coletta, and Iovino, where he had given it to them and on what dates. "This was cash money kickbacks," Steinman said. "We have no record of the kickback money." He said the payments started at twelve or fourteen thousand dollars a month and "it was going up an average of about one thousand dollars a month."

Sol Steinman offered little improvement.

When they had finished, Goldman appealed to U.S. District Judge Henry Werker for a dismissal of all charges. Werker gave it to him. "What you are asking me to say in keeping this indictment alive," Werker told Prosecutor Jones, "is that I can expect that reasonable people will find beyond a reasonable doubt on your proof that in each of those years an average of twenty-three thousand dollars was paid monthly . . . and that Mr. Gamaldi got a third of each of these payments. I think this is too highly speculative and too highly ambiguous because there is no showing as to exactly when and where those payments were made in each of the years. It is a generalized statement. It's too vague in my opinion to be sufficient proof in law."

Thus ended Moe Steinman's only appearance as a witness at a criminal trial of the men he "gave up" to win his own freedom. As a result of Judge Werker's decision, the government dropped its charges against Iovino and Coletta. No one ever mentioned in court that in 1972, Hills became one of Iowa Beef's biggest customers. And Steinman's family collected a commission on every pound.

On Tuesday, November 18, 1975, I was about to leave my office at the *Wall Street Journal* to go listen to Steinman's testimony at the Gamaldi trial when I got a call from another reporter who had covered the Holman case. She had just heard from one of Iowa Beef's own lawyers that Walter Bodenstein had been appointed to a big executive job in Sioux City, helping Holman run the company.

I refused to believe it until I found a small item deep inside our own paper. Closely following an Iowa Beef press release, the item said that Leroy Zider, the executive vice-president and chief operating officer, believed to be heir apparent to the presidency, had resigned. The middle of the story dealt with various disagreements between Zider and Holman that supposedly caused their parting. The fifth and final paragraph read as follows: "The company said that Walter Bodenstein, formerly chairman of C. P. Sales in Paramus, New Jersey [where Bodenstein had moved his office], a sales agency for Iowa Beef, has replaced Mr. Zider as head of the company's processing division. He was given the title of group vice-president." (Iowa Beef later took pains to explain that Bodenstein was *not* given Zider's titles, but did replace him in all functions.)

Interviews with Holman and other Iowa Beef officials later made it clear that Bodenstein's replacement of Zider was more than just a personnel change. It was a policy change. Bodenstein was assigned to set up independent sales agencies around the country similar to the one Steinman's family still owned in Paramus. These independently-owned agencies would replace Iowa Beef's own salesmen, men like Lew Jacobs. It was a policy change that Zider and others at Iowa Beef had vigorously opposed. They argued that the only advantage of such independent sales companies would be that bribe money, if paid, could not be traced directly to Iowa Beef's corporate books. They also objected to something else: it had become clear that Walter Bodenstein was to be rewarded with ownership of the sales agency in New England and possibly other agencies as well. Why was Bodenstein to be favored with these gold mines?

Later that morning, November 18, 1975, during a break in the Gamaldi trial, I asked Steinman about Bodenstein's appointment. He looked surprised. "It's not definite yet, is it?" he said. "I been in jail. I haven't heard a thing about it."

Later that week, however, Steinman made several calls from the federal correctional center in Manhattan to Currier Holman's office in Dakota City. Both Holman and Bodenstein later insisted that the calls were personal to Bodenstein, and that Holman had not talked with Steinman since they were fingerprinted together back in 1973.

In the nearly four years since Steinman had put Bodenstein in charge of C. P. Sales, there was certainly evidence that Bodenstein had turned the concern into a lot more than a mere commission drop. The well-appointed office suite in Paramus contained a classroom where hundreds of meat buyers and dealers were instructed about boxed beef. Bodenstein had learned the system well himself, and had hired a staff of nine salesmen (although several were paid directly by Iowa Beef, and the others, who were paid from C. P. Sales's commission money, also handled brokerage accounts for other meat packers). Wholesalers and buyers have said in interviews that Bodenstein's salesmen provided valuable counseling (though they also said that the meat would have sold itself without the service).

According to Bodenstein, and there's no evidence to the contrary, C. P. Sales didn't pay off anyone. The only dealing with the Mafia Bodenstein said he could recall was one time when his automatic credit-watch system cut off credit for Joseph Castellano's Dial Poultry Company, a customer. Castellano came into the C. P. Sales office with his father, Mafia boss Paul Castellano. Bodenstein says it was the only time in his life he had ever seen Paul, and that he doesn't know why the mobster came along. He says he told the Castellanos, as he would any customer, that if they wanted their credit restored they would have to supply a fuller financial statement. He says they declined to do this, and instead agreed to a reduced credit line of $40,000, only enough for a single carload—an ironic twist, since the government alleged that the Castellanos themselves had millions of dollars in loanshark funds out on the street.

Despite the positive picture Bodenstein presented, however, there were clearly many dark factors. The whole C. P. Sales deal had been set up by Steinman as part of an illegal conspiracy. All its stock was held by Steinman's children and other members of his family. Bodenstein had earlier established a propensity for involving himself in suspicious businesses connected to Steinman or Johnny Dio. He had been questioned in the Securities and Exchange Commission fraud investigations of Dio's dealings, although he hadn't been charged himself. He had been indicted for filing fraudulent quarterly employee income tax returns, and the charge was dropped only as a condition of Moe Steinman's plea bargain, not for any lack of evidence. Although Iowa Beef probably didn't know it, he had gone before the federal grand jury under a grant of immunity in 1973 and confessed to numerous tax violations and "possible" violations of the securities laws. Bodenstein's commissions cost Iowa Beef a lot more than its cost of selling elsewhere. This bothered some Iowa Beef middle managers. ("Money down the goddamn drain," one called it.) Moreover, C. P. Sales had never been audited, which bothered them also.

A team from Iowa Beef's own auditing firm, Touche Ross & Company, had begun an audit at Iowa Beef's request and had failed to complete it for reasons never made clear.

Some of Bodenstein's assistance to Iowa Beef was of a suspicious nature. Two weeks before Bohack supermarkets filed a bankruptcy petition in July 1974, Bohack—two of whose officers were on Steinman's kickback list—suddenly and mysteriously stopped buying from Iowa Beef, previously its main supplier of meat. Bohack switched to Iowa Beef's chief competitor, MBPXL Corp., which, as a result, was stung with the unpaid meat bills when Bohack got protection from creditors under Chapter 11 of the bankruptcy laws. The bills totaled $900,000. Immediately after the bankruptcy filing, when Bohack was operating under court supervision and its payments were guaranteed, Bohack switched back and made Iowa Beef its sole supplier. And who was chairman of the Bohack creditors' committee overseeing this flim-flam? None other than Walter Bodenstein, who happened to be the attorney for Adam Bozzuto, who operated a grocery supply chain that serviced Bohack.

Also while operating C. P. Sales, Bodenstein continued, under a prepaid legal plan, to represent members of the Amalgamated Meat Cutters, which railed against Iowa Beef's labor policies. He represented various other law clients including Bozzuto, Iowa Beef, and Holly Farms, from which he also continued to collect up to $84,000 a year in chicken brokerage commissions. On top of that, he operated a retail meat store that competed with his C. P. Sales's customers.

There's much more. To fill an important position at C. P. Sales, Bodenstein had just brought in William Grunstein, another tie to Steinman and the corrupt past. Grunstein, whose family had owned a Prohibition-era speakeasy, had gone to prison in the early 1950s in the same rotten-meat-to-the-Armed-Forces scandal that sent Sam Goldberger to jail. In fact, Grunstein and Goldberger had bribed the same meat inspector, and did considerable business with each other. In Grunstein's case, according to evidence at his trial, already frozen meat was defrosted in the men's room, out of sight of supervisors, and was sold for fresh. Rejected meat was placed in different cartons and shipped back to more cooperative inspectors until it was accepted.

After prison, still owing the government $600,000 as the compromise settlement of claims over the bad meat, Grunstein started Jefferson Packing Company in Hoboken, New Jersey. It went bankrupt in 1971, with Food Fair supermarkets charging that Grunstein had defrauded it of more than a million dollars by transferring assets to a separate corporation. The corporation that received the assets then hired Grunstein for a high salary after the bankruptcy. (Food Fair eventually dropped the suit, because, its lawyers say, several years of searching failed to locate any seizable assets in Grunstein's name; "he had made himself judgment-proof," one lawyer said.) On the "everybody's-a-crook" tape that Currier Holman made in the New York District Attorney's office in 1973, he singled out Bill Grunstein's Jefferson Packing Company and said he suspected that it gave kickbacks. Yet Holman didn't complain when Bodenstein brought Grunstein onto the Iowa Beef team.

Grunstein and his family also controlled a large share of Tammybrook Country Club, Creskill, New Jersey, which more or less replaced the Block brothers' country club in Connecticut as the scene of New York meat industry affairs, including the annual "Meat Ball" dinner-dance. These affairs were regularly attended by mobsters. At one of them, Currier Holman personally announced Iowa Beef's investment of $25,000 in Israeli bonds, a charity Steinman helped promote. Just as Bodenstein was preparing to go to Sioux City to become a top executive at Iowa Beef, New York dealers were startled to find Grunstein, despite his troubled past, soliciting them to be distributors for Iowa Beef.

Not just Grunstein, but Bodenstein himself occasionally alienated buyers instead of charming them. One major chain, Pathmark (Supermarkets General Corp.), and most of another, Shop-Rite, refused to buy from Iowa Beef in the C. P. Sales commission area because they didn't want to pay Steinman's family.

Shop-Rite actually sent a representative to Dakota City in September, 1972, to try to negotiate an independent purchasing agreement. The representative came back reporting that Iowa Beef had agreed to sell to Shop-Rite directly from the central office, with no commissions being paid to C. P. Sales. The price would be the same, but it was important to Shop-Rite to know that none of its money was going to crooks. In 1974, Shop-Rite learned that C. P. Sales had been getting its commissions all along, because no matter what Iowa Beef promised, the Steinman-Bodenstein contract required a commission for all meat sold within 125 miles of New York. Shop-Rite cancelled its orders.

Yet the strongest argument against Bodenstein—the strongest argument that his efforts at legitimacy were too late if not also too little to permit a respectable career in the meat industry—lay in the words of Judge Burton Roberts as he gave his decision in the Iowa Beef case, September 16, 1974. Just fourteen months before Iowa Beef brought Bodenstein into its executive suite, Judge Roberts debunked Iowa Beef's contention that Steinman had withdrawn from the conspiracy and that Bodenstein was running a clean operation. Wrote the judge,

> Clearly, Steinman's contemplated role was always one that was to be played behind the scenes, distributing the bribe money. Nothing that Bodenstein did on behalf of Cattle Pakt or C. P. Sales indicates that Steinman had abdicated his own particular responsibility.
>
> In direct contradiction of any inference that Steinman had decided to, so to speak, hang up his kick-backing shoes was his announcement at the Hampshire House meeting of his percentage arrangement with the unions and meat buyers and his further declaration that he had made a commitment with the union leaders to "take care" of them for five years. . . . Shortly after these statements were made, the five-year written contract was entered into by both Steinman and Bodenstein

on behalf of Cattle-Pakt. . . . It is absurd to believe that IBP would have made such a deal for nothing more than the legitimate services of Bodenstein selling meat under this quota-less agreement. IBP knew virtually nothing about Bodenstein other than the fact that he was Steinman's son-in-law. Bodenstein knew virtually nothing about the meat business other than that his father-in-law took care of union leaders and meat buyers. But then again, that is all that either one of them had to know. It is clear that the written agreement was nothing more than a front for the secret, illegal services of Steinman and that the conspiracy continued as long as this written agreement was in effect.

The written agreement was not only still in effect in November, 1975, it had actually been renewed and extended during the investigation of Steinman and Iowa Beef. It stayed in effect through 1977.

A story appeared in the *Wall Street Journal* edition of November 19, 1975, pointing out Bodenstein's background and quoting from Judge Roberts's decision. The morning the story appeared, before the securities markets even opened, holders of Iowa Beef stock rushed to sell. The New York Stock Exchange halted trading in the stock. The syndicate of banks that held Iowa Beef's $60 million line of credit expressed concern, and the executives flew to New York to huddle with First National City Bank, now the lead bankers. The American Credit Indemnity Company suspended Iowa Beef's credit insurance (such insurance, which guarantees shippers against nonpayment of bills, is considered indispensible in a volatile industry like cattle).

On November 24, 1975, Holman caved in. He agreed to ask for a resignation from Bodenstein, who went back to Paramus to receive his commissions again. Bodenstein's territory absorbed five million pounds a week; the meat averaged $1 a pound. Two days later, Iowa Beef shares reopened on the New York exchange after a full week's halt; the price had fallen from $26.625 a share to $20.25 a share, despite an announcement by Iowa Beef that its profits for the fiscal year ended November 1, 1975, were a record $23.2 million, or $8.05 a share. (Apparently to try to stem the tide of selling, Iowa Beef rushed out figures still marked as unaudited; usually businesses wait to release audited figures.) Clearly investors, particularly institutional investors, were shunning Iowa Beef stock for reasons other than the company's financial performance. Word had gotten around that Iowa Beef was tied to the Mafia.

The question was why, and it was being asked not only on Wall Street, but on cattle ranches and in meat shops all over the country. Holman had to pay his way into the New York market back in 1970, but that was five years ago. Now he was *in* the market. Why, after renewing and extending the brokerage contract, had he brought Steinman's son-in-law into the executive suite? And why would he change marketing policies and create C. P. Sales-like agencies in other parts of the country? And why would he give them to Bodenstein? Within a few feet of Holman's own office there were people who didn't understand it. Leroy Zider, one of several Iowa Beef executives who lost their jobs after arguing against Bodenstein, said, "The revenues he was receiving were grossly out of line with the cost of doing business, or the value of his service. He was getting commission on business that the guys there [in Sioux City] felt he didn't have anything to do with."

Even in the most kindly light, Bodenstein was still receiving the wages of sin. And, beyond the Bodenstein issue, many in the industry were aware of the unique and lucrative deal that Iowa Beef was giving to Steinman's old pal and trading partner, Sam Goldberger. With his unique supply of Iowa Beef's trimmings at bargain prices, Goldberger, the convicted purveyor of tainted meat, had put a corner on a noticeable chunk of the nation's ground beef market. (Iowa Beef said it was just because he was a smart trader.)

Holman took out full-page advertisements in many newspapers defending Bodenstein and blaming the press, particularly the *Journal,* for unfairly riding Bodenstein out of Sioux City.

Many looked for a deeper motive behind all this—maybe money. Holman had never shown particular interest in amassing a personal fortune. Salaries and office frills for Holman and others at Iowa Beef had always been modest compared to those at other companies of comparable size. Still, some speculated that part of the millions going out of Iowa Beef might be coming back to Holman under the table.

On the other hand, the source of Steinman's continuing hold over Currier Holman may have been protection. Back in 1974, Judge Roberts had predicted that Iowa Beef would suffer from damage suits filed by customers and shareholders, who would claim that prices had been raised and dividends restrained by the cost of bribery. These damage suits never materialized. And perhaps the reason they never materialized was Steinman's continuing insistance that he had never paid a nickel out in bribes on behalf of Iowa Beef.

Everyone involved in the case seemed to go out of his way to pay lip service to Steinman's contrived system of accounting. Long after the trial, Holman and his subordinates at Iowa Beef (including Bodenstein) continued to argue the point at great length. Steinman, in his testimony against George Gamaldi, went far outside the confines of the Gamaldi case to emphasize that the C. P. Sales deal was innocent; he enumerated big bribes he paid to supermarket executives who then bought from Iowa Beef, but from C. P. Sales, he insisted, there were no bribes. Steinman not only rejected all efforts by the state to get him to testify against Holman, he even risked his sweetheart deal with Aronwald by refusing to concede that he had intended to pay bribes on behalf of Iowa Beef. (Judge Roberts had refused to accept his plea on that basis; Judge Fraiman later took it.)

Bill Aronwald, Steinman's patron at the Justice Department, also evidenced this strange concern over whose money the bribes were paid with. At Steinman's sentencing hearing, Judge Metzner had asked Steinman's lawyer, Elkan Abramowitz, the nature of the charge Steinman had pleaded to in state court. Abramowitz replied, "It related to a much broader conspiracy, not only with respect to Iowa Beef, but with respect to the supermarket officials . . . and the union officials who are under indictment." Suddenly Aronwald, the prosecutor, broke in and asked to confer with Abramowitz. As soon as they finished talking, Abramowitz asked to amend the court record to make clear that "there were no actual bribes paid by Mr. Steinman or by anyone in his employ in connection with Iowa Beef."

To argue over just whose money it was that Moe Steinman paid his bribes with and whose money he and his family lived on sounds like so much hairsplitting. Yet everyone seemed to be taking the distinction very seriously. Perhaps the issue was of more legal importance to Holman than others understood, and Steinman, by his obstinance, was earning the riches that Holman would continue to heap on Steinman's relatives and associates.

Or, perhaps, the simple explanation for Holman's largess is that he still needed to pay the right people to get his meat into New York.

In January, 1976, Aronwald was caught from behind again. His last remaining case from the meat investigation was the indictment against Irving Stern, Nicholas Abondolo, and Moe Fliss, the three butchers' union leaders. The charges were, first, conspiracy to travel interstate to commit racketeering, and, second, income tax evasion for the payments they took from Steinman on behalf of supermarket executives and meat dealers. The racketeering charge carried a twenty-year maximum sentence and, importantly, would have brought a mandatory ban on the men's continuation in union office until five years after they completed their sentences.

Yet Aronwald agreed in plea bargaining to drop the toughest charges. Perhaps he was aware now of how weak Moe Steinman's testimony was. He agreed to let Stern, Abondolo, and Fliss plead guilty to a single count of income tax evasion. The charge would be reworded so as to contain no mention of payoffs, or amounts of money, or where the undeclared income came from, so that there would be no five-year ban on continuation in office. But Aronwald planned, he said later, to explain to the judge at sentencing all about the payoffs, so that the judge presumably would take the matter seriously and award prison time. While they wouldn't be barred from union office, the men might at least have some embarrassing explaining to do to the membership.

Then came the sting. In court for the sentencing hearing January 6, 1976, Aronwald found matters not as he had expected them. Without informing him, the three defendants had sent letters to the judge and the probation officer giving their own strange explanations for the guilty pleas.

Stern wrote that he had carried $50,000 in tax exempt bonds in a margin (credit) account at his broker's in 1969. The interest he paid the broker for the margin account amounted to $3,414.66, Stern said. But, Stern confessed, he had deducted this interest payment from his taxable income even though interest deductions aren't allowed on margin accounts in the case of tax-exempt securities. A technicality, but Stern would be a good citizen and plead guilty. "I am ashamed to say so, but regretfully at the time I made these deductions I knew that it was improper to do so," he wrote.

Abondolo wrote that he wanted to clear his conscience by pleading guilty, because "in the early 1960s my father and I entered into a joint business transaction, and we invested approximately two thousand dollars. . . ." The investment was profitable in 1969, but Abondolo didn't report the income. So he was confessing.

Then came Fliss, who said that he, too, had gone into the stock market in 1969 "on a very modest scale." The account had been carried in his brother's name, he said, which is why there was no record of it in his own name. Nevertheless, the profits were returned to Fliss, and now he was confessing that he hadn't paid his taxes. All three defendants adamantly denied taking improper payments from anyone.

Having heard all this, Judge Thomas P. Griesa indicated that he was not about to send three good citizens to jail for such minor transgressions. The flabbergasted Aronwald demanded that the judge throw out the guilty pleas and let the original racketeering case be tried. The defense attorneys, however, argued that they had lived up to their share of the bargain, and the racketeering and other charges would have to be dropped.

After much debate and several postponements, Judge Griesa finally said he would read the grand jury testimony against the three and see how it impressed him.

When the court reconvened in April, 1976, it was a circus. Aronwald and the defense lawyers began debating the whole Moe Steinman case. According to Aronwald, Steinman had led the government to the three miscreants behind the defense table and now it was time to punish them. The defense lawyers still denied that their men had taken payoffs. They accused Steinman of "incredibility and outright fabrication," and said he was using Stern, Abondolo, and Fliss as scapegoats to avoid paying taxes on the money he pocketed for himself, and to draw lightning away from the real villains. Said Abondolo's lawyer, Albert Krieger, Steinman "was able to preserve Currier Holman's position within Iowa Beef Processors, and it could have resulted in his son-in-law being head of IBP. The only reason he [Bodenstein] is not in charge of IBP is because of public outrage. . . ." Only Steinman, he said, was capable of such "Machiavellian thinking." He said the butcher leaders had made a deal, pleaded guilty, and shouldn't be called on now to prove their innocence of other charges.

Judge Griesa began timidly to agree with Aronwald. "I was bothered," he said with considerable understatement, "by what might be an unrealistic coincidence that three officers of the same union were pleading guilty to tax counts for 1969 . . . that had nothing to do with union affairs." It was, he said finally, "simply incredible."

In reference to his examination of the grand jury materials, Griesa got tougher. "What he [Steinman] testified to for pages and pages was just a virtual deluge of money flowing around, of kickbacks to people selling meat and people buying meat. . . . I think it's by and large conceded by everybody seated here that the basic point of what he was saying went on. . . . Can you say that all three of these witnesses [Steinman, Saker and George George] were invalid?" The judge answered his own question by declaring his finding "that each of the defendants . . . did receive payments either directly or indirectly from employees or officers of supermarkets."

Pressed now, the defense tried a more familiar tack. Stern's wife, it was declared, had just had open heart surgery. She was alone at home and needed Stern to care for her. Fliss was sixty-four, had a hernia and ulcers, had twice been hospitalized since the indictment was filed, and on top of that his wife had taken an overdose of sleeping pills and would no doubt kill herself if he went to prison. Anyway, Fliss also had a strict diet for his ulcer and it would be tough on the prison kitchen system to cater to him. Abondolo complained (through his lawyer) that he had already been through two years of "agony" just being indicted. Surely no more punishment was necessary.

Griesa started out as if he was actually going to stand up to this whimpering and punish the crime. "For the law to have even a modest effect to deter this kind of situation, there must be some meaningful punishment at the end of the line," he said. "If businessmen, salesmen, get the idea that all that awaits them is probation," he said, it wouldn't deter them from stealing whatever they could get their hands on. "I see no other meaningful penalty except prison," he concluded. In reference to Stern's wife, he pointed out that the longtime union organizer "has considerable means, and if a member of his family needs a nursing home he can well afford it."

Then he gave Stern and Fliss four months each and Abondolo six.

After all, Moe Steinman himself was already out on the streets again after not serving any longer. And a few years earlier, in the well-publicized case of Four Seasons Nursing Homes, a $200 million securities fraud, Griesa had sentenced Jack L. Clark, the alleged architect of the fraud who had personally profitted by $10 million, to a mere one year in jail, with parole eligibility in four months.

By the end of 1976, Stern, Abondolo, and Fliss were free and back in union office. Fliss retired with full dignity at the end of the year. Abondolo was hailed in 1977 by the butchers' international magazine as a model union officer. Stern gave the keynote speech at the union's 1977 convention in Washington. "People aren't shunning me," Stern commented before the speech. "They aren't walking away from me. I had over five hundred letters in my file on my behalf from various organizations. The record is, I committed tax evasion on unrelated matters."

Stern was the only one of the butchers' leaders in the Stanhope meeting with Steinman to be charged with or convicted of a crime. Like him, the others continued in office, except that one, Albert DeProspoe, had retired and turned the reigns of his local over to his brother, Elmer.

And so the last of the meat investigations ended, thirteen years after the first one had begun. Kenneth Conboy, who replaced Al Scotti as head of the rackets squad, wrote the epitaph for it. "The final results of this were woefully short of what they could have been," he said. "Most of it was rather trivial in terms of ultimate result."

8

Less Justice

Moe Steinman may have extracted something far more important than money from the world's largest meat packer. After his meeting with Holman at the Stanhope in 1970, a moral atmosphere set in at Iowa Beef that seems incredible for a company its size. The departure of half a dozen top executives who disagreed with Holman over his relationships with Moe Steinman and Walter Bodenstein left the executive suite in an unhealthy state of autocracy.

The supposed "outside" directors who would keep watch on the officers were people like David Holtzman, who was getting $35,000 a year plus stock options from Iowa Beef as a financial consultant, and Louis Dinklage, a cattle feeder who counted Iowa Beef as a $12.4 million-a-year customer. There was no one around to say "no" to Currier Holman, and Holman already had cast aside any doubts that the end justified the means.

He and two other executives who stuck with him—J. Fred Haigler and Robert Kemp—got themselves a company-backed stock deal that may be unique in American industry. Instead of an incentive for good management (often an executive gets future rights to buy stock at today's price so that he will benefit if the stock price rises), Iowa Beef gave Holman, Haigler, and Kemp a protective shield against the consequences of bad management. The company agreed to buy back the stock that the three executives already owned, and if the market price was down, the company would pay according to an accounting figure known as "book value" (the purported per-share worth of the buildings, machinery, and other assets). Thus when Iowa Beef stock tumbled to $20 a share because of the Bodenstein incident, the top officers didn't suffer financially along with the other shareholders. Book value remained a healthy $41.69 a share.

The company did still more unusual things to help insiders, even former insiders like Holman's partner Andy Anderson. Anderson had refused to go to New York to testify at Holman's trial, pleading ill health (he had diabetes). It's impossible to say whether there was any connection, but Anderson certainly did well by his old partner.

After leaving Iowa Beef in 1970, and spending a few years in retirement, Anderson founded a pork processing firm called Madison Foods Inc., in partnership with two former vice-presidents at Iowa Beef. Madison's sole operation is an exclusive ten-year contract with Armour & Company under which Armour delivers hogs at one end of the plant and picks up boxes of meat at the other. For its October 25, 1975, fiscal year, Madison reported a modest profit of $371,254, or 58 cents a share, on gross sales of $6.4 million. It listed total assets of $9.7 million, and stockholder equity (assets minus debt) of $1.4 million. Yet soon afterward, Iowa Beef bought Madison Foods at an effective price of $15 million. Anderson and other shareholders received thirteen times their original investment. For Iowa Beef, this amounted to paying more than forty times annual profits* for a company with a seemingly locked-in business.

Moreover, other Iowa Beef insiders including co-chairman Haigler, general counsel William Heubaum (who replaced Nymann) and vice-president Russell Walker also had bought in early on Madison's stock, and apparently stuffed their pockets with the proceeds of the generous buy-out. Holman needed loyal men around him after his ordeal, and evidently he was willing to pay with the stockholders' money to buy them.

In a similar way, Kemp, who also helped the defense at Holman's trial, left Iowa Beef in 1975 and started a slaughterhouse in Pasco, Washington. Iowa Beef kept him on as a paid consultant and bought carcasses from him, and then, in 1977, bought the slaughterhouse itself, though apparently it paid him only the money he had invested (this was after questions had been raised about the Madison deal). Kemp's independent (for a while) slaughterhouse helped Iowa Beef break into the northwestern United States, where cattlemen had fought the inroads of a big packer that might drive local packers out of business, monopolize the market, and control prices.

Labor relations has a long and miserable history at Iowa Beef, but in the years after the Steinman contract, the dealings grew steadily more devious. The Amalgamated Meat Cutters has never successfully organized the Emporia, Kansas, plant, which remains unionfree. In 1974, a huge new Iowa Beef

---

*Corporations usually refer to their profits as "earnings," even though the money occasionally is "earned" by means of fraud, bribery and price-fixing. The author prefers the more neutral term, "profits."

plant opened in Amarillo, Texas. As construction was underway, Iowa Beef signed a contract with a Teamster local that claimed to represent the few hundred construction workers. After the plant opened, Iowa Beef continued to deal with the Teamsters as representative of some two thousand butchers, and contracts have been signed at wages far below those prevailing under Amalgamated Meat Cutter contracts. The Amalgamated itself, for reasons one can only guess at, politely declined to challenge these moves. Kemp's slaughterhouse in Washington also signed up with the Teamsters.

And Iowa Beef was quick to join the parade of major companies that hired Country Wide Personnel Inc., the sweetheart trucking operation described in Part Six run by Eugene Boffa, the convicted bank swindler whose wife bankrolled Salvatore "Sally Bugs" Briguglio while Briguglio was between jobs as an extortionist, counterfeiter, and contract murderer.

But the most devious labor tactics of all may have been used at Dakota City. Shortly before the Amalgamated contract there expired in January 1977, Iowa Beef arranged for a new company called Farm Products Inc., to lease out a large portion of the plant. Farm Products—founded and owned by an executive in Kemp's slaughterhouse venture—had set up shop in a shack out by the Sioux City stockyards, hired half a dozen men, and held an election that established something called the United Industrial Packing & Allied Workers as a bargaining unit. Suddenly, Farm Products showed up in the Iowa Beef plant with several hundred workers, all represented by the U.I.P.A.W., which few had ever heard of, receiving much lower wages than even the existing Amalgamated contract called for.

Iowa Beef then took a stonewall bargaining stance guaranteeing a strike by the Amalgamated, while the plant kept humming under the U.I.P.A.W., and Farm Products Inc. Early in 1978, with an Amalgamated contract still not in sight, the company announced that it was opening up the whole Dakota City plant and hiring scabs. Hundreds of Nebraska state troopers were put at Iowa Beef's disposal to protect the plant and the scab workers from the nearly two thousand union men and women. The Amalgamated local in Dakota City, which had only grudging support from its own international during the whole strike, claimed that Iowa Beef used illegal aliens and other improper tactics (which Iowa Beef denied), and eventually won an unfair labor practice action before the National Labor Relations Board against Farm Products Inc., but to little practical avail. In April, 1978, the local caved in and settled for the same terms Iowa Beef had unilaterally imposed on the scabs—an average 5 percent wage increase a year for four years, a length of contract almost unheard of in organized labor in these inflationary times.

In all of this, the international butchers' union went meekly along.

Iowa Beef's antitrust policies have also come in for heavy government scrutiny in recent years. One set of allegations concerns possible manipulations of the primary national pricing mechanism, to the detriment of cattlemen and consumers alike. This mechanism is a privately-owned publication, known officially as the *National Provisioner*, but universally referred to the "Yellow Sheet" because of its color. The Yellow Sheet's quotations on whole carcass prices are the basis of formulas that determine the prices paid for live cattle and for boxed beef. Many wholesale meat dealers acknowledge privately that they help rig the sheet at the behest of major packers, but none has come forward to testify.

The Yellow Sheet is published out of a ramshackle old house on Chicago's deteriorating near north side by an aging staff of about nine reporters, mostly retired (or at least former) packing company employees. It bases the prices it reports on a tiny fraction—well under 5 percent—of the beef traded. These are supposedly the freely-negotiated on-the-spot trades. Most beef traded, including almost all of Iowa Beef's boxed beef, is sold well in advance of the delivery date. Supermarkets want a firm commitment that meat will be supplied, and packinghouses want to know in advance how many cattle to have on hand. But nobody knows what the fair market price will be on the date of delivery, so they agree that the trade will be made on a price to be determined by the Yellow Sheet quotation that day.

Thus a very small tail—the tiny minority of sales where the price is freely negotiated for on-the-spot delivery—wags a very large dog. And the temptation is great to manipulate the tail. This, it is alleged, can be done by reporting phony trades late in the day. If the packer doing the reporting has agreed to sell large quantities of beef for delivery that day at the sheet price, he will report an inflated trade to the Yellow Sheet to drive the price up. And if the packer has agreed to buy large quantities of cattle for delivery that day at the sheet price, he will report a deflated trade to drive it down. The Yellow Sheet says it requires confirmation of all the trades it reports, but the trade can be confirmed by another packinghouse that is part of the plot, or by a wholesaler who is dependent on the packer for his supply of meat. Or the trade may not be phony at all; it may actually occur, but at a contrived price. Packers can contrive one or two unprofitable trades to determine the closing price on the Yellow Sheet on a given day, and enjoy enormous profits from all the other trades that are already under contract to take place at the sheet price. Since major packinghouses often trade with each other late in the day when one finds itself a little long or short on its carcass needs, such contrived trades can easily be arranged on an I'll-scratch-your-back-and-you-scratch-mine basis.

Even the many critics of the Yellow Sheet don't doubt that Lester Norton, its long-time manager, is honest and well-meaning. They do doubt that he is efficient and accurate. Yet his quotations are depended on by so many large corporations, and are locked into so many contracts, that his occasional would-be competitors find they are knocking their heads against a brick wall. If the system operates to anyone's advantage, that someone is the major packers. And the most major packer of all, by far, is Iowa Beef.

One hears rumors throughout the industry that the executives at Iowa Beef, sometimes the same ones who report prices to the Yellow Sheet, invest in the cattle futures market for their own private accounts on the side. This would be a clear conflict of interest, and a sure way to make money, especially if the Yellow Sheet can be manipulated as easily as many believe. One could simply bet in the futures market as to whether cattle prices were going up or down, and then proceed to report prices to the Yellow Sheet in a manner that would fulfill one's prophecy. The focal point of these rumors was long Alan Booge (pronounced Bogue), head of the team of telephone salesmen who marketed cattle and reported prices at Iowa Beef. Booge, whose title was vice-president for carcass sales, may well have had more to do with determining the daily price of meat at the supermarket than any other person in the United States.

In November, 1976, both Currier Holman and Alan Booge flatly denied to me that private futures trading by executives at Iowa Beef was even possible. Booge also denied allegations made by carcass buyers, who declined to be quoted by name, that he had directed them on occasion to conceal information about cattle sales. (Concealing information about certain sales that take place above or below the desired price can, of course, make the Yellow Sheet price come out lower or higher than it should be.)

In January, 1977, Iowa Beef suddenly demanded and received Booge's resignation. A company spokesman acknowledged that Booge had been trading in the futures market and Holman wouldn't allow it. Iowa Beef wouldn't disclose the details of Booge's trading, and attempts to reach Booge himself were unsuccessful. He was never charged criminally. Later in 1977 he did give a deposition in a civil suit brought in federal court, Iowa, by cattle sellers who accused Iowa Beef of antitrust violations. Lawyers who were there say Booge answered questions about the cattle trading activities of various executives. But, at Iowa Beef's request, the court sealed the contents of the deposition, and refused my written requests to examine it.

Pricing is another item that has drawn the attention of antitrust experts to Iowa Beef. According to internal documents, Iowa Beef struck a deal to sell beef to Waldbaum Inc., Bodenstein's biggest retail customer, for substantially less than it charged other customers. Memos from 1973 indicate that Heubaum, the general counsel, was concerned. One could go to jail, he warned a company official who was on his way to see Waldbaum, if one were "to discriminate in price between different purchasers of similar commodities, where the price differential cannot be attributed to efficiencies in the cost. . . ." The memos don't indicate whether the price differential for Waldbaum ended.

Another internal memo, in 1974, says that other Iowa Beef sales deals might violate antitrust law. And a 1975 memo rather bluntly raises the issue of predatory pricing. "The price cut," an executive instructed, "should be deep enough to force some of our competitors (national packers) out of the production/market segment and some of our competitors (local breakers) out of business. . . . If we are tough and price to the value that this [boxed beef] program is to us, most of our competitors should cede the territory."

After Holman was convicted in 1974, he seemed to take a more tolerant view of others who had suffered the wrath of justice. In 1975, about the time of the Bodenstein hiring, Iowa Beef had decided to employ an exclusive Los Angeles sales agent modeled on Bodenstein in New York. The job was offered to Bill Walmsley, a large Los Angeles meat wholesaler who, a year earlier, had been given a six-month suspended sentence and fined $10,000 after pleading guilty to bribing federal meat inspectors. Walmsley, however, turned the Iowa Beef job down.

After the Bodenstein hiring was aborted, with Zider and other senior executives who opposed Bodenstein already gone, and Haigler nearing retirement age, it became clear to Holman that he needed another, younger face in the executive suite for the role of heir apparent. He picked Dale Tinstman, who became president of the company in 1976. Tinstman had been an outside director of Iowa Beef while running a Lincoln, Nebraska, securities firm, which handled deals for the big meatpacker. In 1974, Tinstman and the securities firm were accused by the Securities and Exchange Commission of misleading the public in a large bond sale. Without admitting or denying guilt, he agreed to a civil court order barring him from work in the securities industry for a substantial time.

Holman immediately fished Tinstman out of the water by giving him a job as Iowa Beef's financial advisor. His former securities firm, which also was charged with misleading the public, was selected to handle Iowa Beef's acquisition of Madison Foods in 1976. On Tinstman's appointment as president, the Des Moines Register called for his resignation, and said the Iowa Beef board "should start making responsible decisions." He did not resign, and a year later became chief executive of Iowa Beef. In February, 1977, while intently charting the course of Iowa Beef's union-busting strike, which had just begun at Dakota City, Currier Holman dropped dead of a heart attack. His estate was valued at $5.3 million. The day after he died, Iowa Beef stock jumped more than a point, and it continued to climb over the next week.

Holman had never shown an ounce of contrition. In an interview with Meat Processing magazine, Holman had reflected on the Moe Steinman deal a year after his conviction for entering that deal: "Faced with the same situation again, I wouldn't know of another way to resolve it. So, yes, I would handle the situation in the same way. No, I would not do things differently."

And yet he died a bitter man. Among his last words to me the previous fall had been these: "They drove nails in the guy for the wrong reasons about two thousand years ago, and I don't think it's stopped very much. . . . We were indicted for a crime of intent. A court two thousand years ago killed one, crucified one of your race, for a crime of—crucified a guy for the crime of intent. It turned out to be wrong. . . . I'll get into heaven a hell of a lot quicker than Judge Roberts, or you, or a lot of people. Because I don't deal in dirt. . . . I think in opposition to the ordinary company that this company will be here for a hundred years. I damn well think that the Midwest needs it. And I know you do. Because you're gonna starve if something happens to us out here, pardner. So whether you know it or not, the basis on which this company is founded are ideals. We didn't break any laws. We didn't conspire. Now or ever. That's the truth. I don't lie."

The Sioux City establishment stayed loyal to the end. The local newspaper was covered with eulogies. But perhaps the best eulogy had been given earlier, while Holman was still alive. When a reporter asked Holman's local banker, John Van Dyke, what the community thought about the scandal, he replied, "Knowing all the circumstances involved and what a highly motivated person he is, I don't blame him at all. He wanted to get the job done and felt that that was the way to do it, and he did it. . . . Besides, what's the difference between a commission and a bribe—I don't know."

Shortly before the Iowa Beef case came to trial in New York in 1974, defense attorneys Richard Wynn and Jeffrey Atlas advised Holman that for the sake of public appearance he ought to remove Sam Goldberger from Iowa Beef's board of directors. He did, though he later said he didn't understand why. Goldberger continued to buy Iowa Beef's meat trimmings for less money than others paid, and to resell the trimmings at a big profit. Iowa Beef employees and others in the industry harbored suspicions about the arrangement, but management insisted that Goldberger was just a shrewd buyer. Roy Zider, the former executive whom Bodenstein briefly replaced, complained particularly that Goldberger was sometimes allowed to do business on what was called "ship to-bill to," an arrangement under which meat could be shipped to a designated warehouse with the bill sent to Goldberger elsewhere. That way it would be difficult to trace exactly what meat was going to Goldberger and what he did with it.

In the mid-1970s, Goldberger also was a partner in a Chinese restaurant in Miami, with Howard Obrunt, son of William Obrunt, the reputed financial genius of the Canadian underworld. William Obrunt, who has served prison time for fraud, forgery, conspiracy and using false documents, and who is close to Canadian Mafia boss Vincent Cotroni, also has longstanding interests in the meat business. The manager of one Obrunt-owned packing plant in Montreal later became the main distributor for Iowa Beef products in eastern Canada, a plum he captured shortly after Steinman and Goldberger entered Iowa Beef's affairs.

In February, 1978, Goldberger was scheduled to go on trial in tax court in Miami on civil charges that he shortchanged Uncle Sam by more than $265,000, largely due to deductions for "meat purchases which were neither received nor included in inventory." There were also puffed-up expenses and unreported income from commissions on food sales, the IRS said. But Goldberger's doctor managed to get the trial postponed. According to an IRS spokesman, Goldberger had "a circulation problem in his leg."

On June 20, 1976, as Benny Moscowitz was unlocking his store in the Fourteenth Street meat district at 6:20 A.M., a man appeared as if from nowhere and stuck a gun on him. Another man reached from behind Moscowitz, extended a knowing hand into exactly the pocket where Moscowitz carried his own gun, and neatly disarmed him. The two men forced Moscowitz to the floor, kicked him for awhile, then shot him in both legs just above the knee and left.

At the time, Moscowitz's store was operating under supervision of a bankruptcy court because of a creditors' suit. The chief creditor in the lawsuit was Ranbar Packing Company, one of the Castellano family's meat firms. A lawsuit seemed a strange method of collection for the Castellanos, several of whom were about to go on trial for allegedly operating a multi-million-dollar loan-shark ring. Moscowitz blamed his financial troubles on the Castellanos' friend, Moe Steinman, who never paid Moscowitz a commission on the Iowa Beef deal (though Steinman did force supermarkets to carry Moscowitz's meat patties).

In August, 1973, the government scored what appeared to be a major breakthrough in its longstanding investigation of the Castellano group. A middle-level operative in the family rackets, Arthur "Fat Artie" Berardelli, who was free on bail while appealing convictions for fraud and selling counterfeit securities, was indicted again for fraud. Bill Aronwald's strike force sized up Berardelli as a man who could be "flipped," or turned into a government witness against others in the Mob. Berardelli was young, the prosecutors reminded him, and could still make a decent life for himself if he would leave his Mafia friends and let the government give him a new name and an honest job somewhere outside New York. Otherwise, he was going to spend many years in prison, and be tied to a miserable lot of people after he was out. Berardelli's lawyer, supplied by Legal Aid, advised him to take the deal. He did.

The mobster began meeting with FBI agent James Kallstrom and IRS agent Frank Frattolillio, two of the best veteran investigators in town. From the beginning, it was clear that he was unreliable. He would make appointments for 4 A.M. in some city park or building plaza, and then leave Kallstrom and Frattolillio up until morning with no one to talk to but each other, and occasionally Jacob Laufer, the government lawyer Aronwald assigned to the case. But he was all that Uncle Sam had to work with, and he was giving good information. He told about the loanshark rackets—where the money came from, how it was put on the street, who collected it. He implicated some big names. He agreed to wear a wire (a small, concealed tape recorder) when talking to his colleagues. And the government promised him it would arrange to lift his pending two-year prison sentence, and not press other charges.

After more than a year, Berardelli produced one highly incriminating tape recording of a meeting with Paul "Little Paul" Castellano. Despite the use of circumspect language, the conversation as a whole left no doubt that Castellano had lent Berardelli large amounts of money, which Berardelli had in turn lent to loanshark clients, and that Castellano expected Berardelli to continue paying the specified return on the outstanding balance even after Berardelli went to jail. Collecting the money from the customers was Berardelli's problem. There were implications on the tape that the other Paul Castellano, "Big Paul," Carlo Gambino's brother-in-law and heir, was overseeing the whole business. Berardelli's taped meetings with "Big Paul" himself, however, failed to produce conclusive admissions of criminal conduct. The meetings continued.

In the summer of 1974, Berardelli's wife found out what he was doing. Berardelli's wife was a Gambino cousin, closely related to some of the gang members Berardelli was giving evidence against. She turned on her husband, called him "a rat," and said she wouldn't join him in his relocation. "If I had gone against her," Berardelli later said, "I would have lost her and the children forever." Berardelli announced that he wouldn't testify for the government. The government agents then told Berardelli that the Mob would kill him if he didn't come under government protection. They said if he didn't testify his wife and children would never see him again, that he would go to prison and never come out alive. They also told his mother this.

Berardelli continued to come to Aronwald's office and wear a wire. The people he was having conversations with, though, may have been informed that they shouldn't say anything revealing in front of Berardelli. At least they didn't. As late as March 19, 1975, Berardelli recorded a conversation between himself and Big Paul Castellano. Everything said was consistent with the notion that Castellano was supervising a loanshark operation involving Berardelli and other persons under discussion. But there were no conclusive admissions.

Later that same day, Berardelli's final appeal was turned down. This forced the government to arrest him and begin the lenient treatment it had promised. His first cell was a room at the Plaza Hotel in Manhattan. Later, for security reasons, he was moved to the Holiday Inn in Huntington, Long Island. On March 26, 1975, he was brought before U. S. District Judge Constance Baker Motley for what the Justice Department thought would be a probationary sentence so Berardelli could be relocated and given a new job. Two other federal judges, Robert L. Carter and Murray Gurfein, who also had Berardelli up for sentencing, had agreed to this deal. But Judge Motley chose to thwart Justice, and threw Berardelli into prison for two years. She denounced the government's whole battle plan against the Mob, declaring that it was wrong to pressure insiders to "flip," or become informers. To the G-men, informers were the only apparent tool left in Syndicate cases after electronic surveillance was severely restricted (first by Johnson Administration policy, then by a 1968 federal law). But now Judge Motley indicated that it was improper for law enforcement to seek cooperation from a convicted defendant. She effectively ordered Berardelli to stay away from government lawyers and stop cooperating in the Castellano case.

On March 31, 1975, Berardelli entered the prison camp at Eglin Air Force Base, Florida—about the nicest accomodations the government has for convicts who must somehow be kept at an institution. He checked in under an assumed name, Alfred Bernstein. Almost immediately he ran into another inmate from New York who greeted him, "Hi, Artie." There went his cover. Unable to get any more out of Beradelli, the government proceeded to convert what he had already told them into formal charges.

On June 30, an indictment came down against nine persons involved in what the government said was a $150 million loanshark ring run by Big Paul Castellano. (No doubt Don Carlo Gambino would have had charge over any such venture, but Big Paul, his brother-in-law, was as high in the organization as a soldier like Berardelli could see.) At least five of the defendants, including Big Paul, Little Paul, and Joseph Castellano, were relatively big fish.

With the usual delays while the defense lawyers built up their fees and kept their clients at large by filing various motions, a year and a half rolled by before anyone felt the pressure of trial. On November 8, 1976, Little Paul faced the fact that the tape recorder had caught him red-handed, and he pleaded guilty. Jake Laufer, the government attorney, tried to be tough. Not only did Little Paul have to plead both to loanshark conspiracy and to perjury in the signing of an income tax form (he had failed to report "substantial" interest income), Laufer also redrew the conspiracy charge so as to place in the record the mechanics of the whole loanshark operation. According to the confession Little Paul was required to make, Big Paul and Joseph Castellano supplied the money, which was then lent out "at interest rates exceeding 100 percent a year" by Little Paul, Angelo Scarpulla, Frank Granato, Victor Li Pari, and Arthur Berardelli; and the collection work was handled by Frank Guglielmi, Joseph Castellano, Robert Herko and Granato, Li Pari and Berardelli.

Despite all the confessions, and despite having one count carrying a maximum of five years in prison and another carrying three, U. S. District Judge John Bartels sentenced Little Paul Castellano to a total of four months in the Manhattan federal correctional center and fined him $5,000.

Little Paul did not agree to testify against his comrades, and it's unlikely he ever would have. So when the Castellano trial opened November 9, 1976, the government's case rested substantially on Berardelli's on-again-off-again cooperation. Some loanshark victims Berardelli had identified were on hand also, but for the most part the only person they knew much about was the man they had dealt with, Berardelli himself, who wasn't on trial in the case.

When the chips were down, Berardelli was back on the side of the Mob. He took the Fifth Amendment. Prosecutor Laufer arranged to immunize him against prosecution, and Judge Bartels then ordered him to testify. He still refused, and the defendants were acquitted.

Berardelli was charged with and convicted of contempt of court, and Judge Bartels sentenced him to five years in prison—fifteen times as long as Little Paul Castellano, Berardelli's boss, got for actually doing what Berardelli, under threat of death, simply wouldn't testify about. While Berardelli was free on appeal, the IRS and FBI, which had devoted thousands of manhours to the case he had torpedoed, still kept track of him. Clearly, his silence had been rewarded. He owned a clothing business with thirteen employees, and drove a new Cadillac leased in the name of the business. The leasing firm was run by one of the defendants he had protected.

Back in 1974, Berardelli had also given testimony to a New York State grand jury, and had provided the names of some loanshark victims to reinforce what he said. This resulted in state indictments against Scarpulla, Herko, and Little Paul Castellano. Under a deal, they pleaded guilty to one count of criminal usery. Judge Martin Evans sentenced them all to probation. He also fined Little Paul $5,620 and Scarpulla $1,000.

In 1977, the Castellanos' Ranbar Packing Inc. was indicted by a federal grand jury in Brooklyn on charges of defrauding the government with counterfeit or stolen food stamps. Specifically mentioned in the indictment were $660,000 in claims filed and mostly paid between February, 1976, and May, 1977. But the Justice Department said that this appeared to be just the tip of the iceberg. Only one individual was indicted, Martin Gitlitz, the secretary-treasurer of Ranbar, who actually submitted the claims to the government. No Castellanos were held responsible.

On December 22, 1977, the Securities and Exchange Commission filed a civil suit seeking to enjoin Ranchers Packing Corp., Peter Castellana and two other men from violating the securities laws. Until 1976, the lawsuit disclosed, Ranchers was losing money because it couldn't interest the supermarkets in its meat and the Army rejected it after placing orders. So Ranchers' owner, Martin Rochman, went to the Castellanos, who effectively took over the company. Legally, Ranchers acquired the Castellanos' Ranbar, which was booming with $30 million in sales and a $1.6 million line of credit frim Citibank, the largest bank in town. But Peter Castellana effectively controlled both firms. In July, 1977, Ranbar, now the subsidiary, sought protection from creditors under the bankruptcy laws, listing debts of $3.4 million (Citibank got most of its money out in time). At this writing, Ranbar is trying to negotiate a deal to pay creditors so-many cents on the dollar and be excused for the rest.

Ranchers, the surviving company, however, was registered with the S.E.C., and its stock was held by the public. The S.E.C. charged that Ranchers had violated the law by failing to disclose to the public shareholders that Castellana was involved (his only title at the company was "chief salesman"), by failing to disclose the shakiness of Ranbar's books, and by including inedible meat in the inventory so as to double the inventory's true value. Without admitting or denying the charges, Ranchers and Castellana consented to an injunction against doing this again, and thus suffered no punishment—a standard S.E.C. procedure.

Johnny Dio remains at this writing a prisoner in the U. S. Penitentiary at Danbury, Connecticut.

On December 12, 1973, he was taken from Danbury—where he was serving a sentence on the kosher meat frauds—to federal court in Manhattan for the trial of one of the stock fraud cases, which resulted in lengthening his sentence. He identified himself in court as a former dress manufacturer whose family now operated an advertising specialty company.

In testimony, however, he also gave some insights into prison life and how he keeps his influence with the seamier Jewish business community. On Jewish holidays, he testified, "outside rabbis" and other guests are invited inside the walls for banquets, which are also attended by the warden and the associate warden. Until Dio arrived, it had been something of a problem to find gentile inmates willing to serve as waiters and busboys for these affairs. As soon as he learned of the problem, however, Dio said he recruited "some of the boys that I had known there," and volunteers were suddenly available. In return, Dio got to sit in on the dinners where he said the food was better than usual.

He comes up for parole in August, 1979. If he makes it, you'd better start looking twice at your salami.

For many years prior to 1974, B & P Packing Company in Newark, New Jersey, employed ten butchers. Now it doesn't employ any. Prior to 1974, B & P was a fabricator—that is, it bought carcasses of meat and butchered them. After 1974, B & P exclusively handled boxed beef.

"I enjoy this much better," says Paul Chanin, the owner. "I don't have any of the headaches. I move the meat in, and I move the meat out." B & P occupies the same space it did before, but now the space is used for storage instead of for meat cutting. A forty-foot trailer comes in and dumps its load of boxes, forty thousand pounds worth. Then B & P's customers—small retail meat store owners—come in and pick up their needs. "It is unprofitable to take a forty-foot trailer and dump off ten boxes of meat to a customer," Chanin explains. "Our function is to take these little guys and get the meat to them."

What happened to B & P is happening all over the meat industry. The boxed beef revolution has arrived. "The demand for meat is here," Paul Chanin says. "I can't possibly fabricate what I'm handling today. I have much better control over my business. I get in boxed weights and I send out boxed weights. I know I'm not getting ripped off. And you can't get reliable people here. If you were depending on people to show up for work Monday morning and they didn't show up, you'd see the incentive."

Interestingly, however, Paul Chanin doesn't handle Iowa Beef. He thinks something funny is going on with Iowa Beef's prices. "It's being footballed around here," he says. "Some companies get a penny a pound cheaper." Moreover, he had complaints about having to use Walter Bodenstein as a middle man (which apparently is no longer necessary under a new marketing system begun in 1978). Chanin buys his meat from Monfort of Colorado, an Iowa Beef immitator and competitor.

Lori Schuller, twenty-four, used to work on a factory assembly line near Sioux City, putting together parts for Zenith radios as the conveyor belt brought them by. Then she got a job on another factory assembly line, breaking down cattle parts for Iowa Beef as the conveyor belt brought *them* by. She did not need the two-year apprenticeship program required of the versatile, old-fashioned butcher. Mrs. Schuller learned her job in less than a week.

Every hour, 636 loin strips rolled past Mrs. Schuller's station in Iowa Beef's cavernous Dakota City plant. That's two for each of the 318 cattle slaughtered at the beginning of the assembly line. As always, it was forty-eight degrees in the plant. The din of voices and machinery swallowed up individual sounds. With special electric saws, Mrs. Schuller and the three other persons at her station trimmed each loin strip twice, first at the bony head, then at the fatty tail. Guidelines were etched into the cutting table to make it easy. Every piece would come out the same size. She took the bone and fat and, like a basketball center shooting a hook shot, caromed it off a metal "backboard" onto another conveyor belt running high overhead. That belt led to a rendering room where the bone and fat was processed for animal food and other uses. Closer to eye level, a middle conveyor belt carried tenderloins, which already had been removed from the strips by other workers upstream from Mrs. Schuller. She ignored the tenderloins as they rolled past, and put her trimmed strips back onto the bottom conveyor belt where she got them from. Just downstream, eleven workers at the next station trimmed fat from the side of the strips down to just one-half inch. They were equipped with knives specially designed for exactly this process. At the end of the line, each strip was vacuum-sealed in plastic to prevent shrinkage, and placed in a cardboard box.

The strips coming into each worker's station were almost the same size, and so were the strips going out. Iowa Beef has standardized the size cattle it sends into the processing room. That's the way the retail chains love it. Surveys have shown that shoppers prefer different sized steaks in different parts of the country, and even in different neighborhoods. Opening an Iowa Beef loin box, a retailer can set his saw for three-quarter-inch, one inch, or whatever, and saw off uniform steaks of the weight he wants without worrying about length and breadth. The same principle holds for chucks, rounds, and ribs, the other standard parts of the cattle. Says Tom Nolting, owner of four supermarkets in southern Indiana, "If we were to bone out a rib and slice off rib-eye steaks like that, we'd probably have to charge $3.49 a pound. This way we just unpack a box of rib-eyes and slice 'em off like bread, and we could probably do it for $2.99 a pound." Small ribbons of lean meat that the retailer used to have to trim for his hamburger machine have already been trimmed at the factory. The retailer simply buys his ground beef trimmings in another box. Even the hides have been started on the tanning process at Dakota City.

Says Lou Havrilla, an assistant vice-president at Iowa Beef, "What you saw down there was a factory. None of us are really in the meat business. We're in the tonnage business. Beef just happens to be our raw material."

Someone else is doing Mrs. Schuller's job now, exactly as she did it. After an Iowa Beef executive and a reporter picked her out at random as a typical employee, she proved how typical she was by quitting before the story appeared in print. The Amalgamated Meat Cutters union says Iowa Beef ran through twenty thousand workers for its two thousand Dakota City butcher jobs before the plant had been open ten years. Then came the 1977 strike, which brought almost total turnover. Even before the strike, fewer than 25 percent of the workforce had been at the plant three years. Such workers obviously earn less than old-line meat companies like Swift and Armour pay their skilled butchers. And they obviously earn *much* less than do the local retail and wholesale butchers around the country whom they are replacing.

Membership in the Amalgamated has dropped to about 525,000 from about 550,000 a few years ago, despite ever-increasing meat consumption. If the automation introduced by Iowa Beef and its immitators had taken full effect, the membership would be down much more. In many midwestern cities, the union still explicitly bans the importation of boxed beef. In some cities, the union has threatened to strike to stop boxed beef, and in Kansas City such a strike actually occurred. Iowa Beef says 16 percent of the American people are still covered by such bans. Even in New York, Philadelphia, and other large cities where boxed beef has been admitted, contracts have been changed to provide that no currently employed full-time butchers can lose their jobs because of it.

When the butchers retire, however, they tend to be replaced by part-time workers, or not to be replaced at all. In Philadelphia, butchers' membership dropped from 5,000 to about 4,750 in the first six years boxed beef was allowed in, though much more meat was being sold. In New York, a training program designed to bring minority group members into the trade was ended. All through the northeast, apprenticeship programs are being eliminated.

Some union officials still rail against boxed beef. "It's no different from the Japanese sending cheap TVs in, undercutting the price," complains David W. Gelios, secretary-treasurer of Local 626 in Toledo. "It doesn't have the bloom, it doesn't have the tenderness" of freshly butchered meat, says Leon Schachter, the butchers' leader in the Washington, D.C., area. But consumer reaction hasn't borne him out.

And Iowa Beef remains by far the biggest benificiary of the boom it started.

Tino De Angelis was paroled in 1972 after serving seven years of his twenty-year sentence for the salad oil swindle. A year later I visited him in his neat, almost ascetically modest one-and-a-half-room apartment on the first floor of a small Jersey City hotel, and then at a hog butchering operation he was supervising in North Bergen, New Jersey. I was completely taken in. He was a charming, grandfatherly little man who spoke in a quiet voice of his regrets for the wrongs he had done and his desire to make a little money to pay back the innocent victims of the salad oil caper (though in his opinion that certainly did not include American Express). He was as polite as could be. At this time I didn't know about his connection with the Merkel Meat scandal, so I didn't ask him about it. His pork operation showed every sign of legitimacy. I saw him bundled up in three sweaters in the cooler room, where he spent his days, patiently and expertly training young immigrant employees in how to quickly strip a bone of its meat without leaving waste. I wrote a rather flattering article about him on the front page of the *Wall Street Journal*, indicating that he seemed to have gone straight, and even offering his own unique view of the salad oil case (he blamed the big grain companies and banks for trying to wipe him, the little guy, out; and he said that the nearly $1 billion he reaped was all poured back into the vegetable oil market as he tried to stay even through declining prices). He wrote me a nice note.

A year later, the Agriculture Department, besieged by Tino's creditors, filed a civil suit against his Rex Pork Company and against Paul H. Boiardi, a longtime friend of Tino's from Milton, Pennsylvania, who owned Rex Pork (Tino was unable to keep any assets in his own name because of outstanding tax judgments against him from the salad oil case). The Agriculture Department suit said Rex Pork had failed to pay for about $3 million of livestock it had slaughtered and sold. Particularly hurt were some pork dealers in the Indianapolis area and the National Farmers Organization of Corning, Iowa. They had dealt with Tino, and said—as was clearly the case—that he was running the operation. Rex Pork and Boiardi consented to a cease-and-desist decree, and the National Farmers Organization got a court order to seize a warehouse full of slaughtered pigs. Meanwhile, the Agriculture Department was moving to take away inspection services from several companies Tino was associated with on the grounds that he was "unfit to engage in any business requiring inspection." Without inspection stamps, of course, Tino would have been hard-pressed to sell his meat. He eventually foxed his way out of this jam by voluntarily withdrawing his companies from the program while seeing to it that his plant was covered by the inspection services provided for another company of which he was not an officer.

While all this was going on in 1975, the *Wall Street Journal* advertising department—which is very conscientious about trying to protect readers from fraudulent sales pitches, though it's fighting an uphill battle—came to the news department with some proposed advertising, which read thus:

BUSINESS OPPORTUNITY

Finish and fatten your own pigs to market weight. We will assist in procurement of 50 lb feeder pigs. All feed requirements. Farmers in Pa, NY corn belt to feed and care for your pigs on custom basis. Hedge pig purchase in future market through sale of grown hogs. Sale of finished hogs for slaughter—3 cycles per year. Excellent opportunity for year round profitable secured operation. Box——.

The *Journal* refused the ad, which was submitted by Miller Pork Packers. The advertising department had recognized the name of Miller's president, Angela Bracconeri (Tino's sister), and of the person who was to receive the responses, Michael De Angelis (Tino's brother), both of whom had been active in the salad oil affair. After all, a *Journal* reporter, Norman "Mike" Miller, now the paper's Washington bureau chief, had won a Pulitzer Prize for reporting on the swindle years ago. Now all this new business, coupled with the recent Agriculture Department actions, which had already been reported inside the paper, was inevitably going to make another page-one feature. It was brought to me because I had interviewed Tino previously and knew his past.

When I called him for comment, the previously polite and grandfatherly Tino exploded in threats and obscenities. The threats—not the obscenities—wound up, as they had to, in the paper as part of the story. He quickly called and wrote, his old polite self again, to apologize to me and also to my wife for any trouble the threats may have caused. If Tino had actually been afraid for his businesses, he should have known better than to think the government, let alone a newspaper, would be able to suppress a spirit like his. Nearly two years later, in 1977, the Justice Department sued three meat companies—Eastern Pork Cutters Inc., Eastern Smoked Meat Inc., and Fem Company Inc.—accusing them of killing a tributary of the Hackensack River by contaminating it with disease-causing bacteria. A government lawyer said the three companies, all operating in one plant, not only had taken all the oxygen out of the creek by releasing meat processing waste, but also had dumped salmonella bacteria downstream causing a public health hazard along the Hackensack. U. S. District Judge Herbert Stern ordered the three firms to start trucking their waste to a site designated by the U. S. Environmental Protection Agency. Not named in the suit was the man who was generally believed to be supervising the plant: Tino De Angelis. Eastern Pork and Eastern Smoked Meat had been founded in 1976 by his family.

Tino's old friend Charlie Anselmo is still operating a meat brokerage at 408 West Fourteenth Street. Lots of people in the market say they see him on the street regularly, but nobody seems to have any idea exactly what he's doing —or want to talk about it.

Nathan Lokietz, after his brief jail term for the Merkel Meat scandal, began operating under the name Dyker Meats on Gansevoort Street, and caused a lot of talk among meat inspectors. One wrote to me in 1974 complaining about Lokietz's operations, but no action was taken on this count before Lokietz's creditors threw him into bankruptcy court shortly thereafter.

Investigation showed that Norman Lokietz was not indeed the head of Dyker Meats—his son, Sheldon, was. Sheldon was the young man who escaped indictment in the Merkel Meat case because his father agreed to testify. Now Sheldon owned all the stock, and his father (and a brother) were simply employees. Sources say, however, that Nat Lokietz was always in command and that ownership was placed in his son's name for appearance's sake.

In 1974, Dyker expanded its operations by taking over a Brooklyn company known as Premier Smoked Meats. On February 4, 1975, Premier's creditors filed suit to place Premier in involuntary bankruptcy, and eventually the company was declared bankrupt. It owed $225,000 in secured debts, $526,594.22 in unsecured debts, and an unknown amount in wages and taxes. Joshua J. Angel, the attorney for the trustee in bankruptcy, wrote at least twice to the Justice Department demanding an investigation of what he said was bankruptcy fraud. He said Premier, under Lokietz's control, had been selling its meat "at prices far less than the cost of same" to potential co-conspirators. "I have strong reason to believe that the bankrupt's affairs were conducted in a criminal manner," Angel wrote. He says the response was perfunctory, and nothing was done.

On April 10, 1978, Robert Nicholson and Jack Carey were waiting for a plane at La Guardia Airport. Off the arriving plane, on which Nicholson and Carey were due to depart, stepped Moe Steinman, just up from Florida. "He almost collapsed when he saw us," Nicholson laughs. "He thought we were waiting there for him!" The startled Steinman readily answered a few general questions thrown up by his curious former pursuers. Steinman said he lived in Fort Lauderdale, but flew into New York on business that Monday afternoon, arriving about 1:30. He was to return at about the same time Thursday, and his remarks led the detectives to suspect that he made the same flights often, perhaps every week. "He was wearing a brown leisure suit, and looked the picture of health," Nicholson recalls. He says they didn't discuss the business.

If they had, it probably would have involved meat. Steinman and his brother Sol continued to operate Trans-World Fabricators, which apparently was still brokering meat to supermarkets from the same office on Gansevoort Street, until Sol, too, retired to Florida in 1977. What Trans-World was replaced with is something this book can't report, though Steinman's continued journeys to New York four days a week make it clear he was keeping his fingers in the pie.

One particular deal he might have told Nicholson about at the airport, had they been talking business, was a move by a couple of Steinman's old money-washing partners on Fourteenth Street to take over the distribution of meat to Chinese and Polynesian restaurants in the New York area. The chief distributor for those restaurants started losing its routes early in 1978 to an upstart firm run by Steinman's old colleagues. A brief struggle ensued, after which the old firm and the new firm merged. Sources in the industry say that Steinman orchestrated the whole affair. Litigation was started by a former officer of the old firm who says he was gypped out of a business with an annual net profit of $342,000. Steinman's name doesn't appear in the court papers, but a principal is quoted in an affidavit as saying that one group agreed to the merger because they were "told by the Mafia they had to sell or else they would be out of business . . . and worse things would happen to them." A lawyer for that group is quoted as saying, "It was just like in the movies. They made us an offer that we could not refuse."

Frank Snitow, the state prosecutor whom Bob Nicholson so admired, and who fought so energetically to keep Moe Steinman from getting off the hook, resigned from the district attorney's office in 1976, and went into private practice. His first major case was the defense of Carmine DeSapio, the Mafia-connected former boss of the Tammany Hall Democratic political machine in New York, who had gone to prison for conspiring to give a cut of city contracts to Anthony "Tony Ducks" Corallo, a member of Johnny Dio's Lucchese mob. DeSapio had been indicted again in 1976 on charges that he committed perjury before a grand jury looking into political corruption. Snitow defended him successfully and the case was thrown out of court.

Snitow wrote me defending his representation of Carmine DeSapio. He said I had "a woefully inadequate sense of justice and little comprehension of the purpose of our court system. The defense of the accused is no less noble a profession than the prosecutorial function," he concluded.

Al Scotti, Snitow's old boss, also left the D.A.'s office for private practice. After decades of serving Frank Hogan as first assistant, Scotti was disappointed at being passed over by the politicians in Albany when it came time to choose Hogan's successor. When he set up his private office, Scotti almost immediately was approached by rackets figures to handle their defense. He was offered, he says, "huge fees." But he steadfastly refused to defend cases involving organized crime figures. "I think it would be a disservice to law enforcement," he says. "I have been identified in the public mind with fighting them all these years, and it might induce cynicism regarding all prosecutions."

In saying so, Scotti almost certainly put his finger on the central problem in prosecution today, and one of the two prime causes of law enforcement's failure to thwart the Mafia (the other, and most important, being judicial sentencing). Most authorities refer to it as the revolving door concept—young lawyers seeking trial experience cut their teeth as prosecutors, not really dedicated to the cause of law enforcement but dedicated to the construction of successful future careers as politicians or defense lawyers. Nothing works more to their own selfish advantage than making easy plea bargains with defendants. It gives them impressive conviction statistics, yet doesn't cause hard feelings. The Snitow view of a lawyer as a gun for hire is much more common than the Scotti view of the lawyer as a dedicated advocate for causes he selects and believes in. In fact, Snitow, by truly dedicating himself even briefly to the cause of law enforcement, and by attempting to take an unyielding stance against the racketeers, was revealing himself as an extraordinary prosecutor. The true, lifelong professional dedication Scotti stands for is almost unheard of. (Some chief prosecutors might have continued professional law enforcement careers had not politics booted them into private practice or less effective government jobs. Robert Morgenthau, the former U.S. Attorney for Manhattan and now the island's district attorney, and Jonathan Goldstein, former U.S. Attorney for New Jersey, come to mind.)

Richard Wynn and Jeffry Atlas had been prosecutors before they defended Holman and Iowa Beef. Former District Attorney Richard Kuh went to work for a law firm representing supermarket officials in the Steinman case. Dennis O'Connor, chief counsel to the New Jersey State Commission of Investigation while the commission was investigating Philadelphia Mafia boss Angelo Bruno, went to work for the Trenton law firm representing Bruno. Former Essex County, New Jersey, Prosecutor Brendan Byrne became a partner in a law firm that represented various Mafia-connected people. Mafia union racketeer Thomas Pecora listed Byrne as his personal attorney on a gambling charge, and Byrne's law firm showed up to bail Pecora out of jail. Byrne is now governor of New Jersey. One of the most respected prosecutors in recent years, Richard Ben Veniste, who jailed Teamster pension fund boss Allen Dorfman and three years later jailed John Mitchell and the Watergate conspirators, then went into private practice representing Alvin Malnik, a prominent borrower of Teamster pension fund money who has frequently had contact with mobsters, and has twice been indicted for large financial crimes, though never convicted. And so on, ad infinitum.

Bill Aronwald, the strike force chief who made the deal with Moe Steinman, went into private practice associated with Hyman Zolotow, who not only does criminal defense work, but whose clients also numbered the Bronx Independent Meat Company, which was at the time the largest distributor in the region for the products of Iowa Beef Processors. Bronx Independent Meat Company, of course, purchased these products through Walter Bodenstein. Daniel P. Hollman, who preceded Aronwald as head of the strike force, then turned to combating the efforts of that very office to rid New York of Joseph Castellano, whom Hollman signed up as a client. Hollman proved better at defense than he had been at prosecution, as has been the case with so many lawyers, and Castellano was acquitted of loanshark charges and went back to the meat business and his other endeavors.

William O. Bittman, a star Justice Department trial lawyer who prosecuted Jimmy Hoffa and Bobby Baker among others, not only turned up later representing Howard Hunt of the Watergate burglary team, but also passing envelopes of White House hush money to the burglars. The Watergate prosecution team accused him of lying to them and withholding an important document.

Rick Wynn, the former prosecutor who defended Currier Holman, departed even farther from law enforcement. In 1977, he pleaded guilty to having set up a pornography ring that dealt in child pornography. He tried to explain that his role consisted only of introducing two of his criminal defense clients to each other so they could make some money to pay legal bills, and he said he really didn't know what they were doing. But sources at the district attorney's office disclosed a tape recording in which a Mob pornographer told Wynn that the films showed "kids pissin' on each other, kids screwing each other. Why would anybody want to buy that stuff?" the racketeer asked in an atmosphere of joviality.

"People will buy anything these days," Wynn replied. He accepted money from the man.

The revolving door sometimes works the other way, too, but with equally unsettling results. Elkan Abramowitz, who brilliantly finagled Moe Steinman off the district attorney's hook, and thus preserved the meat industry empires of Johnny Dio, Chappy Brescia and Paul Castellano, was appointed chief of the criminal division of the United States Attorney's office for the Southern District of New York, the largest and most important regional office in the Justice Department. There is little doubt that Abramowitz is an extremely capable lawyer, and that the government would be getting its money's worth if it paid Abramowitz merely to keep him away from the defense table for a while, even to go on a prolonged vacation if he wanted to. But to make him responsible for planning the use of investigative and prosecutorial resources in the nation's most critical federal district is another matter. It is entirely possible that by keeping his oath of confidentiality to his former clients, he was handcuffing himself and the Justice Department in important areas.

There is, of course, no suggestion intended here that any of the lawyers mentioned above have improperly transferred any specific pieces of information from one office to another, or have violated the generally accepted legal ethics regarding disclosure of confidential information from a former client. The question, rather, is the generally accepted legal ethics themselves, and whether they are best suited to the fair administration of justice.

Lawyers say it's naive to think that they should take any responsibility for the positions they defend in court. The idea of identifying a lawyer with his argument certainly runs counter to the financial interest of lawyers. Nevertheless, it does not necessarily run counter to justice. It is possible to envision a just system in which the best professional debaters do *not* claim an ethical obligation to hire themselves out to whoever has the most money, to defend any argument, no matter how vile, that the person with the money wants defended. Putting the government to its proof is a fine principle, embodied in the Constitution to protect the innocent. Nowadays, however, it is often turned into a game, profitable for lawyers, in which the end seems to be to keep the greatest number of criminals on the street, which is not what the framers of the Constitution had in mind. It may be time to ask ourselves whether justice really requires our best debaters to stretch legal precedent and their own ingenuity to the farthest limits to get their man off regardless of his guilt—or whether it would be adequate justice, even better justice, if a defendant merely had the right to try to persuade a lawyer to take responsibility for his cause.

Under such a different ethic, any lawyer could defend a person he believed to be innocent (or quite possibly innocent). Or he could take the case of a defendant who agreed to plead guilty, and could help make sure the punishment wasn't excessive for the actual crime. But he would not be expected to plead a defendant not guilty unless he truly doubted the defendant's guilt. A lawyer proven wrong would not, of course, have to go to jail with his client; but he *would* have to shoulder some moral responsibility for being wrong. And he could not retain credibility while switching sides on an issue (such as the standards to be met to obtain a wiretap order), according to who is paying him.

Surely every accused person could still find a lawyer willing to take on his cause—or if his cause was so ridiculous that no lawyer would invest his dignity in it, no judge or juror would be likely to either. The point is that under such an ethic no lawyer could claim an obligation to marshal the full resources of his genius to obtain freedom for a man he knew didn't deserve it. And the so-called Mob lawyer—not the lawyer who takes on an individual case where he truly senses injustice, but the lawyer who makes his living impeding law enforcement's fight against the Syndicate—could be labeled for the antisocial character he really is.

There is another moral aspect to all this. Elkan Abramowitz didn't defend Moe Steinman pro bono (without charge, for the public good). He got a lot of money from Steinman. Where could Moe Steinman have obtained this money except from his corrupt deals? Even his salary from Daitch-Shopwell was based on his ability to make these deals. The fact is that Elkan Abramowitz probably spent several years maintaining himself and his family at least in part on money Moe Steinman stole from every meat-eating resident in the greater New York area—the very people whose safety and property Abramowitz was then put in charge of protecting.

This moral taint, of course, is not peculiar to Elkan Abramowitz. It falls on every private defense lawyer who takes on a client who he knows has been engaged in profitable criminal activity. Abramowitz was certainly aware that Steinman was a crook; Abramowitz advised him to plead guilty—and then took his money. Where could the defense money have come from? Even if a client is innocent of a particular charge facing him, but obviously practices criminality as a profession, the defense lawyer, however nobly he may express his devotion to civil liberties and the system of justice, is living off dirty money —and in most cases living very well off it.

Many of those who direct our prosecutors' offices have been living off this dirty money in the recent past. And many of their subordinates who function in the courtroom aspire to live off it in the near future. That is the revolving door. And as long as it keeps revolving—as long as prosecutors are essentially just people on leave of absence from the defense team—then it's likely that dedicated career lawmen in the FBI and other police forces will be dissatisfied, and that justice often won't be done.

In October, 1976, Robert Nicholson resigned from the New York City Police Department to become chief investigator for the State Commission of Investigation. Lou Montello and Jack Carey resigned to join his staff.

Within a few months, Nicholson had organized an undercover operation in Amsterdam, New York, near Schenectady, that exposed how local and county law enforcement officers had been corrupted by gamblers. According to press accounts of the investigation, he found wholesale professional casino-type gambling spots, where he and his investigators observed the police chief, the city judge, an assistant district attorney, a county supervisor, and six policemen enjoying the action. In personal testimony before the commission, he identified five commercial establishments that served as permanent fronts for gambling operations, and he told how a $100,000 fund contributed to by the professional gamblers was cut up among thirty police officers.

In private, friends report, Nicholson still talks bitterly about the Steinman case. For the record, he simply says he is "disappointed." It's no wonder.

The meat kingpin had gotten off, moved to Florida on his pension, and still did business in New York during the week. The butchers' union was run by ex-cons. The son of a convicted former butchers' leader (Frank Kissel) still operated a major regional sausage concern (Eatwell) in the same plant Merkel had used, while another son helped run the butchers' union. Tino, Anselmo, Lokietz, the Castellanos, Brescia, Gerace, remained in business. Johnny Dio was nearing parole, and his son Dominick, brother Tommy, and cousin Thomas Plumeri were still involved in the family businesses, including kosher meats. Nicholson had wanted to start an investigation into the kosher meat business, but there hadn't been time.

In 1976, the district attorney's squad underwent some drastic changes. The squad had once numbered about eighty, and turnover (according to Nicholson and Snitow) was only four or five men a year. Now there are fewer men, many of them are new, and the police department bureaucracy is far more involved. Some of the department brass and other officials had long been jealous of the elite squad. They had resented its independence and prestige. Frank Hogan was a figure they couldn't argue with. But Hogan died. There were budget cuts. There was political pressure to focus on street crime. There was unionization. Detectives demanded overtime pay, and night differential. When they were willing to work without it, other cops pressured them not to. Even their commanding officers had a union. Under the new contracts, they were entitled to early retirements with pensions, and took them, robbing the squad of experience.

This book originally closed with some off-the-cuff remarks about detective work that Nicholson offered late one evening. When he saw them on paper, he asked to substitute a more thoughtful critique of his industry. This is what he wrote:

Investigation of organized crime cases hasn't changed much and never shall. In my opinion, the only successful way to combat organized crime is to identify those involved and then send experienced investigators into the field to surveil them, follow them day and night, everywhere they go, identify the people with whom they associate, and in turn, follow them and so on. Then, maybe after six months, if you're lucky, you might have enough evidence to get a wiretap, if not you just continue on.

Wiretapping is probably the single most important weapon law enforcement has to combat organized crime. When used properly, it can be your entire case. When abused, it can destroy your case. Organized crime figures are creatures of habit like the rest of us. They will many times discuss crimes over a telephone merely because they are too lazy to travel across town. Some would say "aren't they smarter than that"? I don't know, maybe they're not.

Long continuous hours of just waiting for something to happen are an investigator's burden. Patience is his most important device, memory is his most valued asset. Labor union contracts which force the investigator to abandon his pursuit after eight hours simply because his tour has ended truly works against the dedicated investigator. Talk to the "hot shot" detectives and they'll all agree. During the Merkel investigation, we didn't go home for three solid days. We had little food and no sleep, but we never dreamed of asking for relief, instead we were rewarded with good solid evidence and a district attorney who knew he had a strong case, and told us so. Until law enforcement realizes that these tried and proven methods work and return to them, the only winners will be the bad guys.

The bottom line is you've got to send your investigators out to where the crime is. Waiting in a comfortable office for it come to you just doesn't work.

Notes on Libel, Accuracy, Style, and Gratitude

One reason for the delay in publication of this book particularly deserves the reader's attention. A terrible chill has been thrown over the free flow of information in this country by libel laws, by the lack of any consistent court standards of what it's permissible to print (even if one concedes that judges should be able to *decide* what it's permissible to print), and by the power of anyone to threaten a well-intentioned journalist and his publisher with financial ruin.

Newsmen face this threat not just when we make an honest error, as everyone occasionally does, but even when we report with 100 percent accuracy. The problem is not so much that someone might file a valid libel claim and win; none of the dozen or so litigants I have inspired in fifteen years of active journalism has yet won a libel suit or received one penny in settlement from me or on account of anything I have written. The potential for harassment, however, is broad. Legal fees are insanely high to defend even a totally unmeritorious lawsuit. Second, if a slip-up ever does occur, the life savings of a newsman and his family are at stake; libel insurance is not available for authors (some serious dfficulties would arise even if it were). And a third problem is the growing evidence, through a series of decisions in 1978, that a hostile judiciary is declaring war on journalists.

The real losers, of course, are not the journalists, who will keep at it. The losers are the American people. The crooked or acquiescent public officials, businessmen, mobsters, and others who plunder our wealth have found a way through the courts to hobble those who would help the public find out what's going on.

This book was turned down by a major publishing house for the frankly acknowledged reason that the house is reluctant to print works that might attract nuisance libel claims. Other houses have shown evidence of similar fears, and other authors have run into similar problems. Journalistic books must be written under onerous contractual terms, which are standard in book publishing (W.W. Norton & Company, which published this book, has terms a bit more lenient than most). These terms place upon an author, with his meager resources, the implausible burden of indemnifying a large publishing corporation against the vagaries and unfairnesses of the law. The result of this is not that any claimant will get much money, but that the author and his family may be wiped penniless by even a small part of the legal fees for what may have been a single mistake, or may not have been any mistake at all.

Much of this situation may be due to a broad public misunderstanding of the finances of publishing. Over and over in researching this book, I have listened to people say that I was "making a lot of money writing a book"— this to express their resentment at being asked a few simple questions, or at being requested to spend five minutes' time to save me two days' work. One former prosecutor refused to be interviewed unless I made substantial payments to him. He argued that many of his former colleagues on the prosecutors' staff had sold books about their big cases, and he felt entitled to share in the wealth. When I told him what I was receiving for this book, he said his former colleagues had all done better, and that I "went cheap."

It might help if I were to explain briefly here about the "lot of money" that I and other journalist-authors make. The fact is that no sane person would write a book like *Vicious Circles* to get rich. These books require thousands of hours of labor. This book was financed on advance guarantee of $13,500 (after payment of agent's fees) of which $5,400 was in hand before the manuscript was submitted; most journalistic books are financed on less. There is much more money to be made today writing "thriller"-type fiction (I know, because I have made it, and have been offered more of it). Libel laws are no small reason for this. Even the occasional journalist-author one hears of who gets $75,000 or $100,000 to write a book is probably getting it for two or three years of hard work for which he has undergone considerable training. The hourly pay even in these rare success stories is much less than the author could have earned if he had gone to law school and hired himself out as an attorney. Most journalist-authors write for less than the minimum wage; they do it because they think they have learned something that the public ought to know, and because that is their profession.

Some suffer more than poor remuneration. Myron Farber, a reporter for the *New York Times,* was held in jail and accused of "profiteering" and "standing on an altar of greed" by U.S. District Judge Frederick B. Lacey. Farber's crime was having agreed to take $75,000 (of which only about half was safe in hand) for spending two-and-a-half years of his life working eighteen-hour days to write a book about a series of mysterious deaths. The deaths remained mysterious because government prosecutors—who were later promoted to judgeships—failed to investigate them properly when they occurred. Judge Lacy earns $54,500 a year, guaranteed for life. If he augments his income by writing a book based on what he has heard while on the bench, he won't be the first judge to do so.

I have tried earnestly to make every one of these two hundred thousand or so words true. Yet I know full well that even Joe DiMaggio never walked onto a ballfield in April without being sure that several times before the season ended in October he would drop a fly ball, or throw wildly, on a play that any rookie would be expected to handle. So it is almost inevitable that somewhere in these pages I have dropped a ball or two. My last nonfiction book contained two errors that I have been made aware of. I badly misspelled the name of a shoemaker, and I called a law enforcement officer a U.S. marshall when in fact he was—and proud of it—a Treasury agent. Still, I think Joe DiMaggio would have looked back on that as a pretty good season.

For any errors in this book, I sincerely apologize, and if informed of them, I will be glad to apologize publicly and do my best to see that they are corrected in any future editions. I am confident that if any errors exist, they will not be such as to stain the essence of this book; that nobody else could have done it a whole lot better; and that some of the ones I got right were real beauts, and more than make up for any slips.

There has been controversy over the use in some recent books of third-party quotes—that is, the direct quotation of conversation when not everyone involved has confirmed it. My rule has been this: If it's on tape, and the tape came from a reliable source, I went with it. If the verbatim conversation was related to me by one participant or overhearer, and the general gist of it was confirmed elsewhere, I have used it, but have tried to indicate where the quotes came from. If I had reason to believe that a participant in a conversation might dispute the version printed, I made every reasonable effort to consult him and print his side of it, except where a court has already determined that he committed illegal acts along the lines suggested by the remarks.

About the origins of this book:

The "meat" sections resulted from a letter sent to Frederick Taylor, the *Journal*'s executive editor, by John Kennedy of Staten Island, a reader. Mr. Kennedy enclosed a small clipping of an article from deep inside the *New York Times* reporting that the largest meatpacking firm in the world was going on trial in New York for conspiring to pay millions of dollars in bribes to the executives of the area's major supermarkets and officials of the butchers' union. Mr. Kennedy wanted to know what this was all about, and I am deeply grateful to Fred Taylor for asking if I would be interested in finding out.

My interest in the Mafia began many years ago because of two simple facts: I wanted to be a newspaperman, and the best reporters on all the newspapers I saw seemed to be assigned to write about the Mafia (or whatever euphemism it was then called by). This sense dates back to the work of Edward Frank and Carolyn Pickering on the *Indianapolis Star,* and continues through the work and coaching of Henry Price and Gloria Landers on the *(Perth Amboy) News Tribune,* where I got into the business myself, and later to Anthony Scaduto of the *New York Post.*

The "cheese" chapters resulted from a clipping from a publication called the *Farm Journal,* which Les Gapay of the *Wall Street Journal's* Washington bureau was alert enough and kind enough to send me.

The lunch chapter grew out of a lunch I had (but not at a lunchwagon stand) with New York Police Lieutenant Remo Franchesini, who made some offhand reference to what he called "the hot dog case," and when I expressed my ignorance, led me to the right court file.

The "trucking" section—and so much else—probably would never have come about had it not been for the tireless and courageous work of Jim Drinkhall. For a whole decade, Jim carried the ball alone and unsung for a little West Coast truckdrivers' magazine called *Overdrive.* One day in 1974, he called up, introduced himself, and said he wanted to talk about a couple of characters he was looking into whom I had written about in an earlier book. The more we talked, the more curious I became and I finally asked Jim to send me his clippings. They hit me with the force of a Mack truck. My editors were impressed, too. I spent nine months trying to find mistakes in what Drinkhall had done, then gave up and wrote a series of articles in the *Journal* on corruption in the Teamsters' union. Along the way, I learned that Jim had become something of a legend. Justice Department attorneys, who dealt all day with FBI agents, asserted that Drinkhall was the best investigator in the country. They regaled me with stories about how he hung out on the steps of pension fund offices, followed strangers to airports, and took seats beside them on planes to hear their stories.

Now, in 1978, a whole spate of books seems to be coming out about the Teamsters' union. It's safe to say that without Drinkhall, they probably wouldn't exist, at least not in anything like the form they've taken. The same may well be true of the federal government's current push against Teamster corruption. Jim now works for the *Wall Street Journal.* In the purest essence of our profession—the ability to find out important information that powerful people are trying to suppress—he may well be the best reporter in the country.

Much of the material in the banking section was originally developed by Bob Windrem of PROD, a dissident Teamsters' group, and Ann Crawford of the *(Bergen County, New Jersey) Record.* The Joey Franzese case was first brought to me by Stewart Pinkerton, the *Journal's* New York bureau manager. The original tip on liquor industry corruption came from Mary Bralove, who was just about to move from covering the food (and liquor) industry for the *Journal* to become its assistant New York bureau manager.

Once the rest of the book was done, the docks and the garment industry simply demanded their own inclusion.

My in-laws, Mr. and Mrs. Irving Kaplan, deserve special thanks for allowing me to turn their patio into a sometimes cluttered office during my three- and four-week vacations every year.

Great thanks also go to Robert Nicholson, Louis Montello, and Robert Sack (the *Journal*'s libel lawyer) for donating valuable reading time and contributing to substantial changes to help assure the accuracy and legal safety of the book. Still others who made substantial contributions by allowing a 750-page manuscript to intrude on their lives: Tony Scaduto, Starling Lawrence, Ellen Levine, Eric Swenson, Renee Schwartz, Janet Ter Veen, Cynthia Rigg, and David Thaler. And thanks also, out of general principle, to Mike Gartner.

This volume also could not have been produced without the work of these other reporters, whose published stories I have used, and only some of whom could be thanked conveniently in the text:

Norma Abrams, Len Ackland, Leo Adde, David Adlerstein, Michael Alloy, Jack Anderson, George Anthan, Edith Evans Asbury, Michael Auger, Gene Ayres.

David L. Beal, Harry Bernstein, Gregg Blackburn, Howard Blum, Walter Bogdanich, Don Bonafede, C.L. Booth, Ken Botwright, Jon Bradshaw, Mary Bralove, Michael Brody, Leonard Buder.

Charles Calley, Jerry Capeci, James Carberry, William M. Carley, Stephen L. Castner, Martyn Chase, Homer Clance, Nancy Clark, Laurence Collins, Ann Crawford.

Bob Davis, Leslie Davis, Jan deBlieu, Art Delugach, Lee Dembart, Joe Demma, Gary W. Diedrichs, Patrick Dillon, Gene Divine, Bryan Doherty, Dan Dorfman, Tom Downey, Mark Draisen, Dave Drury, Paul Dubois, Elizabeth Duff.

Joel Elson, Sheldon Engelmayer, Christopher Evans, M.A. Farber, Bill Farr, Frank Faso, Ellen Fleysher, Helen Fogel, Phil Fortman, Lacey Fosburgh, Lucinda Franks.

Nicholas Gage, Gil Gaul, Jeff Gerth, George Getschow, Chuck Gloman, Michael Gold, Ray Goldbacher, Gene Goldenberg, Cathy Gradt, Charles Grutzner, John Guinther, Herbert Haddad, Bill Hendrickson, Seymour M. Hersh, Robert D. Hershey Jr., James C. Hyatt, Arlo Jacobson, Elliot Jaspin, Walter Johns Jr., Harry Jones Jr.

Morris Kaplan, Nancy Kesler, Brian B. King, Ron LaBrecque, Hal Lancaster, Jerry Landauer, Jonathan R. Laing, Rudy Larini, Les Ledbetter, Daryl Lembke, Jay Levin, Tamar Lewin, Roger Lewis, Paul Lilley, Tom Lownes, Arnold H. Lubasch, Dick Lynets.

Cathy Sherman Machan, Jim Marino, James M. Markham, Stuart

Marques, Ken Matthews, Robert J. McAuley, Terry McDonald, Ann McDuffie, Robert D. McFadden, Dale McFeatters, Mary Jo Meisner, Paul R. Merrion, Paul Meskil, Al Messerschmidt, Phil Milford, Dan E. Moldea, Paul L. Montgomery, Jack Moore, Sheila Moran, Dan Morgan, Jeff Morgan, Walter Mossberg, Ralph S. Moyed, John Mulligan.

Bill Neikerk, Chuck Neubauer, Jack Newfield, Jean Novotny, John O'-Brien, David B. Offer, Cal Olson, Ralph Orr, John Osbon, Jack Oswald, Patrick Owens, Allan Parachini, Rachelle Patterson, Jim Patton, Mike Pearl, Stanley Penn, Emanuel Perlmutter, Art Petacque, Andy Plattner, Thomas Poster, James T. Prior, Wesley Pruden Jr.

Selwyn Raab, Edward Ranzal, A.H. Raskin, Wendell Rawls, Jr., Robert Rawtich, Tom Renner, James Ricci, Victor Riesel, James Risser, Bill Romano, Jack Roth, Robert Rudolph.

William Safire, Michael Satchell, James Savage, Al Scarth, Ron Scherer, Max H. Seigel, Richard Severo, Peggy Sheldon, Brian Smith, Mark Smolonsky, Denis Sneigr, Damon Stetson, James Strong, Julie Stump, William Styles, Lorana Sullivan, Ronald Sullivan, Jack Taylor, J.F. terHorst, Jo Thomas, Susan Trausch, Philip Z. Trupp, Tony Tucci, Wallace Turner, Trudy Tynan.

Michael Utevsky, Lester Velie, Robert J. Wagman, Martin Waldron, Pete Waldmeir, Bill Wallace, Dave Warsh, Gary Wasserman, Philip Wechsler, Joe Weiler, A.E. Welding, Michael F. Wendland, Ralph D. Wennblom, Jack Wharton, John Whitmarsh, Robert Windrem, Allen Wolper, and Alice Zarrillo.

Index